THE NEW
HIGH
SCHOOL
EQUIVALENCY
DIPLOMA
TESTS

SECONDARY LEVEL TESTS OF
GENERAL EDUCATIONAL DEVELOPMENT

By DAVID R. TURNER, M.S. in Ed.

arco   219 Park Avenue South
New York, N.Y. 10003

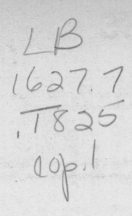
First Edition, B-3507
First Printing

COPYRIGHT © 1978
by Arco Publishing Company, Inc.

Published by ARCO PUBLISHING COMPANY, INC.
219 Park Avenue South, New York, N.Y. 10003

Library of Congress Cataloging in Publication Data

Turner, David Reuben, 1915-
    The new high school equivalency diploma tests.

    1. High school equivalency examination. I. Title.
LB1627.7.T825   373.1'2'62   77-20196
ISBN 0-668-04447-0 (Library Edition)
ISBN 0-668-04451-9 (Paper Edition)

Printed in the United States of America

26

CONTENTS

HOW TO USE THIS INDEX
Slightly bend the right-hand edge
of the book. This will expose
the corresponding Parts
which match the index, below.

PART ONE
STUDY TIPS
TWO VERISIMILAR EXAMS FOR PRACTICE

PART

1

2

3

4

5

6

7

...continued on next page

CONTENTS continued

PART FOUR
SCIENCE

PART FIVE
READING SKILLS

PART SIX
MATHEMATICS

PART

1

2

3

4

5

6

7

...continued on next page

CONTENTS continued

PART SEVEN
ANOTHER EXAM, ANOTHER CHANCE

WHAT THIS BOOK WILL DO FOR YOU

Even though this course of study has been carefully planned to help you get in shape by the day your test comes, you'll have to do a little planning on your own to be successful. And you'll also need a few pointers proven effective for many other good students.

If you want to take an exam but are reluctant for fear that you've been away from school too long, or for fear that your skills are a bit rusty, don't sell yourself short. You'll get the greatest help from this book by understanding how it has been organized, and by using it accordingly. Study carefully this concise, readable treatment of what is required by your exam, and your way will be clear. You will progress directly to your goal. You will not be led off into blind alleys and useless digressions.

We believe that you can improve your exam scores measureably with the help of this "self-tutor." It's a carefully thought-out homestudy course which you can readily review in less than twenty hours. It's a digest which you might have been able to assemble after many hundred hours of laborious digging. Since you'll have quite enough to do without that, consider yourself fortunate that we have done it for you.

To prepare for a test you must motivate yourself . . . get into the right frame of mind for learning from your "self-tutor." You'll have to urge yourself to learn. That's the only way people ever learn. Your efforts to score high will be greatly aided because you'll have to do this job on your own . . . perhaps without a teacher. Psychologists have demonstrated that studies undertaken for a clear goal (which you initiate yourself and actively pursue) are the most successful. You, yourself, want to pass this test. That's why you bought this book and embarked on this program. Nobody forced you to do it, and there may be nobody to lead you through the course. Your self-activity is going to be the key to your success in the forthcoming weeks.

Used correctly, your "self-tutor" will show you what to expect and will give you a speedy brush-up on the major problems crucial to your exam. Even if your study time is very limited, you will:

- gain familiarity with your examination;
- improve your general test-taking skill;

- improve your skill in analyzing and answering questions involving reasoning, judgment, comparison, and evaluation;
- improve your speed and skill in reading and understanding what you read—an important ability in learning, and an important component of most tests.

This book will pinpoint your study by presenting the types of questions you will get on the actual exam. You'll score higher even if you only familiarize yourself with these types.

This book will help you find your weaknesses and find them fast. Once you know where you're weak, you can get right to work (before the exam), and concentrate on those soft spots. This is the kind of selective study which yields maximum results for every hour spent.

This book will give you the *feel* of the exam. Many of our practice questions are taken from previous exams. Since previous exams are not always available for inspection by the public, our sample test questions are quite important for you. The day you take your exam you'll see how closely the book conforms.

This book will give you confidence *now*, while you are preparing for the exam. It will build your self-confidence as you proceed. It will beat those dreaded before-test jitters that have hurt so many other test-takers.

This book stresses the modern, multiple-choice type of question because that's the kind you'll undoubtedly get on your exam. In answering these questions you will add to your knowledge by learning the correct answers, naturally. However, you will not be satisfied with merely the correct choice for each question. You will want to find out why the other choices are incorrect. This will jog your memory . . . help you remember much you thought you had forgotten. You'll be preparing and enriching yourself for the exam to come.

Of course, the great advantage in all this lies in narrowing your study to just those fields in which you're most likely to be quizzed. Answer enough questions in those fields and the chances are very good that you'll meet a few of them again on the actual test. After all, the number of questions an examiner can draw upon in these fields is rather limited. Examiners frequently employ the same questions on different tests for this very reason.

By creating the "climate" of your test, this book should give you a fairly accurate picture of what's involved, and should put you in the right frame of mind for passing high.

Arco Publishing Company has been involved with trends and methods in testing ever since the firm was founded in 1937. We have *specialized* in books that prepare people for exams. Based on this experience it is our modest boast that you probably have in your hands the best book that could be prepared to help *you* score high. Now, if you'll take a little advice on using it properly, we can assure you that you will do well.

PREVIEW AND PROGRAM

Adults who have not completed their high school education now have an opportunity to get a high school diploma without going back to school. All this through a High School Equivalency Diploma, recognized as the equivalent of a four-year high school diploma by business, industry, civil service commissions, U.S. Armed Forces, licensing bureaus, and many institutions of higher education.

This book will tell you what the High School Equivalency Diploma is about and how to prepare yourself for the test. You will find Sample Tests, and answers, to familiarize you with the actual test. You will also find study material designed to make most effective use of your time and effort.

Purpose and Meaning

Many students were forced to leave school during World War II to serve in the armed forces. High School Equivalency Diploma tests were first used to give veterans, a chance to receive high school diplomas. For this purpose the American Council on Education produced the battery of tests called General Educational Development, better known simply as G.E.D. The diploma awarded to those making satisfactory grades on these tests has the same worth as that given to graduates from a four-year high school.

Equivalency programs have now been extended to include civilian adults. Tests are given at regular intervals either by the Education Departments of the different states or by individual high schools, depending on the administrative procedures adopted by each state.

You do not have to attend high school at all in order to get a High School Equivalency Diploma. The age requirement for the examination varies from state to state, but in no state is the minimum age requirement over twenty-one years.

There are great opportunities in our country for those who have educational background. Industry, business, civil service, the armed services, and many colleges extend open arms to those who are educationally qualified. It does not matter whether the educated individual has acquired his education *in* the class room or *outside* the classroom. If he is an educated person, he will be accepted—in fact, he will be welcomed.

The purpose of the High School Equivalency Diploma is to establish that a person who has not attended high school classes has, nevertheless, the educational background of a high school graduate. If he does have that background, in spite of the fact that he has never taken classroom courses, he can now have all the prestige of the high school graduate.

This is as it should be. After all, if a person has traveled widely, and through his travels, has learned quite a bit about history, geography, science, literature, and so many other things that are taught in the classroom, why shouldn't he receive credit and recognition for his ability and achievement?

Regardless of the state where you get the certificate, it is honored everywhere in business, government civil service, and by certain colleges.

Values of a Diploma

"DO YOU HAVE A HIGH SCHOOL DI-PLOMA?" How many times have you heard that question and have had to answer "no"? You probably realize that the lack of a High School Diploma is responsible for holding you back from greater success . . . otherwise you would not be reading this book. Well, the truth of the matter is that a High School Diploma or its equivalent is *one of life's most valuable tools for success*—for it opens up the doors to greater earning power and greater opportunities.

Better, Higher-Paying Jobs

Look around you. A little observation and reflection will quickly convince you that people with High School Diplomas have by far the better positions in all walks of life. The man or woman without a diploma is usually at the bottom of the ladder.

The U.S. Government has made studies which show quite clearly that high school graduates earn nearly $1,000 more each year after the age of 24 than grade school graduates. In plain dollars and cents, a high school diploma or its equivalent can add more than $60,000 to your lifetime earning power.

In Industry

Inspect the want-ad section of the daily newspaper. You will find that the better paying jobs are reserved for the high school and college graduate. A recent study indicates that there are more and more jobs available for the educated person—fewer and fewer jobs for the person who lacks education. Many employment agencies will not even consider an applicant unless he has at least a high school diploma or its equivalent.

In Civil Service

Hundreds of thousands of men and women are needed annually to fill high-paying, secure, lifetime jobs with federal, state, and municipal government units. Firemen, policemen, typists, office clerks, postal carriers, railway mail clerks, etc., are always in demand. A high school diploma or its equivalent is usually required for these positions.

In Our Armed Forces

For anyone in military service, a high school diploma is often an essential for promotion. It is much easier to attain the status of an officer—non-commissioned as well as commissioned—if you possess a diploma. All branches of the armed forces are eager to help servicemen even while they are in service to gain a high school equivalency certificate. The United States Armed Forces Institute (USAFI) has several testing stations just for this purpose.

An applicant who has received a satisfactory score on the High School Equivalency Test while in service does not have to take the test again when he returns to civilian life.

For College Entrance

There are a great many colleges which recognize the High School Equivalency Diploma for college entrance. If you are interested in entering a certain college with your Equivalency Diploma, it would be advisable for you to write to that institution to ask whether it will accept the certificate.

A recent newsletter published by the Commission on Accreditation of the American Council on Education relates the interesting case of a lady from the state of Maryland who says (in her own words): "A few years ago I wrote a letter to the State Department of Education asking them to send me the booklet which explains how an adult may get a high school diploma for college entrance without going to high school. The booklet explained that by passing certain examinations given by the State Board of Education one could get such a diploma. The assumption is that we never stop learning. If you have raised children, the chances are that, without realizing it, you have learned much of their homework by listening to them or helping them. Because of my age, I didn't want to waste time. I studied hard and passed the equivalency examination. With the diploma, I was able to go to college. By this June I shall have earned 107 college credits. I expect to get my diploma from a local university next year, so you see it can be done."

Trade and Vocational Schools

In this age of specialization the skilled person invariably commands a higher salary than the unskilled individual. Many of the better trade and vocational schools where you can acquire skills that are in demand won't enroll you unless you have a high school diploma.

Prestige

Let's face it—a person without a high school diploma is sometimes looked down at by his friends and his community. This may often be unfair, but the sad fact is that a person who has not gone through high school is supposed to have narrow intellectual interests.

A diploma may make a lot of difference in how people consider you. And it is true—isn't it?—that the effort you put into getting that diploma gives you educational growth and a broader knowledge of the world you live in. These benefits will be with you all the rest of your life.

Richer, Fuller, Happier Life

But, a High School Equivalency Diploma can mean even more. It means you can face life with confidence in yourself and your abilities ... you can meet situations, people, problems without having "two strikes" against you before you start. You will command the attention and respect of others—instead of being overlooked or shrugged off with a "what can he know—he didn't even finish high school." And with the increased earnings and better jobs that go with a High School Equivalency Diploma—you will be able to afford some of the finer things you have always wanted ... find more time for play and relaxation. Think of it! A High School Equivalency Diploma can give you all these things. Can you honestly afford to get along without a diploma any longer? Can you willingly pass up this amazing opportunity to get *your* diploma?

When you get that High School Equivalency Diploma, you will have the feeling of satisfaction that comes with obtaining something worthwhile. This will be accompanied by an attitude of confidence as well as a desire to continue your education either in the classroom or outside of it. "There's nothing like success to bring success."

Simple Steps to a High School Diploma

You are now aware that you can get a high school diploma (or equivalency certificate) even if you do not have the school credits that are ordinarily required for the diploma. As an adult, if you pass the High School Equivalency Diploma Test, you are able to get a high school diploma—*even if you do not have the school credits*. The High School Equivalency Diploma is awarded to adults who prove that they have the educational level of the average high school graduate—even though they have not gone to high school.

It may very well be that you have the educational background of a high school graduate. If you have traveled, if you have met many different types of people, if you have read books and articles (in English or in a foreign language), if you have had other experiences in life that have broadened you—it is likely that you have more education than your record indicates. That is what the High School Diploma Eqivalency Test is for — to find out whether you deserve to be called a high school graduate even though you do not have the classroom training.

You Can Do It!

Do not be discouraged if you are not ready to take the High School Diploma Test. This book will help you to prepare for it. Let's suppose that your reading, arithmetic, English and spelling levels are somewhere between the 6th and 9th grades. We are going to try to raise your level so that, eventually, you will have a 12th grade ability—then you will be ready to take the High School Diploma Test.

There's plenty of hard work ahead. But you can do it if you are serious. This book will guide you—it will give you light, and it will help you to find your way.

Nationwide Recognition

Every state in the union (and the Canal Zone, the District of Columbia, Guam, and Puerto Rico) issues and accepts an Equivalency Diploma. In all states the examinations for a diploma are based on the G.E.D. tests. The diploma is recognized as a valid high school equivalency credential by all states.

In no state is attendance at school or classes required.

Who Can Take the Test?

Age requirements vary from state to state. There is, of course, no maximum age; an adult man or woman can take it at any time throughout his life The minimum age is never over twenty-one, and in Arizona and Hawaii, for instance, it is as low as eighteen. In a few states and territories the minimum age is lower for veterans than for non-veterans and service personnel.

Fees

Since Equivalency Diplomas are issued by the individual states, there is no set fee throughout the country for taking the test. The fee not only varies from state to state; it sometimes also varies *within* the state, from one testing center to another.

What About Veterans?

A veteran who has taken and passed the G.E.D. battery of tests while in the service will usually receive his Equivalency Diploma without having to take further tests when he returns to civilian life. He should make application for his diploma to his state Department of Education.

For those who pass the test, some states charge an additional fee for issuance of the Equivalency Diploma while others offer this service free.

Testing Centers

Testing agency centers are located in different parts of each state. The chance is that there will be one not very far from where you live.

The addresses of all testing agency centers in your state usually are listed on the application form, which may be obtained from your state Department of Education at your state capital.

Test Scores

Minimum passing scores are required on each of the five tests as well as a minimum passing average on all the tests. Although the Equivalency Tests are similar in all states, the passing scores differ. They vary between states from a low score of 35 to a high score of 50 required on each test, and from a low combined score of 200 to a high of 250 for the five tests.

In Oklahoma, for instance, a score of 40 or above is required on each of the five tests and an average score of 50—a total of 250—on all five tests. The passing score in Vermont is 35 on each test and an average of 45 is required on all five tests. Virginia and Alaska are among the few states that make no distinction between the passing score in each test and the average score on all five: 40 or above is required in Virginia and 50 or above in Alaska.

When Will I Know?

It takes from six to eight weeks to receive the scores. They are sent directly to the person who took the examination.

A Second State Diploma

In New York State, the holder of an Equivalency Diploma may also go on to earn a Regents High School Diploma. He can qualify for a Regents Diploma by passing Regents tests in all of the following: three units in a major elective subject; either American History and World Background III or American History II and World History; English Comprehensive. Application forms are available at high school offices anywhere in the state.

How to Apply

For an application, write to the Department of Education in the capital city of the state where you reside. Fill out each item of information requested on the application. Follow the directions in regard to the fee and where to mail it.

ALL ABOUT THE TEST

The more you know about the exam you will have to face, the better your chances of success. That's just what this chapter is for. To set the stage for the exam to come and spotlight the steps toward scoring high.

Since 1943 the G.E.D. High School Equivalency Diploma Test has served the adult population by providing the opportunity to demonstrate educational achievement comparable to that of the high school graduate. The test is designed to measure the intellectual skills that are typical of a sound general academic high school education and it serves as a basis for granting a High School Equivalency Diploma to those who complete it successfully.

The holder of a High School Equivalency Diploma, just like a traditional high school graduate, has in his hand the key to advanced educational or vocational doors which are locked to the under-educated.

In April of 1973, the Commission on Educational Credit appointed a committee to study the High School Equivalency Diploma Test with an eye toward constructing a new form of the test which would be more reflective of current trends in high school instructional programs, and at the same time would require less time to administer to candidates. As a result of this study, a new form of the H.S.E.D.T. was developed. Like the older forms of the H.S.E.D.T., the new form consists of a battery of five tests of approximately equal weight. However, the new H.S.E.D.T. is somewhat altered in content and requires only six hours of testing time instead of the original ten hours.

The five subtests in the new H.S.E.D.T. are intended to measure those levels of knowledge and ability which are characteristic of the average high school graduate. The subject and skill areas covered are:

Test 1: Writing Skills
Test 2: Social Studies
Test 3: Science
Test 4: Reading Skills
Test 5: Mathematics

TEST I. WRITING SKILLS

The Writing Skills Test consists of about eighty multiple-choice questions testing your ability to use Standard Written English. Standard Written English is the kind of English commonly found in textbooks and magazines—and the kind of English you are expected to use when writing compositions, reports or business letters.

This test is designed to measure your knowledge of spelling, punctuation, capitalization, grammar, usage, diction, style, sentence structure, logic and organization. It does all this through the use of four different types of multiple-choice questions. A description of each question type and its relative importance in the test as a whole is provided below.

1. Spelling—10%
This test consists of groups of commonly used words with one word in each group misspelled. You are to identify the misspelled word.

2. English Usage—45%
In this test you will be given a sentence containing four underlined and numbered segments followed by a fifth underlined and numbered option which is "no error." You must indicate which underlined segment, if any, contains an error.

Approximately one-third of the English Usage questions are concerned with Punctuation and Capitalization. The Punctuation questions may ask you to demonstrate correct use of the period, comma, question mark, apostrophe, semi-colon, parentheses, quotation marks and exclamation marks. Questions on Capitalization concern the use of capitals in proper names and titles, and to indicate the start of a new sentence.

The other two-thirds of the English Usage questions cover Grammar and Usage. These questions may concern agreement of subjects and verbs, pronouns and antecedents; tenses of verbs; correct usage of nouns, adjectives, adverbs, prepositions and conjunctions.

3. Sentence Correction—30%
This test consists of single sentences with one portion underlined. Following each sentence are five alternatives for the underlined part, one of which is clearly preferable with respect to correctness and effectiveness of expression. You are to choose the alternative which makes the best sentence.

About one-half of the questions are concerned with Diction and Style, measuring your knowledge of vocabulary and effectiveness of expression, and your ability to write clearly and concisely.

The other half of the questions covers Sentence Structure including relationships among clauses, misplaced modifiers, awkward phrases, parallel structure and conversion of short sentences into complex ones.

4. Logic and Organization—15%

In this test you will be presented with brief passages with portions either underlined or numbered. Following each passage are questions testing your comprehension of the pattern and structure of the paragraph, including the relationship between the topic sentence and other sentences in the passage, interrelationships among ideas in the passage, effective use of transitional words and clauses, ordering of ideas, economy and clarity of statements.

TEST II. SOCIAL STUDIES

The Social Studies Test consists of about sixty questions. Most of the questions are based on reading material or data presented in the form of graphs, maps, pictures, cartoons or tables. A small portion of the questions tests recall of specific facts and terms of fundamental importance in the Social Studies.

The passages you will be expected to read and analyze may consist of material from books, newspapers or magazines, including advertisements, sports, news, editorials and feature articles. They may be documents such as job applications or other forms, or they may be step-by-step instructions for getting a particular job done. Each passage will be followed by a group of questions based upon its content.

The subject matter of the Social Studies Test may fall into any of the following five areas of Social Studies Knowledge:

1. Economics—20%

Particularly consumer economics and the practical concepts necessary to understanding current events and conducting personal or business affairs.

2. Geography—15%

Population distribution, migration, climate, natural resources, regions, geographical patterns, spatial associations.

3. Political Science—20%

Government, including its history, processes and functions. Political philosophy, international politics, state and local government, power, and equality.

4. History—25%

Particularly American History with emphasis on the historical roots of major current phenomena. Industrialization, urbanization, social change, conflict and compromise.

5. Behavioral Science—20%

Sociological, anthropological and psychological concepts which emphasize understanding human behavior. Social institutions, organizations and classes. Social structure, tradition and culture. Motivation, role behavior and status.

The questions will test any of the five skills listed below.

1. *Knowledge.* These items test your recall of specific facts and terms, concepts and principles that are essential to the social studies.

2. *Comprehension and Interpretation.* This type of question requires you to demonstrate your ability to understand and evaluate verbal or pictorial material. You may be asked to pick out specific facts from the reading or to determine the main idea of a passage.

3. *Inference.* In this kind of question you may be asked to show your ability to understand the consequences of the data you have been given or to draw conclusions about it. Questions may ask you to make a reasoned guess about what might happen next based upon your knowledge of what came before.

4. *Application.* This type of question tests your ability to apply abstract ideas or concepts to particular cases or given data. You may be asked to decide what might happen in a situation which is similar to, but different from, the one described in the reading.

5. *Evaluation.* Here you will be asked to assess the adequacy of the data you have been given. You may have to determine what is opinion and what is fact or to pinpoint biases in the material presented. You might be asked about the tone of a particular passage or the intent of the author in writing it.

TEST III. SCIENCE

The H.S.E.D.T. Science Test is similar in format to the Social Studies Test. It consists primarily of groups of questions based on reading passages or data presented in graphic form.

As in the Social Studies Test, there will be some questions testing your knowledge of fundamental concepts in science. However, these questions will stress broad scientific principles and their applications rather than the ability to memorize isolated facts.

The reading passages for this test will be brief, yet comprehensive in scope. They may come from magazines, reviews, journals, newspapers or reference books, but not usually from classroom texts.

The test is designed not only to measure your reading ability in the sciences, but also to see how well you can understand, analyze and use the information presented. The Science Test covers four specific subject areas.

1. Biology—50%
    Cells and their structure, genetics, evolution, human anatomy and physiology, health and nutrition, reproduction, photosynthesis and ecology.

2. Earth Science—20%
    Geology, earth history, nature of our water and air, temperature, wind, precipitation, the solar system.

3. Chemistry—15%
    Acids and bases, molecules and molecular theory, atoms and atomic energy.

4. Physics—15%
    Measurement of distance, matter, light and sound, mechanics, gases, electricity, magnetism.

TEST IV. READING SKILLS

The Reading Skills Test focuses on your ability to understand what you read. The test consists of a number of short selections taken from a variety of sources. Each selection is followed by a group of questions based solely on the information provided by the passage. No questions require previous knowledge of the author or his work in order to arrive at the correct answer. The passages you will be asked to read and interpret reflect a wide range in both difficulty and length.

The questions may ask about the meaning of a whole passage or small parts of it. They may be concerned with what is suggested by the selection as well as what is stated in it. You may be asked to define a word or phrase in the context of the passage, to interpret figurative language or to describe the mood of the selection.

The selections used to test your reading skills fall into five categories.

1. General Reading—35%
    Social, scientific or general interest articles commonly found in magazines or newspapers. Textbook material in the fields of social studies or science; editorials and journalistic works.

2. Prose Literature—35%
    Contemporary prose, either expository or creative, of literary quality. An occasional 18th- or 19th-century period piece.

3. Practical Reading—15%
   Instructions, recipes, contracts, outlines, catalog entries, advertisements, newspaper articles and propaganda.

4. Poetry—10%
   Light or serious verse capable of being interpreted without reference to outside sources.

5. Drama—5%
   Comedy, tragedy or social drama.

TEST V. MATHEMATICS

This test consists of approximately fifty multiple-choice questions testing your ability to solve a variety of problems in elementary mathematics with the emphasis on those practical aspects of mathematics necessary to everyday life.

The areas on which you will be tested are divided about as follows:

1. Arithmetic—55%
   Computation involving whole numbers, decimals, fractions and percents. Properties of real numbers. Measurement of length, area, volume, money, time, mass/weight, and liquids. Data interpretation and averages.

2. Algebra—25%
   Coordinate geometry, including the number line, rectangular coordinates, distance between two points using two graphs, slope, ratio and proportion. Use of algebraic formulas. Solution of linear equations and simple linear inequalities. Exponents and quadratic equations at a very simple level. Points of intersection of two lines.

3. Geometry—20%
   Direct and indirect measurement of angles, lines and areas. Identification of similarities between geometric shapes. Interpretation of line graphs, broken line graphs, bar graphs and circular graphs. Application of Pythagorean relationships.

STUDYING AND USING THIS BOOK

Even though this course of study has been carefully planned to help you get in shape by the day your test comes, you'll have to do a little planning on your own to be successful. And you'll also need a few pointers proven effective for many other good students.

SURVEY AND SCHEDULE YOUR WORK

Regular mental workouts are as important as regular physical workouts in achieving maximum personal efficiency. They are absolutely essential in getting top test scores, so you'll want to plan a test-preparing schedule that fits in with your usual program. Use the Schedule on the next page. Make it out for yourself so that it really works with the actual time you have at your disposal.

There are five basic steps in scheduling this book for yourself and in studying each assignment that you schedule:

1. SCAN - the entire job at hand.
2. QUESTION - before reading.
3. READ - to find the answers to the questions you have formulated.
4. RECITE - to see how well you have learned the answers to your questions.
5. REVIEW - to check up on how well you have learned, to learn it again, and to fix it firmly in your mind.

Scan

Make a survey of this whole book before scheduling. Do this by reading our introductory statements and the table of contents. Then leaf through the entire book, paying attention to main headings, sub-headings, summaries, and topic sentences. When you have this bird's eye view of the whole, the parts take on added meaning, and you'll see how they hang together.

Question

As you scan, questions will come to your mind. Write them into the book. Later on you'll be finding the answers. For example, in scanning this book you would naturally change the headline STUDYING AND USING THIS BOOK into *What don't I know about studying? What are my good study habits? How can I improve them? How should I go about reading and using this book?*

Practice the habit of formulating and writing such questions into the text.

Read

Now, by reviewing your questions you should be able to work out your schedule easily. Stick to it. And apply these five steps to each assignment you give yourself in the schedule. Your reading of each assignment should be directed to finding answers to the questions you have formulated and will continue to formulate. You'll discover that reading with a purpose will make it easier to *remember* the answers to your questions.

Recite

After you have read your assignment and found the answers to your questions, close the book and recite to yourself. For example, if your question here was "What are the five basic steps in attacking an assignment?" then your answer to yourself would be scan, question, read, recite, and review. Thus, you check up on yourself and "fix" the information in your mind. You have now seen it, read it, said it, and heard it. The more senses you use, the more you learn.

Review

Even if you recall your answers well, review them in order to "overlearn." "Overlearning" gives you a big advantage by reducing the chances of forgetting. Definitely provide time in your schedule for review. It's the clincher in getting ahead of the crowd. You'll find that "overlearning" won't take much time with this book because the text portions have been written as concisely and briefly as possible. You may be tempted to stop work when you have once gone over the work before you. This is wrong because of the ease with which memory impressions are bound to fade. Decide for yourself what is important and plan to review and overlearn those portions. Overlearning rather than last minute cramming is the best way to study.

19

Your Time is Limited—Schedule Your Study

1. SCOPE OF EXAMINATION

Test Subjects	No. of Questions	Percentage of Total (Weight)
Total:		**100 percent**

SUBJECT
SCHEDULE

2. YOUR KNOWLEDGE OF SUBJECT

Test Subjects	Poor	Fair	Good	Very Good	Excellent

3. DIVIDING YOUR STUDY TIME

Test Subjects	Total Hours	Hours Per Week
Total:		

Total number of weeks for study

Hours per week

Total number of hours

The SUBJECT SCHEDULE is divided into three parts: 1. Scope of Examination; 2. Your Knowledge of Subject; and 3. Dividing Your Study Time. To use your schedule, put down in part 1 all the subjects you will face on your test, the number of questions in each subject, and the "weight," or percentage, given to each subject in the total make-up of the test.

In part 2, again fill in all the test subjects and, with a check mark, rate yourself *honestly* as to your knowledge of each subject.

At the top of part 3, put down the number of weeks you will be able to devote to your studying. Determine the number of hours you will study each week and multiply that figure by the number of weeks to give you the total hours of study.

Again fill in the subjects. Then, take the weight given to each test subject (in part 1) and average it against your knowledge of that subject (as checked in part 2) to arrive at the number of hours you should allow for study of that subject out of your total study hours. In Chapter 2, under the heading "10. Total Time Allowed For Each Subject," you will find a more detailed explanation of how to divide your study time.

After you have fixed the total number of hours to be devoted to each subject, divide them by the number of weeks of study to arrive at the total weekly hours you will study each subject.

STUDY TIMETABLE
PRELIMINARY

Key Letters	Study Subjects
A	
B	
C	
D	
E	
F	

Key Letters	Study Subjects
G	
H	
I	
J	
K	
L	

Mon.

Tues.

Wed.

Thur.

Fri.

Sat.

Sun.

HOW TO USE THE STUDY TIMETABLE

At right is a sample timetable filled in for a whole week to show you how a typical schedule might be arranged. The letters *A, B, C,* etc., are keyed to your study subjects so that, for example, *A* might stand for Vocabulary, *B* for Numerical Relations, and so forth. You will note that each day is divided into nine possible study hours and each hour, in turn, is divided into four 15-minute periods.

	7 AM	12 PM		7 PM	8 PM	9 PM	
Mon.	BB	AA		BBCC	CCEEE	GG	

		12 PM		7 PM	6 PM	4 PM	
Tues.		FF		AAABB	DDDD	GG	

	7 AM	12 PM		7 PM			
Wed.	CC	BB		BBBB			

		12 PM		7 PM	8 PM	9 PM	10 PM
Thur.		A		AA	BBEEE	FFHH	

	7 AM		7 PM	8 PM			
Fri.	AA		FFFEE	CC			

	10 AM	11 AM	12 PM	3 PM	4 PM	
Sat.	DDD	AAAA		BBB	FF	

	1 PM	2 PM	3 PM	4 PM	8 PM	
Sun.	DDD	CCCC	AAHHH	BB		

STUDY TIMETABLE

FINAL

Key Letters	Study Subjects
A	
B	
C	
D	
E	
F	

Key Letters	Study Subjects
G	
H	
I	
J	
K	
L	

Mon.

Tues.

Wed.

Thur.

Fri.

Sat.

Sun.

Plan to study difficult subjects when you can give them your greatest energy. Some people find that they can do their best work in the early morning hours. On the other hand, it has been found that forgetting is less when study is followed by sleep or recreation. Plan other study periods for those free times which might otherwise be wasted . . . for example lunch or when traveling to and from work.

Plan your schedule so that not more than 1½ or 2 hours are spent in the study of any subject at one sitting. Allow at least a half-hour for each session with your book. It takes a few minutes before you settle down to work.

You will find that there is enough time for your study and other activities if you follow a well-planned schedule. You will not only be able to find enough time for your other activities, but you will also accomplish more in the way of study and learning. A definite plan for study increases concentration. If you establish the habit of studying a subject at the same time each day, you will find that less effort is required in focusing your attention on it.

PART ONE

Study Tips

Two Verisimilar Exams for Practice

━THE GIST OF TEST STRATEGY━

HOW TO BE A MASTER TEST TAKER

- APPROACH THE TEST CONFIDENTLY. TAKE IT CALMLY.

- REMEMBER TO REVIEW, THE WEEK BEFORE THE TEST.

- DON'T "CRAM." BE CAREFUL OF YOUR DIET AND SLEEP .. ESPECIALLY AS THE TEST DRAWS NIGH.

- ARRIVE ON TIME . . . AND READY.

- CHOOSE A GOOD SEAT. GET COMFORTABLE AND RELAX.

- BRING THE COMPLETE KIT OF "TOOLS" YOU'LL NEED.

- LISTEN CAREFULLY TO ALL DIRECTIONS.

- APPORTION YOUR TIME INTELLIGENTLY WITH AN "EXAM BUDGET."

- READ ALL DIRECTIONS CAREFULLY. TWICE IF NECESSARY. PAY PARTICULAR ATTENTION TO THE SCORING PLAN.

- LOOK OVER THE WHOLE TEST BEFORE ANSWERING ANY QUESTIONS.

- START RIGHT IN, IF POSSIBLE. STAY WITH IT. USE EVERY SECOND EFFECTIVELY.

- DO THE EASY QUESTIONS FIRST; POSTPONE HARDER QUESTIONS UNTIL LATER.

- DETERMINE THE PATTERN OF THE TEST QUESTIONS. IF IT'S HARD-EASY ETC., ANSWER ACCORDINGLY.

- READ EACH QUESTION CAREFULLY. MAKE SURE YOU UNDERSTAND EACH ONE BEFORE YOU ANSWER. RE-READ, IF NECESSARY.

- THINK! AVOID HURRIED ANSWERS. GUESS INTELLIGENTLY.

- WATCH YOUR WATCH AND "EXAM BUDGET," BUT DO A LITTLE BALANCING OF THE TIME YOU DEVOTE TO EACH QUESTION.

- GET ALL THE HELP YOU CAN FROM "CUE" WORDS.

- REPHRASE DIFFICULT QUESTIONS FOR YOURSELF. WATCH OUT FOR "SPOILERS."

- REFRESH YOURSELF WITH A FEW, WELL-CHOSEN REST PAUSES DURING THE TEST.

- USE CONTROLLED ASSOCIATION TO SEE THE RELATION OF ONE QUESTION TO ANOTHER AND WITH AS MANY IMPORTANT IDEAS AS YOU CAN DEVELOP.

- NOW THAT YOU'RE A "COOL" TEST-TAKER, STAY CALM AND CONFIDENT THROUGHOUT THE TEST. DON'T LET ANYTHING THROW YOU.

- EDIT, CHECK, PROOFREAD YOUR ANSWERS. BE A "BITTER ENDER." STAY WORKING UNTIL THEY MAKE YOU GO.

HIGH SCHOOL EQUIVALENCY DIPLOMA TESTS

TECHNIQUES OF STUDY AND TEST-TAKING

*Although a thorough knowledge of the subject matter is the most impor-
tant factor in succeeding on your exam, the following suggestions could
raise your score substantially. These few pointers will give you the
strategy employed on tests by those who are most successful in this
not-so-mysterious art. It's really quite simple. Do things right . . . right
from the beginning. Make successful methods a habit. Then you'll get
the greatest dividends from the time you invest in this book.*

PREPARING FOR THE EXAM

1. *Budget your time*. Set aside definite hours each day for concentrated
study. Adhere closely to this budget. Don't fritter away your time with excessive
"breaks." A cup of coffee, a piece of fruit, a look out of the window—they're
fine, but not too often.

2. *Study with a friend or a group*. The exchange of ideas that this arrangement affords may be very beneficial. It is also more pleasant getting together in
study sessions. Be sure, though, that you ban "socializing." Talk about friends,
dates, trips, etc. at some other time.

3. *Eliminate distractions*. Psychologists tell us that study efforts will reap
much more fruit when there is little or no division of attention. Disturbances
caused by family and neighbor activities (telephone calls, chit-chat, TV programs,
etc.) will work to your disadvantage. Study in a quiet, private room. Better still,
use the library.

4. *Use the library*. Most colleges and universities have excellent library
facilities. Some institutions have special libraries for the various subject areas:
Physics library, Education library, Psychology library, etc. Take full advantage of
such valuable facilities. The library is free from those distractions that may inhibit
your home study. Moreover, research in your subject area is so much more
convenient in a library since it can provide much more study material than you
have at home.

5. *Answer all the questions in this book*. Don't be satisfied merely with the
correct answer to each question. Do additional research on the other choices which
are given. You will broaden your background to be adequately prepared for the
"real" exam. It's quite possible that a question on the exam which you are going
to take may require you to be familiar with the other choices.

6. *Get the "feel" of the exam.* The sample questions which this book contains will give you that "feel." Gestalt (meaning *configuration* or *pattern*) psychology stresses that true learning results in a grasp of the *entire situation.* Gestaltists also tell us that we learn by "insight." One of the salient facets of this type of learning is that we succeed in "seeing through" a problem as a consequence of experiencing *previous similar situations.* This book contains hundreds of "similar situations"—as you will discover when you take the actual exam.

7. *Take the Sample Tests as "real" tests.* With this attitude, you will derive greater benefit. Put yourself under strict examination conditions. Tolerate no interruptions while you are taking the sample tests. Work steadily. Do not spend too much time on any one question. If a question seems too difficult go to the next one. If time permits, go back to the omitted question.

8. *Tailor your study to the subject matter. Skim or scan.* Don't study everything in the same manner. Francis Bacon (1561-1626) expressed it this way: "Some books are to be tasted, others to be swallowed, and some few to be chewed and digested."

9. *Organize yourself.* Make sure that your notes are in good order—also, that your desk top is neat. Valuable time is consumed unnecessarily when you can't find quickly what you are looking for.

10. *Keep physically fit.* You cannot retain information well when you are uncomfortable, headachy, or tense. Physical health promotes mental efficiency. Guarding your health takes into account such factors as these:

a. Sufficient sleep
b. Daily exercise and recreation
c. Annual physical examination
d. A balanced diet
e. Avoidance of eyestrain
f. Mental health

HOW TO TAKE AN EXAM

1. *Get to the Examination Room about Ten Minutes Ahead of Time.* You'll start better when you are accustomed to the room. If the room is too cold, or too warm, or not well ventilated, call these conditions to the attention of the person in charge.

2. *Make Sure that you Read the Instructions Carefully.* In many cases, test-takers lose credits because they misread some important point in the given directions—example: the *incorrect* choice instead of the *correct* choice.

3. *Be Confident.* Statistics conclusively show that success is likely when you have prepared faithfully. It is important to know that you are not expected to answer every question correctly. The questions usually have a range of difficulty and differentiate between several levels of skill. It's quite possible that an "A" student might answer no more than 60% of the questions correctly.

4. *Skip Hard Questions and Go Back Later*. It is a good idea to make a mark on the question sheet next to all questions you cannot answer easily, and to go back to those questions later. First answer the questions you are sure about. Do not panic if you cannot answer a question. Go on and answer the questions you know. Usually the easier questions are presented at the beginning of the exam and the questions become gradually more difficult.

If you do skip ahead on the exam, be sure to skip ahead also on your answer sheet. A good technique is periodically to check the number of the question on the answer sheet with the number of the question on the test. You should do this every time you decide to skip a question. If you fail to skip the corresponding answer blank for that question, all of your following answers will be wrong.

Each student is stronger in some areas than in others. No one is expected to know all the answers. Do not waste time agonizing over a difficult question because it may keep you from getting to other questions that you can answer correctly.

5. *Guess If You Are Not Sure*. No correction is made for guessing when this exam is scored. Therefore, it is better to guess than to omit an answer.

6. *Mark the Answer Sheet Clearly*. When you take the examination, you will mark your answers to the multiple-choice questions on a separate answer sheet that will be given to you at the test center. If you have not worked with an answer sheet before, it is in your best interest to become familiar with the procedures involved. Remember, knowing the correct answer is not enough! If you do not mark the sheet correctly, so that it can be machine scored, you will not get credit for your answers!

In addition to marking answers on the separate answer sheet, you might also be asked to give your name and other information, including your social security number. As a precaution bring along your social security number for identification purposes.

Read the directions carefully and follow them exactly. If they ask you to print your name in the boxes provided, write only one letter in each box. If your name is longer than the number of boxes provided, omit the letters that do not fit. Remember, you are writing for a machine; it does not have judgment. It can only record the pencil marks you make on the answer sheet.

Use the answer sheet to record all your answers to questions. Each question, or item, has four or five answer choices labeled (A), (B), (C), (D), (E). You will be asked to choose the letter for the alternative that best answers each question. Then you will be asked to mark your answer by blackening the appropriate space on your answer sheet. Be sure that each space you choose and blacken with your pencil is *completely* blackened. If you change your mind about an answer, or mark the wrong space in error, you must erase the wrong answer. Erase as thoroughly and neatly as possible. The machine will "read" your answers in terms of spaces blackened. Make sure that only one answer is clearly blackened. If you erase an answer, erase it completely and mark your new answer clearly. The machine will give credit only for clearly marked answers. It does not pause to decide whether you really meant (B) or (C).

Make sure that the number of the question you are being asked on the question sheet corresponds to the number of the question you are answering on the answer sheet. It is a good idea to check the numbers of questions and answers frequently. If you decide to skip a question, but fail to skip the corresponding answer blank for that question, all your answers after that will be wrong.

7. *Read Each Question Carefully*. The exam questions are not designed to trick you through misleading or ambiguous alternative choices. On the other hand, they are not all direct questions of factual information. Some are designed to elicit responses that reveal your ability to reason, or to interpret a fact or idea. It's up to you to read each question carefully so you know what is being asked. The exam authors have tried to make the questions clear. Do not go too far astray in looking for hidden meanings.

8. *Don't Answer Too Fast*. The multiple-choice questions which you will meet are not superficial exercises. They are designed to test not only rote recall, but also understanding and insight. Watch for deceptive choices. Do not place too much emphasis on speed. The time element is a factor, but it is not all-important. Accuracy should not be sacrificed for speed.

9. *Materials and Conduct At The Test Center*. You need to bring with you to the test center your Admission Form, your social security number, and several No. 2 pencils. Arrive on time as you may not be admitted after testing has begun. Instructions for taking the tests will be read to you by the test supervisor and time will be called when the test is over. If you have questions, you may ask them of the supervisor. Do not give or receive assistance while taking the exams. If you do, you will be asked to turn in all test materials and told to leave the room. You will not be permitted to return and your tests will not be scored.

FIRST VERISIMILAR EXAMINATION

To begin your studies, test yourself now to see how you measure up. This examination is similar to the one you'll get, and is therefore a practical yardstick for charting your progress and planning your course. Adhere strictly to all test instructions. Mark yourself honestly and you'll find where your weaknesses are and where to concentrate your study.

Allow about 6 hours for this Examination.

That's approximately how much time you'll have on the actual exam. Keep a record of your time, especially if you want to break up this practice into several convenient sessions. Then you'll be able to simulate actual exam conditions.

In constructing this Examination we tried to visualize the questions you are *likely* to face on your actual exam. We included those subjects on which they are *probably* going to test you.

Although copies of past exams are not released, we were able to piece together a fairly complete picture of the forthcoming exam.

A principal source of information was our analysis of official announcements going back several years.

Critical comparison of these announcements, particularly the sample questions, revealed the testing trend; foretold the important subjects, and those that are likely to recur.

In making up the Tests we predict for your exam, great care was exercised to prepare questions having just the difficulty level you'll encounter on your exam. Not easier; not harder, but just what you may expect.

The various subjects expected on your exam are represented by separate Tests. Each Test has just about the number of questions you may find on the actual exam. And each Test is timed accordingly.

The questions on each Test are represented exactly on the special Answer Sheet provided. Mark your answers on this sheet. It's just about the way you'll have to do it on the real exam.

As a result you have an Examination which simulates the real one closely enough to provide you with important training.

Proceed through the entire exam without pausing after each Test. Remember that you are taking this Exam under actual battle conditions, and therefore you do not stop until told to do so by the proctor.

Certainly you should not lose time by trying to mark each Test as you complete it. You'll be able to score yourself fairly when time is up for the entire Exam.

Correct answers for all the questions in all the Tests of this Exam appear at the end of the Exam.

Don't cheat yourself by looking at these answers while taking the Exam. They are to be compared with your own answers *after* the time limit is up.

ANALYSIS AND TIMETABLE: VERISIMILAR EXAMINATION I.

This table is both an analysis of the exam that follows and a priceless preview of the actual test. Look it over carefully and use it well. Since it lists both subjects and times, it points up not only what to study, but also how much time to spend on each topic. Making the most of your study time adds valuable points to your examination score.

SUBJECT TESTED	Time Allowed	SUBJECT TESTED	Time Allowed
WRITING SKILLS		SCIENCE	
Spelling	5 min.	Interpretation of Science	60 min.
English Grammar and Usage	15 min.	Readings	
Effectiveness of Expression	15 min.	Science Information	30 min.
Logic and Organization	10 min.		
		READING SKILLS	
		Interpretation of Literary	70 min.
		Materials	
SOCIAL STUDIES		Interpretation of Prose	20 min.
Interpretation of Social	60 min.		
Studies Readings		MATHEMATICS	
Social Studies Knowledge	30 min.	General Mathematical Ability	40 min.
		Graph Interpretation	5 min.

ANSWER SHEET FOR VERISIMILAR EXAMINATION I.

TEST I. SPELLING

TEST II. ENGLISH GRAMMAR AND USAGE

TEST III. EFFECTIVENESS OF EXPRESSION

TEST IV. LOGIC AND ORGANIZATION

TEST V. INTERPRETATION OF SOCIAL STUDIES READINGS

TEST VI. SOCIAL STUDIES KNOWLEDGE

31

TEST VII. INTERPRETATION OF SCIENCE READINGS

This is an answer grid with numbered items 1 through 32, each having bubbles labeled 1 2 3 4 5.

TEST VIII. SCIENCE INFORMATION

This is an answer grid with numbered items 1 through 32, each having bubbles labeled A B C D E.

TEST IX. INTERPRETATION OF LITERARY MATERIALS

This is an answer grid with numbered items 1 through 48, each having bubbles labeled 1 2 3 4 5.

TEST X. INTERPRETATION OF PROSE

This is an answer grid with numbered items 1 through 16, each having bubbles labeled A B C D E.

TEST XI. GENERAL MATHEMATICAL ABILITY

This is an answer grid with numbered items 1 through 32, each having bubbles labeled 1 2 3 4 5.

TEST XII. GRAPH INTERPRETATION

This is an answer grid with numbered items 1 through 8, each having bubbles labeled A B C D E.

TEAR OUT ALONG THIS LINE AND MARK YOUR ANSWERS AS INSTRUCTED IN THE TEXT

PART I. THE WRITING SKILLS TEST

TIME: 45 Minutes. 78 Questions.

TEST I. SPELLING

TIME: 5 Minutes. 12 Questions.

DIRECTIONS: In each of the following groups one word may be misspelled. For each group select the one misspelled word. If you think all four words in the group are correctly spelled, mark the answer 5.

1. 1) disfigurement
    2) essential
    3) ocasion
    4) operator
    5) none misspelled

2   1) asembly
    2) journalist
    3) restrain
    4) funniest
    5) none misspelled

3. 1) chemical
    2) busily
    3) joyous
    4) build
    5) none misspelled

4. 1) penalty
    2) sufficeint
    3) occasionally
    4) exile
    5) none misspelled

5. 1) inseption
    2) representation
    3) conscience
    4) perspired
    5) none misspelled

6. 1) obeying
    2) tactical
    3) inspiration
    4) incedintal
    5) none misspelled

7. 1) sleight
    2) insistent
    3) complesity
    4) proclamation
    5) none misspelled

8. 1) physics
    2) consumne
    3) coating
    4) chiefly
    5) none misspelled

9. 1) proceeded
    2) graphic
    3) decision
    4) importence
    5) none misspelled

10. 1) weathered
    2) steadyness
    3) fertilized
    4) field
    5) none misspelled

11. 1) admittance
    2) recipient
    3) argue
    4) pennetration
    5) none misspelled

12. 1) grammer
    2) oddity
    3) selvedge
    4) nineteenth
    5) none misspelled

END OF TEST

Go on to do the following Test in this Examination, just as you would be expected to do on the actual exam. You will find correct answers for the entire Examination following the last question. Check your answers carefully after you have completed the whole Examination.

S/3060

TEST II. ENGLISH GRAMMAR AND USAGE

TIME: 15 Minutes. 25 Questions.

DIRECTIONS: This is a test of standard written English. The rules may differ from everyday spoken English. Many of the following sentences contain grammar, usage, word choice, and idiom that would be incorrect in written composition. Some sentences are correct. No sentence has more than one error. Any error in a sentence will be underlined and lettered; all other parts of the sentence are correct and cannot be changed. If the sentence has an error, choose the underlined part that is incorrect, and mark that letter on your answer sheet. If there is no error, mark E on your answer sheet.

Correct and explanatory answers are provided at the end of the exam. After you have completed the entire exam, read the explanations carefully. They'll reinforce your strengths and pinpoint your weaknesses so that you know just what to study to raise your score.

1. She <u>gathered up</u> all the apples and, <u>putting</u> them in a basket, <u>carries</u>
        A   B   C
    them <u>into</u> the house. <u>No error.</u>
         D   E

2. There was a time when <u>the Arctic</u> was unknown territory; now scien-
                              A
    tists <u>manning</u> research stations there and the mysteries of <u>this frozen</u>
           B   C
    continent <u>are being</u> revealed. <u>No error.</u>
               D   E

3. Mary was so <u>disinterested</u> in the <u>baseball</u> game <u>that</u> she <u>yawned</u>
                    A   B   C   D
    unashamedly. <u>No error.</u>
                   E

4. Nigeria, a <u>former</u> British colony and <u>protectorate</u>, <u>it is</u> now a member
                A   B   C
    <u>of</u> the British Commonwealth of Nations. <u>No error.</u>
    D   E

5. John Kennedy <u>effected</u> many <u>executive reforms</u> during the <u>tragically</u>
                     A   B   C
    numbered years he served as <u>President</u> of the United States. <u>No error.</u>
                                  D   E

6. Tuck a dish towel over the potatoes to keep them warm and to absorb
   <u>A</u>   <u>B</u>
   steam so they will not become soggily. No error.
        <u>C</u>   <u>D</u>   <u>E</u>

7. The symbolic <u>interpretation</u> of <u>visions</u> <u>renders</u> the interpreter <u>a</u> pro-
                    A   B   C   D
   phet. <u>No error.</u>
          E

8. I loved the <u>morning</u> and <u>should go</u> down the dirt road with my tin <u>pail</u>
                   A   B
   <u>toward</u> the stream where there were <u>gooseberries.</u> <u>No error.</u>
       C   D   E

9. <u>Their</u> are <u>still</u> people who say <u>that it has</u> never been <u>proved</u> that our
      A   B   C   D
   earth is round. <u>No error.</u>
                     E

10. Until <u>nearly</u> the end of the century, the <u>workshop</u> was the <u>quite most</u>
            A   B   C
    popular supplier of madonnas for the <u>public patrons</u> of Florence. <u>No</u>
                                             D
    error.
    E

11. Harvard's football <u>captain</u> could <u>tackle, block</u> and pass better than <u>any</u>
          A   B   C   D
    on the team. <u>No error.</u>
                    E

12. <u>A round and white sun</u> <u>emblazoned</u> at the <u>summit</u> <u>of the sky.</u> <u>No error.</u>
              A   B   C   D   E

13. When the <u>members</u> of the committee are <u>at odds</u> and they\are in the
                A   B
    process of offering <u>their</u> resignations, problems become <u>insoluble.</u> <u>No</u>
                           C   D
    error.
    E

14. <u>One</u> of the requirements <u>was</u> a course in <u>sixteenth</u> <u>centuries</u> literature.
       A   B   C   D
    No error.
       E

15. Further acquaintance with the memoir's of Elizabeth Barrett Brown-
      A   B
   ing and Robert Browning enables us to appreciate the depth of influ-
                    C   D
   ence that two people of talent can have on each other. No error.
                                                      E

16. When my commanding officer first looked up from his desk, he took
              A   B   C
   Lieutenant Baxter to be I. No error.
                D   E

17. Though he had awakened before the birds began to twitter, he laid in
                A   B   C
   bed until long after the sun had arisen. No error.
                        D   E

18. As she dived off the springboard, she was horrified to see that the
          A   B
   water was drained from the pool the night before. No error.
            C   D   E

19. When the reviews appeared in the morning papers, we saw that every-
                                 A
   body but Carolyn and him had received averse notices. No error.
    B   C   D   E

20. The ceremonies were opened by a drum and bugle corps of Chinese
                  A   B
   school children parading up the street in colorful uniforms. No error.
     C   D   E

21. Irregardless of what other members of the board say, I must repeat, as
     A   B
   chairman, that these are the facts concerning the requirements for the
     C   D
   position. No error.
       E

22. There would have been no objections to him joining the party if he had
            A   B
   been amenable to the plans of the group. No error.
    C   D   E

23. I was <u>not at all surprised</u> <u>to hear that</u> Wallace Dolan, one of the <u>most</u>
          A   B

<u>promising</u> young men in the <u>community won</u> the poetry contest. <u>No</u>
 C   D

<u>error.</u>
 E

24. Little Mary, in her <u>naiveté</u>, explained her absence from school with an
       A

<u>incredulous</u> tale <u>in which</u> she played the role of the <u>daring heroine.</u> <u>No</u>
  B   C   D

<u>error.</u>
 E

25. The mourners <u>past</u> <u>solemnly</u> through the great doors of the cathedral <u>in</u>
     A B

<u>keeping with</u> the low <u>tones</u> of the organ. <u>No error.</u>
  C   D   E

END OF TEST

*Go on to do the following Test in this Examination, just as you would be
expected to do on the actual exam.*

TEST III. EFFECTIVENESS OF EXPRESSION

TIME: 15 Minutes. 25 Questions.

DIRECTIONS: A sentence is given, of which one part is under-lined. Following the sentence are five choices. The first (A) choice simply repeats the underlined part. Then you have four additional choices which suggest other ways to express the underlined part of the original sentence. If you think that the underlined part is cor-rect as it stands, write the answer A. If you believe that the under-lined part is incorrect, select from the other choices (B or C or D or E) whichever you think is correct. Grammar, sentence struc-ture, word usage, and punctuation are to be considered in your decision. The original meaning of the sentence must be retained.

1. Society does not *submerge itself under nature* but rather takes control of nature and utilizes its power.

    (A) submerge itself under nature
    (B) submit over itself to nature
    (C) submit itself to nature
    (D) submerge itself under the presence of nature
    (E) submerge itself to the presence of nature

2. We were amazed to see the *amount of people waiting in line to see Santa Claus*.

    (A) amount of people waiting in line to see Santa Claus
    (B) number of people waiting in line to see Santa Claus
    (C) amount of persons waiting in line to see Santa Claus
    (D) amount of people waiting to see Santa Claus
    (E) amount of people waiting in line to Santa Claus

3. The ebullient chairman *was neither in favor of or opposed to the plan*.

    (A) was neither in favor of or opposed to the plan
    (B) was not in favor of or opposed to the plan
    (C) was neither in favor of the plan or opposed to it
    (D) was neither in favor of the plan or opposed to the plan
    (E) was neither in favor of nor opposed to the plan

4. He will probably continue *to go astray among* his shallow and nebu-lous ideals.

    (A) to go astray among
    (B) to wander askance and astray among
    (C) to go askance amonst
    (D) to wander askance amongst
    (E) to wander askance and astray between

5. Of the two candidates, I think *he is the best suited.*
    (A) he is the best suited.
    (B) that he is the best suited.
    (C) he is suited best.
    (D) he is the better suited.
    (E) he's the best suited.

6. Every pupil in the whole class understood the assignment *except I* and that is why I feel so stupid.
    (A) except I
    (B) excepting I
    (C) outside of me
    (D) excepting me
    (E) except me

7. Geronimo, American Indian chief of the Apache tribe, lived to *the age of eighty years old*.
    (A) the age of eighty years old
    (B) the old and ripe age of eighty
    (C) the ripe old age of eighty years old
    (D) be eighty years old
    (E) be a ripe and eighty years old

8. European film distributors originated the art of "dubbing"—*the substitution of lip-synchronized translations* in foreign languages for the original soundtrack voices.
    (A) —the substitution of lip-synchronized translations
    (B) ; the substitution of lip-synchronized translations
    (C) —the substitutions of translations synchronized by the lips
    (D) , the lip-synchronized substitution of translations
    (E) . The substitution of lip-synchronized translations

9. At dawn in the morning of the fiftieth day at sea, *a glimpse of the islands was caught*.
    (A) a glimpse of the islands was caught
    (B) a glimpse of the islands were caught
    (C) we caught a glimpse of the islands
    (D) the islands were caught a glimpse of
    (E) we caught a glimpse of the islands's view

10. *Finally and at long last* the old dog opened both eyes and sniffed the morning air.
    (A) Finally and at long last
    (B) Finally
    (C) But at long last
    (D) So finally
    (E) Yet at long last

11. Sitting around the bonfire on the beach, *mystery stories were told by each of us*.
    (A) mystery stories were told by each of us
    (B) mystery stories were told by all of us
    (C) each of us told mystery stories
    (D) stories of mystery were told by each of us
    (E) there were told mystery stories by each of us

12. "When my husband *will come home*, I'll tell him you called," the housewife sighed into the phone.

    (A) will come home,
    (B) will come home
    (C) will have come home,
    (D) comes home,
    (E) has come home,

13. The pseudonym of Emily Bronte, *the author of Wuthering Heights*, was Ellis Bell.

    (A) , the author of *Wuthering Heights,*
    (B) , the authoress of *Wuthering Heights,*
    (C) (she happens to have written *Wuthering Heights)*
    (D) (she happens to be the authoress of *Wuthering Heights)*
    (E) (she wrote *Wuthering Heights* all by herself)

14. *After he graduated school*, he joined the army.

    (A) After he graduated school,
    (B) After he was graduated from school,
    (C) When he graduated school,
    (D) After he graduated school
    (E) As he was graduated from school,

15. This book has been *laying here for weeks*.

    (A) laying here for weeks
    (B) laying here weeks
    (C) laying down here for weeks
    (D) lieing here for weeks
    (E) lying here for weeks

16. Successful revolution from *the utmost first to the utmost last* is a movement calling for the iron unity of all members.

    (A) the utmost first to the utmost last
    (B) the very first to the very last
    (C) the utmost
    (D) first to last
    (E) the first to the last

17. Inspecting her son's report card, *his mother noted* that he had made good grades in Latin and history.

    (A) his mother noted
    (B) it was noted by his mother
    (C) his mother had noted
    (D) a notation was made by his mother
    (E) Robert's mother noted

18. The loud noise of subway trains and trolley cars *frighten people from the country*.

    (A) frighten people from the country
    (B) frighten country people
    (C) frighten persons from the country
    (D) frightens country people
    (E) frighten people who come from the country

19. George Washington Carver was *an American botanicalist* around the turn of the eighteenth century.
    - (A) an American botanicalist
    - (B) a American botanicalist
    - (C) an American botanist
    - (D) a botanicalist in America
    - (E) a botanist of the United States of America

20. I think they, *as a rule, are much more conniving than us*.
    - (A) as a rule, are much more conniving than us
    - (B) as a rule are much more conniving than us
    - (C) as a rule, are much more conniving than we
    - (D) as a rule; are much more conniving than us
    - (E) are, as a rule, much more conniving than us

21. The old man told *Mary and I* many stories about his childhood in the hills of Scotland.
    - (A) Mary and I
    - (B) Mary and me
    - (C) me and Mary
    - (D) I and Mary
    - (E) Mary together with me

22. The soldiers who left Valley Forge with General Washington *sure enough had won* a spiritual victory.
    - (A) sure enough had won
    - (B) sure had won
    - (C) sure must have won
    - (D) had won
    - (E) will have won

23. I feel *as though I was being borne* bodily through the air.
    - (A) as though I was being borne
    - (B) as though I was being born
    - (C) like I was being borne
    - (D) like as though I was being borne
    - (E) as though I am being borne

24. The wild game hunter stalked the tiger slowly, cautiously, *and in a silent manner*.
    - (A) and in a silent manner
    - (B) and silently
    - (C) and by acting silent
    - (D) and also used silence
    - (E) and in silence

25. Each class, of about an hour's duration, *listened attentively while* the basic principles were explained.
    - (A) listened attentively while
    - (B) listened at attention while
    - (C) listened attentively all the while
    - (D) could listen attentively while
    - (E) listened attentively whereas

END OF TEST

TEST IV. LOGIC AND ORGANIZATION

TIME: 10 Minutes. 16 Questions.

DIRECTIONS: This test consists of brief passages in which each sentence is numbered. Following each passage are questions which refer to the numbered sentences in the passage. Answer each question by choosing the best alternative (A,B,C,D, or E) and blacken the space corresponding to your choice on the Answer Sheet provided.

Explanations of the key points behind these questions appear with the answers at the end of this test. The explanatory answers provide just the help you need to strengthen your ability to master this type of question.

[1]Regarding physical changes that have been and are now taking place on the surface of the earth. [2]The sea and its shores have been the scene of the greatest stability. [3]The dry land has seen the rise, the decline, and even the disappearance and vanishing, of vast hordes of various types and forms. [4]This has occurred within comparatively recent times, geologically talking. [5]But life in the sea is today virtuously what it was when many of the forms now extinct on land had not yet been evolved. [6]Many of these have a marked capacity to cling closely to the substratum. [7]Also, it may be parenthetically stated here, the marine habitat has been biologically the most important in the evolution and development. [8]Its rhythmic influence can still be traced in those animals whose ancestors have long since left the water. [9]Irregardless it is now generally held as an accepted fact that the shore area of an ancient sea was the birthplace of life.

1. What should be done with sentence 1?

    (A) It should be left as it is.
    (B) It should be joined to the beginning of sentence 3 with *since*.
    (C) It should be joined to the beginning of sentence 2.
    (D) It should be joined to the end of sentence 5.
    (E) The part after *place* should be omitted.

2. Sentence 3 would be best if the words *disappearance and vanishing* were

    (A) left as they are
    (B) changed to *disappearing and vanish*
    (C) changed to *disppearance and banishment*
    (D) changed to *disappearance*
    (E) changed to *appearance*

3. In sentence 4, the word *talking* is best

    (A) left as it is
    (B) changed to *chattering*
    (C) changed to *chatting*
    (D) changed to *conversing*
    (E) changed to *speaking*

4. The word *virtuously* in sentence 5 should be

    (A) left as it is
    (B) changed to *virtuous*
    (C) changed to *virtually*
    (D) changed to *vertigo*
    (E) changed to *arduously*

5. What should be done with sentence 6?

    (A) It should be left as it is.
    (B) It should be omitted entirely.
    (C) It should be placed at the end of the passage.
    (D) It should be placed at the beginning of the passage.
    (E) It should be placed after the first sentence.

6. Sentence 7 would be clearest if

    (A) it were left as it is
    (B) it began with *Thusly and also*
    (C) it began *This is the way of things also*
    (D) the part after *important* were omitted
    (E) it ended with *of life on this planet*

7. Sentence 8 is best placed

    (A) where it is now
    (B) before sentence 1
    (C) after sentence 1
    (D) after sentence 10
    (E) after sentence 9

8. Sentence 9 should begin

    (A) as it begins now
    (B) with *For it is*
    (C) with *Thereafter it was*
    (D) with *Thus it shall always be*
    (E) with *Forever it will be*

[1]If Johnny cannot write, one of the reasons may be conditioning based on speed rather then respect for the creative process. [2]Speed is neither a valid test of competence in writing. [3]It makes for murkiness, glibness and disorganization. [4]It takes the good looks out of the language. [5]It rules out respect for the reflective, contemplative and searching thought that should precede expression. [6]It runs along side of the word-by-word and line-by-line reworking that enables a piece to be finely knit. [7]This is not to minimize the value of genuine facility. [8]Withall years of practice, a man may be able to put down words swiftly and expertly. [9]But it is the same kind of swiftness that enables a cellist, after having invested years of effort, to negotiate an intricate passage from Haydn. [10]Speed writing is for stenographers and court reporters, not for anyone who wants to use language with precision and distinction.

9. Sentence 1 would be best if
   (A) it were left as it is
   (B) *rather then* were changed to *rather than*
   (C) *respect for* were changed to *respectful of*
   (D) *creative* were changed to *creation*
   (E) *may be* were changed to *might be*

10. What should be done with sentence 2?
    (A) It should be left as it is.
    (B) The phrase *and a proper preparation for* should be added after *of*.
    (C) The phrase *either a prosperous preparation for* should be added after *of*.
    (D) The phrase *nor a proper preparation for* should be added after *of*
    (E) It should be omitted entirely.

11. In sentence 4, the words *good looks* should be
    (A) left as they are
    (B) changed to *gorgeously*
    (C) changed to *lovely*
    (D) changed to *bounty*
    (E) changed to *beauty*

12. Sentence 5 would be most improved if
    (A) *contemplative and searching* were omitted
    (B) *respect* were changed to *respects*
    (C) *rules out* were changed to *rules over*
    (D) *reflective, contemplative and searching* were omitted.
    (E) *precede* were changed to *proceed*

13. The phrase *along side of* in sentence 6 should be
    (A) left as it is
    (B) changed to *counter to*
    (C) changed to *along beside of*
    (D) changed to *countering of*
    (E) changed to *around*

14. Sentence 8 should begin
    (A) the way it begins now
    (B) with *Understanding years*
    (C) with *Always years*
    (D) with *Years practicing*
    (E) with *With years*

15. Sentence 9 is best placed
    (A) where it is now
    (B) before sentence 1
    (C) after sentence 1
    (D) after sentence 9
    (E) after sentence 12

16. If the passage is to be divided into two paragraphs, the second paragraph should begin with
    (A) sentence 3
    (B) sentence 4
    (C) sentence 7
    (D) sentence 9
    (E) sentence 10

END OF PART

PART II. THE SOCIAL STUDIES TEST

TIME: 90 Minutes. 50 Questions.

TEST V. INTERPRETATION OF SOCIAL STUDIES READINGS

TIME: 60 Minutes. 34 Questions.

This test consists of short reading passages from social science sources followed by multiple-choice questions based on the passages. You may refer to the passages as often as necessary in answering the questions. Although the test requires a background knowledge of social science, it is also intended to test your ability to get at the meaning of what you read.

It does not matter if you have forgotten some details and facts you once knew, as long as you remember the important social science ideas and can use them to help you interpret what you read.

DIRECTIONS: Read each passage to get the general idea. Then reread the passage more carefully to answer the questions based on the passage. For each question read all choices carefully. Then select the answer you consider correct or most nearly correct. Blacken the answer space corresponding to your best choice, just as you would do on the actual examination.

Each state shall appoint, in such manner as the legislature thereof may direct, a number of electors, equal to the whole number of Senators and Representatives to which the state may be entitled in the Congress. But no Senator or Representative, or person holding an office of trust or profit under the United States, shall be appointed an elector.

The electors shall meet in their respective states, and vote by ballot for President and Vice President. They shall make distinct lists of all persons voted for as President, and of all persons voted for as Vice President, and of the number of votes for each, which lists they shall sign and certify, and transmit sealed to the seat of the government of the United States, directed to the President of the Senate. The President of the Senate shall, in the presence of the Senate and House of Representatives, open all certificates and the votes shall then be counted; the person having the greatest number of votes for the President shall be the President, if such number be a majority of the whole number of electors appointed; and if no person have such majority, then from the persons having the highest numbers not exceeding three on the list of those voted for as President, the House of Representatives shall choose immediately, by ballot, the President. But in choosing the President, the votes shall be taken by states, the representation from each state having one vote; a quorum for this purpose shall consist of a member or members from two-thirds of the states, and a majority of all the states shall be necessary to make a choice.

1. The people who actually elect the President are known as the

   1) electorate.
   2) congress.
   3) majority.
   4) electoral college.

2. If a state has 27 members in the House of Representatives its total number of electoral votes would be
   1) 27.
   2) 29.
   3) 54.
   4) dependent on the number of people who voted in the state.

3. The person responsible for opening the electoral ballots is the

1) President of the Congress.
2) Vice President of the United States.
3) majority leader of the House.
4) Chairman of the election committee.

4. Of the following, which one could qualify as an elector?

1) A United States Senator
2) The Secretary of State of the U.S.
3) The Governor of N.Y. State
4) The Vice President of the U.S.

5. If a presidential candidate receives 45 percent of the popular vote

1) he cannot become the next President.
2) he may still win the election.
3) he will receive 45 percent of the electoral vote.
4) his election would be dependent on the Senate.

6. The votes of the electors must be sent to

1) Washington, D.C.
2) the state capitols.
3) the headquarters of the leading candidates.
4) the Republican and Democratic party chairmen.

7. The system of electing the President of the United States is

1) direct representation.
2) indirect representation.
3) majority representation.
4) quorum representation.

8. People who consider this plan "undemocratic" would likely rather see the President elected by

1) the electoral college.
2) congress.
3) popular vote.
4) written ballot.

9. According to the electoral system, the number of people who may be nominated to become President

1) allows for only a two-party system.
2) is limited to three people.
3) must be the candidate of a majority party.
4) is not limited to a set number.

Much has been written in the past about the needless deaths, the untold suffering and the economic destruction brought on by war. While all of this may certainly be true there is another cause where millions of human lives are wasted, billions of dollars spent and suffering as widespread as that of in war is occurring. This cause is disease, a cause which continues in times of peace as well as in times of war.

At a time when we are sending men to the moon, splitting the atom and exploring the last physical outposts of the earth, why is science not being better used to end this problem? One of the reasons is that the money to be made is in the curative end of medicine and not in preventive medicine. The average citizen does not really become concerned about a disease until he is personally involved, and then prevention is too late. Another big problem arises out of the fact that medicine is still largely individualistic and so such items as financial status and geographical location have an almost controlling effect on treatment.

If medicine is to make the progress necessary to end the needless waste of humanity now going on the effort must be cooperative. Since the private sector of medicine is understandably concerned first with profit, we cannot expect research on prevention to be properly conducted by private corporations. Those private organizations concerned with preventive medicine do not get enough in donations from a basically unconcerned society for them to carry the burden. The only remaining way for a cooperative attack to be made is for government to become actively and widely involved in supporting scientific research and development in this field.

10. Which of the following points of view is closest to that of the author?

   1) War is not as dangerous to our society as disease.
   2) Science is unable to find cures for common disease because of lack of concern.
   3) Government must place stricter controls on those who deal with public health.
   4) A national plan of cooperation would do much to improve our health.

11. Those people who might be against the program proposed by the author feel so mainly because

   1) the cost would be too great.
   2) government could place controls on private enterprise.
   3) it would limit research in curative areas.
   4) doctors and hospitals could not be included.

12. Which of the following would be the best example of preventive medicine?

   1) immunization   3) pain killers
   2) bandages   4) operations

DIRECTIONS: Mark questions 13-17 using the following answers:
   1) The author probably would agree.
   2) The author probably would disagree.
   3) It is impossible to tell if the author would agree or disagree.

13. The means of distributing medicine is more advanced than other medical developments.

14. Too much money is being spent on curative medicine.

15. Freedom from government controls is necessary if medicine is to continue to make progress.

16. Modern public health services are adequate for the health needs of our nation.

17. Capitalism and the profit motive will not lead to improvements in medicine.

SPEAKER NUMBER ONE

Many schemes have been devised to strengthen our economy and raise our standard of living. The irony of the situation is that nothing needs to be done. The best method of improving our economy is to rely on human instinct: on the ability of people to pay to have their own wants satisfied and to profit from satisfying the wants of others. The Constitution guarantees the pursuit of happiness, but many of the collectivist schemes try to guarantee happiness itself by the use of handouts. We do not need a super-government dictating what both management and labor need to do to be productive.

If we go back to the old-fashioned competition upon which the country has prospered we will find that the cost of government will drop and we can lower taxes. This will increase the amount of money available for investment and production. The increase in activity is what our economy needs to prosper and give all our people a chance to strive for happiness.

SPEAKER NUMBER TWO

We all agree that it is important to improve our economy and to end the social and economic crises resulting from a faltering economy. Past experience has shown that unless definite controls are placed upon concentrations of economic power the economy will not properly regulate itself. We must not allow monopolies to destroy the freedom of the marketplace. We must protect the purchasing power of our senior citizens through continuation of social security programs. We must control the flow of currency through the use of a graduated income tax. In short, we must use those tools which the science of economics has developed to control our own economy. Only in that way will everyone be able to share in its growth.

18. What was the most basic difference between the two points of view presented here?

   1) whether or not our economy should be made stronger
   2) how much government control should be used in our economic system
   3) whether or not we should have competition in our economy
   4) the place of democracy in our economic system

19. How would Speaker Number One feel about strengthening the Sherman Anti-Trust Act?

   1) He would like it because it strengthens competition.
   2) He would agree only if it proved to be constitutional.
   3) He would oppose it as unnecessary government interference.
   4) He would oppose it because he feels it is undemocratic.

20. How would Speaker Number One feel about strikes which bring industry to a halt?

   1) He would want them settled through government-sponsored mediation.
   2) He would feel strikes should not be allowed if they interrupt our economy.
   3) It is a natural way for differences to be worked out between labor and management.
   4) Strikes are the result of large companies refusing to treat their workers fairly.

21. Which of the following taxes would Speaker Number Two most likely oppose?

   1) a Corporate Tax
   2) an Inheritance Tax
   3) an Income Tax
   4) a Sales Tax

DIRECTIONS: Mark the next five items according to the following:

   1) if both speakers would agree
   2) if neither speaker would agree
   3) if only Speaker Number One would agree
   4) if only Speaker Number Two would agree

22. The control of interest rates should be handled by an impartial committee of private citizens.

23. The more complex our economy becomes the more necessary government controls become.

24. Only government control of all aspects of our economy can protect everyone's interests.

25. Ups and downs in business cycles are not desirable.

26. Monopolies are harmful to the continuing growth of our economy.

The cultures of China two thousand years ago were somewhat similar to those of the ancient Mayans. Both cultures had made great advances in medicine and religion. They both had highly developed social and political structures. Today China remains one of the great cultures of the world, while the Mayan culture has all but disappeared. Yet, during those twenty centuries the geographical conditions around which these cultures developed have not shown much change. It does not seem that their cultures were dependent upon geography for their existence.

There are many cases where peoples living in the same geographical area have developed different cultures. Athens and Sparta, both city states in the same peninsula, are a case in point. Sparta was known for its disciplined soldiers and its slavery. There was little interest in improving business, government or the arts. Although Athens also conquered many smaller communities, they absorbed the inhabitants and made them citizens. They were one of the most forward of people and welcomed change and improvement. Since they both developed under similar geographic conditions it does not seem that social heritage is caused or retarded by climate.

27. As used in this passage the word "culture" means

1) the habits that individuals have developed.
2) those traits for which a society is known.
3) the everyday conduct that shows a good heritage.
4) those understandings and actions which a formal education can teach.

28. Judging from this passage, the Spartan education was concerned primarily with

1) broadening understandings.
2) business and commerce.
3) developing arts and crafts.
4) the military.

29. Judging from this passage, the Athenian education was concerned primarily with

1) broadening understandings.
2) business and commerce.
3) developing arts and crafts.
4) the military.

30. The best title for the passage would be

1) Ancient Cultures and How They Developed.
2) The Differences Between Chinese and Other Ancient Cultures.
3) The Uncreative Role of Geography on Social Development.
4) How Climate Causes Social Development.

31. Both Athens and Sparta were parts of what is now known as

1) Asia.
2) Greece.
3) China.
4) Persia.

32. The author's main purpose is to

1) try to prove a theory of cultural determination.
2) try to discredit a theory of cultural determination.
3) describe some of the ancient culture patterns.
4) show how culture patterns develop.

33. The Mayan civilization developed in what is now

1) Central America.
2) Asia.
3) Africa.
4) Europe.

34. The author's attitude toward a theory that cultures are caused by geographical conditions is one of

1) agreement.
2) disagreement.
3) impartiality.
4) a lack of sufficient knowledge.

END OF TEST

TEST VI. SOCIAL STUDIES KNOWLEDGE

TIME: 30 Minutes. 16 Questions.

DIRECTIONS: For each of the following questions, select the choice which best answers the question or completes the statement.

1. In which of the following ways did the frontier influence American foreign policy?
   (A) it led to foreign alliances
   (B) it led to the development of a policy of isolation
   (C) it encouraged trade agreements with European nations
   (D) it stimulated interest in hemispheric cooperation.

2. The Conservation Movement in the United States of America got its major impetus from Theodore Roosevelt and
   (A) James G. Blaine
   (B) Gifford Pinchot
   (C) Elihu Root
   (D) William Jennings Bryan.

3. Which one of the following has changed from being a part of our "unwritten constitution" to being a part of our written Constitution?
   (A) limiting the number of terms of the presidency
   (B) formation of political parties
   (C) senatorial courtesy
   (D) provision for a President's cabinet.

4. In which one of the following paired events did the first event lead directly to the second?
   (A) bombing of Pearl Harbor—annexing of Hawaii by the United States of America
   (B) purchase of Alaska—cold war with Russia
   (C) failure of the League of Nations—World War I
   (D) assassination of President Garfield—passage of the Pendleton Civil Service Act.

5. Which item below pairs an outstanding American with a noteworthy contribution made by him?
   (A) Benjamin Franklin—leader of the Minutemen
   (B) Samuel Adams—Writs of Assistance
   (C) Haym Solomon—raising of funds to help Washington
   (D) James Otis—Boston Tea Party.

6. The defeat of the Persians by the Greek states may be likened in its effect on future history to the
   (A) defeat of the Moors at Tours
   (B) defeat of the Britons by Roman Legions
   (C) capture of the Philippines by the Japanese
   (D) rout of the Russians at Tannenberg Forest.

7. Which of the following events is the result of the three others mentioned?
   (A) the formation of the Holy Alliance
   (B) pronouncement of the Monroe Doctrine
   (C) revolts in Spanish territories in the Americas
   (D) Russian claims on the Pacific Coast of North America.

8. The stated purposes of UNESCO include all of the following *except*
   (A) to promote collaboration among nations to further human rights
   (B) to achieve freedom for all people without distinction of race, sex, language, or religion
   (C) to aid in the attainment by all peoples of the highest level of health
   (D) to use education, science, and culture to further justice throughout the world.

9. "Dependent on outside sources for iron ore, recent development of hydro-electric power, large consumption of wheat products, rainfall scarce in southern portion"—this description applies chiefly to
   (A) West Germany   (B) Italy
   (C) Sweden   (D) Soviet Union.

10. The difference between the rigorous climate of Labrador and the relatively salubrious climate of Norway is due chiefly to
    (A) prevailing winds and latitude
    (B) latitude and altitude
    (C) altitude and atmospheric pressure
    (D) water currents and prevailing winds.

11. Of the following persons elected to government office, the one whose term of office is longest is
    (A) governor in most states
    (B) president of the United States
    (C) United States senator
    (D) United States congressman.

12. The Constitution of the United States denies to the States the power to
    (A) make treaties   (B) establish courts
    (C) levy taxes   (D) borrow money.

13. "During the decade 1840-1850, they left their native land in large numbers because of the famine and came to the United States to settle for the greater part, in seaboard cities." This description best applies to emigrants from
    (A) Germany   (B) Ireland
    (C) Russia   (D) Italy.

14. Prior to the adoption of the Constitution, we, as a nation, were governed by the
    (A) Mayflower Compact
    (B) Declaration of Independence
    (C) Articles of Confederation
    (D) Fundamental Orders.

15. The chronological order in which the United States acquired the following four possessions is
    (A) Virgin Island, Alaska, Puerto Rico, Panama Canal Zone
    (B) Alaska, Panama Canal Zone, Puerto Rico, Virgin Islands
    (C) Alaska, Puerto Rico, Panama Canal Zone, Virgin Islands
    (D) Virgin Islands, Panama Canal Zone, Puerto Rico, Alaska.

16. A private citizen, slandered by a senator or congressman on the floor of the Senate or House
    (A) can compel an investigation into the charges by the Department of Justice
    (B) can compel a hearing before a tribunal chosen by a Federal District Court
    (C) cannot obtain legal redress because of a law of Congress
    (D) cannot obtain legal redress because of the immunity granted to the office-holder by the Federal Constitution.

END OF PART

Go on to the following Test in the next Part of this Examination, just as you would be expected to do on the actual exam. If you have any available time use it to make sure that you have marked your Answer Sheet properly for this Part. Correct Answers for all Parts of this Exam follow the last question. Derive your scores only after completing the entire Exam.

PART III. THE SCIENCE TEST

TIME: 90 Minutes. 55 Questions.

TEST VII. INTERPRETATION OF SCIENCE READINGS

TIME: 60 Minutes. 29 Questions.

This test places a special emphasis on scientific vocabulary and ability to pay close attention to detail and logic. It consists of a selection of passages from the field of natural sciences at the high school level and a number of questions testing a person's ability to comprehend and to interpret the content of each passage.

DIRECTIONS: *Below each of the following passages of natural science reading material you will find one or more incomplete statements about the passage. Select the words or expressions that most satisfactorily complete each statement in accordance with the meaning of the paragraph.*

Correct answers for these questions appear at the end of this examination, together with the answers to all the other tests.

The pituitary gland is a small gland, about the size of an acorn or cherry, which lies at the base of the brain. It was once thought to be the "master gland" of the body, since its secretions have appeared to influence the activity of all other endocrine glands. However, it is now known that other glands, especially the thyroid and adrenal glands, influence the pituitary gland.

The pituitary gland consists of two lobes: anterior and posterior. The anterior lobe secretes several different hormones. One of these, the somatotropic, or growth hormone, regulates the growth of the skeleton. If an oversecretion of this hormone occurs during the growing years, tremendous height may be attained. This condition is called giantism. Circus giants over 8 feet tall, weighing over 300 pounds and wearing size 30 shoes, are examples of this disorder. If the oversecretion occurs during adult life, the bones of the face and hands thicken, since they cannot grow in length. However, the organs and the soft tissues enlarge tremendously. This condition is known as acromegaly. Victims of this disorder have greatly enlarged jawbones, noses, hands and fingers.

Somatotropic hormone deficiency results in a pituitary dwarf, or midget. These individuals are perfectly proportioned "men in miniature." They are quite different from the thyroid dwarf in that they have normal intelligence.

Another hormone secretion of the anterior lobe of the pituitary gland, the gonadotropic hormone, influences the development of the reproductive organs. It also influences hormone secretion of the ovaries and testes. The gonadotropic hormone, together with the sex hormones, causes the sweeping changes which occur during adolescence, when the child becomes an adult.

Other secretions of the anterior lobe of the pituitary gland include hormones which stimulate the secretion of milk in the mammary glands (lactogenic hormone), the activity of the thyroid gland (thyrotropic hormone) and the parathyrotropic glands (parathyrotropic hormone).

ACTH is a secretion of the anterior lobe of the pituitary gland and stimulates the outer part, or cortex, of the adrenal glands. The adrenals, in turn, secrete hormones which are responsible for the control of certain phases of carbohydrate, fat and protein metabolism and the salt and water balance in the body.

The adrenal cortex also yields hormones which control the production of some types of white corpuscles and the structure of connective tissue. When ACTH is given to patients with leukemia a dramatic but, unfortunately, temporary improvement occurs. Its effects in arthritis treatment are somewhat more encouraging. Good results in the treatment of asthma and other allergies with ACTH have been reported. Even though ACTH may not give permanent cures to these diseases, its use may lead the way to the discovery of their actual causes.

The posterior lobe of the pituitary gland produces two hormones: (1) pitressin, which helps regulate the amount of water in the blood and the blood pressure; and (2) pitocin which stimulates smooth muscles. It is administered following childbirth to cause contraction of the muscles of the uterus, thus preventing blood loss.

1. A hormone is

   1) an important gland.
   2) a type of medicine.
   3) a chemical secretion.
   4) a type of germ.

2. Which of the following is not a secretion of the pituitary gland?

   1) somatotropic
   2) gonadotropic
   3) pitocin
   4) adrenalin

3. Which of the following will affect the age at which a person reaches puberty?

   1) sex hormones
   2) gonadotropic
   3) lactogenic
   4) none of the above

4. Cretinism results in a stunted body and a dull, stupid mentality. It is caused by a defect in which gland?

   1) pituitary
   2) adrenal
   3) thyroid
   4) parathyroid

5. The circus giant of over 8 feet in height probably got too much somatotropic hormone when he was

   1) an infant.
   2) a teenager.
   3) a young adult.
   4) an older adult.

6. A cure for leukemia is

   1) a pituitary hormone.
   2) an adrenal hormone.
   3) a cortexial hormone.
   4) none of the above.

7. A cow who failed to have enough lactogenic hormone would probably

   1) fail to become pregnant.
   2) become overly fat.
   3) lose a lot of weight.
   4) not give any milk.

8. A person admitted to a hospital with swollen limbs due to too much water in the joints may be suffering from

   1) improper functioning of the adrenal gland.
   2) overactivity of the pituitary gland.
   3) underactivity of the pituitary gland.
   4) too much pitressin.

9. The hormones of the pituitary gland reach the necessary parts of the body by means of

   1) a special duct system.
   2) the respiratory system.
   3) the nervous system.
   4) blood vessels.

The total force resulting from the pressure of the atmosphere inward on our bodies is many tons. You might wonder why we do not feel just a bit crushed. That is because this pressure is balanced by an equal and opposite pressure inside our bodies. For the same reason, deep-sea fish escape being crushed by the water, even though they live a mile under the surface where the pressure is more than a ton per square inch. It is said that such fish may blow up and burst if they are brought to the surface too quickly. When we go up in an airplane or an elevator, or travel rapidly up a mountain where the pressure is reduced, we ourselves are aware of a mild sample of this bursting sensation. Our ears seem to close up; then they "pop" as the excess pressure on the eardrum is released. Aviators know that repeated swallowing helps to equalize the pressure inside and outside the body when one is rising or falling rapidly.

Since most gauges measure pressure above atmospheric, and we ourselves are normally unconscious of air pressure, how do we know that the atmosphere really does exert a pressure of 15 (more precisely, 14.7) pounds to the square inch? A barometer solves the problem. The most accurate form is the mercury barometer, which may be constructed in the following fashion: A glass tube, about 3 feet in length and sealed at one end, is filled to overflowing with mercury. Keeping the open end sealed with a finger, the tube is inverted and the open end immersed to a depth of an inch or two in a vessel containing mercury. When the finger is removed, the mercury will not run out of the inverted tube, but the level of the mercury will remain about 30 inches (76 centimeters) above the level in the open vessel. There is a vacuum above the mercury in the closed end of the tube; and the mercury column is supported by atmospheric pressure pushing down on the mercury outside. In other words, a column of mercury 30 inches high produces a pressure of nearly 15 pounds per square inch at its base, just balancing the atmospheric pressure.

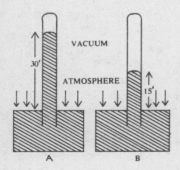

The mercury barometer. (A) A column of mercury 30 inches high is supported by normal atmospheric pressure at sea level. (B) At an altitude of 3 1/2 miles the pressure is only half as great.

The height of the mercury column in the barometer tube will vary as the pressure of the atmosphere varies. Thus, the barometer reading falls as we ascend above sea level. On top of a mountain a mile high, the pressure of the atmosphere is only about 12 pounds per square inch, and the height of the mercury column in the barometer is about 26 inches.

Since the air pressure varies with altitude, barometers serve as altimeters to measure the height above sea level. But a tube containing a mercury column 30 inches high is not a convenient instrument to carry around, and for approximate measurements the mercury barometer is usually replaced by one of the aneroid type. This is simply a flat, evacuated pill box with thin flexible metal walls. Through a system of levers, the motion of the walls is greatly amplified and transmitted to a pointer. As the pressure changes, the walls of the box move in and out, and the pointer moves over a scale that reads either in inches or centimeters by comparison with the mercury barometer. If the instrument is to be used as an altimeter, the scale may read directly in feet elevation. Airplanes are equipped with aneroid barometers of this type.

The barometer is not entirely satisfactory as an altimeter, because the pressure of the atmosphere changes continually, even at sea level. Changes in air pressure frequently predict a change in the weather. Hence, the very feature that makes a barometer unreliable as an altimeter makes it valuable in forecasting the weather. As you undoubtedly know, a falling barometer often indicates an approaching storm; a rising barometer, clear weather. Incidentally, many devices commonly sold as barometers measure only temperature, humidity or some other factor that is not reliable in the prediction of weather changes.

10. Which of the following best describes a barometer?

    1) a tube of mercury 30 inches high
    2) a device which measures atmospheric pressure
    3) an instrument used to predict changes in weather
    4) a gauge which tells the height above sea level

11. What is one of the most common uses of a barometer?

    1) to measure the weight of liquids under varying conditions
    2) to measure the weight of gases under varying conditions
    3) to measure the weight of air at varying heights
    4) to measure the volume of air at varying heights

12. What is the reason mercury is used in a barometer instead of alcohol?
    1) Mercury is heavier than alcohol.
    2) Mercury will not freeze as fast as alcohol.
    3) Alcohol will evaporate faster than mercury.
    4) Alcohol is more dangerous than mercury.

13. Why does the tube used in a mercury barometer have to be at least 30 inches tall?

    1) A shorter tube would be less accurate.
    2) A shorter tube would be more difficult to read.
    3) Mercury weighs 30 lbs. per cubic inch.
    4) Air pressure at sea level will raise a column of mercury 30 inches.

14. Which of the following is the most important reason that mercury rises in a barometer?

    1) It is a liquid.
    2) A vacuum is kept at the top of the tube.
    3) The pressure of the air pushes the mercury up.
    4) The heat causes the mercury to expand.

15. If the atmospheric pressure could be increased to 30 lbs./sq. inch, the height of mercury in a tube would be

    1) 120 inches.   3) 30 inches.
    2) 60 inches.   4) 15 inches.

16. An aneroid barometer can be used as an altimeter because

    1) it is relatively easy to read and to transport.
    2) atmospheric pressure decreases at a known amount as height increases.
    3) it can measure the height of an airplane above ground level.
    4) it is not affected by heat and cold.

17. Why does the inside of an aneroid barometer contain a vacuum?

    1) A vacuum allows the air pressure to move the walls of the container.
    2) A vacuum makes it easier for the dial to move up and down.
    3) A vacuum will amplify any motion caused by air pressure.
    4) A vacuum allows the instrument to be made lighter and more portable.

18. When a person goes to a higher altitude at a rapid rate the pressure on the ear drum is the result of

    1) the decrease in oxygen as height increases.
    2) the air pressure inside the ear being greater than the inside pressure.
    3) the air pressure outside the ear being greater than the inside pressure.
    4) a vacuum developing inside the ear as the air becomes thinner.

19. If the tube of one mercury barometer is 1/8 inch in diameter and the tube of another is 1/4 inch in diameter, the difference in the height of the mercury at sea level will be

    1) 60 inches.   3) 15 inches.
    2) 30 inches.   4) 0 inches.

20. If the atmospheric pressure always remains constant at a given altitude, a barometer could not be used
    1) to forecast weather.
    2) as an altimeter.
    3) to measure atmospheric pressure.
    4) to indicate a drop in air pressure as the height above sea level increases.

The ear is indeed a remarkable mechanism; and it is so complicated that its operation is none too fully understood. Certainly it is extremely sensitive. At the threshold of audibility, the power requirement is inconceivably tiny. If all people in the United States were listening simultaneously to a whisper (20 decibels), the power received by all of their eardrums together would total only a few millionths of a watt—far less than the flying power generated by a single mosquito.

The ear is remarkable, too, for its ability to distinguish between various pitches and qualities of sounds. In the range of frequencies where the ear is most sensitive (500 to 4,000 vibrations per second), changes in pitch of 0.3 percent can be detected. Thus if a singer trying to reach the octave above middle C (512 vibrations per second) is off key by only 1.5 vibrations per second, the fault can be detected.

The normal ear can respond to frequencies ranging from 20 to 20,000 vibrations per second. In this range it is estimated that the ear can distinguish more than half a million separate pure tones; that is 500,000 differences in frequency, loudness or both.

The range varies somewhat from ear to ear and becomes considerably shorter for low-intensity sounds. Above the audible range, air vibrations similar to sound are called supersonic vibrations. These may be generated and detected by electrical devices and are useful for several purposes—especially in depth sounding at sea. The time for the waves to travel from the generator to the bottom of the ocean and back again is a measure of the depth. Supersonic vibrations apparently can be heard by some animals—notably bats. It is believed that bats are guided during flight, not by sight, but by supersonic "sounds" which they emit and reflect back to their ears from various surfaces and obstacles.

The versatility of the ear becomes more wonderful when you remember that many different qualities of sound can be distinguished, even though the many sources (as, for example, the instruments in an orchestra) are all emitting the same fundamental frequency at the same time.

Then, too, we are able to tell approximately the direction from which sound comes. This is possible primarily because we have two ears instead of one. The sound arrives a split second later at one ear than at the other, and the brain by experience interprets this phase difference in terms of direction.

Besides detecting sound, a portion of the ear has another entirely different function: The semicircular canals enable us to maintain our equilibrium.

The mechanism by which the ear accomplishes all these tasks is very complicated and is to a great extent still a matter of speculation. It is easy enough to dissect the ear and see what is in it; it is another matter to find out what makes it work. The methods by which the physical response to sound is telegraphed to the brain along the auditory nerves, and the interpretation placed on these signals by the brain itself, are subjects far too complicated for us to discuss here.

The ear is divided into three parts: the outer ear, the middle ear and the inner ear. The outer ear consists of a canal closed at the inner end by a membrane, the eardrum. The middle ear contains a system of three bone levers, known as the hammer, the anvil and the stirrup. These bones serve to transmit the sound vibrations from the eardrum to the membrane-window covering the inner ear. The principal feature of the inner ear is the cochlea, a peculiar spiral bony enclosure that looks much like a snail shell. Contained in the cochlea is the vital organ of hearing, the basilar membrane, which is about 0.01 inch wide and, when uncoiled, is scarcely more than an inch in length.

Surrounding the basilar membrane is a liquid. The sound vibrations are transmitted to this liquid, and then, apparently, through the liquid a certain distance depending on the frequency. Lower frequencies are transmitted to the farther end of the basilar membrane; higher frequencies are able to penetrate only a short distance through the liquid. Along the basilar membrane are located the auditory nerve endings. When a particular portion of the basilar membrane is stimulated by the sound vibrations, the brain records the disturbance as a certain pitch. More vigorous oscillation is interpreted as a louder sound.

Go on to the next page

21. A dog might be able to hear a whistle that a human cannot hear because

   1) the human hears sounds of a higher frequency.
   2) the dog hears sounds of a higher frequency.
   3) the human hears sounds of a lower frequency.
   4) the dog hears sounds of a lower frequency.

22. It seems that ordinary sounds cause a wave-like vibration in
   1) the outer ear.
   2) the middle ear.
   3) the auditory nerves.
   4) all of the above.

23. Which of the following statements about hearing is true?

   1) All vibrations occur at frequencies of between 20 and 20,000 vibrations per second.
   2) Vibrations below 20 or 20,000 per second cannot be detected.
   3) All human beings can hear sounds if the vibrations are within a range of between 20 and 20,000 vibrations per second.
   4) The average human being cannot hear sounds below 20 or above 20,000 vibrations per second.

24. If a musical instrument had the ability to make a sound at 4,000 vibrations per second, most people would consider the sound was
   1) high pitched.
   2) medium pitched.
   3) low pitched.
   4) inaudible.

25. A sound coming from a person's left would
   1) hit the right ear first.
   2) hit the left ear first.
   3) hit both ears at the same time.
   4) none of the above.

26. Sounds get from the ear to the brain because the auditory nerve

   1) can vibrate faster than 20,000 times per second.
   2) vibrates between 20 and 20,000 times per second.
   3) filters out vibrations higher than 20,000 per second and lower than 20 per second.
   4) reacts to vibrations of between 20 and 20,000 per second.

27. Which of the following sounds would penetrate most deeply into the ear?

   1) a loud high pitched whistle
   2) the squeak of a fingernail on the blackboard
   3) a normal human voice
   4) a softly struck bass drum

28. Which of the following would cause the most vigorous vibration in a human ear?

   1) a supersonic vibration
   2) a police whistle
   3) a loud bass drum
   4) a shot from a cannon

29. The auditory nerve causes the brain to
   1) correctly hear sounds.
   2) correctly locate sounds.
   3) correctly interpret sounds.
   4) none of the above.

END OF TEST

Go on to do the following Test in this Examination, just as you would be expected to do on the actual exam. You will find correct answers for the entire Examination following the last question. Check your answers carefully after you have completed the whole Examination.

TEST VIII. SCIENCE INFORMATION

TIME: 30 Minutes. 26 Questions.

DIRECTIONS: *For each of the following questions, select the choice which best answers the question or completes the statement.*

Correct answers for these questions appear at the end of this examination, together with the answers to all the other tests.

1. Of the following electrical devices found in the home, the one which develops the highest voltage is the
   (A) electric broiler
   (B) radio tube
   (C) television picture tube
   (D) electric steam iron.

2. Most soluble food substances enter the blood stream
   (A) through the small intestine
   (B) through the duodenum
   (C) through the capillaries in the stomach
   (D) through the hepatic vein.

3. Of the following, the animal which is *not* a rodent is the
   (A) beaver   (B) guinea pig
   (C) rabbit   (D) skunk.

4. The "dark" side of the moon refers to the
   (A) craters into which no sunlight has ever reached
   (B) south pole of the moon's axis
   (C) hemisphere which has never reflected the sun's rays on the earth
   (D) moon itself, which is symbolically "dark" because no man has reached it.

5. Whenever possible, children should make simple devices in science rather than use ready-made commercial ones because
   (A) home-made devices are cheaper
   (B) there is learning and pleasure in construction

(C) home-made devices may work better
(D) each child can have his own apparatus.

6. Of the following, the one which is *not* characteristic of poison ivy is that it has
   (A) milky juice   (B) shiny leaves
   (C) three leaflet clusters (D) white berries.

7. Cholesterol is
   (A) a basic part of bone structure
   (B) an alcohol formed in the body
   (C) a substance found in blood
   (D) the cause of colitis.

8. Of the following, the one which most closely approximates the diameter of the moon is
   (A) 2,000 miles   (B) 8,000 miles
   (C) 186,000 miles   (D) 240,000 miles.

9. A man hears the echo from a mountain wall five seconds after he has shouted. Of the following, the one which most nearly expresses the distance of the man from the mountain is
   (A) five miles
   (B) one mile
   (C) nine hundred yards
   (D) 1100 feet.

10. Of the following, the one which is present in greatest amounts in the air we breathe is
    (A) carbon dioxide   (B) oxygen
    (C) water vapor   (D) nitrogen.

11. The vitamin which helps coagulation of the blood is

   (A) C   (B) D
   (C) E   (D) K

12. During what season is hail most likely to occur during thunderstorms?

   (A) fall   (B) winter
   (C) spring   (D) summer.

13. We can see only one side of the moon because the

   (A) earth rotates on its own axis
   (B) moon makes one rotation as it makes one revolution around the earth
   (C) moon has no refractive atmosphere
   (D) sun does not shine on the moon's unseen side.

14. Which of the following parts of the ear is partly responsible for maintaining body balance?

   (A) the middle ear
   (B) the semi-circular canals
   (C) the semi-lunar valves
   (D) the cochlea.

15. Which of the following birds would most probably *not* be found in a wooded area?

   (A) thrush   (B) barred owl
   (C) green heron   (D) towhee.

16. Research undertaken in connection with the International Geophysical Year resulted in all of the following finds *except* that

   (A) Anarctica is a solid land mass
   (B) there is more ice and snow on earth than previously estimated
   (C) there is a vast mineral-rich region in the bed of the Southeast Pacific
   (D) there is more radiation in near-by space than previously estimated.

17. The usual vector in the transmission to humans of rickettsial diseases is

   (A) birds   (B) rodents
   (C) arachnids   (D) insects.

18. Passive immunity to diphtheria may be achieved by taking an injection of

   (A) a vaccine   (B) a toxin
   (C) a toxoid   (D) an antitoxin.

19. Of the following, the only safe blood transfusion would be

   (A) Group A blood into a Group O person
   (B) Group B blood into a Group A person
   (C) Group O blood into a Group AB person
   (D) Group AB blood into a Group B person

20. Blood in the adult human body makes a complete circulation in about

   (A) 10 seconds   (B) 30 seconds
   (C) 1 minute   (D) 3 minutes.

21. The "pacemaker" of the heart is located in the

   (A) left auricle   (B) left ventricle
   (C) right auricle   (D) right ventricle.

22. The most active mixing of many digestive juices occurs in the

   (A) stomach   (B) duodenum
   (C) ileum   (D) jejunum.

23. Grasses are usually pollinated by

   (A) wind   (B) water
   (C) birds   (D) insects.

24. Of the following groups of plants, the one from which coal was largely formed is the

   (A) thallophytes   (B) bryophytes
   (C) pteridophytes (D) spermatophytes.

25. The water-conducting tissue in an angiosperm is

   (A) phloem   (B) xylem
   (C) pith   (D) cambium.

26. The functions of plant roots may normally include all of the following *except*

   (A) photosynthesis   (B) food storage
   (C) absorption   (D) support.

END OF PART

PART IV. THE READING SKILLS TEST

TIME: 90 Minutes. 55 Questions.

TEST IX. INTERPRETATION OF LITERARY MATERIALS

TIME: 70 Minutes. 43 Questions.

This test is based on a selection of passages, both prose and verse. The questions emphasize knowledge and special abilities not frequently needed in ordinary reading. The abilities to interpret figures of speech, to cope with unusual sentence structure and word meaning, and to recognize mood and purpose are often tested, as is an understanding of literary forms.

DIRECTIONS: Below each of the following passages of literature you will find one or more incomplete statements about the passage. Select the words or expressions that most satisfactorily complete each statement in accordance with the meaning of the paragraph.

Correct answers for these questions appear at the end of this examination, together with the answers to all the other tests.

I cannot see the wit of walking and talking at the same time. When I am in the country, I wish to
2 vegetate like the country. I am not for criticizing hedgerows and black cattle. I go out of town in order to
forget the town and all that is in it. There are those who for this purpose go to watering places and carry
4 the metropolis with them. I like more elbow-room and fewer incumbrances. I like solitude, when I give
myself up to it, for the sake of solitude; nor do I ask for a friend in my retreat to whom I may whisper
6 solitude is sweet.

1. In this passage the author is

1) complaining that most people talk too much.
2) explaining why he goes into the country.
3) trying to show that country living is not perfect.
4) saying that he does not like people.

2. Which of the following would the author consider a "watering place"? (line 3)

1) a lake
2) a library
3) a night club
4) any place where you can get a drink

3. The author goes into the country

1) to forget his problems.
2) because he hates city life.
3) for his health.
4) because that is where he works.

4. In the last two lines the author is saying that he

1) wishes his friends could learn to enjoy solitude with him.
2) is being forced to live in solitude without his friends.
3) doesn't like to be with people who talk loudly.
4) doesn't need to share solitude in order to enjoy it.

2   A sound at the window made him turn. It had begun to rain again. He looked dreamily at the large silver drops falling perpendicularly across the street light. He knew it was time for him to begin his trip out West.

4   The radio had been right, rain was general all over the state. It was falling on every part of the western valley, on the green covered hills, falling gently on the vineyards of Laurens and even farther
6 eastward falling into the dark mutinous Atlantic waves. It was falling, also, on every part of the small cemetery on the hill where Mary Spencer lay buried. It had soaked the crooked crosses and gravestones,
8 the iron fence and the barren trees. He listened and heard the rain falling gently throughout the earth and gently falling, like the descent of the Second Coming, upon the living and the dead.

5. The author is concerned here with

   1) actions.   3) thoughts.
   2) dreams.   4) facts.

6. The word "perpendicularly" in line (2) means

   1) slantwise.   3) at a 90° angle.
   2) softly.   4) heavily.

7. The sentence which begins "It was falling on every part of the western valley.............."
(lines 4– 5) is

   1) a quote from the radio forecast.
   2) the author's version of what the radio said.
   3) the beginning of a list of the wettest places of the state.
   4) the way the man pictured the rain falling.

8. "Mutinous Atlantic waves" (line 6) indicates they are

   1) continuous.
   2) defiant and dangerous.
   3) large and lumbering.
   4) peaceful and quiet.

9. The man is thinking about the rain mainly in connection with

   1) his trip.
   2) its beauty.
   3) a scientific curiosity.
   4) a feeling about life.

William Shakespeare was born at Stratford-on-Avon in this country; in whom three eminent poets
2 may seem in some sort to be compounded. Martial, in the warlike sound of his surname (whence some may conjecture him of military extraction) *Hasti-Vibrans*, or Shake-speare. Ovid, the most natural and
4 witty of all poets; and hence it was that Queen Elizabeth, coming into a grammar school, made this extemporary phrase,

6   "Persius a crab-staff, bawdy Martial, Ovid a fine wag."

8   Plautus, who was an exact comedian, yet never any scholar, as our Shakespeare (if alive) would confess himself. Add to all these, that though his genius generally was jocular, and inclining him to
10 festivity, yet he could (when so disposed) be solemn and serious, as appears by his tragedies; so that Heraclitus himself (I mean if secret and unseen) might afford to smile at his comediens, they were so
12 merry; and Democritus scarce forbear to sigh at his tragedies, they were so mournful.

He was an eminant instance of the truth of that rule, *"Poeta non fit sed nascitur"* (one is not made
14 but born a poet). Indeed his learning was very little; so that, as Cornish diamonds are not polished by any lapidary, but are pointed and smooth even as they are taken out of the earth, so nature itself was all the
16 art which was used upon him.

10. This passage would most probably appear in a

    1) seventeenth-century biography.
    2) twentieth-century newspaper.
    3) twentieth-century history text.
    4) modern movie review.

11. The article was apparently written in

    1) The United States.   3) Rome.
    2) England.   4) Greece.

12. In lines (2-3) "whence some may conjecture him of military extraction" indicates some people would think of Shakespeare as coming from a military family because of

    1) his military training.
    2) the military nature of his plays.
    3) his appearance.
    4) the sound of his name.

13. In lines (2-3) "compounded" most nearly means

    1) added to.
    2 made worse.
    3) combined.
    4) improved.

14. This author thought Shakespeare was

    1) very immodest.
    2) lacking in wit.
    3) not serious enough.
    4) very talented.

Hail to thee, blithe spirit!
      Bird thou never wert—
That from heaven or near it
      Pourest thy full heart
In profuse strains of unpremeditated art.

      Higher still and higher
From the earth thou springest,
      Like a cloud of fire;
The blue deep thou wingest,
And singing still dost soar, and soaring ever singest.

15. In this poem the author is writing about a

    1) bird.
    2) ghost.
    3) person.
    4) song.

16. "Unpremeditated" in line (5) means

    1) unskillful.
    2) unplanned.
    3) unknown.
    4) disrespectful.

17. The tone of this poem is

    1) cynical.
    2) serious.
    3) indifferent.
    4) romantic.

18. Line (8), "Like a cloud of fire," indicates the author thinks the subject of the poem is

    1) beautiful.
    2) dangerous.
    3) frightening.
    4) imaginary.

19. The word "art" in line (5) is a

    1) color.   3) odor.
    2) object.   4) sound.

20. The author of this poem probably

    1) believes in God.
    2) doubts that there is a God.
    3) thinks there is nothing beautiful in life.
    4) dislikes all animals.

2 Men in great places are thrice servants: servants of the sovereign or state; servants of fame; and servants of business. So as they have no freedom; neither in their persons, nor in their actions, nor in their times. It is a strange desire, to seek power and to lose liberty: or to seek power over others and to lose
4 power over a man's self. Certainly great persons had need to borrow other men's opinions, to think themselves happy; for if they judge by their own feeling, they cannot find it; but if they think with
6 themselves what other men think of them, and that other men would fain be as they are, then they are happy as it were by report; when perhaps they find the contrary within. For they are the first that find
8 their own griefs, though they be the last that find their own faults. In place there is license to do good and evil; whereof the latter is a curse: for in evil the best condition is not to will; the second, not to can. But
10 power to do good is the true and lawful end of aspiring. For good thoughts (though God accept them) yet towards men are little better than good dreams, except they be put in act; and that cannot be without
12 power and place; as the vantage and commanding ground.

21. The word "fain" (line 6) means

    1) gladly.
    2) never.
    3) dejectedly.
    4) painfully.

22. The word "license" (line 8) means

    1) legal right.
    2) religious command.
    3) formal permission.
    4) freedom.

23. The author of this article believes that for men who are great persons their own good intentions

    1) are what those below them need.
    2) are inspired by God through dreams.
    3) are all that God is interested in from them.
    4) are of almost no value unless they are carried out.

24. The author feels great men are

    1) only happy if they make others happy.
    2) only happy if they have great power.
    3) never really happy.
    4) usually outwardly unhappy.

25. According to this article, great men lose their freedom as a result of

    1) disobeying God.
    2) the circumstances surrounding their position.
    3) mistreating those under them.
    4) being defeated by others seeking their position.

26. The phrase "and that cannot be without power and place; as the vantage and commanding ground" (lines 11–12) means

    1) a great person wants only power and the chance to command.
    2) power has its place but only when giving commands.
    3) power and position are necessary in order to carry out good plans.
    4) good thoughts and ideas are often ruined by power and position.

	CREON:	Fellow citizens, having learned that Oedipus the king lays dire
2		charges against me, I am here, indignant. If, in the present
		troubles, he thinks that he has suffered from me, by word or
4		deed, aught that tends to harm, in truth I crave not my full term
		of years, when I must bear such blame as this. The wrong of this
6		rumor touches me not in one point alone, but has the largest scope,
		if I am to be called a traitor in the city, a traitor, too, by thee and
8		by my friends.
	CHORUS:	Nay, but this taunt came under stress, perchance of anger, rather
10		than from the purpose of the heart.
	CREON:	And the saying was uttered, that my counsels won the seer to utter
12		his falsehoods?
	CHORUS:	Such things were said—I know not with what meaning.
14	CREON:	And was this charge laid against me with steady eyes and steady mind?
	CHORUS:	I know not; I see not what my masters do: but here comes our lord
16		forth from the house.

27. From this passage we know that Creon

1) is plotting against the King.
2) is helping to defend the King.
3) was in charge of the King's court.
4) was being accused of doing something wrong.

28. At this time Creon felt very

1) happy.   3) angry.
2) sorry.   4) sad.

29. Creon said that if he was found to be wrong he would

1) not want to live.
2) willingly accept a jail term.
3) flee the country.
4) ask for the King's pardon.

30. Creon said that the King was a

1) dangerous man.
2) liar.
3) cruel man.
4) traitor.

31. When the King spoke of Creon he did so

1) with deep regret.
2) out of anger.
3) in a spirit of revenge.
4) in a way that was unknown.

32. The word "seer" (line 11) refers to

1) the truth.   3) the King.
2) Creon's ability.   4) the Chorus.

33. In lines (7–8) Creon shows he is concerned about

1) which one of his friends betrayed him.
2) what his friends will think of him.
3) how to get out of the city.
4) whether or not other people will become implicated.

34. From the last line we know that the next person to come on stage is

1) Creon's friend.
2) Oedipus.
3) the King's soldier.
4) a priest.

Who drives the horses of the sun
2 Shall lord it but a day;
Better the lowly deed were done,
4 And kept the humble way.

The rust will find the sword of fame,
6 The dust will hide the crown;
Ay, none shall nail so high his name
8 Time will not tear it down.

The happiest heart that ever beat
10 Was in some quiet breast
That found the common daylight sweet,
12 And left to Heaven the rest.

35. The mood of the poem is one of

1) distrust.
2) ambition.
3) contentment.
4) disappointment.

36. The words "rust" and "dust" in the second verse refer to

1) mistakes.
2) danger.
3) evil.
4) time.

37. "Who drives the horses of the sun . . ." (line 1) refers to

1) God.
2) a person who has become important.
3) an unknown Greek hero.
4) a farmer.

38. The purpose of the second verse is to remind the reader that time

1) heals all wounds.
2) causes people to forget.
3) should not be wasted.
4) waits for no man.

39. The third verse suggests that happiness is

1) doing one's best.
2) only found in heaven.
3) remembering your own childhood.
4) accepting one's role in life.

	ALGER:	Did you hear what I was playing, Lane?
2	LANE:	I didn't think it polite to listen, sir.
4	ALGER:	I'm sorry for that, for your sake. I don't play accurately—anyone can play accurately—but I play with wonderful expression. As far as the piano is concerned, sentiment is my forte. I keep science for Life.
6	LANE:	Yes, sir.
8	ALGER:	And, speaking of the science of Life, have you got the cucumber sandwiches cut for Lady Bracknell?
	LANE:	Yes, sir. (Hands them on a salver.)
10 12	ALGER:	Oh! by the way, Lane, I see from the book that on Thursday night, when Lord Shoreman and Mr. Worthing were dining with me, eight bottles of champagne are entered as having been consumed.
	LANE:	Yes, sir; eight bottles and a pint.
14	ALGER:	Why is it that at a bachelor's establishment the servants invariably drink the champagne? I ask merely for information.
16	LANE:	I attribute it to the superior quality of the wine, sir. I have often observed that in married households the champagne is rarely of a first-rate brand.
18	ALGER:	Good heavens! Is marriage so demoralizing as that?
20	LANE:	I believe it is a very pleasant state, sir. I have had very little experience of it myself up to the present. I have only been married once. That was in consequence of a misunderstanding between myself and a young person.
22	ALGER:	I don't know that I am much interested in your family life, Lane.
	LANE:	No, sir; it is not a very interesting subject. I never think of it myself.
24	ALGER:	Very natural, I am sure. That will do, Lane, thank you.
	LANE:	Thank you, sir.
26 28	ALGER:	Lane's views on marriage seem somewhat lax. Really, if the lower orders don't set us a good example, what on earth is the use of them? They seem, as a class, to have absolutely no sense of moral responsibility.

40. We may infer from this scene that Alger is

1) kind.
2) modest.
3) conceited.
4) angry.

41. Alger's interest in Lane is

1) real concern.
2) a pretense of being concerned.
3) amusement at his comments.
4) only in what Lane can do for him.

42. Alger and Lane are together because

1) Lane works for Alger.
2) Alger works for Lane.
3) they are partners.
4) they both work for the same boss.

43. From this scene we can assume that Alger is a

1) bachelor.
2) musician.
3) politician.
4) philosopher.

END OF TEST

TEST X. INTERPRETATION OF PROSE

TIME: **20** Minutes. 12 Questions.

DIRECTIONS: Below each of the following passages of literature you will find one or more incomplete statements about the passage. Select the words or expressions that most satisfactorily complete each statement in accordance with the meaning of the paragraph.

Correct answers for these questions appear at the end of this examination, together with the answers to all the other tests.

Reading Passage

To keep clear of concealment, to keep clear of the need of concealment, to do nothing which he might not do out on the middle of Boston Common at noonday—I cannot say how more and more it seems to me to be the glory of a young man's life. It is an awful hour when the first necessity of hiding anything comes. The whole life is different thenceforth. When there are questions to be feared and eyes to be avoided and subjects which must not be touched, the the bloom of life is gone. Put off that day as long as possible. Put it off forever if you can.

1. The title below that best expresses the ideas of this passage is
   (A) a time for concealment
   (B) noonday on Boston Common
   (C) a code for living
   (D) penalties for procrastination
   (E) youth vs. age

2. The author recommends
   (A) being aboveboard
   (B) living for the present
   (C) avoiding necessity
   (D) living by example
   (E) being careful in discussion.

Reading Passage

English folk singers have adopted a conventional method of singing. During the performance the eyes are closed, the head is upraised, and a rigid expression of countenance is maintained until the song is finished. A short pause follows the conclusion, and then the singer relaxes his attitude and repeats in his ordinary voice the last line of the song, or its title. This is the invariable ritual on formal occasions. It does not proceed from any lack of appreciation. The English peasant is by nature a shy man and undemonstrative, and on ceremonious occasions, as when he is singing before an audience, he becomes very nervous and restrained, and welcomes the shelter afforded by convention.

3. The title below that best expresses the ideas of this passage is
   (A) country music festivals
   (B) traditional music
   (C) a changing ritual of song
   (D) an unappreciative audience
   (E) a helpful custom.

4. The English folk singer has adopted a conventional method of singing chiefly because of his
   (A) matter-of-fact
   (B) reserved nature
   (C) relaxed attitude
   (D) depressing
   (E) ironic

5. The tone of this passage is best described as
   (A) matter-of-fact   (B) pleading
   (C) argumentative   (D) depressing
   (E) ironic.

Reading Passage

Today, in a time of great confusion and fierce disagreement, and also a time of great opportunity for all who are disposed to make their profit of that confusion, we who use words have a heavy responsibility. We need illimitable boldness in seeking of truth, and great generosity of feeling and imagination in our approach to our task of giving it concrete and moving expression. But we need the greatest care in our choice of the words we use that they may first of all be accurate and fair, that they may meet the classic American test of "justice to all."

6. The title below that best expresses the ideas of this passage is
   (A) taking advantage of confusion
   (B) the need for disagreement
   (C) truth-seeking aspect of words
   (D) confusion and limitation of words
   (E) a duty of writers and speakers.

7. The writer believes that
   (A) most Americans lack imagination
   (B) writers must be fearless
   (C) all Americans stand for justice for all
   (D) "Justice for All" is a classic American essay
   (E) a majority wish to make a profit from confusion.

Reading Passage

Had Leonardo da Vinci seen the plain evidence of upward winds—the evidence of flying leaves and soaring birds—the air age might have begun in his time, and the airplane would have developed along with the sailing vessel. For these upward winds also explain the sailing of gliders. A glider is nothing but a wood-and-fabric replica of a hawk; there is nothing in it that Leonardo could not have designed, built and flown. It used to be that motorless airplanes could fly only over carefully selected sites, where a steep hillside faced a strong wind and deflected it upward. But today, with no new equipment but a clear mental image of these upward winds, men can fly without motors for hundreds of miles across country, even across flat plains, without machine power of any kind on these updrafts.

8. The title below that best expresses the ideas of this passage is:

   (A) updrafts
   (B) a wood and fabric bird
   (C) da Vinci's invention
   (D) the power of imagination
   (E) the limitation of gliders.

9. Gliders can soar only

   (A) over plateaus
   (B) by riding the winds

   (C) for short distances
   (D) in mountainous country
   (E) over carefully surveyed areas.

10. The author's treatment of his material may best be described as

    (A) quaintly humorous
    (B) completely carefree
    (C) predominantly factual
    (D) utterly pessimistic
    (E) bitterly sarcastic.

Reading Passage

Despite the many categories of the historian, there are only two ages of man. The first age, the age from the beginnings of recorded time to the present, is the age of the cave man. It is the age of war. It is today. The second age, still only a prospect, is the age of civilized man. The test of civilized man will be represented by his ability to use his inventiveness for his own good by substituting world law for world anarchy. That second age is still within the reach of the individual in our time. It is not a part-time job, however. It calls for total awareness, total commitment.

11. The title below that best expresses the ideas of this passage is

    (A) the historian at work
    (B) the dangers of all-out war
    (C) the power of world anarchy
    (D) mankind on the threshold
    (E) the decline of civilization.

12. The author's attitude toward the possibility of man's reaching an age of civilization is one of

    (A) limited hope
    (B) complete despair
    (C) marked uncertainty
    (D) complacency
    (E) anger.

END OF PART

Go on to the following Test in the next Part of this Examination, just as you would be expected to do on the actual exam. If you have any available time use it to make sure that you have marked your Answer Sheet properly for this Part. Correct Answers for all Parts of this Exam follow the last question. Derive your scores only after completing the entire Exam.

PART V. THE MATHEMATICS TEST

TIME: 45 Minutes. 36 Questions.

TEST XI. GENERAL MATHEMATICAL ABILITY

TIME: 40 Minutes. 30 Questions.

This test covers topics taught at both the elementary and high school level. Some topics which may be covered are definitions, ratios, percent, decimals, fractions, mathematical symbols, indirect measurement, interpretation of graphs and tables, scale drawings, approximate computation, and units of measurement. Some questions are based on techniques taught in elementary algebra and plane geometry courses. Questions frequently test knowledge of mathematical principles and stress their applications through the performance of mathematical operations and manipulations. The ability to express practical problems in mathematical terms is frequently tested. The test may also include one or two questions based on the concepts of modern mathematics.

Each question in this test has four or five suggested answers numbered (1), (2), (3), (4) or (5). On your answer sheet, blacken the numbered space that is the same as the answer you have selected for each question.

Do not make any marks on the test itself. It is best to work out the solution to each question on a sheet of blank paper before looking at the suggested answers. This will help prevent you from being misled by answers that at first glance may look correct.

EXAMPLE

What is the cost of 7 loaves of bread at 40¢ a loaf?

1) $2.80
2) $2.40
3) $2.00
4) $1.40
5) $1.20

1 2 3 4 5

(The 1 has been marked on the answer sheet because the correct answer is $2.80.)

Correct answers for these questions appear at the end of this examination, together with the answers to all the other tests.

70

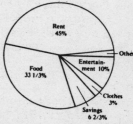

1. Find the sum: 1/2+1/3+3/5+7/10.

1) 12/20
2) 1-5/30
3) 2-2/15
4) 3-1/5
5) 4-1/2

2. X dollars invested at 4% simple interest for 2 years will yield which of the following total interest?

1) .01X
2) .04X
3) .06X
4) .08X
5) .16X

3. Find the sum of 18, −6, −8, 2, −10, 4.

1) 4
2) 0
3) −2
4) −6
5) −8

4. Last year a car dealer sold 125 cars for approximately $3,000 each. How much did the car dealer take in on the sale of these cars?

1) $100,000
2) $125,000
3) $300,000
4) $375,000
5) $475,000

5. What is the next number in the following series?

.25   1.50   2.75

1) 0
2) 1
3) 2
4) 3
5) 4

6. Line AB is parallel to line CD, E, F, G, H and I are vertices of different triangles. CD is divided into 5 equal segments as shown. Which triangle has the greatest area?

1) E
2) F
3) G
4) H
5) I

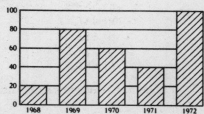

7. The above figure represents how a man spends his weekly salary. What percentage is for other expenses?

1) 1%
2) 2%
3) 3%
4) 4%
5) 5%

Questions 8–10 are based on the bar graph below.

The bar graph represents the percentage of students passing the GED test between 1968 and 1972.

8. The ratio of the percent passing in 1972 to the percent passing in 1968 is

1) 1:5.
2) 1:4.
3) 2:3.
4) 4:1
5) 5:1.

9. 60,000 students took the test in 1970. How many students failed the test?

1) 12,000
2) 24,000
3) 36,000
4) 48,000
5) 60,000

10. Between what two years was the ratio of passing students 1:3?

1) 1968:1970
2) 1969:1971
3) 1970:1972
4) 1968:1971
5) 1970:1971

Questions 11–12 are based on the graph below.

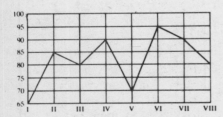

The graph shows the mark for a student's math tests.

11. What was the average for the eight tests?

1) 80
2) 81.2
3) 81.5
4) 81.7
5) 81.8

12. Which 3 tests would yield the lowest average?

1) I II III
2) II III IV
3) III IV V
4) IV V VI
5) V VI VII

13. Two-thirds of a class are girls. If there are 9 boys in the class, how many girls are there?

1) 3
3) 6
3) 18
4) 27
5) 54

14. Which of the following percentages is equivalent to 7/3?

1) 233 1/3%
2) 100 2/3%
3) 90%
4) 70%
5) 30%

15. Simplify the expression x −[2−(x+3)+1].

1) X
2) 2X
3) X−1
4) 2X−1
5) 2X+3

16. The dimensions of a rectangular solid are 2, 3 and 4 inches. If the dimensions are doubled, the ratio between the original solid and the new solid is

1) 1:2.
2) 2:1.
3) 1:8.
4) 2:5.
5) 3:4.

Go on to the next page

17. If x = .2 and y = (1−x), what is the value of 2xy?

1) .32
2) 3.2
3) 1.6
4) 32
5) none of these

18. A salesman receives 33-1/3% commission on all sales. If his commission is $90.00, what were his sales?

1) $90
2) $180
3) $200
4) $270
5) $360

19. Find the square root of .81.

1) .0009
2) .009
3) .09
4) .9
5) none of these

20. During a 10-day museum exhibit the number of spectators doubled each day. If the exhibit opened on Tuesday and the attendance on Friday of the same week was 800, what was the attendance on opening day?

1) 800
2) 400
3) 200
4) 100
5) 50

21. During the past week Mr. White spent the following time studying for the math test:

Mon: 2 hrs. 15 min.
Tues: 3 hrs.
Wed: 45 min.
Thurs: 1 hr. 40 min.
Fri: 2 hrs. 20 min.

What was the average time spent studying math per day?

1) 2 hrs.
2) 4 hrs.
3) 6 hrs.
4) 8 hrs.
5) 10 hrs.

22. Which of these fractions is greater than 1/5?

1) 3/13
2) 8/26
3) 12/39
4) all of these
5) none of these

23. What is the next number in the series 4, 10, 22, 46?

1) 80
2) 94
3) 100
4) 104
5) 110

24. When compared by the square yard, which is a better buy: One yard of carpet A which is 24" wide and sells for $6, or one yard of carpet B which is 36" wide and sells for $9.00?

1) carpet A is $3 less per sq. yd.
2) carpet B is $3 less per sq. yd.
3) carpets A and B are the same price per sq. yard.
4) carpet B is $1 more per sq. yd.
5) impossible to determine

25. The number 83.42 contains two significant digits. How should it be written?

1) 83
2) 83.0
3) 83.00
4) .40
5) .42

Go on to the next page

26. The interest on a bank loan for 36 months is $180. If the loan is paid off in 18 months the interest is only $90. What percent of savings is there in paying the loan during the shorter period?

   1) 100%
   2) 75%
   3) 50%
   4) 25%
   5) 10%

27. One-half of the class is absent on Monday. One-third of those present did not do their homework. Of those present, what fraction of the entire class have their homework?

   1) 2/3
   2) 1/2
   3) 1/3
   4) 1/6
   5) none of these

28. A gas tank is 1/8 full. After ten gallons of gas have been put into the tank it is now 3/4 full. What is the capacity of the gas tank?

   1) 8 gal.
   2) 10 gal.
   3) 12 gal.
   4) 14 gal.
   5) 16 gal.

29. Three neighbors, A, B and C, each have a back yard pool with dimensions as follows:

   A—length 20 ft. width 10 ft. depth 5 ft.
   B—length 15 ft. width 15 ft. depth 5 ft.
   C—length 25 ft. width 5 ft. depth 5 ft.

   Which of the following is necessarily true when the pools are filled to capacity?

   1) pool A holds the most water
   2) pool B holds the most water
   3) pool C holds the most water
   4) all pools hold the same amount of water
   5) none of these

30. What percent of 45 is 90?

   1) 200
   2) 100
   3) 50
   4) 25
   5) none of these

END OF TEST

Go on to do the following Test in this Examination, just as you would be expected to do on the actual exam. You will find correct answers for the entire Examination following the last question. Check your answers carefully after you have completed the whole Examination.

TEST XII. GRAPH INTERPRETATION

TIME: 5 Minutes. 6 Questions.

DIRECTIONS: Read each test question carefully. Each one refers to the following graph, and is to be answered solely on that basis. Select the best answer among the given choices and blacken the proper space on the answer sheet.

Explanations of the key points behind these questions appear with the answers at the end of this test. The explanatory answers provide just the help you need to strengthen your ability to master this type of question.

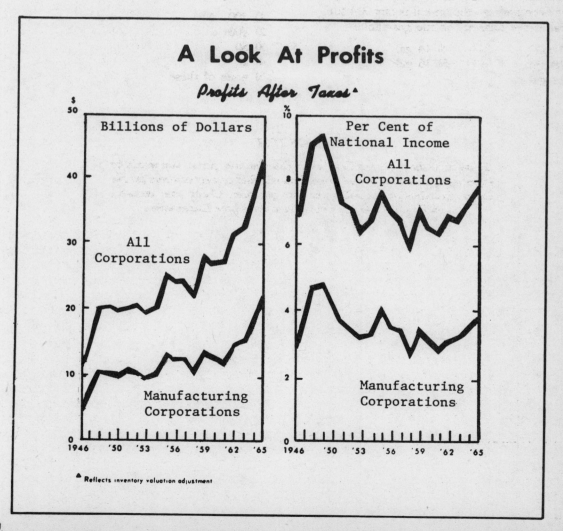

S1131

1. In 1958, the profits of *non*-manufacturing corporations was

   (A) $8 billion   (B) $10 billion
   (C) $12 billion   (D) $14 billion
         (E) none of the above

2. The percents of the National Income for all corporations and for manufacturing corporations show a paired rise or a paired fall in every year *except*

   (A) 1950-1951   (B) 1953-1954
   (C) 1956-1957   (D) 1961-1962
         (E) 1962-1963

3. What was the National Income in 1946?

   (A) $10 billion   (B) $17 billion
   (C) $60 billion   (D) $170 billion
         (E) $6 trillion

4. Between 1948 and 1952, the National Income

   (A) more than doubled
   (B) increased, but did not double
   (C) decreased by more than 50%

(D) decreased by less than 50%
(E) remained practically the same

5. The *average* income of a manufacturing corporation in 1959

   (A) was more than twice that of a non-manufacturing corporation in 1948
   (B) was greater than that of any corporation in 1946
   (C) was less than 4% of the National Income in that year
   (D) was approximately $14 billion
   (E) was greater than 4% of the National Income in that year

6. As the number of corporations doubled between 1946 and 1948, how was the average profit affected?

   (A) It remained fairly constant.
   (B) It rose by about 50%.
   (C) It rose by about 100%.
   (D) It fell by about 50%.
   (E) It fell by about 100%.

END OF EXAMINATION

Now that you have completed the last Test in this Examination, use your available time to make sure that you have written in your answers correctly on the Answer Sheet. Then, after your time is up, check your answers with the Correct Answers we have provided for you. Derive your scores for each Test Category and determine where you are weak so as to plan your study accordingly.

CORRECT ANSWERS FOR VERISIMILAR EXAMINATION I.

TEST I. SPELLING

1.3	3.5	5.1	7.3	9.4	11.4
2.1	4.2	6.4	8.2	10.2	12.1

TEST II. ENGLISH GRAMMAR AND USAGE

1.C	5.E	9.A	13.E	17.C	21.A	25.A
2.B	6.D	10.C	14.D	18.C	22.B	
3.A	7.E	11.D	15.B	19.D	23.D	
4.C	8.B	12.B	16.D	20.E	24.B	

TEST II. EXPLANATORY ANSWERS

1. **(C)** *Carries* is an incorrect verb form and should be *carried*.

2. **(B)** *Manning* is a gerund and should be *man*, the present tense of the verb to man.

3. **(A)** *Disinterested,* which is an adjective meaning unbiased, should be *uninterested* which means having no interest in.

4. **(C)** The pronoun *it* is superfluous in this sentence. Only the verb *is* is required.

5. **(E)**

6. **(D)** *Soggily* is an adverb and should be *soggy,* an adjective which modifies potatoes.

7. **(E)**

8. **(B)** *Should go down* is an incorrect verb form and should be *would go down*.

9. **(A)** *Their* should be the adverb *there* in an impersonal construction where the real subject follows the verb.

10. **(C)** *Quite most* is redundant and should be *quite* or *most*.

11. **(D)** *Any* is the incorrect pronoun and should be *anyone*.

12. **(B)** *Emblazoned* is the incorrect verb choice and should be *blazed*.

13. **(E)**

14. **(D)** *Centuries* is the plural and should be the singular *century*.

15. **(B)** *Memoir's* is possessive and should be the plural *memoirs*.

16. **(D)** *I* is the object of the infinitive to be and should be *me*.

17. **(C)** *Laid*, the past tense of lay when it connotes to set or put, should be *lay* which connotes recline.

18. **(C)** *Was drained* is the incorrect verb tense and should be *had been drained*.

19. **(D)** *Averse* which means unwilling should be *adverse* which means unfavorable.

20. **(E)**

21. **(A)** *Irregardless* is a nonstandard word form and should be *regardless*.

22. **(B)** *Him*, an objective pronoun, should be *his*, a possessive pronoun modifying the gerund joining.

23. **(D)** *Community won* should be *community, won*. The comma is necessary to set off the dependent clause that modifies Wallace Dolan.

24. **(B)** The adjective *incredulous* more appropriately modifies a person and should be *incredible*.

25. **(A)** *Past*, which is an adjective or adverb, should be *passed*, the past tense of the verb to pass.

TEST III. EFFECTIVENESS OF EXPRESSION

1.C	5.D	9.C	13.A	17.A	21.B	25.A
2.B	6.E	10.B	14.B	18.D	22.D	
3.E	7.D	11.C	15.E	19.C	23.E	
4.A	8.A	12.D	16.D	20.C	24.B	

TEST IV. LOGIC AND ORGANIZATION

1.C	3.E	5.B	7.A	9.B	11.E	13.B	15.A
2.D	4.C	6.E	8.B	10.D	12.A	14.E	16.C

TEST IV. EXPLANATORY ANSWERS

1. **(C)** *Sentence relationship.* Sentence 1 is not a complete sentence. When joined to sentence 2 its meaning is fully revealed.

2. **(D)** *Economy.* "Disappearance and vanishing" mean essentially the same thing. Thus the omission of "and vanishing" prevents sentence 3 from being verbose.

3. **(E)** *Diction.* The gerund "speaking" preceded by a certain type of adverb, such as "geologically," forms a figure of speech.

4. **(C)** *Diction.* "Virtuously" is an adverb meaning in a manner indicating moral excellence. "Virtually," an adverb meaning being so in effect, is the appropriate choice for sentence 5.

5. **(B)** *Irrelevancy.* Sentence 6 has no place in the thought pattern of the passage and should be omitted.

6. **(E)** *Clarification.* It is not clear, in sentence 7, as to what is "evolving" and "developing." The addition of "of life on this planet" clarifies this.

7. **(A)** *Ordering.* Sentence 8 in its current position logically develops the train of thought of the passage.

8. **(B)** *Sentence relationship.* "Irregardless" is an adjective that is a substandard and humorous redundancy for "regardless." It should be changed to "For."

9. **(B)** *Sentence relationship.* "Then" is an adverb that generally means at that time. "Than" is a conjunction used to introduce the second element in a comparison. "Than" is thus the correct word to use in conjunction with "rather."

10. **(D)** *Clarification.* Since a phrase begun with "neither" must always be followed by a phrase begun with "nor," the phrase "nor a proper preparation" should be added to sentence 2 to make it complete.

11. **(E)** *Diction.* "Good looks" refers largely to people while "beauty" refers to both animate and inanimate things.

12. **(A)** *Economy.* "Reflective, contemplative and searching" create essentially the same effect. Therefore, only one of these words is

necessary to the sentence. The elimination of "contemplative and searching" is the best alternative.

13. **(B)** *Diction*. "Along side of" is an adverbial phrase meaning beside. "Counter to," an adverbial phrase meaning in opposition or contrary to, more accurately completes the meaning of sentence 6.

14. **(E)** *Sentence relationship*. "Withal," an adverb defined as besides or despite that, should be changed to "with."

15. **(A)** *Ordering*. Sentence 9 completes the train of thought of the two preceding sentences and should remain where it is.

16. **(C)** *Paragraphing*. The first six sentences of the passage discuss the negative aspects of speed writing. Beginning with sentence 7 some of its better aspects are introduced.

TEST V. INTERPRETATION OF SOCIAL STUDIES READINGS

1.4	6.1	11.2	16.2	21.4	26.4	31.2
2.1	7.2	12.1	17.2	22.4	27.2	32.2
3.2	8.3	13.2	18.2	23.4	28.4	33.1
4.3	9.4	14.3	19.3	24.2	29.1	34.2
5.2	10.4	15.2	20.3	25.1	30.3	

TEST VI. SOCIAL STUDIES KNOWLEDGE

1.B	3.A	5.C	7.B	9.B	11.C	13.B	15.C
2.B	4.D	6.A	8.C	10.D	12.A	14.C	16.D

TEST VII. INTERPRETATION OF SCIENCE READINGS

1.3	5.2	9.4	13.4	17.1	21.2	25.2	29.4
2.4	6.4	10.2	14.2	18.2	22.2	26.4	
3.2	7.4	11.3	15.2	19.4	23.4	27.4	
4.3	8.1	12.1	16.2	20.1	24.1	28.4	

TEST VIII. SCIENCE INFORMATION

1.C	5.B	9.C	13.B	17.C	21.C	25.B
2.A	6.A	10.D	14.B	18.D	22.B	26.A
3.D	7.C	11.D	15.C	19.C	23.A	
4.C	8.A	12.D	16.A	20.B	24.C	

TEST IX. INTERPRETATION OF LITERARY MATERIALS

1.2	7.4	13.3	19.4	25.2	31.4	37.2	43.1
2.3	8.2	14.4	20.1	26.3	32.3	38.2	
3.1	9.4	15.1	21.1	27.4	33.2	39.4	
4.4	10.1	16.2	22.4	28.3	34.2	40.3	
5.3	11.2	17.4	23.4	29.1	35.3	41.4	
6.3	12.4	18.1	24.3	30.2	36.4	42.1	

TEST X. INTERPRETATION OF PROSE

1.C	3.E	5.A	7.B	9.B	11.D
2.A	4.B	6.E	8.A	10.C	12.A

TEST XI. GENERAL MATHEMATICAL ABILITY

1.3	5.5	9.2	13.3	17.1	21.1	25.1	29.2
2.4	6.4	10.1	14.1	18.4	22.4	26.3	30.1
3.2	7.2	11.5	15.2	19.4	23.2	27.4	
4.4	8.5	12.1	16.3	20.4	24.3	28.5	

TEST XII. GRAPH INTERPRETATION

1.C	2.E	3.D	4.B	5.C	6.A

TEST XII. EXPLANATORY ANSWERS

1. **(C)** All corporations had a profit of 22 billion. Manufacturing concerns had a profit of 10 billion. The difference is 12 billion.

2. **(E)** From 1962 to 1963 there was a drop in the Per Cent of National Income for All Corporations as well as for Manufacturing Corporations.

3. **(D)** It was 10 billion for All Corporations. All Corporations had 6% of the National Income.

$$\frac{10 \text{ billion}}{X} = \frac{6\%}{100\%}$$

X = approx. 170 billion.

4. **(B)** In 1948, All Corporations had a 20 billion dollar profit. This was 9% of the National Income. In 1952, All Corporations had the same 20 billion dollar profit. This was 7% of the National Income. It is clear, then, that the National Income increased, but did not double, in 1952.

5. **(C)** The *average* income means the income of one of the thousands of Manufacturing Corporations. There is no mathematical possibility that an average corporation exceeded 4% of the National Income.

6. **(A)** Corporations made twice the profit in 1948 than they did in 1946. Since there were twice as many corporations, the profit remained the same.

HIGH SCHOOL EQUIVALENCY DIPLOMA TESTS

SECOND VERISIMILAR EXAMINATION

This Verisimilar Examination is patterned after the actual exam. In all fairness we must emphasize that it is not a copy of the actual exam, which is guarded closely and may not be duplicated. The exam you'll take may have more difficult questions in some areas than you will encounter on this Verisimilar Exam. On the other hand, some questions may be easier, but don't bank on it. This book is supposed to give you confidence ... not over-confidence.

Allow about 6 hours for this Examination.

That's approximately how much time you'll have on the actual exam. Keep a record of your time, especially if you want to break up this practice into several convenient sessions. Then you'll be able to simulate actual exam conditions.

Correct answers for all the questions in all the Tests of this Exam appear at the end of the Exam.

ANALYSIS AND TIMETABLE: A VERISIMILAR EXAMINATION II.		
This table is both an analysis of the exam that follows and a priceless preview of the actual test. Look it over carefully and use it well. Since it lists both subjects and times, it points up not only what to study, but also how much time to spend on each topic. Making the most of your study time adds valuable points to your examination score.		

WRITING SKILLS		SCIENCE	
Spelling	6 min.	Interpretation of Science Readings	60 min.
English Grammar and Usage	20 min.	Science Information	30 min.
Effectiveness of Expression	10 min.		
Logic and Organization	9 min.	READING SKILLS	
		Interpretation of Literary Materials	70 min.
SOCIAL STUDIES		Interpretation of Prose	20 min.
Interpretation of Social Studies Readings	60 min.	MATHEMATICS	
Social Studies Knowledge	30 min.	General Mathematical Ability	40 min.
		Graph Interpretation	5 min.

ANSWER SHEET FOR VERISIMILAR EXAMINATION II.

TEST I. SPELLING

TEST II. ENGLISH GRAMMAR AND USAGE

TEST III. EFFECTIVENESS OF EXPRESSION

TEST IV. LOGIC AND ORGANIZATION

TEST V. INTERPRETATION OF SOCIAL STUDIES READINGS

TEST VI. SOCIAL STUDIES KNOWLEDGE

TEST VII. INTERPRETATION OF SCIENCE READINGS

1 — 1 2 3 4 5	2 — 1 2 3 4 5	3 — 1 2 3 4 5	4 — 1 2 3 4 5	5 — 1 2 3 4 5	6 — 1 2 3 4 5	7 — 1 2 3 4 5	8 — 1 2 3 4 5
9 — 1 2 3 4 5	10 — 1 2 3 4 5	11 — 1 2 3 4 5	12 — 1 2 3 4 5	13 — 1 2 3 4 5	14 — 1 2 3 4 5	15 — 1 2 3 4 5	16 — 1 2 3 4 5
17 — 1 2 3 4 5	18 — 1 2 3 4 5	19 — 1 2 3 4 5	20 — 1 2 3 4 5	21 — 1 2 3 4 5	22 — 1 2 3 4 5	23 — 1 2 3 4 5	24 — 1 2 3 4 5
25 — 1 2 3 4 5	26 — 1 2 3 4 5	27 — 1 2 3 4 5	28 — 1 2 3 4 5	29 — 1 2 3 4 5	30 — 1 2 3 4 5	31 — 1 2 3 4 5	32 — 1 2 3 4 5
33 — 1 2 3 4 5	34 — 1 2 3 4 5	35 — 1 2 3 4 5	36 — 1 2 3 4 5	37 — 1 2 3 4 5	38 — 1 2 3 4 5	39 — 1 2 3 4 5	40 — 1 2 3 4 5

TEST VIII. SCIENCE INFORMATION

1 — A B C D E	2 — A B C D E	3 — A B C D E	4 — A B C D E	5 — A B C D E	6 — A B C D E	7 — A B C D E	8 — A B C D E
9 — A B C D E	10 — A B C D E	11 — A B C D E	12 — A B C D E	13 — A B C D E	14 — A B C D E	15 — A B C D E	16 — A B C D E
17 — A B C D E	18 — A B C D E	19 — A B C D E	20 — A B C D E	21 — A B C D E	22 — A B C D E	23 — A B C D E	24 — A B C D E

TEST IX. INTERPRETATION OF LITERARY MATERIALS

1 — 1 2 3 4 5	2 — 1 2 3 4 5	3 — 1 2 3 4 5	4 — 1 2 3 4 5	5 — 1 2 3 4 5	6 — 1 2 3 4 5	7 — 1 2 3 4 5	8 — 1 2 3 4 5
9 — 1 2 3 4 5	10 — 1 2 3 4 5	11 — 1 2 3 4 5	12 — 1 2 3 4 5	13 — 1 2 3 4 5	14 — 1 2 3 4 5	15 — 1 2 3 4 5	16 — 1 2 3 4 5
17 — 1 2 3 4 5	18 — 1 2 3 4 5	19 — 1 2 3 4 5	20 — 1 2 3 4 5	21 — 1 2 3 4 5	22 — 1 2 3 4 5	23 — 1 2 3 4 5	24 — 1 2 3 4 5
25 — 1 2 3 4 5	26 — 1 2 3 4 5	27 — 1 2 3 4 5	28 — 1 2 3 4 5	29 — 1 2 3 4 5	30 — 1 2 3 4 5	31 — 1 2 3 4 5	32 — 1 2 3 4 5
33 — 1 2 3 4 5	34 — 1 2 3 4 5	35 — 1 2 3 4 5	36 — 1 2 3 4 5	37 — 1 2 3 4 5	38 — 1 2 3 4 5	39 — 1 2 3 4 5	40 — 1 2 3 4 5
41 — 1 2 3 4 5	42 — 1 2 3 4 5	43 — 1 2 3 4 5	44 — 1 2 3 4 5	45 — 1 2 3 4 5	46 — 1 2 3 4 5	47 — 1 2 3 4 5	48 — 1 2 3 4 5

TEST X. INTERPRETATION OF PROSE

1 — A B C D E	2 — A B C D E	3 — A B C D E	4 — A B C D E	5 — A B C D E	6 — A B C D E	7 — A B C D E	8 — A B C D E
9 — A B C D E	10 — A B C D E	11 — A B C D E	12 — A B C D E	13 — A B C D E	14 — A B C D E	15 — A B C D E	16 — A B C D E

TEST XI. GENERAL MATHEMATICAL ABILITY

1 — A B C D E	2 — A B C D E	3 — A B C D E	4 — A B C D E	5 — A B C D E	6 — A B C D E	7 — A B C D E	8 — A B C D E
9 — A B C D E	10 — A B C D E	11 — A B C D E	12 — A B C D E	13 — A B C D E	14 — A B C D E	15 — A B C D E	16 — A B C D E
17 — A B C D E	18 — A B C D E	19 — A B C D E	20 — A B C D E	21 — A B C D E	22 — A B C D E	23 — A B C D E	24 — A B C D E
25 — A B C D E	26 — A B C D E	27 — A B C D E	28 — A B C D E	29 — A B C D E	30 — A B C D E	31 — A B C D E	32 — A B C D E

TEST XII. GRAPH INTERPRETATION

1 — A B C D E	2 — A B C D E	3 — A B C D E	4 — A B C D E	5 — A B C D E	6 — A B C D E	7 — A B C D E	8 — A B C D E

TEAR OUT ALONG THIS LINE AND MARK YOUR ANSWERS AS INSTRUCTED IN THE TEXT

PART I. THE WRITING SKILLS TEST

TIME: 45 Minutes. 78 Questions.

TEST I. SPELLING

TIME: 6 Minutes. 14 Questions.

DIRECTIONS: In each of the following groups one word may be misspelled. For each group select the one misspelled word. If you think all four words in the group are correctly spelled, mark the answer E.

Correct answers for these questions appear at the end of this examination, together with the answers to all the other tests.

1. (A) extraordinary (B) statesmen
    (C) array   (D) financeer
    (E) none wrong

2. (A) materialism   (B) indefatigible
    (C) moribund   (D) rebellious
    (E) none wrong

3. (A) queue   (B) equilibrium
    (C) contemporary   (D) structure
    (E) none wrong

4. (A) acquatic   (B) fascinated
    (C) bogged   (D) accommodations
    (E) none wrong

5. (A) embarrassment (B) sosialization
    (C) imposition   (D) incredulous
    (E) none wrong

6. (A) politisians   (B) psychology
    (C) susceptible   (D) antipathy
    (E) none wrong

7. (A) convincing   (B) vicissetudes
    (C) negligible   (D) foreign
    (E) none wrong

8. (A) characters   (B) veracity
    (C) testimony   (D) apolagetic
    (E) none wrong

9. (A) shriek   (B) carelogue
    (C) impeccable   (D) ruthless
    (E) none wrong

10. (A) ocassions   (B) accomplishment
    (C) assumed   (D) distinguished
    (E) none wrong

11. (A) servicable   (B) preparation
    (C) exceptional   (D) initiative
    (E) none wrong

12. (A) primarely   (B) available
    (C) paragraph   (D) routine
    (E) none wrong

13. (A) ligament   (B) preseding
    (C) mechanical   (D) anecdote
    (E) none wrong

14. (A) judgment   (B) conclusion
    (C) circumlocution (D) convenient
    (E) none wrong

END OF TEST

Go on to do the following Test in this Examination, just as you would be expected to do on the actual exam. You will find correct answers for the entire Examination following the last question. Check your answers carefully after you have completed the whole Examination.

TEST II. ENGLISH GRAMMAR AND USAGE

TIME: 20 Minutes. 34 Questions.

DIRECTIONS: This is a test of standard written English. The rules may differ from everyday spoken English. Many of the following sentences contain grammar, usage, word choice, and idiom that would be incorrect in written composition. Some sentences are correct. No sentence has more than one error. Any error in a sentence will be underlined and lettered; all other parts of the sentence are correct and cannot be changed. If the sentence has an error, choose the underlined part that is incorrect, and mark that letter on your answer sheet. If there is no error, mark E on your answer sheet.

1. What affect the law will have on our drivers and how it
        A   B   C
   will affect our lives remain to be seen. No error.
             D   E

2. If I was you, I should be careful of who my friends are.
       A   B   C   D
   No error.
   E

3. Merrihew, who I never thought was even in the running,
            A   B
   not only won handily but also broke a record. No error.
           C   D   E

4. Although his story had aspects of truth about it, I
       A   B
   couldn't hardly believe what he said. No error.
        C   D   E

5. I would gladly have attended your wedding if you invited
             A   B C   D
   me. No error.
      E

6. Whoever the gods wish to destroy, they first make mad.
       A   B   C   D
   No error.
   E

7. Drawing up the plan promised to be a years' work.
       A   B   C   D
   No error.
   E

8. There are less tramps on the Bowery since the elevated
      A   B   C
   structure was razed. No error.
              D   E

9. Uncle Jack has expressed the belief that lilacs smell more
      A   B   C
   sweetly than roses. No error.
      D   E

10. I shall vote for whichsoever is, in my opinion, best
       A   B   C
    qualified. No error.
       D   E

11. He is always polite not only to his supervisors and

    colleagues but to anyone else he thinks is deserving of
       A   B   C
    kindly consideration. No error.
       D   E

12. I don't understand your fondness for them; I can't stand
       A   B   C
    the both of them. No error.
       D   E

13. A torrential downpour, in addition to long stretches of
       A   B
    road construction that made it necessary to slow down

    to fifteen miles an hour, have so delayed us that we shall
                              C
    not be able to be on hand for the ceremony. No error.
                       D   E

14. The teacher, along with a committee of bright students,
                   A   B   C
    have compiled a reading list. No error.
       C   D   E

15. We buy only purple plums, since we like those kind best.
       A   B   C   D
    No error.
       E

16. It was he, not I, who became nauseous because of the
            A   B   C
    boat's motion. No error.
       D   E

17. Although Richard graduated high school with honors, he
    <u>A</u>   <u>B</u>
    failed three subjects as a college freshman. No error.
    <u>C</u>   <u>D</u>   <u>E</u>

18. If you have read "A Tale of Two Cities," you know that
    <u>A</u>   <u>B</u>
    Jerry Cruncher was aggravated by his wife's praying.
    <u>C</u>   <u>D</u>
    No error.
    <u>E</u>

19. If he would have come when I asked him, he might not
    <u>A</u>   <u>B</u>   <u>C</u>
    have made the error. No error.
    <u>D</u>   <u>E</u>

20. They invited my whole family to the cookout—my father,
    <u>A</u>   <u>B</u>   <u>C</u>
    my mother, my sister and I. No error.
    <u>D</u>   <u>E</u>

21. Why should these newcomers to the club have the same
    <u>A</u>   <u>B</u>
    privileges as we older members? No error.
    <u>C</u>   <u>D</u>   <u>E</u>

22. Being that I arrived first, I helped the hostess prepare
    <u>A</u>   <u>B</u>   <u>C</u>
    the hors d'oeuvres. No error.
    <u>D</u>   <u>E</u>

23. Such a large amount of pupils in the room is bound to
    <u>A</u>   <u>B</u>   <u>C</u>
    cause confusion. No error.
    <u>D</u>   <u>E</u>

24. Saying only that she was a friend of Mary's, she left
    <u>A</u>   <u>B</u>   <u>C</u>   <u>D</u>
    without giving her name. No error.
    <u>E</u>

25. Because they were unaware of his interest in the build-
    <u>A</u>
    ing, they did not understand why he felt so bad about it's
    <u>B</u>   <u>C</u>
    being condemned. No error.
    <u>D</u>   <u>E</u>

26. Two astronauts were disappointed because they had hoped
    $\overline{}$ A   B
    to have made the first trip to the moon. No error.
         C   D   E

27. If you want me to express my opinion, I think that
      A   B
    Report A is equally as good as Report B. No error.
        C   D   E

28. "Frank's dog is still in the yard," my father said, "perhaps
        A   B
    he had better stay there until we have finished our din-
          C   D
    ner." No error.
        E

29. He had a chance to invest wisely, establish his position,
          A   B
    and displaying his ability as an executive. No error.
        C   D   E

30. The snow fell during the night so that it was laying in big
            A   B
    drifts on the highway the next morning. No error.
         C   D   E

31. The coach with his entire team are traveling by plane.
        A   B   C   D
    No error.
      E

32. By his perserverance, he succeeded in overcoming the
         A   B
    apathy of his pupils. No error.
      C   D   E

33. This is one of those tricky questions that has two
      A   B   C   D
    answers. No error.
          E

34. She did the work very well, however, she showed
        A   B
    no interest in anything beyond her assignment. No error.
       C   D   E

END OF TEST

TEST III. EFFECTIVENESS OF EXPRESSION

TIME: 10 Minutes. 15 Questions.

DIRECTIONS: A sentence is given in which one part is under-
lined. Following the sentence are five choices. The first (A) choice
simply repeats the underlined part. The subsequent four choices
suggest other ways to express the underlined part of the original
sentence. If you think that the underlined part is correct as it
stands, write the answer A. If you believe that the underlined part
is incorrect, select from among the other choices (B or C or D or
E) the one you think is correct. Grammar, sentence structure,
word usage, and punctuation are to be considered in your decision,
and the original meaning of the sentence must be retained.

Correct answers for these questions appear at the end of this examina-
tion, together with the answers to all the other tests.

1. Crossing the bridge, a glimpse of the islands was caught.
   - (A) a glimpse of the islands was caught.
   - (B) a glimpse of the islands were caught.
   - (C) we caught a glimpse of the islands.
   - (D) the islands were caught a glimpse of.
   - (E) we caught a glimpse of the islands' view.

2. This book has been laying here for weeks.
   - (A) laying here for weeks.
   - (B) laying here weeks.
   - (C) laying down here for weeks.
   - (D) lieing here for weeks.
   - (E) lying here for weeks.

3. When my brother will come home, I'll tell him you called.
   - (A) will come home,
   - (B) will come home
   - (C) will have come home,
   - (D) comes home,
   - (E) has come home,

4. After he graduated school, he entered the army,
   - (A) After he graduated school,
   - (B) After he was graduated from school,
   - (C) When he graduated school,
   - (D) After he graduated school
   - (E) As he was graduated from school,

5. I think they, as a rule, are much more conniving than us.
   - (A) as a rule, are much more conniving than us.
   - (B) as a rule are much more conniving than us.
   - (C) as a rule, are much more conniving than we.
   - (D) as a rule; are much more conniving than us.
   - (E) are, as a rule, much more conniving than us.

6. Sitting around the fire, mystery stories were told by each of us.
   - (A) mystery stories were told by each of us.
   - (B) mystery stories were told by all of us.
   - (C) each of us told mystery stories.
   - (D) stories of mystery were told by each of us.
   - (E) there were told mystery stories by each of us.

7. The loud noise of the subway trains and the trolley cars frighten people from the country.
   - (A) frighten people from the country.
   - (B) frighten country people.
   - (C) frighten persons from the country.
   - (D) frightens country people.
   - (E) frighten people who come from the country.

8. Inspecting Robert's report card, his mother noted that he had received high ratings in Latin and history.
   - (A) his mother noted
   - (B) it was noted by his mother
   - (C) his mother had noted
   - (D) a notation was made by his mother
   - (E) Robert's mother noted

9. The old man told <u>Mary and I</u> many stories about Europe.
   - (A) Mary and I
   - (B) Mary and me
   - (C) me and Mary
   - (D) I and Mary
   - (E) Mary together with me

10. The wild game hunter stalked the tiger slowly, cautiously, <u>and in a silent manner</u>.
    - (A) and in a silent manner.
    - (B) and silently.
    - (C) and by acting silent.
    - (D) and also used silence.
    - (E) and in silence.

11. European film distributors originated the art of "dubbing"—<u>the substitution of lip-synchronized translations</u> in foreign languages for the original soundtrack voices.
    - (A) —the substitution of lip-synchronized translations
    - (B) ; the substitution of lip-synchronized translations
    - (C) —the substitutions of translations synchronized by the lips
    - (D) , the lip-synchronized substitution of translations
    - (E) . The substitution of lip-synchronized translations

12. Every pupil understood the assignment <u>except I</u>
    - (A) except I.
    - (B) excepting I.
    - (C) outside of me.
    - (D) excepting me.
    - (E) except me.

13. Of the two candidates, I think <u>he is the best suited</u>.
    - (A) he is the best suited.
    - (B) that he is the best suited.
    - (C) he is suited best.
    - (D) he is the better suited.
    - (E) he's the best suited.

14. <u>You need not go unless you want to.</u>
    - (A) You need not go unless you want to.
    - (B) You don't need to go not unless you want to.
    - (C) You need go not unless you want to.
    - (D) You need not go in case unless you want to.
    - (E) You can go not unless you want to.

15. There is <u>no man but would give</u> ten years of his life to accomplish that deed.
    - (A) no man but would give
    - (B) no man but who would give
    - (C) not no man who would not give
    - (D) no man who would but give
    - (E) not any man would give

END OF TEST

Go on to do the following Test in this Examination, just as you would be expected to do on the actual exam. You will find correct answers for the entire Examination following the last question. Check your answers carefully after you have completed the whole Examination.

TEST IV. LOGIC AND ORGANIZATION

TIME: 9 Minutes. 15 Questions.

DIRECTIONS: This test consists of brief passages in which each sentence is numbered. Following each passage are questions which refer to the numbered sentences in the passage. Answer each question by choosing the best alternative (A,B,C,D, or E) and blacken the space corresponding to your choice on the Answer Sheet provided.

Explanations of the key points behind these questions appear with the answers at the end of this test. The explanatory answers provide just the help you need to strengthen your ability to master this type of question.

[1]There is a time in every man's education when he arrives at the conviction that envy is ignorance. [2]And that imitation is suicide. [3]He must take himself for better or for worst at this time. [4]He is able to understand that, though the universe is full of good, everything good that comes to him does so because of his toll. [5]The power that resides in him is new in nature. [6]The other day I found myself wandering through a natural garden. [7]No one but he suspects what he can do, nor does he know until he has tried. [8]Society everywhere is in conspiracy against the manhood of every one of its members, persons and citizens. [9]Society is a joint stock company. [10]The virtue in greatest demand is conformity. [11]Self-reliance is the least. [12]The members in it agree to surrender their liberty and culture for gain. [13]Society's stock company does not love realities and creators, but customs and names.

1. What should be done with sentence 2?

    (A) It should be left as it is.
    (B) It should be joined to the beginning of sentence 3 with *however*.
    (C) It should be made into two sentences.
    (D) It should be joined to the end of sentence 1.
    (E) The part after *imitation* should be omitted.

2. In sentence 3, the word *worst* should be

    (A) left as it is
    (B) changed to *better*
    (C) changed to *worse*
    (D) changed to *worsen*
    (E) changed to *bad*

3. In sentence 4, the word *toll* should be

    (A) left as it is
    (B) changed to *token*
    (C) changed to *tongs*
    (D) changed to *taxes*
    (E) changed to *toil*

4. What should be done with sentence 6?

    (A) It should be left as is
    (B) It should be omitted.
    (C) It should be moved to the end of the passage.
    (D) It should be lengthened to give more information about *gardens*.
    (E) It should be moved to the beginning of the passage.

5. Sentence 8 would be most improved if

    (A) the word *every* were changed to *each*
    (B) it began with *Thus society*
    (C) the part after *members* were omitted
    (D) the part after *manhood* were omitted
    (E) it began with *Regardless*

6. Sentence 12 is best placed

    (A) where it is now
    (B) before sentence 1
    (C) after sentence 1
    (D) after sentence 9
    (E) after sentence 4

7. The meaning of sentence 11 would be clearest if

    (A) the sentence were left as it is
    (B) the sentence ended with *least popular*
    (C) the sentence were made into two
    (D) the sentence ended with *least populous*
    (E) the sentence began with *That is to say*

8. If the passage is to be divided into two paragraphs, the second paragraph should begin with

    (A) sentence 8
    (B) sentence 4
    (C) sentence 3
    (D) sentence 10
    (E) sentence 13

[1]It is not easy to write in a familiar style. [2]Many people mistake a familiar for a vulgar style. [3]Suppose that to write without formality is to write at random. [4]On the contradiction, there is nothing that requires more precision, and if I may say so, purity of expression, than the style I am speaking of. [5]It utterly rejects all meaningless. [6]It does not take the first word that offers itself, but takes the best word in common use. [7]It does not throw words together in any pleasing combination we please, but uses the true idioms of the language. [8]To write in a genuine familiar style is written as anyone would speak in everyday conversation. [9]The familiar style demonstrates a thorough commandment of the English language as it is spoken. [10]Studies are for delight, for ornament and for ability.

9. What should be done with sentence 3?

   (A) It should be left as it is.
   (B) It should be joined to the beginning of sentence 4.
   (C) It should be joined to the end of sentence 2 with *and*.
   (D) It should be made into two sentences.
   (E) The phrase *without formality* should be changed to *informally*.

10. In sentence 4, the word *contradiction* should be

    (A) left as it is
    (B) changed to *contrary*
    (C) changed to *contract*
    (D) changed to *detraction*
    (E) changed to *contradicting*

11. The meaning of sentence 5 would be clearest if

    (A) the sentence were left as it is
    (B) the sentence began with *Nevertheless it*
    (C) the part after *all* were omitted
    (D) the sentence began with *Regardless it*
    (E) *pretensions* were added to the end of the sentence

12. Sentence 7 would be best if

    (A) left as it is
    (B) the part after *idioms* were omitted
    (C) it were made into two sentences
    (D) *true* were omitted
    (E) *pleasing* were omitted

13. The word *written* in sentence 8 should be

    (A) left as it is
    (B) changed to *wrote*
    (C) changed to *had written*
    (D) changed to *to write*
    (E) changed to *composition*

14. In sentence 9 *commandment* should be

    (A) left as it is
    (B) changed to *command*
    (C) changed to *commanding*
    (D) changed to *commandeer*
    (E) changed to *commanded*

15. What should be done with sentence 10?

    (A) It should be left as it is.
    (B) It should be moved to the beginning of the passage.
    (C) It should begin a new paragraph.
    (D) It should be omitted entirely.
    (E) It should follow sentence 5.

END OF PART

PART II. THE SOCIAL STUDIES TEST

TIME: 90 Minutes. 59 Questions.

TEST V. INTERPRETATION OF SOCIAL STUDIES READINGS

TIME: 60 Minutes. 41 Questions.

DIRECTIONS: Read each passage to get the general idea. Then reread the passage more carefully to answer the questions based on the passage. For each question read all choices carefully. Then select the answer you consider correct or most nearly correct.

The development of voting laws in England is important to us because they were the basis of voting laws in Colonial America. As England began to change from an agricultural country to an industrial country the absolute power of the King began to dissolve. Those who began to have economic power also began to have political power. This political power was recognized by the English "Bill of Rights" passed in 1689. In order that this power would not become further diluted, early English voting laws were based on requirements of land ownership and formal education.

While these same restrictions were followed in Colonial America, the effect was different. In England the poor could not own land, but in America land could be acquired by simply clearing and working it. This new political power coupled with independent economic power resulted in a new kind of democracy which eventually led to the Declaration of Independence and the U.S. Constitution.

1. The main purpose of this article is to
   1) describe the parliamentary law of 1689.
   2) show why voting laws are necessary.
   3) explain the voting laws of England.
   4) explain the background of voting laws in America.

2. What does the author cite as an important factor in the changes in voting laws?
   1) changes in economic situations
   2) colonization
   3) modern ideas of government
   4) the growth of world population

3. Which one of the following is the best example of the economic power mentioned in this article?
   1) the ability to buy land
   2) the ability to pay the costs of government
   3) the ability to bribe public officials
   4) the ability to get a formal education

4. Judging from this passage, which one of the following qualifications probably became the most important factor in voting as a result of the 1689 "Bill of Rights"?
   1) religion
   2) money
   3) education
   4) ancestry

5. The first people allowed to vote in England probably gained this right as the result of
   1) religion.
   2) money.
   3) education.
   4) ancestry.

6. The purpose of the "Bill of Rights" of 1689 was to
   1) furnish a pattern for Colonial America
   2) outlaw tyranny of any kind
   3) guard the voting rights of all citizens
   4) formalize the sharing of political power

7. What would be the most likely reason for the King of England signing the 1689 "Bill of Rights?"
   1) He received a great deal of money for doing so
   2) He was forced to sign in order to retain his position
   3) He wanted to share his responsibilities
   4) He felt democracy was the best form of government

Italy supposedly was more fortunate than its former allies, Germany and Austria-Hungary, because it was on the winning side when World War I ended. But many Italians felt that the war had cost Italy more than had been gained. An Italian at the close of the war might well have said: "We have poured out more blood and treasure to gain southern Tyrol and a few coast towns on the Adriatic than we did in all the wars for national liberty and union during the nineteenth century. Our allies begrudge us some of the territory we expected to acquire, such as the city of Fiume. Perhaps we would have done better to remain neutral. Perhaps a stronger government might have won for us richer spoils of victory."

Conditions within Italy were indeed discouraging. Trade and industry were in bad shape. Strikes and riots among workers were common and Communist ideas were making headway among the poor. As in other European countries, there were many political parties, none of which was strong enough to remain in power for any length of time. Because one new cabinet followed another, the government was unable to enact laws that dealt effectively with the growing problems of depression and unemployment. Under these conditions, many Italians longed for a "man on horseback"—a strong leader who would restore order and prosperity.

The man who gave promise of being the strong leader so many Italians desired was Benito Mussolini. The son of a workingman, Mussolini had become a Socialist and a newspaper writer before World War I. But when the Socialist Party opposed Italy's entrance into the war, Mussolini left it and served in the Italian army. After the fighting ceased, Mussolini organized bands of veterans called Fascisti. The Fascists wore black shirts and their emblem was the old Roman symbol of authority, the fasces or bundle of rods bound around an ax. The Fascists were a quarrelsome lot who often got into street fights with Italians holding other political ideas.

In 1922 the Fascists marched on Rome. The King and his ministers made no attempt to break up this parade of Mussolini's black-shirted followers. In fact, King Victor Emmanuel III appointed Mussolini Prime Minister. For a few years the outward forms of constitutional government were kept. All real power, however, was in the hands of Il Duce, or "The Leader," as Mussolini was called.

Soon the barrel-chested, square-jawed, loud-voiced Mussolini felt strong enough to do away with individual freedom and self-government altogether. He abolished all political parties except his own, the Fascist Party. From then on, Italy's voters were presented, as were the Russian voters, with a single list of candidates for office.

Mussolini built roads, drained marshes and expanded industry. He spent huge sums of money on the army, navy and air force. The average Italian felt pride in these national achievements. He also earned more money, but he paid mor for what he bought, and taxes were higher. It may be doubted, then, that the average Italian was any better off for all Mussolini's efforts. And his freedom and importance had been lost.

8. During World War I Italy fought on the side of

1) the Axis.
2) the Allies.
3) Germany.
4) Austria-Hungary.

9. From this passage we may infer that as a dictator Mussolini

1) earned and kept the respect of his people.
2) was opposed by democratic nations abroad.

3) believed that his country should become a democracy as soon as possible.
4) had as his first priority the freedom of Italy.

10. What is the purpose of the first two paragraphs in this article?

1) to show how Italy had been mistreated
2) to show that Italy could not survive without a strong dictator
3) to indicate why Mussolini was able to take over the government
4) to present some of the weaknesses of a democratic government

11. The form of government Mussolini set up was similar to the dictatorship of Adolph Hitler in

    1) Spain.
    2) Germany.
    3) Russia.
    4) Rome.

12. The author of this article characterizes Mussolini as

    1) a strong ruler who bettered the lot of the common people.
    2) a ruthless man who took what he wanted.
    3) a brilliant thinker who unfortunately was a poor leader.
    4) a cautious man concerned with history and tradition.

13. What would be the best title for the third and fourth paragraphs of this article?

    1) Mussolini's Rise to Power
    2) Mussolini's Socialistic Beliefs
    3) Mussolini's Dictatorial Methods
    4) Mussolini's Reform Measures

14. In order to succeed, Mussolini seems to have relied strongly on appeal to Italians' sense of

    1) pride.   3) religion.
    2) fair play.   4) freedom.

15. Judging from this passage, Mussolini seems to have tried hardest to eliminate

    1) poverty.   3) illiteracy.
    2) religion.   4) opposition.

16. Within his own country, Mussolini's greatest opposition probably came from the

    1) church.   3) common people.
    2) Fascists.   4) military.

17. According to this article, Mussolini's greatest accomplishments probably came in his

    1) domestic programs.
    2) military victories.
    3) foreign alliances.
    4) constitutional changes.

From the **Daily Newsprint:**

"To hear some generals tell it, the concept of an all-volunteer Army is an unrealistic dream that has already been shattered by the enlistment statistics of the past months. It is true that since the draft was suspended the Army has failed to meet its enlistment quotas. The shortfall, however, hardly endangers national security, since the Army has managed to fill about 75 percent of its openings.

With enlistment bonuses of up to $2,500 plus a starting salary of over $300 a month we feel that enlistments will increase. It's not just poster rhetoric to point out that the military can indeed be an honorable and attractive alternative to a dead-end civilian job. We feel that it would be premature to reinstitute the draft at this time."

From the **News of Today:**

"Last night's *Daily Newsprint,* (an offshoot of the radical *This Week's News*) blatantly suggests that it is unnecessary to ensure a strong army by using the draft. They state that manpower requirements are down 'only' 25%. This alone should be sufficient reason to reinstitute the draft, for our country cannot afford to be weak at any time and much less in times when our enemy's strengths are increasing. To do so would only invite attack and lead to our possible destruction.

Our Constitution makes provisions for the draft because our forefathers realized the need for a strong, democratic army. The all-volunteer army will become a 'salt and pepper' army—white officers and black enlisted men. It will become an army of the poor, those to whom $3600 a year looks attractive. The draft does not prevent volunteers but it does help to guarantee a strong democratic army and it should be reinstated to keep us from becoming a second class power."

18. The tone of the *News of Today* can best be described as

    1) emotional.
    2) indifferent.
    3) restrained.
    4) impartial.

19. Which branch of the government is responsible for creating draft laws?

    1) Legislative
    2) Executive
    3) Judicial
    4) Military

20. Why does *News of Today* mention that the *Daily Newsprint* is connected with *This Week's News*?

    1) so that the readers will have all the facts
    2) to prove that *Daily Newsprint* is a radical paper
    3) to associate *Daily Newsprint* with a paper they hope their own readers will not like
    4) to strengthen the arguments made by the *Daily Newsprint*

21. What does the *Daily Newsprint* think should be done to improve Army enlistments?

    1) Army life should be made more attractive.
    2) More money should be offered to those who enlist.
    3) The present program should be given time to prove itself.
    4) Army jobs should be more like civilian jobs.

22. Why does the *News of Today* mention the Constitution in its editorial?
    1) to show that its main purpose is support of the Constitution
    2) to prove that the *Daily Newsprint*'s stand is unconstitutional
    3) to add a feeling of authority to its own position
    4) to show that the Constitution is the law of the land

23. A fear that the new draft laws may have a harmful effect on our country was implied

    1) only by the editor of the *Daily Newsprint*.
    2) only by the editor of the *News of Today*.
    3) by both editors.
    4) by neither editor.

24. The statement "Our nation needs a strong army" would be agreed to by
    1) only the editor of the *Daily Newsprint*.
    2) only the editor of the *News of Today*.
    3) both editors.
    4) neither editor.

25. Which of the following groups would be most likely to agree with the position of the *News of Today*?
    1) the generals of the Army
    2) college students who want to avoid the draft
    3) the United Nations
    4) the Congress of the United States

26. According to the opinion of *News of Today*, which of the following was NOT mentioned as a problem resulting from dropping the draft?

    1) a drop in total army inductees
    2) a racial imbalance in the army
    3) a danger to our freedom
    4) an infringement on personal freedoms

27. The *Daily Newsprint* mentioned the viewpoint of the Army generals in order to

    1) show that the military is prejudiced.
    2) make sure that the public knew all the facts.
    3) place anti-military people on their side.
    4) show that they support the Army.

28. What was the major reason for dropping the draft as a means of raising an army?

    1) to reduce the turnover rate of the Army
    2) to improve the pay of the soldiers
    3) to reduce the cost of maintaining an army
    4) The reason was not given in these editorials.

29. According to the Constitution the draft

    1) is not constitutional.
    2) is the only way the size of the Army may legally be increased.
    3) is one legal means of raising an army.
    4) can only be used if volunteers do not meet the demands of the Army.

Questions 30 to 41

DIRECTIONS: *Read each test question carefully. Answer each one on the basis of the following table.*

THE TREND OF TAX COLLECTIONS: 1956-1972

NOTE—The following table may be assumed to be correct.

(In millions of dollars)

Year	Federal	State	Local	Total
1956	24,207	7,830	9,526	41,563
1958	76,361	8,614	9,689	94,664
1960	72,037	9,433	10,210	91,680
1962	74,927	15,309	11,699	101,045
1964	70,681	19,587	15,894	106,162
1966	118,477	22,098	18,664	159,239
1968	124,904	26,675	20,022	171,601
1970	130,622	29,918	25,299	185,839
1972	138,700	32,218	30,621	201,539

30. The difference between the federal tax collection and the local tax collection in 1960 was
   1) sixty-one billion eight hundred twenty-seven million dollars.
   2) six billion one hundred eighty-two million seven hundred thousand dollars.
   3) sixty-one million eight hundred twenty-seven thousand dollars.
   4) sixty-one thousand eight hundred twenty-seven dollars

31. The main source of federal tax dollars is
   1) property tax.
   2) excise tax.
   3) sales tax.
   4) income tax.

32. Of the following statements about federal and state spending, which is most correct?
   1) Large tax collection years are large government spending years.
   2) The amount of taxes collected coincides with the amount of money spent.

   3) The collections of the federal government are more closely related to general business activity than those of state government.
   4) State taxes have increased at a faster percentage rate than federal taxes.

33. The drop in federal taxes between 1960 and 1964 was probably the result of
   1) general elections.
   2) lower government spending.
   3) smaller corporate income taxes.
   4) changes in tax laws.

34. Federal tax laws are drawn up by the
   1) Treasury Department.
   2) Department of Revenue.
   3) President and his Cabinet.
   4) Legislature.

35. Which of the following depend the most on property tax?
   1) federal
   2) state
   3) local
   4) all depend about equally on property tax

DIRECTIONS: Answer the following questions:

1) if the statement is probably true based on the table.
2) if the statement is probably false based on the table.
3) if the truth or falseness of the statement cannot be determined by the table.

36. The government spent less money in 1960 than in 1958.

37. Federal taxes rose greatly during the Vietnam war.

38. Local and state taxes rose at about the same rate between 1962 and 1966.

39. Local taxes are consistently about one-fourth that of federal taxes.

40. Rural people contribute a higher percentage of taxes than city people.

41. Local taxes have gradually been used to take over the jobs done by state taxes.

END OF TEST

Go on to do the following Test in this Examination, just as you would be expected to do on the actual exam. You will find correct answers for the entire Examination following the last question. Check your answers carefully after you have completed the whole Examination.

TEST VI. SOCIAL STUDIES KNOWLEDGE

TIME: 30 Minutes. 18 Questions.

DIRECTIONS: *For each of the following questions, select the choice which best answers the question or completes the statement.*

Correct answers for these questions appear at the end of this examination, together with the answers to all the other tests.

1. A democratic practice that characterized the New England colonies was that
   (A) there was separation of church and state
   (B) a man's qualification for voting was native birth
   (C) the business of local government was conducted at town meetings
   (D) the choice of governors was left to representative state legislatures.

2. The colony of Rhode Island was founded for the purpose of securing
   (A) an asylum for debtors and criminals
   (B) freedom of worship
   (C) mineral wealth
   (D) protection from the Indians.

3. "Excessive bail shall not be required, nor excessive fines imposed, nor cruel and unusual punishment inflicted" is a quotation from the
   (A) Constitution of the United States of America
   (B) Declaration of Independence
   (C) Articles of Confederation
   (D) Charter of the United Nations.

4. The United States House of Representatives has the power to
   (A) make treaties
   (B) appoint judges to the Supreme Court bench
   (C) try impeachments
   (D) originate money bills.

5. The first representative form of government to exist in America was established in 1619 in
   (A) Virginia
   (B) Rhode Island
   (C) Georgia
   (D) Massachusetts.

6. Of the following New England states, the one which does *not* have an Atlantic seaport is
   (A) Vermont
   (B) Rhode Island
   (C) Connecticut
   (D) New Hampshire.

7. The Japan Current affects the climate of Alaska in a way similar to the way in which the Gulf Stream affects the climate of
   (A) Norway
   (B) Labrador
   (C) Scotland
   (D) France.

8. All of the following have been used to help the American farmer since World War II *except*
   (A) a conservation program
   (B) government subsidies
   (C) price-support plans
   (D) export duties.

9. Two nations that fought on the side of the Allies in World War I but on the side of the Axis in World War II were
   (A) Italy and Bulgaria
   (B) Rumania and Hungary
   (C) Turkey and Bulgaria
   (D) Japan and Italy.

10. Theodore Roosevelt applied the term "Muckrakers" at the turn of the century to the
    (A) traction magnates Whitney, Yerkers, and Widener
    (B) writers Tarbell, Sinclair and Steffens
    (C) meat tycoons Armour, Swift and Morris
    (D) steel and oil monopolists Carnegie, Morgan and Vanderbilt.

S1628

11. Immediate and unconditional freeing of the slaves before the Civil War was demanded by
    (A) Stephen A. Douglas
    (B) William Lloyd Garrison
    (C) Andrew Jackson
    (D) Abraham Lincoln.

12. The Northwest Ordinance is significant in part because it provided a framework for the
    (A) organization of city government
    (B) Constitution of the United States
    (C) admission of new states to the union
    (D) Articles of Confederation.

13. President Monroe's primary reason for stating the Monroe Doctrine was to
    (A) make the United States of America a world power
    (B) stop European interference in the already independent countries of America
    (C) give the United States of America control over the Latin American countries
    (D) help in the economic development of Latin America.

14. Invoking the power granted it in the "elastic clause" of the Federal Constitution, Congress authorized the
    (A) formation of the regular army
    (B) establishment of the first Bank of the United States

(C) establishment of the postal system
(D) borrowing of money.

15. The first major industry to come under Federal governmental regulation in the United States was
    (A) mining
    (B) ship building
    (C) railroad transportation
    (D) textile manufacturing.

16. All of the following labor leaders were founders of labor organizations except
    (A) Samuel Gompers
    (B) John L. Lewis
    (C) William Green
    (D) Uriah S. Stephens.

17. "A public office is a public trust" is a statement attributed to
    (A) George Washington
    (B) Abraham Lincoln
    (C) Theodore Roosevelt
    (D) Grover Cleveland

18. Of the following pairs, the one in which the items are incorrectly paired is
    (A) dynamite—Nobel
    (B) elevator—Otis
    (C) safety lamp—Drake
    (D) linotype—Mergenthaler.

END OF PART

Go on to the following Test in the next Part of this Examination, just as you would be expected to do on the actual exam. If you have any available time use it to make sure that you have marked your Answer Sheet properly for this Part. Correct Answers for all Parts of this Exam follow the last question. Derive your scores only after completing the entire Exam.

PART III. THE SCIENCE TEST

TIME: 90 Minutes. 55 Questions.

TEST VII. INTERPRETATION OF SCIENCE READINGS

TIME: 60 Minutes. 35 Questions.

DIRECTIONS: Below each of the following passages of natural science reading material you will find one or more incomplete statements about the passage. Select the words or expressions that most satisfactorily complete each statement in accordance with the meaning of the paragraph.

A colored transparent object, such as a piece of red glass, transmits red light, and absorbs all or most of the other colors that shine on it. But what about opaque (non-transparent) objects? Why is one piece of cloth, for example, red while another is blue? The answer is that we see only the light that is reflected from such an object. White light, which contains all colors, shines on our piece of cloth. The dye in the cloth is of such a nature that it pretty well absorbs all colors except red. The red is then reflected, and that is what we see. If some other color or combination of colors is reflected, then we may get any hue or tint. Incidentally, this gives us a hint as to why many fabrics seem to have one color under artificial light and another color in daylight. The artificial light is of a different composition from daylight, and therefore the amount of each color reflected is different.

Light from an incandescent lamp, for example, contains proportionately more red and yellow than does sunlight, and hence emphasizes the red and yellow hues, weakening the blues and violets by contrast. Strangely enough, though, yellow may appear quite white under an incandescent lamp. This comes about because our eyes, being accustomed to the yellowish light from the lamp, no longer distinguish the lamplight from the real white of sunlight. Therefore, a piece of yellow cloth or paper, reflecting all the colors contained in the lamplight, appears to be white.

1. If an object were manufactured so that all light rays that hit it were reflected away from it, the color of the object would be

   1) white.
   2) black.
   3) iridescent.
   4) transparent.

2. If an object absorbed all of the light that strikes it, the color of the object would be

   1) white.
   2) black.
   3) iridescent.
   4) transparent.

3. If an object were made in such a way that the light striking it was neither reflected nor absorbed, the object would be

   1) white.
   2) black.
   3) iridescent.
   4) transparent.

4. If the light from a blue mercury lamp which contains no red light waves were to illuminate a pure red tie, the tie would appear to be

   1) white.
   2) black.
   3) red.
   4) transparent.

5. The author implies that for an object to be visible

   1) all of the received light must be reflected.
   2) some of the received light must be reflected.
   3) some of the received light must be absorbed.
   4) any of the above situations may occur.

We know that a small permanent magnet, such as a compass needle, will set itself parallel to a magnetic line of force. But an unmagnetized piece of soft iron will do the same thing, and will, furthermore, be attracted to the pole of a permanent magnet just as a compass needle is. Suppose that a nail, for example, is brought near the south pole of a permanent magnet. A north pole is induced in the nail on the end nearer the south pole of a permanent magnet and it becomes, temporarily, a magnet. But it loses most of its induced magnetism as soon as it is removed from the field of the permanent magnet.

Nearly all materials have weak magnetic properties that can be detected and measured by delicate apparatus. But a very few materials—iron, cobalt, nickel and several alloys—show outstandingly large magnetic effects. These ferromagnetic substances, as they are called, are essentially different from the common run of materials. They naturally contain a multitude of tiny magnets which are normally pointing in all the various directions, so that their individual magnetic effects cancel out. When the material is placed in a magnetic field, all the tiny magnets in it turn about and tend to line up with the field and so with one another. As a result, the sample is itself a good magnet, as long as it is in the magnetic field. Once it is removed, the tiny magnets again become disorganized, and the sample no longer acts as a magnet.

Permanent magnets are also made of ferromagnetic materials, but various tricks are employed to keep the tiny elementary magnets in them from getting out of alignment once they have been lined up in a magnetic field. In steel, for example, the elementary magnets are brought into cooperation only with difficulty, but they also find it hard to get out of line with one another after the magnetizing field is removed; a permanent magnet is the result. Even a steel magnet, however, will lose its magnetism if it is heated or severely jarred. In recent years, certain alloys have been used to make extremely powerful permanent magnets.

It is not known why iron, nickel and cobalt naturally contain these tiny magnets, while gold, lead and other metals do not have them. The electrons in metal continually whirl, teetotum-fashion. Both of these motions constitute electric currents, and the magnetic effects of these currents are presumably responsible for the magnetic behavior of the material. In fact, the weak magnetic properties of ordinary materials can be explained quite acceptably by considering in detail how these electron currents will interact with external magnetic fields. The ferromagnetic metals are more of a puzzle. How the travelling and spinning electrons in them cooperate to produce tiny magnetized domains is beginning to be understood, but the picture is not yet complete.

The magnetism of the earth remains essentially unexplained, despite the many theories that have been advanced. The magnetism of both sun and earth appears to be connected with the rotation of these bodies. For many reasons it seems unlikely that the earth's core actually contains a large iron magnet. But why aren't the magnetic poles located at the geographic poles? And why do the magnetic poles gradually shift their positions with the passage of years? At present, the north magnetic pole (that is, the place where a compass needle points vertically downward) is located north of Hudson Bay, well over a thousand miles from the north geographic pole. It is moving westward at the rate of a very few miles per year. The south magnetic pole is in the Antarctic, nearly opposite the north magnetic pole.

The behavior of the earth's magnetic poles is not only mysterious, but most annoying. Compass needles fail to point true north and, what is worse, their error, or declination, changes slightly from year to year in any one locality. In Maine the compass points as much as 23° to the west of true north and in the state of Washington as much as 24° to the east of true north. There is one line in the United States (extending irregularly from South Carolina northward through the middle of Lake Superior) where the compass does point to the true north; but east or west of this line the declination varies between 0° and the maximum of 23° or 24°.

Go on to the next page

6. The south pole of a magnet attracts

    1) the north pole of another magnet.
    2) the south pole of another magnet.
    3) both poles of another magnet.
    4) either pole, but not both poles of another magnet.

7. In an ordinary piece of iron the atomic magnets are probably arranged

    1) with all poles pointing in the same direction.
    2) with poles on either end pointing in the same direction.
    3) so that only the poles in the center neutralize each other.
    4) in a random order.

8. The reason a temporary magnet loses its magnetism is that the atomic groups have

    1) lost their magnetism.
    2) lost their alignment.
    3) become permanent magnets.
    4) become temporary magnets.

9. In order to make a light alloy of aluminum that would be magnetic, it might be best to combine it with

    1) helium.
    2) silver.
    3) gold.
    4) nickel.

10. Which of the following materials would probably be best to use to protect a delicate instrument from magnetism?

    1) iron
    2) copper
    3) rubber
    4) paper

11. If two large magnets were placed together and heated

    1) one magnet would increase in strength and one magnet would decrease.

2) both magnets would increase in strength.
    3) both magnets would decrease in strength.
    4) both magnets would remain unchanged.

12. The causes for the magnetic fields of the earth are probably connected with

    1) materials at the earth's core.
    2) materials located at the earth's poles.
    3) the rotation of the moon around the earth.
    4) the daily rotation of the earth.

13. If a sailor living in Washington corrects his compass so that it points to true north, and then he moves to Maine, his compass would

    1) still be correct.
    2) point 23° west of true north.
    3) point 46° west of true north.
    4) be of no value.

14. If an explorer were to follow his compass south until it pointed directly down he would be

    1) at the south geographic pole.
    2) at the north geographic pole.
    3) 1000 miles from the south geographic pole.
    4) 1000 miles from the north geographic pole.

15. If the north poles of two separate magnets are brought together, their attraction is

    1) negative.
    2) positive.
    3) zero.
    4) alternating.

16. If a compass were corrected today for local use, when would it be necessary to correct it again if it is to be absolutely correct?

    1) next month
    2) next year
    3) next century
    4) never

Go on to the next page

Many important scientific developments came out of World War II, and one of the most important was radar. The word is a contraction of "radio detection and ranging." It works in much the same way as an echo. When you shout toward a cliff or a large building part of the sound bounces back. In radar, short beams are sent out. When they strike an object they bounce back and are picked up by a receiver. The direction of the returning signal indicates the direction of the object, and the time it takes to return indicates how far away the object is. Because different objects reflect radar waves at different densities, objects can be detected in any kind of weather, day or night. Radar waves are not deflected by atmospheric layers and therefore always travel in a straight line.

Radar waves are electromagnetic waves, as are light waves, electric waves, x-rays, cosmic rays and radio waves. All electromagnetic waves travel at 186,000 miles per second, the speed of light. They differ from each other in the number of vibrations per second; this is known as their frequency. They also differ in their wave length. To find the wave length of an electromagnetic wave, the following formula is used:

$$\text{wave length} = \frac{186,000}{\text{frequency}}$$

Thus, a radio station broadcasting at 500 kilocycles (500,000 vibrations per second) would have a wave length of 0.3720 mile or about 1960 feet. If the frequency should go to 100 kilocycles the wave length would be 980 feet.

More and more research is developing other uses for electromagnetic waves. Radar operates at 10 million kilocycles (a wave length of just over 1 inch). Other inventions operate at much lower frequencies (diathermy machines at about 500 kilocycles, etc.). As transmitters are developed which can transmit smaller and smaller wave lengths we will have more uses for electromagnetic waves.

Below is a table giving the range of the approximate wave length of some better known electromagnetic waves.

type of wave	wave length
electric waves	from 1/8 mile–over 600 miles
radio broadcast waves	1/10 mile–15 feet
UHF, television and radar	15 feet–less than 1 inch
infrared heat	0.04–0.00004 inch
visible light	0.00001 inch (red)–0.00001 inch (violet)
x-rays	0.0000004 inch–0.000000004 inch
cosmic rays	0.00000000003 inch–0.000000000000003 inch

17. Radio waves and radar waves have the same
    1) frequency.
    2) wave length.
    3) strength.
    4) speed.

18. A beam having the frequency of 4,000 kilocycles would have a wave length of about
    1) 1960 feet.
    2) 980 feet.
    3) 490 feet.
    4) 245 feet.

19. A radar set could not locate an aircraft if the aircraft was flying
    1) faster than the speed of sound.
    2) above a heavy storm.
    3) above the atmosphere.
    4) below the horizon.

20. It is possible to find the distance an object is located from a radar set because the
    1) wave length of radar is known.
    2) frequency of radar is known.
    3) speed of radar is 186,000 miles per second.
    4) power of each set is known.

21. Does all visible light have the same frequency?

    1) Yes; all light is electromagnetic.
    2) Yes; all light travels at the same speed.
    3) No; red has a higher frequency than violet.
    4) No; violet has a higher frequency than red.

22. If an airplane altimeter uses a wave length of 2 inches, it is using

    1) sound waves.
    2) Ultra High Frequency waves.
    3) light waves.
    4) x-rays.

23. Radio waves will not penetrate the ionosphere, but UHF waves will. Would you expect x-rays to penetrate the ionosphere?

    1) Yes, because they have a shorter wave length than UHF and radio waves.
    2) Yes, because they have a lower frequency than UHF and radio waves.
    3) No, because they travel slower than UHF and radio waves.
    4) No, because they have a different frequency and wave length from either radio or UHF waves.

24. Compared to cosmic rays the frequency of visible light waves is

    1) higher.
    2) lower.
    3) the same.
    4) unable to be told from the information given.

METAL	Potential volts
LITHIUM	−3.05
MAGNESIUM	−2.37
ALUMINUM	−1.66
IRON	−0.44
HYDROGEN	−0.00
TIN	+0.15
COPPER	+0.34
SILVER	+0.80
GOLD	+0.08
COBALT	+1.84

In all cells, the voltage observed arises from two sources: a voltage at the anode (+pole) and a voltage at the cathode (−pole). If either of these voltages was known, the other could be obtained by subtraction. However, it is impossible to measure the voltage of an individual electrode, since any complete circuit necessarily contains two electrodes. We are forced to assign a completely arbitrary voltage to one electrode. The voltage of the other electrode is thereby fixed. For convenience, the voltage of the standard hydrogen electrode is given the value zero. Consequently, in any cell which contains the standard hydrogen electrode, the entire measured voltage is attributed to the half-reaction at the other electrode. Voltages thus assigned are called oxidation potentials.

The chart lists various metals with their oxidation potentials. The voltage given applies when the half-reaction proceeds in the forward direction. For the reverse direction, the sign of the voltage must be changed.

Several interesting observations can be made when elements are arranged in this manner. The farther apart the two elements are on the scale the greater the potential voltage will be when they are made into an electric cell. The elements with negative numbers will be cathode and those with positive potential will be anode. By subtracting the cathode potential from that of the anode we get the potential electromotive force of the cell. A magnesium-silver cell would furnish $(+0.80) − (−2.37)$ or $+3.17$ potential.

A second interesting and important fact is that any metal

in solution will replace any metal above it. For instance, if an aluminum coin was placed in a proper silver sulphate solution the aluminum would go into solution as the silver was being deposited on the coin.

Another observation of interest is the reaction these elements have to hot acid. While acid will dissolve most metals, when it dissolves those above hydrogen the reaction is simple. The hydrogen is driven off and the metal replaces it, forming a salt. When those metals below hydrogen are dissolved in acid, water is formed and the more complicated compounds of the metal and the acid are formed.

The metals below hydrogen are found in a free state, while those below copper will not rust in the open air. Those metals above hydrogen are secured by electrical or roasting methods and thus are likely to be relatively cheap.

As can be seen, the more positive the voltage potential the less likelihood there is of chemical activity taking place.

25. In a solution tin would displace
    1) only iron.
    2) only aluminum.
    3) neither iron nor aluminum.
    4) both iron and aluminum.

26. If magnesium is placed in hot nitric acid
    1) no chemical reaction will take place.
    2) magnesium sulphate is formed.
    3) water is formed.
    4) hydrogen is formed.

27. The voltage potential of an hydrogen-aluminum cell should be
    1) −1.66 volts.
    2) −3.32 volts.
    3) +1.66 volts.
    4) +3.32 volts.

28. The voltage potential of a copper-iron cell should be
    1) −0.10 volt.
    2) +0.10 volt.
    3) +0.78 volt.
    4) −0.78 volt.

29. Which of the following cells will produce the greatest potential voltage?
    1) aluminum-iron
    2) silver-cobalt
    3) gold-magnesium
    4) copper-iron

30. The fact that one metal will replace another in a solution is most important in
    1) making alloys.   3) blacksmithing.
    2) electro-plating.   4) iron smelting.

31. When a piece of iron is placed in a copper sulphite solution
    1) copper is deposited.
    2) iron is deposited.
    3) copper goes into solution.
    4) hydrogen is freed to form water.

32. When tin is placed in hot sulphuric acid
    1) hydrogen is formed.
    2) water is formed.
    3) tin nitrate is formed.
    4) no reaction takes place.

33. Which kind of table would place metals in the same order as the table showing the potential voltage?
    1) a chemical activity chart
    2) a chart listing chemicals by their importance
    3) a chart listing chemicals by their cost
    4) a chart listing chemicals by their weight

34. Why does hydrogen show a voltage potential of 0.00?
    1) cells cannot be made using hydrogen
    2) hydrogen is not chemically active
    3) hydrogen has no weight
    4) hydrogen is used only as a basis of comparison

35. The oxidation potential of a metal is the same as the
    1) atomic weight.
    2) chemical strength.
    3) voltage potential.
    4) atomic number.

END OF TEST

TEST VIII. SCIENCE INFORMATION

TIME: 30 Minutes. 20 Questions.

DIRECTIONS: For each of the following questions, select the choice which best answers the question or completes the statement.

Correct answers for these questions appear at the end of this examination, together with the answers to all the other tests.

1. The time that it takes for the earth to complete a 60 degree rotation is
   (A) 1 hour
   (B) 4 hours
   (C) 6 hours
   (D) 24 hours.

2. Of the following, the most common metal found in the earth's crust is
   (A) iron
   (B) copper
   (C) aluminum
   (D) tin.

3. Of the following, the gas which is needed for burning is
   (A) carbon dioxide
   (B) oxygen
   (C) nitrogen
   (D) argon.

4. Of the following, the process which will result in water that is the most nearly chemically pure is
   (A) aeration
   (B) chlorination
   (C) distillation
   (D) filtration.

5. The number of degrees on the Fahrenheit thermometer between the freezing point and the boiling point of water is
   (A) 100 degrees
   (B) 180 degrees
   (C) 212 degrees
   (D) 273 degrees.

6. Of the following planets, the one which has the largest number of satellites is
   (A) Jupiter
   (B) Mercury
   (C) Neptune
   (D) Pluto.

7. The Beaufort Scale indicates
   (A) temperature
   (B) air pressure
   (C) wind force
   (D) wind direction.

8. Of the following, the string with the lowest pitch would be a
   (A) tight, thick string
   (B) loose, thick string
   (C) tight, thin string
   (D) loose, thin string.

9. Washing soda is composed of the chemical elements sodium, oxygen and
   (A) nitrogen
   (B) chlorine
   (C) sulfur
   (D) carbon.

10. One is most likely to feel the effects of static electricity on a
    (A) cold, damp day
    (B) cold, dry day
    (C) warm, humid day
    (D) warm, dry day.

11. The biologist who first artificially induced mutations by means of irradiation was
    (A) Morgan
    (B) Muller
    (C) Curie
    (D) DeVries.

12. In backcrossing, a hybrid is always mated with
    (A) its own parent
    (B) another hybrid
    (C) a pure dominant
    (D) a pure recessive.

13. All of the following concepts in genetics were first clearly stated by Gregor Mendel *except*
    (A) dominance
    (B) independent assortment
    (C) segregation
    (D) hybrid vigor.

14. The Santa Gertrudis breed of cattle was developed by using
    (A) selection
    (B) inbreeding
    (C) outbreeding
    (D) all of the above.

S1627

15. Differences in feather color in Andalusian chickens illustrate the genetic principle of
    (A) independent assortment (B) dominance
    (C) blending inheritance (D) linkage.

16. Albinism is caused by
    (A) deficiency of Vitamin D
    (B) an unknown environmental factor
    (C) a hereditary factor
    (D) a neoplasm.

17. Of the following, a human blood disease which has been definitely shown to be due to a hereditary factor or factors is
    (A) pernicious anemia (B) sickle cell anemia
    (C) polyscythemia (D) lukemia.

18. Of the following human traits, the one which is under both genetic and hormonal control is
    (A) hemophilia (B) color blindness
    (C) baldness (D) cytological sex.

19. Kallikak is the
    (A) name of a type of orange
    (B) pseudonym of an American family
    (C) term for a type of congenital nerve disorder
    (D) name of a neurotropic virus.

20. The relation between termites and their intestinal protozoa is an example of
    (A) saprophytism (B) parasitism
    (C) symbiosis (D) commensalism.

END OF PART

Go on to the following Test in the next Part of this Examination, just as you would be expected to do on the actual exam. If you have any available time use it to make sure that you have marked your Answer Sheet properly for this Part. Correct Answers for all Parts of this Exam follow the last question. Derive your scores only after completing the entire Exam.

PART IV. THE READING SKILLS TEST

TIME: 90 Minutes. 53 Questions.

TEST IX. INTERPRETATION OF LITERARY MATERIALS

TIME: 70 Minutes. 42 Questions.

DIRECTIONS: Below each of the following passages of literature you will find one or more incomplete statements about the passage. Select the words or expressions that most satisfactorily complete each statement in accordance with the meaning of the paragraph.

For several days the captain seemed very much out of humor. Nothing went right, or fast enough for
2 him. He quarreled with the cook, and threatened to flog him for throwing wood on deck; and he had a
dispute with the mate about reeving a Spanish burton,—the mate saying he was right, and had been
4 taught how to do it by a man who was a sailor! This, the captain took in dudgeon, and they were at
swords' points at once.

6   But his displeasure was chiefly turned against a large, heavy-molded fellow from the Middle States
who was called Sam. This man hesitated in his speech, and was rather slow in his motions, but was a
8 pretty good sailor, and always seemed to do his best; but the captain took a dislike to him, thought he
was surly and lazy; and "if you once give a dog a bad name"—as the sailor phrase is—"he may as well
10 jump overboard." The captain found fault with everything this man did, and hazed him for dropping a
marline spike from the main yard, where he was at work. This, of course, was an accident, but it was set
12 down against him.

The captain was on board all day Friday, and everything went on hard and disagreeably. "The more
14 you drive a man, the less he will do" was as true with us as with any other people. We worked late Friday
night and were turned-to early Saturday morning. About ten o'clock the captain ordered our new officer,
Russell, who by this time had become thoroughly disliked by all the crew, to get the gig ready to take him
ashore.

1. At the time this was written the ship was

  1) tied up to a dock.   3) out at sea.
  2) riding at anchor.   4) just being built.

2. From this passage we know that the ship was a

  1) sailing ship.   3) passenger ship.
  2) steam ship.   4) war ship.

3. The word "dudgeon" (line 4) means nearly the same as

  1) exciting.   3) complimentary.
  2) confusion.   4) anger.

4. Sam was from

  1) England.   3) Spain.
  2) The United States.   4) Africa.

5. The writing in this passage may best be described as

  1) matter of fact.   3) make believe.
  2) humorous.   4) ornate.

6. From this description we know that the crew of the ship was

  1) untrained.
  2) ready for mutiny.
  3) being punished for making a mistake.
  4) being overworked.

7. The person telling the story felt that the captain was

  1) unfair and brutal.
  2) justifiably angry.
  3) strict but fair.
  4) lacking the knowledge needed to be a captain.

Thou blossom bright with autumn dew,
2 And colored with the heaven's own blue,
That openest when the quiet light
4 Succeeds the keen and frosty night,

Thou comest not when violets lean
6 O'er wandering brooks and springs unseen,
Or columbines, in purple dressed,
8 Nod o'er the ground-bird's hidden nest.

Thou waitest late and com'st alone,
10 When woods are bare and birds are flown,
And frosts and shortening days portend
12 The aged year is near his end.

Then doth thy sweet and quiet eye
14 Look through its fringes to the sky,
Blue—blue—as if that Sky let fall
16 A flower from its cerulean wall.

I would that thus, when I shall see
18 The hour of death draw near to me,
Hope, blossoming within my heart,
20 May look to heaven as I depart.

8. The mood of this poem is best described as

1) sad and afraid.
2) fearful and angry.
3) respectful and hopeful.
4) unhappy and doubtful.

9. The flower discussed in the poem blooms in

1) early spring, just after the snow melts.
2) early summer, when it is getting hot.
3) early fall, when harvest has begun.
4) late fall, when everything else is dead.

10. In line (11) "portend" most nearly means

1) announce.
2) protect.
3) cause.
4) hide.

11. In the last verse the poet is writing about the

1) sadness of seeing the flowers die.
2) beauty found in the flowers.
3) hope he has for the coming year.
4) way he wants to feel about death.

12. The poet compares "hope" with the

1) time of year.
2) flower.
3) soul.
4) birds.

13. The flowers mentioned in the second verse are for the purpose of

1) comparing good and evil.
2) contrasting beauty and ugliness.
3) showing how unusual is the flower he describes.
4) indicating some flowers are wild and others domesticated.

ROSE: Can it be possible you love me so?
2   No, no, within those eyeballs I espy
           Apparent likelihoods of flattery.
4   Pray now, let go my hand.

HAM: Sweet Mistress Rose,
6   Misconstrue not my words, nor misconceive
           Of my affection, whose devoted soul
8   Swears that I love thee dearer than my heart.

ROSE: As dear as your own heart? I judge it right;
10   Men love their hearts best when th'are out of sight.

HAM: I love you, by this hand.

12 ROSE: Yet hands off now!
           If flesh be frail, how weak and frail's your vow!

14 HAM: Then by my life I swear.

ROSE: Then do not brawl;
16   One quarrel loseth wife and life and all.
          Is not your meaning thus?

18 HAM: In faith, you jest.

ROSE: Love loves to sport, therefore leave love, y' are best.

20 HAM: Sweet Rose, be not so strange in fancying me.
          Nay, never turn aside, shun not my sight;
22   I am not grown so fond, my love
          On any that shall quit it with disdain;
24   If you will love me, so—if not—farewell.

14. Judging from this passage, it would seem that

1) Rose has caught Ham in a lie.
2) Rose is angry with Ham and wants him to leave her alone.
3) Ham is trying to convince Rose of his love.
4) Ham is having fun teasing Rose.

15. In line (8) Ham most likely means by the word "heart"

1) life.
2) soul.
3) sweetheart.
4) mind.

16. In line (9) Rose most likely means by the weard "heart"

1) life.
2) soul.
3) sweetheart.
4) mind.

17. What does Rose mean in line (17) by "Is not your meaning thus"?

1) Because life is unsure, your love is unsure.
2) No one loves someone else more than himself.
3) If you really loved me you wouldn't fight.
4) You drink and quarrel too much for me to trust you.

18. "In faith, you jest" (line 18) means

    1) have more faith in me.
    2) I'm sorry you find my love humorous.
    3) faith is not a joking matter.
    4) I'm sure you must be teasing me.

19. In his last speech, Ham tells Rose

    1) if you won't forgive me, I'll kill myself.
    2) if you won't accept my love and return it I'm leaving.

    3) I'm tired of you and you may as well leave.
    4) no matter what you say I'm never going to give up.

20. Rose could best be described as being

    1) cautious.
    2) modest.
    3) submissive.
    4) dramatic.

 I crossed one swell of living turf after another, looking for a place to sit down and draw. Do not, for
2 heaven's sake, imagine I was going to sketch from nature. I was going to draw devils and seraphim,
and blind old gods that men worshipped before the dawn of right, and saints in robes of angry crimson,
4 and seas of strange green, and all the sacred or monstrous symbols that look so well in bright colors
on brown paper. They are much better worth drawing than nature; also they are much easier to draw.
6 When a cow came slouching by in the field next to me, a mere artist might have drawn it; but I always
get wrong in the hind legs of quadrupeds. So I drew the soul of the cow; which I saw there plainly walking
8 before me in the sunlight; and the soul was all purple and silver, and had seven horns and the mystery
that belongs to all the beasts. But though I could not with a crayon get the best out of the landscape, it
10 does not follow that the landscape was not getting the best out of me. And this, I think, is the mistake
that people make about the old poets who lived before Wordsworth, and were supposed not to care very
12 much about nature because they did not describe it much.

21. This passage probably came from

    1) a romantic novel.
    2) an article on painting technique.
    3) a humorous essay.
    4) a biography of a great painter.

22. The drawing was done in

    1) a field.
    2) a studio.
    3) the artist's home.
    4) a city.

23. What seems to be the most likely reason that the author did not draw pictures of nature?

    1) It is not the kind of thing that inspires artists.
    2) He didn't think it was enough of a challenge.
    3) He did not like nature.
    4) He could not draw well enough.

24. The author apparently

    1) likes art and draws well.
    2) likes art but draws poorly.
    3) dislikes art and draws poorly.
    4) dislikes art but likes poetry.

25. The author indicates (lines 9–10) that the landscape was

    1) interesting but common.
    2) uninteresting and lifeless.
    3) quite easily reproduced.
    4) an inspiration to his work.

26. In this article the author is really

    1) laughing at himself.
    2) bragging about his artistic ability.
    3) making excuses for himself.
    4) making fun of art and artists.

A ride of two hundred and odd miles in severe weather is one of the best softeners of a hard bed that
2 ingenuity can devise. Perhaps it is even a sweetener of dreams, for those which hovered over the rough
couch of Nicholas, and whispered their airy nothings in his ear, were of an agreeable and happy kind. He
4 was making his fortune very fast indeed, when the faint glimmer of an expiring candle shone before his
eyes, and a voice he had no difficulty in recognizing as part and parcel of Mr. Squeers, admonished him
that it was time to rise.

6 "Past seven, Nickleby," said Mr. Squeers.
"Has morning come already?" asked Nicholas, sitting up in bed.
8 "Ah! that has it," replied Squeers, "and ready iced too. Now, Nickleby, come; tumble up, will you?"

Nicholas needed no further admonition, but "tumbled up" at once, and proceeded to dress himself by
10 the light of the taper which Mr. Squeers carried in his hand.

27. What was the probable relationship between Nicholas and Mr. Squeers?

1) father and son
2) business partners
3) employee and employer
4) doctor and patient

28. "He was making his fortune very fast indeed ..." (lines 4-5) refers to the

1) amount of money he inherited.
2) success of a business trip.
3) salary Mr. Squeers paid him.
4) things he was dreaming about.

29. What kind of a morning was it that greeted Nickleby?

1) hot
2) cold
3) stormy
4) beautiful

30. The "taper" mentioned in line (10) is a

1) candle.
2) small lamp.
3) flashlight.
4) mirror.

Go on to the next page

But Mr. Burke appears to have no idea of principles when he is contemplating governments. "Ten
2 years ago," says he, "I could have felicitated France on her having a government, without inquiring what
the nature of that government was or how it was administered." Is this the language of a rational man? Is
4 it the language of a heart feeling as it ought to feel for the rights and happiness of the human race? On
this ground, Mr. Burke must compliment all the governments in the world, while the victims who suffer
6 under them, whether sold into slavery or tortured out of existence, are wholly forgotten. It is power, and
not principles, that Mr. Burke venerates; and under this abominable depravity, he is disqualified to judge
8 between them. This much for his opinion as to the occasions of the French Revolution. I now proceed to
other considerations.

10   I know of a place in America called Point-no-Point because, as you proceed along the shore, gay and
flowery as Mr. Burke's language, it continually recedes, and presents itself at a distance before you; but
12 when you have got as far as you can go, there is no point at all. Just thus it is with Mr. Burke's three
hundred and fifty-six pages. It is therefore difficult to reply to him. But as the points he wishes to establish
14 may be inferred from what he abuses, it is in his paradoxes that we must look for his arguments.

31. The tone of this passage is

1) warm praise.
2) mild satire.
3) disinterested comment.
4) bitter attack.

32. The word "felicitated" in line (2) means

1) attacked.
2) congratulated.
3) warned.
4) consulted.

33. "Paradoxes" as used in line (14) most nearly
means

1) contradictions.
2) illustrations.
3) speeches.
4) explanations.

34. The purpose of this article is to

1) present a political point of view.
2) review a book.
3) introduce a history book.
4) encourage a student.

35. The author thinks that Mr. Burke's style of
writing is

1) scholarly and exact.
2) crude but effective.
3) elegant but shallow.
4) sloppy and illiterate.

36. The author would probably most approve of a
government that was

1) concerned about the welfare of its citizens.
2) built on long established traditions.
3) opposed to war under any conditions.
4) strong and strict.

37. The author suggests that Mr. Burke would
approve of

1) only strong dictatorial governments.
2) only democratic governments.
3) only some form of socialist or communistic
governments.
4) any of the above mentioned forms of
government.

Go on to the next page

The merchant, to secure his treasure,
2 Conveys it in a borrowed name;
Euphelia serves to grace my measure,
4 But Chloe is my real flame.

My softest verse, my darling lyre,
6 Upon Euphelia's toilet lay—
When Chloe noted her desire
8 That I should sing, that I should play.

My lyre I tune, my voice I raise,
10 But with my numbers mix my signs;
And whilst I sing Euphelia's praise,
12 I fix my soul on Chloe's eyes.

Fair Chloe blushed; Euphelia frowned;
14 I sung, and gazed; I played, and trembled;
And Venus to the Loves around
16 Remarked how ill we all dissembled.

38. In line (1), "secure" most nearly means

1) hide.
2) get.
3) sell.
4) store.

39. Lines (3) and (4) mean that he

1) can't decide which girl he really loves.
2) is in love with two girls at the same time.
3) sings about Euphelia but loves Chloe.
4) sings about Chloe but loves Euphelia.

40. Line (10) means that he

1) has become tired of playing and singing.
2) keeps getting the words of the song mixed up.
3) is putting all of his feelings into the words of the song.
4) is singing one thing but thinking another.

41. Which of the two girls seems to be interested in the singer?

1) Chloe
2) Euphelia
3) neither
4) both

42. The tone of this poem is

1) extremely serious.
2) unemotional.
3) despairing.
4) somewhat light.

END OF TEST

Go on to do the following Test in this Examination, just as you would be expected to do on the actual exam. You will find correct answers for the entire Examination following the last question. Check your answers carefully after you have completed the whole Examination.

TEST X. INTERPRETATION OF PROSE

TIME: 20 Minutes. 11 Questions.

DIRECTIONS: Below each of the following passages of literature you will find one or more incomplete statements about the passage. Select the words or expressions that most satisfactorily complete each statement in accordance with the meaning of the paragraph.

Correct answers for these questions appear at the end of this examination, together with the answers to all the other tests.

Reading Passage I

"Sticks and stones can break my bones, But names will never hurt me." No doubt you are familiar with this childhood rhyme; perhaps, when you were younger, you frequently invoked whatever protection it could offer against unpleasant epithets. But like many popular slogans and verses, this one will not bear too close scrutiny. For names *will* hurt you. Sometimes you may be the victim, and find yourself an object of scorn, humiliation, and hatred just because other people have called you certain names. At other times you may not be the victim, but clever speakers and writers may, through name calling, blind your judgment so that you will follow them in a course of action wholly opposed to your own interests or principles. Name calling can make you gullible to propaganda which you might otherwise readily see through and reject.

1. The title below that best expresses the ideas of this passage is
   (A) an object of scorn
   (B) an unusual course of action
   (C) the foolishness of rhymes
   (D) verbal assassination
   (E) the clever speaker.

2. Name calling may make you more susceptible to
   (A) childhood rhymes
   (B) biased arguments
   (C) sticks and stones
   (D) invoked protection
   (E) enpleasant epithets.

3. The author evidently feels that slogans and verses are frequently
   (A) invoked by gullible writers
   (B) humiliating to their authors
   (C) disregarded by children
   (D) misunderstood by clever speakers
   (E) an over-simplification of a problem.

Reading Passage II

The Greek language is a member of the Aryan or Indo-European family and its various dialects constitute the Hellenic group. It was probably spoken in Europe and Asia, at least 1,500 years before the Christian Era, by Greeks with classical learning. Later it was a universal language among the cultured classes, just as Latin afterward became the medium of international communication. During the Dark Ages, Greek was little known to Western Europe, except in monasteries, although it remained the language of the Byzantine Empire. The emigration of the Greeks to Italy after the fall of Constantinople, and during the century preceeding, gave a new impetus to the study of the Greek language, and the revival of learning gave it the place it has ever since occupied.

4. The title below that best expresses the ideas of this passage is
   (A) the Greek language
   (B) Greece, past and present
   (C) importance of the Greek dialects
   (D) Greek, the universal language
   (E) an interesting language.

5. A result of Greece's being the center of classical learning was that
   (A) it built great schools
   (B) its citizens were all cultured
   (C) Greek was the universal language among the cultured classes

   (D) Greek was not important during the Dark Ages
   (E) Greek displaced Latin.

6. The Greek language
   (A) was probably spoken in Europe as early as 1500 B.C.
   (B) was introduced into Europe by way of Constantinople
   (C) was responsible for the revival of learning
   (D) became dominant in Italy
   (E) had more dialects than Latin.

Reading Passage III

The hearty laugh, Chesterton maintained, cannot be had without touching the heart. I do not know why touching the heart should always be connected only with the idea of touching it to compassion or a sense of distress. The heart can be touched to joy and triumph; the heart can be touched to amusement. But all our comedians are tragic comedians. These later fashionable writers are so pessimistic in bone and marrow that they never seem able to imagine the heart ever having any concern with mirth. When they speak of the heart, they always mean the pangs and disappointments of the emotional life. When they say that a man's heart is in the right place, they mean, apparently, that it is in his boots.

7. The title below that best expresses the ideas of this passage is
   (A) arousing compassion
   (B) the right place for a man's heart
   (C) laughter and sympathy
   (D) tragic humor
   (E) touching the heart.

8. References to the heart should always be connected with
   (A) the pangs and disappointments of the emotional life

   (B) genuine emotional experience
   (C) feelings of joy and triumph
   (D) compassion or a sense of distress
   (E) extreme gaiety.

9. Fashionable writers today always produce
   (A) pessimistic, heartless pangs
   (B) sarcasm mixed with joy
   (C) witticisms and pangs of regret
   (D) comedy and pessimism
   (E) sad or unhappy emotional effects.

Reading Passage IV

The English are a heterogeneous and contradictory race with conservative tendencies. While progress is the aim of every Englishman, he nevertheless distrusts and resents change. When he goes to bed, he insists that his mattress shall be supported by a symphony of springs that is the newest word in comfort, but when he wakes up in the morning he requires that the view from his bedroom window shall be the same as it was yesterday and for centuries of yesterdays before that. Thus it is that Great Britain is a land in which the past is always becoming the present, in which history is inescapably part of the picture of today, and thus it is that Great Britain has become a storehouse of treasures that are both the work of nature and the work of man.

10. The title below that best expresses the ideas of this passage is:
   (A) history and the British
   (B) the losing battle of the past
   (C) the contradictory British
   (D) Great Britain, noblest work of nature and of men
   (E) no escape from tradition.

11. The passage implies that Englishmen
   (A) oppose progress
   (B) are careless of their ancient natural beauties
   (C) are favorable to changes
   (D) are a race of few and unvaried characteristics
   (E) enjoy luxuries.

END OF PART

Go on to the following Test in the next Part of this Examination, just as you would be expected to do on the actual exam. If you have any available time use it to make sure that you have marked your Answer Sheet properly for this Part. Correct Answers for all Parts of this Exam follow the last question. Derive your scores only after completing the entire Exam.

PART V. THE MATHEMATICS TEST

TIME: 45 Minutes. 34 Questions.

TEST XI. GENERAL MATHEMATICAL ABILITY

TIME: **40** Minutes. 30 Questions.

This test covers topics taught at both the elementary and high school level. Some topics which may be covered are definitions, ratios, percent, decimals, fractions, mathematical symbols, indirect measurement, interpretation of graphs and tables, scale drawings, approximate computation, and units of measurement. Some questions are based on techniques taught in elementary algebra and plane geometry courses. Questions frequently test knowledge of mathematical principles and stress their applications through the performance of mathematical operations and manipulations. The ability to express practical problems in mathematical terms is frequently tested. The test may also include one or two questions based on the concepts of modern mathematics.

DIRECTIONS: Study each of the following problems and work out your answers in the blank space at the right. Below each problem you will find a number of suggested answers. Select the one that you have figured out to be right and mark its letter on the answer sheet. In the sample questions provided, the correct answers are: $S1 = A$; $S2 = C$.

Correct answers for these questions appear at the end of this examination, together with the answers to all the other tests.

Samples:

S1. If the area of a square is 62 square inches, find to the nearest tenth of an inch the length of one side.

A. 7.9 C. 6.2
B. 9.7 D. 2.6.

S2. Solve the following equation for a: $5a + 3b = 14$

A. $14 - 3b + 5$ C. $\dfrac{14 - 3b}{5}$
B. $3b - 14 \times 5$ D. $3b - 14$.

DO YOUR FIGURING HERE

1. Solve for x and y. $5x - 2y = 19$
   $7x - 4y = 29$

   A. $x = -3, y = -2$ C. $x = 3, y = -2$
   B. $x = 2, y = 3$ D. $x = -2, y = -3$.

S1964

121

2. Mr. Brown makes deposits and writes checks as follows:

May 1, $375 deposit
May 6, $150 check
May 10, $35 check
May 11, $42 deposit
May 20, $140 check
May 26, $18 check.

Mr. Brown's bank balance on April 30 was $257. What is his balance on May 31?

A. $465
B. $331
C. $185
D. $165.

DO YOUR FIGURING HERE

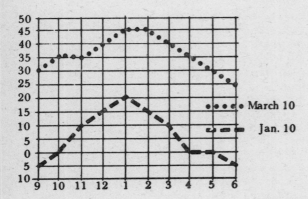

3. The above graph shows the temperatures in a certain city for 2 different dates. How many degrees higher was the lowest temperature on March 10 than the lowest temperature on January 10?

A. 35°
B. 30°
C. 25°
D. 45°.

4. From the same graph estimate the temperature at 3:30 on March 10.

A. 37-1/2°
B. 42-1/2°
C. 30°
D. 5°.

5. From the same graph determine the times on January 10 when the temperature was 5°.

A. 11:30 and 3:30
B. 10:30 and 2:30
C. 10:30 and 3:30
D. 11:30 and 2:30.

DO YOUR FIGURING HERE

6. A student had averages of 87, 90, 80, 85, and 75 for the first 5 terms in school. What must be his average for the sixth term in order for his overall average for the six terms to be 85%?

    A. 93%
    B. 85%
    C. 87%
    D. 90%.

7. In a class of 36 students, 28 passed an examination, 4 failed and the rest were absent. What percent of the class was absent?

    A. 14-2/7%
    B. 11-1/9%
    C. 75%
    D. 33-1/3%.

8. How many digits are there to the right of the decimal point in the square root of 74859.2401?

    A. 4
    B. 2
    C. 3
    D. 1.

9. The scale of a map is 3/8"=100 miles. How far apart are 2 cities 2-1/4" apart on the map?

    A. 1200 miles
    B. 300 miles
    C. 600 miles
    D. 150 miles.

10. Tom is preparing a circle graph to show that 1/12 of the local income tax is spent in payment of public debts. How big an angle must he measure at the center of the circle to represent this fact?

    A. 30°
    B. 15°
    C. 12°
    D. 60°.

11. The diagram at the right shows the side view of a house. What is the distance from E to AB?

    A. 41'
    B. 25'
    C. 20'
    D. 39'.

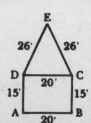

12. A weather bureau reported the following temperatures on a certain day:

1 A.M.—5°
5 A.M.—2°
9 A.M. 0°
1 P.M. 10°
5 P.M. 10°
9 P.M. 5°

What was the average temperature for the day?

A. −3°
B. 0°
C. +3°
D. +6°

13. If you have 3 hrs. and 20 minutes to travel 150 miles, what is the average speed at which you must travel?

A. 60 mph
B. 45 mph
C. 50 mph
D. 70 mph.

14. What is the square root of .0004?

A. .0002
B. .002
C. .16
D. .02.

15. The side of a square is 18″. What is its area in square feet?

A. 324
B. 9
C. 2.25
D. 3/2.

16. Reduce to its simplest form: $\dfrac{x^2 - y^2}{(x - y)^2}$

A. $x+y$
B. $\dfrac{x - y}{x + y}$

C. $x-y$
D. $\dfrac{x + y}{x - y}.$

17. Find ∠ x, where the central angles are as shown

A. 15°
B. 70°
C. 30°
D. 35°

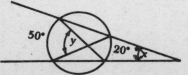

18. In the same diagram, find ∠ y.

   A. 15°
   B. 70°
   C. 30°
   D. 35°.

19. If the sides of a parallelogram are 8″ and 10″ and
     the included angle is 60°, find its area.

   A. 80 square inches
   B. 40 $\sqrt{2}$ square inches
   C. 40 square inches
   D. 40 $\sqrt{3}$ square inches.

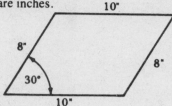

20. If the numerical value of the circumference of a
     circle is equal to the numerical value of its area,
     find its radius.

   A. 4
   B. 1
   C. 8
   D. 2.

21. A tower casts a shadow of 40′ at the same time
     that a yardstick casts a shadow of 2′. How high
     is the tower?

   A. 80′
   B. 40′
   C. 60′
   D. 100′.

22. How high must a box be if its base is 5″ by 6″, and
     its contents must be 135 cubic inches?

   A. 9″
   B. 4″
   C. 5″
   D. 4-1/2″.

23. What is the probability that a random selection
     from a box containing 6 black balls and 4 white
     balls will be a white ball?

   A. 4:6
   B. 6:10
   C. 4:10
   D. 6:4.

24. What common fraction is the equivalent of .625?

   A. 3/5
   B. 5/8
   C. 4/5
   D. 2/3.

25. What is the value of the following expression when reduced to its simplest form?

$$\left(\frac{x}{y} - \frac{y}{x}\right) \div \left(\frac{x-y}{xy}\right)$$

   A. 1
   B. $x-y$
   C. $y-x$
   D. $x+y$.

26. A rectangular tabletop is 30″ by 48″. How many square feet of glass will it take to cover it?

   A. 20 square feet
   B. 5 square feet
   C. 15 square feet
   D. 10 square feet.

27. What will $2000 amount to after 2 years if invested at 5% interest, compounded annually?

   A. $2100
   B. $2205
   C. $2500
   D. $2700.

28. A is 20 miles east of B. C is 15 miles north of A. What is the shortest airline distance from B to C?

   A. 35 miles
   B. 25 miles
   C. 30 miles
   D. 20 miles.

29. Mr. A paid $90 a share for stock, the par value of which was $100. After he had the stock for a year, the company paid him a $9 dividend. What rate of interest did he make on his investment?

   A. 9%
   B. 10%
   C. 18%
   D. 20%.

30. If $V = 1/3\pi r^2 h$, express h in terms of π, V and r.

   A. $h = \dfrac{3\pi r}{V}$

   B. $h = \dfrac{\pi r}{3V}$

   C. $h = \dfrac{3V}{\pi r^2}$

   D. $h = \dfrac{3r^2}{\pi V}$.

DO YOUR FIGURING HERE

END OF TEST

TEST XII. GRAPH INTERPRETATION

TIME: 5 Minutes.   4 Questions.

DIRECTIONS: Read each test question carefully. Each one refers to the following graph, and is to be answered solely on that basis. Select the best answer among the given choices and blacken the proper space on the answer sheet.

Correct and explanatory answers are provided at the end of the exam. After you have completed the entire exam, read the explanations carefully. They'll reinforce your strengths and pinpoint your weaknesses so that you know just what to study to raise your score.

Characteristics of
U.S. Travelers Abroad . . .

Based on Passports Issued
and Renewed in 1965

Occupation△
1.2 Million = 100%

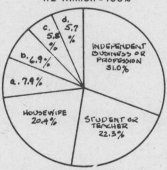

a. Skilled, Clerical, Technical
   or Sales Workers
b. Other
c. Retired
d. Civilian Government and Military

△ Based on 1st nine months only

Note: Due to rounding, figures may not add up to 100%

Age
1.3 Million = 100%

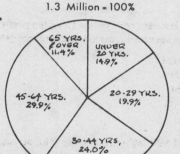

Residence
1.3 Million = 100%

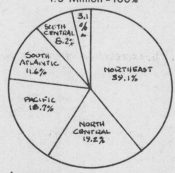

△Mountain

1. How many persons aged 29 or younger traveled abroad in 1965?

   (A) 175,000   (B) 245,000
   (C) 385,000   (D) 455,000
           (E) 550,000

2. Of the people who did *not* live in the Northeast, what percent came from the North Central states?

   (A) 19.2%   (B) 19.9%
   (C) 26.5%   (D) 31.5%
           (E) 40.2%

3. The fraction of travelers from the four smallest groups of occupation is equal to the fraction of travelers

   (A) under 20 and over 65 combined
   (B) from the North Central and mountain states
   (C) between 45 and 64 years of age
   (D) from the housewife and "other" categories
   (E) from the Pacific and South Central states

4. If the South Central, Mountain and Pacific sections were considered as a single classification, how many degrees would its sector include?

   (A) 30°   (B) 67°
   (C) 108°   (D) 120°
           (E) 150°

END OF EXAMINATION

Now that you have completed the last Test in this Examination, use your available time to make sure that you have written in your answers correctly on the Answer Sheet. Then, after your time is up, check your answers with the Correct Answers we have provided for you. Derive your scores for each Test Category and determine where you are weak so as to plan your study accordingly.

CORRECT ANSWERS FOR VERISIMILAR EXAMINATION II.

TEST I. SPELLING

1.D	3.E	5.B	7.B	9.B	11.A	13.B
2.B	4.A	6.A	8.D	10.A	12.A	14.E

TEST II. ENGLISH GRAMMAR AND USAGE

1.A	6.A	11.E	16.C	21.E	26.C	31.C
2.A	7.D	12.D	17.A	22.A	27.D	32.A
3.E	8.A	13.C	18.C	23.B	28.B	33.D
4.C	9.D	14.C	19.A	24.E	29.C	34.B
5.D	10.E	15.D	20.D	25.C	30.B	

TEST III. EFFECTIVENESS OF EXPRESSION

1.C	3.D	5.C	7.D	9.B	11.A	13.D	15.A
2.E	4.B	6.C	8.A	10.B	12.E	14.A	

TEST IV. LOGIC AND ORGANIZATION

1.D	3.E	5.C	7.B	9.C	11.E	13.D	15.D
2.C	4.B	6.D	8.A	10.B	12.E	14.B	

TEST IV. EXPLANATORY ANSWERS

1. **(D)** *Sentence relationship*. Sentence 2 is not a complete sentence. When added to the end of sentence 1, a concise and informative sentence is created.

2. **(C)** *Diction*. "Worst" is a superlative. The figure of speech in sentence 3, "for better or for. . .," must be completed with a comparative. "Worse" is that comparative.

3. **(E)** *Diction*. "Toll" is a noun defined as a tax or charge for a privilege. "Toil," a noun defined as hard and exhausting work, most accurately completes the meaning of sentence 4.

4. **(B)** *Irrelevancy*. The action of sentence 6, "walking through a natural garden," has no place in the development of the passage.

5. **(C)** *Economy*. "Members, persons and citizens" imply essentially the same relationship to "society." Thus the elimination of the latter two prevents sentence 8 from being overly wordy.

6. **(D)** *Ordering*. Sentence 12 fits neatly into the train of thought developed in sentence 9. Its current placement is much weaker.

7. **(B)** *Clarification*. Sentence 11, as it stands, is vague. The addition of "popular" defines "self-reliance" in terms of the "society" being discussed, and completes the comparison begun in sentence 10.

8. **(A)** *Paragraphing*. Sentence 8 introduces the subject of "society" and therefore introduces the second paragraph of the passage.

9. **(C)** *Sentence relationship*. Sentence 3 as it stands is an imperative statement that does not fit into the grammatical structure of the paragraph. When joined to the end of sentence 2 with "and" it is well integrated into the paragraph.

10. **(B)** *Diction*. "Contradiction," which is defined as the assertion of the opposite of, should be "contrary," which is defined as quite different. "On the contrary" is a figure of speech.

11. **(E)** *Clarification*. "Meaningless" is an adjective without a noun to modify. The addition of the noun, "pretensions," reveals the full meaning of the sentence.

12. **(E)** *Diction*. "We please" and the gerund, "pleasing," both convey essentially the same meaning. The omission of "pleasing" prevents sentence 7 from being verbose.

13. **(D)** *Diction*. "Written" is the past participle of the verb to write. It must be changed to the infinitive "to write" to be grammatically correct.

14. **(B)** *Diction*. "Commandment" is a noun defined as an order or direction. "Command," a noun implying possession of authority or control over, most accurately completes the meaning of sentence 9.

15. **(D)** *Ordering*. Sentence 10, whose subject is "studies" rather than "a familiar style of writing," does not belong in the passage.

TEST V. INTERPRETATION OF SOCIAL STUDIES READINGS

1.4	7.2	13.1	19.1	25.1	31.4	37.1
2.1	8.2	14.1	20.3	26.4	32.3	38.2
3.2	9.2	15.4	21.3	27.3	33.3	39.2
4.2	10.3	16.1	22.3	28.4	34.4	40.3
5.4	11.2	17.1	23.2	29.3	35.3	41.3
6.4	12.2	18.1	24.3	30.3	36.3	

TEST VI. SOCIAL STUDIES KNOWLEDGE

1.C	4.D	7.C	10.B	13.B	16.C
2.B	5.A	8.D	11.B	14.B	17.D
3.A	6.A	9.D	12.C	15.C	18.C

TEST VII. INTERPRETATION OF SCIENCE READINGS

1.1	6.1	11.3	16.1	21.4	26.4	31.1
2.2	7.4	12.4	17.4	22.2	27.3	32.2
3.4	8.2	13.3	18.1	23.1	28.3	33.1
4.2	9.4	14.3	19.4	24.2	29.3	34.4
5.4	10.1	15.1	20.3	25.4	30.2	35.3

TEST VIII. SCIENCE INFORMATION

1.B	4.C	7.C	10.B	13.D	16.C	19.B
2.C	5.B	8.B	11.B	14.D	17.B	20.C
3.B	6.A	9.D	12.D	15.C	18.C	

TEST IX. INTERPRETATION OF LITERARY MATERIALS

1.2	7.1	13.3	19.2	25.3	31.4	37.4
2.1	8.3	14.3	20.4	26.1	32.2	38.1
3.4	9.4	15.2	21.3	27.3	33.1	39.3
4.2	10.1	16.3	22.1	28.4	34.2	40.4
5.1	11.4	17.1	23.4	29.2	35.3	41.4
6.4	12.2	18.4	24.2	30.1	36.1	42.4

TEST X. INTERPRETATION OF PROSE

1.D	3.E	5.C	7.E	9.E	11.E
2.B	4.A	6.A	8.B	10.C	

TEST XI. GENERAL MATHEMATICAL ABILITY

1.C	5.C	9.C	13.B	17.A	21.C	25.D	29.B
2.B	6.A	10.A	14.D	18.D	22.D	26.D	30.C
3.B	7.B	11.D	15.C	19.D	23.C	27.B	
4.A	8.B	12.C	16.D	20.D	24.B	28.B	

TEST XII. GRAPH INTERPRETATION

1.D	2.D	3.A	4.C

TEST XII. EXPLANATORY ANSWERS

1. **(D)** 19.9% + 14.9% = 34.8%.
34.8% of 1.3 million = (approx.) 455,000.

2. **(D)** 100% minus 39.1% = 60.9% did not live in the Northeast. 19.2 is approximately 31.5% of 60.9.

3. **(A)** 7.9 + 6.9 + 5.8 + 5.7 = 26.3.
14.9 + 11.4 = 26.3.

4. **(C)** 8.2 + 3.1 + 18.7 = 30%.
30% of 360 degrees = 108 degrees.

2

PART TWO

Writing Skills

The emphasis in this test is upon ability to avoid errors in spelling, punctuation, capitalization, and grammatical usage. Consideration is also given to ability to choose the best words or phrases and to organize ideas in clear, well-balanced sentences.

DIRECTIONS FOR ANSWERING QUESTIONS

For each question read all the choices carefully. Then select that answer which you consider correct or most nearly correct. Write the letter preceding your best choice next to the question

Should you want to answer on the kind of answer sheet used on machine-scored examinations, we have provided several such facsimiles. Tear one out if you wish, and mark your answers on it . . . just as you would do on an actual exam.

In machine-scored examinations you should record all your answers on the answer sheet provided. Don't make the mistake of putting answers on the test booklet itself.

On some machine-scored exams you are instructed to "place no marks whatever on the test booklet."

In other examinations you may be instructed to mark your answers in the test booklet. In such cases you should be careful that no other marks interfere with the legibility of your answers.

It is always best NOT to mark your booklet unless you are sure that it is permitted.

It is most important that you learn to mark your answers clearly and in the right place.

To help you understand the procedure, the following sample item is given:

SAMPLE O: The sum of 5 and 3 is

(A) 11   (B) 8   (C) 9   (D) 2   (E) 10.

The sum of 5 and 3 is 8, so that the acceptable answer is shown thus on your answer sheet:

	A	B	C	D	E
SAMPLE O	||	■	||	||	||

Practice Using Answer Sheets

Alter numbers to match the practice and drill questions in each part of the book.
Make only ONE mark for each answer. Additional and stray marks may be counted as mistakes.
In making corrections, erase errors COMPLETELY. Make glossy black marks.

TOP SCORES IN SPELLING

The material in this chapter has appeared repeatedly on past examinations. It's all quite relevant, and well worth every minute of your valuable study time. Beginning with basic rules and a concise text, it proceeds to an illuminating presentation of a wide variety of questions and answers that exemplify the basic text while they strengthen your ability to answer actual test questions quickly and accurately.

THE importance of spelling cannot be overestimated. Bad spelling is a principal cause of failure among examinees.

It is impossible in this brief resume to supply a set of easy rules for all cases and all exceptions. However, we can give you some guidance that will almost certainly raise your test score.

We offer here a set of rules and a word list based on our study of many tests. After working through the sample test questions with these rules in mind, we suggest that you make a list of any words which you have misspelled. Further study of this list should then give you a big boost.

We also suggest that you find in your local library such books as "Words Frequently Misspelled," and "Spelling Word Lists," for supplementary work.

A FEW RULES THAT REALLY HELP

1. EI or IE

I COMES BEFORE *E*

Examples: friend, belief, niece, grieve

EXCEPT AFTER *C*

Examples: deceit, ceiling, conceive, receipt

OR WHEN SOUNDED LIKE *AY*

Examples: vein, neighbor, feign, heinous

Exceptions: either, neither, height, foreign, sovereign, forfeit, seize, counterfeit, financier

2. S or ES

ADD *ES*
  TO WORDS ENDING IN *S, SH, X* OR *Z*

Examples: rush, rushes; success, successes; bench, benches; fox, foxes

AND TO WORDS ENDING IN *Y* AFTER A CONSONANT, BUT FIRST CHANGE *Y* TO *I*

Examples: try, tries; artery, arteries; community, communities

ADD *S* ALONE
  TO ANY OTHER WORDS WHERE *S* IS NEEDED

Examples: boy, boys; chair, chairs; friend, friends; want, wants; decide, decides

3. L or LL

FINAL *L* IS DOUBLED
FOLLOWING A SINGLE VOWEL IN WORDS OF ONE SYLLABLE

Examples: fall, bell, sill, doll, hull

FOLLOWING A SINGLE VOWEL IN WORDS OF MORE THAN ONE SYLLABLE, WHEN THE STRESS FALLS ON THE LAST SYLLABLE

Examples: recall, fortell, distill

FINAL *L* IS SINGLE
FOLLOWING MORE THAN ONE VOWEL IN WORDS OF ONE SYLLABLE

Examples: bail, real, soul, feel

FOLLOWING MORE THAN ONE VOWEL IN WORDS OF MORE THAN ONE SYLLABLE WHEN THE STRESS FALLS ON THE LAST SYLLABLE

Examples: conceal, ideal, detail

FOLLOWING A SINGLE VOWEL IN WORDS OF MORE THAN ONE SYLLABLE, WHEN THE STRESS FALLS *BEFORE* THE LAST SYLLABLE

Examples: marginal, alcohol, dismal

4. SUFFIXES

These are syllables that are added to a base word to make a new word.

Some common suffixes:

able	less
ed	ly
er	ment
ful	ness
ing	ous

You can add these suffixes to some base words without changing the spelling of either the base word or the suffix.

Base Word	Suffix	New Word
expend	able	expendable
roar	ed	roared
read	er	reader
use	ful	useful
sink	ing	sinking
count	less	countless
love	ly	lovely
arrange	ment	arrangement
glad	ness	gladness
peril	ous	perilous

However, some base words must be changed slightly before you can add the suffix. Here are some rules for these changes.

IN WORDS ENDING IN *E*
DROP THE *E* WHEN THE SUFFIX BEGINS WITH A VOWEL

Examples: like, likable; love, loved; trace, tracer

OR AFTER *DG*

Examples: judge, judgment; acknowledge, acknowledging

IN WORDS ENDING IN *Y*
CHANGE *Y* TO *I* AFTER A CONSONANT IN WORDS OF MORE THAN ONE SYLLABLE

Examples: lovely, lovelier; accompany, accompaniment; tardy, tardiness; levy, levied

BUT KEEP THE *Y* WHEN YOU ADD *ING*

Examples: rally, rallying; fry, frying; reply, replying; destroy, destroying

AND WHEN YOU ADD *LY* OR *NESS* TO WORDS OF ONE SYLLABLE

Examples: sly, slyly, slyness; shy, shyly, shyness; dry, dryly, dryness

Exceptions: day, daily; lay, laid; say, said; slay, slain; pay, paid

IN WORDS ENDING IN A CONSONANT
DOUBLE THE FINAL CONSONANT IF IT FOLLOWS A SINGLE VOWEL IN WORDS OF ONE SYLLABLE, AND IF THE SUFFIX BEGINS WITH A VOWEL

Examples: fat, fatter; hop, hopping; wed, wedding

OR IF IT FOLLOWS A SINGLE VOWEL IN WORDS OF MORE THAN ONE SYLLABLE AND THE STRESS REMAINS ON THE SAME SYLLABLE

Examples: refer, referred; control, controlled

5. PREFIXES

These are syllables that go in front of a base word to make a new word.

Some common prefixes:

ab	com	en	ir	per
ac	con	il	mal	pro
ad	de	im	mis	re
bi	dis	in	over	under

You can add any prefix to a base word without changing the spelling of either the prefix or the base word.

Examples:

Prefix	Base Word	New Word
ab	normal	abnormal
ac	company	accompany
ad	join	adjoin
bi	lateral	bilateral
com	mission	commission
con	dense	condense
de	centralize	decentralize
dis	organize	disorganize
en	lace	enlace
il	legible	illegible
im	possible	impossible
in	sincere	insincere
ir	rational	irrational
mis	spell	misspell

Prefix	Base Word	New Word
mal	formed	malformed
over	do	overdo
per	form	perform
pre	text	pretext
pro	noun	pronoun
re	flex	reflex
under	go	undergo

We listed the foregoing rules in the order of their importance for you. Should they seem more than you can handle, we suggest that you memorize *at least* the following: all three points of (1); the first two points of (2) (the third point is practically self-evident); and the first two points of (3) (because if you know when to double the final *l*, you can leave it single for all the words that do not fit into these rules).

If you memorize these eight short statements, you will have taken a big step towards success in any spelling examination. Then study (4) carefully, and try to think of additional words you can make by using a base word and a suffix. Check your result, and if you have made mistakes, study it again until getting the right answer comes naturally. Go over (5), too, but you needn't put so much effort into it. The important thing here is to be able to recognize a prefix when you see it.

WORDS FREQUENTLY MISSPELLED

aberration
abeyance
abscess
abundance
accessible
accumulation
acquaint
across
actually
adage
addressee
adjunct
adoption
advise
aggravate
allege
amendment
amplify
ancient
anecdote
anemia
angle
annoyance
antipathy
apologetic
apparatus
appellate
appetite
aquatic
arouse
arraignment
ascertain
assessment
aversion

baccalaureate
bankruptcy
beatitude
beleaguered
belligerent
biased
biscuit
blamable
bookkeeping
bounteous
bureau

capitol
carburetor
category
cemetery
chamois
character
chauffeur
circumstantial
citation
clamorous
clique
colossal
column
commandant
commemorate
committal
community
compel
complacency
conciliatory
confectionery
connoisseur
consummation
controller
conversant
coroner
corporal
correlation
correspondence
corrugated
criticism
crucial
crystallized
currency

dearth
deceive
deferred
deliberate
demurrage
denunciatory
derogatory
description
desecration
detrimental
dilapidated

diocese
diphtheria
disappearance
dissatisfied
distinguished

ecstasy
eczema
effects
elaborate
electrolysis
embarrass
eminently
emolument
emphasis
emphatically
ephemeral
equilibrium
equinoctial
equipped
essential
exaggerate
exceed
exercise
exhortation
existence
extraordinary

facilitation
fallibility
fascinated
feudal
financier
foreign
forfeit
function

gelatin
grandeur

harass
hearth
heinous
heritage
hindrance
histrionic
hygienic

illegitimate
imminent
impartiality
impeccable
impromptu
incongruity
indictment
individual
ingenuous
inimitable
innocuous
integrity
intelligence
intercede
interruption
irreparably

jeopardy
journal
judgment
judiciary

laboratory
labyrinth
lacquer
liquidate
loose
lucrative

mackerel
maintenance
maneuver
marital
masquerade
matinee
mechanical
medallion
medieval
mediocrity
memoir
midget
mischievous
moribund
murmuring
myriad
negligible
nevertheless

nickel
ninth
occur
official
ordinance

pacifist
pamphlet
panicky
parliament
patient
patronize
peculiar
permissible
picnicking
piquancy
plagiarism
pneumonia
policy
possession
prairie
preceding
precious
predatory
predilection
preferably
preparation
presumptuous
previous
principal
proletarian
promissory
propaganda
psychology
publicity
punctilious

queue

realize
reasonable
recognizable
regrettable
rehearsal
relevant
renascence
repetitious

resilience
resonance
responsibility
rheostat
rhetorical
rhythm
routine

sacrilegious
salable
salient
sandwich
scissors
scripture
secretary
senior
similar
sobriquet
sophomore
source
sovereign
specialized
specifically
staunch
stretch
subversive
succeed
summarize
surfeit
surgeon
symmetrical
tariff
temperament
thorough
transaction
transient
tremendous

vacillate
vacuum
vengeance

warrant
whether
wholly
wield

yacht

TEST I. SPELLING

TIME: 16 Minutes. 48 Questions.

DIRECTIONS: *This test gives four suggested spellings for each word listed. Choose the spelling you know to be correct and mark your answer accordingly.*

Correct Answers are consolidated after the last question.

1. (A) transeint   (B) transient
    (C) trancient   (D) transent

2. (A) heratage   (B) heritage
    (C) heiritage   (D) heretage

3. (A) exibition   (B) exhibition
    (C) exabition   (D) exhebition

4. (A) intiative   (B) enitiative
    (C) initative   (D) initiative

5. (A) similiar   (B) simmilar
    (C) similar   (D) simuler

6. (A) sufficiantly   (B) sufisiently
    (C) sufficiently   (D) suficeintly

7. (A) anticipate   (B) antisipate
    (C) anticapate   (D) antisapate

8. (A) intelligence   (B) inteligence
    (C) intellegence   (D) intelegence

9. (A) referance   (B) referrence
    (C) referense   (D) reference

10. (A) conscious   (B) consious
    (C) conscius   (D) consceous

11. (A) paralell   (B) parellel
    (C) parellell   (D) parallel

12. (A) abundence   (B) abundance
    (C) abundants   (D) abundents

13. (A) spesifically   (B) specificaly
    (C) specifically   (D) specefically

14. (A) elemanate   (B) elimenate
    (C) elliminate   (D) eliminate

15. (A) resonance   (B) resonnance
    (C) resonence   (D) reasonance

16. (A) benaficial   (B) beneficial
    (C) benefitial   (D) bennaficial

17. (A) retrievable   (B) retreivable
    (C) retrievible   (D) retreavable

18. (A) collosal   (B) colossal
    (C) colosal   (D) collossal

19. (A) inflameable   (B) inflamable
    (C) enflamabel   (D) inflammable

20. (A) auxillary   (B) auxilliary
    (C) auxilary   (D) auxiliary

21. (A) corregated   (B) corrigated
    (C) corrugated   (D) coregated

22. (A) accumalation   (B) accumulation
    (C) acumulation   (D) accumullation

23. (A) consumation   (B) consummation
    (C) consumeation   (D) consomation

24. (A) retorical   (B) rhetorical
    (C) rhetorrical   (D) retorrical

25. (A) inimitable   (B) iminitable
    (C) innimitable   (D) inimitible

26. (A) proletarian   (B) prolletarian
    (C) prolatarian   (D) proleterian

27. (A) appelate   (B) apellate
   (C) appellate   (D) apelate

28. (A) esential   (B) essencial
   (C) essential   (D) essantial

29. (A) assessment   (B) assesment
   (C) asessment   (D) assesmant

30. (A) ordinence   (B) ordinnance
   (C) ordinanse   (D) ordinance

31. (A) disapearance   (B) disappearance
   (C) disappearense   (D) disappearence

32. (A) attendence   (B) attendanse
   (C) attendance   (D) atendance

33. (A) acertain   (B) assertain
   (C) ascertain   (D) asertain

34. (A) specimen   (B) speciman
   (C) spesimen   (D) speceman

35. (A) relevant   (B) relévent
   (C) rellevent   (D) relavant

36. (A) anesthetic   (B) aenesthetic
   (C) anestitic   (D) annesthetic

37. (A) foriegn   (B) foreign
   (C) forriegn   (D) forreign

38. (A) interuption   (B) interruption
   (C) interrupsion   (D) interrupcion

39. (A) acquiesence   (B) acquiescence
   (C) aquiescense   (D) acquiesance

40. (A) exceed   (B) exsede
   (C) exseed   (D) excede

41. (A) maneuver   (B) manuver
   (C) maneuvere   (D) manneuver

42. (A) correlation   (B) corrolation
   (C) corellation   (D) corralation

43. (A) hinderence   (B) hindranse
   (C) hindrance   (D) hindrence

44. (A) existence   (B) existance
   (C) existense   (D) existince

45. (A) bankrupcy   (B) bankruptcy
   (C) bankruptsy   (D) bankrupsy

46. (A) receipts   (B) receits
   (C) reciepts   (D) recieps

47. (A) impromtu   (B) inpromtu
   (C) impromptu   (D) impromptue

48. (A) pronounciation   (B) pronunciatun
   (C) pronunciation   (D) pronounciatun

END OF TEST

Go on to do the following Test in this Examination, just as you would be
expected to do on the actual exam.

CONSOLIDATE YOUR KEY ANSWERS HERE

Practice using Answer Sheets. Make ONE mark for each answer. Additional and stray marks may be counted as mistakes. In making corrections erase errors COMPLETELY. Make glossy black marks. To arrive at an accurate estimate of your ability and progress, cover the Correct Answers with a sheet of white paper while you are taking this test.

CORRECT ANSWERS TO THE FOREGOING PRACTICE QUESTIONS

Now compare your answers with these Correct Answers to the Practice Questions. If your answers differ from these, go back and study those questions to see where and how you made your mistakes.

1.B	7.A	13.C	19.D	25.A	31.B	37.B	43.C
2.B	8.A	14.D	20.D	26.A	32.C	38.B	44.A
3.B	9.D	15.A	21.C	27.C	33.C	39.B	45.B
4.D	10.A	16.B	22.B	28.C	34.A	40.A	46.A
5.C	11.D	17.A	23.B	29.A	35.A	41.A	47.C
6.C	12.B	18.B	24.B	30.D	36.A	42.A	48.C

TEST II. SPELLING

13 Minutes. 40 Questions.

DIRECTIONS: *In this test all words but one of each group are spelled correctly. Indicate the misspelled word in each group.*

Correct Answers are consolidated after the last question.

1. (A) proscenium (B) resillient
   (C) biennial (D) connoisseur

2. (A) queue (B) equable
   (C) ecstacy (D) obsequious

3. (A) quizes (B) frolicking
   (C) maelstrom (D) homonym

4. (A) pseudonym (B) annihilate
   (C) questionaire (D) irascible

5. (A) diptheria (B) annular
   (C) acolyte (D) descendant

6. (A) truculant (B) rescind
   (C) dilettante (D) innuendo

7. (A) prevalence (B) discrete
   (C) efrontery (D) admissible

8. (A) igneous (B) annullment
   (C) dissipate (D) abattoir

9. (A) quiescent (B) apologue
   (C) myrrh (D) inocuous

10. (A) propoganda (B) gaseous
    (C) iridiscent (D) similar

11. (A) supercede (B) tyranny
    (C) beauteous (D) victuals

12. (A) geneology (B) tragedy
    (C) soliloquy (D) prejudice

13. (A) remittance (B) shoeing
    (C) category (D) gutteral

14. (A) catarrh (B) parlamentary
    (C) villain (D) omitted

15. (A) vengeance (B) parallel
    (C) nineth (D) mayoralty

16. (A) changeable (B) therefor
    (C) incidently (D) dissatisfy

17. (A) orifice (B) deferrment
    (C) harass (D) accommodate

18. (A) picnicking (B) proceedure
    (C) hypocrisy (D) seize

19. (A) vilify (B) efflorescence
    (C) sarcophagus (D) sacreligious

20. (A) paraphenalia (B) apothecaries
    (C) occurrence (D) plagiarize

21. (A) irreparably (B) comparitively
    (C) lovable (D) audible

22. (A) nullify (B) siderial
    (C) salability (D) irrelevant

23. (A) asinine (B) dissonent
    (C) opossum (D) indispensable

24. (A) discomfit (B) sapient
    (C) exascerbate (D) sarsaparilla

25. (A) valleys (B) maintainance
    (C) abridgment (D) reticence

26. (A) tolerance (B) circumferance
    (C) insurance (D) dominance

27. (A) diameter (B) tangent
    (C) paralell (D) perimeter

28. (A) providential (B) personal
    (C) accidental (D) diagonel

29. (A) development (B) retarded
    (C) homogenious (D) intelligence

30. (A) noticeable (B) forceible
    (C) practical (D) erasable

31. (A) heroes (B) folios
    (C) sopranos (D) usuel

32. (A) typical (B) descend
    (C) summarize (D) continuel

33. (A) courageous (B) recomend
    (C) omission (D) eliminate

34. (A) compliment (B) illuminate
    (C) auxilary (D) installation

35.   (A) preliminary   (B) aquainted
     (C) syllable   (D) analysis

36.   (A) accustomed   (B) negligible
     (C) interupted   (D) bulletin

37.   (A) summoned   (B) managment
     (C) mechanism   (D) sequence

38.   (A) comittee   (B) surprise
     (C) noticeable   (D) emphasize

39.   (A) occurrance   (B) likely
     (C) accumulate   (D) grievance

40.   (A) obstacle   (B) particuliar
     (C) baggage   (D) fascinating

END OF TEST

*Go on to do the following Test in this Examination, just as you would be
expected to do on the actual exam.*

CONSOLIDATE YOUR KEY ANSWERS HERE

*Practice using Answer Sheets. Make ONE mark for each answer. Additional and stray
marks may be counted as mistakes. In making corrections erase errors COMPLETELY.
Make glossy black marks. To arrive at an accurate estimate of your ability and progress,
cover the Correct Answers with a sheet of white paper while you are taking this test.*

CORRECT ANSWERS TO THE FOREGOING PRACTICE QUESTIONS

*Now compare your answers with these Correct Answers to the Practice Questions.
If your answers differ from these, go back and study those questions to see where
and how you made your mistakes.*

1.B	6.A	11.A	16.C	21.B	26.B	31.D	36.C
2.C	7.C	12.A	17.B	22.B	27.C	32.D	37.B
3.A	8.B	13.D	18.B	23.B	28.D	33.B	38.A
4.C	9.D	14.B	19.D	24.C	29.C	34.C	39.A
5.A	10.A	15.C	20.A	25.B	30.B	35.B	40.B

TEST III. SPELLING

30 Minutes. 100 Questions.

DIRECTIONS: *In the following list, some words are spelled correctly, some misspelled. On your practice sheet, write CORRECT for those words properly spelled; spell out the word correctly for those misspelled.*

Correct Answers are consolidated after the last question.

1. unparalleled
2. gastliness
3. mediocrity
4. exibition
5. posessing
6. lucritive
7. corresspondence
8. accellerated
9. labirynth
10. duplisity
11. repitious
12. jepardy
13. impartiallity
14. sobriquet
15. accesable
16. incredible
17. connoisseurs
18. fallibility
19. litagation
20. piquansy
21. fuedal
22. predetory
23. desparado
24. incongruity
25. delibarate

26. competetive
27. beleaguered
28. leiutenant
29. equinoxial
30. derogatory
31. denuncietory
32. panickey
33. calendar
34. belligerents
35. abolition
36. predjudice
37. propoganda
38. adolesents
39. irresistible
40. exortation
41. renascence
42. counsil
43. bullitin
44. aberation
45. integraty
46. cristallized
47. irrepairably
48. punctillious
49. catagory
50. parlament

51. medalion
52. bountious
53. aggrevate
54. midgit
55. wierd
56. elliminate
57. murmering
58. hystrionic
59. goverment
60. clamerous
61. garantee
62. presumptious
63. comemmerate
64. indispensible
65. bookeeping
66. disatisfied
67. tremendious
68. interseed
69. inaugerate
70. rehersel
71. nucleous
72. benefiting
73. wholy
74. discription
75. alright

76. representitive
77. mischievious
78. ingenuous
79. accidently
80. exilerate
81. pronounciation
82. fourty
83. mackeral
84. rescind
85. kleptomania
86. summerize
87. resillience
88. regretable
89. questionaire
90. privelege
91. judgment
92. plagiarism
93. vengence
94. subpoena
95. rythm
96. derth
97. impromtue
98. incumbant
99. forfiet
100. maintainance

END OF TEST

Go on to do the following Test in this Examination, just as you would be expected to do on the actual exam.

S1259

CONSOLIDATE YOUR KEY ANSWERS HERE

1. _____ 2. _____ 3. _____ 4. _____ 5. _____ 6. _____ 7. _____ 8. _____
9. _____ 10. _____ 11. _____ 12. _____ 13. _____ 14. _____ 15. _____ 16. _____
17. _____ 18. _____ 19. _____ 20. _____ 21. _____ 22. _____ 23. _____ 24. _____
25. _____ 26. _____ 27. _____ 28. _____ 29. _____ 30. _____ 31. _____ 32. _____
33. _____ 34. _____ 35. _____ 36. _____ 37. _____ 38. _____ 39. _____ 40. _____
41. _____ 42. _____ 43. _____ 44. _____ 45. _____ 46. _____ 47. _____ 48. _____
49. _____ 50. _____ 51. _____ 52. _____ 53. _____ 54. _____ 55. _____ 56. _____
57. _____ 58. _____ 59. _____ 60. _____ 61. _____ 62. _____ 63. _____ 64. _____
65. _____ 66. _____ 67. _____ 68. _____ 69. _____ 70. _____ 71. _____ 72. _____
73. _____ 74. _____ 75. _____ 76. _____ 77. _____ 78. _____ 79. _____ 80. _____
81. _____ 82. _____ 83. _____ 84. _____ 85. _____ 86. _____ 87. _____ 88. _____
89. _____ 90. _____ 91. _____ 92. _____ 93. _____ 94. _____ 95. _____ 96. _____
97. _____ 98. _____ 99. _____ 100. _____

CORRECT ANSWERS TO THE FOREGOING PRACTICE QUESTIONS

Now compare your answers with these Correct Answers to the Practice Questions. If your answers differ from these, go back and study those questions to see where and how you made your mistakes.

1. correct
2. ghastliness
3. correct
4. exhibition
5. possessing
6. lucrative
7. correspondence
8. accelerated
9. labyrinth
10. duplicity
11. repetitious
12. jeopardy
13. impartiality
14. correct
15. accessible
16. correct
17. correct
18. correct
19. litigation
20. piquancy
21. feudal
22. predatory
23. desperado
24. correct
25. deliberate
26. competitive
27. correct
28. lieutenant
29. equinoctial
30. correct
31. denunciatory
32. panicky
33. correct
34. correct
35. correct
36. prejudice
37. propaganda
38. adolescents
39. correct
40. exhortation
41. correct
42. counsel
43. bulletin
44. aberration
45. integrity
46. crystallized
47. irreparably
48. punctilious
49. category
50. parliament
51. medallion
52. bounteous
53. aggravate
54. midget
55. weird
56. eliminate
57. murmuring
58. histrionic
59. government
60. clamorous
61. guarantee
62. presumptuous
63. commemorate
64. indispensable
65. bookkeeping
66. dissatisfied
67. tremendous
68. intercede
69. inaugurate
70. rehearsal
71. nucleus
72. correct
73. wholly
74. description
75. correct
76. representative
77. mischievous
78. correct
79. accidentally
80. exhilarate
81. pronunciation
82. forty
83. mackerel
84. correct
85. correct
86. summarize
87. resilience
88. regrettable
89. questionnaire
90. privilege
91. correct
92. correct
93. vengeance
94. correct
95. rhythm
96. dearth
97. impromptu
98. incumbent
99. forfeit
100. maintenance

THE SIMPLE RULES OF GRAMMAR

Jimmy: *Teacher, ain't it time for lunch?*

Teacher: *Say, "Isn't it time for lunch."*

(After several minutes of teacher explanation and pupil drill on verb forms and conjugations . . .)

Jimmy: *Isn't it time for lunch? I ain't never been so hungry.*

PERHAPS the reason that Jimmy repeated the error in the conversation above is that he didn't care to learn grammar—at least, not the way his teacher taught it.

Grammar, though, is really easy—provided you learn it scientifically.

Research has indicated that a great many errors in grammar may be traced to a lack of understanding of simple grammatical principles —and these principles may be learned thoroughly and conclusively by any person of average intelligence in a surprisingly short period of time. Yet torturous days and weeks and months have been spent in classrooms in the drilling of unnecessary grammatical ideas into the poor heads of little boys like Jimmy. This takes place in spite of the fact that pupils have remembered and used a very small percentage of the abstruse grammar to which they have been subjected.

Attributive genitives, periphrastic conjugations and the rest of the hoity-toity crowd of grammar nuisances have little or no place in a Good English instruction program unless the student is interested in the technical aspects of the language—and since so very few individuals are so inclined, why torment the great majority of those who wish to learn just plain, good, simple English? Why force them to absorb useless concepts? The simple rules are enough. Here they are.

Note: The best way to learn these rules is by the *felt need* method. Wait till you have a grammar problem—then study the rule which solves that problem. You will learn the rules with thorough understanding by using this procedure.

PARTS OF SPEECH

A NOUN is a person, place or thing: *teacher, city, desk* or *king*.

PRONOUNS substitute for nouns: *she* for Helen, *those* for gowns.

AN ADJECTIVE describes a noun: *warm* or *cold, blue* or *brown*.

A VERB has action or state of being: they *yell*, you *feel* and all *are seeing*.

An ADVERB qualifies the verb: run *fast*, walk *slowly, hardly* disturb.

CONJUNCTIONS join in many ways: in *and* out, night *or* day.

A PREPOSITION has its place before a noun: *in* outerspace.

The INTERJECTION notes surprise: *My!* how lovely! *"Help!"* he cries.

Nouns

A noun is a name of anything
A NOUN is a person, place or thing:
teacher, city, desk or *king.*

A. There are several kinds of nouns.

COMMON (refers to a general group)— *cat, health, girl, sincerity.*

PROPER (distinguishes one from others)—*Chicago, Jack, Central Park.*

These "name" nouns are always capitalized.

COLLECTIVE (denotes several combined into one)— *team, crowd, organization, Congress.*

Note: A *group* of teachers from England *is visiting* our school. The collective noun, *group*, is singular; therefore, verb, *is visiting*, is singular.

CONCRETE (refers to something material)—*pail, steel, desk.*

ABSTRACT (refers to something that is not material)—*hope, weakness, education.*

B. Nouns have NUMBER. Note the tricky plurals for some nouns:

SINGULAR	PLURAL
alumnus	alumni
analysis	analyses
archipelago	archipelagoes
axis	axes
basis	bases
brother-in-law	brothers-in-law
crisis	crises
embryo	embryos
louse	lice
monkey	monkeys
oasis	oases
phenomenon	pheonomena
portfolio	portfolios
salmon	salmon
spoonful	spoonfuls
swine	swine
tomato	tomatoes
veto	vetoes
r	r's
3	3's

add *'s* to form plural of letters and numbers.

C. Nouns have GENDER

MASCULINE	FEMININE
bull	cow
cock	hen
czar	czarina
drake	duck
executor	executrix
gander	goose
marquis	marchioness
rajah	ranee
ram	ewe
stallion	mare

Note: There is also a NEUTER GENDER for nouns denoting inanimate objects (example: rocks, chair, silence, street, etc.) and a COMMON GENDER for nouns signifying either sex (example: citizen, pedestrian, customer, cousin, etc.).

D. Nouns have CASE

NOMINATIVE (when the noun is the subject of the thought).

OBJECTIVE (when the noun is the object of the thought).

POSSESSIVE (when the noun shows that it possesses something).

E. A noun is in the NOMINATIVE CASE when it is used as follows:

1. SUBJECT — The name or thing about which an assertion is made: The *girl* powdered her face.
   Note: A subject always answers the question WHAT or WHO.
2. PREDICATE NOUN—The noun that comes after a copulative verb (see COPULATIVE VERB).
   Note: The predicate noun means the same as the subject.
   Babe Ruth was a great *hitter*.
3. DIRECT ADDRESS: *Jack*, please pick up the papers.

4. NOMINATIVE ABSOLUTE (independent idea): The *plane* having departed, we left the airport.

5. NOMINATIVE BY APPOSITION (explanatory adjunct): My instructor, a learned *man*, is now on leave.

F. A noun is in the OBJECTIVE CASE when it is used as follows:

1. DIRECT OBJECT — A noun which receives the action of a transitive verb (see TRANSITIVE VERB)
Note: The direct object answers the question WHAT or WHOM: The child ate the *cookie*.

2. OBJECTIVE COMPLEMENT — A noun that explains the direct object: They elected Kennedy *president*.

3. OBJECTIVE BY APPOSITION: We met Jack, an old *friend*.

4. ADVERBIAL OBJECTIVE — A noun that denotes distance, time, manner, etc.): My uncle stayed a *week*.

5. OBJECT OF PREPOSITION — A noun which is introduced by a preposition: They have gone to the *game*.

6. SUBJECT OF THE INFINITIVE: We believed the *boys* to be honest.

7. INDIRECT OBJECT

1. comes after a verb of "giving."

2. "to" or "for" is expressed or understood.

3. Must accompany a DIRECT OBJECT.
Examples: Please lend *Wilson* a nickel.
Give my love to your *brother*.

8. RETAINED OBJECT — a noun which was the object of the active verb and is held over as the object of the same verb in the Passive Voice: He was offered some *advice* by me. Sentence formerly: I offered him some *advice*. See ACTIVE and PASSIVE VOICE.

G. A noun is in the POSSESSIVE CASE when it is used to express possession, source or origin.
Charles' book (not Charle's).
doctor's visit (one doctor)
doctors' visit (more than one doctor)
children's shoes
baby's bottle
babies' bottle (hardly a sanitary example)
mother-in-law's house (apostrophe is placed in last element of hyphenated noun)
Kenyon and Knott's book (one book by two authors)
Jack's and Sam's cars (one owned by each)

Pronouns

A pronoun is used in place of a noun.
PRONOUNS substitute for nouns: *she* for
Helen, *those* for gowns.

A. EXPLETIVE PRONOUN — *it* or *there*.
An expletive pronoun is followed by the subject.
The subject is *men* in this sentence. *There* were three *men* on the bench.
The subject is *they* in this sentence: *It is they* who are going.

B. ANTECEDENT OF THE PRONOUN — The noun to which a pronoun refers. Picasso is the *artist whom* we all admire. (*artist* is the antecedent of the pronoun *whom*.) See WHO and WHOM.

Note: A pronoun must agree with its antecedent in GENDER, PERSON, and NUMBER. Everyone must have *his* own pen. (*their* is *incorrect*).

C. KINDS OF PRONOUNS

1. DEMONSTRATIVE PRONOUN — *this* and *that*, *these* and *those*.

2. INDEFINITE PRONOUN — *all, any, nobody*, etc.

3. INTERROGATIVE PRONOUN — *who, which, what*.

who refers to persons.
what refers to animals and things.
which (selectively used) refers to persons or animals or things.

Who broke the cup?
Which of the two children broke the cup?
Which of the puppies do you want?
Which of the apples tastes sweetest?
What is that noise?
What is that annoying creature?

4. **PERSONAL PRONOUN** — No other part of speech has as many forms or changes as the personal pronoun.

Note 1: The apostrophe is *not* used in POSSESSIVE CASE forms of the personal pronouns. Don't write this is *your's*.

Note 2: *It's* means *it is*. *It's* is *not* a personal pronoun.

Note 3: The Nominative form must be used in the following constructions:

It is *I.*
It is *she*.   Underlined pronouns are all
I am *he*.   Predicate Nouns.

She is younger than *we*. This really means . . .
"than we are"; "we" is a subject -- therefore *we* is in the Nominative Case.
He likes Joan better than *I*. This means . . .
"better than I like Joan"
He likes Joan better than *me*. This means . . .
"He likes Joan better than he likes me."

Note 4. The objective form must be used in the following constructions:

. . between you and *me*.
. . with John and *her*.   (see Object of Preposition)
. . from Mary and *us*.

		NOMINATIVE CASE	OBJECTIVE CASE	POSSESSIVE CASE
SINGULAR	1st person	I	me	mine
	2nd person	you	you	yours
	3rd person	he, she, it	him, her, it	his, hers
PLURAL	1st person	we	us	ours
	2nd person	you	you	yours
	3rd person	they	them	theirs

5. **REFLEXIVE PRONOUN** — *myself, yourselves, oneself*, etc.

6. **RELATIVE PRONOUN** — *who, which, that, what.*
who refers to persons.
which refers to animals and things.
that refers to persons, animals, and things.
what (that which) refers to things.

Example: Tell me *what* you know.

Note 1: Infrequently, *as* and *but* may be used as relative pronouns:
He gave us such food *as* he had.
There is no one *but* considers him a genius. (*but* in this case, means *other than the person who*).

Note 2: More errors are made in the use of *who* and *whom* than in the use of any other word pairs in our language.

Adjectives

An adjective usually modifies a noun
AN ADJECTIVE describes a noun: *warm*
or *cold, blue* or *brown.*

He is a *tall* man.
A *soft* answer turneth away wrath.

A. Do not use an adjective to modify a verb.
(See ADVERBS)
She sings *good* is *incorrect.* (SAY, *well*)

B. There are two other adjective uses besides
the use of noun modifier.

PREDICATE ADJECTIVE – comes after
a copulative verb (see COPULATIVE
VERB).

Note: We feel *bad.* (We're troubled) *Bad*
is an adjective. *We feel badly.* (There
is something wrong with our sense of
touch.) *Badly* is an adverb.

OBJECTIVE COMPLEMENT (see Objective Complement under NOUN).
Jack painted the car *pink.*

Note: *AN ARTICLE* is another name for
the following three adjectives: *the,
a, an.*

DEFINITE ARTICLE – *the*

INDEFINITE ARTICLE – *a, an*
a desk (Before a consonant)
an apple (Before a vowel)

C. Adjectives change in form by COMPARI-
SION. There are three degrees of comparison.

POSITIVE DEGREE – no comparison is
made. The *sweet* peach.

COMPARATIVE DEGREE – The *sweet-
er* peach. (one of two peaches)

SUPERLATIVE DEGREE – The *sweetest*
peach. (One of three or more peaches).

Verbs

A Verb Usually Expresses Action
A VERB has action or state of being: they
yell, you *feel* and all *are seeing.*

A. There are three major types of verbs.

TRANSITIVE	1) has action and 2) takes a direct object He *killed* the cat.
INTRANSI-TIVE	1) has action but 2) takes no direct object. She *fell* down.
COPULATIVE	1) has no action and 2) may take a predicate noun or adjective. Jim *is* captain. (*captain* is predicate noun ... also called predicate nomina-tive)

A COPULATIVE VERB may be:

1) any part of the verb BE (*was, is,* etc.)
2) one of the *sensate* verbs (*smell, feel, taste,* etc.)
3) one of the "*appear*" verbs (*appear, be-come, seem,* etc.)

Mary *was* ill. (*ill* is predicate adjective)

We *are going.* (*are going* is not a copulative verb -- it's intransitive).

The candy *tastes* sweet. (If you say
sweetly, you are giving the candy
tasting ability).

He *feels* strong about this matter.
(*strongly* is incorrect.)

B. TENSES – There are six tenses.

	SIMPLE FORM	PROGRESSIVE FORM	EMPHATIC FORM
1. PRESENT	Roger Maris hits	is hitting	does hit (a home run.)
2. PAST	hit	was hitting	did hit (a home run.)
3. PRESENT PERFECT	has hit	has been hitting	
4. FUTURE	will hit	will be hitting	
5. PAST PERFECT	had hit	had been hitting	
6. FUTURE PERFECT	will have hit	will have been hitting	

WHEN TO USE THE PAST PERFECT

Consider the sentence — "The foreman *asked* what *had happened* to my eye." (Don't say what *happened* in this case.) The action *had happened* and the action *asked* are both *past*. The PAST PERFECT tense (*had happened*) is used because it is "more past" than the action *asked*.

WHEN TO USE THE PRESENT PERFECT.

Consider the sentence —- "I'm glad you're here at last — I *have* waited an hour for you to arrive." (Don't say I *waited* in this case.) The action *have waited* began in the *past* and extended to the *present*. In this case we use the PRESENT PERFECT.

WHEN TO USE THE FUTURE PERFECT.

Consider the sentence — "When I reach Chicago tonight, my uncle *will have left* for Los Angeles."
The action *will have left* is going to take place before the action *reach*, although both actions are in the future. When there are two future actions, the action completed first is expressed in the FUTURE PERFECT tense.

C. A PRINCIPAL verb is that part of a verb combination that expresses the action.

I do *believe*. (*do* is the AUXILIARY verb,…*believe* is the PRINCIPAL verb)
You may *enter*. (*may* is the AUXILIARY verb . . . *enter* is the PRINCIPAL verb.

In the past tense, say *might have entered*).

We shall *eat*. (*shall* is the AUXILIARY verb . . . *eat* is the PRINCIPAL verb).

D. PRINCIPAL PARTS – There are three principal parts. From these we get all parts of the verb. The principal parts are the following:
1. Present
2. Past
3. Present perfect

The other three tenses come from the three Principal Parts:

The FUTURE tense is derived from the Present . . . The FUTURE PERFECT tense and the PAST PERFECT tense are both derived from the Present Perfect tense.

Learn the Principal Parts of the following irregular verbs. You will then know every form of each irregular verb.

E. MOOD (or MODE) . . . is the manner in which the action or the state of the verb is expressed. There are three Moods.

> INDICATIVE MOOD is factual.
>
> Example: We *are* going to the concert.
> There are six tenses in the Indicative Mood. (see TENSES).
>
> SUBJUNCTIVE MOOD is used for *orders, supposition, contrary to fact* conditions.
>
> Examples: The principal ordered that there *be* a fire drill. (OR-DER)
> They are frightened lest they be *attacked* on the way home. (SUPPOSITION)
> If I *were* rich, I'd be in Paris now. (CONTRARY TO FACT PRESENT CONDITION)
> If the student *had studied*, he would have passed. (CONTRARY TO FACT PAST CONDITION)
> Note that there are two Contrary to Fact Tenses (Present and Past.)
>
> IMPERATIVE MOOD is used for *commands* and *wishes*.
>
> Examples: *Leave* the premises at once! (COMMAND)
> *Bless* your heart! (WISH)
> The Imperative Mood has only one tense . . . the *Present*.

F. VOICE . . . There are two Verb Voices.

1. ACTIVE VOICE — the *subject* of the sentence is the *doer* of action.

2. PASSIVE VOICE — the *subject* is act-ed upon.

   Examples: Pittsburgh *won* the pennant. (ACTIVE VOICE)

The pennant *was won* by Pittsburgh. (PASSIVE VOICE)

Only *transitive* verbs may be converted from the Active Voice to the Passive Voice.

A Passive Verb may sometimes act as a COPU-LATIVE verb.

Examples: He *is considered* a genius. ("genius" here is a predicate nominative . . . see)

The lady *was made* ill by the pill. ("ill" is a predicate adjective . . . see)

G. NUMBER and PERSON . . . A verb must agree with its subject in Number and Person.

Examples:

He doesn't know. ("don't" is incorrect)

Neither Mary nor Helen *is coming*. ("are coming" is incorrect).

Neither Jim nor we *are going*.
Either he or I *am leaving*. } verb agrees with LAST subject

None of them *is* missing. (subject "none" is singular)

He and she *are* going. (subject is plural)

It is I who *am* the most willing. ("who," like its antecedent "I," is in the first person singular)

She as well as I *is* going. ("she" is the subject)

Smith together with Jones and Jackson *is* arriving. ("Smith" is the subject)

Three and three *is* six. ("Three and three" comprise a unit)

That man, not we, *is* guilty. (Second subject "we" is parenthetical.
Verb here agrees with the first subject)

Four-fifths of the task *is* accomplished. (Unity of the subject "four-fifths" is conveyed by the object of the preposition "task")

SOME IRREGULAR VERBS

PRESENT	PAST	PRESENT PERFECT
abide	abode	has abode
arise	arose	has arisen
bear (carry)	bore	has borne
bear (bring forth)	bore	has borne
bid	bade	has bid, bidden
bide	bode, bided	has bode, bided
bleed	bled	has bled
broadcast	broadcast, broadcasted (radio and TV)	has broadcast (ed)
burst	burst	has burst
chide	chid, chidded	has chid, chidded, chidden
choose	chose	has chosen
cleave (adhere)	cleaved	has cleaved
cleave (split)	cleft, cleaved	has cleft, cleaved, cloven
cling	clung	has clung
drown	drowned	has drowned
drink	drank	has drunk
flee	fled	has fled
fling	flung	has flung
fly	flew	has flown
flow	flowed	has flowed
forsake	forsook	has forsaken
freeze	froze	has frozen
grind	ground	has ground
hang (a picture)	hung	has hung
hang (a person)	hanged	has hanged
lay (place)	laid	has laid
lead	led	has led
lend	lent	has lent
lie (rest)	lay	has lain
light	lit, lighted	has lit, lighted
raise	raised	has raised
rid	rid, ridded	has rid, ridded
ring	rang	has rung
set	set	has set
sew	sewed	has sewed, sewn
shrink	shrank or shrunk	has shrunk, shrunken
sink	sank, sunk	has sunk
sit	sat	has sat
ski	skied (rhymes with seed)	has skied
slay	slew	has slain
slide	slid	has slid or slidden
sling	slung	has slung
slink	slunk	has slunk
smite	smote	has smitten
spring	sprang or sprung	has sprung
sting	stung	has stung
stink	stank, stunk	has stunk
stride	strode	has stridden
strive	strove	has striven
swing	swung	has swung
thrust	thrust	has thrust
weave	wove	has woven
wring	wrung	has wrung

Adverbs

An Adverb Usually Modifies A Verb
An ADVERB qualifies the verb: run *fast*,
walk *slowly, hardly* disturb.

A. Adverbs commonly answer questions WHY? HOW? WHERE? WHEN? TO WHAT DEGREE?

Examples: Since it is snowing, I shall stay *here*. (WHERE)
Please do it *now*. (WHEN)
We *wholly* agree with you. (TO WHAT DEGREE)
She played the selection *beautifully*. (HOW)
He dived *for the pearl*. (WHY ...adverbial phrase)

B. Two special types of adverbs follow:
1. RELATIVE ADVERB . . . introduces adjective and adverbial clauses (see).

Examples: This is the place where he broke his leg. ("Where" begins the adjective clause) I'll phone you *when* I arrive. ("when" begins the adverbial clause)

2. INTERROGATIVE ADVERB . . . introduces questions.

Examples: *When* do you expect to leave?
How are we to save ourselves?

Prepositions

A preposition shows relationship between the word that follows it and the idea that precedes the preposition.
A PREPOSITION has its place before a
noun: *in* outerspace.

A. The most common prepositions are *with, to, on, of, in, from, for, by, at*.

B. Do *not* omit prepositions.

Example: Play it *in* this way. (play it this way is *incorrect*).

C. Use no unnecessary prepositions.

Example: It fell *off* the table. ("off of" is incorrect)

D. A preposition may be used at the end of a sentence . . . unless such use is awkward.

Example: Whom did he give the book to? (correct)
She is the nurse whom I was helped by. (awkward)

IDIOMS

English, like other languages, has its own
idioms—that is, its own way of saying something.
Here, below, is a list of frequently used (or shall
we say "misused") idioms in which the correct
preposition is important.

IDIOM	EXAMPLE
ABOUND IN (or WITH)	This letter ABOUNDS IN mistakes.
ACCOMPANIED BY (a person)	The salesman was ACCOMPANIED BY the buyer.
ACCOMPANIED WITH (a present)	He ACCOMPANIED the closing of the contract WITH a gift.
IN ACCORDANCE WITH	Act in ACCORDANCE WITH the regulations.
ACQUIESCE IN (ak-wee-ESS)	The executives were compelled to ACQUIESCE IN the director's policy.
ACQUIT OF	The office boy was ACQUITTED OF the charge of stealing pencils.
ADEPT IN (or AT)	The store manager is ADEPT IN typing.
AGREE TO (an offer)	The firm AGREES TO your payment of $100 in settlement of the claim.
AGREE WITH (a person)	I AGREE WITH Mr. Smith on that point.
AGREE UPON-or ON-(a plan)	We must AGREE UPON the best method.
ALLERGIC TO	The patient is ALLERGIC TO chocolate.
ANGRY AT (a situation) ANGRY WITH (a person)	The customer is ANGRY WITH the clerk AT being detained.
APPROPRIATE FOR (meaning *suitable to*)	This gown is also APPROPRIATE FOR a dinner dance.
AVAILABLE FOR (a purpose) AVAILABLE TO (a person)	These typewriters are now AVAILABLE TO offices FOR essential use.
AVERSE TO	The President is AVERSE TO increasing his staff.
COGNIZANT OF	He was not COGNIZANT OF dissension among his workers.
COINCIDE WITH	Your wishes in this matter COINCIDE WITH mine.
COMMENSURATE WITH (kum-MEN shure-it).	What you earn will be COMMENSURATE WITH how much effort you put into the job.
COMPARE TO (shows similarity between things that have different forms)	A man's life may be COMPARED TO a play.
COMPARE WITH (shows difference between things of like form)	How can you COMPARE a mink coat WITH a beaver?
COMPATIBLE WITH	The ideas of the section manager should be COMPATIBLE WITH those of the buyer.
COMPLY WITH	If you do not wish to COMPLY WITH our request, please submit your resignation.

IDIOM	EXAMPLE
CONDUCIVE TO	The employer's kindness is CONDUCIVE TO good work.
CONFORM TO (or WITH)	The average person CONFORMS TO the will of the majority. It is necessary to CONFORM WITH these rules.
CONVERSANT WITH	A salesman should be fully CONVERSANT WITH the articles he is selling.
DESIROUS OF	Some people are DESIROUS OF a price increase.
DIFFER WITH (an opinion) DIFFER FROM (a thing)	I DIFFER WITH you in regard to its quality. This machine DIFFERS FROM the old one in many respects.
DISSUADE FROM	We should DISSUADE him FROM making that investment.
EMPLOYED AT (a definite salary)	Our secretary is EMPLOYED AT $85 a week.
EMPLOYED IN (certain work)	My father is EMPLOYED IN blueprint reading.
ENVIOUS OF	Some of the employees are ENVIOUS OF his promotion.
IDENTICAL WITH (or TO)	These stockings are IDENTICAL WITH those I showed you last week.
INFER FROM	I INFER FROM his remarks that he is dissatisfied.
OBLIVIOUS OF (or TO)	The typist is OBLIVIOUS OF the construction noise outside.
OPPOSITE TO (or FROM) (meaning contrary)	Your point of view is OPPOSITE TO mine.
PERTINENT TO	This sales talk must be PERTINENT TO the item to be sold.
PREFER TO	I PREFER nylon TO silk.
PRIOR TO	I want a deposit PRIOR TO final settlement.
VIE WITH	The salesmen are VYING WITH one another for this week's prize.

Conjunctions

A conjunction connects words, phrases and clauses.
CONJUNCTIONS join in many ways: in *and* out, night *or* day.

There are three types of CONJUNCTIONS:

1. CO-ORDINATE CONJUNCTIONS... connect words, phrases, independent (main) clauses of EQUAL VALUE. (see CLAUSES)

   Examples: Mary *and* Jane (WORDS are connected)

   Into the village *or* through the woods (PHRASES are connected)

   You may go to the park *but* wear your rubbers. (INDEPENDENT CLAUSES are connected)

2. SUBORDINATE CONJUNCTIONS... connect dependent clauses to independent clauses. (see CLAUSES)

   Examples: *Although* he felt better, he refused to leave the house.

   (Note that the *Subordinate Conjunction* may start the sentence)

   We shall leave *since* there is nothing for us to do.

3. CORRELATIVE CONJUNCTIONS... are used in pairs.

   Examples: *Both* men *and* women are needed for the job.

   Neither Jim *nor* Jack is going.

Interjections

An interjection expresses strong feeling.
The INTERJECTION notes surprise: *My!* how lovely! *"Help!"* he cries.

O denotes wishing. It is used in Direct Address (see).

It is not directly followed by a comma or by any other punctuation mark.

Example: O mother of mine!

Oh denotes sorrow, hope, surprise, pain.

It may be followed by a comma or by an exclamation mark.

Example: Oh, I'm in real trouble!

UNITS OF THOUGHT

There are three ways to express a thought:

PHRASE — *has no subject or verb*. A phrase is an *incomplete* thought.

Example: *in the park*

CLAUSE — *has a subject and a verb*. A clause is an *incomplete* thought.

Example: *after they had left*

SENTENCE — *has* a subject and a verb. A sentence is a *complete* thought.

Example: *We saw you.*

KINDS OF SENTENCES

SIMPLE . . . one main clause.

Example: I feel fine.

COMPOUND . . . two or more main clauses.

Example: Symphonic music stimulates some persons to noble thoughts, but others are lulled to sleep by it.

COMPLEX . . . one main and one subordinate clause.

Example: Because snow had closed the airport, the pilot made a forced landing.

COMPOUND – COMPLEX . . . two main clauses and one (or more) subordinate clauses.

Example: You prefer art and I prefer music although I am an art major.

Note: A *main* clause is the same as an *independent* clause.

A *subordinate clause* is the same as a *dependent* clause.

PHRASES AND CLAUSES

. . . There are three kinds of phrases
. . . There are three kinds of clauses

THREE KINDS OF PHRASES
NOUN PHRASE (takes place of noun)
e.g. *"On to Paris"* was the cry of the enemy.
ADJECTIVE PHRASE (takes place of adjective)
e.g. The girl *in the red bathing suit* is my sister.
ADVERBIAL PHRASE (takes place of adverb)
e.g. He ran *into the house*.

Note: All of the foregoing phrases are also PREPOSITIONAL PHRASES. A prepositional phrase is so called because it is introduced by a *preposition*.

Other types of phrases (according to what they are introduced by) are:

INFINITIVE PHRASES (see INFINITIVE)

PARTICIPIAL PHRASES (see PARTICIPLE)

GERUND PHRASES (see GERUND)

THREE KINDS OF CLAUSES
NOUN CLAUSE (takes place of noun)
e.g. *That he was talented* was obvious.
ADJECTIVE CLAUSE (takes place of adjective)
e.g. The child *who fell down* is my cousin.
ADVERBIAL CLAUSE (takes place of adverb)
e.g. He arrived *after I had left*.

VERBALS

A verbal is a form of the verb — it is NOT a verb.

There are THREE VERBALS (Infinitive - Participle - Gerund)

INFINITIVE — to go, to run, to see, etc. . . . may be noun *or* adjective *or* adverb.

e.g.   I like *to swim.* (noun)

e.g.   A book *to read* is what the child wants. (adjective)

e.g.   He went *to play* ball (adverb)

PARTICIPLE

   a. Present Participle — going, seeing, feeling, etc.
   b. Past Participle — having gone, having seen, having felt, etc.
   . . . a participle is ALWAYS AN ADJECTIVE.

e.g. *Going* to the store, Joe slipped.

GERUND — knowing, running, hearing, etc.
   . . . a gerund is ALWAYS A NOUN.

e.g.   He enjoys *running.*

Verbal Phrases

INFINITIVE PHRASE

To study hard is sometimes necessary. (also a *noun phrase*)

He had a job *to do quickly.* (also an *adjective phrase*)

She was too emotional *to drive the car.* (also an *adverbial phrase*)

Note: Avoid the *split infinitive.* This is an infinitive which is "split" by an adverb.
INCORRECT: We decided *TO carefully CONSIDER* the matter.
SAY, we decided *TO CONSIDER* the matter *carefully.*

PARTICIPIAL PHRASE

Running to the store, the boy tripped. (also *adjective phrase*)
Feeling very ill, the party was called off. (This is incorrect because "feeling" has nothing to modify . . . it certainly does not modify "party." Every participle — since it is an adjective — must have a noun to modify. If the participle does not modify, it is DANGLING. A *dangling participle is always wrong.*)

GERUND PHRASE

She likes *dancing in the dark.* (also a *noun phrase*)

MISPLACED MODIFIERS

The modifiers in the English language are:

Adjectives
Adjective Phrases } They modify
Adjective Clauses } *nouns* or *pronouns.*

Adverbs
Adverbial Phrases } They modify *verbs,*
Adverbial Clauses } *adjectives* and other *adverbs.*

Occasionally, these modifiers are misplaced. Let us consider the modifying word *only.* It may be an adjective or adverb. Note the various meanings of the following sentence by your placing *only* in the positions indicated by arrows.

I   saw   Jones   shoot   Smith.

Try this MISPLACED MODIFIER test. Preserve the meaning that was originally intended.

Test On Misplaced Modifiers

1. Does a person live here with one eye named Wilson?
2. The musician played the piano with wooden legs. (three possibilities).
3. Mrs. Jones was injured while preparing her husband's supper in a horrible manner.
4. While enjoying lunch, the gong sounded.
5. A strange man was strolling down Broadway with a red beard.
6. At the age of six, her mother died and left four children.
7. Mrs. McGillicuddy resigned from the Women's League after belonging fifteen years with much disappointment on the part of the members.
8. While eating oats, they took the horse out of the stable.
9. The flames were put out before any damage was done by the Fire Department.
10. While paddling, a huge fish leaped into the canoe.
11. The child watched the St. Patrick's Day Parade sitting in a carriage.
12. Have you read about the girl who was run over in the newspaper?
13. I wish to sell a brand-new house by an expert builder of the best concrete block.
14. He sold the watch to the young lady with the Swiss movement.
15. The girl went to the party with the young man wearing a low-cut gown.
16. We found a description of the crocodile in the dictionary.
17. They read about the arrest of the gangster who had intimidated his victims with relief.
18. I found it pleasant studying about knights in shining armor in the library.
19. The old man went to the barn to milk the cow with a cane.
20. The table was delivered by the driver with the wooden top.

Answers to Misplaced Modifier Test

1. Does a one-eyed person named Wilson live here?
2. A. The musician with wooden legs played the piano.
   B. The musician played the piano which had wooden legs.
   C. The musician played the piano by using wooden legs.
3. Mrs. Jones was injured in a horrible manner while preparing her husband's supper.
4. While we were enjoying lunch, the gong sounded.
5. A strange man with a red beard was strolling down Broadway.
6. When the girl was six, her mother died and left four children.
7. With much disappointment on the part of the members, Mrs. McGillicuddy resigned from the Women's League after belonging fifteen years.
8. They took the horse out of the stable while he was eating his oats.
9. The flames were put out by the Fire Department before any damage was done.
10. While we were paddling, a huge fish leaped into the canoe.
11. Sitting in a carriage, the child watched the St. Patrick's Day Parade.
12. Have you read in the newspaper about the girl who was run over?
13. I wish to sell a brand-new house made by an expert builder who used the finest concrete block.
14. He sold the watch with the Swiss movement to the young lady.
15. Wearing a low-cut gown, the girl went to the party with the young man.
16. In the dictionary, we found a description of the crocodile.
17. With relief, we read about the arrest of the gangster who had intimidated his victims.
18. I found it pleasant studying in the library about knights in shining armor.
19. The old man with the cane went to the barn to milk the cow.
20. The table with the wooden top was delivered by the driver.

Punctuation Rules

*These are the simple rules of Punctuation. They
are really easy to learn.*

1. APOSTROPHE (')

1. to indicate possession.
Bob's hat; Burns' poems; Jones's houses;
Note: Use *apostrophe only* (without the s)
for certain words that end in *s*:

a. When *s* or *z* sound comes before the
final *s*:
Moses' journey
Cassius' plan

b. After a plural noun:
girls' shoes
horses' reins

Where to place the Apostrophe

These (ladie's, ladies') blouses are on
sale.

The apostrophe means *belonging* to
everything to the *left* of the apostrophe:

ladie's (l a d i e ' s)
belonging to ladie (no such word)
ladies' (l a d i e s ')
belonging to ladies (correct)

These (childrens', children's) coats are
size 8.

One could not say belonging to childrens (c h i l d r e n s ');
therefore, children's (c h i l d r e n ' s)-
belonging to children - is correct.

Also Note:
a. When two or more names comprise one
firm, possession is indicated in the last
name.

Lansdale, Jackson and Roosevelt's law
firm.
Sacks and Company's sale.

b. In a compound noun, separated by
hyphens, apostrophe belongs in last syllable - *father-in-law's*

In this connection, it is worthwhile noting
that the plurals of compound nouns are
formed by adding the s (no apostrophe,
of course) to the first syllable - I have
three *brothers-in-law*. Those are my
brothers-in-law's cars.

The apostrophe has two other uses besides
indicating possession:

2. for plurals of letters and figures
three d's; five 6's

3. to show that a letter has been left out
let's (for *let us*)

Note a: ours, yours, his, hers, its, theirs and
whose -
though possessive - have no apostrophe.

Note b: The apostrophe is omitted occasionally in titles.
Teachers College, Actors Equity Association.

2. COLON (:)

The colon is used

1. after such expressions as *the following, as
follows*, and their equivalents.

"The sciences studied in high schools
are as follows: biology, chemistry, and
physics."

2. after the Salutation in a Business Letter

Gentlemen:
Dear Mr. Jones:

Note: A comma (see below) is used after
the Salutation in a Friendly Letter -

Dear Ted,

3. COMMA (,)

In general, the comma is used in writing just as you use a pause in speaking. Here are the specific situations in which commas are used.

1. *direct address*
   Mr. Adams, has the report come in yet?

2. *apposition*
   Sam, our buyer, gave us some good advice.

3. *parenthetical expressions*
   We could not, however, get him to agree.

4. *letter*
   Sincerely,
   Truly yours,

5. *dates, addresses*
   November 11, 1918
   Cleveland 2, Ohio

6. *series*
   We had soup, salad, ice cream, and milk for lunch.
   Note: Comma before the "and" in a series is not necessary.

7. *phrase or clause at beginning of sentence* (if the phrase or clause is long)
   As I left the room in order to go to school, my mother called me.

8. *separating clauses of long sentence*
   We asked for Mr. Smith, but he had already left for home.

9. *clearness*
   After planting, the farmer had his supper.

10. *direct quotation*
    Mr. Arnold blurted out, "This is a fine mess!"

11. *modifier expressions that do not restrict the meaning of the thought which is modified.*
    Air travel, which may or may not be safe, is an essential part of our way of life.
    Note: Travel which is on the ground is safer than air travel. (NO COMMAS)

4. DASH (—)

The dash is about twice as long as the hyphen (see next column). The dash is used

1. *to break up a thought*
   There are five—remember I said five—good reasons to refuse their demands.

2. *instead of parentheses* (see below)
   A beautiful horse—Black Beauty is its name—is the hero of the book.

5. EXCLAMATION MARK (!)

The exclamation mark is used after an expression of *strong feeling*.
Ouch! I hurt my thumb.

6. HYPHEN (-)

The hyphen divides a word.

mother-in-law

Note: The number words, twenty-one through ninety-nine, are hyphenated.

7. PARENTHESES ( )

1. Parentheses set off that part of the sentence that is not absolutely necessary to the completeness of the sentence:

   I was about to remark (this may be repetition) that we must arrive there early.

2. Parentheses are also used to enclose figures, letters, signs and dates in a sentence:

   Shakespeare (1564-1616) was a great dramatist.

   The four forms of discourse are a) narration b) description c) exposition d) argument.

8. PERIOD (.)

The period is used

1. *after a complete thought unit*
   The section manager will return shortly.
2. *after an abbreviation*
   Los Angeles, Calif.

9. QUESTION MARK (?)

The question mark is used after a *request for information*.

When do you leave for lunch?

10. QUOTATION MARKS (" ")

Quotation marks are used

1. to enclose what a person says *directly*
   "No one could tell," she said, "that it would occur."
   He exclaimed, "This is the end!"
   "Don't leave yet," the boss told her.

2. to enclose a title
   I have just finished reading "Arrowsmith."

11. SEMICOLON (;)

The semicolon is not used much. It is to be avoided where a comma or a period will suffice. Following, however, are the common uses of the semicolon:

1. *to avoid confusion with numbers*
   Add the following; $1.25; $7.50; and $12.89.

2. *before explanatory words or abbreviations - namely, e.g., etc.*
   We are able to supply you with two different gauges of nylon stockings; namely, 45 and 51.

Note: the *semicolon* goes *before* the expression (namely) - a *comma follows* the expression.

3. *to separate short statements of contrast*
   War is destructive; peace is constructive.

Capitalization Rules

1. *The first word of a sentence*
   With cooperation, a depression can be avoided.

2. *All proper names*
   America, Santa Fe Chief, General Motors, Abraham Lincoln.

3. *Days of the week and months.*
   The check was mailed on *Thursday.*

   Note: The seasons are not capitalized
   Example: In Florida, *winter* is mild.

4. *The word* <u>dear</u> *when it is the first word in the salutation of a letter.*

   Dear Mr. Jones:
     but
   My *dear* Mr. Jones:

5. *The first word of the complimentary close of a letter*

   Truly yours,
     but
   Very *truly* yours,

6. *The first, and the important words in a title*
   The *Art* of *Salesmanship*

7. *A word used as part of a proper name*
   William *Street* (but-That *street* is narrow.)
   Morningside *Terrace* (but - We have a *terrace* apartment.)

8. *Titles, when they refer to a particular official or family member.*
   The report was read by *Secretary* Marshall.
   (but - Miss Shaw, our *secretary*, is ill.)
   Let's visit *Uncle* Harry.
   (but - I have three *uncles*.)

9. *Points of a compass, when they refer to particular regions of a country.*
   We're going *South* next week. (but - New York is *south of Albany*.)

   Note: Write - the Far West, the Pacific Coast, the Middle East, etc.

10. *The first word of a direct quotation.*
    It was Alexander Pope who wrote, "A little learning is a dangerous thing."

    Note: When a direct quotation sentence is broken, the *first* word of the *second half* of the sentence is not capitalized.

"Don't phone," Lily told me, "*because* they're not in yet."

GRAMMAR FOR TEST TAKERS

Grammar is a classic stumbling block on the road to lofty examination scores. This section attempts to remove that block, or at least to minimize its damaging effects, by concentrating on material relevant to examination questions.

Immediately below is a series of sentences which are grammatically correct or incorrect. Confronted with a similar series on a test, the candidate would be required to indicate whether or not they were correct. That is exactly what should be done here. Do not guess. If you aren't sure whether a sentence is correct or not, mark it as such. And if you mark a sentence as being correct that isn't, be sure you understand why you made the mistake.

GRAMMAR FUNDAMENTALS IMPARTED BY THE QUESTION AND ANSWER METHOD

EXPLANATIONS OF KEY POINTS BEHIND THESE QUESTIONS ARE GIVEN WITH THE ANSWERS WHICH FOLLOW THE QUESTIONS

All these sentences are followed by judgments of their accuracy in accordance with grammatical principles. These explanations will give you an accurate measure of your strengths and weaknesses in this important test subject.

1. They are as old as us.

2. She is older than him.

3. Whom do you suppose paid us a visit.

4. Punish whomever is guilty.

5. It is me.

6. Can it be them?

7. Can it be her?

8. It would be impossible for you and I.

9. This is the death knell for we individualists.

10. He had a great deal of trouble with the store's management.

11. I, who's older, know better than you.

12. The mans hair is gray.

13. Is there any criticism of Arthur going?

14. Everybody tried their hardest.

15. I do not like these sort of cakes.

16. The government are unanimously agreed upon this action.

17. The government is unanimously agreed upon this action.

18. She don't like to engage in such activity.

19. The use of liquors are dangerous.

20. The district attorney, as well as many of his aides, have been involved in the investigation.

21. Either the fifth or the seventh of the courses they have laid open are to be accepted.

22. The fighting and wrestling of the two men is excellent.

23. The worst feature of the play were the abominable actors.

24. There is present a child and two dogs.

25. I shall go. You will go. He will go. We shall go. You will go. They will go.

26. I will; I repeat, I will. You shall; I say you shall. He shall; I say he shall. We will; we say we will. You shall; I say you shall. They shall; I say they shall.

27. When he saw me he says his prayers.

28. If I only knowed what the results of my action would be I would have restrained myself.

29. He spoke slow and careful.

30. The sun shines bright on my old Kentucky home.

31. She looks beautiful.

32. A Washington Street car accident resulted in two deaths.

33. The man gave the wrong reply.

34. The boy answered wrong.

35. He always has and will do it.

36. We hoped that you would have come to the party.

37. I intended to have gone.

38. In the parlor, my cousin kept a collection of animals which he shot.

39. He said that Venus was a planet.

40. If he was here, I should be happy.

41. I wish that I was a man.

42. By giving strict obedience to commands, a soldier learns discipline, and consequently would have steady nerves in time of war.

EXPLANATORY ANSWERS—GRAMMAR FUNDAMENTALS

Most of the 42 statements are grammatically incorrect. The errors are those of CASE, AGREEMENT, NUMBER, or PRINCIPAL PARTS. The proper form for each incorrect statement is given below. Following the proper form is a brief explanation of the grammatical principle underlying the correction.

STATEMENTS INVOLVING CASE

1. They are as old as we (are).

2. She is older than he (is).
   PRINCIPLE: (1, 2) The subject of a verb is in the nominative case, even when the verb is remote, or understood (not expressed).

   NOTE: T H A N and AS are conjunctions, not prepositions. When they are followed by a pronoun merely, this pronoun is not their object, but part of a clause, the rest of which may be understood. The case of this pronoun is determined by its relation to the rest of the unexpressed clause. Sometimes the understood clause calls for the objective: "I like his brother better than (I like) him."

3. Who do you suppose paid us a visit?
   PRINCIPLE: Guard against the improper attraction of who into the objective case by intervening expressions.

4. Punish whoever is guilty.
   PRINCIPLE: Guard against the improper attraction of who or whoever into the objective case by preceding verbs or prepositions.

5. It is I.

6. Can it be they?

7. Can it be she?

PRINCIPLE: (5, 6, 7) Nouns or pronouns connected by the verb to be (in any of its forms: is, was, were, be, etc.) agree in case. To be never takes an object, because it does not express action.

8. It would be impossible for you and me.

9. This is the death knell for us individualists.
   PRINCIPLE: (8, 9) The object of a preposition or a verb is in the objective case.

10. He had a great deal of trouble with the management of the store.
    PRINCIPLE: It is usually awkward and slightly illogical to attribute possession to inanimate objects.

11. I, who am older, know better than you.
    PRINCIPLE: A pronoun agrees with its antecedent in person, number and gender, but not in case.

12. The man's hair is gray.
    PRINCIPLE: A noun or pronuon used to express possession is in the possessive case. Do not omit the apostrophe from nouns, or from pronouns which require it, such as one's.

13. Is there any criticism of Arthur's going?
    PRINCIPLE: A noun or pronoun linked with a gerund should be in the possessive case.

STATEMENTS INVOLVING NUMBER

14. Everybody tried his hardest.
    PRINCIPLE: Each, every, every one, everybody, anybody, either, neither, no one, nobody, and similar words are singular.

15. I do not like this sort of cakes.
    PRINCIPLE: Do not let this or that, when modifying kind or sort, be attracted into the plural by a following noun.

16, 17. Both statements are correct.
    PRINCIPLE: (16, 17) Collective nouns may be regarded as singular or plural, according to the meaning intended.

18. She doesn't like to engage in such activity.
    PRINCIPLE: Do not use don't in the third person singular. Use doesn't. Don't is a contraction of do not.

STATEMENTS INVOLVING AGREEMENT

19. The use of liquors is dangerous.
    PRINCIPLE: A verb agrees in number with the subject. A verb should not agree with a noun which intervenes between it and the subject.

20. The district attorney, as well as many of his aides, has been involved in the investigation.
    PRINCIPLE: The number of the verb is not affected by the addition to the subject of words introduced by: with, together with, no less than, as well as, etc.

21. Either the fifth or the seventh of the courses they have laid open is to be accepted.
    PRINCIPLE: Singular subjects joined by nor, or, take a singular verb.

22. The fighting and wrestling of the two men are excellent.
    PRINCIPLE: A subject consisting of two or more nouns joined by and takes a plural verb.

23. The worst feature of the play was the abominable actors.
    PRINCIPLE: A verb should agree in number with the subject, not with a predicate noun.

24. There are present a child and two dogs.
    PRINCIPLE: In "there is" and "there are," the verb should agree in number with the noun that follows it.

25. The conjugation is correct.
    PRINCIPLE: To express simple futurity or mere expectation, use shall with the first person (both singular and plural) and will with the second and third.

26. All the sentences are correct.
    PRINCIPLE: To express resolution or emphatic assurance, reverse the usage: that is, use will with the first person (both singular and plural) and shall with the second and third.

STATEMENTS INVOLVING PRINCIPAL PARTS

27. When he saw me he said his prayers.

28. If I only knew what the results of my action would be, I would have restrained myself.
    PRINCIPLE: Use the correct form of the past tense and the past participle. Avoid come, done, bursted, knowed, says, for the past tense; and (had) eat, (had) froze, (have) ran, (has) wrote, (are) suppose, for the past participle.

NOTE: Memorize the principal parts of the most common "irregular" verbs. The principal parts are the infinitive (*play*), the first person of the past tense (*played*), and the past participle (*played*). This sample (*play*) is a "regular" verb; that is, the past tense and past participle are formed by adding *ed* to the infinitive. This is not the case with "irregular" verbs. One way to recall the principal parts of "irregular" verbs is to repeat as follows: today I choose; yesterday I chose; often in the past I have chosen. Thus, the principal parts of choose are: choose (infinitive); chose (past tense); and chosen (past participle).

29. He spoke slowly and carefully.
    PRINCIPLE: Do not use an adjective to modify a verb.

30. The statement is correct because BRIGHT modifies SUN.
    PRINCIPLE: In such sentences as "He stood firm," and "The cry rang clear," the modifier should be an adjective if it refers to the subject, an adverb if it refers to the verb.

31. Statement is correct grammatically.
    PRINCIPLE: After a verb pertaining to the senses, an adjective is used to denote a quality pertaining to the subject. (An adverb is used only when the reference is clearly to the verb.)

32. A street car accident in Washington resulted in two deaths.
    PRINCIPLE: Use "made" adjectives with caution. When an adjective phrase which normally follows the noun is condensed and placed before the noun as an attributive modifier, the result may be awkward, or even confusing.

33, 34. Both are correct.
    PRINCIPLE: Certain adverbs do not differ in form from adjectives. When form does not indicate which of the two parts of speech is intended, the word must be classified according to its use in the sentence.

35. He always has done it, and always will do it.
    PRINCIPLE: Do not use a verb, conjunction, preposition, or noun in a double capacity when one of the uses is ungrammatical.

36. We hoped that you would come to the party. (The principal verb HOPED indicates a past time. In that past time our hope was that you WOULD come, not that you WOULD HAVE come.)
    PRINCIPLE: In dependent clauses and infinitives, the tense is to be considered in relation to the time expressed in the principal verb.

37. I intended to go. (The principal verb INTENDED indicates a past time. In that past time I intended to do something. What? Did I intend to GO, or to have gone.)

38. In the parlor, my cousin kept a collection of animals which he had shot.
    PRINCIPLE: When narration in the past tense is interrupted for reference to a preceding occurrence, the past perfect tense is used.

39. He said that Venus is a planet.
    PRINCIPLE: General statements equally true in the past and in the present are usually expressed in the present tense.

40. If he were here, I should be happy.

41. I wish that I were a man.
    PRINCIPLE: The subjunctive mode of the verb to be is used to express a condition contrary to fact, or a wish.

42. By giving strict obedience to commands, a soldier learns discipline, and consequently WILL HAVE steady nerves in time of war. war.
    PRINCIPLE: Use the correct auxiliary. Make sure that the tense, mode, or aspect of successive verbs is not altered without reason.

TEST I. CORRECT USAGE

DIRECTIONS: Each of the following questions is of the type you may expect to find on your test. Select the letter next to the sentence that best completes the statement. Following each question is the rule of grammar that applies. Each correct answer is explained.

1. The most acceptable of the following sentences is:

   (A) It is us you meant.
   (B) It is us whom you meant.
   (C) It is us who you meant.
   (D) It is we you meant.

   RULE: The nominative or subject case follows the verb "to be." Nominative pronouns are: I, we, she, they, it and who.

   EXPLANATION: Since US is in the objective case, the only correct choice is "D."

2. The most acceptable of the following sentences is:

   (A) This is entirely between you and he.
   (B) This is completely between you and he.
   (C) This is between you and him.
   (D) This is between he and you.

   RULE: The objective case follows a preposition. Pronouns used in the objective case are: me, us, you, him, her, it, them and whom.

   EXPLANATION: Since BETWEEN is a preposition, it must be followed by objective pronouns. Therefore, "C" is the only correct choice.

3. The most acceptable of the following sentences is:

   (A) As I said, neither of them are guilty.
   (B) As I said neither of them are guilty.
   (C) As I said neither of them is guilty.
   (D) As I said, neither of them is guilty.

   RULE: A singular, indefinite pronoun must be used with a singular verb. Singular pronouns include: anyone, someone, each, neither, everyone, another, somebody, no one.

   EXPLANATION: Eliminate "A," since NEITHER is singular and cannot be used with "are," which is plural. Eliminate "B" for the same reason. Eliminate "C," since a comma should properly be inserted after SAID. "D" is the correct answer since IS is a singular verb.

4. The most acceptable of the following sentences is:

   (A) What kind of a substance is insulin?
   (B) What kind of substance is insulin?
   (C) What kind a substance is insulin?
   (D) Of what kind of substance is insulin?

   RULE: Before a noun, use "kind of."

   EXPLANATION: KIND A and KIND OF A are corruptions and may not properly be used preceding a noun. "B" is the correct answer.

5. The most acceptable of the following sentences is:

   (A) Your pen is different from mine.
   (B) Your pen is different to mine.
   (C) You pen is different than mine.
   (D) Your pen is different with mine.

   RULE: "Different from" is preferred to "different than." Therefore, "A" is the correct answer.

6. The most acceptable of the following sentences is:

 (A) The lawyer's client sat besides him.
 (B) The client sat beside the lawyer.
 (C) The client sat besides the lawyer.
 (D) His client sat besides him.

RULE: Do not confuse "beside" with "besides." The former means "by the side of;" the latter means "in addition to."

EXPLANATION: Since the sentences refer to position, BESIDE, meaning "by the side of," is the desired word. Therefore, "B" is the correct answer.

7. The most acceptable of the following sentences is:

 (A) The prisoners went back to their cells, like they were ordered.
 (B) The prisoners have went back to their cells as they were ordered.
 (C) The prisoners went back to their cells, as they were ordered.
 (D) The prisoners have gone back to their cells, like they were ordered.

RULE: "Like" means "similar to," and takes an object. It is often incorrectly substituted for "as" and "as if." "Like" may not introduce a clause, while "as" may introduce a subject and a verb.

EXPLANATION: Eliminate "A" because LIKE may not introduce a subject and a verb. Eliminate "B" because the past participle of TO GO is GONE and not WENT. "C" is the correct answer because WENT is the correct form of the past tense of TO GO, and AS is properly used here, introducing a subject and a verb.

8. The most acceptable of the following sentences is:

 (A) These problems had been laying dormant for centuries.
 (B) These problems has been laying dormant for centuries.
 (C) These problems had been lain dormant for centuries.
 (D) These problems had been lying dormant for centuries.

RULE: The verb "lie" does not take an object. It means "to rest or stay." Its principal parts are: lie, lay, lying, lain. The verb "lay" takes an object. It means the actual putting down of something. Its principal parts are: lay, laid, laying, laid.

EXPLANATION: Eliminate "A" since the correct form of the required present participle is LYING. Eliminate "B" for the same reason. Eliminate "C", since LAIN is incorrectly used. "D" is the correct answer, since LYING is correctly used.

9. The most acceptable of the following sentences is:

 (A) The draperies were not hanged well.
 (B) The draperies were not hanged good.
 (C) The draperies were not hung well.
 (D) The draperies were not hung good.

RULE: "Hanged" is only used when referring to death by hanging. In other cases, "hung" is used. Its principal parts are: hang, hung, hung.

EXPLANATION: Eliminate "A" since HANGED is improperly used. Eliminate "B" for the same reason. "C" is the correct answer. Eliminate "D," since good is an adjective and cannot modify a verb. WELL is an adverb and is properly used to modify a verb.

TEST II. CORRECT USAGE

TIME: 20 Minutes. 33 Questions.

DIRECTIONS: In each of the following groups of sentences, select the one sentence that is grammatically INCORRECT. Mark the answer sheet with the letter of that incorrect sentence.

Explanations of the key points behind these questions appear with the answers at the end of this test. The explanatory answers provide the kind of background that will enable you to answer test questions with facility and confidence.

(A) His speed was equal to that of a racehorse.
(B) His failure was due to weak eyes.
(C) His love for war is contemptuous.
(D) Of course, my opinion is worth less than a lawyer's.

2

(A) In spite of the fact that it had not been refrigerated for several hours, the milk was still sweet.
(B) No sooner had he finished his studies when he dashed out to play.
(C) "Will you ride to the game with me?" asked John.
(D) To see is to believe, but one must be sure that one sees clearly.

3

(A) There goes the last train with American soldiers.
(B) Such talk aggravates me.
(C) The scene opens quickly, and in walk John and Mary.
(D) I cough continually in the winter.

4

(A) Everyone was present but him for whom the meeting was called.
(B) The citizen was wholly within his rights.
(C) Not only did I eat too much, but I also drank to excess.
(D) Let's meet around six o'clock.

5

(A) He lost considerable in Wall Street.
(B) Last night, in a radio address, the President urged us to subscribe to the Red Cross.
(C) In the evening, light spring rain cooled the streets.
(D) "Un-American" is a word which has been used even by those whose sympathies may well be pro-Nazi.

6

(A) The professor finished the unit inside of a month.
(B) After stealing the bread, he ran like a thief.
(C) Swimming is more enjoyable than dancing.
(D) The scouts walked a mile further than they had intended.

7

(A) The meal was meant to be theirs.
(B) We all prefer those other kinds of candy.
(C) Has either of you a sharp pencil?
(D) That was a great bunch of people.

8

(A) Bob Kennedy was the choice of many.
(B) Bring all these books to the library.
(C) We are desirous of serving you.
(D) Anyone may attend.

9

(A) I beg leave to call upon you in case of an emergency.
(B) Do not deter me from carrying out the demands of my office.
(C) Please see me irregardless of the time of day.
(D) The attorney for the slayer insisted his client was innocent.

(A) It is the noise made by the crickets that you hear.
(B) She told us that she would be at home on Sunday.
(C) The Democratic Convention was about to drop Chicago as its site because of a telephone strike.
(D) Sandy is a very cute girl.

11

(A) In brief, jurors must exercise their very best judgment.
(B) If we can make a deal, I'll buy your paintings.
(C) The letter, having been corrected, was ready for his signature.
(D) Their disagreement soon developed into a bitter fight.

12

(A) I think that Report A is equally as good as Report B.
(B) Not only John but also his brothers have applied for admission to college.
(C) This book is more valauble than any other book in my library.
(D) My cousin said that he intended to go to camp with me.

13

(A) I prefer these kind of books to those.
(B) Did he say, "The test will be on Saturday"?
(C) When we reviewed the report, we felt that we oughtn't to incur any further expenses.
(D) It's time to give the baby its bath.

14

(A) Working hard at school during the day and in the post office during the night, he seemed to be utterly indefatigable.
(B) Do you think she is liable to win the fellowship?
(C) I found "Ode to a Skylark" in an anthology called "Singing Winds."
(D) Their stories being unintelligible, it's hard to say who's to blame for the disturbance.

15

(A) Many artisans participated in the building of the Sistine Chapel.
(B) The contrast between the two parties is patent.
(C) Although Richard graduated high school with honors, he failed three subjects as a college freshman.
(D) Neither the teacher nor the students have found the reference.

16

(A) I can read almost anything, but these childlike books disgust me.
(B) Neither of the candidates was able to secure a plurality of the votes.
(C) To keep abreast of current events requires that one read conscientiously at least two newspapers daily.
(D) There would have been bitter opposition to the plan had its provisions been publicized.

17

(A) His tone clearly inferred that he was bitterly disappointed.
(B) Having lain on the beach all afternoon, he suffered a severe sunburn.
(C) We cannot but suspect his motive.
(D) The family groups chosen to represent our town were the Browns, the Evanses, and the Granbards.

18

(A) The zinnia has the more vivid color, but the violet is the sweeter-smelling.
(B) No sooner had he begun to speak when the audience started to boo.
(C) About three-fourths of the review was a summary of the story; the rest criticism.
(D) I shall insist that he not be accepted as a member.

19

(A) In China today, there is insistence upon the doctor's giving greater attention to traditional medicine.
(B) No one in the audience dares refrain from hearty applause.
(C) We sure hope you will be able to come to the meeting.
(D) Lest the traveler concentrate too much on his stomach, the author has included notes on history.

20

(A) We ought to have prepared the group for the excitement which followed.
(B) Award the cup to whoever receives the majority of the judges' votes.
(C) She was promoted because she was more discrete than the other secretary.
(D) All he said was, "Please set it down over there."

21

(A) What you earn is nobody's business.
(B) Swimming is a healthful pastime.
(C) Mr. Brown was accidentally omitted when the invitations were issued.
(D) The boss insisted on no one else for the assignment but you.

22

(A) Do you think that the alumnae are helpful?
(B) I suggest that you send the document to the local library.
(C) Their comments being so indistinct, it's hard to say who's correct.
(D) They were happy to hear that the young piano student was liable to win the Tschaikovsky competition.

(23)

(A) He had a reputation for being an outstanding administrator, but he was not happy about being faced with too many dilemmas.
(B) Harry wants to be a good athlete like his older brother.
(C) We are quite enthused about his Ph.D.
(D) Maria is one of those pupils who frequently spend a good deal of their time in the detention room.

(24)

(A) Mary Lou incurred the enmity of the class when she revealed the secret.
(B) Being that she was a newcomer, Rose was shy.
(C) Though cleverer than her sisters, Louise is less trustworthy than they.
(D) Harassment of his employees is the mark of a tyrannical employer.

(25)

(A) The lecture finished, the audience began asking questions.
(B) Any man who could accomplish that task the world would regard as a hero.
(C) Our respect and admiration are mutual.
(D) George did like his mother told him, despite the importunities of his playmates.

(26)

(A) Oliver Wendell Holmes, Jr., decided to become a writer being that his father was a successful author.
(B) Adult Westerns on TV have neglected the great tradition of bronco-busting in the Old West.
(C) Nothing would satisfy him but that I bow to his wishes.
(D) The two companies were hopeful of eventually effecting a merger, if the government didn't object.

(27)

(A) Mrs. Mary Johnson Aldrich, only daughter of the late Senator Aldrich, disclosed today plans for her third marriage, to Dr. H. Walter Sloan.
(B) An excellent grade of synthetic rubber was discovered in 1954 by Goodrich-Gulf scientists.
(C) It's now clear that the largest number of votes may go to the incumbent.
(D) In the entire group, none was able to bear the heavy burden better than he.

(28)

(A) Few studied hard enough to achieve success in this challenging field.
(B) That there statue is one of the many that needs a good scrubbing.
(C) Larry practiced for a long time; consequently, he became quite proficient.
(D) His attempting to drive over the icy road surprised all of us.

(29)

(A) Look! Here comes Bruce and the rest of the team.
(B) Our students must write theses to qualify for the M.A. degree.
(C) You swim faster than he, but not so gracefully.
(D) Now kick your feet in the water like Gregory just did.

(30)

(A) After waiting for two hours, the audience left the hall, angry and disillusioned because of the author's failure to appear.
(B) In spite of the expense, it seems likely that more American men and women will be graduated from college this year than ever before.
(C) If you study for the test, you may get a good mark.
(D) If you do not know who owns the purse, leave the usher keep it until the owner appears.

(31)

(A) Michael has been taking accordion lessons for more than two years.
(B) Betty and Sue formed the nucleus of the group.
(C) Several players complimented each other as they came off the field.
(D) The tragedy of Leningrad dwarfs even that of the Warsaw ghetto or Hiroshima.

(32)

(A) The professor wanted to do advanced work in hydrodynamics, in which he had taken his Doctor of Philosophy degree.
(B) Eisenhower preferred to use the word "finalize" even though it was proscribed by precise grammarians.
(C) Would that I had been allowed to stay a minute longer!
(D) No sooner had the batter stepped into the box when a fastball came right at his head.

(33)

(A) It was probably an innocuous remark, but can you blame me for feeling resentful?
(B) It is generally conceded that Lincoln's address at Gettysburg is an American masterpiece.
(C) Enclosed herewith is one copy of the book you ordered.
(D) Despite elaborate preparations, the plan soon failed.

CONSOLIDATE YOUR KEY ANSWERS HERE

Practice using Answer Sheets. Make ONE mark for each answer. Additional and stray marks may be counted as mistakes. In making corrections erase errors COMPLETELY. Make glossy black marks. To arrive at an accurate estimate of your ability and progress, cover the Correct Answers with a sheet of white paper while you are taking this test.

CORRECT KEY ANSWERS TO THE PRACTICE QUESTIONS

Now compare your answers with these Correct Key Answers. If your answers differ from these, go back and study the Practice Questions to see where and how you made your mistakes. In doing this, the following Explanatory Answers should prove helpful. They provide concise clarifications of the basic points behind the Key Answers. Even where your Key Answers are the same as ours, go over the explanations carefully because they may be quite useful in helping you pick up extra points on the exam.

1.C	6.D	11.B	16.A	21.D	26.A	31.C
2.B	7.D	12.A	17.A	22.D	27.B	32.D
3.B	8.B	13.A	18.B	23.C	28.B	33.C
4.D	9.C	14.B	19.C	24.B	29.D	
5.A	10.D	15.C	20.C	25.D	30.D	

EXPLANATORY ANSWERS CLARIFYING CARDINAL POINTS

Here you have the heart of the Question and Answer Method. . .getting help when and where you need it. Where one of your Key Answers differs from ours you have a problem which can easily be remedied by reading the explanation. Then, if you have time, you might be able to pick up points on the exam by reading the other explanations, even where you wrote the Key Answers correctly. These explanations stress fundamental facts, ideas, and principles which just might pop up as questions on future exams.

1. C   His love for war is **contemptible**. REASON: **contemptuous** means feeling contempt.

2. B   No sooner had he finished his studies **than** he dashed out to play. REASON: **No sooner . . . than** is the correct expression.

3. B   Such talk **irritates** me. REASON: to **aggravate** means to make serious; **to irritate** means to annoy.

4. D   Let's meet **about** six o'clock. REASON: **around** is incorrect for the idea of "approximately."

5. A   He lost a **considerable amount** in Wall Street. REASON: Don't use **considerable** as a noun.

6. D   The scouts walked a mile **farther** than they had intended. REASON: **farther** is used for concrete distance—**further** for abstract distance (**I'll explain further**).

7. D   That was a great **crowd** of people. REASON: We speak of people as a **crowd**—bananas, grapes, etc., as a bunch.

8. B   **Take** all these books to the library. REASON: We **bring to the speaker**—we **take from the speaker**.

9. C   Please see me **regardless** of the time of day. REASON: There is no such word as **irregardless**.

10. D   Sandy is a very **attractive** girl. REASON: Avoid this over-used word (**cute**).

11. B   If we can make an **arrangement**, I'll buy your paintings. REASON: **deal** means quantity.

12. A   I think that Report A is as good as Report B. REASON: **equally** should be omitted since it is redundant—or replace **equally** with **just**.

13. A   I prefer **this kind** of books to that kind. REASON: **kind**, being singular, requires the singular demonstrative adjective (**this**).

14. B   Do you think she is **likely** to win the fellowship? REASON: **liable** means subject to some undesirable action.

15. C   Although Richard **graduated from** high school with honors, he failed three subjects as a college freshman. REASON: We **graduate from** a school—also **are graduated from** a school. The verb **graduate**, when followed by a direct object, means to mark with divisions, as a thermometer.

16. A   I can read almost anything, but these **childish** books disgust me. REASON: **childlike** means **innocent**.

17. A   His tone clearly **implied** that he was bitterly disappointed. REASON: The speaker **implies**—the listener **infers**

18. B   No sooner had he begun to speak **than** the audience started to boo. REASON: The correlative conjunction is **no sooner . . . than**.

19. C   We **surely** hope you will be able to come to the meeting. REASON: **sure** may not be used as an adverb.

20. C   She was promoted because she was more **discreet** than the other secretary. REASON: **discrete** means **separate**.

21. D   The boss insisted on **no one** for the assignment but you. REASON: **else** is superfluous here.

22. D   They were happy to hear that the young piano student was **likely** to win the Tschaikovsky competition. REASON: **liable** implies harm; **likely** refers to probable occurrence.

23. C   We are quite **enthusiastic** about his Ph.D. REASON: **enthused** is poor usage.

24. B   **Since** she was a newcomer, Rose was shy. REASON: **Being that** is incorrect because **Being**, a participle, does not modify a noun in the sentence.

25. D   George did **as** his mother told him, despite the importunities of his playmates. REASON: The conjunction **as** (not the preposition **like**) must be used to connect the main clause and the subordinate clause.

26. A   Oliver Wendell Holmes, Jr., decided to become a writer **since** his father was a successful author. REASON: **being that** is incorrect as a substitute for **since**.

27. B   An excellent grade of synthetic rubber was **invented** in 1954 by Goodrich-Gulf scientists. REASON: Man **discovers** what has already been there—he **invents** something that had no prior existence.

28. B   **That statue** is one of the many that needs a good scrubbing. REASON: The expressions **that there** and **this here** are unacceptable.

29. D   Now kick your feet in the water **as** Gregory just did. REASON: **as** is used as a conjunction which is required since the verb **did (kick)** follows. The preposition **like** is incorrect when a verb follows.

30. D   If you do not know who owns the purse, **let** the usher keep it until the owner appears. REASON: An infinitive does not follow **leave**—an infinitive such as **(to) keep** does follow **let**.

31. C   Several players complimented **one another** as they came off the field. REASON: **one another** refers to three or more—**each other** refers to two.

32. D   No sooner had the batter stepped into the box **than** a fastball came right at his head. REASON: The correct expression is **no sooner . . . than . . .**

33. C   Enclosed is one copy of the book you ordered. REASON: **herewith** is unnecessary in this case.

ENGLISH USAGE

In this test of standard written English the questions consist of a sentence with four of its parts underlined and lettered (A) (B) (C) (D) and (E). (E) consists of the words "No error." In most of the questions one of the underlined parts of the sentence is incorrect by the standards of written English. On your Answer Sheet you are to blacken the letter that corresponds with the incorrect, underlined part. In some of the questions all of the underlined parts are correct. For such questions, blacken the letter (E) that goes with "No error." Some of the sentences are quite difficult in that the underlined parts present fairly complex problems of usage. So, before you decide which letter to mark on your Answer Sheet, look carefully at all the underlined parts. The error, if there is one, is underlined and lettered. All other elements of the sentence are correct and may not be changed.

You'll get the idea if you study carefully the typical directions and illustrations given below. The directions should be no problem for you now because you can take your time to be sure that you understand them perfectly. They'll be quite familiar to you when you encounter them on the actual exam and you'll zip right through. After you've gotten the directions in hand, go on to test yourself with the predictive questions that follow. Check your answers with those provided at the end of the mini-test. At that time you'll know you have a good grasp of English Usage.

Illustrations:

I. He strode swiftly and firmly
         A   B
toward we judges. No error
       C   D   E

II. He labors every hour
       A   B
so that he would become
   C
politically acceptable
   D
to his party. No error
                 E

Correct Answers

TEST I. ENGLISH USAGE

TIME: 6 Minutes. 9 Questions.

DIRECTIONS: This is a test of standard written English. The rules may differ from everyday spoken English. Many of the following sentences contain grammar, usage, word choice, and idiom that would be incorrect in written composition. Some sentences are correct. No sentence has more than one error. Any error in a sentence will be underlined and lettered; all other parts of the sentence are correct and cannot be changed. If the sentence has an error, choose the underlined part that is incorrect, and mark that letter on your answer sheet. If there is no error, mark E on your answer sheet.

1. The chairman had ruled against the petitioner's
   A   B
   motion; yet no one was more dedicated than him.
                        C   D
   No error
   E

2. Every time he rotates the discus in his sinewy
      A   B   C
   hands, the biceps of his huge arms rolled
   smoothly under his taut shirt. No error
   D   E

3. Admiral Dewey's pennant was risen at Santiago
                    A   B
   as an indication of the beginning of the
   C   D
   engagement. No error
               E

4. Mayor Hargrove, whom the voters respected,
                   A   B
   had given Commissioner Newland neither open
   C
   or implied support. No error
   D   E

5. Placing the longbow on the lush grass at his
                A   B
   feet, Robin Hood, who had had an exciting
                            C
   day, threw hisself down to rest. No error.
              D   E

6. The Amazons, a race of female warriors, were
       A
   not, however, devoid of female feelings. No
        B   C   D
   error.
   E

7. The representative of the film industry was
                                           quoted as saying, "You may sneer if you wish,
   A
   but if it weren't for Westerns, there would be
            B   C
   few television sponsors today." No error.
   D   E

8. Because Johnny was interested in semaphore
   A   B
   code, he joined the Boy Scouts to learn these
                                              C
   kind of signaling. No error.
       D   E

9. In the future I shall include neither you or your
   A   B   C   D
   sister in my plans. No error.
                       E

CONSOLIDATE YOUR KEY ANSWERS HERE

Practice using Answer Sheets. Make ONE mark for each answer. Additional and stray marks may be counted as mistakes. In making corrections erase errors COMPLETELY. Make glossy black marks. To arrive at an accurate estimate of your ability and progress, cover the Correct Answers with a sheet of white paper while you are taking this test.

CORRECT KEY ANSWERS TO THE PRACTICE QUESTIONS

Now compare your answers with these Correct Key Answers. If your answers differ from these, go back and study the Practice Questions to see where and how you made your mistakes. In doing this, the following Explanatory Answers should prove helpful. They provide concise clarifications of the basic points behind the Key Answers. Even where your Key Answers are the same as ours, go over the explanations carefully because they may be quite useful in helping you pick up extra points on the exam.

1.D	3.B	5.D	7.E	9.D
2.B	4.D	6.D	8.C	

EXPLANATORY ANSWERS CLARIFYING CARDINAL POINTS

Here you have the heart of the Question and Answer Method. . .getting help when and where you need it. Where one of your Key Answers differs from ours you have a problem which can easily be remedied by reading the explanation. Then, if you have time, you might be able to pick up points on the exam by reading the other explanations, even where you wrote the Key Answers correctly. These explanations stress fundamental facts, ideas, and principles which just might pop up as questions on future exams.

1. **(D)** The chairman had ruled against the petitioner's motion; yet no one was more dedicated *than he*.

2. **(B)** Every time *he rotated* the discus in his sinewy hands, the biceps of his huge arms rolled smoothly under his taut shirt.

3. **(B)** Admiral Dewey's pennant *was raised* at Santiago as an indication of the beginning of the engagement.

4. **(D)** Major Hargrove, whom the voters respected, had given Commissioner Newland neither open *nor* implied support.

5. **(D)** *hisself* is not a word. It should be *himself*.

6. **(D)** *female* describes the sex. It should be *feminine*, an adjective used for qualities associated with the sex.

7. **(E)** No error.

8. **(C)** *these* should be *this* to agree with singular noun code.

9. **(D)** *or* should be *nor* because neither is always paired with nor.

TEST II. EFFECTIVE EXPRESSION

TIME: 8 Minutes. 15 Questions.

The following are representative examination type questions. They should be carefully studied and completely understood. The actual test questions will probably not be quite as difficult as these.

DIRECTIONS: *This is a test of standard written English. The rules may differ from everyday spoken English. Many of the following sentences contain grammar, usage, word choice, and idiom that would be incorrect in written composition. Some sentences are correct. No sentence has more than one error. Any error in a sentence will be underlined and lettered; all other parts of the sentence are correct and cannot be changed. If the sentence has an error, choose the underlined part that is incorrect, and mark that letter on your answer sheet. If there is no error, mark E on your answer sheet.*

Correct key answers to all these test questions will be found at the end of the test.

1. If he had had the forethought to arrange an appointment,
        A   B   C
   his reception would have been more friendly. No error.
                 D   E

2. His education had filled him with anger against those
                           A
   whom he believed had hurt or humiliated him. No error.
     B   C   D   E

3. The train having stopped several times during the night,
              A
   we couldn't even lay down to sleep. No error.
     B   C   D   E

4. Admirers of American ballet have made the claim that
      A
   its stars can dance as well or better than the best of the
    B   C   D
   Russian artists. No error.
           E

5. Rather than go with John, he decided to stay at home.
   A   B   C   D
   No error.
   E

    5. A B C D E

6. You telling the truth in the face of such dire consequences
   A   B
   required great moral courage. No error.
   C   D   E

    6. A B C D E

7. The following description, together with the drawings,
                              A
   present a master plan for the development of the airport.
   B   C   D
   No error.
   E

    7. A B C D E

8. For conscience' sake he gave himself up, though no sus-
       A   B   C
   picion had been directed toward him. No error.
          D   E

    8. A B C D E

9. I am depending on the medicine being delivered without
         A   B   C
   delay. No error.
   D   E

    9. A B C D E

10. His father was disturbed to find that the boy had lied
    A   B   C
    rather than telling the truth. No error.
           D   E

    10. A B C D E

11. Neither tears or protests effected the least change in their
                  A   B   C
    parents' decision. No error.
    D   E

    11. A B C D E

12. We thought the author of the letter to Aunt Mame to
           A   B   C
    be him. No error.
    D   E

    12. A B C D E

13. The victim's mother, besides herself with grief, could
        A   B   C
    give no coherent account of the accident. No error.
            D   E

    13. A B C D E

14. The children smiled at him, the laborer's greeted him by
    $\overline{\quad}$
    A   B

    waving their hats, and even the dogs licked his hand.
    $\overline{\quad}$
    C   D

    No error.
    E

14   A   B   C   D   E

15. Every sheet of ruled paper and every sheet of unruled
    A   B   C

    paper is carefully examined before it is returned.
    D

    No error.
    E

15   A   B   C   D   E

CONSOLIDATE YOUR KEY ANSWERS HERE

Practice using Answer Sheets. Make ONE mark for each answer. Additional and stray marks may be counted as mistakes. In making corrections erase errors COMPLETELY. Make glossy black marks. To arrive at an accurate estimate of your ability and progress, cover the Correct Answers with a sheet of white paper while you are taking this test.

	A B C D E		A B C D E		A B C D E		A B C D E		A B C D E		A B C D E		A B C D E		A B C D E
1		2		3		4		5		6		7		8	

	A B C D E		A B C D E		A B C D E		A B C D E		A B C D E		A B C D E		A B C D E
9		10		11		12		13		14		15	

CORRECT ANSWERS TO THE FOREGOING PRACTICE QUESTIONS

Now compare your answers with these Correct Answers to the Practice Questions. If your answers differ from these, go back and study those questions to see where and how you made your mistakes.

1.E	3.C	5.E	7.B	9.B	11.A	13.B	15.E
2.B	4.C	6.A	8.E	10.D	12.E	14.B	

TEST III. EFFECTIVE EXPRESSION

TIME: 8 Minutes. 15 Questions.

The following are representative examination type questions. They should be carefully studied and completely understood. The actual test questions will probably not be quite as difficult as these.

DIRECTIONS: This is a test of standard written English. The rules may differ from everyday spoken English. Many of the following sentences contain grammar, usage, word choice, and idiom that would be incorrect in written composition. Some sentences are correct. No sentence has more than one error. Any error in a sentence will be underlined and lettered; all other parts of the sentence are correct and cannot be changed. If the sentence has an error, choose the underlined part that is incorrect, and mark that letter on your answer sheet. If there is no error, mark E on your answer sheet.

Correct key answers to all these test questions will be found at the end of the test.

1. I saw Mr. Davis, him whom you pointed out last evening.
   A   B   C   D
   No error.
   E

2. When you have done your report, will you return this
            A   B
   memoranda as soon as possible? No error.
   C   D   E

3. This applicant lacks a few months' experience, otherwise
        A   B   C
   he is qualified for the position. No error.
         D   E

4. That scientist must be ingenuous to be able to arrive at
   A   B   C
   such valid conclusions. No error.
   D   E

5. She flouts her mink coat whenever she goes out with us
   $\underline{}$ $\underline{}$
   A   B
   so that we'll think she's very wealthy. No error.
       C   D   E

   5 A B C D E

6. Granting this to be true, what would you imply from the
     A   B   C
   statement which he has made? No error.
      D   E

   6 A B C D E

7. We objected to him scolding us for our good, especially
         A   B
   when he said it hurt him more than us. No error.
          C   D   E

   7 A B C D E

8. I was quite disappointed in his words, for I had always
         A   B   C
   treated him like he was my brother. No error.
         D   E

   8 A B C D E

9. Precisely the same thought sent the three of us into two
     A
   different directions—they to West Berlin and me to
      B   C   D
   Paris. No error.
       E

   9 A B C D E

10. Many a box of oranges have been sent to New York by
       A   B   C
    enthusiastic Californians. No error.
        D   E

    10 A B C D E

11. Let me say once and for all that between you and I
      A   B
    there can be no further friendship. No error.
       C   D   E

    11 A B C D E

12. He proved to his own satisfaction that he was as shrewd as,
       A   B   C
    if not shrewder than, she. No error.
       D   E

    12 A B C D E

13. The award should go to the pupil who we think the
       A   B
    parents had intended it for. No error.
       C   D   E

    13 A B C D E

14. We insist upon your telling us who else's signature ap-
    $\overline{}$ $\overline{}$ $\overline{}$
    A   B   C
    peared on this petition besides yours. No error.
              $\overline{}$ $\overline{}$
              D   E

14 A B C D E

15. The child felt very bad when his teacher criticized him
              $\overline{}$ $\overline{}$
              A   B
    before the entire class. No error.
    $\overline{}$ $\overline{}$ $\overline{}$
    C   D   E

15 A B C D E

CONSOLIDATE YOUR KEY ANSWERS HERE

Practice using Answer Sheets. Make ONE mark for each answer. Additional and stray marks may be counted as mistakes. In making corrections erase errors COMPLETELY. Make glossy black marks. To arrive at an accurate estimate of your ability and progress, cover the Correct Answers with a sheet of white paper while you are taking this test.

CORRECT ANSWERS TO THE FOREGOING PRACTICE QUESTIONS

Now compare your answers with these Correct Answers to the Practice Questions. If your answers differ from these, go back and study those questions to see where and how you made your mistakes.

1.B 3.C 5.A 7.A 9.C 11.B 13.B 15.E
2.E 4.B 6.C 8.D 10.B 12.E 14.C

TEST IV. EFFECTIVE EXPRESSION

TIME: 8 Minutes. 15 Questions.

The following are representative examination type questions. They should be carefully studied and completely understood. The actual test questions will probably not be quite as difficult as these.

DIRECTIONS: This is a test of standard written English. The rules may differ from everyday spoken English. Many of the following sentences contain grammar, usage, word choice, and idiom that would be incorrect in written composition. Some sentences are correct. No sentence has more than one error. Any error in a sentence will be underlined and lettered; all other parts of the sentence are correct and cannot be changed. If the sentence has an error, choose the underlined part that is incorrect, and mark that letter on your answer sheet. If there is no error, mark E on your answer sheet.

Correct key answers to all these test questions will be found at the end of the test.

1. Interested in semaphore code, Betty joined the
   A   B
   Girl Scouts to learn these kind of signals. No error.
      C   D   E

2. Harvard's football captain could tackle, block and pass
   A   B   C
   better than anyone on the team. No error.
          D   E

3. You may sneer if you wish, but if it weren't for Westerns,
                        A   B
   there would be few television sponsors today. No error.
          C   D   E

4. Though Larry had awakened before the birds began to
              A
   twitter, he laid in bed until long after the sun
       B   C
   had arisen. No error.
       D   E

5. As Martha <u>dived</u> off the springboard, she was <u>horrified</u> to
           A   B
   see that the water <u>was drained</u> from the pool the night
                    C
   <u>before.</u> <u>No error.</u>
     D   E

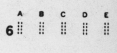

6. <u>Their</u> are <u>still</u> people who say that it has never <u>really</u>
     A   B   C
   been <u>proved</u> that the earth was round. <u>No error.</u>
        D   E

7. John Kennedy <u>effected</u> many <u>executive</u> reforms during
                 A   B
   the <u>tragically</u> few years that he served as <u>President.</u>
         C   D
   <u>No error.</u>
     E

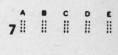

8. Mary was so <u>disinterested</u> in the <u>baseball</u> game <u>that</u> she
                A   B   C
   yawned <u>unashamedly.</u> <u>No error.</u>
           D   E

9. <u>Today's *Times*</u> has headlines about another girl <u>who has</u>
     A   B
   just <u>swam</u> the English <u>Channel.</u> <u>No error.</u>
        C   D   E

10. Placing his <u>longbow</u> on the grass <u>beside</u> him, Robin Hood,
              A   B
    who <u>had had</u> an exciting day, <u>laid</u> down to rest. <u>No error.</u>
          C   D   E

11. I was not <u>at all</u> surprised <u>to hear</u> of Jim <u>Dolan</u> winning
              A   B   C
    the poetry <u>contest.</u> <u>No error.</u>
            D   E

12. There was a time when the <u>far</u> North was unknown ter-
                             A
    ritory; <u>however,</u> American soldiers <u>manning</u> radar stations
            B   C
    there now wave to Boeing jet planes <u>zooming</u> by over-
                                              D
    head. <u>No error.</u>
          E

13. While I <u>was crossing</u> the Atlantic on the <u>Queen Eliza-</u>
$\qquad\qquad$ A

beth, <u>I busied</u> myself by <u>reading</u> Golding's "Lord of the
$\qquad$ B $\qquad$ C

<u>Flies".</u> <u>No error.</u>
$\quad$ D $\qquad$ E

$\qquad\qquad\qquad\qquad\qquad\qquad\qquad\qquad\quad$ A $\quad$ B $\quad$ C $\quad$ D $\quad$ E
$\qquad\qquad\qquad\qquad\qquad\qquad\qquad\qquad$ 13 :: :: :: :: ::

14. That angry outburst of <u>Father's</u> last night <u>resulted</u> in our
$\qquad\qquad\qquad\qquad\quad$ A $\qquad\qquad$ B

<u>guests</u> packing up and <u>leaving</u> this morning. <u>No error.</u>
$\quad$ C $\qquad\qquad\qquad$ D $\qquad\qquad\qquad$ E

$\qquad\qquad\qquad\qquad\qquad\qquad\qquad\qquad\quad$ A $\quad$ B $\quad$ C $\quad$ D $\quad$ E
$\qquad\qquad\qquad\qquad\qquad\qquad\qquad\qquad$ 14 :: :: :: :: ::

15. We have a new <u>snobbery</u> in the theater, <u>made up</u> of
$\qquad\qquad\qquad$ A $\qquad\qquad\qquad$ B

<u>that kind</u> of people who will not sit <u>beyond</u> a certain
$\quad$ C $\qquad\qquad\qquad\qquad\qquad$ D

<u>row.</u> No error.
$\quad$ E

$\qquad\qquad\qquad\qquad\qquad\qquad\qquad\qquad\quad$ A $\quad$ B $\quad$ C $\quad$ D $\quad$ E
$\qquad\qquad\qquad\qquad\qquad\qquad\qquad\qquad$ 15 :: :: :: :: ::

CONSOLIDATE YOUR KEY ANSWERS HERE

Practice using Answer Sheets. Make ONE mark for each answer. Additional and stray marks may be counted as mistakes. In making corrections erase errors COMPLETELY. Make glossy black marks. To arrive at an accurate estimate of your ability and progress, cover the Correct Answers with a sheet of white paper while you are taking this test.

CORRECT ANSWERS TO THE FOREGOING PRACTICE QUESTIONS

Now compare your answers with these Correct Answers to the Practice Questions. If your answers differ from these, go back and study those questions to see where and how you made your mistakes.

1.D	3.E	5.C	7.E	9.C	11.C	13.D	15.E
2.D	4.C	6.A	8.A	10.D	12.A	14.C	

SENTENCE CORRECTION

The questions contained in this section are designed to test your knowledge of grammar, sentence structure, correct usage and punctuation, and to point out some of the main sources of errors that have confounded candidates on past examinations.

In Sentence Correction you will be asked to choose the best way of phrasing a sentence, rather than to identify unacceptable usage. Part of the sentence or the entire sentence is underlined. In some of the questions the underlined part of the sentence falls below the standards of written English, and therefore must be rephrased. In other questions the underlined part of the sentence is correct.

Please bear in mind the requirements of "standard written English" so that you choose the answer which yields the most effective sentence....the one which is unambiguous, clear, exact, and free of awkwardness.

TEST I. SENTENCE CORRECTION

TIME: 3 Minutes. 5 Questions.

DIRECTIONS: A sentence is given, of which one part is underlined. Following the sentence are five choices. The first (A) choice simply repeats the underlined part. Then you have four additional choices which suggest other ways to express the underlined part of the original sentence. If you think that the underlined part is correct as it stands, write the answer A. If you believe that the underlined part is incorrect, select from the other choices (B or C or D or E) whichever you think is correct. Grammar, sentence structure, word usage, and punctuation are to be considered in your decision. The original meaning of the sentence must be retained.

1. You need not go unless you want to.

    (A) You need not go unless you want to.
    (B) You don't need to go not unless you want to.
    (C) You need go not unless you want to.
    (D) You need not go in case unless you want to.
    (E) You can go not unless you want to.

2. I believe there is no man but would give ten years of his life to accomplish such a lofty goal.

    (A) no man but would give
    (B) no man but who would give
    (C) not no man who would not give
    (D) no man who would but give
    (E) not any man would give

3. Often the young couple stood <u>enfolding each other together</u> in the dark and sweet smelling barn.

   (A) enfolding each other together
   (B) enfolding each other
   (C) each enfolding with the other
   (D) enfolding together
   (E) each folding together

4. <u>I don't do well in those kinds of tests.</u>

   (A) I don't do well in those kinds of tests.
   (B) I don't do well in those kind of tests.
   (C) I don't do good in those kinds of tests.

   (D) I don't do good in those kind of tests.
   (E) I don't do good in tests like those.

5. <u>Honor as well as profit are to be gained by this work.</u>

   (A) Honor as well as profit are to be gained by this work.
   (B) Honor also profit is to be gained by this work.
   (C) Honor in addition to profit are to be gained by this work.
   (D) Honor, as well as profit, are to be gained by this work.
   (E) Honor as well as profit is to be gained by this work.

CONSOLIDATE YOUR KEY ANSWERS HERE

Practice using Answer Sheets. Make ONE mark for each answer. Additional and stray marks may be counted as mistakes. In making corrections erase errors COMPLETELY. Make glossy black marks. To arrive at an accurate estimate of your ability and progress, cover the Correct Answers with a sheet of white paper while you are taking this test.

CORRECT KEY ANSWERS TO THE PRACTICE QUESTIONS

Now compare your answers with these Correct Key Answers. If your answers differ from these, go back and study the Practice Questions to see where and how you made your mistakes. In doing this, the following Explanatory Answers should prove helpful. They provide concise clarifications of the basic points behind the Key Answers. Even where your Key Answers are the same as ours, go over the explanations carefully because they may be quite useful in helping you pick up extra points on the exam.

1. A   2. A   3. B   4. A   5. E

EXPLANATORY ANSWERS CLARIFYING CARDINAL POINTS

1. **(A)** *You need not go unless you want to.*

2. **(A)** *I believe there is no man but would give ten years of his life to accomplish such a lofty goal.*

3. **(B)** Often the young couple stood *enfolding each other* in the dark and sweet smelling barn.

4. **(A)** I don't do well *in those kinds of tests.*

5. **(E)** Honor as well as profit *is to be gained* by this work.

TEST II. SENTENCE CORRECTION

TIME: 25 Minutes. 45 Questions.

DIRECTIONS: A sentence is given, of which one part is under-lined. Following the sentence are five choices. The first (A) choice simply repeats the underlined part. Then you have four additional choices which suggest other ways to express the underlined part of the original sentence. If you think that the underlined part is cor-rect as it stands, write the answer A. If you believe that the under-lined part is incorrect, select from the other choices (B or C or D or E) whichever you think is correct. Grammar, sentence struc-ture, word usage, and punctuation are to be considered in your decision. The original meaning of the sentence must be retained.

Correct key answers to all these test questions will be found at the end of the test.

1. We can't do their job since <u>its difficult to do even ours.</u>
   - (A) its difficult to do even ours.
   - (B) its difficult to do even our's.
   - (C) its' difficult to do even ours'.
   - (D) it's difficult to do even ours.
   - (E) its difficult to do ours even.

2. Do you think that Alice has shown <u>more progress than any girl in the class?</u>
   - (A) more progress than any girl in the class?
   - (B) greater progress than any girl in the class?
   - (C) more progress than any girl in the class has shown?
   - (D) more progress than any other girl in the class?
   - (E) more progress from that shown by any girl in the class?

3. She insisted <u>on me going.</u>
   - (A) on me going.
   - (B) on I going.
   - (C) for me to go.
   - (D) upon me going.
   - (E) on my going.

4. <u>Everyone, including Anne and Helen, was there.</u>
   - (A) Everyone, including Anne and Helen, was there.
   - (B) Everyone including Anne and Helen, was there.
   - (C) Everyone, including Anne and Helen, were there.
   - (D) Everyone including Anne, and Helen, was there.
   - (E) Everyone including Anne and Helen was there.

5. I was really very much excited <u>at the news, that's why</u> I dropped the vase.
   - (A) at the news, that's why
   - (B) by the news, that's why
   - (C) at the news; that's why
   - (D) at the news, that is why
   - (E) at the news that's why

6. <u>He supposed me to be him.</u>
   - (A) He supposed me to be him.
   - (B) He supposed me to be he.
   - (C) He supposed I to be him.
   - (D) He supposed I to be he.
   - (E) He thought me to be he.

7. With a sigh of contentment, <u>she set her doll in the carriage; then she herself laid down</u> and fell asleep.
   - (A) she set her doll in the carriage; then she herself laid down
   - (B) she sat her doll in the carriage; then she herself laid down
   - (C) she sat her doll in the carriage; then she herself lay down
   - (D) she set her doll in the carriage; then she herself lay down
   - (E) she set her doll in the carriage; then her-self she laid down

8. Is the climate of Italy <u>somewhat like Florida?</u>
   - (A) somewhat like Florida?
   - (B) somewhat similar to Florida?
   - (C) somewhat like that of Florida?
   - (D) something like Florida?
   - (E) similar to Florida?

S1363

9. Everyone except Ruth and I knows her.
   (A) Everyone except Ruth and I knows her.
   (B) Everyone except Ruth and I know her.
   (C) Everyone besides Ruth and me knows her.
   (D) Everyone except I and Ruth knows her.
   (E) Everyone except Ruth and me knows her.

10. The reason I plan to go is because she will be disappointed if I don't.
    (A) because she will be disappointed
    (B) that she will be disappointed
    (C) because she will have a disappointment
    (D) on account of she will be disappointed
    (E) because she shall be disappointed

11. Our teacher won't leave us come into the room after the gong sounds.
    (A) Our teacher won't leave us come
    (B) Our teacher won't let us come
    (C) Our teacher refuses to leave us come
    (D) Our teacher won't leave us enter
    (E) Our teacher won't allow that we come

12. Being an intelligent person, the slur was disregarded by him.
    (A) Being an intelligent person the slur was disregarded by him.
    (B) Being that he was an intelligent person, the slur was disregarded by him.
    (C) Being an intelligent person, he disregarded the slur.
    (D) Being that he was an intelligent person, he disregarded the slur.
    (E) As an intelligent person, the slur was disregarded by him.

13. Instead of him going home, he went to a movie.
    (A) Instead of him going home
    (B) Instead that he went home
    (C) Instead of him going on home
    (D) Instead of his going home
    (E) Instead that he was going home

14. If the parent would have shown more interest, her daughter would have been in college today.
    (A) If the parent would have shown more interest
    (B) If the parent had shown more interest
    (C) If the parent would have showed more interest
    (D) If the parent would have been showing more interest
    (E) Should the parent have shown more interest

15. Having eaten a hearty luncheon, the judge was ready to seriously consider the circumstances.
    (A) to seriously consider the circumstances.
    (B) seriously to consider the circumstances.
    (C) to consider seriously the circumstances.
    (D) to consider the circumstances seriously.
    (E) with seriousness to consider the circumstances.

16. Such of his stories as was original were accepted.
    (A) Such of his stories as was original were accepted.
    (B) Such of his stories as were original was accepted.
    (C) Such of his stories as were original were accepted.
    (D) Such of his stories as were original were excepted.
    (E) His stories such as were original were excepted.

17. I could not but help feel that her reasons for coming here were not honest.
    (A) I could not but help feel
    (B) I could not but feel
    (C) I couldn't help only to feel
    (D) I could not help feel
    (E) I could but not feel

18. She never has and she never will do any work.
    (A) She never has and she never will do any work.
    (B) She never has and she never will do no work.
    (C) She never has, and she never will do any work.
    (D) Never has she and never will she do any work.
    (E) She never has done and she never will do any work.

19. He is not as talented as his wife.
    (A) He is not as talented as his wife.
    (B) He is not so talented as his wife.
    (C) He is not talented like his wife is.
    (D) As his wife, he is not as talented.
    (E) He doesn't have the talent as his wife.

20. Did you see James's hat?
    (A) Did you see James's hat?
    (B) Did you see James hat?
    (C) Have you seen Jame's hat?
    (D) Have you seen James hat?
    (E) Have you saw James hat?

DIRECTIONS: *A passage is given in which words or phrases are underlined. Following the passage are five choices for each word or phrase underlined. The first (A) choice simply repeats the underlined part. Then you have four additional choices which suggest to you other ways to express the underlined part of the original sentence. If you think that the underlined part is correct as it stands, write the answer A.   If you believe that the underlined part is incorrect, select from the other choices (B or C or D or E) whichever you think is correct. Grammar, sentence structure, word usage, and punctuation are to be considered in your decision. The original meaning of the sentence must be retained.*

Questions 21–30

Some people choose one way of solving their

personal <u>problems. While</u> others choose other ways.
₂₁

You can <u>get</u> a good idea of a <u>persons</u> character by
₂₂ ₂₃

the way he tries <u>to solve</u> his problems. If <u>a individ-</u>
₂₄ ₂₅

ual gets very <u>mad</u> and gives all kinds of nonsensical
₂₆

excuses, you may conclude that he is living in an

unreal world. He needs help to get back to the real

world—the world of <u>thinkers' and scientists'</u>. He
₂₇

may need encouragement to work hard in order to

be part <u>of</u> reality. Maybe he is trying to accomplish
₂₈

the impossible and needs a task that is possible

<u>to be performed</u>. That person is <u>wise</u> if he can learn
₂₉ ₃₀

what the world expects from him in order to get

along in the world.

21. (A) problems. While
    (B) problems while
    (C) problems the while
    (D) problems; while
    (E) problems, while

22. (A) get
    (B) cop
    (C) arrive in
    (D) get up
    (E) visualize

23. (A) persons
    (B) person
    (C) persons'
    (D) persons's
    (E) person's

24. (A) to solve
    (B) in solving
    (C) in the solution of
    (D) for the solution of
    (E) solving

25. (A) a individual
    (B) an individual
    (C) a guy
    (D) a fella
    (E) a human

26. (A) mad
    (B) angered
    (C) aggravated
    (D) much angry
    (E) angry

27. (A) thinkers' and scientists'
    (B) thinker's and scientist's
    (C) thinkers' and scientists
    (D) thinkers and scientists
    (E) thinkers' and of scientists'

28. (A) of
    (B) from
    (C) in
    (D) with
    (E) as to

29. (A) to be performed
    (B) for performing
    (C) to perform
    (D) for performance
    (E) in performing

30. (A) wise
    (B) smart
    (C) hep
    (D) knowledged
    (E) of wisdom

Questions 31–40

The coast of <u>north Africa</u> is <u>allmost</u> as pleasant
            31   32

as <u>southern California</u>, with hot, dry summer and
    33

heavy rains in winter. The mountains of <u>Morocco's</u>

and <u>Algeria's</u> have a heavy winter snowfall and
    34

excellent <u>ski grounds.</u> Temperatures in the coast
        35

land's higher altitudes <u>are falling below</u> freezing
                 36

on <u>winter's nights.</u> South of the mountains the true
    37

desert begins. It is not a continuous sea of <u>land,</u>
                               38

<u>some</u> parts are great stretches of sand, but <u>others</u>
                                39

are rock and gravel. One may travel for days and

<u>not see scarcely</u> any sand.
    40

31. (A) north Africa
    (B) north africa
    (C) North Africa
    (D) Northafrica
    (E) North-Africa

32. (A) allmost
    (B) almost
    (C) all most
    (D) al most
    (E) most

33. (A) southern California
    (B) southern california
    (C) Southern California
    (D) South California
    (E) the South of California

34. (A) Morocco's and Algeria's
    (B) Morocco and Algeria's
    (C) Morocco's and Algeria
    (D) Morocco and Algeria
    (E) Morocco's and of Algeria's

35. (A) ski grounds
    (B) skier grounds
    (C) skiing grounds
    (D) grounds to ski
    (E) ski ground

36. (A) are falling below
    (B) is falling below
    (C) fall below
    (D) has been falling below
    (E) fall under

37. (A) winter's nights
    (B) winter nights
    (C) Winter's nights
    (D) Winter nights
    (E) Winter Nights

38. (A) land, some
    (B) land some
    (C) land; some
    (D) land and some
    (E) land since some

39. (A) others
    (B) other's
    (C) others'
    (D) other ones
    (E) other stretches

40. (A) not see scarcely
    (B) not see scarcely no
    (C) see scarcely no
    (D) see not scarcely
    (E) see scarcely any

Questions 41–45

If you want to see a <u>collection of junk</u> from all
                                 41

over the world, go to the Caledonian Market in

London. Here rubbish is something which is sold

and looking for rubbish is a <u>pass time.</u> You learn
                                       42

here what unbelievable human needs and desires there are. People hunt about, with open-mouthed curiosity, <u>at</u> the leftovers from thousands of attic
₄₃
rooms and basements. The Market is the <u>next to last</u>
₄₄
resting place of unwanted vases, musical instru-ments that will not play, sewing machines that will not sew, baby carriages that will not roll, bicycles <u>whose wheels</u> will not turn.
₄₅

42. (A) pass time
    (B) passtime
    (C) pastime
    (D) past time
    (E) passer of time

43. (A) at
    (B) upon
    (C) between
    (D) among
    (E) into

44. (A) next to last
    (B) next-to-last next but one
    (C) next to a last
    (D) next from last
    (E) next but one next-to-last

41. (A) collection of junk
    (B) collection in junk
    (C) junky collection
    (D) collection with junk
    (E) collection made of junk

45. (A) whose wheels
    (B) who's wheels
    (C) wheels of which
    (D) wheels of whom
    (E) which wheels

CONSOLIDATE YOUR KEY ANSWERS HERE

Practice using Answer Sheets. Make ONE mark for each answer. Additional and stray marks may be counted as mistakes. In making corrections erase errors COMPLETELY. Make glossy black marks. To arrive at an accurate estimate of your ability and progress, cover the Correct Answers with a sheet of white paper while you are taking this test.

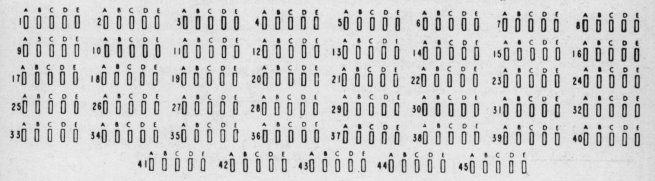

CORRECT ANSWERS TO THE FOREGOING PRACTICE QUESTIONS

Now compare your answers with these Correct Answers to the Practice Questions. If your answers differ from these, go back and study those questions to see where and how you made your mistakes.

1.D	7.D	13.D	19.B	25.B	31.C	37.B	43.D
2.D	8.C	14.B	20.A	26.E	32.B	38.C	44.A
3.E	9.E	15.C	21.E	27.D	33.A	39.A	45.A
4.A	10.B	16.C	22.A	28.A	34.D	40.E	
5.C	11.B	17.B	23.E	29.C	35.C	41.A	
6.A	12.C	18.E	24.A	30.A	36.C	42.C	

TEST III. SENTENCE CORRECTION

TIME: 5 Minutes. 10 Questions.

DIRECTIONS: A passage is given in which words or phrases are underlined. Following the passage are four choices for each word or phrase underlined. The first (A) choice simply repeats the underlined part. Then you have four additional choices which suggest to you other ways to express the underlined part of the original sentence. If you think that the underlined part is correct as it stands, write the answer A. If you believe that the underlined part is incorrect, select from the other choices (B or C or D) whichever you think is correct. Grammar, sentence structure, word usage, and punctuation are to be considered in your decision. Regardless which choice you make, the original meaning of the sentence must be retained.

The six year old child is about the best kind of
                    1
example that can be found of that type of inquisitive-
        2
ness that cause some aggravated adults to exclaim,
           3   4   5
"curiosity killed the cat." To him, the world is a
fascinating place to be explored and investigated
with great thoroughness, but such a world is bounded
              6
by the environment in which he or the people who
                                                7
he knows live. It is constantly expanding through
new experiences. Which bring many eager questions
                    8
from members of any group of first-graders, as each
one tries to figure out new relationships—to know
and accept their place within the family, the school,
              9
and the community—to understand all around him.
There are adults who find it quite annoying to be
presented with such rank inquisitiveness. But this
is no purposeless prying, no idle curiosity! It is that
quality characteristic of the successful adult, inherent
                            10
in the good citizen—intellectual curiosity.

1. (A) old child (C) old
   (B) oldster (D) old-child

2. (A) kind of example (C) sort of example
   (B) kinds of example (D) example

3. (A) cause (C) exhort
   (B) causes (D) exhorts

4. (A) aggravated (C) irritated
   (B) mad (D) gravitated

5. (A) exclaim, "curiosity (C) exclaim; "curiosity
   (B) exclaim, "Curiosity (D) exclaim! "Curiosity

6. (A) with great thoroughness
   (B) with a great thoroughness
   (C) quite thoroughly
   (D) in a manner that is very thorough

7. (A) who (C) which
   (B) whom (D) what

8. (A) experiences. Which (C) experiences; which
   (B) experiences: Which (D) experiences, which

9. (A) their (C) his
   (B) there (D) each

10. (A) of (C) on
    (B) to (D) in

CORRECT ANSWERS FOR THE FOREGOING QUESTIONS.

1.C   2.D   3.B   4.C   5.B   6.C   7.B   8.D   9.C   10.A

HIGH SCHOOL EQUIVALENCY DIPLOMA TESTS

LOGIC AND ORGANIZATION

The test of Logic and Organization provides a measure of your ability to write clearly, concisely and correctly without asking you to write anything of your own. It does this by presenting one or more passages of about 200 words in length and then posing questions about each passage. The questions require you to make decisions regarding the relevancy of ideas expressed, the relationship of the sentences in the passage, diction, economy and clarity of statement, ordering of ideas and paragraphing.

The test of Logic and Organization consists of brief passages or groups of sentences followed by multiple-choice questions about the underlined or numbered parts of the passage. The questions are designed to measure your knowledge of the pattern and structure of paragraphs. They test your ability to extract and categorize ideas, to determine relationships among the sentences in the passage, to use transitional words and sentences effectively, to differentiate between relevant and irrelevant ideas, to make effective use of comparison and contrast, cause and effect, and time and space.

The Sample Questions that follow illustrate the seven types of questions you may be asked in the test of Logic and Organization. The complete explanations provided after the last question will help you learn to identify and correct common errors made in English Composition.

DESCRIPTION OF THE TEST AND SAMPLE QUESTIONS

Here are some sample questions for you to do. Mark your answers on the Sample Answer Strip, making sure to keep your mark inside the correct box. If you want to change an answer, erase the mark you don't want to count. Then mark your new answer. Use a No. 2 (medium) pencil.

SAMPLE TEST. LOGIC AND ORGANIZATION

TIME: **6 Minutes. 7 Questions.**

DIRECTIONS: This test consists of brief passages in which each sentence is numbered. Following each passage are questions which refer to the numbered sentences in the passage. Answer each question by choosing the best alternative (A,B,C,D, or E) and blacken the space corresponding to your answer.

[1]Do students learn from programmed instruction? [2]The research leaves us in no doubt of this. [3]These objections are well taken. [4]They do, indeed, learn. [5]They learn and they do so quickly from linear programs, from branching programs, from scrambled books and from programs in texts. [6]Many kinds of students learn—college, high school, secondary, preschool, military, etc. [7]The limits of the topics which can be studied meticulously by means of programs are not yet known. [8]For each of the kinds of subject matter and the kinds of students, experiments have demonstrated that a considerable amount of learning can be derived from programs. [9]Nevertheless, the learning has been measured either by comparing pre- and post-tests or the time and trials needed to reach a set of criteria for each performance. [10]The question cannot be answered quite so confidently. [11]How well do students learn from programs as compared to how well they learn from other kinds of instruction?

1. What should be done with sentence 3?

    (A) It should be left as it is.
    (B) It should be omitted.
    (C) It should be moved to the end of the passage.
    (D) It should begin the passage.
    (E) It should be lengthened to give more information.

    (B)   This item falls into the first of the seven question categories in Logic and Organization—*Irrelevancy*. In this category you must determine whether or not a sentence or an idea has a place in the logical order of the passage. Sentence 3 bears no logical relation to the sentences before or after it and thus should be omitted.

2. Sentence 5 would be best if

    (A) it were left as it is
    (B) it were made into two sentences, the new one beginning after *quickly*
    (C) everything in the sentence after *quickly* were omitted
    (D) *and they do so quickly* were omitted
    (E) it were made into two sentences, the new one beginning after *so*.

(D) This item illustrates the second question category—*Economy*. In this type of question you are asked to recognize excess verbiage and reduce it by combining ideas or making one longer sentence out of two brief ones. The phrase "and they do so quickly" is excessively wordy and thus should be omitted.

3. In sentence 7, *meticulously* is best

    (A) left as it is
    (B) changed to *exuberantly*   (D) changed to *wisely*
    (C) changed to *inefficiently*   (E) changed to *efficiently*

(E) This item falls into the third question category—*Diction*. In this category you are expected to choose the appropriate word with respect to both meaning and style of the passage. "Meticulously," which means in a manner that is scrupulous or finicky, should be changed to "efficiently," which means in a manner that produces the desired results with a minimum of effort, expense or waste. "Efficiently" is more suited to the overall meaning of the passage.

4. The meaning of sentence 8 would be clearest if

    (A) left as is
    (B) *mentioned above* were added after *students*
    (C) *have demonstrated* were changed to *could have demonstrated*
    (D) *mentioned below* were added after *subject matter*
    (E) *can be* were changed to *could have been*

(B) This item demonstrates the fourth question category—*Clarification*. In this type of question you must show that you can avoid ambiguity or expand an idea to clarify its meaning or its relationship to the other sentences in the passage. Thus, "mentioned above" should be added after "students" to make it clear which subject matter and which students are being referred to.

5. Sentence 9 should begin

    (A) the way it begins now
    (B) with *However, that learning*
    (C) with *This learning*
    (D) with *Besides this, the learning*
    (E) with *The learning, therefore,*

(C) This item illustrates the fifth question category—*Sentence Relationship*. In this category you are asked to demonstrate the correct use of transition words or other connectives to establish the relationship between ideas or sentences. "Nevertheless" is an inappropriate word to complete the transition between sentences 8 and 9.

6. Sentence 10 is best placed

(A) where it is now
(B) after sentence 8
(C) after sentence 7
(D) before sentence 11
(E) after sentence 11

(E) This item falls into the sixth question category—*Ordering*. You are asked to select the best order for the sentences in the passage. Sentence 10, since it refers to the question stated in sentence 11, most appropriately follows sentence 11.

7. If the passage is to be divided into two paragraphs, the second paragraph should begin with

(A) sentence 8
(B) sentence 4
(C) sentence 9
(D) sentence 3
(E) sentence 7

(A) This item falls into the seventh and last question category—*Paragraphing*. In this category you are asked to divide the passage into appropriate paragraphs. Sentence 8 marks the beginning of the second paragraph in the passage since it introduces a new subject—the research that has been done on programmed instruction.

HOW TO PROFIT FROM THE PRACTICE TESTS

On the following pages you are furnished practice tests consisting of questions like those on the actual exam. The time limit here is just about what you may expect. Take these tests as a series of dress rehearsals strengthening your ability to score high on this type of question. For each test use the Answer Sheet provided to mark down your answers. If the Answer Sheet is separated from the questions, tear it out so you can mark it more easily. As you finish each test, go back and check your answers to find your score, and to determine how well you did. This will help you discover where you need more practice.

TEST I. LOGIC AND ORGANIZATION

TIME: 7 Minutes. 8 Questions.

DIRECTIONS: This test consists of brief passages in which each sentence is numbered. Following each passage are questions which refer to the numbered sentences in the passage. Answer each question by choosing the best alternative (A,B,C,D, or E) and blacken the space corresponding to your choice on the Answer Sheet provided.

Explanations of the key points behind these questions appear with the answers at the end of this test. The explanatory answers provide just the help you need to strengthen your ability to meet and master this type of question.

[1]As the world's population grows, the part played by man in inducting plant life becomes more and more important. [2]In such regions, the influence of man on plant life is in large measure a beneficial one. [3]In old and densely populated countries, as in central Europe, man determines almost wholly what shall grow and what shall not grow. [4]Laws, often centuries old, protect plants of economic value and preserve soil fertility. [5]In newly settled countries the situation is unfortunately quite the opposite reverse. [6]The pioneer's life is too strenuous a one for man to think of posterity. [7]However, some years ago, Mt. Mitchell, the highest summit east of the Mississippi, was covered with a magnificent forest. [8]A lumber company was given full rights to fell the trees. [9]Those not cut down were crushed. [10]The mountain was left a wasted area where fire would rage and erosion would too. [11]Wasteful cutting of bushes is the first step. [12]There was no stopping the devastation of the forest, for the contract had been given. [13]In a more enlightened civilization this could not have happened.

1. The word *inducting* in sentence 1 should be

    (A) left as it is
    (B) changed to *deducting*
    (C) changed to *influencing*
    (D) changed to *fluctuating*
    (E) changed to *humbling*

2. Sentence 2 is best placed

    (A) where it is now
    (B) after sentence 5
    (C) after sentence 8
    (D) after sentence 6
    (E) after sentence 3

3. What should be done with sentence 5?

(A) It should be left as it is.

(B) It should be shortened to *The situation is the opposite*.

(C) The phrase *the opposite reverse* should be shortened to *the opposite*.

(D) The phrase *the opposite reverse* should be lengthened to *the opposing opposite reverse*.

(E) The part after *unfortunately* should be omitted.

4. In sentence 6, the word *posterity* is best

(A) left as it is

(B) changed to *prostration*

(C) changed to *provender*

(D) changed to *sensibility*

(E) changed to *prosecution*

5. Sentence 10 would be most improved if the

(A) sentence were left as it is

(B) sentence were changed to *erosion would complete the destruction*

(C) sentence were omitted entirely

(D) entire sentence were joined to the end of sentence 9 with *and*

(E) sentence were changed to *erosion would compete with destruction*

6. What should be done with sentence 11?

(A) It should be left as it is.

(B) It should be shortened to *Wasteful cutting of bushes comes first*.

(C) It should be combined with sentence 10.

(D) The word *Wasteful* should be omitted.

(E) It should be omitted entirely.

7. Sentence 12 is best placed

(A) where it is now

(B) after sentence 13

(C) after sentence 7

(D) after sentence 14

(E) after sentence 5

8. If the passage is to be divided into two paragraphs, the second paragraph should be begin with

(A) sentence 5

(B) sentence 12

(C) sentence 8

(D) sentence 7

(E) sentence 3

END OF TEST

Go on to do the following Test in this Examination, just as you would be expected to do on the actual exam.

CONSOLIDATE YOUR KEY ANSWERS HERE

Practice using Answer Sheets. Make ONE mark for each answer. Additional and stray marks may be counted as mistakes. In making corrections erase errors COMPLETELY. Make glossy black marks. To arrive at an accurate estimate of your ability and progress, cover the Correct Answers with a sheet of white paper while you are taking this test.

	A B C D E	A B C D E	A B C D E	A B C D E	A B C D E	A B C D E	A B C D E	A B C D E
	1 □□□□□	2 □□□□□	3 □□□□□	4 □□□□□	5 □□□□□	6 □□□□□	7 □□□□□	8 □□□□□

CORRECT KEY ANSWERS TO THE PRACTICE QUESTIONS

1.C   2.E   3.C   4.A   5.B   6.E   7.A   8.D

EXPLANATORY ANSWERS CLARIFYING CARDINAL POINTS

Here you have the heart of the Question and Answer Method. . .getting help when and where you need it. Where one of your Key Answers differs from ours you have a problem which can easily be remedied by reading the explanation. Then, if you have time, you might be able to pick up points on the exam by reading the other explanations, even where you wrote the Key Answers correctly. These explanations stress fundamental facts, ideas, and principles which just might pop up as questions on future exams.

1. **(C)** *Diction.* "Inducting," which means to place formally in an office, a society, etc., should be changed to "influencing," which means to have effect upon.

2. **(E)** *Ordering.* Sentence 2 should follow sentence 3 since "such regions" refers to "old and densely populated countries."

3. **(C)** *Economy.* The phrase "the opposite reverse" is verbose since "opposite" and "reverse" have similar meanings.

4. **(A)** *Diction.* "Posterity" is defined as all future generations and accurately completes the meaning of the sentence.

5. **(B)** *Clarification.* The phrase "erosion would complete the destruction" clarifies the meaning of the sentence in the most comprehensive way.

6. **(E)** *Irrelevancy.* The sentence, which refers to the "cutting of bushes" is irrelevant to the passage.

7. **(A)** *Ordering.* Sentence 12, after the omission of sentence 11, appropriately follows sentence 10.

8. **(D)** *Paragraphing.* Sentence 7 begins the topic of Mt. Mitchell, which specifically illustrates the theme introduced in the first paragraph.

S3616

TEST II. LOGIC AND ORGANIZATION

TIME: 7 Minutes. 8 Questions.

DIRECTIONS: This test consists of brief passages in which each sentence is numbered. Following each passage are questions which refer to the numbered sentences in the passage. Answer each question by choosing the best alternative (A,B,C,D, or E) and blacken the space corresponding to your choice on the Answer Sheet provided.

Explanations of the key points behind these questions appear with the answers at the end of this test. The explanatory answers provide just the help you need to strengthen your ability to meet and master this type of question.

¹When television is good, nothing—not the theater, not the magazines or newspapers—nothing is inferior. ²But when television is bad, nothing is worse. ³I invite you to sit down in front of your television set when your station goes on the air and stay there without a book, magazine, newspaper, or anything else to distract you. ⁴Keep your eyes glued to that set until the station signs off. ⁵There are many people in this great country, and radio stations must serve all of us. ⁶I can assure you that you will observe a vast wasteland. ⁷They are game shows, violence, audience participation shows and formula comedies about totally unbelievable families. ⁸Followed by blood and thunder, mayhem, more violence, sadism, murder, Western badmen, Western goodmen, private eyes, gangsters, still more violence, and cartoons. ⁹And, endlessly, there are commercials that scream and cajole and offend without end. ¹⁰True, you will see a few things you will enjoy. ¹¹And most of all, there is boredom. ¹²But they will be very, very few. ¹³And if you think I exaggerate and overstate the matter, try it.

1. The word *inferior* in sentence 1 should be

    (A) left as it is
    (B) changed to *worse*
    (C) changed to *the best*
    (D) changed to *anterior*
    (E) changed to *better*

2. What should be done with sentence 5?

    (A) It should be left as it is.
    (B) It should follow sentence 1.
    (C) It should be omitted entirely.
    (D) It should be made into two separate sentences.
    (E) It should follow sentence 8.

3. The word *wasteland* in sentence 6 should be

    (A) left as it is
    (B) changed to *baseball park*
    (C) changed to *ocean*
    (D) changed to *alley*
    (E) changed to *football field*

4. The meaning of sentence 7 would be clearest if

    (A) left as it is
    (B) the phrase *They are* is changed to *You will see*
    (C) the phrase *They are* is changed to *They will see*
    (D) the word *totally* is omitted
    (E) everything after *comedies* is omitted

5. What should be done with sentence 8?

    (A) It should be left as is.   (D) It should begin with *Thus*.
    (B) It should be joined to sentence 7.   (E) It should end with *therefore*.
    (C) It should be divided into 2 sentences.

6. Sentence 9 would be most improved if

    (A) *and offend* were omitted
    (B) *without end* were omitted
    (C) *and advertisements* were added after *commercials*
    (D) *ceaselessly* were substituted for *endlessly*
    (E) *cajole* were changed to *cavort*

7. Sentence 11 is best placed

    (A) after sentence 6   (D) after sentence 5
    (B) after sentence 13   (E) after sentence 12
    (C) after sentence 9

8. Sentence 13 would be best if the phrase *exaggerate and overstate the matter* were

    (A) left as it is
    (B) changed to *exaggerate and understate the matter*
    (C) changed to *magnify and overstate*
    (D) changed to *multiply the matter*
    (E) changed to *exaggerate*

END OF TEST

Go on to do the following Test in this Examination, just as you would be
expected to do on the actual exam.

CONSOLIDATE YOUR KEY ANSWERS HERE

Practice using Answer Sheets. Make ONE mark for each answer. Additional and stray
marks may be counted as mistakes. In making corrections erase errors COMPLETELY.
Make glossy black marks. To arrive at an accurate estimate of your ability and progress,
cover the Correct Answers with a sheet of white paper while you are taking this test.

CORRECT KEY ANSWERS TO THE PRACTICE QUESTIONS

Now compare your answers with these Correct Key Answers. If your answers differ from these, go back and study the Practice Questions to see where and how you made your mistakes. In doing this, the following Explanatory Answers should prove helpful. They provide concise clarifications of the basic points behind the Key Answers. Even where your Key Answers are the same as ours, go over the explanations carefully because they may be quite useful in helping you pick up extra points on the exam.

1.E   2.C   3.A   4.B   5.B   6.B   7.C   8.E

EXPLANATORY ANSWERS CLARIFYING CARDINAL POINTS

Here you have the heart of the Question and Answer Method. . .getting help when and where you need it. Where one of your Key Answers differs from ours you have a problem which can easily be remedied by reading the explanation. Then, if you have time, you might be able to pick up points on the exam by reading the other explanations, even where you wrote the Key Answers correctly. These explanations stress fundamental facts, ideas, and principles which just might pop up as questions on future exams.

1. **(E)** *Diction.* "Inferior," which is an adjective meaning poor in quality or below average, should be changed to "better," a comparative adjective meaning more excellent.

2. **(C)** *Irrelevancy.* The subject of sentence 5 is "radio stations" and since the subject of the passage is "television," the sentence should be omitted.

3. **(A)** *Diction.* "Wasteland," a noun defined as barren land or unproductive activity, accurately completes the meaning of sentence 6.

4. **(B)** *Clarification.* "You will see" is consistent with the imperative tone of the passage.

5. **(B)** *Sentence relationship.* Sentence 8 is not a complete sentence and, since it completes the train of thought of sentence 7, should be joined to sentence 7.

6. **(B)** *Economy.* "Without end," which carries the same meaning as "endlessly," should be omitted to make sentence 9 less wordy.

7. **(C)** *Ordering.* Sentence 11 completes the train of thought running throughout sentences 7, 8 and 9, and thus should follow sentence 9.

8. **(E)** *Economy.* The phrase, "exaggerate and overstate the matter," is verbose and should be simply "exaggerate."

TEST III. LOGIC AND ORGANIZATION

TIME: 7 Minutes. 8 Questions.

DIRECTIONS: This test consists of brief passages in which each sentence is numbered. Following each passage are questions which refer to the numbered sentences in the passage. Answer each question by choosing the best alternative (A,B,C,D, or E) and blacken the space corresponding to your choice on the Answer Sheet provided.

Explanations of the key points behind these questions appear with the answers at the end of this test. The explanatory answers provide just the help you need to strengthen your ability to meet and master this type of question.

[1]With increasing prosperity, West European youth is having a fling that is creating distinctive consumer and cultural patterns. [2]The increasing emergence in Europe of that phenomenon well known in America as the "youth market." [3]This is a market in which enterprising businesses cater to the demands of teenagers and older youths. [4]The Norwegians have simply adopted the English word "teenager." [5]In the United States, the market is large, successful, wide-ranging and well established. [6]Moreover, in Western Europe, the youth market may appropriately be said to be in its diapers. [7]In some countries, such as Britain, West Germany and France, it is more advanced than in the others. [8]Some manifestations of the market, chiefly sociological, have been recorded. [9]But they are only just beginning to be the subject of organized consumer research and promotion.

1. In sentence 1, *having a fling* is best

    (A) left as it is
    (B) changed to *making an ascent*
    (C) changed to *throwing a party*
    (D) changed to *racing with time*
    (E) changed to *having a flight*

2. The meaning of sentence 2 would be clearest if the sentence is

    (A) left as it is
    (B) begun with *The hope will be*
    (C) ended with *and often grandparents*
    (D) begun with *The result has been*
    (E) ended with *and that is all*

3. What should be done with sentence 4?

    (A) It should be left as it is.
    (B) It should be made into two separate sentences.
    (C) It should be the topic sentence of the second paragraph.
    (D) The word *simply* should be omitted.
    (E) It should be omitted entirely.

4. Sentence 5 would be most improved if

   (A) it were left as it is
   (B) *In the United States* were omitted
   (C) *large, successful* were omitted
   (D) the entire sentence were joined to the end of sentence 4
   (E) the entire sentence were joined to the end of sentence 3 with *and*

5. Sentence 6 should begin

   (A) the way it begins now
   (B) with *Western Europe*
   (C) with *Outside of Western Europe*
   (D) with *In Western Europe*
   (E) with *In Western Europe, therefore*

6. The word *diapers* in sentence 6 should be

   (A) left as it is
   (B) changed to *infancy*
   (C) changed to *winter*
   (D) changed to *insanity*
   (E) changed to *prison*

7. Sentence 7 is best placed

   (A) where it is now
   (B) after sentence 3
   (C) before sentence 3
   (D) after sentence 9
   (E) after sentence 8

8. If the passage is to be divided into three paragraphs, the third paragraph should begin with

   (A) sentence 6
   (B) sentence 8
   (C) sentence 4
   (D) sentence 2
   (E) sentence 7

END OF TEST

*Go on to do the following Test in this Examination, just as you would be
expected to do on the actual exam.*

CONSOLIDATE YOUR KEY ANSWERS HERE

*Practice using Answer Sheets. Make ONE mark for each answer. Additional and stray
marks may be counted as mistakes. In making corrections erase errors COMPLETELY.
Make glossy black marks. To arrive at an accurate estimate of your ability and progress,
cover the Correct Answers with a sheet of white paper while you are taking this test.*

```
    A B C D E      A B C D E      A B C D E      A B C D E      A B C D E      A B C D E      A B C D E      A B C D E
1 [] [] [] [] []  2 [] [] [] [] []  3 [] [] [] [] []  4 [] [] [] [] []  5 [] [] [] [] []  6 [] [] [] [] []  7 [] [] [] [] []  8 [] [] [] [] []
```

CORRECT KEY ANSWERS TO THE PRACTICE QUESTIONS

1.A   2.D   3.E   4.C   5.D   6.B   7.A   8.B

EXPLANATORY ANSWERS CLARIFYING CARDINAL POINTS

Here you have the heart of the Question and Answer Method. . .getting help when and where you need it. Where one of your Key Answers differs from ours you have a problem which can easily be remedied by reading the explanation. Then, if you have time, you might be able to pick up points on the exam by reading the other explanations, even where you wrote the Key Answers correctly. These explanations stress fundamental facts, ideas, and principles which just might pop up as questions on future exams.

1. **(A)** *Diction*. The phrase, "having a fling," is defined as having a brief time of wild pleasures. It most accurately completes the meaning of the sentence.

2. **(D)** *Clarification*. Sentence 2 is not a complete sentence. The addition of the phrase, "The result has been," completes the sentence and integrates it into the passage.

3. **(E)** *Irrelevancy*. The topic of the sentence, the Norwegian word for teenagers, is irrelevant to the topic of the paragraph which is the Western European youth market. The sentence should thus be omitted.

4. **(C)** *Economy*. "Large, successful, wide-ranging and well established" are all adjectives that convey approximately the same meaning. The elimination of "large" and "successful" prevents verbosity.

5. **(D)** *Sentence relationship*. "Moreover" is an adverb that means in addition to what has been said. It is an inappropriate transition word. Therefore the sentence should begin with "In Western Europe."

6. **(B)** *Diction*. "Diapers" is inappropriate to the meaning of the sentence. "The youth market" is being personified and "infancy" is the word most appropriate to this figure of speech.

7. **(A)** *Ordering*. Sentence 7 accurately completes the train of thought of sentence 6.

8. **(B)** *Paragraphing*. The second paragraph should begin with sentence 5. The third paragraph, which introduces the research done on the subject explained in the first two paragraphs, must begin with sentence 8.

TEST IV. LOGIC AND ORGANIZATION

TIME: 7 Minutes. 8 Questions.

DIRECTIONS: This test consists of brief passages in which each sentence is numbered. Following each passage are questions which refer to the numbered sentences in the passage. Answer each question by choosing the best alternative (A,B,C,D, or E) and blacken the space corresponding to your choice on the Answer Sheet provided.

Explanations of the key points behind these questions appear with the answers at the end of this test. The explanatory answers provide just the help you need to strengthen your ability to meet and master this type of question.

¹A Polish proverb claims that fish, to taste right, should swim three times. ²To taste right it should swim in water, in butter and in wine. ³The early efforts of scientists in the food industry were directed at improving the preparation, preservation and distribution. ⁴Our memories of certain foodstuffs eaten during the Second World War suggest that, although these might have been nutritious. ⁵They certainly did not taste good nor were they particularly appealing in appearance or smell. ⁶With regard to touch, systems of classification are of little value because of the extraordinary sensitivity of the skin. ⁷This neglect of the sensory appeal of foods is happily becoming a thing of the past. ⁸A book grew out of this course. ⁹Indeed, in 1957, the University of California considered the subject of such main importance to set up a course in the analysis of foods by sensory methods. ¹⁰The authors hope that it will be useful to food technologists in industry. ¹¹They also hope to help others researching the problem of the sensory evaluation of foods according to sight, taste and smell.

1. Sentence 2 would be best if

   (A) it were left as it is
   (B) the part after *swim* were joined with sentence 1
   (C) the part after *swim* were omitted
   (D) the part after *swim* were joined to sentence 1 with *since*
   (E) it were made into two sentences, the new one beginning after *swim*

2. Sentence 3 would be most improved if

   (A) it began with *At that time*
   (B) it ended with *of fish in butter and wine*
   (C) it ended with *of nutritious food*
   (D) the part after *preparation* were omitted
   (E) the word *preservation* were omitted

3. What should be done with sentence 4?

   (A) It should be left as it is.
   (B) It should be joined to sentence 3 with *since*.
   (C) It should be joined to sentence 2 with *and*.
   (D) It should begin with *Thus*.
   (E) It should be joined to sentence 5.

4. What should be done with sentence 6?

   (A) It should be left as it is.
   (B) It should follow sentence 3.
   (C) It should be made into two separate sentences.
   (D) It should be made into three separate sentences.
   (E) It should be omitted entirely.

5. Sentence 8 is best placed

   (A) after sentence 6
   (B) after sentence 3
   (C) after sentence 9
   (D) after sentence 11
   (E) after sentence 12

6. In sentence 9, *such main* is best

   (A) left as it is
   (B) changed to *charitable*
   (C) changed to *sufficient*
   (D) changed to *insufficient*
   (E) changed to *such suffering*

7. What should be done with sentence 11?

   (A) It should be left as it is.
   (B) It should begin with *Thus*.
   (C) The part after *foods* should be omitted.
   (D) It should end with *forever*.
   (E) The part after *sight* should be omitted.

8. If the passage is to be divided into two paragraphs, the second paragraph should begin with

   (A) sentence 7
   (B) sentence 6
   (C) sentence 11
   (D) sentence 5
   (E) sentence 3

END OF TEST

CONSOLIDATE YOUR KEY ANSWERS HERE

Practice using Answer Sheets. Make ONE mark for each answer. Additional and stray marks may be counted as mistakes. In making corrections erase errors COMPLETELY. Make glossy black marks. To arrive at an accurate estimate of your ability and progress, cover the Correct Answers with a sheet of white paper while you are taking this test.

CORRECT KEY ANSWERS TO THE PRACTICE QUESTIONS

Now compare your answers with these Correct Key Answers. If your answers differ from these, go back and study the Practice Questions to see where and how you made your mistakes. In doing this, the following Explanatory Answers should prove helpful. They provide concise clarifications of the basic points behind the Key Answers. Even where your Key Answers are the same as ours, go over the explanations carefully because they may be quite useful in helping you pick up extra points on the exam.

1.B	2.C	3.E	4.E	5.C	6.C	7.C	8.A

EXPLANATORY ANSWERS CLARIFYING CARDINAL POINTS

Here you have the heart of the Question and Answer Method. . .getting help when and where you need it. Where one of your Key Answers differs from ours you have a problem which can easily be remedied by reading the explanation. Then, if you have time, you might be able to pick up points on the exam by reading the other explanations, even where you wrote the Key Answers correctly. These explanations stress fundamental facts, ideas, and principles which just might pop up as questions on future exams.

1. **(B)** *Sentence relationship.* Sentence 2 is not a complete sentence. The addition of "in water, in butter and in wine" to sentence 1 amplifies the meaning of sentence 1 and eliminates the unnecessary repetition of the phrase, "To taste right it should swim."

2. **(C)** *Clarification.* As sentence 3 stands it is not clear exactly what is being prepared, preserved and distributed. The addition of "of nutritious food" clarifies this.

3. **(E)** *Sentence relationship.* Sentence 4 is not a complete sentence until joined with sentence 5.

4. **(E)** *Irrelevancy.* Sentence 6 discusses the sense of "touch" which is largely irrelevant to the sensory evaluation of food, the subject of the paragraph.

5. **(C)** *Ordering.* Sentence 8 is an extension of the train of thought in sentence 9 and thus should follow it.

6. **(C)** *Diction.* The adjective, "sufficient," is defined as enough or adequate and most accurately completes the meaning of sentence 9.

7. **(C)** *Economy.* The adjective, "sensory," and the phrase, "according to sight, taste and smell," convey the same meaning. Thus, the elimination of the phrase makes this a better sentence.

8. **(A)** *Paragraphing.* Sentence 7 introduces the research currently being done on the theme set forth in the first six sentences.

PART THREE

Social Studies

This test measures ability to read with understanding and to evaluate critically reading selections concerning social, political, economic, and cultural problems and issues. Since ability to evaluate depends upon a person's background in a field, the test indirectly measures the individual's understanding of ideas and knowledge of the social studies.

TOP SCORES ON READING TESTS

In the following pages you'll find every proven technique for succeeding with the reading comprehension question, the pitfall of many a test-taker. These methods have worked beautifully for thousands of ambitious people and they are certain to help you. They are well worth all the time you can afford to devote to them.

Students must be able to read the paragraphs quickly, and still be able to answer questions correctly. The more correct answers you can give, the better your score will be. But if there are twenty paragraphs, and you are able to finish only ten because you read slowly, obviously, you are going to get a score of 50 percent, even if you answer all the questions correctly. On the other hand, if you finish all the paragraphs but can only answer half of the questions correctly, you will still get only 50 percent. Your goal, then, is to build up enough speed to finish all the paragraphs, and at the same time give as many correct answers as possible.

Our goal is to help you reach your goal—and then some. We want you to get the best score possible on any test of reading comprehension; and we also want you to be able to read with enough speed and understanding so that your studying time is cut in half, and your pleasure reading time is multiplied.

You *can* upgrade your reading ability—but you must have a plan—a procedure—a method. First,

let us understand that there are two aspects of success in reading interpretation:

1. READING SPEED
   and
2. UNDERSTANDING WHAT YOU READ.

But these two aspects are not separate. As a matter of fact, they are totally dependent on each other. You can improve your speed by improving your comprehension—and then your comprehension will improve further because you have improved your speed. What you are improving, therefore, is your *speed of comprehension*. Your eyes and your mind must work together. As your mind begins to look for ideas rather than words, your eyes will begin to obey your mind. Your eyes will start to skim over words, looking for the ideas your mind is telling them to search for. Good reading is good thinking—and a good thinker will be a good reader. Speed and comprehension work together.

For convenience, however, let us divide our discussion into two parts—increasing reading speed and improving reading comprehension.

Increasing Reading Speed

A great many people read very slowly and with little comprehension, yet are completely unaware of just how badly they do read. Some people pronounce the words to themselves as they read, saying each word almost as distinctly as though reading aloud; or they think each one separately.

The reason for this is that many people have not gone quite far enough in their "learning to read" process. When you were first taught to read, you learned the sounds of each letter. Then you learned that if you put the letters together, they would make words. But that is where many people stop. Reading, to them, is reading words. But try reading a sentence out loud, saying each word as

though it were a separate unit. How does it sound? Pretty meaningless! A more mature reader will put words together to make phrases. And the most mature reader will put phrases together to make ideas. A writer uses words to state ideas—and that is what a good reader looks for—those ideas. This will affect the way his eyes work. Let's see how.

HOW YOUR EYES WORK IN READING

As you learn to read phrases and thoughts, you will find that your eyes are increasing their *span*. This means that your eyes are seeing several words at a time as you are reading, not just one.

Your eyes work as a camera does. When you want to take a picture, you hold the camera still and snap the shutter. If you move the camera, the picture will blur. When you read, your eyes take pictures of words—and, like a camera, when they are "photographing," they are standing still. Each time your eyes "picture" words in a line of print, they stop—and each stop is called a *fixation*. Watch someone read, and you will see how his eyes make very quick stops across the line. You know he has finished a line when you see his eyes sweep back to the beginning of the next line.

EYE SPAN AND FIXATION

The more words your eyes take in with one fixation, the larger the eye span. And the larger the eye span, the fewer stops your eyes will have to make across the line. Thus, you will be reading faster.

For example, let's divide a sentence the way a slow, word-by-word reader would:

You/ will/ find/ that/ you/ can/ read/ faster/ if/ you/ per/ mit/ your/ eyes/ to/ see/ large/ thought/ units/.

The reader's eyes have made at least nine stops on each line.

This is the way a fast reader would divide the same sentence:

You will find that/ you can read faster/ if/ you permit/ your eyes to see/ large thought/ units.

This reader's eyes have stopped only three times on each line, so of course he will be able to read much faster. Also, reading thought units will enable him to grasp the meaning more effectively. Now here are some exercises to help you increase your eye span.

EXERCISES FOR INCREASING EYE-SPAN

1.
```
0..............0..............0..............0
0..............0..............0..............0
0..............0..............0..............0
0..............0..............0..............0
0..............0..............0..............0
0..............0..............0..............0
```

In the above "paragraph," the dots stand for letters and each 0 is one eye fixation. "Read" a line, forcing your eyes to shift from 0 to 0. When you finish the first line, let your eyes swing back to the next line. Try to get an even rhythm. Now you can feel what your eyes should be doing as they read a line in four fixations. Is this different from the way they usually feel when you read? Keep practicing this "paragraph" until it feels comfortable, and then try to read a line of print in the same way. You can make up your own "paragraph" with only three fixations and practice.

2. Here is a list of three-word phrases, with a line drawn down the center. Focus your eyes on the line, and look at the three words at once. Remember, only *one* fixation. Do not read each word separately. If you have trouble at first, read the phrases through once in your usual way, and then practice the one fixation.

at the store
day and night
box of candy
come with me
in the house
bring my paper
time to finish
make every effort
all the questions
read very fast

3. Choose a newspaper column on a subject that interests you, and read it through. Then draw two vertical lines equally distant from each other down the center. Reread the column fixating on first one vertical line, then the next—two fixations per line. When you get very good at this, try drawing just one line down the center and fixating once. You can practice this daily.

VOCALIZING CAN SLOW YOU DOWN

Some readers move their lips or whisper while they read "silently." This habit is called vocalizing. It is caused by the fact that your earliest reading was done aloud, and the habit of hearing each word as you read it, persists.

It would be physically impossible for you to speak at the rate of speed at which a good reader can read—say 350 words per minute. And if you could, no one could understand you. If you read only as fast as you can talk, you will never be a fast reader.

Obviously, then, you must stop vocalizing. Your

lips and vocal cords must not be permitted to interfere in the exchange of ideas between eyes and mind. Even if you are not obviously vocalizing, you may be subvocalizing. Your lips are not moving, your vocal cords are not involved, but you are hearing each word as you read it. This is as much a deterrent to reading speed as actual vocalizing. Most people *do* subvocalize.

HOW TO STOP VOCALIZING

1. Put your fingers on your lips. Make sure your lips do not move as you read. If they do, put a pencil or a rubber eraser between your teeth. Then read. If you start to vocalize, the pencil will drop out. If you are reading in public you might be embarrassed to appear with a pencil in your mouth. In that case, just clench your teeth hard—and keep reading.

2. Only *you* will know if you are subvocalizing—and be honest with yourself. If you are subvocalizing (and you probably are) try this exercise. Before you start to read, repeat these nonsense syllables to yourself for 30 seconds: da-rum, da-rum, da-rum, da-rum, etc. Now begin to read and continue to repeat da-rum as you read. If you are doing this, then you cannot subvocalize what you are reading. At first you will find this extremely difficult to do, but if you keep practicing, soon you will find that there is a direct connection between written word and thought—with no intervening vocalizing.

VARY YOUR READING SPEED

One should adjust his reading speed to what he is reading. Some paragraphs will be easier for you than others, possibly because you are more interested in the subject matter, or know something about it. Other paragraphs, particularly those that deal with factual or technical material, may have to be read more slowly.

Flexibility should be employed so that the reader will change his speed from paragraph to paragraph—even from sentence to sentence, just as a driver would vary his driving speed depending on where he is driving. Some passages are open highways while others are crowded city thoroughfares.

For example, read the following passage:

It was a sunny Sunday afternoon in December. Some people were at the movies; some were out walking; and some were at home listening to the radio. Suddenly an announcement was broadcast—and the United States was plunged into war.

On December 7, 1941, the Japanese Air Force attacked Pearl Harbor, destroying battleships, aircraft carriers, planes, and a strategic military base, leaving the United States without the military arsenals needed for anti-aircraft activity and civilian protecton.

Which of these paragraphs is the "highway"? Which is the crowded city thoroughfare? Where can you breeze through? Where will you need to slow down to absorb every detail. You're right! The first paragraph is a simple introduction. A glance should suffice. The second paragraph is fact-packed, so you will need to slow down.

OTHER PHYSICAL FACTORS

Don't neglect the obvious reading aids. Good eyesight is essential. When was your last eye checkup? If glasses were prescribed, are you using them? Make sure that you are physically comfortable, sitting erect wlth head slightly inclined. You should have good direct and indirect light, with the direct light coming from behind you and slightly above your shoulder. Hold your reading matter at your own best reading distance so that you don't have to stoop or squint.

FORCE YOURSELF TO FASTER READING

Now that you know the elements that make for fast reading, you must continue to force yourself to read as quickly as you can. Use a stop-watch to time yourself. You can figure your rate of speed by dividing the number of words on a page into the number of seconds it took you to read it, and then multiplying by 60. This will give you your rate in words-per-minute. Since no one rate of speed is possible for all reading material, your rate will vary. But an average reading speed of 350 words-per-minute should be possible for uncomplicated, interesting, straightforward material. If you are already reading that fast, then try for 500 words-per-minute. You should be able to answer correctly at least 80 per cent of the questions following a reading passage.

Practice reading quickly. Move your eyes rapidly across the line of type, skimming it. Don't permit your eyes to stop for individual words. Proceed quickly through the paragraph without backtracking. If you think you don't understand what you are reading, then reread two or three times—but always read quickly. You will be amazed to discover how much you actually do understand.

Improving Reading Comprehension

Many readers are afraid of not understanding what they read quickly. But the old idea that slow readers make up for their slowness by better comprehension of what they read has been proven untrue. Your ability to comprehend what you read will keep pace with your increase in speed. You will absorb as many ideas per page as before, and get many more ideas per unit of reading time.

It has been demonstrated that those who read quickly also read best. This is probably due to the fact that heavier concentration is required for rapid reading; and concentration is what enables a reader to grasp important ideas contained in the reading material.

GETTING THE MAIN IDEA

A good paragraph generally has one central thought—and that thought is usually stated in one sentence. That sentence, the *topic sentence,* is often the first sentence of the paragraph, but it is sometimes buried in the middle, or it can be at the end. Your main task is to locate that sentence and absorb the thought it contains while reading the paragraph. The correct interpretation of the paragraph is based on that thought *as it is stated,* and not on your personal opinion, prejudice, or preference about that thought.

Here are several examples of paragraphs. Read them quickly and see if you can pick out the topic sentence. It is the key sentence. The rest of the paragraph either supports or illustrates it. The answers follow the paragraphs.

1. Pigeon fanciers are firmly convinced that modern inventions can never replace the carrier pigeon. "A pigeon gets through when everything else fails," they say. In World War II, one pigeon flew twenty miles in twenty minutes to cancel the bombing of a town. Radios may get out of order and telephone lines may get fouled up, but the pigeon is always ready to take off with a message.

2. When a piece of paper burns, it is completely changed. The ash that is left behind does not look like the original piece of paper. When dull-red rust appears on a piece of tinware, it is quite different from the gleaming tin. The tarnish that forms on silverware is a new substance unlike the silver itself. Animal tissue is unlike the vegetable substance from which it is made. A change in which the original substance is turned into a different substance is called a chemical change.

3. A child who stays up too late is often too tired to be successful in school. A child who is allowed to eat anything he wishes may have bad teeth and even suffer from malnutrition. Children who are rude and disorderly often suffer pangs of guilt. Children who are disciplined are happy children. They blossom in an atmosphere where they know exactly what is expected of them. This provides them with a sense of order, a feeling of security.

Answers: In paragraph 1, the first sentence is the topic sentence. In paragraph 2, the last sentence is the topic sentence. In paragraph 3, it is the fourth sentence—"Children who are disciplined. . . . ".

If a selection consists of two or more paragraphs, the correct interpretation is based on the central idea of the entire passage. The ability to grasp the central idea of a passage can be acquired by practice—practice that will also increase the speed with which you read.

Reading for a Purpose—The Survey Method

Many readers don't know what they are looking for when they read. They plunge into a page full of words, and often that is what they end up with —just words. It's like walking into a supermarket without having made a list of what you want to buy. You wander aimlessly up and down the aisles and end up with a basketful of cookies and fruit and pickles—and nothing for a main dish.

It is extremely important to have a purpose in mind *before* you start to read—to make a "list" before you start shopping. Good readers use the *survey* method. By "survey" we mean a quick over-view of what you are going to read before you actually start reading. It is like looking at a road map before you start on a trip. If you know in what direction you are going, you are apt to get there sooner, and more efficiently. This is what you do.

1. Read the title. Think about what the selection will probably be about. What kind of information can you expect to obtain? Gear your mind to look for the central thought.

2. Think about the kind of vocabulary you will meet. Will it be technical? Are you familiar with the subject, or will you have to prepare yourself to meet many new words? After a quick glance, you may decide to skip this selection and go back to it later. (Remember, on a timed reading test you want to give yourself a chance to sample *all* the selections. The one at the end may be easier for you than the one in the middle, but you won't know if you never get to the end.) The difficulty of the vocabulary may be the deciding factor.

3. If there are subheadings, read them. They can provide a skeleton outline of the selection.

4. Read the first sentence of each paragraph. It usually contains the most important ideas in the selection. The topic sentence is more often found in the beginning of a paragraph than in any other position.

5. READ THE QUESTIONS BASED ON THE SELECTION. The questions are there to test whether or not you understand the most important ideas in the selection. If you read them first, they will steer you through your reading in the most effective way possible. Now you really know what to look for! In any kind of reading, whether on test or in texts, always look at the questions first (unless you are directed not to do so).

The survey method can be applied to all kinds of reading, particularly textbook reading. In addition to the above, you should include the following in your textbook survey:

(a) Read the preface quickly. It states the author's purpose in writing the book.

(b) Look at the publication date (on the copyright page). This can tell you if the information is up-to-date.

(c) Look through the table of contents. See what the author has included, and the order in which it appears. Some tables of contents can serve as an outline for the book.

(d) If there are chapter or part summaries, read through them quickly. They'll give you a forecast of what's to come.

(e) Look at illustrations, maps, graphs, etc. These are meant to help you visualize essential information. Remember, one picture can be worth a thousand words.

Increase Your Vocabulary

In order to understand what you are reading, you must know the meaning of the words that are used. Very often you can guess at the meaning from the rest of the sentence, but that method is not completely reliable. The sentence itself is important for determining which of the word's several meanings is intended, but you usually have to have some idea of the word itself.

How can you build a larger vocabulary? You could sit down with a long list of words and try to memorize it, or perhaps go through the diction-ary page by page. This would be very time consuming—and very boring! Memorizing words is probably the *least* successful way of building a vocabulary.

Words are best remembered when they are understood and used, when they are part of your own experience. Here are some ways in which you can do this.

1. Learn a little etymology. You already know a lot, because approximately 70 per cent of the words we use consist of roots and prefixes de-

rived from Latin and Greek. There are 84 roots and 44 prefixes that are the mainstay of our language. If you learn those you will have a clue to the meaning of thousands of words. For example, the Latin root *voc* (meaning "to call") appears in the words advocate, vocation, irrevocable, vociferous, etc. The root *port* (meaning "to carry") is found in the words report, export, support, porter, etc.

Learn to look for the roots of words, and for familiar parts of words you meet.

2. Read—everything, anything. Even signs and posters sometimes have new words in them. Try to find at least one new word every day.

3. Use the dictionary—frequently and extensively. Look up the meaning of a word you don't know, and see if you can identify its root.

4. Play word games—like Anagrams, Scrabble. And do Crossword Puzzles.

5. Listen to people who speak well. Don't be afraid to ask them the meaning of a word they use that is unfamiliar to you. They'll be flattered.

6. Make a personal word list of your new words. Make it on index cards so that you can play a "flash-card" game with yourself.

7. Look for special word meanings in special subject areas. Since most reading comprehension passages deal with science, literature, or social studies, a weakness in the vocabulary used in these subjects can put you at a great disadvantage. Be sure you know the meaning of the terms that are frequently used.

8. Use the new words you learn each day. Don't save them for a rainy day—by then they may be lost. When you talk or write, try to use as many new words as you can. A word used is a word remembered!

Cues and Clues For Readers

Examination points may be unnecessarily lost by ignoring the author's hints as to what *he* thinks is most important. Be on the lookout for such phrases as "Note that . . ." "Of importance is . . ." "Don't overlook . . ." These give clues to what the writer is stressing. Beware of negatives and all-inclusive statements. They are often put in to trip you up. Words like *always, never, all, only, every, absolutely, completely, none, entirely, no,* can sometimes turn a reasonable statement into an untrue statement. For example look at the following sentence:

When you get caught in the rain, you catch cold.

True? Of course. Now look at this sentence:

When you get caught in the rain, you *always* catch cold.

Different, isn't it? Not *always* true.

PUNCTUATION

Other hints which you should also watch for are those given by punctuation. Here are a few points to keep in mind:

1. QUOTATION MARKS—When a statement is quoted, it may not necessarily represent the author's opinion, or the main thought of the passage. Be sure you make this distinction if it is called for.

2. EXCLAMATION POINT—This mark is often used to indicate an *emphatic* or *ironical* comment. It's the author's way of saying, "This is important!"

3. COMMAS—Watch those commas. They can change the meaning of a sentence. For example:

As I left the room, in order to go to school John called me.

As I left the room in order to go to school, John called me.

In each sentence, a different person is going to school.

4. PARENTHESES—These are often used to set off a part of the sentence that is not absolutely necessary to the sentence. But don't ignore them in reading comprehension tests. Sometimes they give vital information. For example:

Shakespeare (whose life spanned the sixteenth and seventeenth centuries) was a great dramatist.

5. COLON—Often used to emphasize a sequence in thought between two independent sentences. For example:

Science plays an important role in our civilization: thus we should all study physics, chemistry, and biology.

6. ELLIPSES—Three dots often found in quoted material which indicates that there has been an omission of material from the original quotation. Often the material omitted is not important, but a good, critical reader should be aware of the omission.

A Systematic Plan

You can't sit down the night before a test in reading comprehension and "cram" for it. The only way you can build up your reading skill is to practice systematically. The gains you make will show up not only in an increased score on a reading comprehension test, but also in your reading for study and pleasure.

Trying to change reading habits that you have had for a long time can be difficult and discouraging. Do not attempt to apply *all* of the suggestions we have given to *all* your reading *all* at once. Try to follow a program like the one below.

1.   Set aside 15 minutes a day to practice new reading techniques.

2.   Start off with a short, easy-to-read article for a magazine or newspaper—and time yourself. At the end of your practice session, time yourself on another short article, and keep a record of both times.

3.   Select a news story. Read it first, and then practice an eye-span exercise. Work towards reducing your eye fixations to no more than two for a line, the width of a newspaper column.

4.   Read an editorial, book review, or movie or drama review in a literate magazine or newspaper. This type of article always expresses the author's (or the paper's) point of view and is therefore good practice for searching out the main idea. After you read, see whether you can write a good title for the article and jot down in one sentence the author's main idea. Also, you can try making up a question based on the article with five alternate answers (the kind you find on reading comprehension tests). This is excellent practice for determining main ideas, and you can use the questions to test your friends.

5.   Find one new word and write the sentence in which it appears. Guess at its meaning from the context. Then look up the definition in a dictionary and try to make up a sentence of your own, using the word. Then try to use the word in your conversation at least twice the following day.

If you follow this program daily, you will soon find that you can extend to more and more reading the skills you are building, and your reading comprehension test score will show the great gains you have made.

A SAMPLE QUESTION ANALYZED

Here is a sample question followed by an analysis. Try to understand the process of arriving at the correct answer.

Reading Passage

"Too often, indeed, have scurrilous and offensive allegations by underworld creatures been sufficient to blast the career of irreproachable and incorruptible executives who, because of their efforts to serve the people honestly and faithfully, incurred the enmity of powerful political forces and lost their positions."

(1) Judging from the contents of the preceding paragraph, you might best conclude that

(A) the larger majority of executives are irreproachable and incorruptible

(B) criminals often swear in court that honest officials are corrupt in order to save themselves

(C) political forces are always clashing with government executive

(D) underworld creatures make scurrilous and offensive allegations against incorruptible executives

(E) false statements by criminals sometimes cause honest officials the loss of their positions or the ruin of their careers.

Analysis of Choices

(A) can generally be said to be a true statement, but it cannot be derived from the paragraph. Nothing is said in the paragraph about "the larger majority" of executives.

(B) may also be a true statement and can to a certain extent be derived from the paragraph. However, the phrase "in order to save themselves" is not relevant to the sense of the paragraph, and even if it were, this choice does not sum up its central thought.

(C) cannot be derived from the paragraph. The catch-word "always" makes this choice entirely invalid.

(D) This choice is true as derived from the sense of the paragraph. It is open, however, to two exceptions. First, this choice is in the form of a general statement whereas the paragraph starts with the restrictive phrase "too often," thereby precluding a generality. Secondly, this choice does not summarize the central idea of the paragraph which may be better expressed in the remaining choice.

(E) is the *best* conclusion that could be drawn from the contents of the paragraph in the light of the five choices given. It is open to no exceptions and adequately sums up the central thought of the paragraph.

TEN SUCCESS STEPS

Here are proven techniques for getting the right
answer to *any* Reading Interpretation question.

Survey Selection

1. Read the selection through quickly to get the
general sense.
2. Reread the selection, concentrating on the central idea.
3. Can you now pick out the *topic sentence* in
each paragraph?
4. If the selection consists of more than one paragraph, determine the *central idea* of the entire
selection.

Survey Stems
Concentrate on Each Question

5. Examine the five choices carefully, yet rapidly.
Eliminate immediately those choices which are *farfetched, ridiculous, irrelevant, false,* or *impossible*.
6. Eliminate those choices which may be true, but
which have nothing to do with the sense of the
selection.
7. Check those few choices which now remain as
possibilities.

Reread Selectively
Shuttle Back to Selection

8. Refer back to the original selection and determine which one of these remaining possibilities
is best in view of

a) specific information in the selection
 or
b) implied information in the selection

Reread only the part of the selection that applies
to the question, and make your decision as to the
correct choice based on these considerations:

(a) A choice must be based on fact actually
given or definitely understood (and not on your
personal opinion or prejudice.) Some questions require making a judgment—and this judgment also
must be based on the facts as given.

(b) In questions involving the central thought
of the passage (for example: "The best title for
this selection . . .") the choice must accurately
reflect the entire thought—not too narrow, and not
too general.

9. Be sure to consider only the facts *given* or
definitely understood some place in the selection.

10. Be especially careful of trick expressions or
"catch-words" which sometimes destroy the validity
of a seemingly acceptable answer. These include
the expressions: "under all circumstances," "at all
times," "never," "always," "under no conditions,"
"absolutely," "completely," and "entirely."

AVOID THE TRAPS

Trap #1—Sometimes the question cannot
be answered on the basis of the stated facts.
You may be required to make a deduction
from the facts given.
Trap #2—Eliminate your personal opinions.

Trap #3—Search out significant details that
are nestled in the paragraph. Reread the
paragraph as many times as necessary (with
an eye on your watch).

USING THE "SUCCESS STEPS" WITH A PRACTICE PASSAGE

DESCRIPTION OF THE TEST AND SAMPLE QUESTIONS
Here are some sample questions for you to do. Mark your answers on the Sample Answer Sheet, making sure to keep your mark inside the correct box. If you want to change an answer, erase the mark you don't want to count. Then mark your new answer. Use a No. 2 (medium) pencil.

HERE'S HOW YOU SHOULD ANSWER THESE READING QUESTIONS. Each one is made up of a paragraph, followed by four or five statements based on the paragraph. You may never have seen the paragraph before, but you must now read it carefully so that you understand it. Then read the statements following. Any one of them might be right. You have to choose the one that is most correct. Try to pick the one that's most complete, most accurate . . . the one that is best supported by and necessarily flows from the paragraph. Be sure that it contains nothing false so far as the paragraph itself is concerned. After you've thought it out, write the capital letter preceding your best choice in the margin next to the question. When you've answered all the questions, score yourself faithfully by checking with our answers that follow the last question. But please don't look at those answers until you've written your own. You just won't be helping yourself if you do that. Besides, you'll have ample opportunity to do the questions again, and to check with our answers, in the event that your first try results in a low score. If you'd really like to get into the swing of the thing while practicing, you might want to answer on facsimiles of the kind of answer sheets provided on machine-scored examinations. For practice purposes we have provided such facsimiles.

Let us, now, demonstrate with an actual exam-type reading interpretation selection how to apply the ten "success steps":

Reading Passage

Vacations were once the prerogative of the privileged few, even as late as the 19th century. Now they are considered the right of all, except for such unfortunate masses as, for example, the bulk of China's and India's population, for whom life, save for sleep and brief periods of rest, is uninterrupted toil.

They are more necessary now than once because the average life is less well-rounded and has become increasingly departmentalized. I suppose the idea of vacations, as we conceive it, must be incomprehensible to primitive peoples. Rest of some kind has of course always been a part of the rhythm of human life, but earlier ages did not find it necessary to organize it in the way that modern man has done. Holidays, feast days, were sufficient.

With modern man's increasing tensions, with the stultifying quality of so much of his work, this break in the year's routine became steadily more necessary. Vacations became mandatory for the purpose of renewal and repair. And so it came about that in the United States, the most self-indulgent of nations, the tensest and most departmentalized, vacations have come to take a predominant place in domestic conversation.

STEP-BY-STEP EXPLANATIONS

STEP 1—We read the selection through quickly to get the general sense.

STEP 2—We reread the selection concentrating on the central idea.

STEP 3—We discover that the topic sentence of each paragraph of this selection is the first sentence of each paragraph. This order is almost always the case: the topic sentence is the first sentence of a paragraph.

STEP 4—The central idea of the selection consists of various aspects of vacations.

1. The title below that best expresses the ideas of this passage is:
   a. Vacation Preferences
   b. Vacations: the Topic of Conversation
   c. Vacations in Perspective
   d. The Well-Organized Vacation
   e. Renewal, Refreshment and Repair

Explanation of Question

STEP 5—Question 1. . . . We eliminate Choice D immediately because it is irrelevant. The selection refers in no way to organization of a vacation.

STEP 6—Eliminate Choice B. Vacations are often a topic of conversation—not so in this selection, however.

STEP 7—Since Choices A, C, and E remain as possible correct choices, we check them.

STEP 8—Choice C is an all-inclusive title. Choices A and E are not all-inclusive. Therefore, C is the correct choice as the best title for the passage.

STEP 9—In arriving at the correct answer, we have considered only the facts given or definitely understood.

STEP 10—We were on the alert for trick expressions and "catch-words." There were none in Question 1.

Proceed in the same "10-Step" manner in answering questions 2, 3 and 4 of the sample selection.

2. We need vacations now more than ever before because we have
   A. a more carefree nature
   B. much more free time
   C. little diversity in our work
   D. no emotional stability
   E. a higher standard of living

Explanation of Question

We concentrate on Question 2 and its five possible answers. We remember that first reading indicated that the answer to this question is in the beginning of paragraph 2, so we reread just that part of the selection, which deals with the necessity for vacations. Choice A is irrelevant and ridiculous, and we eliminate it. Choice B may be a true statement, but it does not pertain to the *need* for vacations. Choice C looks like a good possibility, because a less well-rounded life that is increasingly departmentalized indicates little diversity—but better to check further. We eliminate Choice D immediately because of the word "no," one of our trick expressions. Choice E, like Choice B, does not refer to need. So we return to Choice C as the best possible answer.

3. It is implied in the passage that the lives of Americans are very
   A. habitual   C. patriotic
   B. ennobling   D. varied
        E. independent

Explanation of Question

We concentrate on Question 3 with its five possible answers, remembering that the answer is to be found in paragraph 3—so we go directly to that paragraph. The word "implied" in the stem of the question tells us that we may not find a direct answer but will have to do some thinking. The paragraph tells us that much work is stultifying, that there is much routine, and that vacations are necessary for renewal and repair. We can conclude, then, that life is pretty dull and we will look at the choices to find a word that is synonymous with "dull." Choice A is certainly a possibility, but we look quickly at the remaining choices just to be sure, and discover that there is no other possible choice; B, C, and E are irrelevant, and D is the exact opposite. Choice A is our answer.

4. As used in the passage, the word "prerogative" (line 1) most nearly means
   A. habit   C. request
   B. distinction   D. demand
        E. hope

Explanation of Question

Concentrating on Question 4 we find that it calls for the definition of a word which is located in line 1, so we go to that portion of the paragraph. Word definitions can often be answered by a careful reading of the sentence in which the word appears, and often the following sentence as well. If we read the sentence in which "prerogative" appears and look at the five possible answers, any one of them might be correct. However, if we read the first part of the second sentence in paragraph 1, we see the clue word *now*. In other words, at this time, as contrasted with the past, vacations are the right of all instead of the right of a few. We can thus conclude that the word "prerogative" is synonymous with the word "right." We look at the five possible choices in this light. We can eliminate A and E immediately since they are in no way synonymous with "right."

Choice C, while a possible synonym, is really too mild a word if we substitute it in the sentence. Choices B and D are possible, with Choice D seeming to be the most likely. But if we substitute it in the sentence for the word prerogative, it does not make as much sense as does Choice B, for vacations were not actually a demand of the privileged few—but more a distinction. Since the stem of our question asks for the nearest meaning, we can be most comfortable in choosing B.

STEP 8—*Shuttle back to the selection.* We check to see that we have answered each question and marked the answer in accordance with the directions specified at the beginning of the examination.

If you follow the outlined procedure for answering reading comprehension questions, you will find that you are answering questions correctly and quickly. Most passages will require at least two readings—one for general sense and one for answering the questions. The important thing is to know where to spot the answers, and to remain calm and collected when examining the possible choices. Don't panic—you can be pretty sure that if a question is hard for you it will be hard for everyone else, too.

HOW TO PROFIT FROM THE PRACTICE TESTS

On the following pages you are furnished practice tests consisting of questions like those on the actual exam. The time limit here is just about what you may expect. Take these tests as a series of dress rehearsals strengthening your ability to score high on this type of question. For each test use the Answer Sheet provided to mark down your answers. If the Answer Sheet is separated from the questions, tear it out so you can mark it more easily. As you finish each test, go back and check your answers to find your score, and to determine how well you did. This will help you discover where you need more practice.

INTERPRETATION OF READING MATERIALS IN THE SOCIAL STUDIES

This test measures ability to read with understanding and to evaluate critically reading selections concerning social, political, economic, and cultural problems and issues. Since ability to evaluate depends upon a person's background in a field, the test indirectly measures the individual's understanding of ideas and knowledge of the social studies.

DIRECTIONS: Read each passage to get the general idea. Then reread the passage more carefully to answer the questions based on the passage. For each question read all choices carefully. Then select the answer you consider correct or most nearly correct. Blacken the answer space corresponding to your best choice, just as you would do on the actual examination.

To explain exactly how to answer this type of social studies question we show you a social studies passage and three sample questions. The correct answers are: S1 = A; S2 = D; S3 = D.

Sample:

It is not always necessary to travel great distances to foreign lands to bring back interesting and valuable scientific results. Right here in the United States there are treasures to be sought which in a few years may be past obtaining. The frontier is gone but even today there are areas of no inconsiderable magnitude practically unexplored; and one need not even go so far as our newer West, for, though they are becoming scarce, little-explored regions still exist along the Atlantic seaboard and in the Mississippi Valley. Among the treasures today sought by expeditions from museums and universities are photographs of native wild birds and recordings of their voices — particularly of birds which, because of the development of civilization, are becoming rare.

S1. The writer points out that the Atlantic states provide
A. a rich field for scientific investigation
B. a high level of civilization
C. opportunities for travel
D. great museums and universities.

S2. The writer mentions museum expeditions sent out to
A. create bird sanctuaries
B. domesticate wild birds
C. kill and retrieve birds for exhibits
D. take pictures of rare birds.

S3. The kind of treasure to which this paragraph refers is
A. buried gold
B. new territory
C. museum collections
D. exact knowledge of wild life.

TEST I. INTERPRETATION OF SOCIAL STUDIES READINGS

TIME: 25 Minutes. 15 Questions.

DIRECTIONS: Below each of the following passages of social science reading material you will find one or more incomplete statements about the passage. Select the words or expressions that most satisfactorily complete each statement in accordance with the meaning of the paragraph.

Correct key answers to all these test questions will be found at the end of the test.

Reading Passage

History has long made a point of the fact that the magnificent flowering of ancient civilization rested upon the institution of slavery, which released opportunity at the top for the art and literature which became the glory of antiquity. In a way, the mechanization of the present-day world produces the condition of the ancient in that the enormous development of labor-saving devices and of contrivances which amplify the capacities of mankind affords the base for the leisure necessary to widespread cultural pursuits. Mechanization is the present-day slave power, with the difference that in the mechanized society there is no group of the community which does not share in the benefits of its inventions.

1. The title below that best expresses the ideas of this passage is
   (A) Slavery in the ancient world
   (B) Today's community
   (C) Worthwhile use of leisure
   (D) Ancient culture
   (E) Modern slave power.

2. Which factor has produced more leisure time?
   (A) the abolition of slavery
   (B) the glory of antiquity
   (C) the development of art and literature
   (D) an increase in inventions
   (E) the development of the community.

3. The flowering of any civilization has always depended on

(A) the galley slave
(B) leisure for the workingman
(C) mechanical power
(D) leisure for cultural pursuits
(E) transportation.

4. The author's attitude toward mechanization is one of
   (A) awe   (D) fear
   (B) acceptance   (E) devotion.
   (C) distrust

Reading Passage

John Greenleaf Whittier was the "Quaker Puritan" scion of Massachusetts farmers. For this frail young man, however, farm life was too tough an existence. His early interest in books and legends led him toward journalism, with poetry as a pleasant side line. He became a Quaker firebrand and agitator, the politician among abolitionists, and a gadfly to New England Congressmen during the original "Great Debate." His impassioned prose and poetry against slavery were often directed at a clergy whose acceptance of it he fought as a Quaker and a Christian.

Only after the Civil War, when emancipation had been at least nominally won, did the aging Whittier emerge as the genial, easygoing "folkbard" remembered today. Until recently the prominence given this last phase of his literary life by scholarly circles has obscured his earlier contributions to American literature and political freedom and tolerance.

5. The author of this passage indicates that Whittier's
   (A) lifetime was one of invalidism
   (B) nature caused him to detest farm life
   (C) early writings were overlooked for some time
   (D) ideas are similar to Robert Frost's
   (E) chief desire was to lead the quiet life of the Quakers.

6. The passage implies that Whittier showed a kind of personal courage when he
   (A) fought in the Civil War
   (B) attacked men in high places with his writings
   (C) worked on the family farm in spite of his dislike for farming
   (D) toned down his style because of his Quaker background
   (E) gave up poetry to write political tracts.

7. From reading the passage, we may infer that if Whittier were alive today he would most probably take up his pen in support of
   (A) segregation
   (B) politicians
   (C) the United Nations
   (D) desegregation
   (E) folk literature.

Reading Passage

Fortunately it is as yet only through fantasy that we can see what the destruction of the scholarly and scientific disciplines would mean to mankind. From history we can learn what their existence has meant. The sheer power of disciplined thought is revealed in practically all the great intellectual and technological advances which the human race has made. The ability of the man of disciplined mind to direct this power effectively upon problems for which he was not specifically trained is proved by examples without number. The real evidence for the value of liberal education lies in history and in the biographies of men who have met the valid criteria of greatness. These support overwhelmingly the claim of liberal education that it can equip a man with fundamental powers of decision and action, applicable not only to boy-girl relationship, to tinkering hobbies, or to choosing the family dentist, but to all the great and varied concerns of human life—not least, those that are unforeseen.

8. The title below that best expresses the ideas of this passage is
   (A) The destruction of thinking
   (B) The advance of the human race
   (C) Facts vs. fantasies
   (D) The disciplined mind
   (E) The power of thought.

9. The author indicates that the person with a liberal education has the ability to
   (A) read with more discernment than others
   (B) apply general principles
   (C) develop a clearer understanding of history than others
   (D) imagine a world without thought
   (E) gain prestige.

10. According to the passage, one of the evidences of the results of truly disciplined minds is found in
    (A) history
    (B) education itself
    (C) science
    (D) intellectual freedom
    (E) the beliefs of philosophers.

11. In this passage, the author stresses the importance of
    (A) increased interest in the study of history
    (B) technological advances
    (C) education for living
    (D) more training for students
    (E) satisfying the desire for security.

12. Which characteristic of great men is implied most strongly in the passage?
    (A) social consciousness
    (B) intellectual pride
    (C) self-respect
    (D) self-confidence
    (E) flexibility.

Reading Passage

Once every year Kansas City is host to a convention of the world's largest aggregation of juvenile capitalists. On no other occasion is so much teen-age wealth seen under one roof. The 8,000 youngsters from forty-eight states and territories who assemble here every October are delegates of Future Farmers of America, a national organization composed of 340,000 members. The prosperous boys who meet here have accumulated their own wealth as farmers and farm operators. Their individual net worth ranges through varying degrees of affluence up to as much as $50,000 for some of the boys.

What's more, they earned it during their high school years or immediately afterwards. Each boy is eligible to be a member of Future Farmers until he reaches twenty-one. He enters the ranks by enrolling in an agricultural class under a well-trained teacher in the school he is attending.

13. The title below that best expresses the ideas of this passage is
(A) Prosperity
(B) Young capitalists
(C) Farming enterprises
(D) Agriculture aids education
(E) The need for more agriculture education.

14. The author implies that
(A) all high schools offer agricultural training

(B) many of the boys have earned $50,000 since graduation
(C) a boy does not necessarily have to be a trained farmer
(D) the entire United States is represented in this organization
(E) "juvenile capitalists" is the world's largest organization.

15. The author states that
(A) 340,000 is the maximum number of members
(B) each year the convention is held in the same city
(C) only boys earning a certain amount may be delegates
(D) once a member, a boy is always a member until he becomes 21
(E) any boy between 18 and 21 years of age may join the organization.

CONSOLIDATE YOUR KEY ANSWERS HERE

Practice using Answer Sheets. Make ONE mark for each answer. Additional and stray marks may be counted as mistakes. In making corrections erase errors COMPLETELY. Make glossy black marks. To arrive at an accurate estimate of your ability and progress, cover the Correct Answers with a sheet of white paper while you are taking this test.

CORRECT KEY ANSWERS TO THE PRACTICE QUESTIONS

Now compare your answers with these Correct Key Answers. If your answers differ from these, go back and study the Practice Questions to see where and how you made your mistakes. In doing this, the following Explanatory Answers should prove helpful. They provide concise clarifications of the basic points behind the Key Answers. Even where your Key Answers are the same as ours, go over the explanations carefully because they may be quite useful in helping you pick up extra points on the exam.

| 1.E | 3.D | 5.C | 7.D | 9.B | 11.C | 13.B | 15.B |
| 2.D | 4.B | 6.B | 8.D | 10.A | 12.E | 14.D | |

TEST II. INTERPRETATION OF SOCIAL STUDIES READINGS

TIME: 15 Minutes. 10 Questions.

DIRECTIONS: *Below each of the following passages of social science reading material you will find one or more incomplete statements about the passage. Select the words or expressions that most satisfactorily complete each statement in accordance with the meaning of the paragraph.*

Correct key answers to all these test questions will be found at the end of the test.

Reading Passage

Disregard for odds and complete confidence in one's self have produced many of our great successes. But every young man who wants to go into business for himself should appraise himself as a candidate for the one percent to survive. What has he to offer that is new or better? Has he special talents, special know-how, a new invention or service, or more capital than the average competitor? Has he the most important qualification of all, a willingness to work harder than anyone else? A man who is working for himself without limitation of hours or personal sacrifice can run circles around any operation that relies on paid help. But he must forget the eight-hour day, the forty-hour week, and the annual vacation. When he stops work, his income stops unless he hires a substitute. Most small operations have their busiest day on Saturday, and the owner uses Sunday to catch up on his correspondence, bookkeeping, inventorying, and maintenance chores. The successful self-employed man invariably works harder and worries more than the man on a salary. His wife and children make corresponding sacrifices of family unity and continuity; they never know whether their man will be home or in a mood to enjoy family activities.

1. The title below that best expresses the ideas of this passage is
   (A) Overcoming obstacles
   (B) Running one's own business
   (C) How to become a success
   (D) Young men in industry
   (E) Why small businesses fail.

2. This passage suggests that
   (A) small businesses are the ones that last
   (B) salaried workers are untrustworthy
   (C) a willingness to work will overcome loss of income

(D) small business failures cause depressions
(E) working for one's self may lead to success.

3. The author of this passage would most likely believe in
   (A) individual initiative
   (B) socialism
   (C) corporations
   (D) government aid to small business
   (E) nonunion labor.

Reading Passage

While the poll takers are most widely known for their political surveys, the greatest part of their work is on behalf of American business. There are three kinds of commercial surveys. One is public relations research, such as that done for banks, which finds out how the public feels about a company. Another is employee-attitude research, which learns from rank-and-file workers how they really feel about their jobs and their bosses, and which can avert strikes by getting to the bottom of grievances quickly. The third, and probably most spectacular, is marketing research, testing public receptivity to products and designs. The investment a company must make for a new product is enormous—$5,000,000 to $10,000,000, for instance, for just one new product. Through the surveys a company can discover in advance what objections the public has to competing products, and whether it really wants a new one. These surveys are actually a new set of signals permitting better communication between business and the general public— letting them talk to each other. Such communication is vital in a complex society like our own. Without it, we would have not only tremendous waste but the industrial anarchy of countless new unwanted products appearing and disappearing.

4. The title below which best expresses the ideas of this passage is
   (A) The poll taker
   (B) Business asks questions
   (C) Behind the scenes in business
   (D) Our complex business world
   (E) Averting industrial anarchy.

5. The passage states that polls can benefit industry by
   (A) reducing waste
   (B) establishing fair prices
   (C) strengthening people's faith in business
   (D) saving small businesses
   (E) serving as a new form of advertising.

6. This paragraph is developed by means of
   (A) cause and effect
   (B) contrast
   (C) illustrations
   (D) anecdotes
   (E) vivid description.

7. Which is *not* mentioned as an area in which polls have been conducted?
   (A) new products
   (B) politics
   (C) public relations
   (D) labor-management relationships
   (E) family relationships.

8. The passage leads the reader to believe that for business purposes surveys are
   (A) overrated
   (B) too widely used
   (C) often deceptive
   (D) necessary
   (E) costly.

Reading Passage

I have heard it suggested that the "upper class" English accent has been of value in maintaining the British Empire and Commonwealth. The argument runs that all manner of folk in distant places, understanding the English language, will catch in this accent the notes of tradition, pride and authority and so will be suitably impressed. This might have been the case some five or six decades ago but it is certainly not true now. The accent is more likely to be a liability than an asset.

It is significant that the Royal Family in their speeches and broadcasts use a considerably modified form of the accent. The public English of George V was magnificently free from all affectations. His children and grandchildren have done their best to follow his example.

9. The title below that best expresses the ideas of this passage is
   (A) The "King's English"
   (B) The affected language of royalty
   (C) The decline of the British Empire
   (D) Changed effects of "British accent"
   (E) Prevention of the spread of Cockney.

10. According to the author, the "upper class" English accent
   (A) has been imitated all over the world
   (B) may have helped to perpetuate the British Empire before 1900
   (C) has been strongly opposed by British royalty
   (D) has brought about the destruction of the British Commonwealth
   (E) may have caused arguments among the folk in distant corners of the Empire.

CONSOLIDATE YOUR KEY ANSWERS HERE

CORRECT ANSWERS TO THE FOREGOING PRACTICE QUESTIONS

Now compare your answers with these Correct Answers to the Practice Questions. If your answers differ from these, go back and study those questions to see where and how you made your mistakes.

1.B	3.A	5.A	7.E	9.D
2.E	4.B	6.C	8.D	10.B

TEST III. INTERPRETATION OF SOCIAL STUDIES READINGS

TIME: 12 Minutes.   9 Questions.

DIRECTIONS: *Below each of the following passages of social science reading material you will find one or more incomplete statements about the passage. Select the words or expressions that most satisfactorily complete each statement in accordance with the meaning of the paragraph.*

Correct key answers to all these test questions will be found at the end of the test.

Reading Passage

Foreign propagandists have a strange misconception of our national character. They believe that we Americans must be hybrid, mongrel, undynamic; and we are called so by the enemies of democracy because, they say, so many races have been fused together in our national life. They believe we are disunited and defenseless because we argue with each other, because we engage in political campaigns, because we recognize the sacred right of the minority to disagree with the majority and to express that disagreement even loudly. It is the very mingling of races, dedicated to common ideals, which creates and recreates our vitality. In every representative American meeting there will be people with names like Jackson and Lincoln and Isaacs and Schultz and Kovacs and Sartori and Jones and Smith. These Americans with varied backgrounds are all immigrants or the descendants of immigrants. All of them are inheritors of the same stalwart tradition of unusual enterprise, of adventurousness, of courage—courage to "pull up stakes and git moving." That has been the great compelling force in our history. Our continent, our hemisphere, has been populated by people who wanted a life better than the life they had previously known. They were willing to undergo all conceivable hardships to achieve the better life. They were animated, just as we are animated today, by this compelling force. It is what makes us Americans.

1. The title below that best expresses the ideas of this selection is
   (A) No common ideals
   (B) America's motivating force
   (C) American immigrants
   (D) The evils of foreign propaganda
   (E) Defenseless America.

2. According to the paragraph, our national character thrives because we have
   (A) immigrant blood   (B) majority groups

   (C) overcome hardships
   (D) driving ambition   (E) minority rights.

3. Foreign propagandists believe that Americans
   (A) are enemies of democracy
   (B) lack a common heritage
   (C) have a unified national character
   (D) refuse to argue with each other
   (E) are ashamed of foreign descent.

4. Foreign propagandists and the author both agree that Americans
   (A) are disunited
   (B) have no common tradition
   (C) come from varied backgrounds
   (D) have the courage of their convictions
   (E) are deeply religious.

Reading Passage

History is a fable agreed upon. At best, it is only a part-told tale. The conquerors tell their own story. The stagehands never get the spotlight. The janitor and the night watchman remain in darkness. The names of the kings and caudillos monopolize attention.

When Jerusalem fell, who wielded the hammer and trowel to raise its walls again? Who actually watered the Hanging Gardens of Babylon? Were there no cooks and foot soldiers and ditch diggers and road makers in the conquering armies of the Caesars? Who taught Shakespeare the alphabet? Who thinks of the unknown heroes who created the alphabet itself and gave signs to sounds and made possible the memory of mankind in our libraries? The Presidents we know; the peasants are anonymous.

The locomotive engineer and the bus driver do their job to get us where we want to go—all unknown soldiers unless accident and death break the journey. Who ever thinks of the man in the front cab of the subway train unless a sudden jerk reminds us that he is human too? Can we spell out the debt we owe to those who give as well as get and put necessities and luxury within our reach? At least we should remember sometimes our collective debt to those who work in obscurity.

5. The title that best expresses the ideas of this passage is
   (A) Heroes of history
   (B) A look at the past
   (C) Anonymous makers of history
   (D) The debts we owe
   (E) Our unknown soldiers.

6. The author indicates that
   (A) man has a long memory
   (B) most people do not know their history very well
   (C) those who serve others are important to the world
   (D) it is useless to expect recognition for one's work
   (E) it is too bad that people have neglected historical records so shamefully.

7. This passage was probably written in observance of
   (A) Thanksgiving Day
   (B) Veterans Day
   (C) Father's Day
   (D) Independence Day
   (E) Labor Day.

Reading Passage

In the gush of admiration for the beautifully redone interior of the White House the public has largely lost sight of the new look about its eighteen acres of grounds. Old cedars and elms dating back to John Quincy Adams' occupancy of the White House have been refurbished. New trees, bushes, gardens and walks have appeared where shacks and building materials marred the landscape during the four years of the restoration. Although one group of tourists recently complained of a few stalks of onion grass in the pansy beds, most Washington visitors agree that the White House grounds never looked more colorful and impressive.

8. The title below that best expresses the ideas of this passage is
   (A) The White House gardens
   (B) A flaw in the landscape
   (C) Refurbishing the gardens
   (D) Improved setting for the White House
   (E) The new White House interior.

9. The writer indicates that
   (A) tourists complain about the plantings
   (B) the old gardens were more attractive than the new
   (C) the White House is visited by more tourists than before
   (D) some of the trees go back to the days of an early president
   (E) reconstruction of the White House was a very expensive undertaking.

CONSOLIDATE YOUR KEY ANSWERS HERE

Practice using Answer Sheets. Make ONE mark for each answer. Additional and stray marks may be counted as mistakes. In making corrections erase errors COMPLETELY. Make glossy black marks. To arrive at an accurate estimate of your ability and progress, cover the Correct Answers with a sheet of white paper while you are taking this test.

CORRECT ANSWERS TO THE FOREGOING PRACTICE QUESTIONS

Now compare your answers with these Correct Answers to the Practice Questions. If your answers differ from these, go back and study those questions to see where and how you made your mistakes.

1. B	3. B	5. C	7. E	9. D
2. D	4. C	6. C	8. D	

TEST IV. INTERPRETATION OF SOCIAL STUDIES READINGS

TIME: 18 Minutes. 12 Questions.

DIRECTIONS: Below each of the following passages of social science reading material you will find one or more incomplete statements about the passage. Select the words or expressions that most satisfactorily complete each statement in accordance with the meaning of the paragraph.

Reading Passage

Somewhere between 1860 and 1890, the dominant emphasis in American literature was radically changed. But it is obvious that this change was not necessarily a matter of conscious concern to all writers. In fact, many writers may seem to have been actually unaware of the shifting emphasis. Moreover, it is not possible to trace the steady march of the realistic emphasis from its first feeble notes to its dominant trumpet-note of unquestioned leadership. The progress of realism is, to change the figure, rather that of a small stream, receiving accessions from its tributaries at unequal points along its course, its progress now and then balked by the sand bars of opposition or the diffusing marshes of error and compromise. Again, it is apparent that any attempt to classify rigidly, as romanticists or realists, the writers of this period is doomed to failure, since it is not by virtue of the writer's conscious espousal of the romantic or realistic creed that he does much of his best work, but by virtue of that writer's sincere surrender to the atmosphere of the subject.

1. The title that best expresses the ideas of this passage is
   (A) Classifying American writers
   (B) Leaders in American fiction
   (C) The sincerity of writers
   (D) The values of realism
   (E) The rise of realism.

2. Which characteristic of writers does the author praise?
   (A) their ability to compromise
   (B) their allegiance to a "school"
   (C) their opposition to change
   (D) their awareness of literary trends
   (E) their intellectual honesty.

3. As used in the last sentence, by virtue of most nearly means
   (A) in spite of
   (B) by rejection of
   (C) because of moral excellence
   (D) through the force of
   (E) connection with.

4. In this passage, which statement does the author make about realism?
   (A) It is too strong a force in current literature.
   (B) It is to be preferred to romanticism.
   (C) Its advocates are vitally concerned with its progress.
   (D) Its origins are obscure.
   (E) Its writers are very skillful.

5. One may infer from reading this selection that its author
   (A) favors a return to realism in writing
   (B) has little knowledge of the romantic movement in American literature
   (C) views literature from a broad perspective
   (D) is annoyed by the inconsistent approaches of American writers to their subjects
   (E) finds American writers very easy to classify.

Reading Passage

A critic of politics finds himself driven to deprecate the power of words, while using them copiously in warning against their influence. It is indeed in politics that their influence is most dangerous, so that one is almost tempted to wish that they did not exist, and that society might be managed silently, by instinct, habit and ocular perception, without this supervening Babel of reports, arguments and slogans.

6. The title below that best expresses the ideas of this passage is
   (A) Words and their influence
   (B) Critics of politics
   (C) Fanatical language
   (D) Thought control
   (E) Government by slogans.

7. The author implies that critics of misused language
   (A) become fanatical on this subject
   (B) are guilty of what they criticize in others
   (C) are clever in contriving slogans
   (D) tell the story of the Tower of Babel
   (E) rely too strongly on instincts.

8. Which statement is true according to the passage?
   (A) Critics of politics are often driven to take desperate measures.
   (B) Words, when used by politicians, have the greatest capacity for harm.
   (C) Politicians talk more than other people.
   (D) Society would be better managed if mutes were in charge.
   (E) Reports and slogans are not to be trusted.

Reading Passage

The man in the street speaks vaguely of "the olden times," for he has but one epithet to apply to all the ages which lie between the dawn of history and the invention of the locomotive. If he thinks of them at all, Julius Caesar and Queen Elizabeth are to him essentially contemporaries, and from his point of view he is quite justified in thinking of them as such, since to one who judges of the value of life by the comforts amidst which it is passed, it is hardly worth while to make any distinction except that between a way of life which comes up to the 19th century standard and one which does not. All ages except the present were alike in being compelled to get along without the things of which he is most proud, and what he calls "progress" did not begin until a very short time ago.

9. The title below that best expresses the ideas of this passage is
   (A) Evaluating one's contemporaries
   (B) The comforts of the past
   (C) History, short-term view
   (D) The 19th century
   (E) The true nature of progress.

10. The average man's knowledge of history is
    (A) limited   (D) scholarly
    (B) theoretical   (E) wide.
    (C) profound

11. As used in the passage, the word "epithet" (line 2) most nearly means
    (A) statement   (D) characteristic
    (B) question   (E) expression.
    (C) reason

12. The author implies that the average man
    (A) considers progress an outdated notion
    (B) often thinks of past ages
    (C) has a narrow set of values
    (D) has a historical perspective
    (E) is purposely vague about history.

CONSOLIDATE YOUR KEY ANSWERS HERE

Practice using Answer Sheets. Make ONE mark for each answer. Additional and stray marks may be counted as mistakes. In making corrections erase errors COMPLETELY. Make glossy black marks. To arrive at an accurate estimate of your ability and progress, cover the Correct Answers with a sheet of white paper while you are taking this test.

CORRECT ANSWERS TO THE FOREGOING PRACTICE QUESTIONS

Now compare your answers with these Correct Answers to the Practice Questions. If your answers differ from these, go back and study those questions to see where and how you made your mistakes.

1.E	3.D	5.C	7.B	9.C	11.E
2.E	4.D	6.A	8.B	10.A	12.C

TEST V. INTERPRETATION OF SOCIAL STUDIES READINGS

TIME: 20 Minutes. 12 Questions.

DIRECTIONS: Below each of the following passages of social science reading material you will find one or more incomplete statements about the passage. Select the words or expressions that most satisfactorily complete each statement in accordance with the meaning of the paragraph.

Reading Passage

For India, starting its independent life only in the recent past, there were alarming problems to be faced immediately if the country were to survive at all as an entity—overwhelming questions involving a working constitution, food, industrialization, integration of the princely states, civil and social services and the establishment of the first free relations with the rest of the world. It is hard to imagine a less auspicious beginning for the birth of a nation. Special solutions had to be evolved for special conditions. "At short notice (India) had to carry out a series of simultaneous telescoped revolutions which, in the Western nations, had been spread over several centuries." Consequently, in keeping with its ideal of "this *and* that," India worked out its individual parliamentary system, its social, economic and political patterns, borrowing from all over the world, adapting to its own needs.

1. The title below that best expresses the ideas of this passage is
   (A) India before independence
   (B) India's economic system
   (C) Indian dependence on other nations
   (D) Complexities of Indian independence
   (E) The unification of India.

2. The expression "this *and* that" (line 15) implies that India is
   (A) accepting Western ideas exclusively
   (B) dissatisfied with its place among nations
   (C) carrying on a violent revolution
   (D) having difficulty with integration
   (E) anxious to solve all of its problems.

3. The passage implies that, until thirteen years ago, India
   (A) had been in close contact with other nations (B) was a highly unified nation
   (C) had a primitive economy
   (D) had an independent parliament
   (E) had borrowed extensively from other countries.

4. The changes which took place in India were
   (A) selected by the Western powers
   (B) comprehensive in scope
   (C) favorable toward the Indian princes
   (D) contrary to the Western parliamentary system
   (E) accomplished at great loss in prestige.

Reading Passage

It was Robert Frost's function to mediate between New England and the mind of the rest of the nation, so skeptical of New England, yet so solicitous also, eager for its welfare, willing to believe in it, but not without proofs of its probity, its sanity, its health. Robert Frost afforded these proofs. In him the region was born again—it seemed never to have lost its morning vigour and freshness; and one felt behind his local scene the wide horizons of a man whose sympathies and experiences were continental. He had himself discovered New England after a boyhood in California, and he had tramped through the Carolinas and wandered over the West; and he knew how to say that "Yankees are what they always were" in a way that commanded affection as well as respect. A true folk-mind, Frost was a mystical democrat, compassionately filled with a deep regard for the dignity of ordinary living; and he was an artist as well as a poet; a lover of goodness and wisdom, who found them, not by seeking them, but rather along the path of gaiety.

5. The title that best expresses the ideas of this passage is
   (A) Frost's travels throughout America
   (B) Frost's contributions as a poet
   (C) The conflict between New England and the rest of the nation
   (D) The functions of poets
   (E) Contrasts between Frost's childhood and his adulthood.

6. Frost's poems caused others to regard New England with
   (A) scorn
   (B) uneasiness
   (C) compassion
   (D) respect
   (E) envy.

7. The passage implies that Frost's poems reveal his
   (A) patriotism
   (B) love of travel
   (C) diplomacy
   (D) reawakening
   (E) art of living.

Reading Passage

The Mideast lives amid vanished glories, present prejudices and future fears. Scrabble in its soil with a hoe and you will find relics of empires long, long gone—birthplaces of civilization that have waxed and waned—and monuments to religions almost as old as recorded history.

From the Nile to the Euphrates, where trans-world air routes now cover much the same trails as the plodding camel caravans of the past, Man—persistent, passionate, prejudiced—carries on the age-old plot of the human drama. All has altered, yet nothing has changed in the Middle East since centuries before Christ.

Palmyra, the caravan city of Queen Zenobia, is now a magnificent but melancholy reminder of the dreams of men long dead. Baalbek, where even the gods of yesterday have died, is but a tourist attraction, though today no tourists come. The Pyramids themselves, grandiose monuments to Man's eternal hope of immortality, are scuffed and wrinkled now—cosmetically patched against the inexorability of the centuries.

Yet, essentially nothing has changed. Man and his emotions, Man and his ignorance and knowledge, Man in his pride, Man at war with other men, sets the scene and dominates the stage of the turbulent Middle East.

8. The title below that best expresses the ideas of this passage is
   (A) The old *vs.* the new
   (B) The appeal of the Pyramids
   (C) The unchanging Mideast
   (D) New routes to the Mideast
   (E) The birthplace of empires.

9. According to the passage, problems in the Middle East have been due to the
   (A) waning of civilization
   (B) lack of tourist trade
   (C) collapse of former civilizations
   (D) disappearance of belief in immortality
   (E) weaknesses of man.

10. The passage suggests that
    (A) man's nature does not change
    (B) man will eventually triumph over ignorance
    (C) man's destiny has changed
    (D) man's nature has improved in the last thousand years
    (E) man's prejudices against others will gradually disappear.

11. The passage suggests that men of the ancient Middle East were
    (A) irreligious
    (B) vain
    (C) melancholy
    (D) poor
    (E) unimaginative.

12. The reader may conclude from the passage that ancient civilizations
    (A) existed before Christianity
    (B) embraced one God
    (C) relied upon agriculture as their industry
    (D) were interested in the drama
    (E) were democratic in nature.

CONSOLIDATE YOUR KEY ANSWERS HERE

Practice using Answer Sheets. Make ONE mark for each answer. Additional and stray marks may be counted as mistakes. In making corrections erase errors COMPLETELY. Make glossy black marks. To arrive at an accurate estimate of your ability and progress, cover the Correct Answers with a sheet of white paper while you are taking this test.

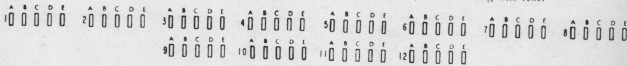

CORRECT ANSWERS TO THE FOREGOING PRACTICE QUESTIONS

1. D	3. C	5. B	7. E	9. E	11. B
2. E	4. B	6. D	8. C	10. A	12. A

SOCIAL STUDIES GLOSSARY

This is some of the language you're likely to see on your examination. You may not need to know all the words in this carefully prepared glossary, but if even a few appear, you'll be that much ahead of your competitors. Perhaps the greater benefit from this list is the frame of mind it can create for you. Without reading a lot of technical text you'll steep yourself in just the right atmosphere for high test marks.

This glossary was created to help you master some of the key words and terms you will meet in the Social Studies section of the test. You will notice that certain words or phrases have been italicized in the definitions. This means those words or phrases are defined in the glossary.

[A]

age   An historical period. The Elizabethan Age, for example, refers to the time when Queen Elizabeth I was on the throne of England. Also see *era* and *epoch*.

American Federation of Labor and Congress of Industrial Organizations (AFL-CIO)   A group of American labor *unions* joined together in a huge federation. AFL-CIO is the unification of two federations, the American Federation of Labor (AFL) with the Congress of Industrial Organizations (CIO). The AFL began in 1881. The CIO was formed in 1935. The merger of the two groups took place in 1955.

anarchist   A believer in the idea that any government is an evil institution and should be eliminated.

Antarctic Circle   An imaginary line around the earth which is about 23½ degrees from the South *Pole*. See *Arctic Circle*.

anthropology   The study of man, how he lives and his customs.

archaeology   The study of how man lived in the past. This is usually done by investigating ancient buildings, household articles, etc.

Arctic Circle   An imaginary line about 23½ degrees south of the North *Pole*. See *Antarctic Circle*.

aristocracy (1) government by a group of people who are considered to be the highest social *class*; (2) a social class with special privileges.

atomic An adjective that in social studies refers to the splitting of the atom to produce energy, as exemplified by the atomic bomb, *hydrogen bomb*, and nuclear energy.

automation The replacement of the work of people by machines.

[B]

ballot A vote in elections.

Bill of Rights The first ten amendments to the *Constitution* of the United States, in which the *rights* of citizens are specifically stated.

Bolshevik A Russian communist. This term was used in the first half of the 20th century, but is not commonly used now. See *communism*.

bureaucracy A term usually referring to the institutions and power of the federal government.

[C]

cabinet In the United States, a body of people specially chosen by the President to advise him and to manage certain branches of the government.

capitalism An *economic* system in which companies or individuals own and manage most or all of a nation's economic activity.

caucus A meeting of politicians who decide on the policies and candidates of their *political party*.

Central Intelligence Agency (CIA) An agency of the United States government which collects and evaluates secret data of other countries.

civic An adjective referring to citizenship. "Voting is a civic duty" means each citizen should vote in elections.

civics The study of citizenship, dealing especially with the *rights* and duties of citizens.

civil disobedience The doctrine that citizens do not have to obey unjust laws, and have the *right* and duty to demonstrate against them in order to have them eliminated.

civil rights The *rights* belonging to all citizens. In recent years in the United States, the term has mainly referred to the struggle of black people, especially in the South, to obtain the *right* to vote and to equal opportunities.

civilization A social system which is highly developed and complex, as opposed to primitive society which is simple and centers around a small group of people, or a tribe. *Western Civilization* refers to the *culture* of the nations of Europe and the American continents. *Eastern Civilization* refers to the culture of the nations of Asia.

class Usually in social studies, this term refers to social class. According to some people, *society* is divided into several distinct groups, such as the working class, aristocracy, etc.

Cold War Following World War II, hostility developed between the communistic nations led by the Soviet Union and the more democratic nations of *Western Civilization*, led by the United States. This period has been called "the Cold War."

colony A land area owned and ruled by a nation usually separated by distance. The United States, for example, was once a colony of Great Britain.

confederation A banding together of various groups for specific reasons, such as defense, trade, etc.

Congress of the United States A term referring to the *House of Representatives* and the *Senate of the United States*.

Congress of Industrial Organizations (CIO) See *American Federation of Labor and Congress of Industrial Organizations (AFL-CIO)*.

conservative A person who believes in maintaining existing social and governmental institutions with little or no change. This word is also an adjective. "A conservative person" is one with conservative views. See *radical* and *liberal*.

Continental Congress (1) First Continental Congress: The group of American delegates from the 13 *colonies* who met before the American Revolution to discuss and protest British laws. (2) Second Continental Congress: The group of delegates from the 13 colonies that conducted the American Revolution. See *Declaration of Independence*.

constituents Those people who are represented by a representative or representatives in a legislative body. For example, all the people living in a Congressional District are constituents of the member of the *House of Representatives* elected from that district.

Constitution Rules that form the duties and rights of a particular social or governmental body. The Constitution of the United States sets forth the structure of the federal government, its responsibilities, limits of power, and rights of citizens.

communism The idea that in the perfect *society* all goods will be owned commonly by all citizens. For more than one hundred years, communism has usually meant the doctrine held by Karl Marx. See *Marxism*. Certain nations, such as the Soviet Union, are referred to as communist nations.

Counter-Reformation An *era* in the history of the Roman Catholic Church (1545–1648) in which clerical leaders reformed the church. This was done as a result of the *Reformation*.

culture The total of the customs, beliefs, arts, skills and practices of a *society* or *civilization*.

[D]

Dark Ages   An *era* in Europe following the breakdown of the *Roman Empire* and lasting until about 1000. Government in this period was either chaotic or almost nonexistent, and barbarians looted cities at will with little resistance.

Declaration of Independence   A paper written mainly by Thomas Jefferson at the direction of the Second *Continental Congress*. It set forth the reasons that the American *colonies* decided to break away from Great Britain. It is considered one of the greatest documents stating human *rights* ever written.

deflation   A general lowering in the prices for goods and services. See *inflation*.

defranchisement   The taking away of the *right* to vote.

democracy   To the Ancient Greeks, this term meant direct rule of the people in which all governmental policies would be decided at a meeting of all citizens. This meaning has been modified to denote representative government in which elected representatives of the people decide governmental policies. The United States is a democracy in this last sense.

democrat   (1) A believer in *democracy*. (2) A member of the Democratic *political party* of the United States.

depression   In social studies, a period in which there is widespread unemployment due to an acute reduction in business activity and industrial production. See *prosperity* and *recession*.

dictator   An absolute ruler of a country, either one legally elected who declares that an emergency necessitates his absolute rule, or one who seizes power by force.

diplomacy   In social studies, the method by which nations negotiate with each other.

dynasty   A series of rulers, usually lasting for at least one hundred years, of the same family.

[E]

Eastern Civilization   See *civilization*.

Eastern Hemisphere   See *hemisphere*.

ecology   A biological science dealing with the balance of nature, or the delicate relationship between living things and their *environments*.

economics   A social science that is the study of the way man produces, distributes and uses goods.

electorate   The people who have the *right* to vote in an election.

empire   A group of different nations ruled by a single powerful nation. See *Roman Empire*.

enfranchisement   (1) The act of freeing slaves. (2) The granting of the *rights* of citizenship.

environment   Surroundings.

epoch   An historical period of importance. See *era* and *age*.

Equator   An imaginary line extending around the earth. It lies exactly halfway between the North and South *Poles*.

era   An important historical period. See *epoch* and *age*.

ethnic   An adjective referring to the identification of people with the same language, customs, etc., into one group.

[F]

Fair Deal   A social reform program of President Harry S. Truman.

fascism   A particular kind of government that controls all activities of a nation. Italy under the *dictator* Benito Mussolini and Germany under the *dictator* Adolf Hitler are examples of fascist governments. Unlike *democracy*, in a fascist government all political, social and religious opposition to the government is ruthlessly crushed.

federalism   A political union among various states or regions in which much of the political power is given to a national government.

Federalist Party   A *political party* of the United States which advocated a strong national government. It lasted until 1816.

feudalism   A social, political and economic system that flourished throughout most of Europe during the *Middle Ages*. It had a rigid *class* system. Governments were controlled by chiefs or lords. The people ruled by the lords were called vassals. Vassals owed absolute obedience to the lord who made and enforced laws and levied taxes. The lord, on the other hand, owed the vassal protection against outside invaders. In this period, nations were weak.

[G]

geography   The study of the physical world and man's relationship to it.

Gettysburg Address   A moving speech by President Abraham Lincoln at the dedication of the cemetery at Gettysburg, Pennsylvania, on November 19, 1863. The cemetery was the burial ground for Union soldiers who had been killed at the Battle of Gettysburg.

graft   The getting of money dishonestly, usually by bribery. This term specifically refers to political dishonesty.

Gross National Product   The total value of all goods produced and services rendered in a country over one year.

[H]

hemisphere   Half of the globe or earth. All the earth north of the *Equator* is called the Northern Hemisphere. All the earth south of the *Equator* is called the Southern Hemisphere. The half of the globe that contains North and South America is called the Western Hemisphere. The half of the earth containing Europe, Asia, Africa and Australia is called the Eastern Hemisphere.

House of Representatives   The more numerous legislative body of the United States, in which representation is based on the population of each state. Together with the *Senate*, it forms the *Congress* of the country.

hydrogen bomb   An extremely powerful *atomic* bomb set off by the fusion of hydrogen atoms.

[I]

ideology   A system of strongly held beliefs. *Communism* is an ideology, as is *democracy.*

immigrant   A person who has left the country of his birth to live in another country.

incumbent   A person who holds a political office.

indenture   In social studies, a contract by which one promises to work for a specified period. In colonial America, a person wishing to come to the English *colonies* would promise to work for an American for a time (usually seven years) in return for the cost of the sea voyage. The indentured servant, as such an *immigrant* was called, had few *rights*. He or she was little more than a slave. Unlike a slave, though, he or she received freedom when the contract was finished.

Industrial Revolution   A period in history beginning in the eighteenth century, and, according to some historians, still going on today. In this *era*, man has invented many machines to aid him in his work and make his life more comfortable. The *epoch* has also seen the creation of the factory system as opposed to the making of goods at home.

inflation   A general rise in the prices for goods and services. See *deflation.*

isolationism   In social studies, the belief that a nation best conducts its affairs by avoiding becoming involved in the affairs of other countries.

[L]

League of Nations   An organization of nations created in 1920 with the purpose of avoiding world war by open negotiation. The League is considered a failure since World War II broke out in 1939. It was discontinued in 1946 when the United Nations came into existence.

left   In social studies, the body of people who are *liberals*, socialists, communists and *anarchists*. See *socialism* and *communism*. In other words, the left is made up of people who believe in changing national institutions. See *right*.

liberal   A person who believes in modifying national institutions by peaceful methods. The word is also an adjective. A "liberal person" is one holding liberal views. See *conservative*.

[M]

Marxism   Named after Karl Marx, a German, who founded this theory of *socialism*. He believed the working class was underpaid and did not get a fair share of what it produced. This would eventually lead to world revolution, after which a new communistic world *society* would be born. See *communism*. Many nations follow Marx's theories, the leader being the Soviet Union.

medieval   An adjective referring to the *Middle Ages*.

metropolitan   An adjective referring to the city and its surrounding area. See *urban* and *suburban*.

Middle Ages   A period of stability in Europe following the *Dark Ages*. *Feudalism* prevailed in this *era* which lasted approximately from 1000 to 1450. Some historians include the Dark Ages in the Middle Ages.

militarism   A view that the military forces ought to be the strongest institution in *society*, perhaps even lead the government.

monarchist   A person who believes the best form of government is one headed by a king or queen.

monopoly   Absolute control or ownership of a product by a single individual, a small group of people, or a corporation.

Monroe Doctrine   A doctrine set forth by President James Monroe in 1823, warning European nations not to make any more colonies in the *Western Hemisphere*. See *colony*.

[N]

National Socialism   Another term for *Nazism*.

nationalism   A belief in the superiority of one's nation above all other nations.

Nazism   The form *fascism* took in Germany from 1933 to 1945 under the *dictator* Adolf Hitler. In Nazism, all rights of dissent or mild opposition were brutally suppressed. The Nazi Party was the only *political party*. Nazis believed the "race" they belonged to was superior to all others. For this reason, they killed millions of Jews and other minority peoples during their cruel reign. Led by Hitler, Germany began World War II and was finally defeated in 1945. See *racism*, *National Socialism*.

New Deal   A program of social reform carried out by President Franklin Roosevelt during his terms of office (1933–1945).

New Frontier   A program of social reform stated as an aim of his administration by President John F. Kennedy in 1961 and partly carried out by himself and his successor, President Lyndon B. Johnson.

North Atlantic Treaty Organization (NATO)   A *confederation* of nations in Western Europe and North America, bound together in a defense pact to protect any or all of the members against an attack by the Soviet Union or any communist nation. See *communism*.

North Pole   See *poles*.

Northern Hemisphere   See *hemisphere*.

[O, P].

oligarchy   A government ruled by a very small body of people.

parliament   A legislative body. The best known is the British Parliament, consisting of a House of Commons (somewhat like our *House of Representatives)* and a House of Lords.

party (political)   A group of people bound together and dedicated to winning control of a government so they can put their ideas into force. The two leading parties in the United States are the Democratic Party and the Republican Party.

peonage   A system in which a person, usually a farm worker, is forced to work in order to pay off a debt. This system was long in use in Latin America, and was little better than slavery.

physical map   A map showing the physical features of the land. Colors usually indicate elevation.

plutocracy   Control of government by rich people.

poles   The two ends of the axis the earth revolves on. The northern axis end is called the *North Pole*. The southern axis end is called the *South Pole*.

political map   A map emphasizing political units. Usually the colors on such maps stand for different countries, states, or other political units.

political science   The study of government.

politics   (1) The management of government. (2) The contests of *political parties* for power.

primary elections   Elections held by one *political party* in various states, in which the candidates are selected to run against candidates of the other party or parties.

propaganda   The spreading of certain political ideas, usually in printed form or by TV, radio, or film.

prosperity   In social studies, a time when there is little unemployment and most people have enough money to purchase goods and services in substantial amounts. See *depression* and *recession*.

public ownership The ownership and management by government of certain services. The postal system is an example of public ownership.

public works program Projects run and paid for by government. This kind of program is usually begun by governments in times of *depression* or *recession* in order to reduce unemployment.

[R]

racism A false viewpoint, which believes that one group of people are superior in all ways to other groups of peoples. For example, the Nazis believed that people of German stock were superior to all other peoples of the world. See *Nazism*.

radical A person who holds extreme positions on either the *right* or *left*, and would like to see his views adopted without delay and possibly with violence. This word is also an adjective, as in "holding radical views."

ratify To approve. The Senate of the United States has to approve or ratify all treaties with other nations. See *treaty*.

reactionary A person who would like to see government or *society* in general return to methods, laws, and customs that have been discarded. This is also an adjective, as in "holding reactionary views."

recession A limited period when unemployment rises and business activity and industrial output slow down. A period of *recession* is not as long, nor is it as devastating, as a *depression*. See *prosperity*.

Reformation An historical *era* of the Sixteenth Century. Generally recognized as the person who began the Reformation *Age*, Martin Luther, a German monk, protested the corruption that had crept into many areas of the Roman Catholic Church. The protest led to the formation of Protestant sects throughout Europe. See *Counter-Reformation*.

Renaissance An historical period in Europe (from about 1300 to 1600) that marked a shift from the God-centered life of the *Middle Ages* to greater emphasis upon man and his place in the universe. It was a remarkably creative *era* in all fields, including art, science, exploration, and religious thought.

republic A type of government in which the people govern through their elected representatives. Today republic has the same meaning as *democracy*.

republican (1) A believer in the republican form of government. (2) A member of the Republican *political party* of the United States.

right (1) In social studies, the body of people who are *conservatives*, *reactionaries*, and *fascists*. See *reactionary* and *fascism*. In other words, the right is made up of people who wish no changes in *society*, or wish to return to discarded institutions or methods, or wish to impose a dictatorial type of government. See *left* and *dictator*. (2) A right is also used to refer to a privilege that is the property of every citizen, such as the right to vote in the United States.

Roman Empire   A period in Roman history dating from 27 B.C. to 395 A.D. during which the Romans conquered and ruled a large area of Europe as well as portions of Africa and Asia. See *empire.*

rural   An adjective referring to areas which are not part of a *metropolitan* region.

[S]

Senate   (1) The general meaning is one body of a two-body legislature, such as the Roman Senate. (2) The Senate of the United States consists of two members representing each state, or 100 members in all. See *House of Representatives.*

socialism   A social system by which all the people own or control industries and public services. Many people look upon Karl Marx as the founder of socialism, as he was of communism. However, there were advocates of socialism before Marx. Socialists in general are considered *democratic,* preferring to gain their ends by peaceful means as opposed to advocates of *communism* who would resort to violent means to impose their system if peaceful means failed. See *Marxism.*

society   The social order of a nation. See *culture.*

sociology   A science which studies man's behavior when he is in a *society.*

South Pole   See *poles.*

Southern Hemisphere   See *hemisphere.*

strike   In social studies, the refusal of employees to work until they achieve certain conditions. Usually a strike is organized by a labor *union.* A strike might be called in order to gain higher pay or better working conditions or special benefits, such as pensions for workers when they retire.

suburb   A community near a city from which many people go to the city to work. A suburb is considered to be in a metropolitan area. See *urban* and *rural.*

suburban   An adjective referring to communities near a city from which many people go to the city to work. A *suburb* is considered to be within a *metropolitan* area. See *urban* and *rural.*

[T]

tariff   A tax levied on goods entering one nation from another.

theocracy   A government ruled by members of the clergy.

topography   The physical features of the earth. See *physical map.*

totalitarianism   Any form of government which is dictatorial in nature and allows the citizen few, if any, *rights.* Communist and fascist governments are examples of totalitarian governments. See *communism, fascism,* and *Nazism.*

trade route   A route over which goods are sent in great numbers. Trade routes may be by water or by land.

treaty   An agreement between nations. See *diplomacy* and *ratify*.

Tropic of Cancer   An imaginary line extending around the earth at 23½ degrees north of the *Equator*. See *Tropic of Capricorn, Arctic Circle*, and *Antarctic Circle*.

Tropic of Capricorn   An imaginary line extending around the earth at 23½ degrees south of the *Equator*. See *Tropic of Cancer, Arctic Circle*, and *Antarctic Circle*.

[U, V]

union   (1) A banding together of separate political units to gain certain ends. The United States is a union of fifty states. See *federalism*. (2) A *labor* union is an organization of workers formed to protect individual *rights* and gain better working conditions. See *American Federation of Labor* and *Congress of Industrial Organizations*.

urban   An adjective referring to a city. See *rural, suburb, suburban* and *metropolitan*.

veto   A *right* to forbid a law or proposed action of a legislative body from taking effect. The President of the United States can veto a proposed law passed by the *Senate* and *House of Representatives*. However, a two-thirds vote in favor of the proposed law by the members present in the Senate and House of Representatives can overturn the veto.

[W]

welfare   A system by which poor people who are unemployed can receive assistance from government in the form of money, housing, and food.

Western Civilization   See *civilization*.

Western Hemisphere   See *hemisphere*.

Whig Party   A *political party* of the United States which opposed the Democratic Party. It started in 1832 and had disappeared by 1860.

HIGH SCHOOL EQUIVALENCY DIPLOMA TESTS

SOCIAL STUDIES QUIZZER

The following tests are carefully constructed to simulate your exam. The questions deal with history, geography, political science, and economics. They cover past as well as current events. "The past furnishes a base from which to understand the present." After you take the tests, a critical comparison will enable you to discover which of the four major social science areas need additional study.

TEST I. SOCIAL STUDIES

TIME: 25 Minutes. 17 Questions.

DIRECTIONS: *Select from the choices offered in each of the following, the one which is correct or most nearly correct.*

Correct key answers to all these test questions will be found at the end of the test.

1. Basic to the idea of a federal system of government is the
   (A) existence of a strong executive
   (B) division of power between national and state governments
   (C) distribution of powers between two branches of the legislature
   (D) existence of a Supreme Court.

2. Of the following, the European nation that dominated trade in Asia and the East Indies during the sixteenth century was
   (A) Portugal   (B) Spain
   (C) Holland   (D) England.

3. Of the following statements, the one which best describes the term "gerrymandering" is:
   (A) Organized pressure on legislators to pass certain legislation
   (B) The rearrangement of election districts in the states so that the party in power gains control of as many as possible.
   (C) A practice whereby legislators secure support for the enactment of laws by trading votes with their colleagues.
   (D) A clamoring for war or aggressive policy in foreign affairs.

4. Of the following, the event directly associated with the early history of New York State was
   (A) Shay's Rebellion
   (B) the publication of The Liberator
   (C) the Whiskey Rebellion
   (D) the trial of John Peter Zenger.

5. The United States has declared war at some time or other against all of the following countries *except*
   (A) England   (B) Russia
   (C) Spain   (D) Italy.

6. "In the field of world policy, I would dedicate this nation to the policy of the good neighbor" is a quotation from the speeches of
   (A) Franklin D. Roosevelt
   (B) Theodore Roosevelt
   (C) Abraham Lincoln
   (D) Calvin Coolidge.

7. All of the following were included in Woodrow Wilson's "Fourteen Points" *except*
   (A) freedom of the press
   (B) freedom of the seas
   (C) reduction of armaments
   (D) the establishment of a general federation of nations.

8. During the entire period from 1800 to 1850, the greatest number of immigrants to the United States came from
(A) Germany
(B) England
(C) Scandinavia
(D) Ireland.

9. Voting qualifications in the United States are
(A) determined by the states, subject to constitutional restrictions
(B) established by Congress, subject to constitutional restrictions
(C) enumerated in the Bill of Rights
(D) specifically defined in the Federal Constitution.

10. Of the following pairs, the one which *incorrectly* attributes a river system to a country is
(A) Yellow—China
(B) Vistula—Italy
(C) Murray-Darling—Australia
(D) Loire—France.

11. The Domesday Book was a(n)
(A) census of population and property
(B) volume detailing religious practices
(C) example of the rise of vernacular literature
(D) manual of court procedure.

12. Of the following, the one which names two countries in the United Arab Republic is
(A) Egypt and Lebanon
(B) Egypt and Syria
(C) Syria and Lebanon
(D) Egypt and Jordan.

13. In the United States government, one of the powers possessed by the Senate and not the House of Representatives is the power to
(A) approve the appointment of ambassadors
(B) override the president's veto
(C) impeach the president
(D) originate revenue bills.

14. The prevention of unfair practices in conducting television programs is under the jurisdiction of the
(A) Public Service Commission
(B) Federal Trade Commission
(C) Interstate Commerce Commission
(D) Federal Communications Commission.

15. Each of the following leaders is correctly matched with a country *except*
(A) Prime Minister Nehru—India
(B) President Sukarno—Jordan
(C) President Nasser—United Arab Republic
(D) President Nkrumah—Ghana.

16. The Mesabi Range is famous for its rich deposits of
(A) coal
(B) copper
(C) iron
(D) uranium.

17. The Pendleton Act of 1883 was a long overdue attempt to eliminate the evils of the
(A) Tariff of Abominations
(B) Specie Circular
(C) Squatter sovereignty
(D) Spoils system.

CONSOLIDATE YOUR KEY ANSWERS HERE

Practice using Answer Sheets. Make ONE mark for each answer. Additional and stray marks may be counted as mistakes. In making corrections erase errors COMPLETELY. Make glossy black marks. To arrive at an accurate estimate of your ability and progress, cover the Correct Answers with a sheet of white paper while you are taking this test.

CORRECT ANSWERS TO THE FOREGOING PRACTICE QUESTIONS

Now compare your answers with these Correct Answers to the Practice Questions. If your answers differ from these, go back and study those questions to see where and how you made your mistakes.

1.B	4.D	7.A	10.B	13.A	16.C
2.A	5.B	8.A	11.A	14.D	17.D
3.B	6.A	9.A	12.B	15.B	

TEST II. SOCIAL STUDIES

TIME: 25 Minutes. 17 Questions.

DIRECTIONS: *For each of the following questions, select the choice which best answers the question or completes the statement.*

Correct key answers to all these test questions will be found at the end of the test.

1. Of the following, the one which had the greatest influence upon the development of the American legal system is the
   (A) Roman law
   (B) judicial system set up in colonies
   (C) British common law
   (D) ideas of John Locke.

2. The idea of Ptolemy that the sun revolved around the earth was disproved by
   (A) Newton   (B) Copernicus
   (C) Galileo   (D) Roger Bacon.

3. The Senate Investigating Committee, chaired by Senator McClellan, was concerned with the problem of
   (A) racketeering practices in labor unions and management
   (B) agricultural surpluses
   (C) Civil Rights legislation
   (D) limiting the treaty-making powers of the President.

4. The role of the Cabinet in American Government is
   (A) defined in the Constitution
   (B) based on the ideas of Alexander Hamilton
   (C) an example of a practice that developed through custom
   (D) analogous to the system of government prevailing in England in the 18th century.

5. The main purpose of the Truman Doctrine was to
   (A) give economic and technical aid to needy countries outside of the Communist orbit
   (B) develop supremacy over the Soviet Union in the building of atomic weapons
   (C) encourage dissension in the satellite countries of the Soviet Union
   (D) contain communism by aiding Greece and Turkey.

6. The "Great Compromise" was finally adopted by the Constitutional Convention because
   (A) the small states threatened to bolt the Convention unless representation was made equal in both houses
   (B) the Southern states would not have ratified the Constitution without it
   (C) the membership of Congress would have been too large and unwieldy to be able to function effectively
   (D) an agreement was also made to include a Bill of Rights in the Constitution.

7. Of the following matched items, the one that is *incorrectly* paired is
   (A) Thomas Jefferson—Louisiana Purchase
   (B) John Marshall—strict interpretation of the Constitution
   (C) John Quincy Adams—Monroe Doctrine
   (D) Roger Taney—Dred Scott Decision.

8. The great political leader of Athens during the Golden Age of Greece was
   (A) Phidias   (B) Plato
   (C) Pericles   (D) Aristides.

9. The loss of Chicago's claim to the title "Hog Butcher for the World" is due mainly to the
   (A) growth of major cities on the west coast and development of superhighways for trucks
   (B) automation in the meat industry
   (C) increase in importation of meat from other countries
   (D) decrease in the consumption of meat products.

10. When Thoreau advocated passive resistance to the tyranny of government he was anticipating the program of
    (A) Sun Yat Sen   (C) Mahatma Gandhi
    (B) Jan Masaryk   (D) Susan B. Anthony.

S1628

11. Despite the fact that England is farther north than any point in the United States, its winters are generally warmer than those in northern United States because
 (A) England has a Mediterranean climate
 (B) England's shores are warmed by the Gulf Stream
 (C) England is warmed by the breezes that blow from Africa
 (D) the winds that influence England's climate are the prevailing easterlies.

12. The city which is sometimes described as the "Pittsburgh of the South" because of its high production of steel is
 (A) Birmingham, Alabama
 (B) Nashville, Tennessee
 (C) Richmond, Virginia
 (D) Atlanta, Georgia.

13. The term "manifest destiny" would most likely be found in the chapter of an American history textbook dealing with
 (A) immigration
 (B) the Industrial Revolution
 (C) expansion
 (D) foreign affairs.

14. The most important factor in England's rise to power in the 16th Century was the
 (A) riches brought home through expeditions to the New World
 (B) destruction of the Spanish naval power
 (C) world trip of Sir Francis Drake
 (D) conquest of New Amsterdam.

15. The Foreign Ministers Conference of Geneva, held in early 1959, dealt mainly with the problem of
 (A) West Berlin and the unification of Germany
 (B) the limitation of armaments
 (C) the withdrawal of Allied troops from Europe
 (D) international trade.

16. Of the following, the body of water that is completely land-locked is the
 (A) Black Sea   (B) Tyrrhenian Sea
 (C) Ionian Sea   (D) Caspian Sea.

17. The current government of France is known as the
 (A) Second Republic   (B) Third Republic
 (C) Fourth Republic   (D) Fifth Republic.

CONSOLIDATE YOUR KEY ANSWERS HERE

Practice using Answer Sheets. Make ONE mark for each answer. Additional and stray marks may be counted as mistakes. In making corrections erase errors COMPLETELY. Make glossy black marks. To arrive at an accurate estimate of your ability and progress, cover the Correct Answers with a sheet of white paper while you are taking this test.

CORRECT ANSWERS TO THE FOREGOING PRACTICE QUESTIONS

Now compare your answers with these Correct Answers to the Practice Questions. If your answers differ from these, go back and study those questions to see where and how you made your mistakes.

1. C	4. C	7. B	10. C	13. C	16. D
2. B	5. D	8. C	11. B	14. B	17. D
3. A	6. A	9. A	12. A	15. A	

TEST III. SOCIAL STUDIES

TIME: 20 Minutes. 15 Questions.

DIRECTIONS: Select from the choices offered in each of the following, the one which is correct or most nearly correct.

Correct key answers to all these test questions will be found at the end of the test.

1. The term "savanna" best describes large
   (A) forest areas of central Africa
   (B) swamp areas in the southern part of the United States
   (C) grassland regions of Brazil
   (D) constellations in the Milky Way.

2. The practical effect on persons traveling westward across the International Date Line would be to place them in time
   (A) back 24 hours   (B) ahead 12 hours
   (C) back 12 hours   (D) ahead 24 hours.

3. An excerpt from a biographical dictionary which reads as follows: "A great compromiser, author of the 'American System', member of the War-Hawk group during the War of 1812" would best fit
   (A) Henry Clay   (B) Daniel Webster
   (C) John C. Calhoun (D) Stephen Douglas.

4. A third party in the 20th century which drew most of its support from the Republicans was the
   (A) Populist Party
   (B) American Labor Party
   (C) Liberal Party
   (D) Progressive Party.

5. All of the following countries have recently experienced coups d'etat led by military men, *except*
   (A) Sudan   (B) Lebanon
   (C) Pakistan   (D) Iraq.

6. The Jacquerie was a
   (A) peasant uprising
   (B) French feudal system
   (C) society in Paris
   (D) medieval monastery.

7. Hoover Dam is located on the
   (A) Colorado River   (B) Tennessee River
   (C) Missouri River   (D) Columbia River.

8. The ruling of the Supreme Court of the United States of America that racial segregation in public schools is unconstitutional is based on the
   (A) 5th Amendment (B) 13th Amendment
   (C) 14th Amendment (D) 15th Amendment.

9. The Eisenhower Doctrine empowered the President of the United States to
   (A) construe an attack upon any member nation of NATO as an attack upon the United States
   (B) grant military aid to any SEATO nation according to the terms set forth in the agreement
   (C) use armed force to assist any nation in the Middle East that requests it to put down acts of Communist aggression upon that nation
   (D) withdraw financial aid granted an underdeveloped nation if that nation should fall within the Communist orbit.

10. In the United States of America, the most important factor among the following for the development of economic life since the Civil War has been the
    (A) acquisition of new territory
    (B) development of mass production
    (C) growth of the merchant marine
    (D) reforms in state banking.

11. The right of the United States Supreme Court to pass upon the constitutionality of laws is
    (A) expressly stated in the Federal Constitution
    (B) the result of Congressional action
    (C) assumed by the Supreme Court as a necessary function
    (D) the result of an amendment to the Federal Constitution.

S1628

12. The seating of an elected United States Senator or Representative follows his election except when
   (A) two-thirds of the membership of the House to which he was elected disallows it
   (B) a majority of both Houses sitting in joint session disallows it
   (C) disapproval by the legislature of his home state is sustained by the Judiciary Committee of the House to which he was elected
   (D) the governor of his state finds good cause for invalidating the election.

13. Which of the following features of our federal government can be traced most directly to our heritage of government in the English fashion?
   (A) our written constitution
   (B) our bicameral legislature
   (C) the supremacy of our federal judiciary
   (D) our system of checks and balances.

14. When a condition exists in which there is a decline in employment and an increase in government spending for relief, one would probably also find
   (A) an increase in bank loans
   (B) a decline in imports
   (C) an increase in installment buying
   (D) a reduction in bond purchases as compared with purchases of stocks.

15. New York ranks among the first ten states in the production of
   (A) dairy products, fruits, potatoes
   (B) dairy products, wheat, sugar beets
   (C) corn, wheat, sugar beets
   (D) fruits, corn, potatoes.

CONSOLIDATE YOUR KEY ANSWERS HERE

Practice using Answer Sheets. Make ONE mark for each answer. Additional and stray marks may be counted as mistakes. In making corrections erase errors COMPLETELY. Make glossy black marks. To arrive at an accurate estimate of your ability and progress, cover the Correct Answers with a sheet of white paper while you are taking this test.

CORRECT ANSWERS TO THE FOREGOING PRACTICE QUESTIONS

Now compare your answers with these Correct Answers to the Practice Questions. If your answers differ from these, go back and study those questions to see where and how you made your mistakes.

1.C	3.A	5.B	7.A	9.C	11.C	13.B	15.A
2.D	4.D	6.A	8.C	10.B	12.A	14.B	

TEST IV. AMERICAN HISTORY

TIME: 60 Minutes. 44 Questions.

DIRECTIONS: For each question in this test, read carefully the stem and the five lettered choices that follow. Choose the answer which you consider correct or most nearly correct. Mark the answer sheet for the letter you have chosen: A, B, C, D, or E.

Explanations of the key points behind these questions appear with the answers at the end of this test. The explanatory answers provide the kind of background that will enable you to answer test questions with facility and confidence.

(1)

Which event occurred in the United States during the Critical Period (1781-1789)?

(A) Whiskey Rebellion
(B) Shay's Rebellion
(C) Hartford Convention
(D) Closing of the port of Boston
(E) Meeting of the Second Continental Congress

(2)

One reason for the importance of the Northwest Ordinance (1787) was that it provided for

(A) the government of Texas
(B) the sale of western lands
(C) free navigation on the Great Lakes
(D) the eventual admission of territories as equal states
(E) the judicial system of the United States

(3)

Some of the best arguments in support of the adoption of the United States Constitution are found in

(A) *Common Sense*
(B) the Articles of Confederation
(C) *The New Freedom*
(D) the Freeport Doctrine
(E) *The Federalist*

(4)

Which of the following was a result of the other three?

(A) Alien and Sedition Acts
(B) Disappearance of the Federalist Party
(C) Hartford Convention
(D) Increase in democratic spirit in the United States
(E) None of these

S1339

(5)

The idea that the federal government was a compact or contract among the states was expressed in

(A) Lee's Resolutions
(B) the theory of "manifest destiny"
(C) South Carolina's "Exposition and Protest"
(D) Webster's reply to Hayne
(E) the Freeport Doctrine

(6)

The Treaty of 1795 with Spain was most popular with

(A) western farmers using the Mississippi River for shopping
(B) northern fur trappers seeking the removal of British troops from the Northwest Territory
(C) patriotic Americans attempting to stop the impressment of seamen
(D) New England merchants seeking to reopen triangular trade
(E) southerners seeking new markets for tobacco

(7)

Which statement best describes the reaction of many American colonists toward British colonial policy following the French and Indian War?

(A) They refused to accept the idea of Parliament's right to manage their internal affairs.
(B) They petitioned the British Parliament for immediate independence.
(C) They urged the colonial legislatures to enforce the taxation program of the British Parliament.
(D) They opposed the withdrawal of British troops from the Ohio Territory.
(E) They advocated higher taxes to cover the costs of the war.

8

The friendship between the United States and France can be traced back to

(A) the Alliance of 1778
(B) the activities of Citizen Genêt
(C) French aid during the War of 1812
(D) French support of the North during the Civil War
(E) the gift of the Statue of Liberty

9

On which issue did Thomas Jefferson reverse his opinion as to strict construction of the Constitution?

(A) The Bank of the United States
(B) The purchase of the Louisiana Territory
(C) The moving of the capital to Washington, D.C.
(D) The appointment of the "midnight judges"
(E) The election of 1800

10

One reason why Great Britain supported the Monroe Doctrine in 1823 was that she

(A) had declared war on Spain
(B) wished to support the Holy Alliance
(C) had developed trade with the Latin American countries
(D) followed a policy of supporting democratic revolutions
(E) wished to curry favor with the United States

11

An important result of the Napoleonic Wars in Europe was the

(A) spread of the Industrial Revolution
(B) success of the Continental system
(C) rise of a spirit of nationalism
(D) elimination of monarchies
(E) military supremacy of France

Base your answers to questions **12** - **13** *on information given in the graph below.*

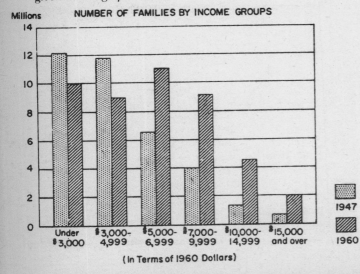

NUMBER OF FAMILIES BY INCOME GROUPS

Millions

(In Terms of 1960 Dollars)

1947

1960

12

Which trend is indicated during the period 1947-1960?

(A) The average family income increased.
(B) The number of families with incomes over $15,000 declined.
(C) The number of families earning between $3,000 and $4,999 increased.
(D) In 1960, 35 percent of the families in the United States earned $10,000-$15,000 per year.
(E) In 1947, more than half of United States families earned less than $3,000.

13

In which income group was there the greatest increase in the number of families?

(A) $3,000-$4,999   (B) $5,000-$6,999
(C) $7,000-$9,999   (D) $10,000-$14,999
              (E) $15,000 and over

Questions **14** - **16**

Directions: Match each of the numbered quotations below with the appropriate lettered document.

(A) Albany Plan of Union
(B) Gettysburg Address
(C) Declaration of Independence
(D) Mayflower Compact
(E) United States Bill of Rights

14

"We hold these truths to be self-evident, that all men are created equal, that they are endowed by their Creator with certain inalienable rights..."

15

"It is for us the living, rather, to be dedicated here to the unfinished work which they who fought here have thus far so nobly advanced."

16

"No Soldier shall, in time of peace be quartered in any house, without the consent of the Owner, nor in time of war, but in a manner to be prescribed by law."

17

The theory of "manifest destiny" is best illustrated in the

(A) Good Neighbor Policy
(B) slogan "Fifty-four forty or fight"
(C) selection of the parallel 36° 30' in the Missouri Compromise
(D) granting of independence to the Philippines
(E) Emancipation Proclamation

(18)

One direct result of the passage of the Kansas-Nebraska Act was the

(A) rise of the abolition movement
(B) migration of settlers from the Kansas-Nebraska territory
(C) formation of the Republican party
(D) organizing of the first "underground railroad"
(E) Missouri Compromise

(19)

The chief reason for the opposition of the South to the election of Abraham Lincoln in 1860 was his

(A) resistance to secession
(B) demand for the immediate abolition of slavery
(C) hostility to the extension of slavery
(D) insistence on equal education for Negroes and whites
(E) unsophisticated appearance

(20)

The presidential candidacies of John C. Breckinridge in 1860 and Theodore Roosevelt in 1912 were similar in that

(A) both men were Republicans
(B) their campaigns split their parties and allowed the election of President by a minority vote
(C) both men announced support for high protective tariffs for industry
(D) both failed to gain any electoral votes
(E) both were opposed by agrarian interests

(21)

In which pair is the first item an *immediate* cause of the second?

(A) Assassination of James Garfield—Pendleton Act
(B) Election of John Quincy Adams—Twelfth Amendment
(C) Assassination of Alexander Hamilton—End of the Federalist Party
(D) Sinking of the *Lusitania*—Entry of the United States into World War I
(E) Hitler's attack on Poland—United States' entry into World War II

Questions **(22)**-**(26)** are concerned with the following discussion on Imperialism.

Speaker I: It is our duty to extend the blessings of Christianity and civilization to backward peoples. If we are to fulfill our duty, we must govern them.

Speaker II: The United States must be a major power in the world. Therefore, we will have to have a powerful navy and merchant fleet. To service these fleets, we need to acquire naval bases in various parts of the world.

Speaker III: We need overseas areas where American businessmen can safely invest surplus capital and find new markets as well as raw materials.

Speaker IV: If we should become involved in creating a world empire, we might find that in the process, democracy at home has been hurt.

(22)

Which speaker would have been most apt to support the Open Door Policy?

(A) I   (B) II
(C) III   (D) IV

(23)

Before the Spanish-American War, most Americans shared the views of Speaker

(A) I   (B) II
(C) III   (D) IV

(24)

Alfred T. Mahan's views are best expressed by Speaker

(A) I   (B) II
(C) III   (D) IV

(25)

The objectives of "dollar diplomacy" in the Caribbean are best expressed by Speaker

(A) I   (B) II
(C) III   (D) IV

(26)

After a brief revolution in 1893, Americans who shared the ideas of Speakers I and III urged Congress to annex

(A) Hawaii   (B) Jamaica
(C) Bermuda   (D) the Virgin Islands

(27)

Which of the following statements about the North Atlantic Treaty Organization (NATO) are true?

I. Originally, it was an outgrowth of the Brussels Treaty organization for defense against Soviet encroachment.
II: It had the effect of bringing the United States and a number of additional nations—(not all European)—into association for the purpose of Western European defense.
III. For the United States, membership was a drastic reversal of foreign policy in that, for the first time in history, the United States entered into a European military alliance in peacetime.

IV. Aside from its military implications, NATO has also been intended as a major means for the advancement of European political unity.

(A) I, II, III, and IV
(B) II, III, and IV
(C) I, II, and IV
(D) I, II, and III
(E) I, III, and IV

(28)

Samuel Gompers attempted to win gains for labor by

(A) uniting skilled and unskilled workers into one union
(B) organizing industrial or vertical unions
(C) forming craft unions of skilled workers
(D) campaigning actively for the election of AFL members to public office
(E) urging civil disobedience as a means to win public support

(29)

In the period 1887-1890, Congress passed major legislation to regulate abuses in

(A) local governments
(B) industrial combinations
(C) union methods
(D) farm credit
(E) governmental hiring practices

(30)

The Embargo and Non-Intercourse Acts passed by the United States in the early nineteenth century illustrate the

(A) unsuccessful attempt of the United States to isolate itself from a European conflict
(B) success of the United States in obtaining recognition of neutral rights
(C) temporary submergence of sectionalism as an issue
(D) overwhelming support given by members of Congress to President Jefferson's policy
(E) desire of the United States to ally itself with Napoleon

Questions (31) - (34)

Directions: Match each numbered statement with the appropriate map projection.

(A) Mercator   (B) Sinusoidal
(C) Goode's Interrupted   (D) Azimuthal Equidistant
              (E) Orthographic

(31)

This projection is most favored for aircraft navigation.

(32)

This projection cannot be used for a world map.

(33)

This is the most favored projection for marine charts because all compass directions appear as straight lines.

(34)

This projection is excellent for land areas but poor for oceans.

(35)

The pre-Civil War South objected to protective tariffs because they

(A) increased the cost of slaves
(B) kept the price of cotton low
(C) increased the prices of manufactured goods
(D) aided western farmers at the planters' expense
(E) destroyed the market for tobacco

(36)

In 1786, which of the following individuals would most probably have been in favor of Shays' Rebellion?

(A) A Boston merchant
(B) A New England sea captain
(C) A Massachusetts Senator
(D) A Massachusetts farmer
(E) A Virginia Representative

(37)

Henry Clay is classified as both

(A) a "muckraker" and a "mugwump"
(B) a "war hawk" and a great compromiser
(C) a member of the Virginia dynasty and a presidential nominee
(D) an ambassador to France and a Secretary of State
(E) a "whig" and a defender of the South

(38)

Both Andrew Carnegie and John D. Rockefeller, Sr., may be classified as

(A) leaders in industrial consolidation in the nineteenth century
(B) organizers of the Republican Party
(C) individuals favoring strict government regulation of railroads
(D) opponents of the principle of philanthropy
(E) inheritors of great wealth

(39)

The election of Lincoln in 1860 helped to bring about secession because

(A) Lincoln had promised to free the slaves
(B) a disappointed Douglas urged the South to seek revenge
(C) the South had now lost control of both houses of Congress and of the executive branch
(D) Lincoln ordered an attack on Fort Sumter
(E) Lincoln ordered the South out of the Union

(40)

Sharecropping emerged in the post-Civil War South as a means by which

(A) southern planters exchanged crops for northern manufactured goods
(B) more than one crop shared the available land on the plantation
(C) former slaves formed cooperative credit associations to share costs of entering farming
(D) impoverished planters and former slaves supplied each other's need for labor and land
(E) religious persons shared what they grew with those less fortunate

(41)

Which was a result of the Homestead Act of 1862?

(A) Increased desertions from the Confederate Army by soldiers hoping to obtain free land
(B) Increased speculation in western lands
(C) Increased public awareness of the need for conservation of natural resources
(D) Increased criticism of the Republican Party for failure to fulfill a pledge made in the 1860 campaign
(E) Hastened settlement of New Mexico

(42)

The aim of Napoleon's Continental System was to

(A) crush revolutions in Central Europe
(B) codify the legal systems of all European nations
(C) close European ports to English manufactured goods and colonial commodities
(D) extend the benefits of the French Revolution to other European nations
(E) extend French military rule over the entire continent

(43)

The denunciation by farmers of what they called the "Crime of '73" reflected the demand for

(A) an increased regulation of railroads
(B) an increase in aid to the land-grant colleges
(C) federal regulation of stock market transactions
(D) higher prices through currency expansion
(E) return of federal farm supports

(44)

According to the "South Carolina Exposition and Protest," a federal law could be nullified by a state because the federal government was

(A) created by the states
(B) dependent on the states for taxes
(C) composed of men elected or appointed from the states
(D) limited in its use of power by the Bill of Rights
(E) a temporary organization with annual membership

CONSOLIDATE YOUR KEY ANSWERS HERE

Practice using Answer Sheets. Make ONE mark for each answer. Additional and stray marks may be counted as mistakes. In making corrections erase errors COMPLETELY. Make glossy black marks. To arrive at an accurate estimate of your ability and progress. cover the Correct Answers with a sheet of white paper while you are taking this test.

SAMPLE ANSWER SHEET

CORRECT KEY ANSWERS TO THE PRACTICE QUESTIONS

Now compare your answers with these Correct Key Answers. If your answers differ from these. go back and study the Practice Questions to see where and how you made your mistakes. In doing this, the following Explanatory Answers should prove helpful. They provide concise clarifications of the basic points behind the Key Answers. Even where your Key Answers are the same as ours, go over the explanations carefully because they may be quite useful in helping you pick up extra points on the exam.

1.B	7.A	13.C	19.C	25.C	31.D	37.B	43.D
2.D	8.A	14.C	20.B	26.A	32.E	38.A	44.A
3.E	9.B	15.B	21.A	27.A	33.A	39.C	
4.B	10.C	16.E	22.C	28.C	34.C	40.D	
5.C	11.C	17.B	23.D	29.B	35.C	41.B	
6.A	12.A	18.C	24.B	30.A	36.D	42.C	

```
SCORE  ............................  %
      NO. CORRECT  ÷
      NO. OF QUESTIONS ON THIS TEST
```

TEST I. EXPLANATORY ANSWERS

Here you have the heart of the Question and Answer Method. . .getting help when and where you need it. Where one of your Key Answers differs from ours you have a problem which can easily be remedied by reading the explanation. Then, if you have time, you might be able to pick up points on the exam by reading the other explanations, even where you wrote the Key Answers correctly.

(1)

(B) Shays' Rebellion took place in 1786.

(2)

(D) The Northwest Ordinance provides for the formation of "no less than three nor more than five states" from the territory and that these states would be "on an equal footing with the original states in all respects whatever."

(3)

(E) *The Federalist* was a series of essays by Alexander Hamilton, James Madison, and John Jay, setting forth reasons for the adoption of the new Constitution.

(4)

(B) The increased spirit of democracy led to objection to the Alien and Sedition Acts and the proposals of the Hartford Convention. The cumulative effect was the demise of the Federalists as a political party.

(5)

(C) South Carolina's "Exposition and Protest" was patterned after the Virginia and Kentucky Resolutions and advocated that the Union was formed by compact among sovereign states and could be dissolved at will.

(6)

(A) The treaty provided for the "right of deposit" at New Orleans and free navigation of the Mississippi.

(7)

(A) They felt that they had earned the right to self-government by their part in the war.

(8)

(A) The Alliance of 1778 with France helped provide the margin of victory in the American Revolution.

(9)

(B) The need for prompt action to confirm the Louisiana Purchase made a constitutional amendment impractical. Therefore, Jefferson had to reverse his position and accept a loose interpretation.

(10)

(C) Britain's trade with the newly independent countries of Latin America was of even greater volume than ours. She feared that the return of Spain would mean an end to her trade.

(11)

(C) Nationalism was fostered as a device to defeat Napoleon by urging the subject peoples to demand their own government.

(12)

(A) The graph shows that in 1947 about 24 million families earned less than $5,000, and in 1960 the number had dropped to 19 million. At the same time the families earning over $5,000 increased from about 13 million to over 26 million.

(13)

(C) This group more than doubled. It had an increase of 5 million.

(14)

(C) This principle of the "natural rights of man," formulated by Locke and advocated by Rousseau in France, was written by Thomas Jefferson in the Declaration of Independence.

(15)

(B) This statement is from Lincoln's most famous short speech—the Gettysburg Address.

(16)

(E) This is the Third Amendment of the Bill of Rights.

(17)

(B) The slogan, "Fifty-four forty [54° 40'] or fight," implied that we were unwilling to settle for less than complete control of the Oregon Territory.

(18)

(C) One of the pledges in the original program of the Republican Party was to favor repeal of the Kansas-Nebraska Act.

51339

19

(C) Lincoln had steadfastly maintained that he would not interfere with slavery in the states, but opposed its extension into the territories.

20

(B) In 1860 Lincoln was elected with about 40 percent of the vote. In 1912 Wilson received about 45 percent. Both were elected.

21

(A) Garfield was shot by a rejected job-seeker in 1881. The Pendleton Act of 1883 set up a fair merit system for government employees.

22

(C) The Open Door Policy enabled the United States to invest in other countries' spheres of influence.

23

(D) The United States was too busy at home to look elsewhere.

24

(B) Mahan was a strong advocate of sea power.

25

(C) "Dollar diplomacy" implies a profit motive.

26

(A) Americans living in Hawaii wanted United States control to protect themselves.

27

(A) All the statements are correct.

28

(C) Gompers learned from the earlier failures in union organizing and limited himself to skilled workers.

29

(B) In 1887 Congress passed the Interstate Commerce Act, and in 1890 the Sherman Anti-Trust Act was passed.

30

(A) The United States attempted to avoid both England and France. Since we (New England) existed on trade with both, we could not afford to lose the friendship of either.

31

(D) The Azimuthal Equidistant projection is accurate for Great Circle arcs.

32

(E) Since the Orthographic projection is based on visual perception of a sphere, only one side (hemisphere) can be shown at a time.

33

(A) Mercator projections distort land masses at the upper and lower ends of the map, but compass directions remain fixed.

34

(C) The interruptions in Goode's Interrupted projection occur at points that cut into the sea areas. Thus the oceans cannot be viewed in their entirety.

35

(C) Southern needs for manufactured goods were most usually filled by England, and protective tariffs became a burden to southern planters.

36

(D) Shays' Rebellion was organized in behalf of the debtor classes, which included the farmers.

37

(B) Henry Clay was a "war hawk" in the Congress prior to 1812, and he was called the "Great Compromiser" for his efforts at ameliorating sectional differences by moderating legislation.

38

(A) Both men were "Captains of Industry"—Carnegie in steel, and Rockefeller in oil.

39

(C) The South felt that it had no voice in the government of the Union and thus had to leave.

40

(D) The absence of cash and the inability to get credit forced the planter and former slave into the sharecropper relationship.

41

(B) Most of the homestead lands were held by speculators because of the difficulties of working a homestead.

42

(C) Napoleon wanted to force Britain out of the European trading picture.

43

(D) Farmers, being debtors, favored inflation as a way of wiping out their indebtedness. They reasoned that the return of silver in currency would increase cheap money.

44

(A) South Carolina argued that, since the Union was created by the states, it could be dissolved by them.

PART FOUR

Science

4

This test places a special emphasis on scientific vocabulary and ability to pay close attention to detail and logic. It consists of a selection of passages from the field of natural sciences at the high school level and a number of questions testing a persons's ability to comprehend and to interpret the content of each passage.

INTERPRETATION OF READING MATERIALS IN NATURAL SCIENCE

This test places a special emphasis on scientific vocabulary and ability to pay close attention to detail and logic. It consists of a selection of passages from the field of natural sciences at the high school level and a number of questions testing a persons's ability to comprehend and to interpret the content of each passage.

DIRECTIONS: Read each passage to get the general idea. Then reread the passage more carefully to answer the questions based on the passage. For each question read all choices carefully. Then select the answer you consider correct or most nearly correct. Blacken the answer space corresponding to your best choice, just as you would do on the actual examination.

To show you exactly how to answer this type of natural science question, we give you a representative natural science passage and suggest that you answer the two sample questions based on it. The correct answers are: S1=D; S2=C.

Sample: Influenza travels exactly as fast as man. In oxcart days its progress was slow. In 1918 man could girdle the globe in eight weeks, and that is exactly the time it took influenza to complete its encirclement of the earth. Today, by jet, man moves at higher speed. This modern speed makes influenza's advent unpredictable from day to day. It all means that our control over the disease must be proportionately swifter.

S1. The title below that best expresses the ideas of this paragraph is:
A. Influenza Around the World
B. Influenza Epidemic of 1918
C. Unpredictability of Influenza
D. The Effect of Speed on the Spread of Influenza.

S2. The author states that more adequate control of influenza is necessary nowadays because
A. it may occur at any time
B. it may occur anywhere
C. man carries it about more quickly
D. germs can travel as fast as an airplane.

TEST I. INTERPRETATION OF SCIENCE READINGS

TIME: 25 Minutes. 15 Questions.

DIRECTIONS: Below each of the following passages of natural science reading material you will find one or more incomplete statements about the passage. Select the words or expressions that most satisfactorily complete each statement in accordance with the meaning of the paragraph.

Correct key answers to all these test questions will be found at the end of the test.

Reading Passage

Self-contained diving suits have made it possible for a diver to explore the depths without the local authorities' knowing very much about it. Should he be lucky enough to discover a wreck, a diver can recover the less cumbersome fragments, bronzes, marble, or bits of statuary, without attracting official attention. Today one can indulge in a secret treasure hunt right down to the seabed with the added advantage that it is far harder to keep a watch on sunken treasure than it is to protect excavations on shore. So the modern despoiler is as great a pest to the serious archaeologist at sea as he is on land. In Egypt and Syria he has deprived us of invaluable data. He nearly always ransacks his objective to take away some portable trophy which he thinks valuable, he keeps his treasure house a secret, and we must blame him for the appearance of various objects impossible to date or catalog.

1. The title below that best expresses the ideas of this passage is
   (A) Recovering ships
   (B) Modern diving suits
   (C) The irresponsible explorer
   (D) Cataloging long-lost objects
   (E) Concealing the truth in the Near East.

2. The passage suggests that the author is
   (A) opposed to excavations on shore
   (B) sympathetic to the officials
   (C) sympathetic to the divers
   (D) opposed to investigations in Syria and Egypt
   (E) opposed to the despoilers' cataloging their finds.

3. It is to the amateur archaeologist's advantage that local authorities
   (A) protect his findings on land
   (B) allow him to keep portable treasures

(C) provide catalogs of underwater treasures
(D) are sometimes unaware of his diving activities
(E) are ignorant of the true value of sunken treasures.

Reading Passage

The white man lapsed easily into an Indian. The mountain man's eye had the Indian's alertness, forever watching for the movement of boughs or grasses, for the passage of wildlife downwind, something unexplained floating in a stream, dust stirring in a calm, or the configuration of mere scratches on a cottonwood. His ear would never again hear church bells or the noises of a farm, but, like the Indian's, was tuned to catch any sound in a country where every sound was provisionally a death warning. He dressed like an Indian, in blankets, robes, buckskins, and moccasins. He lived like an Indian in bark huts or skin lodges. He thought like an Indian, propitiating the demons of the wild, making medicine, and consulting the omens.

4. The title below that best expresses the ideas of this passage is
   (A) Signs of an enemy
   (B) In praise of the Indian
   (C) Characteristics of a traitor
   (D) The white man turned Indian
   (E) Disadvantages of Indian life.

5. The author states that the mountain man was
   (A) homesick   (D) alert
   (B) patriotic   (E) learned.
   (C) humble

6. This passage suggests that the Indian is
   (A) careless
   (B) antisocial
   (C) contemptuous of the whites
   (D) a lover of his family
   (E) superstitious.

Reading Passage

We were about a quarter mile away when quiet swept over the colony. A thousand or more heads periscoped. Two thousand eyes glared. Save for our wading, the world's business had stopped. A thousand avian personalities were concentrated on us, and the psychological force of this was terrific. Contingents of homecoming feeders, suddenly aware of four strange specks moving across the lake, would bank violently and speed away. Then the chain reaction began. Every throat in that rookery let go with a concatenation of wild, raspy, terrorized trumpet bursts. With all wings now fully spread and churning, and quadrupling the color mass, the birds began to move as one, and the sky was filled with the sound of judgment day.

7. The title below that best expresses the idea of this passage is
   (A) Our shore birds
   (B) A quiet colony
   (C) Judgment day
   (D) Waiting
   (E) An unwelcome intrusion.

8. The passage indicates that the writer
   (A) was a psychologist
   (B) observed the fear of the flying birds
   (C) was terrified at the sounds
   (D) crossed the lake by boat
   (E) went alone to the rookery.

9. According to the passage, when they first noticed the visitors, the birds of the colony
   (A) flew away
   (B) became very quiet
   (C) churned their wings
   (D) set up a series of cries
   (E) glared at the homecoming birds.

10. The reaction of the visitors to the experience described in this passage was probably one of
    (A) impatience   (D) awe
    (B) fear   (E) sadness.
    (C) anger

Reading Passage

Lumbering in the Northwest in the early days was often a two-fisted business, in which one would say that neither the lumber barons nor the lumberjacks had learned a thing from the wastage, the fires, the boom-and-bust days, and stump counties of eastern history. Nothing, that is, except greatly increased efficiency at whirlwind exploitation. But that was in a cruder age, in the days when labor troubles went to the shooting stage, when pirates on Puget Sound stole whole rafts of timber, when fires burned over forests the size of many a European principality, and when the Forest Service was jeered at and obstructed. Those days are gone. Progressive companies now hire their own trained foresters and follow practical conservation. Well-located lumber towns have become permanent cities with fine schools and churches. Employees are usually married, eat the best food, and own their homes. Fire is fought like the Devil.

11. The title below that best expresses the ideas of this passage is
    (A) Forestry today
    (B) The good old days
    (C) Lessons of history
    (D) Lumber baron and lumberjack
    (E) Improvement in the lumber industry.

12. Early methods of lumbering were
    (A) unplanned   (D) extravagant
    (B) impractical   (E) magnificent.
    (C) pugnacious

Reading Passage

The six year old is about the best example that can be found of that type of inquisitiveness that causes irritated adults to exclaim, "Curiosity killed the cat." To him, the world is a fascinating place to be explored and investigated quite thoroughly, but such a world is bounded by the environment in which he or the people he knows live. It is constantly expanding through new experiences, which bring many eager questions from members of any group of first graders, as each one tries to figure out new relationships—to know and accept his place within the family, the school, and the community—to understand all around him. There are adults who find it quite annoying to be presented with such rank inquisitiveness. But this is no purposeless prying, no idle curiosity! It is that quality, characteristic of the successful adult, inherent in the good citizen—intellectual curiosity.

13. The title below that best expresses the ideas of this passage is
    (A) A new-found world
    (B) New relationships
    (C) Wonders of growth
    (D) Purposeless prying
    (E) Curiosity—six-year-old style.

14. The author states that a successful adult inherently exhibits
    (A) irritation
    (B) questioning
    (C) curiosity
    (D) comprehension of change
    (E) understanding of machines.

15. In this passage the author's attitude toward children is one of
    (A) despair
    (B) confidence
    (C) indifference
    (D) sharp criticism
    (E) exaggerated optimism.

CONSOLIDATE YOUR KEY ANSWERS HERE

Practice using Answer Sheets. Make ONE mark for each answer. Additional and stray marks may be counted as mistakes. In making corrections erase errors COMPLETELY. Make glossy black marks. To arrive at an accurate estimate of your ability and progress, cover the Correct Answers with a sheet of white paper while you are taking this test.

CORRECT ANSWERS TO THE FOREGOING PRACTICE QUESTIONS

Now compare your answers with these Correct Answers to the Practice Questions. If your answers differ from these, go back and study those questions to see where and how you made your mistakes.

1.C	3.D	5.D	7.E	9.B	11.E	13.E	15.B
2.B	4.D	6.E	8.B	10.D	12.D	14.C	

TEST II. INTERPRETATION OF SCIENCE READINGS

TIME: 15 Minutes. 10 Questions.

DIRECTIONS: *Below each of the following passages of natural science reading material you will find one or more incomplete statements about the passage. Select the words or expressions that most satisfactorily complete each statement in accordance with the meaning of the paragraph.*

Correct key answers to all these test questions will be found at the end of the test.

Reading Passage

Observe the dilemma of the fungus: it is a plant, but it possesses no chlorophyl. While all other plants can put the sun's energy to work for them combining the nutrients of ground and air into body structure, the chlorophylless fungus must look elsewhere for an energy source. It finds it in those other plants which, having received their energy free from the sun, relinquish it at some point in their cycle either to other animals (like us humans) or to fungi.

In this search for energy the fungus has become the earth's major source of rot and decay. Wherever you see mold forming on a piece of bread, or a pile of leaves turning to compost, or a blown-down tree becoming pulp on the ground, you are watching a fungus eating. Without fungus action the earth would be piled high with the dead plant life of past centuries. In fact certain plants which contain resins that are toxic to fungi will last indefinitely; specimens of the redwood, for instance, can still be found resting on the forest floor centuries after having been blown down.

1. The title below that best expresses the ideas of this passage is
   (A) Life without cholorophyl
   (B) The source of rot and decay
   (C) The harmful qualities of fungi
   (D) The strange world of the fungus
   (E) Utilization of the sun's energy.

2. The statement ". . . you are watching a fungus eating" is best described as
   (A) figurative
   (B) ironical
   (C) parenthetical
   (D) joking
   (E) contradictory.

3. The author implies that fungi
   (A) are responsible for all the world's rot and decay
   (B) cannot live completely apart from other plants
   (C) attack plants in order to kill them
   (D) are poisonous to resin-producing plants
   (E) can survive indefinitely under favorable conditions.

4. The author uses the word "dilemma" to indicate that
   (A) the fungus is both helpful and harmful in its effects
   (B) no one really understands how a fungus lives
   (C) fungi are not really plants
   (D) the function of chlorophyl in producing energy is a puzzle to scientists
   (E) the fungus seems to have its own biological laws.

Reading Passage

It is here, perhaps, that poetry may best act nowadays as corrective and complementary to science. When science tells us that the galaxy to which our solar system belongs is so enormous that light, traveling at 186,000 miles per second, takes between 60,000 and 100,000 years to cross from one rim to the other of the galaxy, we laymen accept the statement but find it meaningless—beyond the comprehension of heart or mind. When science tells us that the human eye has about 137 million separate "seeing" elements, we are no less paralyzed, intellectually and emotionally. Man is appalled by the immensities and the minuteness which science has disclosed for him. They are indeed unimaginable. But may not poetry be a possible way of mediating them to our imagination?—of scaling them down to imaginative comprehension? Let us remember Perseus, who could not look directly at the nightmare Gorgon without being turned to stone, but could look at her image reflected in the shield the goddess of wisdom lent him.

5. The title below that best expresses the ideas of this passage is
   (A) Poetry and imagination
   (B) A modern Gorgon
   (C) Poetry as a mediator
   (D) The vastness of the universe
   (E) Imaginative man.

6. According to the passage, the average man
   (A) should have a better memory
   (B) is impatient with science
   (C) cannot trust the scientists
   (D) is overwhelmed by the discoveries of science
   (E) does not understand either science or poetry.

7. Perseus was most probably
   (A) a scientist
   (B) a legendary hero
   (C) an early poet
   (D) a horrible creature
   (E) a minor god.

8. This passage is chiefly developed by means of
   (A) examples   (D) definition
   (B) cause and effect   (E) anecdotes.
   (C) narration

Reading Passage

Hail is at once the cruelest weapon in Nature's armory, and the most incalculable. It can destroy one farmer's prospects of a harvest in a matter of seconds; it can leave his neighbor's unimpaired. It can slay a flock of sheep (it has killed children before now) in one field, while the sun continues to shine in the next. To the harassed meteorologist its behavior is even more Machiavellian than that of an ice storm. Difficult as it undoubtedly is for him to forecast the onset of an ice storm, he knows pretty well what its course and duration will be once it has started; just about all he can do with a hailstone is to measure the size of the stones—and they have a habit of melting as soon as he gets his hands on them. He is not even too sure any more about the way in which hail forms—and until he knows this, of course, he isn't likely to stumble upon any very satisfactory prognostic rules.

9. The title below that best expresses the ideas of this passage is
   (A) Forecasting ice storms
   (B) The way that hail forms
   (C) The harassed meteorologist
   (D) The unpredictability of hailstorms
   (E) Hail—the killer.

10. As used in the passage, the word "prognostic" (last line) most nearly means
    (A) restraining   (D) foretelling
    (B) breakable   (E) regular.
    (C) day-by-day

CONSOLIDATE YOUR KEY ANSWERS HERE

Practice using Answer Sheets. Make ONE mark for each answer. Additional and stray marks may be counted as mistakes. In making corrections erase errors COMPLETELY. Make glossy black marks. To arrive at an accurate estimate of your ability and progress, cover the Correct Answers with a sheet of white paper while you are taking this test.

CORRECT ANSWERS TO THE FOREGOING PRACTICE QUESTIONS

Now compare your answers with these Correct Answers to the Practice Questions. If your answers differ from these, go back and study those questions to see where and how you made your mistakes.

1. D	3. B	5. C	7. B	9. D
2. A	4. E	6. D	8. A	10. D

TEST III. INTERPRETATION OF SCIENCE READINGS

TIME: 15 Minutes. 10 Questions.

DIRECTIONS: Below each of the following passages of natural science reading material you will find one or more incomplete statements about the passage. Select the words or expressions that most satisfactorily complete each statement in accordance with the meaning of the paragraph.

Correct key answers to all these test questions will be found at the end of the test.

Reading Passage

Lamarck's theory of evolution, although at one time pretty generally discredited, has now been revived by a number of prominent biologists. According to Lamarck, changes in an animal occur through use and disuse. Organs which are specially exercised become specially developed. The need for this special exercise arises from the conditions in which the animal lives; thus a changing environment, by making different demands on an animal, changes the animal. The giraffe, for instance, has developed his long neck in periods of relative scarcity by endeavoring to browse on higher and higher branches of trees. On the other hand, organs that are never exercised tend to disappear altogether. The eyes of animals that have taken to living in the dark grow smaller and smaller, generation after generation, until the late descendants are born eyeless.

The great assumption made by this theory is that the effects of personal, individual effort are transmitted to the offspring of that individual. This is a doctrine that is very much in dispute among modern biologists.

1. The title below that best expresses the ideas of this passage is
   (A) Why Lamarck's theory is valid
   (B) A changing environment
   (C) The modern biologist
   (D) The Lamarckian theory
   (E) An attack on Lamarck's theory.

2. According to the passage, most scientists today regard Lamarck's theory of evolution as
   (A) controversial   (D) important
   (B) disproved   (E) misunderstood.
   (C) accepted

3. The author's chief purpose in writing this passage was to
   (A) discredit other theories of evolution
   (B) indicate how heredity influences environment
   (C) show why animals become extinct
   (D) explain a concept of biology
   (E) encourage the acceptance of Lamarck's theory.

4. Which pattern do the ideas of this passage follow?
   (A) general to particular, only
   (B) particular to general, only
   (C) general to particular to general
   (D) particular to particular to general
   (E) general to general to particular.

Reading Passage

The problems we face in conserving natural resources are laborious and complex. The preservation of even small bits of marshlands or woods representing the last stands of irreplaceable biotic communities is interwoven with the red tape of law, conflicting local interests, the overlapping jurisdiction of governmental and private conservation bodies, and an intricate tangle of economic and social considerations. During the time spent in resolving these factors, it often happens that the area to be preserved is swallowed up. Even more formidable is the broad-scale conservation problem raised by the spread of urban belts in such places as the northeastern part of the United States. The pressures of human growth are so acute in such instances that they raise issues which would tax the wisdom of Solomon.

5. The title below that best expresses the ideas of this passage is
   (A) Conservation's last stand
   (B) The encroaching suburbs
   (C) Hindrances to conservation
   (D) How to preserve our resources
   (E) An insoluble problem.

6. The most perplexing problem of conservationists is the one involving
   (A) population growth
   (B) public indifference
   (C) favorable legislation
   (D) division of authority
   (E) increased taxes.

7. The author's attitude toward the situation he describes is
   (A) optimistic   (D) illogical
   (B) realistic   (E) combative.
   (C) bitter

Reading Passage

It is perfectly clear that nature had no intention that any of her children would be monkeying around with radioactive elements, else she would have provided us with some sixth sense to protect us from running headlong into dangerous amounts of radiation. No, she evidently expected us to take our daily dose of cosmic and earth's radiation as we take the cuts and bruises of ordinary living. The idea of getting them out in the form of concentrated extracts was man's, and since the day when the Curies isolated radium from pitchblende, men have had to extend their perceptive capacities by means of various devices.

The earliest device, which indeed first aroused the Curies to pioneer the wilderness of radioactivity, was the fogging of photographic emulsion. Today it is still a very practical method of detecting radiation and is used universally by people working with radioactivity. Film, of course, is no good as a warning device. It can merely tell you later, when developed and compared to a standard, how much radiation you have been exposed to.

8. The title that best expresses the ideas of this passage is
   (A) Our sixth sense
   (B) The Curies' discovery
   (C) Detecting radiation
   (D) The wilderness of radioactivity
   (E) Radioactive elements.

9. The author implies that ever since the Curies isolated radium it has been necessary for scientists to
   (A) avoid radioactive elements
   (B) protect themselves from cosmic radiation
   (C) learn more about the art of photography
   (D) extend their use of concentrated extracts
   (E) be careful about overdoses of radiation.

10. The paragraph which follows this selection most probably deals with
   (A) further dangers in radioactive materials
   (B) a second device for measuring radioactivity
   (C) an explanation of the use of films as warning devices
   (D) the sources of pitchblende
   (E) the standard used to measure radioactivity.

CONSOLIDATE YOUR KEY ANSWERS HERE

CORRECT ANSWERS TO THE FOREGOING PRACTICE QUESTIONS

Now compare your answers with these Correct Answers to the Practice Questions. If your answers differ from these, go back and study those questions to see where and how you made your mistakes.

| 1.D | 3.D | 5.C | 7.B | 9.E |
| 2.A | 4.C | 6.A | 8.C | 10.B |

TEST IV. INTERPRETATION OF SCIENCE READINGS

TIME: 15 Minutes. 11 Questions.

DIRECTIONS: Below each of the following passages of natural science reading material you will find one or more incomplete statements about the passage. Select the words or expressions that most satisfactorily complete each statement in accordance with the meaning of the paragraph.

Correct key answers to all these test questions will be found at the end of the test.

Reading Passage

Throughout extensive areas of the tropics the tall and stately primeval forest has given way to eroded land, scrub and the jumble of secondary growth. Just as the virgin forests of Europe and North America were laid low by man's improvidence, so those of the tropics are now vanishing—only their destruction may be encompassed in decades instead of centuries. A few authorities hold that, except for government reserves, the earth's great rain forests may vanish within a generation. The economic loss will be incalculable, for the primary rain forests are rich sources of timber (mahogany, teak) and such by-products as resins, gums, cellulose, camphor and rattans. No one, indeed, can compute their resources, for of the thousands of species that compose the forest cover, there are only a few whose physical and chemical properties have been studied with a view to commercial use.

Most important of all, the primeval rain forest is a reservoir of specimens, a dynamic center of evolution whence the rest of the world's plant life has been continually enriched with new forms. These extensive reserves must be defended from the acquisitive hand of man, whose ruthless ax would expose them to the ravages of sun and rain.

1. The title below that best expresses the idea of this passage is
   (A) Scene of evolution
   (B) Virgin forests today
   (C) Products of the rain forests
   (D) Importance of the rain forests
   (E) Man's waste of natural resources.

2. Concerning the rain forests, man still lacks knowledge of their
   (A) rate of disappearance
   (B) exact geographic locations
   (C) value as sources of timber
   (D) need for protective foliage
   (E) potential commercial development.

3. The resources of the rain forests are
   (A) incalculable
   (B) purely chemical
   (C) somewhat limited
   (D) uncommercial
   (E) of interest only to scientists.

4. The second sentence of the passage suggests that
   (A) man has been unlucky
   (B) no virgin forests have been replanted
   (C) man has become more wasteful
   (D) tropical rain forests have vanished
   (E) forests in North America were destroyed in a period of ten years.

5. The primary reason for conservation of the great rain forests is that they
   (A) are areas of botanical evolution
   (B) are not ready for man's ruthless ax
   (C) are the chief source of income for governments
   (D) provide major sources of material for chemical industries
   (E) need further development before they can be utilized commercially.

6. As used in the passage, the word "primeval" (second paragraph, first line) means
   (A) of first importance (D) untouched
   (B) commercial (E) thick.
   (C) gorgeous

7. The ideas of the author would probably be most strongly supported by
   (A) lumber company representatives
   (B) conservationists and botanists
   (C) chemical manufacturers
   (D) government representatives
   (E) the "man on the street."

Reading Passage

All museum adepts are familiar with examples of *ostrakoi*, the oystershells used in balloting. As a matter of fact, these "oystershells" are usually shards of pottery, conveniently glazed to enable the voter to express his wishes in writing. In the Agora a great number of these have come to light, bearing the thrilling name, Themistocles. Into rival jars were dropped the ballots for or against his banishment. On account of the huge vote taken on that memorable day, it was to be expected that many ostrakoi would be found, but the interest of this collection is that a number of these ballots are inscribed in an *identical* handwriting. There is nothing mysterious about it! The Boss was on the job, then as now. He prepared these ballots and voters cast them—no doubt for the consideration of an obol or two. *The ballot box was stuffed.*

How is the glory of the American boss diminished! A vile imitation, he. His methods as old as Time!

8. The title below that best expresses the ideas of this passage is
   (A) An odd method of voting
   (B) Themistocles, an early dictator
   (C) Democracy in the past
   (D) Political trickery—past and present
   (E) The diminishing American politician.

9. An obol, as used in the passage, is evidently
   (A) an oystershell
   (B) a Greek coin
   (C) a promise of bread
   (D) a complimentary remark
   (E) an appointive public office.

10. The author suggests that the verdict against Themistocles was to a certain extent
    (A) justified (D) unpopular
    (B) mysterious (E) unimportant.
    (C) predetermined

11. The tone of the last paragraph is
    (A) matter-of-fact (D) insincere
    (B) self-righteous (E) sarcastic.
    (C) complimentary

CONSOLIDATE YOUR KEY ANSWERS HERE

Practice using Answer Sheets. Make ONE mark for each answer. Additional and stray marks may be counted as mistakes. In making corrections erase errors COMPLETELY. Make glossy black marks. To arrive at an accurate estimate of your ability and progress, cover the Correct Answers with a sheet of white paper while you are taking this test.

CORRECT ANSWERS TO THE FOREGOING PRACTICE QUESTIONS

Now compare your answers with these Correct Answers to the Practice Questions. If your answers differ from these, go back and study those questions to see where and how you made your mistakes.

1.D	3.A	5.A	7.B	9.B	11.E
2.E	4.C	6.D	8.D	10.C	

TEST V. INTERPRETATION OF SCIENCE READINGS

TIME: 15 Minutes. 10 Questions.

DIRECTIONS: *Below each of the following passages of natural science reading material you will find one or more incomplete statements about the passage. Select the words or expressions that most satisfactorily complete each statement in accordance with the meaning of the paragraph.*

Correct Answers for this Test are consolidated after the last question.

Reading Passage

The Sky Survey is the first comprehensive mapping of the universe ever attempted. The end result of this gigantic project will be a sky atlas of 1,870 photographs showing celestial objects to a depth and space of some 600 million light-years. It is expected that this atlas will provide a guide for astronomers' research for nearly a century to come. Objects discovered for the first time in the course of this mapping of the heavens range from tiny planetoids to a thousand clusters of nebulae infinitely far out in space. Sky Survey astronomers have made scores of important discoveries, including the fact that our universe is probably twice as old and eight times as voluminous as previously believed. The Sky Survey has found that all stellar systems beyond the earth's galaxy are twice as far as previous knowledge indicates, and that the universe is probably more than 4 billion years old instead of 2 billion.

1. The title below that best expresses the ideas of this passage is
   (A) To the stars and back
   (B) Our stellar system
   (C) Planetoids to nebulae
   (D) A survey of the stars
   (E) New theories of the universe.

2. The importance of the sky atlas is that it will
   (A) contain nearly 2,000 photographs
   (B) prove the universe to be eight times as large as previously believed
   (C) furnish the basis for further study of the universe
   (D) show celestial objects to a depth of 600 light-years
   (E) prove the universe is 4 billion years old.

3. Which statement concerning the Sky Survey is true?
   (A) It is the only mapping of the universe ever attempted.
   (B) It is the most extensive undertaking of its kind.
   (C) It will soon be outdated.
   (D) Its purpose is to disprove present theories concerning the universe.
   (E) It has collected many three-dimensional photographs.

Reading Passage

Windstorms have recently established a record which meteorologists hope will not be equaled for many years to come. Disastrous tornadoes along with devastating typhoons and hurricanes have cost thousands of lives and left property damage totaling far into the millions. The prominence these storms have held in the news has led many people to ask about the difference between the three. Is a typhoon the same as a hurricane? Is a tornado the same as a typhoon? Basically, there is no difference. All three consist of wind rotating counterclockwise (in the Northern Hemisphere) at a tremendous velocity around a low-pressure center. However, each type does have its own definite characteristics. Of the three the tornado is certainly the most treacherous. The Weather Bureau can, with some degree of accuracy, forecast the typhoon and the hurricane; it is impossible to determine where or when the tornado will strike. And out of the three, if one had a choice, perhaps it would be safer to choose to withstand the hurricane.

4. The title below that best expresses the ideas of this passage is
   (A) Recent storms
   (B) Record-breaking storms
   (C) Predicting windstorms
   (D) Treacherous windstorms
   (E) Wind velocity and direction.

S1261

5. Which is *not* common to all of the storms mentioned?
   (A) fairly accurate forecasting
   (B) violently rotating wind
   (C) high property damage
   (D) loss of human lives
   (E) public interest.

6. The author indicates that
   (A) typhoons cannot be forecast
   (B) the Southern Hemisphere is free from hurricanes
   (C) typhoons are more destructive than hurricanes
   (D) hurricanes are not really dangerous
   (E) tornadoes occur around a low-pressure center.

Reading Passage

We now know that what constitutes practically all of matter is empty space; relatively enormous voids in which revolve with lightning velocity infinitesimal particles so utterly small that they have never been seen or photographed. The existence of these particles has been demonstrated by mathematical physicists and their operations determined by ingenious laboratory experiments. It was not until 1911 that experiments by Sir Ernest Rutherford revealed the architecture of the mysterious atom. Moseley, Bohr, Fermi, Millikan, Compton, Urey, and others have also worked on the problem. Matter is composed of molecules whose average diameter is about 1/125 millionth of an inch. Molecules are composed of atoms so small that about five million could be placed in a row on the period at the end of this sentence. Long thought to be the ultimate, indivisible constituent of matter, the atom has been found to consist roughly of a proton, the positive electrical element in the atomic nucleus, surrounded by electrons, the negative electric elements swirling about the proton.

7. The title below that best expresses the ideas of this passage is
   (A) The work of Sir Ernest Rutherford
   (B) Empty spaces in matter
   (C) Atoms, molecules and space
   (D) Notable scientists
   (E) The structure of matter.

8. The center of the atom, according to this passage,
   (A) contains one electron
   (B) has not yet been seen by the naked eye
   (C) was seen as early as 1911
   (D) is about the size of a period
   (E) might be photographed under microscopes.

9. The paragraph indicates that the atom
   (A) is the smallest particle
   (B) is very little larger than a molecule
   (C) has been seen
   (D) is composed of several particles
   (E) is empty space.

10. Scientists agree that molecules are
    (A) huge compared with electrons
    (B) voids
    (C) the most mysterious particles
    (D) not divisible
    (E) not basically composed of electric elements.

CONSOLIDATE YOUR KEY ANSWERS HERE

Practice using Answer Sheets. Make ONE mark for each answer. Additional and stray marks may be counted as mistakes. In making corrections erase errors COMPLETELY. Make glossy black marks. To arrive at an accurate estimate of your ability and progress, cover the Correct Answers with a sheet of white paper while you are taking this test.

CORRECT ANSWERS TO THE FOREGOING PRACTICE QUESTIONS

Now compare your answers with these Correct Answers to the Practice Questions. If your answers differ from these, go back and study those questions to see where and how you made your mistakes.

1.D	3.B	5.A	7.E	9.D
2.C	4.D	6.E	8.B	10.A

TEST VI. INTERPRETATION OF SCIENCE READINGS

TIME: 15 Minutes. 10 Questions.

DIRECTIONS: Below each of the following passages of natural science reading material you will find one or more incomplete statements about the passage. Select the words or expressions that most satisfactorily complete each statement in accordance with the meaning of the paragraph.

Correct key answers to all these test questions will be found at the end of the test.

Reading Passage

Many men can be of greatest service to a company by remaining in the laboratory. A single outstanding discovery may have a far greater impact on the company's profit picture five years hence than the activities of even the most able administrator. It is simply good sense—and good economics—to allow qualified researchers to continue their work. Granting these men maximum freedom to explore their scientific ideas is also eminently good sense.

Some years ago, the theory was rampant that after the age of about 40 the average researcher began losing his creative spark. The chance of his making a major discovery was believed to drop off sharply. Hence, there really wasn't much point to encouraging a man of 45 or 50 to do research.

In recent years, however, this theory has fallen into wide disrepute. Companies find that many researchers continue to be highly productive throughout their careers. There is every reason to allow these men to continue their pioneering work.

Companies are also convinced that the traditional guideposts in establishing salaries are not completely valid. In former years, the size of a man's paycheck was determined primarily by such factors as the number of men he supervised or the size of his annual budget. On this basis, the researcher—however brilliant—who had perhaps one assistant and never spent much money made an extremely poor showing. Companies now realize that the two very important criteria that must also be considered are a man's actual contributions to the company and his creative potential.

In today's era of scientific manpower shortages, companies have more reason than ever to encourage scientists to do the work for which they are most qualified. They also have greater reason than ever to provide within the laboratory the environment in which the creative processes of research can be carried out most effectively.

1. According to the passage, research workers need
   (A) less supervision by administrators
   (B) good working conditions
   (C) smaller budgets
   (D) more assistants
   (E) equal share in the company's profits.

2. The author implies that the administrators are
   (A) underpaid
   (B) envious of the research workers
   (C) well appreciated by the company
   (D) able to hire sufficient research workers
   (E) participating actively in research projects.

3. Which factor once helped to determine the salary a research worker received?
   (A) his contributions to research
   (B) the profits made on his discovery
   (C) administrative considerations
   (D) his creativeness
   (E) the number of administrators.

4. The author's purpose in writing this passage is to
   (A) describe a significant development in industry
   (B) explore scientific ideas
   (C) gain administrative responsibility for research workers
   (D) encourage further education for research workers
   (E) defend the company administrators.

S1261

5. According to the passage, companies should make the most effective use of research workers because
   (A) otherwise America's scientific future is in danger
   (B) research work is more important than any other kind of work
   (C) the research worker's productive period is short
   (D) research personnel are in short supply
   (E) the public needs must be satisfied.

6. The author's tone in the passage is one of
   (A) fierce indignation   (D) sarcasm
   (B) complaint   (E) unconcern.
   (C) calm appraisal

7. Which idea is implied by the passage?
   (A) A company must adapt itself to the times.
   (B) A company's profits really are not as important as good human relations.
   (C) A company's annual budget is unnecessary.
   (D) Men above 40 are a poor employment risk.
   (E) Most research workers are brilliant.

Reading Passage
   In the ordinary course of nature, the great beneficent changes come slowly and silently. The noisy changes, for the most part, mean violence and disruption. The roar of storms and tornadoes, the explosions of volcanoes, the crash of thunder, are the result of a sudden break in the equipoise of the elements; from a condition of comparative repose and silence they become fearfully swift and audible. The still small voice is the voice of life and growth and perpetuity . . . In the history of a nation it is the same.

8. The title below that best expresses the ideas of this passage is
   (A) Upsetting nature's balance
   (B) Repose and silence
   (C) The voice of life and growth
   (D) Nature's intelligence
   (E) The violent elements.

9. As used in the passage, the word "equipoise" (line 6) most nearly means
   (A) stress   (D) slowness
   (B) balance   (E) condition.
   (C) course

10. The author implies that growth and perpetuity in nature and in history are the result of
    (A) quiet changes
    (B) a period of silence
    (C) undiscovered action
    (D) storms and tornadoes
    (E) violence and disruptions.

CONSOLIDATE YOUR KEY ANSWERS HERE

Practice using Answer Sheets. Make ONE mark for each answer. Additional and stray marks may be counted as mistakes. In making corrections erase errors COMPLETELY. Make glossy black marks. To arrive at an accurate estimate of your ability and progress, cover the Correct Answers with a sheet of white paper while you are taking this test.

	A	B	C	D	E
1					
2					
3					
4					
5					
6					
7					
8					
9					
10					

CORRECT ANSWERS TO THE FOREGOING PRACTICE QUESTIONS

Now compare your answers with these Correct Answers to the Practice Questions. If your answers differ from these, go back and study those questions to see where and how you made your mistakes.

1.B	3.C	5.D	7.A	9.B
2.C	4.A	6.C	8.C	10.A

NATURAL SCIENCE GLOSSARY

This is some of the language you're likely to see on your examination. You may not need to know all the words in this carefully prepared glossary, but if even a few appear, you'll be that much ahead of your competitors. Perhaps the greater benefit from this list is the frame of mind it can create for you. Without reading a lot of technical text you'll steep yourself in just the right atmosphere for high test marks.

This glossary was created to help you master some of the key words you will meet in the Natural Science section of the test. Generally, the test deals with four natural sciences: astronomy, biology, chemistry, and physics. You should know that astronomy is the study of celestial bodies, biology the study of living things, chemistry the study of the composition of different kinds of matter and the changes that happen to them, and physics the study of the actions of objects and the reasons behind their actions.

In the glossary, you will usually find a science in parenthesis after the word. This means that the word is by and large identified with that science. That does not mean that the word might not be used in other sciences, though. The word *element* refers to a chemical element and is used, of course, in connection with chemistry. But uranium is an element which is most important in nuclear fission, which is usually considered part of the field of physics.

You will notice that certain words or phrases have been italicized. These italicized words are defined in the glossary.

[A]

absolute zero   (physics) The lowest temperature to which a gas can get. This is 460 degrees below zero on the *Fahrenheit* scale and 273 degrees below zero on the *centigrade* scale.

acceleration   (physics) A change in the speed of an object. If the object goes faster, this is called positive acceleration. If the object goes slower, it is called negative acceleration.

acid   (chemistry) A *compound* that dissolves in water, has a sour taste, and changes blue *litmus paper* to red.

alchemy (chemistry) The *theory* that less valuable metals can be transformed into gold or silver. This idea, popular during the Middle Ages, was false, but the *experiments* of alchemists laid the foundation of modern *chemistry*.

alkali (chemistry) A *base* that dissolves in water, has a bitter taste, and changes red *litmus paper* to blue.

alkaline (chemistry) The adjective form of *alkali*.

ampere (physics) A measurement of the *velocity* of electric current. It was named after a French scientist, Andre Marie Ampère.

Ampère, Andre Marie (physics) A French scientist (1775–1836) whose work and *theory* laid the foundation for the science of electrodynamics. His name lives on in the electrical measurement *ampere*, and its abbreviation, amp.

amphipods (biology) A *crustacean* group that includes sand fleas.

anatomy (biology) The study of the structure of living things. Usually anatomy refers to the structure of the human body.

anemone (biology) A sea animal that resembles the flower of the same name.

aphid (biology) A small insect which is destructive to crops. A fluid produced by aphids is eaten by ants.

aquatic (biology) An adjective referring to water, such as "aquatic sports" (diving, swimming, etc.)

Aristotle (biology) An ancient Greek philosopher whose active mind pondered all aspects of life and its processes. He is often called the "Father of Biology."

asteroids (astronomy) Small *planet*-like bodies that orbit around the sun.

astrology (astronomy) A false *theory* that the position of the stars, sun, moon and planets influence people's lives. Although this is false, the study of astrology was most helpful to the development of *astronomy*.

astronomer (astronomy) A person who studies the movements of *celestial* bodies.

astronomy The study of the movements of *celestial* bodies. This is a major science.

atmosphere (general) The air mass surrounding the earth.

atom (physics and chemistry) A small particle of matter. See *atomic energy*. Once it was thought that the atom was the smallest particle of matter that existed, but now it is known that atoms are made up of *protons, neutrons* and *electrons*.

atomic energy (physics) Power released when *atoms* are split or united. This is also called *nuclear* energy. Also see *nuclear fission* and *nuclear fusion*.

[B]

bacteria (biology) Tiny *organisms* with one *cell*.

bacteriology (biology) The study of *bacteria*. Bacteriology is a branch of *biology*.

base (chemistry) A compound that can combine with an *acid* to make a *salt*.

biochemistry (biology and chemistry) The study of the chemical makeup of *organisms*. This science is a branch of both *chemistry* and *biology*.

biology The study of living things. This is a major science.

botany (biology) The study of plant life. Botany is a branch of *biology*.

Brahe, Tycho (astronomy) A Danish *astronomer* (1546–1601) who made the first systematic study of the movement of *celestial* bodies. He is often referred to only as Tycho.

[C]

carbohydrate (biology) A food substance made up of *carbon, hydrogen* and *oxygen*.

carbon (chemistry) An important chemical *element*.

carbon dioxide (chemistry) A gas made up of *carbon* and *oxygen*.

celestial (astronomy) An adjective referring to the sky.

cell (biology) The basic and smallest part of living things.

centigrade (physics) A system of measurement of temperature. On the centigrade scale, the freezing point of water is zero degrees. The boiling point of water is 100 degrees. Another generally used temperature measurement is the *Fahrenheit* scale.

chemistry The study of the composition of different kinds of matter and the changes that happen to them. This is a major science.

chlorophyll (biology) The green coloring matter in the cells of living plants, caused by sunlight. Chlorophyll is the means by which all regular absorption and digestion of plant food is made.

chromosome (biology) The part of *cells* that determines heredity. Chromosomes contain *genes*.

colloid (chemistry) A substance that does not pass through *membranes* very quickly and may not pass through them at all.

compound (chemistry) The combining of two or more *elements* into a single unit.

conduction (physics) The process by which heat is carried from *molecule* to molecule.

conservation of energy (chemistry) The idea that *energy* changes its form but cannot be created or destroyed.

conservation of matter (chemistry) The idea that matter can change its form but cannot be created or destroyed.

constellation (astronomy) A particular grouping of stars.

copepod (biology) A small *crustacean* which is in the *plankton* family.

Copernicus, Nicholas (astronomy) A Polish astronomer (1473–1543) who put forth the idea that the earth moved through space. It was generally believed in this time that the earth was the center of the *universe* and did not move through space at all.

cosmic year   (astronomy) The time it takes the sun to go around its *galaxy*.

crop rotation   (biology) A method by which crops in an area are changed each year. This helps maintain the *fertility* of the soil.

crustacean   (biology) A group of *aquatic* animals with a hard covering. They are often called "shellfish."

crystal   (chemistry) The form many inanimate objects take.

[D]

Dalton, John   (physics) An English scientist (1766–1844) who set forth the idea that matter was made up of *atoms*.

Darwin, Charles   (biology) The English scientist (1809–1883) who developed a *theory* of *evolution*.

deforestation   (biology) The process by which land is cleared of forests.

dorso-ventral   (biology) An adjective referring to the dorsal vertebrae. These are a set of bones which are found in the spinal column of the human body near the chest.

[E]

eclipse   (astronomy) The blotting out of light when one *celestial* object moves in front of another celestial object. When the moon comes between the earth and the sun it casts a shadow or an eclipse on part of the earth. During this time, the sun cannot be seen on that part of the earth. This is known as a *solar eclipse*. When the earth comes between the sun and the moon, it casts a shadow on the moon. The moon cannot be seen during this time. This is a *lunar eclipse*.

Einstein, Albert   (physics) A German scientist (1879–1955) who lived the last years of his life in the United States. His *theories* changed the field of *physics*. He, more than any other scientist, was responsible for *nuclear fission*.

electron   (physics) The smallest electrical charge known. It is part of every *atom*. See *proton* and *neutron*.

electronics   (physics) The study of the motion of *electrons*.

element   (chemistry) One of 102 known basic substances. These substances, or combinations of them, make up all matter as far as is known.

embryology   (biology) The study of the early development of *organisms*, usually plant and animal.

energy   (physics) The capacity to do *work*.

enzyme   (biology) An *organic* substance that acts as an agent of change within cells.

eugenics   (biology) A system it is thought will improve the human race by mating so-called superior men and women.

evolution, theory of (biology) Usually refers to *Darwin's theory* that living things change from generation to generation. Furthermore, the living things that survive, according to Darwin, manage to do so because they have acquired certain characteristics that make them more powerful or adaptable than others of their kind.

evaporation (biology and chemistry) The process by which liquids and solids change to gases.

experiment (general) A test to see if an idea is true or false.

[F]

Fahrenheit (physics) The system of measurement of temperature which is generally used in the United States. It was developed by Gabriel Fahrenheit (1686–1736), a German scientist. On the Fahrenheit scale, 32 degrees is the freezing point of water and 98.6 degrees is the average temperature of the human body. Another widely used temperature measurement is the *centigrade* scale.

Faraday, Michael (physics) An English scientist (1791–1867) who discovered electricity could move through metal by the use of a magnet.

fertility (biology) The ability to reproduce. See *reproduction*.

force (physics) That which stops or creates motion, or changes the *velocity* of motion.

friction (physics) The resistance objects have when they are moved across other objects.

fungi (biology) A group of simple plants. Fungi do not have any leaves, flowers or color. Because they have no *chlorophyll*, they must feed on plants, animals or decaying matter.

fungicides (biology) Chemicals which kill *fungi*.

[G]

galaxy (astronomy) A grouping of stars. Our sun is a star in the galaxy called the Milky Way.

Galileo (astronomy and physics) An Italian scientist (1564–1642) who made many contributions to science. He discovered that objects of different weights and shapes fall to the ground at the same rate of speed, attracted by *gravity*. He was a strong believer in *Copernicus'* theory that the earth moved in space and was persecuted for this belief.

gene (biology) A part of the *cell* found in the chromosome. Genes determine the traits of *heredity*.

genetics (biology) The study of the differences and similarities between living things and those living things that have reproduced them. See *reproduction*.

geology   (general) The study of how the earth has changed since its beginning.

gravitation   (physics and astronomy) The tendency of objects in space to move towards each other.

gravity   (physics and astronomy) Usually the tendency of smaller objects to move towards the earth.

[H]

Harvey, William   (biology) An English scientist (1578–1657) who discovered the way blood moves through the body.

heat   (physics) The measurement of *kinetic energy*.

hemoglobin   (biology) A substance that gives blood its red color.

heredity   (biology) The way traits are carried from generation to generation.

hormone   (biology) An *organic* substance produced by the body. Hormones are responsible for many bodily functions.

hydrogen   (chemistry) One of the most important chemical *elements*.

hypothesis   (general) An unproved explanation of something that has happened or might happen.

[I]

inorganic   (biology) An adjective meaning "not organic." See *organic*.

insecticides   (biology) Chemical combinations used to destroy harmful insects.

interstellar   (astronomy) An adjective meaning "between the stars."

isotopes   (physics) Atoms that belong to the same chemical element, but are different in weight or mass.

[K]

Kepler, Johannes   (astronomy) A German *astronomer* (1571–1630) who made important discoveries about the *orbits* of *planets*.

kinetic energy   (physics) *Energy* that is in motion. The motion of the baseball between the pitcher's hand and the catcher's glove is an example of kinetic energy. See *potential energy*.

Koch, Robert   (biology) A German doctor (1843–1910) who studied bacteria. He and *Louis Pasteur* are considered the founders of the science of *bacteriology*.

[L]

Lamarck, Chevalier de (biology) A French scientist (1744–1829) who developed a *theory* of *evolution*. See *Darwin*.

Lavoisier, Antoine (chemistry) A French scientist (1743–1794) who made important discoveries concerning fire and *conservation of matter*.

light year (astronomy) The distance it takes light to travel through *interstellar* space in one year.

Linnaeus, Carolus (biology) A Swedish scientist (1707–1778) best-known for developing a system to name animals and plants.

litmus paper (chemistry) A special paper used by chemists to test for *acid* and *alkalies*.

lunar (astronomy) An adjective referring to the moon. A lunar *eclipse* is an eclipse of the moon. See *solar*.

[M]

marine (biology) An adjective meaning "of the sea." Example: "Fish are a form of marine life."

molecule (physics and chemistry) A basic unit of matter made up of *atoms*.

mechanics (physics) The study of the effect force has on moving or motionless bodies. This is a branch of *physics*.

membrane (biology) Soft, thin sheet of tissue in an *organism*. A membrane acts as a wall between two different parts of the organism, or it covers a particular part of the organism.

Mendel, Gregor Johann (biology) An Austrian monk and scientist (1822–1844) who made important discoveries concerning *heredity*.

metabolism (biology) The process used by all living *organisms* to change food into tissue and *energy*.

mercury (chemistry) An important chemical *element*.

meteorology (general) A science that studies the weather and the *atmosphere*.

mollusks (biology) A family of animals usually found in water. Mollusks have no bones. Examples of mollusks are snails, oysters, and octopuses.

mutation (biology) A change from the parents in an offspring. If a rat was born with no tail although its parents had tails, this change would be a mutation.

[N]

nebula (astronomy) A cloudy and gaseous mass found in *interstellar* space.

neutron (physics and chemistry) A small particle that is part of the *atom* and has no electrical charge. See *electron* and *proton*.

Newton, Isaac   (physics and astronomy) An English scientist (1642–1727) who made major discoveries in *astronomy* and *physics*. His most important work was in his study of *gravitation* and *optics*.

nuclear   (physics) An adjective referring to the *nucleus* of the *atom*.

nuclear fission   (physics) The splitting of an *atom* in order to produce *energy*.

nuclear fusion   (physics) The joining together of light-weight *atoms* resulting in the releasing of *energy*.

nucleus   (physics and chemistry) The center or core of an object, necessary to maintain human life.

[O]

observatory   (astronomy) A specially constructed building containing one or more telescopes for observation of the heavens.

optics   (physics) The study of light and its effect. Optics is a branch of *physics*.

orbit   (astronomy) The route that an object in space (such as the moon) takes around another body (such as the earth).

organic   (biology) An adjective referring to living things. See *inorganic*.

organism   (biology) Living things, such as people, plants or animals.

oxide   (chemistry) A compound made up of *oxygen* and another *element*. Water, for example, is a compound made up of 2 *atoms* of *hydrogen* for each atom of oxygen.

oxygen   (chemistry) A very important chemical element. Oxygen, a gaseous element, makes up about 20% of air and is the supporter of ordinary combustion.

[P]

Pasteur, Louis   (biology) A French scientist (1822–1895) who made major discoveries in *chemistry* and *biology*, especially in the control of many diseases. He and Robert Koch were the founders of the science of *bacteriology*.

physics   The study of the action of objects and the reasons behind these actions.

phytogeographic map   (biology) A map showing plant life.

Planck, Max   (physics) A German scientist (1858–1947) who did notable work in *thermodynamics*.

planet   (astronomy) A large body that moves around the sun. The earth is a planet.

plankton   (biology) A group of sea life—both plant and animal—which drifts with tides and currents. Jellyfish are an example of plankton.

potential energy   (physics) *Energy* that is available for use. The baseball in the pitcher's hand is an example of potential energy. It becomes *kinetic energy* when it is thrown.

Priestley, Joseph (chemistry) The English chemist (1738–1804) who discovered *oxygen*.

primeval (general) An adjective meaning "the first" or "early."

protein (biology) A class of food necessary for life. Proteins build tissues and provide *energy*.

proton (physics) An electrically charged particle found in all *atoms*. See *electron* and *neutrons*.

protoplasm (biology) A substance necessary for life found in the *cells* of all *organisms*.

[R]

radio astronomy (astronomy) The study of radio waves received from outer space.

regeneration (biology) The capacity of an *organism* to create new parts of itself.

reproduction (biology) The process by which *organisms* create offspring of their own species.

[S]

salinity (chemistry) The degree of salt present. Usually refers to the amount of salt in a fluid.

salt (biology) A substance that is formed when an *acid* is mixed with a *base*.

satellite (astronomy) An object that *orbits* around a *planet*, such as a moon. In recent years, the earth has had man-made satellites.

soluble (chemistry) Able to be dissolved in a fluid. See *solute*, *solvent* and *solution*.

solar (astronomy) An adjective referring to the sun. A solar *eclipse* is an eclipse of the sun. See *lunar*.

solar system (astronomy) The sun, the *planets*, *satellites*, and the *asteroids*.

solute (chemistry) What is dissolved in a fluid to form a *solution*. See *solution*, *soluble*, and *solvent*.

solution (chemistry) A solution occurs when a liquid, solvent or gas mixes completely in a fluid. For example, when sugar is completely dissolved in hot water, the result is a solution. See *solute*, *solvent*, and *soluble*.

solvent (chemistry) The fluid in which a *solute* is dissolved to form a *solution*. Also see *soluble*.

sonic (physics) An adjective referring to sound.

spawn (biology) A noun referring to the eggs of certain *aquatic* animals, such as fish. Also a verb meaning to lay eggs, usually used in connection with fish.

stimulus (general) That which brings a response. If a person is hungry, the sight of food might make his mouth water. The stimulus is food, and the response, the watering of the mouth.

substratum (geology) A layer lying beneath the top layer.

supersonic (physics) An adjective meaning "faster than sound."

[T, U]

theory (general) An unproved explanation of something that has happened or might happen.

thermodynamics (physics) The study of the actions of *heat*.

ultrasonic (physics) An adjective referring to sound no person can hear because of its high frequency.

unicellular (biology) An adjective meaning "one-celled." See *cell*.

universe (astronomy) All things that exist in space taken as a whole.

[V]

velocity (physics) The rate of motion.

Vesalius, Andreas (biology) An Italian scientist (1514–1564) who studied the body. His discoveries were so important that he is often referred to as "The Father of Anatomy." See *anatomy*.

virus (biology) A tiny germ that attacks body *cells* and causes disease.

vitamins (biology) Name for many special substances found in food which are necessary for the operation of particular functions of the body and to maintain health.

[W, X, Y, Z]

water table (general) The level nearest to the surface of the ground where water is found.

work (physics) In science, work is what occurs when a *force* moves an object.

zoology (biology) The study of animals. This science is a branch of *biology*.

SCIENCE QUIZZER

Most people, like yourself, who take exams are busy people. They cannot afford to waste time; that is why you bought this book, to help provide you with the best preparation possible. This chapter material will help do just that. It is a workable plan for broadening your background in a subject likely to occur on your exam.

TEST I. SCIENCE

TIME: 25 Minutes. 20 Questions.

The following are representative examination type questions. They should be carefully studied and completely understood. The actual test questions will probably not be quite as difficult as these.

DIRECTIONS: *For each of the following questions, select the choice which best answers the question or completes the statement.*

1. The normal height of a mercury barometer at sea level is
   (A) 15 inches (B) 30 inches
   (C) 32 feet (D) 34 feet.

2. Of the following phases of the moon, the invisible one is called
   (A) crescent (B) full moon
   (C) new moon (D) waxing and waning.

3. Of the following, the statement that best describes a "high" on a weather map is
   (A) the air extends farther up than normal
   (B) the air pressure is greater than normal
   (C) the air temperature is higher than normal
   (D) the air moves faster than normal.

4. The nerve endings for the sense of sight are located in the part of the eye called the
   (A) cornea (B) sclera
   (C) iris (D) retina.

5. Of the following, the one which causes malaria is
   (A) a bacterium (B) a mosquito
   (C) a protozoan (D) bad air.

6. A 1000-ton ship must displace a weight of water equal to
   (A) 500 tons (B) 1000 tons
   (C) 1500 tons (D) 2000 tons.

7. Of the following instruments, the one that can convert light into an electric current is the
   (A) radiometer (C) electroylsis apparatus
   (B) dry cell (D) photo-electric cell.

8. On the film in a camera, the lens forms an image which, by comparison with the original subject, is
   (A) right side up and reversed from left to right
   (B) upside down and reversed from left to right
   (C) right side up and not reversed from left to right
   (D) upside down and not reversed from left to right.

9. Of the following, the plant whose seeds are *not* spread by wind is the
   (A) cocklebur   (B) maple
   (C) dandelion   (D) milkweed.

10. Of the following, the insect which is harmful to man's food supply is the
    (A) dragonfly   (B) grasshopper
    (C) ladybug   (D) praying mantis.

11. Of the following, the one which is fall-blooming generally is the
    (A) azalea   (B) hickory
    (C) tulip   (D) witch hazel.

12. At the beginning of a community succession, the first of the following living things to get a foothold on bare rocks, other things being equal, are
    (A) mosses   (B) ferns
    (C) algae   (D) lichens.

13. Ciliated male gametes may be found in the cells of
    (A) bread mold   (B) gingko
    (C) protococcus   (D) slime mold.

14. The shape of which of the following does the vibrio shape of certain bacteria most closely resemble?
    (A) bacilli   (B) spirilla
    (C) cocci   (D) Rickettsia.

15. Nutrition in mushrooms is
    (A) symbiotic   (B) saprophytic
    (C) parasitic   (D) holophytic.

16. In a demonstration in class of a test for vitamin C, one might effectively use
    (A) acetic acid   (B) brom thymol blue
    (C) congo red   (D) indophenol.

17. Rod-shaped bacteria are classified as
    (A) bacilli   (B) cocci
    (C) vibrios   (D) spirilla.

18. A stain used in classifying pathogenic bacteria is
    (A) Gram's   (B) Wright's
    (C) Loeffler's   (D) Giemsa.

19. Bacteriophage is a type of
    (A) enzyme   (B) toxin
    (C) bacterium   (D) virus.

20. Coral is formed by
    (A) marine algae
    (B) a mollusc found in the Caribbean
    (C) an animal related to the sea anemone
    (D) a seed plant.

CONSOLIDATE YOUR KEY ANSWERS HERE

Practice using Answer Sheets. Make ONE mark for each answer. Additional and stray marks may be counted as mistakes. In making corrections erase errors COMPLETELY. Make glossy black marks. To arrive at an accurate estimate of your ability and progress, cover the Correct Answers with a sheet of white paper while you are taking this test.

CORRECT ANSWERS TO THE FOREGOING PRACTICE QUESTIONS

1.B	4.D	7.D	10.B	13.B	16.D	19.D
2.C	5.C	8.B	11.D	14.B	17.A	20.C
3.B	6.B	9.A	12.D	15.B	18.A	

TEST II. SCIENCE

TIME: 10 Minutes. 10 Questions.

DIRECTIONS: *For each of the following questions, select the choice which best answers the question or completes the statement.*

1. One-celled animals belong to the group of living things known as
   (A) protozoa   (B) porifera
   (C) annelida   (D) arthropoda.

2. Spiders can be distinguished from insects by the fact that spiders have
   (A hard outer coverings
   (B) large abdomens
   (C) four pairs of legs
   (D) biting mouth parts.

3. An important ore of uranium is called
   (A) hematite   (B) bauxite
   (C) chalcopyrite   (D) pitchblende.

4. Of the following, the lightest element known on earth is
   (A) hydrogen   (B) helium
   (C) oxygen   (D) air.

5. Of the following gases in the air, the most plentiful is
   (A) argon   (B) nitrogen
   (C) oxygen   (D) carbon dioxide.

6. The time it takes for light from the sun to reach the earth is approximately
   (A) four years   (B) four months
   (C) eight minutes   (D) sixteen years.

7. Of the following types of clouds, the ones which occur at the greatest height are called
   (A) cirrus   (B) cumulus
   (C) nimbus   (D) stratus.

8. The time that it takes for the earth to rotate 45° is
   (A) one hour   (B) three hours
   (C) four hours   (D) ten hours.

9. Of the following glands, the one which regulates the metabolic rate is the
   (A) adrenal   (B) salivary
   (C) thyroid   (D) thymus.

10. All of the following are Amphibia *except* the
    (A) salamander   (B) lizard
    (C) frog   (D) toad.

CONSOLIDATE YOUR KEY ANSWERS HERE

Practice using Answer Sheets. Make ONE mark for each answer. Additional and stray marks may be counted as mistakes. In making corrections erase errors COMPLETELY. Make glossy black marks. To arrive at an accurate estimate of your ability and progress, cover the Correct Answers with a sheet of white paper while you are taking this test.

CORRECT ANSWERS TO THE FOREGOING PRACTICE QUESTIONS

Now compare your answers with these Correct Answers to the Practice Questions. If your answers differ from these, go back and study those questions to see where and how you made your mistakes.

1.A	3.D	5.B	7.A	9.C
2.C	4.A	6.C	8.B	10.B

TEST III. SCIENCE

TIME: 10 Minutes. 8 Questions.

DIRECTIONS: For each of the following questions, select the choice which best answers the question or completes the statement.

1. Of the following planets, the one which has the shortest revolutionary period around the sun is
   (A) Earth
   (B) Mercury
   (C) Jupiter
   (D) Venus.

2. A popular shrub that produces bell-shaped, yellow flowers in early spring is the
   (A) tulip
   (B) azalea
   (C) forsythia
   (D) flowering dogwood.

3. A circuit breaker is used in many homes instead of a
   (A) switch
   (B) fuse
   (C) fire extinguisher
   (D) meter box.

4. Of the following, which is closest to the speed of sound in air at sea level?
   (A) 1/5th of a mile per second
   (B) 1/2 mile per second
   (C) 1 mile per second
   (D) 5 miles per second.

5. In the production of sounds, the greater the number of vibrations per second
   (A) the greater the volume
   (B) the higher the tone
   (C) the lower the volume
   (D) the lower the tone.

6. Of the following media, the one in which the speed of sound is greatest is
   (A) cold air
   (B) warm air
   (C) steel
   (D) water.

7. What is the name of the negative particle which circles the nucleus of the atom?
   (A) neutron
   (B) proton
   (C) meson
   (D) electron.

8. Which of the following rocks can be dissolved with a weak acid?
   (A) sandstone
   (B) granite
   (C) gneiss
   (D) limestone

CONSOLIDATE YOUR KEY ANSWERS HERE

Practice using Answer Sheets. Make ONE mark for each answer. Additional and stray marks may be counted as mistakes. In making corrections erase errors COMPLETELY. Make glossy black marks. To arrive at an accurate estimate of your ability and progress, cover the Correct Answers with a sheet of white paper while you are taking this test.

```
    A B C D E      A B C D E      A B C D E      A B C D E      A B C D E      A B C D E      A B C D E      A B C D E
1 | | | | | |   2 | | | | | |   3 | | | | | |   4 | | | | | |   5 | | | | | |   6 | | | | | |   7 | | | | | |   8 | | | | | |
```

CORRECT ANSWERS TO THE FOREGOING PRACTICE QUESTIONS

Now compare your answers with these Correct Answers to the Practice Questions. If your answers differ from these, go back and study those questions to see where and how you made your mistakes.

| 1.B | 2.C | 3.B | 4.A | 5.B | 6.C | 7.D | 8.D |

TEST IV. SCIENCE

TIME: 10 Minutes. 8 Questions.

DIRECTIONS: *For each of the following questions, select the choice which best answers the question or completes the statement.*

1. Of the following, the scientist who originated and developed the system of classifying the plants and animals of the earth was
(A) Linnaeus   (B) Darwin
(C) Mendel   (D) Agassiz.

2. Of the following substances, the one which is non-magnetic is
(A) iron   (B) nickel
(C) aluminum   (D) cobalt.

3. A scientist noted for his work in the field of antibiotics is:
(A) Salk   (B) Koch
(C) Banting   (D) Waksman.

4. The vascular system of the body is concerned with:
(A) respiration   (B) circulation of blood
(C) sense of touch   (D) enzymes.

5. The "bite," that is, the meeting of the teeth of the upper and lower jaws is described as:
(A) junction   (B) fixation
(C) occlusion   (D) mastication.

6. The transparent, slightly bulging tissue which covers the front sixth of the eyeball and is frequently referred to as the "window of the eyes" is the:
(A) iris   (B) cornea
(C) sciera   (D) retina.

7. The technical term for "cross-eyes" is
(A) myopia   (B) hyperopia
(C) strabismus   (D) trachoma.

8. A boy caught Japanese beetles, large and small, in an insect trap. One would be correct in assuming that the small ones:
(A) had been in the trap for a long time
(B) had recently hatched from eggs
(C) were adults
(D) were younger than the large ones.

CONSOLIDATE YOUR KEY ANSWERS HERE

Practice using Answer Sheets. Make ONE mark for each answer. Additional and stray marks may be counted as mistakes. In making corrections erase errors COMPLETELY. Make glossy black marks. To arrive at an accurate estimate of your ability and progress, cover the Correct Answers with a sheet of white paper while you are taking this test.

	A	B	C	D	E
1	☐	☐	☐	☐	☐
2	☐	☐	☐	☐	☐
3	☐	☐	☐	☐	☐
4	☐	☐	☐	☐	☐
5	☐	☐	☐	☐	☐
6	☐	☐	☐	☐	☐
7	☐	☐	☐	☐	☐
8	☐	☐	☐	☐	☐

CORRECT ANSWERS TO THE FOREGOING PRACTICE QUESTIONS

Now compare your answers with these Correct Answers to the Practice Questions. If your answers differ from these, go back and study those questions to see where and how you made your mistakes.

1.A   2.C   3.D   4.B   5.C   6.B   7.C   8.C

TEST V. SCIENCE

TIME: 20 Minutes. 15 Questions.

DIRECTIONS: For each question in this test, read carefully the stem and the five lettered choices that follow. Choose the answer which you consider correct or most nearly correct. Mark the answer sheet for the letter you have chosen: A, B, C, D, or E.

Explanations of the key points behind these questions appear with the answers at the end of this test. The explanatory answers provide the kind of background that will enable you to answer test questions with facility and confidence.

1. A definition of pure science is

   (A) the application of scientific data
   (B) laboratory experimentation
   (C) the accumulation of scientific data
   (D) research done to further man's understanding of nature
   (E) discovery of scientific facts

2. The definition of applied science is

   (A) laboratory research
   (B) field experiments
   (C) technology
   (D) publication of scientific discoveries
   (E) basic research

3. Of the following men, which one is usually identified as a philosopher of science?

   (A) Fromm
   (B) Whitehead
   (C) Euclid
   (D) James
   (E) Marx

4. Which of the following is NOT a valid problem for science research?

   (A) What was the origin of the universe?
   (B) How did the universe evolve?
   (C) Why does the universe exist?
   (D) Is the universe expanding?
   (E) Are we the only intelligent life in the universe?

5. The processes which make up the scientific method include: 1) experimentation, 2) definition of a problem, and 3) formulation of a hypothesis. The order in which these should occur in a scientific study is

   (A) 2, 3, 1   (D) 1, 2, 3
   (B) 3, 1, 2   (E) 2, 1, 3
   (C) 3, 2, 1

6. Which answer best summarizes the difference between a *hypothesis* and a *theory*?

   (A) A hypothesis is a statement of fact and a theory is a statement of belief.
   (B) A theory is a hypothesis that has been rigorously tested so that scientists accept its probability.
   (C) A theory is a hypothesis that has been tested and proved to be correct.
   (D) A hypothesis is an informed guess while a theory is based on facts.
   (E) There is no difference between a hypothesis and a theory.

7. Homeostasis is often referred to as the end result of the action of numerous negative feedback systems because

   (A) a condition of stability is the end result of negative feedback
   (B) positive feedback never occurs in physiological systems
   (C) negative feedback systems produce oscillatory behavior
   (D) negative feedback systems produce variations with changes in environment
   (E) homeostasis is a mathematically linear system

S3265

Questions 8 to 11

An historian of science has defined "scientific awareness" as comprising three principles throughout history: belief that the earth is round, belief in evolution and belief in the earth's revolving around the sun. By the use of historical records the historian calculated the percentage of people believing in these three principles at different times in history. The data is presented below.

Year	Percentage of people believing the earth is round	Percentage of people believing in evolution	Percentage of people believing in earth's rotation
1200 A.D.	5	1	2
1400	6	1	3
1600	10	1	8
1800	50	1	25
1975	98	90	96

8. Which of the following graphs would best picture a plot of "scientific awareness" against time?

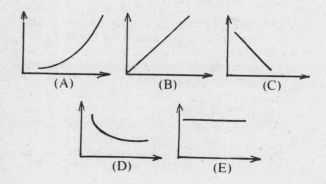

9. Which of the following statements regarding the data is *false*?

   (A) Belief in evolution lagged behind belief in the other two criteria.
   (B) The scientific awareness of people has increased rapidly in the past 200 years.
   (C) Belief in evolution has grown most dramatically since 1800.
   (D) Belief that the earth is round was the hardest of the three criteria to accept.
   (E) There were some people who believed in evolution during all of the periods.

10. During the American Revolution (1776) which of the following statements regarding scientific awareness is most accurate?

    (A) No person believed in science.
    (B) Science was non-existent.
    (C) Scientific awareness was definitely on the rise.
    (D) Scientific awareness was at an all time low.
    (E) The large belief in evolution was surprising.

11. Which of the following statements regarding the state of scientific awareness in the year 2000 is most accurate?

    (A) Scientific awareness will probably increase.
    (B) People will no longer believe in evolution.
    (C) The scientific method will be seriously challenged.
    (D) New evidence will dispel the idea of evolution.
    (E) There will be a larger proportional increase in scientific awareness between 1975 and 2000 than ever before in history.

12. Which of the following is the BEST experimental design to test the hypothesis that vitamin C prevents the common cold?

   (A) Send questionnaires to a representative sample of the population, half of whom regularly take vitamin C and half of whom take no extra vitamins, requesting information about the number of colds each person has had per year.

   (B) In a representative sample of the population, give half 500 mg of vitamin C daily and administer a placebo to the remaining half. Record the number of colds each person has had during one year.

   (C) In a representative sample of the population, give half 500 mg of vitamin C daily and the other half a placebo in such a manner that neither the subjects nor the person administering the medication know who is being medicated. Inject both groups with cold virus and record the number of persons becoming ill.

   (D) Give vitamin C tablets to all your friends and relatives and see how many colds they have during one year.

   (E) Inject a group of rats with vitamin C. A control group would not be medicated. Both groups would then be injected with cold virus and the number becoming ill would be tabulated.

13. Which of the following is the best example of secondary induction?

   (A) A scientist crosses plant P-tall with plant P-short and notes that all the progeny are tall. He records this observation and states, "In plant P, the factor tall is dominant over the factor short."

   (B) The same scientist allows the tall progeny of the above experiment to self-pollinate. He finds that out of 100 offspring, 77 are tall and 23 are short. He states, "Whenever the first generation of a cross between P-tall and P-short are allowed to self-pollinate, short plants will appear in the second generation in a ratio of 1 short to 3 tall."

   (C) A scientist observes the results of many test crosses between plant P-tall and plant P-short, noting that the progeny are always tall. He also allows the first generation to self-pollinate and observes that one-third of the plants are always short. He states, "The factor for short in plant P is not lost in the first generation since short plants appear in the second generation."

   (D) A scientist notes that when plant P-tall is crossed with plant P-short the progeny are always tall. When these tall first generation plants are allowed to self-pollinate, one-third of the offspring are short. He states, "Factors occur in pairs within the sex cells. These pairs separate when gametes are formed."

   (E) A scientist crosses plant P-white with plant P-red. The progeny are all pink. He states, "The factors which cause color in plant P do not exhibit dominance."

14. Many of our bodily functions operate on the basis of a feed back control system. Which of the following are characteristic of such a control system?

   I. Operating energy is needed to make the system work.

   II. Response to a need is in small, repeated steps, rather than one large all-correcting step.

   III. Very often the control will over-shoot the optimal condition, and then will naturally correct in the reverse direction, oscillating toward the optimal condition.

   IV. A perfectly operating system will be subconscious.

   (A) I and II only
   (B) II and III only
   (C) III and IV only
   (D) I, II, and III only
   (E) I, II, III, and IV

15. The continual aim of the natural sciences is to uncover the natural laws that govern the world and the universe. For the scientist the most important value in discovering a natural law is that such a law can be used to

   (A) predict the outcome or consequence of a given event
   (B) prove that a particular theory is correct
   (C) demonstrate an experimental technique
   (D) discover new ways to control nature
   (E) solve scientific equations

END OF TEST

CONSOLIDATE YOUR KEY ANSWERS HERE

Practice using Answer Sheets. Make ONE mark for each answer. Additional and stray marks may be counted as mistakes. In making corrections erase errors COMPLETELY. Make glossy black marks. To arrive at an accurate estimate of your ability and progress, cover the Correct Answers with a sheet of white paper while you are taking this test.

CORRECT KEY ANSWERS TO THE PRACTICE QUESTIONS

Now compare your answers with these Correct Key Answers. If your answers differ from these, go back and study the Practice Questions to see where and how you made your mistakes. In doing this, the following Explanatory Answers should prove helpful. They provide concise clarifications of the basic points behind the Key Answers. Even where your Key Answers are the same as ours, go over the explanations carefully because they may be quite useful in helping you pick up extra points on the exam.

1.D	3.B	5.A	7.A	9.D	11.A	13.D	15.A
2.C	4.C	6.B	8.A	10.C	12.C	14.E	

EXPLANATORY ANSWERS CLARIFYING CARDINAL POINTS

1. **(D)** Pure science is research done to further man's understanding of nature.

2. **(C)** Applied science is another term for technology. The purpose of technology is to use scientific information to make practical changes in nature.

3. **(B)** Although all of the men are philosophers of some renown, Whitehead is the one that is best known as a philosopher of science.

4. **(C)** The question of existence is left for philosophers and theologians because it cannot be empirically studied.

5. **(A)** In the scientific method, the first step is to question the universe—to find a problem to be investigated. Once this problem has been accurately defined, a hypothesis is stated . . . a guess, trying to predict how the universe will behave. Finally comes the experiment to see if the guess is correct.

6. **(B)** The words "correct" and "fact" are too definite to be used in a discussion of theories and hypotheses.

7. **(A)** To answer this question correctly, you must understand feedback systems as well as the meaning of homeostasis. Positive feedback results in uncontrolled behavior and instability because output follows input. If negative feedback increases, stability follows suit. Homeostasis refers to the maintenance of physiological constancy.

8. **(A)** According to the data presented, scientific awareness increased slowly at first and then much more rapidly (this type of increase is called an *exponential* increase). Options (C) and (D) portray situations of a decrease in awareness with time, and option (E) shows no change. Option (B) is incorrect since it shows an increase at a constant rate.

9. **(D)** According to the data options (A), (B), and (E) are obviously true. Option (C) is also true since in 1800 only 1% of the people believed in it while in 1975 90% believed in it. Therefore the correct answer is option (D) since it was harder for people to accept evolution (only 1% until 1975) than the earth's roundness (50% in 1800).

10. **(C)** Option (A) is wrong since some people believed in science while options (B) and (E) are obviously incorrect. Option (D) is wrong since science was not at an all time low as evidenced by the data which show lower figures for earlier years. The correct answer is therefore (C) since the figures show increasing scientific awareness.

11. **(A)** From the data (and the graph in question 1) we can deduce that there will be more scientific awareness in 2000. Therefore option (A) is correct. Options (B), (C) and (D) are obviously incorrect. Option (E) is wrong since there cannot be a larger *proportional* increase since almost all people (greater than 90%) accept the criteria of scientific awareness. There can only be an increase of less than 10%.

12. **(C)** Choice (C) represents a double blind experiment which is considered the most reliable procedure in determining the effectiveness of drugs.

13. **(D)** Primary induction is a statement about observations plus an attempt to define laws derived from the observed phenomena. Secondary induction is dependent on numerous instances of primary induction and results in theories which cover a larger field of investigations. All the choices but (D) illustrate primary induction.

14. **(E)** All of the choices are characteristics of a physiological feedback control system.

15. **(A)** The most important value for the scientist in discovering a natural law is that such a law can be used to predict the outcome or consequence of a given event.

TEST VI. BIOLOGICAL SCIENCE

TIME: 10 Minutes. 15 Questions.

DIRECTIONS: For each question in this test, read carefully the stem and the five lettered choices that follow. Choose the answer which you consider correct or most nearly correct. Mark the answer sheet for the letter you have chosen: A, B, C, D, or E.

Explanations of the key points behind these questions appear with the answers at the end of this test. The explanatory answers provide the kind of background that will enable you to answer test questions with facility and confidence.

1. The halving of the chromosome complement during meiotic division of the sex cells lends credence to the Darwinian theory of evolution because

   (A) it prevents doubling the chromosome complement during fertilization
   (B) it separates like chromosomes
   (C) it provides a means of genetic variation
   (D) sex cells differ
   (E) mutations may be lost

2. Organisms in temperate zones are able to time their activites by cues given by the photoperiod, since

   (A) all organisms need time to rest
   (B) light is a limiting factor
   (C) all organisms have a biological clock
   (D) day length is always constant for a specific locality and season
   (E) some plants need long days in order to bloom

3. Which of the following properties make water indispensable to life as we know it?

   (A) Water expands at temperatures below 4°C.
   (B) Water has an extremely high surface tension.
   (C) Water has a very high heat capacity, heat of vaporization and heat of fusion.
   (D) Water has a high dielectric constant.
   (E) All of the above.

4. Which of the following statements characterize the field of biology?

   I. Biology relates organic structures and activity to underlying chemical and physical activities.
   II. Biology relates organic structure and activity to their functions in and for organisms.
   III. Biology relates organic structure and activity to their evolutionary origin.

   (A) I only
   (B) II only
   (C) I and II only
   (D) II and III only
   (E) I, II, and III

5. Which of the following is true of enzyme catalysis but is not true of inorganic catalysis?

   (A) The catalyst speeds up the reaction.
   (B) The catalyst itself undergoes no change in the reaction.
   (C) The catalyst is subject to cellular controls.
   (D) Only a small amount of the catalyst is necessary.
   (E) The effect of the catalyst is similar to an increase in temperature, pressure or concentration.

6. The cell seems to be the basic unit of life for the following reason(s).

   I. All cells are self-reproductive without a host.
   II. All cells have the same general size and shape.
   III. All cells are self-regulating.

   (A) I only
   (B) II only
   (C) III only
   (D) I and II only
   (E) I and III only

7. Final cellular differentiation within a developing embryo is

   (A) determined by the physical and chemical environment surrounding the cell
   (B) entirely dependent upon the germ layer from which the cell is derived
   (C) dependent upon the specific chromosomes the cell receives
   (D) controlled by the cytoplasm of the unfertilized egg
   (E) determined before gastrulation of the embryo

8. Sharks and porpoises have a remarkably similar appearance and both give birth to live young, yet the shark is a fish and the porpoise is a mammal. This phenomenon can be attributed to which of the following?

   (A) Divergence, as two subdivisions of the same species ceased to interbreed; resulting in speciation and eventual separation.

(B) Adaptation, as the porpoise, which was originally a fish, developed mammalian characteristics to insure survival of the young.

(C) Convergence, as animals of different origins became adapted to similar environments and habits.

(D) Parallelism, as closely related organisms evolved along similar lines.

(E) Cryptic speciation, as two parts of a population have ceased interbreeding without developing any discernable differences.

9. The living material comprising the bulk of a cell is called the

(A) chloroplast
(B) protoplasm
(C) cytochrome
(D) genes
(E) hormones

10. The condition known as goiter is best described by which of the following statements?

(A) It is caused by a deficiency of iron.
(B) It is an enlarged thyroid gland.
(C) It is caused by a deficiency of insulin.
(D) It is caused by an excess of sugar.
(E) It is an abnormally small pineal gland.

11. Which of the following parts of the human eye regulates the amount of light admitted to the eye?

(A) The vitreous humor
(B) The retina
(C) The iris
(D) The optic nerve
(E) The cornea

12. Which of the following statements best describes the method used by female moths to attract male moths?

(A) The female moths use certain sound frequencies.
(B) The female moths fly in certain patterns.
(C) The female moths fly in the vicinity of certain flowers.
(D) The female moths send out certain chemical sex attractants.
(E) The female moths reflect light from their wings.

13. Which of the following items could best be called biodegradable?

(A) Phosphate detergents
(B) Polystyrene cups
(C) Polyvinylchloride pipes
(D) Cellulose
(E) Aluminum

14. Animals pass on traits to their offspring through which of the following units?

(A) Genes
(B) Proteins
(C) Plasmas
(D) Polysaccharides
(E) Corpuscles

15. The existence of microorganisms in the human gastric system is an example of

(A) symbiosis
(B) parisititis
(C) meiosis
(D) phylesis
(E) variance

END OF TEST

Go on to do the following Test in this Examination, just as you would be expected to do on the actual exam.

CONSOLIDATE YOUR KEY ANSWERS HERE

Practice using Answer Sheets. Make ONE mark for each answer. Additional and stray marks may be counted as mistakes. In making corrections erase errors COMPLETELY. Make glossy black marks. To arrive at an accurate estimate of your ability and progress, cover the Correct Answers with a sheet of white paper while you are taking this test.

CORRECT KEY ANSWERS TO THE PRACTICE QUESTIONS

Now compare your answers with these Correct Key Answers. If your answers differ from these, go back and study the Practice Questions to see where and how you made your mistakes. In doing this, the following Explanatory Answers should prove helpful. They provide concise clarifications of the basic points behind the Key Answers. Even where your Key Answers are the same as ours, go over the explanations carefully because they may be quite useful in helping you pick up extra points on the exam.

1.C	3.E	5.C	7.A	9.B	11.C	13.D	15.A
2.D	4.E	6.E	8.C	10.B	12.D	14.A	

EXPLANATORY ANSWERS CLARIFYING CARDINAL POINTS

1. **(C)** Hereditary variation provides for adaptation to differing environmental conditions. Adaptation and resultant natural selection are basic to evolutionary theories proposed by Darwin. Answer (C) is the only one which expresses this idea.

2. **(D)** Only answers (D) and (E) are directly related to cues which are given by the photoperiod. However, answer (E) is too limited while (D) encompasses all activities in all plants. Thus, (D) is the correct choice.

3. **(E)** Water just below the freezing point (A) is denser than ice, therefore, it sinks, protecting bottom dwelling organisms from freezing. High surface tension (B) causes water to rise unusually high in capillary tubes, which is very important in plant physiology. High heat capacity (C) causes water to act as a thermal buffer. High heats of vaporization and fusion also help in keeping environmental temperatures stable. A high dielectric constant (D) makes water a solvent for a large variety of molecules which are necessary for the chemical functioning of organisms. Since all the properties mentioned are indispensable to life, the correct answer is (E).

4. **(E)** There are three types of explanations in biology: 1) the physiological, (I); 2) the teleonomic, (II); 3) the historical, (III). Therefore the correct answer includes all three.

5. **(C)** Enzyme catalysis takes place in living systems and therefore is subject to cellular controls. This is not true of inorganic catalysis which is a laboratory procedure. Therefore (C) is the correct choice.

6. **(E)** There are many one-celled organisms which are self regulating and self reproductive but one need only compare the yolk of a chicken egg and a rod-shaped bacteria to realize that cells come in many sizes and shapes. The correct answer, (E), only includes the first two possibilities.

7. **(A)** Experiments with the embryos of animals such as frogs have shown that final cellular differentiation depends upon the milieu of the cell. In early stages of gastrulation, cells which are in the location of the cell mass from which the eye arises have been transplanted to the region behind the mouth and there they develop into gills. These experiments have been widely published and familiarity with these ideas will lead to a correct answer of (A).

8. **(C)** Sharks and porpoises are not closely related. One would have to go back to the Paleozoic Era to find a common ancestor. This leads to choice (C) as the correct one.

9. **(B)** This question concerns the biology of all living organisms. Options (A), (C) and (D) are specific entities which are located in the cell. Option (E) concerns certain chemicals found in the body. The correct answer is option (B) the protoplasm, which is common to both plant and animal cells.

10. **(B)** A goiter is a large lump in the area below the neck and is caused by a deficiency of iodine. The iodine deficiency causes the enlargement of the thyroid gland. The correct answer is therefore option (B).

11. **(C)** This is a question from the field of human physiology. Option (A), the vitreous humor, is the fluid material which fills the eye. Option (B), the retina, is at the rear of the eye and option (E), the cornea, is the protective lens at the front of the eye. Neither of these parts functions to regulate the amount of light admitted to the eye. The optic nerve, option (D), transmits the light signal to the brain. Therefore the correct answer is option (C), the iris.

12. **(D)** This question from the field of insect behavior can be answered if the candidate realizes that insects communicate via certain chemical scents (*pheromones*). This type of communication is also true of sex attraction which is accomplished by a class of materials known as insect sex attractants. The correct answer is option (D).

13. **(D)** A biodegradable substance is one that can be recycled by nature. Options (A) and (B) will not be recycled by the environment but remain to pollute it. This is also true for options (C) and (E). The correct answer is option (D). As a general rule artificial materials such as plastics are not biodegradable while natural materials, such as starch or wood, are.

14. **(A)** This question concerns the science of heredity. Genes are individual chemical units which determine how tall we are or what color hair and eyes we have. Each gene has a different job to perform. The correct answer is (A).

15. **(A)** This question from biology can be answered by knowing that options (C) (disease), (D) (hormonal deficiency) and (E) (genetic throwback) are not pertinent to the existence of microorganisms in the human gastric system since this is not only a normal situation but a necessary one. When two organisms exist together and each derives a benefit from the relationship the situation is called *symbiosis*. If one suffers at the expense of the other the situation is called *parasitisis*. The correct answer is therefore (A).

PART FIVE

Reading Skills

This test is based on a selection of passages, both prose and verse. The questions emphasize knowledge and special abilities not frequently needed in ordinary reading. The abilities to interpret figures of speech, to cope with unusual sentence structure and word meaning, and to recognize mood and purpose are often tested, as is an understanding of literary forms.

PREFACE TO LITERATURE QUESTIONS

A great deal depends on your examination score, as you know. And this book will help you achieve your highest possible score. You'll get plenty of practice with relevant test subjects and questions. But first we want you to pick up a few facts about the test which may make things easier for you. Forgive us if some of these facts seem self-evident. Our experience has shown that this kind of information is sometimes overlooked . . . to the candidate's detriment.

In the section of the examination entitled Interpretation of Literary Materials, each group of questions is made up of a literary selection followed by one or more incomplete statements about the passage of prose, poetry or drama.

These numbered statements are called "stems" because from each of them depends, like the petals of a flower, the balance of each question. Each "stem" is followed by four or five possible, plausible answers, called "foils." In multiple choice questions they are meant to *foil* the unwary or unwise.

The Literature Section of the High School Equivalency Test usually takes 1½ hours to complete. The test measures your ability to read, understand, and interpret selections from English and American Literature. The selections could cover almost any period in literature, but most excerpts will probably be from modern authors. The questions cover the interpretation of poetry, drama, fiction and non-fiction.

The questions are Multiple Choice, with four possible answers. You may be asked to find: the meaning of a word, phrase, or line; or the theme of a selection. You might be asked to "infer" (identify) various aspects of characterization — mood, motivation, or point of view. You may be asked to identify the plot or setting of a passage, or perhaps recognize the author's viewpoint or writing style. Some questions will deal with "genres" (types of literature), poetic forms, structures, and figures of speech.

Questions rarely follow the order of the passage. You will have to hunt through it for your answer. Many answers are not stated directly in the selection. You may have to "infer" the answer on the basis of "clues." Some questions are based on an impression gained through reading the entire passage.

HERE'S HOW YOU SHOULD ANSWER
THESE LITERARY READING QUESTIONS

Although you may never have seen the literary selection before, you must now read it carefully so that you understand it. Read slowly and try to visualize the entire plot and setting. Try to get the whole story . . . what the author really means, and how he conveys his meaning through his characters, tone, style, rhetorical devices, and language both literal and figurative.

Skim the stems. See if you can figure out what the examiners are getting at. Re-read the passage before answering each question. From the emotions and feelings expressed, choose the best foil for each question. Any one of them might be right. You have to choose the one that's most correct. Try to pick the one that's most complete, most accurate . . . the one that is best supported by and necessarily flows from the selection. Be sure that it contains nothing false so far as the selection itself is concerned.

After you've thought it out, mark your answer in the verisimilar answer boxes provided at the end of the test . . . just as you will do on the actual exam.

Answer all questions. Blank spaces are marked *wrong*. So *guess* if necessary. You will lose nothing. You may gain valuable points.

When you've answered all the questions, score yourself faithfully by checking with the correct, key answers . . . also at the end of the test. But please don't look at those answers until you've written your own. You just won't be helping yourself if you do that. Besides, you'll have ample opportunity to do the questions again and to check with our answers, in the event that your first try results in a low score.

analysis showing you why the others were less correct.

And now, "to the marriage of true minds."

The following study section has been designed to give you the knowledge of literary materials needed to pass the High School Equivalency Examination. It has also been designed to give you experience in answering the kind of questions you will meet.

Your greatest improvement will come from finding out why you erred. Just read the Explanatory Answers for those questions you scored incorrectly. You'll not only find out which foil was correct, but you'll get a differential analysis showing you why the others were less correct.

THE INTERPRETATION OF POETRY

This test is based on a selection of passages, both prose and verse. The questions emphasize knowledge and special abilities not frequently needed in ordinary reading. The abilities to interpret figures of speech, to cope with unusual sentence structure and word meaning, and to recognize mood and purpose are often tested, as is an understanding of literary forms.

Although the Interpretation of Literary Materials is essentially a reading exercise, it demands that you do more than merely skim the surface of a selection. You must infer the author's real meaning from his style and point of view; from the plot and setting; from the intentions and personalities with which he endows his characters; from his opinions and feelings; from the figurative devices he uses; from all the rhetorical nuances described in these pages. Correct answers come from the clues you can piece together and from the unifying thread strung by the author through each passage.

Practically everyone can recognize a poem. When you see the following sentences,

1   I never saw a purple cow,
2   I never hope to see one;
3   But I can tell you anyhow,
4   I'd rather see than be one.

you know you have read a poem. Yet for hundreds of years people have been trying to come up with a precise definition of poetry . . . and have failed. If you think of poetry as rhyming (the last words of lines having similar sounds), then the following selection by William Shakespeare does *not* fit your definition:

1   Our revels now are ended. There our actors,
2   As I foretold you, were all spirits and
3   Are melted into air, into thin air:
4   And, like the baseless fabric of this vision,
5   The cloud-capp'd towers, the gorgeous palaces,
6   The solemn temples, the gorgeous palaces,
7   Yea, all which it inherit, shall dissolve
8   And, like this insubstantial pageant faded,
9   Leave not a rock behind. We are such stuff
10   As dreams are made on, and our little life
11   Is rounded with a sleep.

Yet this *is* poetry, and has been recognized as poetry for almost three hundred years.

Then, if poetry is not necessarily rhymed, might it be a literary form that has a certain rhythm apparent in each line? If that is so, what are we to make of the following selection by the great American poet Walt Whitman?

> A child said, What is the grass? fetching it to me with full hands,
> How could I answer the child? I do not know what it is any more than he.
> I guess it must be the flag of my disposition, out of hopeful green
> stuff woven.
> Or I guess it is the handkerchief of the Lord.
> A scented gift and remembrancer designedly dropt,
> Bearing the owner's name some way in the corners, that
> we may see and remark, and say Whose?

This is also poetry, although it doesn't have a set rhythm.

VERSE, as distinguished from prose, is the name given to the peculiar structure of language employed in *poetry*.

The word *verse* derived from the stem *vers* -turn, and is so called because when the writer has written a certain number of syllables he *turns,* as it were, and commences a new line. Originally, the word was applied only to a *line* of poetry. It is now, however, used to designate the general structure of poetry, as well as a group of lines of poetry, and even one of the subdivisions of a chapter in the Bible.

The chief distinction between *verse* and *prose* is that the former is marked by the recurrence, at regular intervals, of syllables that must be accented by the voice in reading. This regular recurrence of accent is called RHYTHM.

The word *rhythm* comes from a Greek word, meaning *measured motion*.

The best way to learn about poetry is not to try to make an airtight definition, but to understand the "tools" the poet uses in order to produce a poetic effect. You will be asked questions about these tools, and also questions designed to see if you understand the meaning of the poems.

Let us first examine the tools of the poet.

The Tools of the Poet

Meter: Most poets use rhythm. Poetic rhythm is called *meter*. The basic unit of meter is the *foot*. Don't let this term frighten you. It only refers to the way the poet stresses certain syllables. Imagine that the desk or table on which you are working is a drum. You could strike the drum several times, giving each beat a value equal to each of the other beats. It would sound something like this:

BOOM . . . BOOM . . . BOOM . . . BOOM!

But you could get a little variety into your "music" by making some of the beats heavy and some light — and making a certain order in doing so. The following is an example of such a pattern:

BOOM-boom-BOOM-boom-BOOM-boom-BOOM-boom

You will notice when you do this beat that it tends to break down into groups that go like this:

BOOM-boom / BOOM-boom / BOOM-boom / BOOM-boom

One "BOOM-boom" makes a foot. The above line then has four feet, and the first beat of eacn foot is a heavy one. We call this heavy beat a *stress*. The light beat is *unstressed*.

If we look at the third line of the little poem at the beginning of this section, we can see that line breaks down to our four-foot, second-beat-stressed, example.

But I/ can TELL/ you A/ nyHOW

This rhythm, the way the beat occurs—is called meter. This particular boom-BOOM foot is called the *iambic* foot and is one of the most common in English poetry.

Poets use a wide variety of poetic meters. They use a boom-boom-BOOM foot, such as

If you CAN'T/ be a PINE/ on the TOP/ of the HILL

Be a SCRUB/ in the VAL/ley — but r'

The BEST/ little SCRUB/ by the SIDE/ of the RILL;

Be a BUSH/ if you CAN'T/ be a TREE.

You probably noticed that the poet changed the beat in the foot at the beginning of the third line. But he kept the "boom-boom-*BOOM*" rhythm in the rest of the poem. This is called the *anapestic* foot.

TYPES OF POETIC FEET YOU SHOULD STUDY ARE LISTED BELOW WITH EXAMPLES.

BEAT	NAME OF FOOT	EXAMPLE
boom-BOOM	iambic	When I / am dead / you'll find / it hard Said he
boom-boom-BOOM	anapestic	Being born in the cell- ar of Hell / . . . On the pave- ment, on stairs at the door /
BOOM-boom-boom	dactylic	Hail to the chief who in triumph ad/ vances (the last foot is a trochaic foot)
BOOM-boom	trochaic	Hate goes. / loves comes, / all is / blissful
BOOM-BOOM	spondaic	Blow, blow, thou win- ter wind! Freeze, freeze, thou bit-/ ter sky (the first feet in both lines are spondaic feet)

Kinds of Feet

Feet are divided into dissyllabic and trisyllabic.

The dissyllabic feet are the IAMBUS and the TROCHEE.

In classical poetry a third dissyllabic foot, called the SPONDEE, consisting of two long syllables, is used.

An IAMBUS is a dissyllabic foot accented on the second syllable; as, *adore*.

Some prefer to use the technical terms of classical poetry and to speak of an unaccented syllable as *short* [marked thus ($\smile$)], and of an accented syllable as *long* [marked thus (—)].

A TROCHEE is a dissyllabic foot accented on the first syllable; as, *rosy* (— $\smile$).

The word comes from the Greek *trochos*, a running, and the foot is so called from the tripping, sprightly movement it imparts to the verse.

The trisyllabic feet are the ANAPEST, the DACTYL, and the AMPHIBRACH.

The ANAPEST is a trisyllabic foot, accented on the third syllable; as *intercede* ($\smile\smile$ —).

The anapest (*ana* - back, and *paistos* - struck) is so called because it is the reverse of the dactyl.

The DACTYL is a trisyllabic foot accented on the first syllable; as, *holiness* (— ᴗᴗ).

The dactyl (Greek *daktylos,* a finger) is so called, because, like a finger, it has one long joint and two short joints.

The AMPHIBRACH is a trisyllabic foot, having the accent on the middle syllable; as *coeval* (ᴗ — ᴗ).

The amphibrach (*amphi* - on both sides, and *brachys* - short) is so called because there is an unaccented syllable on each side of an accented syllable.

Verses are classified according to the kind of foot and the number of feet occurring in each line. According to the kind of foot, verse may be *iambic, trochaic, anapestic, dactylic,* or *amphibrachic.* According to the number of feet, a verse is *monomdter,* if of one foot; *dimeter,* if of two feet; *trimeter,* if of three feet; *tetrameter,* if of four feet; *pentameter,* if of five feet, and *hexameter,* if of six feet.

If a verse has a syllable more than the regular measure, it is called *hypermeter;* if a syllable less, *catalectic.*

Dissyllabic Verse Iambic Measures

In *iambic* measures the accents generally fall on the even syllables, the second, fourth, etc.

(a) Lines in *Iambic Monometer* are rarely found.

(b) Iambic Dimeter
With ráv|ished éars
The món|arch héars.
   —Dryden.

(c) Iambic Trimeter
Alóft | in áw|ful státe
The gód|like hé|ro sát.
   —Dryden.

Iambic Trimeter Hypermeter
In ró|ses Cú|pid peép|ing
Distúrbed | a beé | a sleéping.

(d) Iambic Tetrameter
A pér|fect wó|man, nó|bly plánned
To wárn, | to cóm|fort, ánd | commánd;
And yet a spirit still and bright
With something of an angel light.
   —Wordsworth.

This is the measure in which most of Sir Walter Scott's longer poems are written. He often varies it by introducing triplets, and dimeters or trimeters.

(e) Iambic Pentameter

Achíl|les' wráth, | to Greéce | the díre|ful spring
Of wóes | unnúm|bered, heáv'n|ly gód|dess, sing.

—Pope.

This is what is generally called Heroic Measure. Unrhymed iambic pentameters constitute the most common form of blank verse. Milton's "Paradise Lost" and most of Shakespeare's plays are written in *pentameter blank verse,* though many of the lines are either *hypermeter* or *catalectic.*

The *elegiac stanza* is a variety of this measure. It consists of four heroic lines, rhyming alternately; as,

> The curfew tolls the knell of parting day,
> The lowing herd winds slowly o'er the lea,
> The plowman homeward plods his weary way,
> And leaves the world to darkness and to me.
> —Gray.

The *Spenserian stanza,* in which Spenser's "The Faerie Queene" and Byron's *"Childe Harold"* are written, consists of eight heroic lines, followed by an *Alexandrine.* The rhyming lines are the first and third; the second, fourth, fifth, and seventh; and the sixth, eighth, and ninth.

(f) Iambic Hexameter

A needless Alexandrine ends the song,
Which, líke | a wound|ed snáke, | drags íts , slow léngth | alóng.
—Pope.

This measure is called *Alexandrine.*

(g) Iambic Heptameter

Now gló|ry tó | the Lórd | of hósts, | from whóm | all gló|ries áre!
And glory to our Sovereign Liege, King Henry of Navarre!
—Macaulay.

This measure is often called *Service, Ballad,* or *Common Meter.* It is very generally used for hymns and ballads, and is often written in lines of four and three feet alternately, the latter being the only ones that rhyme; as,

> With slow and steady step there came
> A lady through the hall,
> And breathless silence chained the lips
> And touched the hearts of all.
> —H. G. Bell.

Trochaic Measures

In *trochaic* measures the accents usually fall on the odd syllables; as, the first, third, etc.

(a) Trochaic Dimeter
Rích the   tréasure,
Swéet the   pléasure.
—Dryden.

(b) Trochaic Trimeter
Whén a roúnd thee   lying,
Aútumn | leáves are | dying.

Trochaic Trimeter Hypermeter
Cóme, and   tríp it,   ás you   go,
On the | líght fan tástic | toe.
—Milton.

This is the most commonly used trochaic measure.

(c) Trochaic Tetrameter
Wíth a | fúll but | sóft e|mótion,
Líke the   swéll of   súmmer's ócean.
—Byron.

(d) Trochaic Pentameter
Lów vo lúptuous | músic | winding | trémbled
—Tennyson

(e) Trochaic Hexameter
Holy! Holy! Holy! all the saints adore Thee.
—Heber

(f) Trochic Heptameter
Leaflets on the hollow oak still as greenly quiver.
—Lytton.

Trisyllabic Verse Anapestic Measures

In anapestic measures the accent, as a rule, falls on every third syllable.

(a) Anapestic Monometer
As ye sweép
Through the deép.
—Campbell.

(b) Anapestic Dimeter
In my ráge | shall be seén
The revénge | of a queen.
—Addison.

(c) Anapestic Trimeter
Iam món|arch of áll | I survéy.
—Cowper.

(d) Anapestic Tetrameter
'Tis the voíce of the slúg|gard, I héard | him compláin.

In anapestic measures, lines are frequently hypermetrical, and an iambus is sometimes substituted for an anapest, as in the following:

'Tis the lást | rose of súm|mer
Left bloóm|ing a lóne;
All her lóve|ly compán|ions
Are fá|ded and góne.
—Moore.

Dactylic Measures

In dactylic measures, the accent, as a rule, falls upon the first, fourth, seventh, and tenth syllables.

(a) Dactylic Monometer
Mérrily,
Cheérily.

(b) Dactylic Dimeter
Toúch her not | scórnfully
Think of her | moúrnfully.
—Hood.

(c) Dactylic Trimeter Hypermeter
Mérrily, | mérrily, | sháll I live | now
Únder the | blóssom that | hángs on the | bough.
—Shakespeare.

(d) Dactylic Hexameter

Dactylic Hexameter, borrowed from Greek and Latin poetry, is used by Longfellow in "Evangeline" and "Miles Standish." It consists of six feet. The last foot is either a spondee or a trochee; and the foot preceding the last is invariably a dactyl. The other four feet are generally dactyls, though a trochee is occasionally introduced; as

> Yé who be|liéve in af|féction that | hópes, and en|dúres and is | patient.
> Yé who be|liéve in the | béauty and | stréngth of wóman's de|votion.

Another way of scanning dactylic lines is to read the first two syllables as a trochee, and to consider the remainder of the line amphibrachic.

Amphibrachic Measures. In amphibrachic measures the accent, as a rule, falls upon the second, fifth, eighth, and eleventh syllables.

Amphibrachic Tetrameter

> There cáme to | the béach a | poor éxile | of Erin,
> The déw on | his thin robe | was héavy | and chill.
> —Campbell.

Another way of scanning this measure is to read the first two syllables as an iambus, and to consider the remainder of the line anapestic.

Mixed Meter

Poets frequently vary the structure of their verse by introducing a variety of feet, as in the following:

> Thére be | nóne of | béauty's | dáughters
> With a má|gic like thée:
> And like | músic | ón the | wáters
> Is they | sweet voíce | to mé.

With regard to some poems, such as Coleridge's "Christabel" and Byron's "Siege of Corinth," we can say only that there is a uniform number of accents in each line.

318 / *High School Equivalency Diploma Tests*

The lines in a poem have their names, too. These names refer to the number of feet in the line. You should learn to recognize and identify the most common because they may appear on your test.

NUMBER OF FEET IN LINE	NAME OF LINE	EXAMPLE
two	dimeter	What should / I say, Since faith / is dead, And truth / away From you / is fled?
three	trimeter	I arise / from dreams / of thee In the first / sweet sleep / of night,
four	tetrameter	My heart's / in the Highlands, / my heart 　is not here; My heart's / in the High- / lands, 　a-chas-/ing the deer /
five	pentameter	A jug / of Wine, / a Loaf / of Bread—/ 　and Thou
six	hexameter	Laurel / is green / for a sea-/son, and 　love is sweet / for a day;/

Usually, the kind of foot and the type of line are referred to together. The following line

<blockquote>When I consider how my life is spent</blockquote>

can be analyzed as

<blockquote>When I consid- er how my life is spent.</blockquote>

You can see at once that the poetic line has five feet and thus is a pentameter. The beat throughout is boom-BOOM, or iambic. So the line is said to be *iambic pentameter*. The following line

<blockquote>And many skeletons shook their heads</blockquote>

is an *iambic tetrameter*. Why?

Analyze the following lines and see if you can discover what they are:

1) Along the heath and near his favorite tree
2) Where the weeds that grew green from the graves of its roses
3) My heart leaps up when I behold
4) Love is all I wish to know and learn on

The first line is iambic pentameter. The second line is anapestic tetrameter. The third line is iambic tetramater. The fourth line is trochaic pentameter. How did you do?

RHYME consists in the similarity of sound in the final syllable or syllables of two or more words. Three things are essential to a perfect *rhyme:*

1. The vowel sounds of the rhyming syllables, and, if the vowels are followed by consonants, the consonant sounds, must be the same; as *try* and *cry*, *light* and *sprite*. Identity of sound, not of letters, is required. *Lose* and *close* do not rhyme.

2. The consonant sounds preceding the vowels must be different; as *way* and *day, sour* and *power.*

3. Similarity of accent; as, *sing* and *fling. Singing* and *fling* do not rhyme.

In *single rhymes,* one syllable rhymes with another; as, *hand* and *band.* In *double rhymes,* two syllables rhyme with two other syllables; as, *crying* and *trying.* In *triple rhymes,* three syllables rhyme with three other syllables. In *double* and *triple* rhymes, the first rhyming syllables must conform to the rules for single rhymes; the other syllables should be identical in sound.

Rhyming syllables usually occur at the ends of lines; the last syllable of a line may, however, be made to rhyme with one in the middle of the line; as,

> Ho, trumpets, sound a war-note!
> Ho, lictors, clear the *way!*
> The knights will *ride,* in all their pride,
> Along the streets to-*day*.
>
> —Macaulay.

Lines whose final syllables rhyme should have the same *indention;* that is, should be commenced, in writing or printing, at an equal distance from the margin. Thus:

> Ring out the old, ring in the new,
> Ring, happy bells, across the snow:
> The year is going, let him go,
> Ring out the false, ring in the true.
>
> —Tennyson.

Forms: The poet has an almost endless variety of poetic forms he can use. He may even invent a new form. You should know a few essential things about forms, though, for your test.

A COUPLET is composed of two consecutive lines, the final syllables of which rhyme. A TRIPLET is composed of three such lines.

In **BLANK VERSE** there is rhythm, but not rhyme; as,

> Of man's first disobedience, and the fruit
> Of that forbidden tree, whose mortal taste
> Brought Death into the world, and all our woe,
> With loss of Eden, till one greater Man
> Restore us, and regain the blissful seat,
> Sing, heav'nly Muse.

The poet *might* break up his poem into various parts. Usually, all parts have the same number of lines and rhyme scheme. Here is an example:

> 1 Under the wide and starry sky
> 2 Dig the grave and let me lie:
> 3 Glad did I live and gladly die,
> 4 And I laid me down with a will.
>
> 5 This be the verse you grave for me:
> 6 Here he lies where he longed to be;
> 7 Home is the sailor, home from the sea,
> 8 And the hunter home from this hill.

The poem is divided into parts. Each part has four lines. The first three lines of each part rhyme with each other. The fourth lines of each part also rhyme with each other. These parts are called *stanzas*.

Another important form you should know is the *sonnet*. A sonnet is a fourteen-line poem, usually iambic pentameter. The following selection is a good example of a sonnet.

> Let me not to the marriage of true minds
> Admit impediments. Love is not love
> Which alters when it alteration finds,
> Or bends with the remover to remove:
> Oh, no! it is an ever-fixed mark
> That looks on tempests and is never shaken;
> It is the star to every wandering bark,
> Whose worth's unknown, although his height be taken.
> Love's not Time's fool, though rosy lips and cheeks
> Within his bending sickle's compass come;
> Love alters not with his brief hours and weeks,
> But bears it out even to the edge of doom.
> If this be error and upon me proved,
> I never writ, nor no man ever loved.

FIGURES OF SPEECH

A poet uses words, of course, but he uses them in very special ways to get particular effects, as a painter uses color. You may be questioned on these special ways, and you should become thoroughly acquainted with them. They are not difficult, and you use many of them in your everyday speech.

Simile and Metaphor. If you are arguing with someone who refuses to see your point of view and you say in the heat of your discussion, "You're like a mule!", you are using a simile. A simile is a comparison that uses "like" or "as" or some other similar expression of comparison. You mean, of course, that the person you are arguing with is as stubborn as a mule.

Poets rely heavily on similes, as you can see by the following lines taken from various poems:

1) And the sheen of their spears was like stars on the sea
2) My love is like a red red rose
3) My love is like to ice, and I to fire
4) Oh, thou art fairer than the evening star

If the poet compares one thing to another *without* using "like", "as", or some similar term implying comparison, this is called a *metaphor*. If, instead of saying, "You're like a mule!", you say instead to the person arguing with you, "You're a mule!", or "You mule!", you are using a metaphor. Here are some examples of poetic metaphor:

1) It is the east, and Juliet is the sun!
2) Or I guess the grass is itself a child
3) Spring, the sweet Spring, is the year's pleasant king
4) Love is a sickness full of woes
5) Her eyes be sapphires plain
6) That little tent of blue which prisoners call the sky

You will notice that in some of these examples the poets treat things as having human qualities, or of being human. Walt Whitman states that the grass is a child. Thomas Nashe says that spring is the king of the year. This treatment of certain objects or abstractions as having human qualities or as being human is called *personification*. Here are some examples:

1) When Faith is kneeling by his bed of death
2) Oft, in the stilly night, ere Slumber's chain has bound me
3) This city now doth like a garment wear
   The beauty of the morning

When a poet uses what is called an *apostrophe*, he goes a step beyond personification. Not only has he given human qualities to objects or emotions or other non-living things, he talks to them as if they were present. Here are some examples:

1) With how sad steps, O Moon, thou climb'st the skies!
3) O Wild West Wind, thou breath of Autumn's being
3) Time, you thief, who love to get
   Sweets into your list, put that in!
4) Oh Life, thou Nothing's younger brother!
5) These pleasures, Melancholy, give,
   And I with thee will choose to live.

GLOSSARY OF LITERARY TERMS

This is some of the language you're likely to see on your examination. You may not need to know all the words in this carefully prepared glossary, but if even a few appear, you'll be that much ahead of your competitors. Perhaps the greater benefit from this list is the frame of mind it can create for you. Without reading a lot of technical text you'll steep yourself in just the right atmosphere for high test marks.

Having studied the Forms and Tools of poetry, you are well advised to review the poetic and literary terms which might prove to be important. They might appear on your test.

allegory: A poem or story in which the characters, objects, places, etc. may stand for certain ideas or ideals. For example, in *The Pilgrim's Progress,* a book by John Bunyan, the leading character, Christian, is really any man who struggles through life searching for goodness.

alliteration: Sometimes poets create a certain effect when they use the same consonant in quick repetition. This is called *alliteration.* Usually, the consonant used appears as the first letter of the words, as you will see in the following examples:

"The mother of months in meadow or plain."
"And watching his luck was the girl he loved,
The lady that's known as Lou."

In the first example, the poet created an alliterative effect by the repetition of the letter "m" in "mother," "months," and "meadow."

The second poet used the letter "l" to get an alliterative effect. Can you pick out the alliterative words?

apostrophe: a direct address to a dead or absent person or thing. Examples:

"O Spirit, that dost prefer the upright heart and pure."
"O Captain! my Captain! rise up and hear the bells."

assonance: Assonance is a cousin to alliteration. It is the appearance of the same vowel sounds in quick repetition. Here are examples:

"Mid hushed, cool-rooted flowers fragrant-eyed"
"A weed by the stream
Put forth a seed
And made a new breed"

In the first example, the sound of "oo" occurs twice. In the second example, the poet used the sound of "ee" and "ea" four times.

ballad: A story in poetic form. Somtimes this form is called a *narrative*.

cliche: A word or phrase which has been used so often in common speech that it has lost its freshness, its "spark."

colloquialism: A word or phrase that is identified with a certain locality. For example the phrase, "How you'all" is identified with the southern part of the United States.

dirge: A sad poem in which the poet speaks of a dead friend, hero, or relative. Another term for dirge is *elegy*.

euphemism: a substitution of a mild expression for a harsh one. Examples:

> The departed (for the dead).
> A slow student (for a stupid one).

foot: a group of two or three syllables upon one of which the accent, or stress of the voice, falls in reading.

Free verse: Poetry that is not necessarily rhymed nor has any special meter.

hyperbole: An exaggeration which the reader knows is not true. Examples:

> "He was the best card player that ever was or ever will be."
> "We are immensely obliged."
>
> "I'd walk a million miles for one of your smiles."

imagery: The poet often tries to arouse in the reader certain pictures or feelings, which is summed up as imagery. For example, when you read the lines,

> The Owl and the Pussy-cat went to sea
> > In a beautiful pea-green boat,

the poet hopes that you will see this ridiculous scene in your mind.

Sometimes a poet may wish you to feel rather than to see. The poet wishes you to feel cold when you read the following lines:

> Talk of your cold! Through the jacket's fold
> It stabbed like a driven nail.
> If our eyes we'd close, then the lashes froze
> Till sometimes we couldn't see.

inversion: The changing of the usual order of words. Usually this is done in order to maintain the meter of the poem. Examples of inversion are:

> "Holy, fair, and wise is she"
> *(the usual order would be "She is holy, fair, and wise.")*

> "Let me not to the marriage of true minds
> Admit impediments. . ."
> *(The usual order would be "Let me not admit there are impediments to the marriage of true minds.")*

irony: says something but means the opposite. Examples:

> "Here's a pretty how-d'ye-do (if one gets a cold shoulder.)"
> "You must love me (if one hates you.)"

limerick: A short humorous poem with a characteristic meter and rhyme structure:

> There was a young lady of Niger
> Who smiled as she rode on a tiger:
> > They came back from the ride
> > With the lady inside
> And the smile on the face of the tiger.

litotes: an understatement in which the negative of the opposite meaning is used: Examples:

> Not bad at all.
> A matter of no slight importance.
> Not entirely unsatisfactory.

metaphor: a comparison between persons or things without the use of like or as. Examples:

> The road was a ribbon of moonlight.
> He was a lion in strength.

metonymy: a figure by which a thing is designated, not by its own name, but by the name of something that resembles or suggests it. Examples:

> glasses (for spectacles)
> the knife (for surgery)

monologue: A story told by one person.

mood: The feeling that the poet wishes the reader to achieve when reading his work. For example, the poet wishes you to have a feeling of well-being and happiness after you read

> The year's at the spring,
> And day's at the morn;
> Morning's at seven;
> The hill-side's dew-pearl'd;
> The lark's on the wing;
> The snail's on the thorn;
> God's in His Heaven—
> All's right with the world!

onomatopoeia: Certain words are supposed to imitate the events they represent. Here are a few examples:

> "Crack! was the sound of the rifle in the night!"
> "The fire bells clanged their alarm."
> "The ball plopped into the water."
> "Crack!", "clanged", and "plopped" are examples of *onomatopoeia*.

oxymoron: Words that seemingly are opposed, such as "a wickedly moral man" and "thunderous silence."

paradox: A statement which seems to contradict itself. However, upon close investigation, it turns out to have an element of truth.

personification: a figure in which an inanimate object is given human qualities. Examples:

Old Sol is really shining today.
Death, be not proud!

scan a line: to mark the feet and tell what kind they are.

simile: a comparison between persons or things with the use of like or as. Examples:

He is as restless as a windshield wiper.
The sky looks like a burning ship.

stanza: a regularly recurring group of lines. For examples of stanzas, see Longfellow's "Psalm of Life" and "Village Blacksmith."

synechdoche: a figure of speech in which a part is used for the whole. Examples:

The cutthroat (for murderer) was finally caught.
This ranch has sixty head (of cattle).

Now, push forward! Test yourself and practice for your test with the carefully constructed quizzes that follow. Each one presents the kind of question you may expect on your test. And each question is at just the level of difficulty that may be expected. Don't try to take all the tests at one time. Rather, schedule yourself so that you take a few at each session, and spend approximately the same time on them at each session. Score yourself honestly, and date each test. You should be able to detect improvement in your performance on successive sessions.

TEST I. INTERPRETATION OF POETRY

TIME: 10 Minutes. 6 Questions.

DIRECTIONS: Below each of the literary passages you will find one or more incomplete statements about the passage of prose, poetry, or drama. Each "stem" is followed by four or five "foils." Read each passage slowly, visualizing the plot, setting, action, characters, meaning, tone, and style. Re-read the passage before answering each question. From the emotions and attitudes expressed, choose the BEST "foil." Blacken the corresponding space on the answer sheet.

Explanations of the key points behind these questions appear with the answers at the end of this test. The explanatory answers provide the kind of background that will enable you to answer test questions with facility and confidence.

Words and Terms You Might Not Know

2) **chaired you through the market-place:** carried him through town on a chair on their shoulders

9) **betimes:** quickly

11) **laurel:** laurel is a symbol for victory

17) **rout:** crowd

19) **renown:** fame

23) **lintel:** top of a door or window

28) **garland:** a wreath

Poetry Passage

1   The time you won your town the race
2   We chaired you through the market-place;
3   Man and boy stood cheering by,
4   And home we brought you shoulder-high.

5   Today, the road all runners come,
6   Shoulder-high we bring you home,
7   And set you at your threshold down,
8   Townsman of a stiller town.

9 Smart lad, to slip betimes away
10 From fields where glory does not stay,
11 And early though the laurel grows
12 It withers quicker than the rose.

13 Eyes the shady night has shut
14 Cannot see the record cut,
15 And silence sounds no worse than cheers
16 After earth has stopped the ears.

17 Now you will not swell the rout
18 Of lads that wore their honors out
19 Runners whom renown outran
20 And the name died before the man.

21 So set, before its echoes fade,
22 The fleet foot on the sill of shade,
23 And hold to the low lintel up
24 The still-defended challenge-cup.

25 And round that early-laurelled head
26 Will flock to gaze the strength less dead,
27 And find unwithered on its curls
28 The garland briefer than a girl's.

—A. E. Housman, "To An Athlete Dying Young"

DIRECTIONS: *Read and answer each question carefully. Select the best answer and blacken the proper space on the answer sheet.*

1. The athlete was a
   (A) runner
   (B) football player
   (C) basketball star
   (D) girl

2. "Threshold" in the third line of the second stanza is a metaphor for
   (A) the grave
   (B) sports
   (C) home
   (D) life

3. "Stiller town" in the last line of the second stanza is a metaphor for
   (A) a country village
   (B) old age
   (C) death
   (D) love

4. The first three feet of line three of the first stanza are
   (A) dactylic
   (B) iambic
   (C) trochaic
   (D) anapestic

5. The poet praises the athlete for
   (A) dying young
   (B) winning the race
   (C) wearing the laurel of victory
   (D) breaking a record

6. An advantage of the athlete's death in the view of the poet is that he
   (A) had slowed down recently, although he was still fast.
   (B) had been forgotten and his death was therefore a mercy
   (C) had been very ill and had suffered a great deal
   (D) had died when he still had fame.

CONSOLIDATE YOUR KEY ANSWERS HERE

Practice using Answer Sheets. Make ONE mark for each answer. Additional and stray marks may be counted as mistakes. In making corrections erase errors COMPLETELY. Make glossy black marks. To arrive at an accurate estimate of your ability and progress, cover the Correct Answers with a sheet of white paper while you are taking this test.

	A	B	C	D	E		A	B	C	D	E		A	B	C	D	E		A	B	C	D	E		A	B	C	D	E		A	B	C	D	E
1	▯	▯	▯	▯	▯	2	▯	▯	▯	▯	▯	3	▯	▯	▯	▯	▯	4	▯	▯	▯	▯	▯	5	▯	▯	▯	▯	▯	6	▯	▯	▯	▯	▯

CORRECT ANSWERS TO THE FOREGOING PRACTICE QUESTIONS

Now compare your answers with these Correct Answers to the Practice Questions. If your answers differ from these, go back and study those questions to see where and how you made your mistakes.

1.A	2.A	3.C	4.C	5.A	6.D

EXPLANATORY ANSWERS CLARIFYING CARDINAL POINTS

Here you have the heart of the Question and Answer Method. . .getting help when and where you need it. Where one of your Key Answers differs from ours you have a problem which can easily be remedied by reading the explanation. Then, if you have time, you might be able to pick up points on the exam by reading the other explanations, even where you wrote the Key Answers correctly. These explanations stress fundamental facts, ideas, and principles which just might pop up as questions on future exams.

1. **(A)** The poet states the athlete "won your town the race" and several times refers to running. The athlete is not a girl because he calls him a "smart lad".

2. **(A)** You know by the title of the poem that the athlete has died. The whole implication of the second stanza is that he is being carried on his funeral day.

3. **(C)** If this is the athlete's funeral day, it becomes obvious that death stands for a "stiller town".

4. **(C)** Trochaic. They have a BOOM-boom beat. The line could be diagrammed as

Mán aňd / bóy stoŏd / chéering / bý

5. **(A)** The poet states that the athlete won the big race in the first stanza, that he broke the record in the fourth stanza, and since he is the champion, the laurel of victory is his. But he does not necessarily praise him for these things. However, he calls him a "smart lad, to slip betimes away" to die.

6. **(D)** **A** and **B** are obviously false. We don't know if **C** is true or not. But the poet states that "Now you will not swell the rout of lads that wore their honors out" and says the athlete is smart to leave "fields where glory does not stay."

TEST II. INTERPRETATION OF POETRY

TIME: 8 Minutes. 5 Questions.

DIRECTIONS: Below each of the literary passages you will find one or more incomplete statements about the passage of prose, poetry, or drama. Each "stem" is followed by four or five "foils." Read each passage slowly, visualizing the plot, setting, action, characters, meaning, tone, and style. Re-read the passage before answering each question. From the emotions and attitudes expressed, choose the BEST "foil." Blacken the corresponding space on the answer sheet.

Explanations of the key points behind these questions appear with the answers at the end of this test. The explanatory answers provide the kind of background that will enable you to answer test questions with facility and confidence.

Words and Terms You Might Not Know

4) **lure:** something which attracts
5) **fretful:** to be worried and peevish
8) **endure:** to last for a long time or forever

Poetry Passage

1 We are not sure of sorrow,
2   And joy was never sure;
3 Today will die tomorrow;
4   Time stoops to no man's lure;
5 And love, grown faint and fretful,
6 With lips but half regretful
7 Sighs, and with eyes forgetful
8   Weeps that no loves endure.

9 From too much love of living,
10   From hope and fear set free,
11 We thank with brief thanksgiving
12   Whatever gods may be
13 That no life lives for ever;
14 That dead men rise up never;
15 That even the weariest river
16   Winds somewhere safe to sea.

—Algernon Charles Swinburne, "The Garden of Proserpine"

DIRECTIONS: Read and answer each question carefully. Select the best answer and blacken the proper space on the answer sheet.

1. Lines 1, 3, and 5, of the first stanza, contain examples of

    (A) oxymoron
    (B) free verse
    (C) alliteration
    (D) onomatopoeia

2. The way in which the poet uses "today" in line three is an example of

    (A) paradox
    (B) simile
    (C) onomatopoeia
    (D) personification

3. The second line of the second stanza is an example of

    (A) trochaic hexameter
    (B) anapestic trimeter
    (C) iambic trimeter
    (D) iambic pentameter

4. The poet

    (A) believes in an after-life
    (B) states that one cannot change fate
    (C) celebrates life
    (D) welcomes death

5. Love in the last four lines of the first stanza is represented as

    (A) a state of mind
    (B) a living being
    (C) a storm
    (D) a flower

CONSOLIDATE YOUR KEY ANSWERS HERE

Practice using Answer Sheets. Make ONE mark for each answer. Additional and stray marks may be counted as mistakes. In making corrections erase errors COMPLETELY. Make glossy black marks. To arrive at an accurate estimate of your ability and progress, cover the Correct Answers with a sheet of white paper while you are taking this test.

```
   A B C D E      A B C D E      A B C D E      A B C D E      A B C D E
 1 ﹝﹞﹝﹞﹝﹞﹝﹞﹝﹞   2 ﹝﹞﹝﹞﹝﹞﹝﹞﹝﹞   3 ﹝﹞﹝﹞﹝﹞﹝﹞﹝﹞   4 ﹝﹞﹝﹞﹝﹞﹝﹞﹝﹞   5 ﹝﹞﹝﹞﹝﹞﹝﹞﹝﹞
```

CORRECT ANSWERS TO THE FOREGOING PRACTICE QUESTIONS

1.C   2.D   3.C   4.D   5.B

EXPLANATORY ANSWERS CLARIFYING CARDINAL POINTS

Here you have the heart of the Question and Answer Method. . .getting help when and where you need it. Where one of your Key Answers differs from ours you have a problem which can easily be remedied by reading the explanation. Then, if you have time, you might be able to pick up points on the exam by reading the other explanations, even where you wrote the Key Answers correctly. These explanations stress fundamental facts, ideas, and principles which just might pop up as questions on future exams.

1. **(C)** The poet achieves alliterative effects by using the words, sure, sorrow, today, tommow, faint and fretful.

2. **(D)** When the poet states that "Today will die tomorrow," he is giving "Today" human qualities.

3. **(C)** The line has three feet, which identifies it as a trimeter. Its beat is boom-BOOM. The line could be diagrammed as follows:

    From hope / and love / set free

4. **(D)** We know the poet does not believe in an after-life since he says. "no life lives forever" and "dead men rise up never". He never hints that a person cannot change fate. He certainly doesn't celebrate life. He thanks "Whatever gods may be" that there is death.

5. **(B)** Love sighs, has eyes, weeps, and grows faint and fretful. It has been given human qualities or has been personified.

TEST III. INTERPRETATION OF POETRY

TIME: 8 Minutes. 5 Questions.

DIRECTIONS: *Below each of the literary passages you will find one or more incomplete statements about the passage of prose, poetry, or drama. Each "stem" is followed by four or five "foils." Read each passage slowly, visualizing the plot, setting, action, characters, meaning, tone, and style. Re-read the passage before answering each question. From the emotions and attitudes expressed, choose the BEST "foil." Blacken the corresponding space on the answer sheet.*

Explanations of the key points behind these questions appear with the answers at the end of this test. The explanatory answers provide just the help you need to strengthen your ability to master this type of question.

Words and Terms You Might Not Know

2) **temperate:** calmer and less changeable
11) **shade:** in the land of death

Poetry Passage

1   Shall I compare thee to a summer's day?
2   Thou art more lovely and more temperate:
3   Rough winds do shake the darling buds of May,
4   And summer's lease hath all too short a date:
5   Sometime too hot the eye of heaven shines,
6   And often is his gold complexion dimm'd;
7   And every fair from fair sometime declines,
8   By chance or nature's changing course untrimm'd;
9   But thy eternal summer shall not fade,
10   Nor lose possession of that fair thou owest;
11   Nor shall Death brag thou wander'st in his shade,
12   When in eternal lines to time thou grow'st:
13   So long as men can breathe, or eyes can see,
14   So long lives this, and this gives life to thee.

—William Shakespeare, "Shall I Compare Thee To A Summer's Day"

DIRECTIONS: *Read and answer each question carefully. Select the best answer and blacken the proper space on the answer sheet.*

1. The poem is

 (A) a dirge
 (B) a sonnet
 (C) a limerick
 (D) a dimeter form

2. The poet likened his love to

 (A) eternal summer
 (B) the eye of heaven
 (C) a summer's day
 (D) the darling buds of May

3. The poet claims his loved one will never really die because

 (A) he loves her
 (B) he will keep her alive by writing this poem

 (C) she is too beautiful
 (D) death won't find her

4. By ''eternal lines,'' the poet refers to

 (A) life
 (B) the lines of his loved one's body
 (C) the lines in his loved one's hand
 (D) his poetry

5. The way the poet used ''Death'' in the tenth line is an example of

 (A) onomatopoeia
 (B) assonance
 (C) personification
 (D) hyperbole

CONSOLIDATE YOUR KEY ANSWERS HERE

Practice using Answer Sheets. Make ONE mark for each answer. Additional and stray marks may be counted as mistakes. In making corrections erase errors COMPLETELY. Make glossy black marks. To arrive at an accurate estimate of your ability and progress, cover the Correct Answers with a sheet of white paper while you are taking this test.

CORRECT ANSWERS TO THE FOREGOING PRACTICE QUESTIONS

1.B   2.A   3.B   4.D   5.C

EXPLANATORY ANSWERS CLARIFYING CARDINAL POINTS

1. **(B)** This certainly is not a dirge, since the poet's love is not dead. It does not have the construction of a limerick, nor is it humorous. There are five feet per line, which means that the poem is in pentameter form. If it had three feet per line, it would be in trimeter form. The poem has fourteen lines and is in iambic pentameter form, which fits our definition of a sonnet.

2. **(A)** The ''eye of heaven'' refers to the sun. The poet tells us in the second line the difference between his love and a summer's day. He tells us in the third line that ''rough winds do shake the darling buds of May'' and changes them and other aspects of summer. But he states to his loved one that ''thy eternal summer shall not fade.'' Thus, she is not like any ordinary summer.

3. **(B)** A is incorrect because he does not actually state that he loves her, although this is obvious. **C** is also wrong. He appreciates the fact that she is beautiful, but that is not why she will be immortal. **D** is incorrect since he never says that Death will not find her, only that Death will not ''brag thou wander'st in his shade.'' **B** is right as you can see by reading the last three lines again.

4. **(D)** The poet states emphatically that his ''eternal lines,'' which will last as long as ''eyes can see,'' will ''give life to thee.'' He may be right, for people have been reading this poem for nearly three hundred years.

5. **(C)** If Death can brag, then Death has been given human qualities, or has become personified.

INTERPRETING FICTION SELECTIONS

Although the Interpretation of Literary Materials is essentially a reading exercise, it demands that you do more than merely skim the surface of a selection. You must infer the author's real meaning from his style and point of view; from the plot and setting; from the intentions and personalities with which he endows his characters; from his opinions and feelings; from the figurative devices he uses; from all the rhetorical nuances described in these pages. Correct answers come from the clues you can piece together and from the unifying thread strung by the author through each passage.

Fiction is telling a story in print. It is an imaginary tale, even though it may have true-to-life characters.

The two major forms of fiction are the short story and the novel.

On your test you probably will be given excerpts from novels or short stories. You will be asked to determine if you

a) know what is happening in the story

b) can understand the characters

c) can detect the attitude of the author towards the characters and his viewpoint towards the story (whether he sees it as amusing or tragic, etc.)

It is important to know that the writer of fiction employs many of the tools the poet uses. In the excerpts you read, you will notice similes, metaphors, onomatopoeia, allegory, cliches, colloquialisms, hyperbole, monologues, oxymorons, and paradoxes. You should review these so you can answer the questions on fiction.

Tools of the fiction writer which you know about are:

Irony

Irony is the difference between what is said and what is meant, which might be very different from the uttered words. For example, in the following excerpt from the story *War* by Luigi Pirandello, an old man talks of his son, killed in battle:

Everyone should stop crying; everyone should laugh, as I do . . . or at least thank God—as I do—because my son, before dying, sent me a message saying that he was dying satisfied at having ended his life in the best way he could have wished. That is why, as you see, I do not even wear mourning. . . .

But later it turns out that the old man is truly agonized over his son's death. Therefore, the speech given above is an example of the use of irony.

Irony also is the difference between what seems to be happening and what really happens. In the story *The Birthmark* by Nathaniel Hawthorne, a man marries a woman he deeply loves. She is very beautiful, but has a large red birthmark on her face. It is the only thing that mars her almost-perfect beauty. Her husband performs a skillful operation on her and manages to remove the mark. However, now having reached perfection, she dies. That he did not anticipate her death emphasizes the ironic tone of the author.

Satire

In a satire, an author mocks human hopes, institutions, and supposed virtues. A satirical author usually is cynical and believes mankind does not really practice what it preaches.

KNOWING WHAT IS GOING ON

On your test, you will probably be asked many questions designed to see if you understand what has happened or exactly what the author has said. You must read each excerpt in the test carefully, rereading those parts you are not quite sure you understand.

Some of the questions will not be difficult if you have read carefully and thoroughly. Many of the questions, however, will ask you to make assumptions about parts of the excerpt. In other words, you will have to *infer* what the author is driving at, although he does not come right out and tell you what he means.

For example, if you read,

The pitcher wound up. The ball came in a big sweeping curve. The batter swung . . . and hit only air.

you can infer that the author is writing about a baseball game and that the batter has missed the ball and has one strike.

If you read,

Jones ran towards me, swinging the club in his hand. "You rat!" he cried. "I'll get you for this!"

you can infer that Jones is very angry at the narrator and means to hit him.

The two passages above are fairly obvious. The inference questions on your test will not be so obvious. Usually, they will ask you to draw certain conclusions from much longer selections. You will be able to practice answering inference questions with the sample selections and questions on the next few pages.

UNDERSTANDING THE CHARACTERS

On your test, you will be asked some questions concerning the characters in a story. Most of these will be inference questions. The author probably will not state "Smith was a cruel man." But he might very well state, as James Joyce did at the end of his story "Counterparts,"

> The little boy cried, "O, Pa!" and ran whimpering round the table, but the man followed him and caught him by the coat. The little boy looked about him wildly but, seeing no way of escape, fell upon his knees.
>
> "Now, you'll let the fire out the next time!" said the man, striking at him vigorously with the stick. "Take that, you little whelp!"

From this passage, you can infer that the man is cruel.

Now you can apply what you have learned in the three following selections and accompanying questions. You will be given the answers and the explanations for the answers.

Now, push forward! Test yourself and practice for your test with the carefully constructed quizzes that follow. Each one presents the kind of question you may expect on your test. And each question is at just the level of difficulty that may be expected.

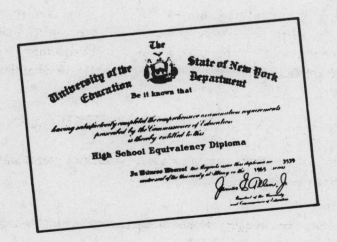

This is the kind of official diploma your State Department of Education will issue to you. It is the legal equivalent of the diploma awarded to students who have graduated from a four-year high school.

TEST IV. INTERPRETATION OF FICTION

TIME: 10 Minutes. 8 Questions.

DIRECTIONS: Below each of the literary passages you will find one or more incomplete statements about the passage of prose, po- etry, or drama. Each "stem" is followed by four or five "foils." Read each passage slowly, visualizing the plot, setting, action, characters, meaning, tone, and style. Re-read the passage before answering each question. From the emotions and attitudes expressed, choose the BEST "foil." Blacken the corresponding space on the answer sheet.

Explanations of the key points behind these questions appear with the answers at the end of this test. The explanatory answers provide just the help you need to strengthen your ability to master this type of question.

Fiction Passage

One night as he was walking about the prison he noticed some earth falling out from under one of the beds attached to the walls. He stopped to see what it was. Suddenly Makar Semyonitch crept out from under the bed. He looked at Aksyonof, frightened.

Aksyonof pretended not to see him, but Makar seized him and said that he had dug a hole under the wall. He had put the dirt into his boots. Each day he had emptied it out on the road when the prisoners were driven to their work.

"Just keep your mouth shut, old man, and you'll get out, too. If you talk, they'll whip me to death, but I'll kill you first."

Aksyonof trembled with anger. He freed himself from the grip, and said, "I don't want to escape. Kill me, will you? You killed me long ago! Maybe I will tell on you, maybe I won't. It is up to God."

Next day, when the convicts were led out to work, the prison guards noticed that a prisoner emptied dirt out of his boots. However, they did not see which one did it. Nonetheless, they questioned all the prisoners to find out who was trying to escape. None of them would tell on Makar Semyonitch because they knew it might mean his death. At last the warden turned to Aksyonof, whom he trusted, and said:

"You always tell the truth. Who dug the hole?"

Makar Semyonitch appeared casual and unconcerned. He looked slyly at the warden and did not even glance at Aksyonof. Aksyonof's lips and hands trembled. For a long time he could not utter a word. "Why should I protect the man who ruined my life?'' he wondered. ''Let him pay for what he has done to me. But if I tell, they will probably whip him to death. Also, I might be wrong about him. And, after all, what good would it do me?''

''Well, old man,'' said the warden, ''who has been digging?''

Aksyonof glanced at Makar Semyonitch, and said, ''I cannot tell you. It is not God's will that I should. Punish me as you wish. I am in your power.''

The warden tried hard, but Aksyonof wouldn't talk any more. Finally the warden dropped the matter.

That night when Aksyonof was almost asleep, someone approached softly. He peered through the darkness and recognized Makar.

''What do you want?'' asked Aksyonof. ''Why have you come?''

Makar Semyonitch said nothing. Aksyonof sat up and said, ''What do you want? Go away, or I will call the guard!''

Makar Semyonitch leaned down and whispered, ''Ivan Dmitritch, forgive me!''

''What for?'' asked Aksyonof.

''I killed the merchant and hid the knife in your bag. I meant to kill you too, but I heard a noise, so I hid the knife and jumped out of the window.''

Aksyonof did not know what to say.

Makar Semyonitch knelt upon the ground beside the bed. ''Ivan Dmitritch, forgive me! For the love of God, forgive me! I will confess I murdered the merchant. You will be set free and can go home.''

''That's easy enough to say,'' said Aksyonof, ''but I have suffered for you a long time. Where could I go now? My wife is probably dead. My sons have forgotten me. I haven't any place to go.''

Makar Semyonitch hit his head on the floor, again and again. ''Ivan Dmitritch, forgive me!'' he cried. ''When they whipped me before sending me here, it was not as painful as seeing you now. Yet you pitied me, and wouldn't tell. For the love of Christ, forgive me.'' He began to cry.

Aksyonof also wept.

''God will forgive you!'' said he. ''Probably I'm much worse than you.''

As he said this, his cares faded. He no longer wished to leave. He only looked forward to death.

Nonetheless, Makar Semyonitch confessed the murder to the warden. But when the time came to set him free, Aksyonof had died.

—Leo Tolstoy, ''God Sees the Truth but Waits''

DIRECTIONS: *Read and answer each question carefully. Select the best answer and blacken the proper space on the answer sheet.*

1. Aksyonof was in prison for

   (A) theft
   (B) murder
   (C) spying
   (D) refusing to fight in a war

2. When Aksyonof says "Kill me, will you? You killed me long ago!" we can infer that

   (A) Aksyonof is really a ghost
   (B) Semyonitch has stolen from Aksyonof
   (C) Semyonitch has destroyed Aksyonof's family
   (D) Aksyonof suspects that Semyonitch framed him

3. We can infer that

   (A) Semyonitch was in prison before Aksyonof
   (B) Aksyonof and Semyonitch have known each other a long time
   (C) Aksyonof likes Semyonitch
   (D) Aksyonof has been in prison many years

4. It is obvious from the way the warden treats him that Aksyonof is

   (A) respected
   (B) disliked
   (C) suspected of trying to escape
   (D) unknown to the warden

5. Aksyonof won't tell on Semyonitch because he

   (A) wants to punish Semyonitch himself
   (B) isn't sure that Semyonitch dug the hole
   (C) doesn't want Semyonitch to die by his action
   (D) is afraid of Semyonitch

6. Semyonitch comes to Aksyonof's bed to

   (A) kill him
   (B) confess he committed the crime for which Aksyonof was imprisoned
   (C) threaten Aksyonof not to talk to the warden any more
   (D) persuade Aksyonof to help him escape

7. Aksyonof does not wish to go home because

   (A) he can't face his old friends
   (B) he feels guilty about the murder of the merchant
   (C) his family has forgotten him
   (D) he has become accustomed to prison

8. Aksyonof's cares faded because

   (A) Semyonitch has confessed and Aksyonof will be freed
   (B) he has forgiven Semyonitch for digging the hole
   (C) he knows how to escape
   (D) he wouldn't judge Semyonitch for his crime

CONSOLIDATE YOUR KEY ANSWERS HERE

Practice using Answer Sheets. Make ONE mark for each answer. Additional and stray marks may be counted as mistakes. In making corrections erase errors COMPLETELY. Make glossy black marks. To arrive at an accurate estimate of your ability and progress, cover the Correct Answers with a sheet of white paper while you are taking this test.

CORRECT KEY ANSWERS TO THE PRACTICE QUESTIONS

Now compare your answers with these Correct Key Answers. If your answers differ from these, go back and study the Practice Questions to see where and how you made your mistakes. In doing this, the following Explanatory Answers should prove helpful. They provide concise clarifications of the basic points behind the Key Answers. Even where your Key Answers are the same as ours, go over the explanations carefully because they may be quite useful in helping you pick up extra points on the exam.

1. B   2. D   3. D   4. A   5. C   6. B   7. C   8. D

EXPLANATORY ANSWERS CLARIFYING CARDINAL POINTS

Here you have the heart of the Question and Answer Method. . .getting help when and where you need it. Where one of your Key Answers differs from ours you have a problem which can easily be remedied by reading the explanation. Then, if you have time, you might be able to pick up points on the exam by reading the other explanations, even where you wrote the Key Answers correctly. These explanations stress fundamental facts, ideas, and principles which just might pop up as questions on future exams.

1. **(B)** Semyonitch in his confession admits that he had "killed the merchant." Then he states that he put the knife in Aksyonof's bag and framed him for the murder.

2. **(D)** The passage tells us nothing to establish the validity of foils **A, B,** or **C.** So we must conclude on the basis of what Aksyonof says to Semyonitch in question 2, that he suspects Semyonitch of having framed him.

3. **(D)** A might be right, for all we know, but we are not told when Semyonitch came to prison. We are not told how long Semyonitch and Aksyonof have known each other, but they do not act as if they have known each other too long. It is obvious that Aksyonof doesn't like Semyonitch But Aksyonof says he has suffered for Semyonitch for "a long time," which implies he has been in prison many years.

4. **(A)** We are told that the warden trusts Aksyonof, and he states that the old man always tells the truth. Also, he would not punish Aksyonof when the prisoner refuses to tell on Semyonitch.

5. **(C)** Aksyonof thinks to himself while being questioned by the warden that if he tells that Semyonitch is the prisoner who is trying to escape, Semyonitch will be whipped to death. He does know that Semyonitch has dug the hole, since his enemy admitted it to him. He does not act in fear of Semyonitch, and there is no indication that he wishes to punish Semyonitch, although he dislikes the man.

6. **(B)** If you didn't get this question, you did not read carefully enough, and you had better reread the selection.

7. **(C)** Aksyonof tells Semyonitch he has no place to go if he leaves prison, since his wife is probably dead and his sons have forgotten him.

8. **(D)** Aksyonof's cares faded because he did not stand in judgment of Semyonitch. He cares nothing for freedom, he doesn't think about escape, and he never was too concerned about Semyonitch digging the hole.

TEST V. INTERPRETATION OF FICTION

TIME: 8 Minutes. 5 Questions.

DIRECTIONS: Below each of the literary passages you will find one or more incomplete statements about the passage of prose, poetry, or drama. Each "stem" is followed by four or five "foils." Read each passage slowly, visualizing the plot, setting, action, characters, meaning, tone, and style. Re-read the passage before answering each question. From the emotions and attitudes expressed, choose the BEST "foil." Blacken the corresponding space on the answer sheet.

Explanations of the key points behind these questions appear with the answers at the end of this test. The explanatory answers provide just the help you need to strengthen your ability to master this type of question.

Words You Might Not Know

deferential: respectful

social weight: the way a person is regarded by those who know him

heroism: bravery

recital: the telling of a story

scandal: an event which brings disgrace to one or more people

magnificent: wonderful

soberly: seriously and quietly

abstractly: without thought or knowledge (as is used in this story)

reflections: thoughts (as is used in this story)

idol: hero

stout: strong (as is used in this story)

idealism: seeing the world and the people in it as good (as used in this story)

Fiction Passage

"Could you see the whites of their eyes?" said the man who was seated on a soapbox.

"Nothing of the kind," replied old Henry warmly. "Just a lot of flitting figures, and I let go at where they 'peared to be the thickest. Bang!"

"Mr. Fleming," said the grocer—his deferential voice expressed somehow the old man's exact social weight—"Mr. Fleming, you never was frightened much in them battles, was you?"

The veteran looked down and grinned. Observing his manner, the entire group tittered. "Well, I guess I was," he answered finally. "Pretty well scared, sometimes. Why, in my first battle I thought the sky was falling down. I thought the world was coming to an end. You bet I was scared."

Everyone laughed. Perhaps it seemed strange and rather wonderful to them that a man should admit the thing, and in the tone of their laughter was probably more admiration than if old Fleming had declared that he had always been a lion. Moreover, they knew that he had ranked as an orderly sergeant, and so their opinion of his heroism was fixed. None, to be sure, knew how an orderly sergeant ranked, but then it was understood to be somewhere just shy of a major general's stars. So when old Henry admitted that he had been frightened, there was a laugh.

"The trouble was," said the old man, "I thought they were all shooting at me. Yes, sir, I thought every man in the other army was aiming at me in particular, and only me. And it seemed so darned unreasonable, you know. I wanted to explain to 'em what an almighty good fellow I was, because I thought then they might quit all trying to hit me. But I couldn't explain, and they kept on being unreasonable—blim-blam!-bang! So I run!"

Two little triangles of wrinkles appeared at the corners of his eyes. Evidently he appreciated some comedy in this recital. Down near his feet, however, little Jim, his grandson, was visibly horror-stricken. His hands were clasped nervously, and his eyes were wide with astonishment at this terrible scandal, his most magnificent grandfather telling such a thing.

"That was at Chancellorsville. Of course, afterward I got kind of used to it. A man does. Lots of men, though, seem to feel all right from the start. I did, as soon as I 'got on to it,' as they say now; but at first I was pretty flustered. Now, there was young Jim Conklin, old Si Conklin's son—that used to keep the tannery—you none of you recollect him—well, he went into it from the start just as if he was born to it. But with me it was different. I had to get used to it."

When little Jim walked with his grandfather he was in the habit of skipping along on the stone pavement in front of the three stores and the hotel of the town and betting that he could avoid the cracks. But upon this day he walked soberly, with his hand gripping two of his grandfather's fingers. Sometimes he kicked abstractedly at dandelions that curved over the walk. Anyone could see that he was much troubled.

"There's Sickles's colt over in the medder, Jimmie," said the old man. "Don't you wish you owned one like him?"

"Um," said the boy, with a strange lack of interest. He continued his reflections. Then finally he ventured: "Grandpa—now—was that true what you was telling those men?"

"What?" asked the grandfather. "What was I telling them?"

"Oh, about your running."

"Why, yes, that was true enough, Jimmie. It was my first fight, and there was an awful lot of noise, you know."

Jimmie seemed dazed that this idol, of its own will, should so totter. His stout boyish idealism was injured.

Presently the grandfather said: "Sickles's colt is going for a drink. Don't you wish you owned Sickles's colt, Jimmie?"

The boy merely answered: "He ain't as nice as our'n." He lapsed then into another moody silence.

—Stephen Crane, "The Veteran"

DIRECTIONS: Read and answer each question carefully. Select the best answer and blacken the proper space on the answer sheet.

1. The reader quickly learns that Henry is

   (A) a storekeeper
   (B) owner of a tannery
   (C) an ex-soldier
   (D) a major general

2. One might say that the old man's leading characteristic is

   (A) hypocrisy
   (B) pride
   (C) honesty
   (D) unfriendliness

3. When Mr. Fleming admitted that he had been afraid in battle, the adult listeners' attitude toward him was

   (A) one of amusement because they knew he had had never been in a war
   (B) was that of bitterness
   (C) remained one of admiration
   (D) changed to disgust

4. The old man does not seem to be aware that

   (A) his grandson is horrified by his admission of fear
   (B) little Jim never knew he had fought in a war
   (C) the listeners think he is a fool
   (D) his grandson was listening

5. The most important point that the author wishes the reader to understand is that

   (A) the boy doesn't like his grandfather
   (B) Henry was afraid in battle
   (C) the boy's image of his grandfather as a hero has been destroyed
   (D) Henry is highly regarded by his town's people

CONSOLIDATE YOUR KEY ANSWERS HERE

Practice using Answer Sheets. Make ONE mark for each answer. Additional and stray marks may be counted as mistakes. In making corrections erase errors COMPLETELY. Make glossy black marks. To arrive at an accurate estimate of your ability and progress, cover the Correct Answers with a sheet of white paper while you are taking this test.

```
     A B C D E     A B C D E     A B C D E     A B C D E     A B C D E
   1 |0 0 0 0 0  2 0 0 0 0 0   3 0 0 0 0 0   4 0 0 0 0 0   5 0 0 0 0 0
```

CORRECT KEY ANSWERS TO THE PRACTICE QUESTIONS

Now compare your answers with these Correct Key Answers. If your answers differ from these, go back and study the Practice Questions to see where and how you made your mistakes. In doing this, the following Explanatory Answers should prove helpful. They provide concise clarifications of the basic points behind the Key Answers. Even where your Key Answers are the same as ours, go over the explanations carefully because they may be quite useful in helping you pick up extra points on the exam.

1. C   2. C   3. C   4. A   5. C

EXPLANATORY ANSWERS CLARIFYING CARDINAL POINTS

Here you have the heart of the Question and Answer Method. . .getting help when and where you need it. Where one of your Key Answers differs from ours you have a problem which can easily be remedied by reading the explanation. Then, if you have time, you might be able to pick up points on the exam by reading the other explanations, even where you wrote the Key Answers correctly. These explanations stress fundamental facts, ideas, and principles which just might pop up as questions on future exams.

1. **(C)** Henry is talking about a battle and war in general. We are not told what job he has in civilian life. We are specifically told that Henry was an "orderly sergeant."

2. **(C)** The old man is honest in the description of his fears; therefore, he is no hypocrite. He does not seem to have pride in himself and is certainly not unfriendly.

3. **(C)** His fellow townsmen just won't believe that Henry is anything less than a hero. There is no indication that they believe him a liar or that they are bitter or disgusted.

4. **(A)** Jim, we are told, is "horror-stricken" at his grandfather's admission that he was afraid in battle. Perhaps Jim didn't know the old man was a soldier, but we are not told so. The probability is that he did know, since his grandfather is his hero. As they walked home together, they probably also came to the store together, and so Henry knew little Jim was present and listening. The listeners don't regard Henry as a fool; that is obvious from their respectful attitude towards him.

5. **(C)** We can eliminate **A**, for it is apparent that little Jim worships his grandfather. **B** and **D** are true statements. Henry was afraid in battle and admitted it, and he is highly regarded by his townspeople. But the author focuses his—and our—attention upon Jim's reaction to what his grandfather said, so we can *infer* that the rest of the story will deal with this relationship.

TEST VI. INTERPRETATION OF FICTION

TIME: 10 Minutes. 6 Questions.

DIRECTIONS: Below each of the literary passages you will find one or more incomplete statements about the passage of prose, poetry, or drama. Each "stem" is followed by four or five "foils." Read each passage slowly, visualizing the plot, setting, action, characters, meaning, tone, and style. Re-read the passage before answering each question. From the emotions and attitudes expressed, choose the BEST "foil." Blacken the corresponding space on the answer sheet.

Explanations of the key points behind these questions appear with the answers at the end of this test. The explanatory answers provide just the help you need to strengthen your ability to master this type of question.

Words You Might Not Know

air: manner (as is used in this story)
introductory: beginning
oilskins: waterproof cloth used to keep rain off sailors
malignantly: with evil
discoloration: a mark
divine: understand (as is used in this story)
imperatively: with command
animated: living
aggregation: collection
compounded: made up of
impelled: urged on
portion: share

nobility: acting with honor and kindness
ideals: rules of goodness to live by
pauper: one who is poor
doctrine: system
expediency: necessity (as is used in this story)
ferment: mixture
prerogative: right
expelled: let out
audible: able to be heard
expiration: act of letting out (as is used in this story)
revolting: disgusting

Fiction Passage

"Johnson," Wolf Larsen said, with an air of dismissing all that had gone before as introductory to the main business in hand, "I understand you're not quite satisfied with those oilskins?"

"No, I am not. They are no good, sir."

"And you've been shooting off your mouth about them."

"I say what I think, sir," the sailor answered courageously, not failing at the same time in ship courtesy, which demanded that "sir" be appended to each speech he made.

It was at this moment that I chanced to glance at Johansen. His big fists were clenching and unclenching, and his face was positively fiendish, so malignantly did he look at Johnson. I noticed a black discoloration, still faintly visible, under Johansen's eye, a mark of the thrashing he had received a few nights before from the sailor. For the first time I began to divine that something terrible was about to be enacted—what, I could not imagine.

"Do you know what happens to men who say what you've said about my slop-chest and me?" Wolf Larsen was demanding.

"I know, sir," was the answer.

"What?" Wolf Larsen demanded, sharply and imperatively.

"What you and the mate there are going to do to me, sir."

"Look at him, Hump," Wolf Larsen said to me, "look at this bit of animated dust, this aggregation of matter that moves and breathes and defies me and thoroughly believes itself to be compounded of something good; that is impressed with certain human fictions such as righteousness and honesty, and that will live up to them in spite of all personal discomforts and menaces. What do you think of him, Hump? What do you think of him?"

"I think that he is a better man than you are," I answered, impelled, somehow, with a desire to draw upon myself a portion of the wrath I felt was about to break upon his head. "His human fictions, as you choose to call them, make for nobility and manhood. You have no fictions, no dreams, no ideals. You are a pauper."

He nodded his head with a savage pleasantness. "Quite true, Hump, quite true. I have no fictions that make for nobility and manhood. A living dog is better than a dead lion, say I with the preacher. My only doctrine is the doctrine of expediency, and it makes for surviving. This bit of the ferment, only dust and ashes, will have no more nobility than any dust and ashes, while I shall still be alive and roaring."

"Do you know what I am going to do?" he questioned. I shook my head.

"Well, I am going to exercise my prerogative of roaring and show you how fares nobility. Watch me."

Three yards away from Johnson he was, and sitting down. Nine feet! And yet he left the chair in full leap, without first gaining a standing position. He left the chair, just as he sat in it, squarely, springing from the sitting posture like a wild animal, a tiger, and like a tiger covered with intervening space. It was an avalanche of fury that Johnson strove vainly to fend off. He threw one arm down to protect the stomach, the other arm up to protect the head; but Wolf Larsen's fist dove midway between, on the chest, with a crushing, resounding impact. Johnson's breath, suddenly expelled, shot from his mouth and as suddenly checked, with the forced, audible expiration of a man wielding an axe. He almost fell backward, and swayed from side to side in an effort to recover his balance.

I cannot give the further particulars of the horrible scene that followed. It was too revolting. It turns me sick even now when I think of it. Johnson fought bravely enough, but he was no match for Wolf Larsen, much less for Wolf Larsen and the mate.

—Jack London, *The Sea Wolf*

DIRECTIONS: Read and answer each question carefully. Select the best answer and blacken the proper space on the answer sheet.

1. We can infer that the scene takes place

   (A) in a court of law
   (B) in the street
   (C) in a boxing ring
   (D) on a ship

2. Wolf Larsen obviously is a

   (A) sailor with the same status as Johnson
   (B) man who is in authority
   (C) the first mate of the ship
   (D) policeman

3. Judging from the selection, Hump is

   (A) a person who has no strong feelings
   (B) a strong person who is able to defeat Larsen
   (C) a man who is able to argue with Larsen
   (D) an out-and-out coward

4. When Hump says "You are a pauper," he means

   (A) Larsen has no money.

   (B) Larsen is too much of an idealist and pays no attention to the realities of life.
   (C) Larsen is poor because he has none of the thoughts that make life worth living.
   (D) Larsen's oilskins in his slop-chest are worthless.

5. Larsen's idea of the doctrine of expediency is

   (A) not to worry about right or wrong but to survive by any means
   (B) to cheat everyone when possible
   (C) to never admit he was wrong in any situation
   (D) to follow the ideals of nobility only when it suits him to do so

6. Larsen might be characterized as man who is

   (A) brutal and stupid
   (B) cynical and cruel
   (C) intellectual and lenient
   (D) wise but stern

CONSOLIDATE YOUR KEY ANSWERS HERE

Practice using Answer Sheets. Make ONE mark for each answer. Additional and stray marks may be counted as mistakes. In making corrections erase errors COMPLETELY. Make glossy black marks. To arrive at an accurate estimate of your ability and progress, cover the Correct Answers with a sheet of white paper while you are taking this test.

```
   A B C D E      A B C D E      A B C D E      A B C D E      A B C D E      A B C D E
1 [][][][][]  2 [][][][][]  3 [][][][][]  4 [][][][][]  5 [][][][][]  6 [][][][][]
```

CORRECT KEY ANSWERS TO THE PRACTICE QUESTIONS

Now compare your answers with these Correct Key Answers. If your answers differ from these, go back and study the Practice Questions to see where and how you made your mistakes. In doing this, the following Explanatory Answers should prove helpful. They provide concise clarifications of the basic points behind the Key Answers. Even where your Key Answers are the same as ours, go over the explanations carefully because they may be quite useful in helping you pick up extra points on the exam.

1. D   2. B   3. C   4. C   5. A   6. B

EXPLANATORY ANSWERS CLARIFYING CARDINAL POINTS

Here you have the heart of the Question and Answer Method. . .getting help when and where you need it. Where one of your Key Answers differs from ours you have a problem which can easily be remedied by reading the explanation. Then, if you have time, you might be able to pick up points on the exam by reading the other explanations, even where you wrote the Key Answers correctly. These explanations stress fundamental facts, ideas, and principles which just might pop up as questions on future exams.

1. **(D)** There are several hints that this scene takes place on a ship, such as the use of "sir" towards Larsen, the reference to ship courtesy, and Johansen being described as "mate."

2. **(B)** Larsen is the leader, and has authority over Johnson, as Johnson admits. We do not know exactly what rank Larsen has, though, but we can guess he is the captain. He does not act nor talk like a policeman on duty.

3. **(C)** We know that Hump has strong feelings because he has argued bitterly against Larsen. He is not a coward because it is apparently dangerous to argue with Larsen. Yet we can infer Hump is not a strong man since he does not go to Johnson's defense in the fight.

4. **(C)** Hump says that Larsen is a pauper because he has "no dreams, no ideals." Therefore, Larsen cannot be an idealist. We don't know if Larsen has money or not, or if his oilskins are worthless.

5. **(A)** **B** is nearly correct, but is only part of Larsen's system of life. He might admit he was wrong if such a confession didn't threaten him. He certainly has no use for the ideals of nobility. Therefore, it is **A** which sums up what he believes in.

6. **(B)** The other three answers are partly right, but only **B** is completely true. Larsen is brutal, but he is not stupid. He is intellectual, but he is not lenient. He is stern, but not gentle. He has a low opinion of men so he is cynical. That he is cruel is obvious.

INTERPRETING DRAMA QUESTIONS

This test is based on a selection of passages, both prose and verse. The questions emphasize knowledge and special abilities not frequently needed in ordinary reading. The abilities to interpret figures of speech, to cope with unusual sentence structure and word meaning, and to recognize mood and purpose are often tested, as is an understanding of literary forms.

Although the Interpretation of Literary Materials is essentially a reading exercise, it demands that you do more than merely skim the surface of a selection. You must infer the author's real meaning from his style and point of view; from the plot and setting; from the intentions and personalities with which he endows his characters; from his opinions and feelings; from the figurative devices he uses; from all the rhetorical nuances described in these pages. Correct answers come from the clues you can piece together and from the unifying thread strung by the author through each passage.

A play is a story that is meant to be acted. Plays are the basis of movies and television. Drama may be written in prose or in poetry. Practically all modern dramas are written in everyday language. On your test, however, you will probably encounter a few questions concerning Shakespeare's plays, which are, of course, poetical.

You will be asked questions to see if you have understood what has taken place in the dramatic selections. You will also be asked questions about the characters. You should also expect to find questions which ask you to judge the personal qualities of the characters.

If you can master questions on fiction, you probably will do as well on drama, since the questions on both are quite similar.

Following are three dramatic selections with typical questions.

TEST VII. DRAMATIC INTERPRETATION

TIME: 8 Minutes. 5 Questions.

DIRECTIONS: Below each of the literary passages you will find one or more incomplete statements about the passage of prose, poetry, or drama. Each "stem" is followed by four or five "foils." Read each passage slowly, visualizing the plot, setting, action, characters, meaning, tone, and style. Re-read the passage before answering each question. From the emotions and attitudes expressed, choose the BEST "foil." Blacken the corresponding space on the answer sheet.

Explanations of the key points behind these questions appear with the answers at the end of this test. The explanatory answers provide just the help you need to strengthen your ability to master this type of question.

Words You Might Not Understand

profiteer: someone who makes money from a business
mutilation: the act of damaging
amiable: pleasant
fragments: pieces
receptacles: containers
morality: the ideals a person believes in
aerial: of the air

Dramatic Passage

Undershaft. One moment, Mr. Lomax. I am rather interested in the Salvation Army. Its motto might be my own: Blood and Fire.
Lomax (shocked). But not your sort of blood and fire, you know.
Undershaft. My sort of blood cleanses: my sort of fire purifies.
Barbara. So do ours. Come down tomorrow to my shelter—the West Ham shelter—and see what we're doing. We're going to march to a great meeting in the Assembly Hall at Mile End. Come and see the shelter and then march with us: It will do you a lot of good. Can you play anything?

Undershaft. In my youth I earned pennies, and even shillings occasionally, in the streets and in public house parlors by my natural talent for stepdancing. Later on, I became a member of the Undershaft orchestral society, and performed passably on the tenor trombone.

Lomax (scandalized—putting down the concertina). Oh I say!

Barbara. Many a sinner has played himself into heaven on the trombone, thanks to the Army.

Lomax (to Barbara, still rather shocked). Yes; but what about the cannon business, don't you know? *(To Undershaft)* Getting into heaven is not exactly in your line, is it?

Lady Britomart. Charles!!!

Lomax. Well; but it stands to reason, don't it? The cannon business may be necessary and all that: we can't get on without cannons; but it isn't right, you know. On the other hand, there may be a certain amount of tosh about the Salvation Army—I belong to the Established Church myself—but still you can't deny that it's religion; and you can't go against religion, can you? At least unless you're downright immoral, don't you know.

Undershaft. You hardly appreciate my position, Mr. Lomax—

Lomax (hastily). I'm not saying anything against you personally—

Undershaft. Quite so, quite so. But consider for a moment. Here I am, a profiteer in mutilation and murder. I find myself in a specially amiable humor just now because, this morning, down at the foundry, we blew twenty-seven dummy soldiers into fragments with a gun which formerly destroyed only thirteen.

Lomax (leniently). Well, the more destructive war becomes, the sooner it will be abolished, eh?

Undershaft. Not at all. The more destructive war becomes the more fascinating we find it. No, Mr. Lomax: I am obliged to you for making the usual excuse for my trade; but I am not ashamed of it. I am not one of those men who keep their morals and their business in watertight compartments. All the spare money my trade rivals spend on hospitals, cathedrals, and other receptacles for conscience money, I devote to experiments and researches in improved methods of destroying life and property. I have always done so; and I always shall. Therefore your Christmas card moralities of peace on earth and goodwill among men are of no use to me. Your Christianity, which enjoins you to resist not evil, and to turn the other cheek, would make me a bankrupt. My morality—my religion—must have a place for cannons and torpedoes in it.

Stephen (coldly—almost sullenly).   You speak as if there were half a dozen moralities and religions to choose from, instead of one true morality and one true religion.

Undershaft.   For me there is only one true morality; but it might not fit you, as you do not manufacture aerial battleships. There is only one true morality for every man; but every man has not the same true morality.

—G. B. Shaw, *Major Barbara*

DIRECTIONS: Read and answer each question carefully. Select the best answer and blacken the proper space on the answer sheet.

1. Barbara asked her father do do all these following things except one, which is

    (A) march to a meeting
    (B) give up making munitions
    (C) visit a Salvation Army Center
    (D) play a musical instrument

2. When Lomax says "There may be a certain amount of tosh about the Salvation Army," he means

    (A) It is not good to join the Salvation Army.
    (B) A lot of nonsense is said about the Salvation Army.
    (C) The Salvation Army soldiers give away a lot of tosh, which is sort of a candy.
    (D) The Salvation Army is an organization made up of young, wealthy people.

3. Undershaft states that he is

    (A) sorry he made mistakes

    (B) should give more to charity
    (C) hates the Salvation Army
    (D) was poor when he was young and gave street performances to make money

4. Lomax's statement that "We can't get on without cannons; but it isn't right, you know." may be considered

    (A) cynical
    (B) idealistic
    (C) metaphorical
    (D) hypocritical

5. Undershaft believes that mankind

    (A) likes war
    (B) hates war
    (C) will eventually create permanent peace
    (D) would be better off if it followed one morality

CONSOLIDATE YOUR KEY ANSWERS HERE

Practice using Answer Sheets. Make ONE mark for each answer. Additional and stray marks may be counted as mistakes. In making corrections erase errors COMPLETELY. Make glossy black marks. To arrive at an accurate estimate of your ability and progress, cover the Correct Answers with a sheet of white paper while you are taking this test.

CORRECT KEY ANSWERS TO THE PRACTICE QUESTIONS

Now compare your answers with these Correct Key Answers. If your answers differ from these, go back and study the Practice Questions to see where and how you made your mistakes. In doing this, the following Explanatory Answers should prove helpful. They provide concise clarifications of the basic points behind the Key Answers. Even where your Key Answers are the same as ours, go over the explanations carefully because they may be quite useful in helping you pick up extra points on the exam.

1. B   2. B   3. D   4. D   5. A

EXPLANATORY ANSWERS CLARIFYING CARDINAL POINTS

Here you have the heart of the Question and Answer Method. . .getting help when and where you need it. Where one of your Key Answers differs from ours you have a problem which can easily be remedied by reading the explanation. Then, if you have time, you might be able to pick up points on the exam by reading the other explanations, even where you wrote the Key Answers correctly. These explanations stress fundamental facts, ideas, and principles which just might pop up as questions on future exams.

1. **(B)** In her first speech, Barbara asked her father to visit her Salvation Army Center, march to a meeting, and play an instrument. But nowhere did she ask him to give up making munitions.

2. **(B)** **(A)** is incorrect. Lomax apparently does not think highly of the Salvation Army, but he says "you can't go against religion." Nor does he use the word "tosh" as a kind of candy. There is no indication that he regards the Salvation Army as an organization of wealthy people.

3. **(D)** Undershaft does not appear to be sorry about anything. He doesn't seem to hate the Salvation Army, since he did not refuse his daughter's invitation to visit her center. He stresses the fact that he spends his spare money on making better weapons, rather than giving it to charity.

4. **(D)** Lomax does not seem to be cynical, since he doesn't believe making cannons is right. Yet he is not idealistic because he accepts the idea that there should be cannons, rather than trying to destroy them. There are no metaphors in his statement. But he is hypocritical because he says he believes in religion, yet in the same breath says that "We can't get on without cannons."

5. **(A)** Undershaft says "The more destructive war becomes the more fascinating we find it." By "we" he means mankind in general. Since A is true, B and C are incorrect. D is wrong: Undershaft says "There is only one true morality for every man; but every man has not the same morality."

TEST VIII. DRAMATIC INTERPRETATION

TIME: 12 Minutes. 7 Questions.

DIRECTIONS: Below each of the literary passages you will find one or more incomplete statements about the passage of prose, poetry, or drama. Each "stem" is followed by four or five "foils." Read each passage slowly, visualizing the plot, setting, action, characters, meaning, tone, and style. Re-read the passage before answering each question. From the emotions and attitudes expressed, choose the BEST "foil." Blacken the corresponding space on the answer sheet.

Explanations of the key points behind these questions appear with the answers at the end of this test. The explanatory answers provide just the help you need to strengthen your ability to master this type of question.

Words You Might Not Know

darker: deeper (as is used in this play)

dowers: gifts, usually marriage gifts from parents

amorous: loving

sojourn: visit

champains: stretches of flat land

meads: fields

felicitate: made happy (as is used in this play)

hereditary: family

interress'd: enter a claim

opulent: rich

mar: hurt

plight: promise (as is used in this play)

orbs: planets and stars

propinquity: kinship

Dramatic Passage

Lear. Meantime we shall express our darker purpose.
Give me the map there. Know that we have divided
In three our kingdom; and 'tis our fast intent

To shake all cares and business from our age,
Conferring them on younger strengths, while we
Unburthen'd crawl toward death. Our son of Cornwall,
And you, our no less loving son of Albany,
We have this hour a constant will to publish
Our daughters' several dowers, that future strife
May be prevented now. The Princes, France and Burgundy,
Great rivals in our youngest daughter's love,
Long in our court have made their amorous sojourn,
And here are to be answer'd. Tell me, my daughters,
Since now we will divest us both of rule,
Interest of territory, cares of state,
Which of you shall we say doth love us most?
That we our largest bounty may extend
Where nature doth with merit challenge. Goneril,
Our eldest-born, speak first.

Goneril. Sir, I love you more than words can wield the matter,
Dearer than eye-sight, space and liberty,
Beyond what can be valued, rich or rare,
No less than life, with grace, health, beauty, honour,
As much as child e'er lov'd or father found;
A love that makes breath poor and speech unable;
Beyond all manner of so much I love you.

Cordelia. *(aside).* What shall Cordelia do? Love, and be silent.

Lear. Of all these bounds, even from this line to this,
With shadowy forest and with champains rich'd,
With plenteous rivers and wide-skirted meads,
We make thee lady. To thine and Albany's issue
Be this perpetual. What says our second daughter,
Our dearest Regan, wife to Cornwall? Speak.

Regan. I am made of that self metal as my sister,
And prize me at her worth. In my true heart
I find she names my very deed of love;
Only she comes too short: that I profess
Myself an enemy to all other joys
Which the most precious square of sense possesses,
And find I am alone felicitate
In your dear highness' love.

Cordelia. *(aside).* Then poor Cordelia!
And yet not so, since I am sure my love's
More ponderous than my tongue.

Lear.   To thee and thine hereditary ever
Remain this ample third of our fair kingdom,
No less in space, validity, and pleasure,
Than that conferr'd on Goneril. Now, our joy,
Although the last, not least, to whose young love
The vines of France and milk of Burgundy
Strive to be interress'd, what can you say to draw
A third more opulent than your sisters? Speak.

Cordelia.   Nothing, my lord.

Lear.   Nothing!

Cordelia.   Nothing.

Lear.   Nothing will come of nothing: speak again.

Cordelia.   Unhappy that I am, I cannot heave
My heart into my mouth: I love your majesty
According to my bond; nor more nor less.

Lear.   How, how, Cordelia! Mend your speech a little,
Lest you may mar your fortunes.

Cordelia.   Good my lord,
You have begot me, bred me, loved me: I
Return those duties back as are right fit,
Obey you, love you, and most honour you.
Why have my sisters husbands, if they say
They love you all? Haply, when I shall wed,
That lord whose hand must take my plight shall carry
Half my love with him, half my care and duty:
Sure, I shall never marry like my sisters
To love my father all.

Lear.   But thy heart with this?

Cordelia.   Ay, my good lord.

Lear.   So young, and so untender?

Cordelia.   So young, my lord, and true.

Lear.   Let it be so; thy truth then be thy dower:
For, by the sacred radiance of the sun,
The mysteries of Hecate, and the night;
By all the operation of the orbs
From whom we do exist and cease to be;
Here I disclaim all my paternal care,
Propinquity and property of blood,
And as a stranger to my heart and me
Hold thee from this for ever.

—William Shakespeare, *King Lear*

DIRECTIONS: *Read and answer each question carefully. Select the best answer and blacken the proper space on the answer sheet.*

1. Lear divides his kingdom among his daughters and sons-in-law because

    (A) he is afraid of them
    (B) they force him to
    (C) he is going to leave England and invade France
    (D) he no longer wishes the responsibility of ruling

2. Before Lear gives away his lands he

    (A) tests his children by making them tell how much they love him
    (B) says Cordelia will marry the Prince of Burgundy
    (C) states that words will have no influence upon his decision
    (D) is told by his children that he should not do so

3. In Lear's first speech the reader learns that

    (A) Lear is fairly young
    (B) Lear is an old man
    (C) Cordelia is married
    (D) Lear dislikes Cordelia

4. Cordelia states that her sisters did not give all their love to Lear because

    (A) they then would not want the lands

    (B) they desire his death
    (C) they told her that they would speak falsely
    (D) they married

5. Cordelia's reasons she cannot give Lear all her love are because

    (A) he has given the best land to her sisters and their husbands
    (B) she must give some of her love to her future husband
    (C) her father does not love her in return
    (D) no one can just demand a person to love

6. The impression the playright wishes to create is that

    (A) Lear is cynical and hypocritical.
    (B) Cordelia truly hates her father.
    (C) Cordelia is honest and speaks what she feels.
    (D) Lear is a humble, understanding man.

7. In the end, Lear

    (A) disowns Cordelia
    (B) forgives Cordelia because he recognizes the truth of her words
    (C) takes back his promise to give away his lands
    (D) forbids Cordelia to marry

CONSOLIDATE YOUR KEY ANSWERS HERE

Practice using Answer Sheets. Make ONE mark for each answer. Additional and stray marks may be counted as mistakes. In making corrections erase errors COMPLETELY. Make glossy black marks. To arrive at an accurate estimate of your ability and progress, cover the Correct Answers with a sheet of white paper while you are taking this test.

```
    A B C D E    A B C D E    A B C D E    A B C D E    A B C D E    A B C D E    A B C D E
1   [] [] [] [] [] 2 [] [] [] [] [] 3 [] [] [] [] [] 4 [] [] [] [] [] 5 [] [] [] [] [] 6 [] [] [] [] [] 7 [] [] [] [] []
```

CORRECT KEY ANSWERS TO THE PRACTICE QUESTIONS

Now compare your answers with these Correct Key Answers. If your answers differ from these, go back and study the Practice Questions to see where and how you made your mistakes. In doing this, the following Explanatory Answers should prove helpful. They provide concise clarifications of the basic points behind the Key Answers. Even where your Key Answers are the same as ours, go over the explanations carefully because they may be quite useful in helping you pick up extra points on the exam.

1.D   2.A   3.B   4.D   5.B   6.C   7.A

EXPLANATORY ANSWERS CLARIFYING CARDINAL POINTS

Here you have the heart of the Question and Answer Method...getting help when and where you need it. Where one of your Key Answers differs from ours you have a problem which can easily be remedied by reading the explanation. Then, if you have time, you might be able to pick up points on the exam by reading the other explanations, even where you wrote the Key Answers correctly. These explanations stress fundamental facts, ideas, and principles which just might pop up as questions on future exams.

1. **(D)** **A** is incorrect because he does not seem to be frightened of his daughters and their husbands; rather, he seems to order them around. **B** is wrong since he is the person who comes up with the plan for dividing his kingdom. **C** is not right because he says nothing about leaving England. But he does say " 'tis our fast intent to shake all cares and business . . .," which means that **D** is the right answer.

2. **(A)** Lear states towards the end of his first speech that he will give his kingdom away according to how much his daughters say they love him. Lear says that Burgundy is interested in marrying his youngest daughter, Cordelia, but he didn't say this will take place. None of his children tell him he should not divide his kingdom.

3. **(B)** Lear says he wants to "shake all cares and business from our age,/Conferring them on younger strengths, while we unburthen'd crawl toward death." Thus, he is old and not young. He also says Cordelia is being courted by the princes of France and Burgundy. He doesn't dislike Cordelia until he flies into a rage towards the end. Before this, he calls her "our joy,/Although the last, not least . . ."

4. **(D)** Cordelia says, "Why have my sisters husbands, if they say/They loved you all?" She also says she will give her husband half her love when she marries. That is her only comment about her sister's speeches.

5. **(B)** If you got the answer to 4, you should get this one. She knows her father loves her and says so, and she says she loves her father. She is not too concerned about receiving part of his kingdom.

6. **(C)** Lear is not cynical and hypocritical; he loves his daughters and believes they should show their love to him. He is not humble, either, or he wouldn't demand they prove their affection. He is not understanding or he wouldn't become angry when Cordelia speaks her mind. Nor does Cordelia hate her father. But she is certainly an honest girl.

7. **(A)** Lear, by uttering all kinds of oaths, makes it obvious that he disowns Cordelia, and that she will be from that time on "a stranger to my heart."

TEST IX. DRAMATIC INTERPRETATION

TIME: 12 Minutes. 9 Questions.

DIRECTIONS: Below each of the literary passages you will find one or more incomplete statements about the passage of prose, poetry, or drama. Each "stem" is followed by four or five "foils." Read each passage slowly, visualizing the plot, setting, action, characters, meaning, tone, and style. Re-read the passage before answering each question. From the emotions and attitudes expressed, choose the BEST "foil." Blacken the corresponding space on the answer sheet.

Explanations of the key points behind these questions appear with the answers at the end of this test. The explanatory answers provide just the help you need to strengthen your ability to master this type of question.

Dramatic Passage

Luka (*pointing to window*). He's laughing! (*pause*) Well, children, God be with you! I'll leave you soon . . .

Pepel. Where are you going to?

Luka. To the Ukraine—I heard they discovered a new religion there—I want to seek—yes! People are always seeking—they always want something better—God grant them patience!

Pepel. You think they'll find it?

Luka. The people? They will find it! He who seeks, will find! He who desires strongly, will find!

Natasha. If only they could find something better—invent something better . . .

Luka. They're trying to! But we must help them, girl—we must respect them . . .

Natasha. How can I help them? I am helpless myself!

Pepel (*determined*). Again—listen—I'll speak to you again, Natasha—here —before him—he knows everything . . . run away with me?

Natasha. Where? From one prison to another?

Pepel. I told you—I'm through with being a thief, so help me God! I'll quit! If I say so, I'll do it! I can read and write—I'll work—He's been telling me to go to Siberia on my own hook—let's go there together, what do you say? Do you think I'm not disgusted with my life? Oh—Natasha—I know . . . I see . . . I console myself with the thought that there are lots of people who are honored and respected—and who are bigger thieves than I! But what good is that to me? It isn't that I repent . . . I've no conscience . . . but I do feel one thing: One must live differently. One must live a better life . . . one must be able to respect one's own self . . .

Luka. That's right, friend! May God help you! It's true! A man must respect himself.

Pepel. I've been a thief from childhood on. Everybody always called me "Vaska—the thief—the son of a thief." Oh—very well—I am a thief—just imagine—now, perhaps, I'm a thief out of spite—perhaps I'm a thief because no one ever called me anything different . . . Well, Natasha . . .?

Natasha (sadly). Somehow I don't believe in words—and I'm restless today—my heart is heavy . . . as if I were expecting something . . . it's a pity, Vassily, that you talked to me today . . .

Pepel. When should I? It isn't the first time I speak to you . . .

Natasha. And why should I go with you? I don't love you so very much—sometimes I like you—and other times the mere sight of you makes me sick . . . it seems—no—I don't really love you . . . when one really loves, one sees no fault . . . But I do see . . .

Pepel. Never mind—you'll love me after a while! I'll make you care for me . . . if you'll just say yes! For over a year I've watched you . . . you're a decent girl . . . you're kind—you're reliable—I'm very much in love with you . . .

(Vassilisa, in her best dress, appears at window and listens.)

Natasha. Yes—you love me—but how about my sister . . .?

Pepel (confused). Well, what of her? There are plenty like her . . .

Luka. You'll be all right, girl! If there's no bread, you have to eat weeds . . .

Pepel (gloomily). Please—feel a little sorry for me! My life isn't all roses—it's a hell of a life . . . little swamps were sucking me under . . . and whatever I try to catch and hold on to is rotten . . . it breaks . . . Your sister—Ooh—I thought she was different . . . if she weren't so greedy after money . . . I'd have done anything for her sake, if she were only all mine . . . but she must have someone else . . . and she has to have money—and freedom . . . because she doesn't like the straight and narrow . . . she can't help me. But you're like a young fir tree . . . you bend, but you don't break . . .

Luka. Yes—go with him, girl, go! He's a good lad—he's all right! Only tell him every now and then that he's a good lad so that he won't forget it—and he'll believe you. Just you keep on telling him "Vasya, you're a good man—don't you forget it!" Just think, dear, where else could you go except with him? Your sister is a savage beast . . . and as for her husband, there's little to say of him! He's rotten beyond words . . . and all this life here, where will it get you? But this lad is strong . . .

Natasha. Nowhere to go—I know—I thought of it. The only thing is—I've no faith in anybody—and there's no place for me to turn to . . .

—Maxim Gorky, *The Lower Depths*

DIRECTIONS: *For each of the following questions, select the choice which best answers the question or completes the statement.*

1. The reader gets the impressions that Luka is

   (A) younger than Pepel and Natasha
   (B) a thief
   (C) Natasha's brother-in-law
   (D) older than Pepel and Natasha

2. Luka seems to be a

   (A) seeker after truth
   (B) hypocrite
   (C) cynic
   (D) pessimist

3. Pepel wishes to go to

   (A) a swamp
   (B) Siberia
   (C) the Ukraine
   (D) prison

4. Pepel admits that he has been a

   (A) policeman
   (B) murderer
   (C) thief
   (D) soldier

5. What bothers Natasha about Pepel's statement that he loves her is that

   (A) he often lies
   (B) he wants to go to Siberia without her

   (C) he does not seem to be serious
   (D) he has been her sister's lover

6. Natasha's problem seems to be that she

   (A) doesn't like Siberia
   (B) has another lover
   (C) has no faith in anyone
   (D) is afraid of her sister

7. Natasha admits she

   (A) doesn't love Pepel
   (B) loves Pepel very much
   (C) is too satisfied with her present life to think about leaving
   (D) would like to go with Pepel

8. Pepel wishes to give up his criminal life because

   (A) the police are after him
   (B) he loves Natasha
   (C) he feels he must live differently
   (D) he is sorry he has been a thief

9. The tone of this selection of the play seems to be

   (A) ironic
   (B) satirical
   (C) tragic
   (D) comical

CONSOLIDATE YOUR KEY ANSWERS HERE

	A	B	C	D	E
1	☐	☐	☐	☐	☐
2	☐	☐	☐	☐	☐
3	☐	☐	☐	☐	☐
4	☐	☐	☐	☐	☐
5	☐	☐	☐	☐	☐
6	☐	☐	☐	☐	☐
7	☐	☐	☐	☐	☐
8	☐	☐	☐	☐	☐
9	☐	☐	☐	☐	☐

CORRECT KEY ANSWERS TO THE PRACTICE QUESTIONS

Now compare your answers with these Correct Key Answers. If your answers differ from these, go back and study the Practice Questions to see where and how you made your mistakes. In doing this, the following Explanatory Answers should prove helpful. They provide concise clarifications of the basic points behind the Key Answers. Even where your Key Answers are the same as ours, go over the explanations carefully because they may be quite useful in helping you pick up extra points on the exam.

1.D	3.B	5.D	7.A	9.C
2.A	4.C	6.C	8.C	

EXPLANATORY ANSWERS CLARIFYING CARDINAL POINTS

Here you have the heart of the Question and Answer Method. . .getting help when and where you need it. Where one of your Key Answers differs from ours you have a problem which can easily be remedied by reading the explanation. Then, if you have time, you might be able to pick up points on the exam by reading the other explanations, even where you wrote the Key Answers correctly. These explanations stress fundamental facts, ideas, and principles which just might pop up as questions on future exams.

1. **(D)** When Pepel and Natasha speak to Luka, it is with respect, and they look to him for advice. Also, he calls them "children." Thus, it can be inferred that he is older than they are. There is no evidence that he is a thief. He is not her brother-in-law, as he says that her sister's "husband . . . is rotten beyond words".

2. **(A)** Luka does not seem to be a hypocrite, for he doesn't say one thing and practice the opposite. He is neither a cynic nor a pessimist, as he speaks his hope for mankind. He is a seeker after truth; he is going to the Ukraine just to observe a new religion.

3. **(B)** Pepel states he does want to go to Siberia with Natasha. He describes his present life as a swamp he wishes to escape from. He is not sorry for his crimes, he says, and he does not indicate he would like to go to prison for them. It is Luka, not Pepel, who wishes to go to the Ukraine.

4. **(C)** Pepel makes a great point of having been a thief, but he does not say or hint that he has murdered anyone. He certainly is not a policeman or a soldier.

5. **(D)** There seem to be many reasons Natasha doesn't believe Pepel's statement that he loves her, but she seems most disturbed by the fact that he has been her sister's lover.

6. **(C)** Natasha has no faith in anyone, including herself. She says she is "helpless" and "there's no place for me." She does not say or even hint that she loves someone else. Nor does she say she is afraid of her sister.

7. **(A)** Natasha doesn't love Pepel. If she did, she says, she wouldn't see any fault in him. She doesn't seem too thrilled by going to Siberia, but at the same time it is obvious she is unhappy with her present life.

8. **(C)** Time and time again, Pepel hits at this theme. He says "One must live differently. One must live a better life . . . one must be able to respect one's own self." He is not sorry, though, for what he has done, nor does he say the police are after him. He does love Natasha, it is true, but that is not the reason he wishes to go ·to Siberia and begin a new life.

9. **(C)** Although the author seems to see Luka as a character of hope, the helplessness and aimlessness of Natasha, on one hand, and Pepel's yearning towards a better life, on the other, mark the selection as tragic.

INTERPRETING NON-FICTION MATERIAL

Although the Interpretation of Literary Materials is essentially a reading exercise, it demands that you do more than merely skim the surface of a selection. You must infer the author's real meaning from his style and point of view; from the plot and setting; from the intentions and personalities with which he endows his characters; from his opinions and feelings; from the figurative devices he uses; from all the rhetorical nuances described in these pages. Correct answers come from the clues you can piece together and from the unifying thread strung by the author through each passage.

Nonfiction prose is anything other than fiction, poetry, and drama. Like drama and fiction, a nonfictional piece of literature may tell a story. Unlike drama and fiction, though, the story it tells is true; it actually happened. It might be a description of a battle, a space flight, or a football game. When you read news in a newspaper, you are reading nonfiction.

When a person writes about the life of someone else, it is called *biography*. If a person writes about his own life, it's an *autobiography*. Both are important forms of nonfiction.

Nonfiction also includes the writing of a person's opinions.

The nonfiction writer uses many of the tools of the fiction writer and the poet. On your test, you will be asked questions on nonfictional selections that are quite similar to those you were asked about fiction.

Read the following nonfictional selections and answer the questions after each selection.

HOW TO PROFIT FROM THE PRACTICE TESTS
On the following pages you are furnished practice tests consisting of questions like those on the actual exam. The time limit here is just about what you may expect. Take these tests as a series of dress rehearsals strengthening your ability to score high on this type of question. For each test use the Answer Sheet provided to mark down your answers. If the Answer Sheet is separated from the questions, tear it out so you can mark it more easily. As you finish each test, go back and check your answers to find your score, and to determine how well you did. This will help you discover where you need more practice.

TEST X. INTERPRETATION OF NON-FICTION

TIME: 10 Minutes. 6 Questions.

DIRECTIONS: Below each of the literary passages you will find one or more incomplete statements about the passage of prose, poetry, or drama. Each "stem" is followed by four or five "foils." Read each passage slowly, visualizing the plot, setting, action, characters, meaning, tone, and style. Re-read the passage before answering each question. From the emotions and attitudes expressed, choose the BEST "foil." Blacken the corresponding space on the answer sheet.

Explanations of the key points behind these questions appear with the answers at the end of this test. The explanatory answers provide just the help you need to strengthen your ability to master this type of question.

Words You Might Not Know

precaution: something done to prevent
something else from happening
ell: 45 inches (as is used in this story)
converted: changed
to bestow upon: to give
urchins: poor children
testimonial: a token of regard
prudence: carefulness
offence: crime
console: comfort

Nonfiction Passage

From this time I was most narrowly watched. If I was in a separate room any considerable length of time, I was sure to be suspected of having a book, and was at once called to give an account of myself. All this, however, was too late. The first step had been taken. Mistress, in teaching me the alphabet, had given me the inch, and no precaution could prevent me from taking the ell.

The plan which I adopted, and the one by which I was most successful, was that of making friends of all the little white boys whom I met in the street. As many of these as I could, I converted into teachers. With their kindly aid, obtained at different times and in different places, I finally succeeded in learning to read. When I was sent on errands, I always took my book with me, and by doing one part of my errand quickly, I found time to get a lesson before my return. I used also to carry bread with me, enough of which was always in the house, and to which I was always welcome; for I was much better off in this regard than many of the poor white children in our neighborhood. This bread I used to bestow upon the hungry little urchins, who, in return, would give me that more valuable bread of knowledge. I am strongly tempted to give the names of two or three of those little boys, as a testimonial of the gratitude and affection I bear them; but prudence forbids;—not that it would injure me, but it might embarrass them; for it is almost an unpardonable offence to teach slaves to read in this Christian country. It is enough to say of the dear little fellows that they lived on Philpot Street, very near Durgin and Bailey's ship-yard. I used to talk this matter of slavery over with them. I would sometimes say to them, I wished I could be as free as they would be when they got to be men. "You will be free as soon as you are twenty-one, but I am a slave for life! Have not I as good a right to be free as you have?" These words used to trouble them; they would express for me the liveliest sympathy, and console with the hope that something would occur by which I might be free.

—Frederick Douglass, *Narrative of the Life of Frederick Douglass*

1. Douglass is writing

    (A) about an experience he had when he was an old man
    (B) about a time shortly after he had been freed
    (C) a biography
    (D) about when he was a boy

2. Douglass' great desire in the selection was to

    (A) escape to the North
    (B) work for his living
    (C) learn to read
    (D) obtain bread for himself and his friends

3. The selection took place

    (A) before the Civil War
    (B) only in Douglass' mind, as it is an imaginary story
    (C) after the Civil War
    (D) recently

4. Douglass learned to read

    (A) by his own efforts only
    (B) from his mistress
    (C) in school
    (D) by using white boys as teachers

5. The reason Douglass does not give the names of his white friends is that

    (A) they might be punished
    (B) they asked him not to
    (C) he never knew what they were called
    (D) he has forgotten their names

6. Judging from the selection, you might sum up Douglass' character as one of

    (A) bravery but of an unforgiving nature
    (B) courage and determination
    (C) cowardice and bitterness
    (D) laziness and selfishness

CONSOLIDATE YOUR KEY ANSWERS HERE

Practice using Answer Sheets. Make ONE mark for each answer. Additional and stray marks may be counted as mistakes. In making corrections erase errors COMPLETELY. Make glossy black marks. To arrive at an accurate estimate of your ability and progress, cover the Correct Answers with a sheet of white paper while you are taking this test.

A B C D E   A B C D E   A B C D E   A B C D E   A B C D E   A B C D E
1 ☐ ☐ ☐ ☐ ☐   2 ☐ ☐ ☐ ☐ ☐   3 ☐ ☐ ☐ ☐ ☐   4 ☐ ☐ ☐ ☐ ☐   5 ☐ ☐ ☐ ☐ ☐   6 ☐ ☐ ☐ ☐ ☐

CORRECT KEY ANSWERS TO THE PRACTICE QUESTIONS

Now compare your answers with these Correct Key Answers. If your answers differ from these, go back and study the Practice Questions to see where and how you made your mistakes. In doing this, the following Explanatory Answers should prove helpful. They provide concise clarifications of the basic points behind the Key Answers. Even where your Key Answers are the same as ours, go over the explanations carefully because they may be quite useful in helping you pick up extra points on the exam.

1. D   2. C   3. A   4. D   5. A   6. B

EXPLANATORY ANSWERS CLARIFYING CARDINAL POINTS

Here you have the heart of the Question and Answer Method. . .getting help when and where you need it. Where one of your Key Answers differs from ours you have a problem which can easily be remedied by reading the explanation. Then, if you have time, you might be able to pick up points on the exam by reading the other explanations, even where you wrote the Key Answers correctly. These explanations stress fundamental facts, ideas, and principles which just might pop up as questions on future exams.

1. **(D)** The implication in the entire selection is that Douglass is writing about a time when he was a youth. He made friends with "little white boys." He also compares his life with theirs, saying "You will be free as soon as you are twenty-one, but I am a slave for life!" He certainly was a not a free person at this time, but a slave. He is not writing a biography because he tells the reader that this was his own experience. When an author is writing about his own life, he is writing an autobiography.

2. **(C)** D is incorrect, for the only reason he took bread from the house was to bribe the white boys into teaching him to read, and he says nothing about wishing to work for his living. A is also wrong, although the reader is told that he is most bitter about being a slave. The selection deals mainly with his desire to learn to read.

3. **(A)** C and D are incorrect because the selection deals with a time when there were slaves in the United States, which was before the Civil War. **B** is incorrect as this is an autobiography.

4. **(D)** He learned the alphabet from Mistress, but she apparently did not teach him to read. C is wrong because he did not go to school. He did not learn to read by his own efforts only, because he tells the reader that he bribed the white boys to teach him.

5. **(A)** He did know their names and he has not forgotten them because he says that "I am strongly tempted to give the names of two or three of those little boys." He does not mention that they asked him not to reveal their names. But he does say "It is almost an unpardonable offence to teach slaves to read . . ."

6. **(B)** C is incorrect. He was bitter about being a slave, but he was no coward since it appears to have been fairly dangerous for him to try to learn to read. Nor does he seem to be lazy or selfish. He was brave, but he did not appear to be unforgiving, although he hated being a slave.

TEST XI. INTERPRETATION OF NON-FICTION

TIME: 10 Minutes. 6 Questions.

DIRECTIONS: Below each of the literary passages you will find one or more incomplete statements about the passage of prose, poetry, or drama. Each "stem" is followed by four or five "foils." Read each passage slowly, visualizing the plot, setting, action, characters, meaning, tone, and style. Re-read the passage before answering each question. From the emotions and attitudes expressed, choose the BEST "foil." Blacken the corresponding space on the answer sheet.

Explanations of the key points behind these questions appear with the answers at the end of this test. The explanatory answers provide just the help you need to strengthen your ability to master this type of question.

Words You Might Not Know

throng: crowd
disembarked: got off a ship or boat
caissons: ammunition wagons
accouterments: equipment
pallor: paleness
shriveled: dried up
contracted: tightened
beseeching: pleading

Nonfiction Passage

The First Brigade, after pushing its way through the throng at the river with the point of the bayonet, was already forming on the crest of the hill. Now and then we heard the pattering sound of bullets, stragglers from the leaden storm above, falling upon the roofs of the boats. Our horses were quickly disembarked, and with the First Brigade in columns closed in mass, leaving orders for the rest of the Division to follow as soon as landed, we moved toward the point indicated by the firing. Directly we saw evidences of close and terrible fighting. Artillery horses dead, cannon dismounted, caissons abandoned, muskets broken, accouterments torn and bloody, appeared everywhere. The first dead soldier we saw had fallen in the road; our artillery had crushed and mangled his limbs, and ground him into the mire. He lay a bloody, loathsome mass, the scraps of his blue uniform furnishing the only distinguishable evidence that a hero there had died. At this sight I saw a manly fellow gulp down his heart, which swelled too closely into his throat. Near him lay a slender rebel boy—his face in the mud, his brown hair floating in a bloody pool. Soon a dead Major, then a Colonel, then the lamented Wallace, yet alive, were passed in quick and sickening success. The gray gloaming of the misty morning gave a ghostly pallor to the faces of the dead. The disordered hair, dripping from the night's rain, the distorted and passion-marked faces, the stony, glaring eyes, the blue lips, the glistening teeth, the shriveled and contracted hands, the wild agony of pain and passion in the attitudes of the dead—all the horrid circumstances with which death surrounds the brave when torn from life in the whirlwind of battle—were seen as we marched over the field, the beseeching cries of the wounded from their bloody and miry beds meanwhile saluting our ears and cutting to our hearts.

—Daniel McCook, *The Second Division At Shiloh*

DIRECTIONS: Read and answer each question carefully. Select the best answer and blacken the proper space on the answer sheet.

1. The selection is a description of

   (A) a battlefield
   (B) a forest fire
   (C) a town after a terrible flood has swept over it
   (D) the author's imaginary visit to Hell

2. At the beginning of the selection, the First Brigade

   (A) is retreating
   (B) is in boats
   (C) is on shore
   (D) has been wiped out

3. The author's attitude towards his dead enemy, the rebel boy, seems to be one of

   (A) pity and sorrow
   (B) disgust and hatred
   (C) scorn and revulsion
   (D) humor and delight

4. It is apparent that

   (A) the battle has been going on for some time and is still continuing
   (B) the battle was over
   (C) the First Brigade has been fighting in the battle for many hours
   (D) the battle has just begun

5. The writer is

   (A) a sailor
   (B) a reporter
   (C) a soldier
   (D) a prisoner

6. We can infer by the author's style (the way he writes) that

   (A) war disgusts and horrifies him
   (B) he glories in combat
   (C) he regards battle as a comical sort of adventure
   (D) he wishes to run away

CONSOLIDATE YOUR KEY ANSWERS HERE

Practice using Answer Sheets. Make ONE mark for each answer. Additional and stray marks may be counted as mistakes. In making corrections erase errors COMPLETELY. Make glossy black marks. To arrive at an accurate estimate of your ability and progress, cover the Correct Answers with a sheet of white paper while you are taking this test.

CORRECT KEY ANSWERS TO THE PRACTICE QUESTIONS

Now compare your answers with these Correct Key Answers. If your answers differ from these, go back and study the Practice Questions to see where and how you made your mistakes. In doing this, the following Explanatory Answers should prove helpful. They provide concise clarifications of the basic points behind the Key Answers. Even where your Key Answers are the same as ours, go over the explanations carefully because they may be quite useful in helping you pick up extra points on the exam.

1.A   2.C   3.A   4.A   5.C   6.A

EXPLANATORY ANSWERS CLARIFYING CARDINAL POINTS

Here you have the heart of the Question and Answer Method. . .getting help when and where you need it. Where one of your Key Answers differs from ours you have a problem which can easily be remedied by reading the explanation. Then, if you have time, you might be able to pick up points on the exam by reading the other explanations, even where you wrote the Key Answers correctly. These explanations stress fundamental facts, ideas, and principles which just might pop up as questions on future exams.

1. (A) If you read the selection carefully it would be obvious to you that this is a battle.

2. (C) The First Brigade has apparently been on boats just before the beginning of the selection, but that it is on shore now is pointed up in the first sentence.

3. (A) The author's attitude towards all the dead soldiers is one of pity and sorrow. He shows no hatred or disgust towards the rebel youth. He certainly doesn't regard any of the dead, either friend or foe, with humor or delight.

4. (A) The battle must have been going on for some time because of the dead and wounded soldiers lying about and the wreckage of equipment. It is still continuing since the author says that the First Brigade is going towards the firing. The First Brigade, though, has not been fighting since it just got off the boats.

5. (C) If the author were a sailor, he would not be marching with the First Brigade, but would remain at the boats. He is obviously not a prisoner since he is marching towards the battle, apparently to fight. A reader might assume that the author is a reporter if it were not for the statement "leaving orders for the rest of the Division to follow as soon as landed, we moved towards the point indicated by the firing."

6. (A) The author's description of the dead soldiers and the battlefield in general is proof that war disgusts and horrifies him. He certainly does not glory in it, nor does he see any humor. Yet he does not seem to wish to run away, since he advances with the other soldiers towards the place where the fighting is.

INTERPRETING DRAMA, POETRY, FICTION AND NON-FICTION

Although the Interpretation of Literary Materials is essentially a reading exercise, it demands that you do more than merely skim the surface of a selection. You must infer the author's real meaning from his style and point of view; from the plot and setting; from the intentions and personalities with which he endows his characters; from his opinions and feelings; from the figurative devices he uses; from all the rhetorical nuances described in these pages. Correct answers come from the clues you can piece together and from the unifying thread strung by the author through each passage.

In the Diploma Exam entitled Interpretation of Literary Materials, each group of questions is made up of a literary selection followed by one or more incomplete statements about the passage of prose, poetry or drama. These numbered statements are called "stems" because on each of them depends, like the petals of a flower, the possible answers for each question. Each "stem" is followed by four or five possible, plausible answers, called "foils." In multiple-choice questions they are meant to *foil* the unwary or unwise.

Although you may never have seen the literary selection before, you must now read it carefully so that you understand it. Read slowly and try to visualize the entire plot and setting. Try to get the whole story . . . what the author really means, and how he conveys his meaning through his characters, tone, style, rhetorical devices, and language, both literal and figurative.

Skim the stems. See if you can figure out what the examiners are getting at. Reread the passage before answering each question. From the emotions and feelings expressed, choose the best foil for each question. Any one of them may be right. You have to choose the one that's most correct. Try to pick the one that's most complete, most accurate . . . the one that is best supported by and necessarily flows from the selection. Be sure that it contains nothing false so far as the selection itself is concerned.

After you've thought it out, mark your answer in the answer boxes provided at the end of the test . . . just as you will do on the actual exam.

S1958

TEST XII. INTERPRETATION OF LITERARY MATERIALS

TIME: 25 Minutes. 20 Questions.

DIRECTIONS: Below each of the literary passages you will find one or more incomplete statements about the passage of prose, poetry, or drama. Each "stem" is followed by four or five "foils." Read each passage slowly, visualizing the plot, setting, action, characters, meaning, tone, and style. Re-read the passage before answering each question. From the emotions and attitudes expressed, choose the BEST "foil." Blacken the corresponding space on the answer sheet.

Correct key answers to all these test questions will be found at the end of the test.

Fiction Passage I.

The crimson hand, which at first had been strongly visible upon the marble paleness of Georgiana's cheek, now grew more faintly outlined. She remained not less pale than ever; but the birthmark, with every breath that came and went, lost somewhat of its former distinctness. Its presence had been awful; its departure was more awful still. Watch the stain of the rainbow fading out the sky, and you will know how the mysterious symbol passed away.

"By Heaven! it is well-nigh gone!" said Aylmer to himself, in almost irrepressible ecstasy. "I can scarcely trace it now. Success! Success! And now it is like the faintest rose color. The lightest flush of blood across her cheek would overcome it. But she is so pale!"

He drew aside the window curtain and suffered the light of natural day to fall into the room and rest upon her cheek. At the same time he heard a gross, hoarse chuckle, which he had long known as his servant Aminadab's expression of delight.

"Ah, clod! ah, earthly mass!" cried Aylmer, laughing in a sort of frenzy. "You have served me well! Matter and spirit—earth and heaven—have both done their part in this! Laugh, thing of the senses! You have earned the right to laugh."

These exclamations broke Georgiana's sleep. She slowly unclosed her eyes and gazed into the mirror which her husband had arranged for that purpose. A faint smile flitted over her lips when she recognized how barely perceptible was now that crimson hand which had once blazed with such disastrous brilliancy as to scare away all their happiness. But then her eyes sought Aylmer's face with a trouble and anxiety that he could by no means account for.

"My poor Aylmer!" murmured she.

"Poor? Nay, richest, happiest, most favored!" exclaimed he. "My peerless bride, it is successful! You are perfect!"

"My poor Aylmer," she repeated with a more than human tenderness, "you have aimed loftily; you have done nobly. Do not repent that with so high and pure a feeling, you have rejected the best the earth could offer. Aylmer, dearest Aylmer, I am dying!"

—Nathaniel Hawthorne, "The Birthmark"

DIRECTIONS: *Read and answer each question carefully. Select the best answer and blacken the proper space on the answer sheet.*

1. We can infer that Aylmer

   (A) does not love Georgiana
   (B) wishes to kill his wife
   (C) is disappointed at first
   (D) has done something to his wife

2. The birthmark is in the shape of

   (A) a crimson hand
   (B) a crimson rose
   (C) a rainbow
   (D) a butterfly

3. The birthmark

   (A) does not change
   (B) becomes redder
   (C) fades away
   (D) fades and then comes back

4. In Aylmer's opinion, Georgiana now is

   (A) ugly
   (B) perfect

   (C) doesn't appreciate his efforts
   (D) still has one flaw

5. The word "symbol" in line six refers to

   (A) Georgiana's cheek
   (B) the rainbow
   (C) Georgiana
   (D) the birthmark

6. Georgiana says in so many words she will die because

   (A) Aylmer does not love her
   (B) she is now too perfect for earth
   (C) the operation was not successful
   (D) she does not love Aylmer

7. The theme probably is

   (A) perfection does not belong on earth
   (B) power can be abused
   (C) do not try to change what is
   (D) love conquers all

Poetry Passage II.

I saw GOD! Do you doubt it?
Do you dare to doubt it?
I saw the Almighty Man! His hand
Was resting on a mountain! And
He looked upon the World, and all about it:
I saw Him plainer than you see me now
—You mustn't doubt it!

He was not satisfied!
His look was all dissatisfied!
His beard swung on a wind, far out of sight
Behind the world's curve! And there was light
Most fearful from His forehead! And He sighed—
—That star went always wrong, and from the start
I was dissatisfied!—

He lifted up His hand
I say He heaved a dreadful hand
Over the spinning earth! Then I said,—Stay,
You must not strike it, God! I'm in the way!
And I will never move from where I stand!—
He said,—Dear child, I feared that you were dead,—
. . . And stayed His hand!

—James Stephens, "What Tomas Said at the Pub"

8. The poem taken as a whole might be considered all but *one* of these

(A) hyperbole
(B) narrative
(C) monologue
(D) sonnet

9. The poem is an example of

(A) free verse
(B) an ode
(C) an elegy
(D) an allegory

10. God raised the hand to

(A) to stroke his head
(B) to strike the earth
(C) to pick up Tomas
(D) to pray for the earth

11. Tomas could be described as a man who

(A) is always having visions
(B) thinks highly of himself
(C) has a low opinion of himself
(D) is timid

12. By the way the poem is written, the reader could infer that the poet looks upon Tomas

(A) with awe at Tomas' vision
(B) as a scoundrel
(C) as a blasphemer
(D) with amusement

Dramatic Passage III.

Gottlieb (comes back. In the entry-room, out of breath). I've seen them, I've seen them! *(To a woman)* They're here, auntie, they're here! *(At the door)* They're here, father, they're here! They've got bean-poles, an' ox-goad, an' axes. They're standin' outside the Dittrich's, kickin' up an awful row. I think he's payin' them money. O Lord! whatever's goin' to happen? What a crowd! Oh, you never saw such a crowd! Dash it all—if once they make a rush, our manufacturers'll be hard put to it.

Old Hilse. What have you been runnin' like that for? You'll go racin' till you bring on your old trouble, and then we'll have you on your back again, strugglin' for breath.

Gottlieb (almost joyously excited). I had to run, or they would have caught me an' kept me. They were all roarin' to me to join them. Father Baumert was there too, and says he to me: You come an' get your sixpence with the rest—you're a poor starving weaver too. An' I was to tell you, father, from him, that you were to come an' help to pay out the manufacturers for their grindin' of us down. Other times is coming, he says. There's going to be a change of days for us weavers. An' we're all to come an' help to bring it about. We're to have our half-pound of meat on Sundays, and now and again on a holiday sausage with our cabbage. Yes, things is to be quite different, by what he tells me.

Old Hilse (with repressed indignation). An' that man calls himself your god-father! and he bids you take part in such works of wickedness? Have nothing to do with them, Gottlieb. They've let themselves be tamped by Satan, and it's his works they're doin'.

Luise (no longer able to restrain her passionate excitement, vehemently). Yes, Gottlieb, get into the chimney corner, an' take a spoon in your hand, an' a dish of skim milk on your knee, an' put on a petticoat an' say your prayers, an' then father'll be pleased with you. And he sets up to be a man!

(Laughter from the people in the entry-room.)

Old Hilse (quivering with suppressed rage). An' you set up to be a good wife, eh? You call yourself a mother, an' let your evil tongue run away with you like that? You think yourself fit to teach your girl, you that would egg on your husband to crime an' wickedness?

Luise (has lost all control of herself). You an' your piety an' religion—did they serve to keep the life in my poor children? In rags an' dirt they lay, all the four—it didn't as much as keep them dry. Yes! I set up to be a mother, that's what I do—an' if you'd like to know it, that's why I would send all the manufacturers to hell—because I'm a mother!—Not one of the four could I keep in life! It was cryin' more than breathin' with me from the time each poor little thing came into the world till death took pity on it. The devil a bit you cared! You sat there prayin' and singin', and let me run about till my feet bled, tryin' to get one little drop o' skim milk. How many hundred nights have I lain an' racked my head to think what I could do to cheat the churchyard of my little one? What harm has a baby like that done that it must come to such a miserable end—eh? An' over there at Dittrich's they're bathed in wine and washed in milk. No! you may talk as you like, but if they begin here, ten horses won't hold me back. An' what's more—if there's a rush on Dittrich's, you'll see me in the forefront of it—an' pity the man as tries to prevent me—I've stood it long enough, so now you know it.

Old Hilse. You're a lost soul—there's no help for you.

Luise (frenzied). It's you there's no help for! tatter-breeched scarecrows—that's what you are—an' not men at all. Whey-faced gutterscrapers that take to your heels at the sound of a child's rattle. Fellows that say ''thank you'' to the man as gives you a hidin'. They've not left that much blood in you as that you can turn red in the face. You should have the whip taken to you, and a little pluck flogged into your rotten bones. *(She goes out quickly.)*

(Embarrassed pause.)

—Gerhart Hauptmann, *The Weavers*

13. As the scene opens, we become aware that

(A) the weavers are happy
(B) the rioters are on the march
(C) the police are after Gottlieb
(D) Luise has gone crazy

14. The real clash of wills in this scene is between

(A) Gottlieb and Hilse
(B) Gottlieb and Luise
(C) Luise and Baumert
(D) Luise and Hilse

15. Baumert is

(A) Hilse's brother
(B) Gottlieb's godfather
(C) Luise's grandfather
(D) a manufacturer

16. The reader can infer that

(A) Luise will take no part in the battle against the manufacturers
(B) Gottlieb will stay with his father
(C) Luise has lost respect for Gottlieb
(D) The weavers cause is not just

17. Of Luise's children

(A) all have died
(B) one of the four had died
(C) were bathed in wine and washed in milk
(D) were with the rioters

18. Old Hilse believes the rioters are

(A) pitiful
(B) born to be killed
(C) right
(D) sinful

19. The reader can infer that Dittrich is a

(A) manufacturer
(B) weaver
(C) police inspector
(D) minister

20. Gottlieb has

(A) joined the rioters
(B) been cruel to his wife
(C) opposed his father
(D) been ill

CONSOLIDATE YOUR KEY ANSWERS HERE

Practice using Answer Sheets. Make ONE mark for each answer. Additional and stray marks may be counted as mistakes. In making corrections erase errors COMPLETELY. Make glossy black marks. To arrive at an accurate estimate of your ability and progress, cover the Correct Answers with a sheet of white paper while you are taking this test.

CORRECT ANSWERS TO THE FOREGOING PRACTICE QUESTIONS

Now compare your answers with these Correct Answers to the Practice Questions. If your answers differ from these, go back and study those questions to see where and how you made your mistakes.

1. D	4. B	7. A	10. B	13. B	16. C	19. A
2. A	5. D	8. D	11. B	14. D	17. A	20. D
3. C	6. B	9. A	12. D	15. B	18. D	

PART SIX

Mathematics

6

This test covers topics taught at both the elementary and high school level. Some topics which may be covered are definitions, ratios, percent, decimals, fractions, mathematical symbols, indirect measurement, interpretation of graphs and tables, scale drawings, approximate computation, and units of measurement. Some questions are based on techniques taught in elementary algebra and plane geometry courses. Questions frequently test knowledge of mathematical principles and stress their applications through the performance of mathematical operations and manipulations. The ability to express practical problems in mathematical terms is frequently tested. The test may also include one or two questions based on the concepts of modern mathematics.

APPROXIMATE CONVERSION FACTORS FOR CHANGING FROM CUSTOMARY UNITS TO METRIC UNITS.

Symbol	When You Know	Multiply by	To Find	Symbol
LENGTH				
in	inches	2.54	centimeters	cm
ft	feet	30	centimeters	cm
yd	yards	0.9	meters	m
mi	miles	1.6	kilometers	km
AREA				
in^2	square inches	6.5	square centimeters	cm^2
ft^2	square feet	0.09	square meters	m^2
yd^2	square yards	0.8	square meters	m^2
mi^2	square miles	2.6	square kilometers	km^2
	acres	0.4	hectares	ha
MASS (weight)				
oz	ounces	28	grams	g
lb	pounds	0.45	kilograms	kg
	short tons (2000 lb)	0.9	tonnes	t
VOLUME				
tsp	teaspoons	5	milliliters	ml
Tbsp	tablespoons	15	milliliters	ml
fl oz	fluid ounces	30	milliliters	ml
c	cups	0.24	liters	l
pt	pints	0.47	liters	l
qt	quarts	0.95	liters	l
gal	gallons	3.8	liters	l
ft^3	cubic feet	0.03	cubic meters	m^3
yd^3	cubic yards	0.76	cubic meters	m^3
TEMPERATURE (exact)				
°F	Fahrenheit temperature	5/9 (after subtracting 32)	Celsius temperature	°C

inches

°F 32 98.6 °F 212
-40   0   40   80   120   160   200
-40 -20   0   20   40   60   80   100
°C   37   °C

MATH MADE SIMPLE

To help you learn to solve problems, references to earlier explanations are given in the form of a number which is enclosed in parentheses. If you go back to the original explanation, you will find it very easy to understand the problem at hand. Each chapter is followed by a short test. And each test is followed by the correct answers and clear-cut solutions to help you arrive at those answers.

FRACTIONS

1. A fraction is part of a unit, such as ½, ¾, etc.
   a. A fraction has a numerator and a denominator.
   Example: In the fraction ¾. 3 is the numerator, and 4 is the denominator.
   b. In any fraction, the numerator is being divided by the denominator.
   Example: The fraction $\frac{2}{7}$ indicates that 2 is being divided by 7.

2. A mixed number is an integer together with a fraction, such as $2\frac{3}{5}$, $7\frac{3}{8}$, etc. The integer is the integral part, and the fraction is the fractional part.

3. An improper fraction is one in which the numerator is greater than the denominator, such as $\frac{19}{6}$, $\frac{25}{4}$, etc.

4. To change a mixed number to an improper fraction:
   a. Multiply the denominator of the fraction by the integer.
   b. Add the numerator to this product.
   c. Place this sum over the denominator of the fraction.

Illustration: Change $3\frac{4}{7}$ to an improper fraction.

SOLUTION:
$$7 \times 3 = 21 \qquad (4a)$$
$$21 + 4 = 25 \qquad (4b)$$
$$3\tfrac{4}{7} = \tfrac{25}{7} \qquad (4c)$$

Answer: $\frac{25}{7}$

5. To change an improper fraction to a mixed number:

a. Divide the numerator by the denominator. The quotient, disregarding the remainder, is the integral part of the mixed number.
b. Place the remainder, if any, over the denominator. This is the fractional part of the mixed number.

Illustration: Change $\frac{36}{13}$ to a mixed number.

$$
\begin{array}{r}
2 \qquad\qquad (5a)\\
SOLUTION:\ 13{\overline{)\,36}}\\
26\\
\overline{10\ \text{remainder}}
\end{array}
$$

$$\tfrac{36}{13} = 2\tfrac{10}{13} \qquad (5b)$$

Answer: $2\frac{10}{13}$

6. The numerator and denominator of a fraction may be changed by multiplying both by the same number, without affecting the value of the fraction.
   Example: The value of the fraction $\frac{2}{5}$ will not be altered if the numerator and the denominator are multiplied by 2, to result in $\frac{4}{10}$.

7. The numerator and the denominator of a fraction may be changed by dividing both by the same number, without affecting the value of the fraction.
   Example: The value of the fraction $\frac{3}{12}$ will not be altered if the numerator and denominator are divided by 3, to result in ¼.

8. As a final answer to a problem:
   a. Improper fractions should be changed to mixed numbers.
   b. Fractions should be reduced as far as possible.

ADDITION OF FRACTIONS

9. Fractions cannot be added unless the denominators are all the same. If they are, add all the numerators and place this sum over the common denominator. In the case of mixed numbers, follow the above rule for fractions and then add the integers.
Example: The sum of $2\frac{3}{8}$, $3\frac{1}{8}$, and $\frac{5}{8}$ is $5\frac{9}{8}$ or $6\frac{1}{8}$. (8a). If the denominators are not the same, the fractions, in order to be added, must be converted to ones having the same denominator. In order to do this, it is first necessary to find the lowest common denominator.

10. The lowest common denominator (henceforth called the L.C.D.) is the lowest number which can be divided evenly by all the given denominators.
If no two of the given denominators can be divided by the same number, then the L.C.D. is the product of all the denominators.
Example: The L.C.D. of $\frac{1}{2}$, $\frac{1}{3}$, and $\frac{1}{5}$ is $2 \times 3 \times 5 = 30$.

11. To find the L.C.D. when two or more of the given denominators can be divided by the same number:
a. Write down the denominators, separated a little from each other.
b. Select the lowest number by which any two or more of these denominators can be divided evenly.
c. Divide the denominators by this number, copying down those which cannot be divided evenly. Place this number to one side.
d. Repeat this, placing each divisor to one side until there are no longer any denominators that can be divided evenly by any selected number.
e. Multiply all the divisors to find the LCD.
Illustration: Find the L.C.D. of $\frac{1}{5}$, $\frac{1}{7}$, $\frac{1}{10}$, and $\frac{1}{14}$.

```
Solution:  2)5  7  10  14    (11a)
                             (11b)
           5)5  7   5   7    (11c)
                             (11b)
           7)1  7   1   7    (11c)
                             (11b)
             1  1   1   1    (11c)
           7 × 5 × 2 = 70    (11e)
```
Answer: The L.C.D. is 70

12. Having learned how to find the L.C.D., we are now prepared to add fractions and mixed numbers when the denominators are not the same. The system presented here involves the drawing of a diagram which will be explained in the method that follows.
To add fractions and mixed numbers:

a. List them one under the other.

b. Draw a diagram to add the fractions.

```
         A
      ┌─────
      │ B
      └─────
         C/A
```

c. Find the L.C.D. and write it in at (A).

d. Ascertain the new numerators by dividing the L.C.D. by each denominator and multiplying this quotient by the old numerator. These new numerators are written in at (B).

e. Add up the new numerators and place this sum over the L.C.D. (C/A in the diagram.)

f. Reduce this fraction and change it to a mixed number if possible.

g. Add this reduced fraction (or mixed number) to the sum of the whole numbers for the final answer.

Illustration: Add $29\frac{7}{12}$, $51\frac{5}{6}$, $37\frac{3}{5}$, and $21\frac{3}{4}$.

SOLUTION:

```
                         60        (11, 12c)
        29 7/12 ┐
        51 5/6  │
        37 3/5  │                  (12a, 12b)
        21 3/4  ┘
                      ┌─── 60 ───
        29 7/12       35
        51 5/6        50
        37 3/5        36
        21 3/4        45
          138      166/60 = 83/30 =
    +  )               2 23/30
       )                          (7, 5, 12e, 12f)
            2 23/30
          140 23/30               (12g)
```

Answer: $140\frac{23}{30}$

SUBTRACTION OF FRACTIONS

Illustration: Subtract $16\frac{4}{5}$ from $29\frac{1}{3}$.

SOLUTION: $29\frac{1}{3} = \frac{88}{3}$, $16\frac{4}{5} = \frac{84}{5}$ (4, 14a)

L.C.D. = 15 (10, 14b)

$\frac{88}{3} - \frac{84}{5} = \frac{440}{15} - \frac{252}{15}$ (6, 12d, 14c)

$= \frac{188}{15}$ (14d)

$= 12\frac{8}{15}$ (14e, 5, 8a)

Answer: $12\frac{8}{15}$

13. a. More than two numbers may be added at the same time. In subtraction, however, only two numbers are involved. In subtraction, as in addition, the denominators must be the same.

b. One must be careful to determine which term is first. The second term is always subtracted from the first, which should be the larger quantity.

To Subtract Fractions

14. a. Change the mixed numbers, if any, to improper fractions.
b. Find the L.C.D.
c. Change both fractions to ones having the L.C.D. as the denominator.
d. Subtract the numerator of the second fraction from the numerator of the first, and place this difference over the L.C.D.
e. Reduce if possible.

MULTIPLICATION OF FRACTIONS

15. a. To be multiplied, fractions need not have the same denominators.
b. A whole number has the denominator 1 understood.

16. To Multiply Fractions:
a. Change the mixed numbers, if any, to improper fractions.
b. Multiply all the numerators, and place this product over the product of the denominators.
c. Reduce, if possible.

Illustration: Multiply $\frac{2}{3} \times 2\frac{4}{7} \times \frac{5}{9}$.

SOLUTION: $2\frac{4}{7} = \frac{18}{7}$ (4, 16a)

$\frac{2}{3} \times \frac{18}{7} \times \frac{5}{9} = \frac{180}{189}$ (16b)

$= \frac{20}{21}$ (7, 8b, 16c)

Answer: $\frac{20}{21}$

17. When a whole number is multiplied by a mixed number.
a. Multiply the whole number by the fractional part of the mixed number.
b. Multiply the whole number by the integral part of the mixed number.
c. Add both products.

Illustration: Multiply $23\frac{3}{4}$ by 95.

SOLUTION: $95 \times \frac{3}{4} = \frac{285}{4}$ (16, 17a)

$= 71\frac{1}{4}$ (5)

$95 \times 23 = 2185$ (17b

$2185 + 71\frac{1}{4} = 2256\frac{1}{4}$ (17c)

Answer: $2256\frac{1}{4}$

18. Cancellation is a device to facilitate multiplication. To cancel means to divide a numerator and a denominator by the same number. *Example:* In the problem $\frac{4}{7} \times \frac{5}{6}$, the numerator 4 and the denominator 6 may be divided by 2.

$$\frac{\overset{2}{\not{4}}}{7} \times \frac{5}{\underset{3}{\not{6}}} = \frac{10}{21}$$

19. The word "of" is often used to mean "multiply."

Example: $\frac{1}{2}$ of $\frac{1}{2} = \frac{1}{2} \times \frac{1}{2} = \frac{1}{4}$.

DIVISION OF FRACTIONS

20. In division, as in subtraction, only two terms are involved. It is very important to determine which term is first. If the problem reads, "$\frac{2}{3}$ divided by 5," then $\frac{2}{3}$ is the first term, and 5 is the second. If it reads, "How many times is $\frac{1}{2}$ contained in $\frac{1}{3}$?", then $\frac{1}{3}$ is first, and $\frac{1}{2}$ is second.

21. The reciprocal of a number is that number inverted.

a. Since every whole number has the denominator 1 understood, the reciprocal of a whole number is a fraction having 1 as the numerator and the number itself as the denominator.
Example: The reciprocal of 5 ($\frac{5}{1}$) is $\frac{1}{5}$.
b. When a fraction is inverted, the numerator becomes the denominator and the denominator becomes the numerator.

Example: The reciprocal of $\frac{3}{8}$ is $\frac{8}{3}$.
Example: The reciprocal of $\frac{1}{3}$ is $\frac{3}{1}$, or simply 3.

22. To divide fractions:

a. Change all the mixed numbers, if any, to improper fractions.

b. Invert the second fraction and multiply.

c. Reduce, if possible.

Illustration: **Divide $2/3$ by $2\frac{1}{4}$**

SOLUTION: **$2\frac{1}{4} = 9/4$ (22a, 4)**

$2/3 \div 9/4 = 2/3 \times 4/9$

$= 8/27$ (22b, 16)

Answer: **$8/27$**

23. A mixed fraction is one that has a fraction as the numerator, or as the denominator, or as both.

Example: **$\dfrac{2/3}{5}$ is a mixed fraction.**

24. To clear a mixed fraction:

a. Divide the numerator by the denominator.

b. Reduce, if possible.

(The longer line indicates the point of division.)

Illustration: **Clear $\dfrac{3/7}{5/14}$**

SOLUTION: **$3/7 \div 5/14 = 3/7 \times 14/5 = 42/35$ (24a)**

$= 6/5$ (7)

$= 1\frac{1}{5}$ (24b, 8a)

Answer: **$1\frac{1}{5}$**

25. Fractions—General Facts.

a. If two fractions have the same denominator, the one with the larger numerator is the greater fraction.

Example: **$3/7$ is greater than $2/7$.**

b. If two fractions have the same numerator, the one with the larger denominator is the smaller fraction.

Example: **$5/12$ is smaller than $5/11$.**

26. In a fractional problem, the whole is 1, which may be expressed by a fraction in which the numerator and the denominator are the same number.

Example: **If the problem involves $1/8$ of a quantity, then the whole quantity is $8/8$, or 1.**

PRACTICE PROBLEMS IN FRACTIONS

1. Find the L.C.D. of $1/8$, $1/7$, $1/6$, and $1/10$.
(a) 800 (b) 860 (c) 840 (d) 830.

2. Add $16\frac{3}{8}$, $4\frac{4}{5}$, $12\frac{3}{4}$, and $23\frac{5}{6}$.
(a) $57\frac{91}{120}$ (b) $57\frac{1}{4}$ (c) 58 (d) 59.

3. Subtract $27\frac{5}{14}$ from $43\frac{1}{6}$.
(a) 15 (b) 16 (c) $15\frac{8}{21}$ (d) $15\frac{17}{21}$.

4. Multiply $17\frac{5}{8}$ by 128.
(a) 2200 (b) 2305 (c) 2356 (d) 2256.

5. What is the sum of $12\frac{1}{6} - 2\frac{3}{8} - 7\frac{2}{3} + 19\frac{3}{4}$.
(a) 21 (b) $21\frac{7}{8}$ (c) $21\frac{1}{8}$ (d) 22.

6. By how much does $\dfrac{6}{7/8}$ exceed $\dfrac{6/7}{8}$?
(a) 1 (b) 8 (c) $6\frac{1}{4}$ (d) $6\frac{3}{4}$.

7. During one week, a man traveled $3\frac{1}{2}$, $1\frac{1}{4}$, $1\frac{1}{6}$, and $2\frac{3}{8}$ miles. The next week he traveled $1/4$, $3/8$, $9/16$, $3\frac{1}{16}$, $2\frac{5}{8}$, and $3\frac{3}{16}$ miles. How many more miles did he travel the second week?
(a) $1\frac{37}{48}$ (b) $1\frac{1}{2}$ (c) $1\frac{1}{16}$ (d) 1.

8. Four men cat a pie. The first three men eat $1/4$, $2/7$, and $3/11$ of the pie respectively. How much of the pie did the fourth man eat?
(a) $59/308$ (b) $70/308$ (c) $1/3$ (d) $1/4$.

9. A, B, and C are bcqueathed an inheritance. A gets $1/6$, B gets $1/8$, and C gets the rest. When the estate was finally adjusted, A had to give $2/3$ of his share to C, and C then gave $3/4$ of his share to B. What part of the estate had B finally?
(a) $3/4$ (b) $71/96$ (c) $75/95$ (d) $76/96$.

10. Clock A loses 1 minute a day, and clock B gains $2\frac{3}{4}$ minutes per day. If clock B is 15 minutes ahead of clock A, how many days will it take clock B to be 30 minutes ahead of clock A?
(a) 7 (b) 4 (c) 6 (d) 8.

Correct Answers

1. c	3. d	5. b	7. a	9. b
2. a	4. d	6. d	8. a	10. b

PROBLEM SOLUTIONS

by Sister Mary Mark Zimmerman, O. P.
(Dominican Sisters, Sparkill, New York)

The solutions to the problems in Mathematics are given to help the student in every possible way. There are other solutions to these problems, but those contained in this book, I feel, are the clearest and most direct way to solve them.

This book is not a magic wand. The solutions and suggestions, combined with a spirit of perseverance and hard work, will make it possible for any student to learn the mathematics needed. To supplement the brief explanations given on the various types of problems, the student could use a junior high arithmetic book, an algebra book and a geometry text. These books can be obtained at the public library.

I wish to extend my gratitude to the Sisters of my Community, and Miss Elizabeth Lanigan, M.A., for their help and suggestions in solving the problems contained in this book; to Mrs. Anthony Agathen, B.S., Ph.M., for her excellent illustrations and careful proof reading; and to Sr. Jean Barbara, O.P., Miss Isabella Powell, Mrs. Vernon Haug, and Miss Mary Zimmerman, for countless hours spent in typing this manuscript. For his experienced advice and assistance, I also wish to thank Mr. Alexander J. Burke, Editor-in-Chief, Language Arts Department, Webster Division, McGraw-Hill Publishing Company, St. Louis, Mo. For their cooperation in the preparation of this book, my sincere appreciation is extended to Mr. Frank McKeon and Mr. Anthony Ahrens.

Sister Mary Mark, O.P.

PROBLEM SOLUTIONS   Fractions

1. Find the L.C.D. of $\frac{1}{8}$, $\frac{1}{7}$, $\frac{1}{6}$, $\frac{1}{10}$
   SOLUTION: Multiply Divisors to find L.C.D.
   2)8-7-6-10   (2 is a factor of 8-6-10)
   3)4-7-3-5   (3 is a factor of 3)
   4)4-7-1-5   (4 is a factor of 4)
   5)1-7-1-5   (5 is a factor of 5)
   7)1-7-1-1   (7 is a factor of 7)
   1-1-1-1   Will have 1-1-1-1
   L.C.D. = 2 x 3 x 4 x 5 x 7 = 840
   (c) Answered in text.

   ANSWER: L.C.D. = 840

2. Add: $16\frac{3}{8}$, $4\frac{4}{5}$, $12\frac{3}{4}$, $23\frac{5}{6}$
   SOLUTION: L.C.D. = 120
   $16\frac{3}{8} = 16\frac{45}{120}$
   $4\frac{4}{5} = 4\frac{96}{120}$
   $12\frac{3}{4} = 12\frac{90}{120}$
   $23\frac{5}{6} = 23\frac{100}{120}$
   $55\frac{331}{120} = 57\frac{91}{120}$ (a)

   ANSWER: Sum = $57\frac{91}{120}$

3. Subtract $27\frac{5}{14}$ from $43\frac{1}{6}$
   SOLUTION: L.C.D. = 42
   $$43\frac{1}{6} = 43\overset{42}{\cancel{43}}\frac{49}{42}$$
   $$-27\frac{5}{14} = 27\frac{15}{42}$$
   $$15\frac{34}{42} = 15\frac{17}{21} \quad (d)$$

   ANSWER: Difference = $15\frac{17}{21}$

4. Multiply $17\frac{5}{8}$ by 128.
   SOLUTION:
   $17\frac{5}{8}$ x 128
   $$\frac{141}{\cancel{8}} \times \frac{\cancel{128}^{16}}{1} = 2256 \ (d)$$

   141
   $\times 16$
   846
   141
   2256

   ANSWER: Product = 2256

5. What is the sum of $12\frac{1}{6} - 2\frac{3}{8}$
   $- 7\frac{2}{3} + 19\frac{3}{4}$.

   SOLUTION:　　　　L.C.D. = 24

   $$12\frac{1}{6} = 12\frac{11\ 28}{24}$$
   $$- 2\frac{3}{8} = 2\frac{9}{24}$$
   $$\frac{}{9\frac{19}{24} = 9\frac{19}{24}}$$
   $$- 7\frac{2}{3} = -7\frac{16}{24}$$
   $$\frac{}{2\ \frac{3}{24} = 2\frac{1}{8}}$$
   $$+ 19\frac{3}{4} = +19\frac{6}{8}$$
   $$\frac{}{21\frac{7}{8}} \quad (b)$$

   Explanation
   Reduced $2\frac{3}{24} = 2\frac{1}{8}$
   L.C.D. = 8

   ANSWER: $21\frac{7}{8} =$ Sum

6. By how much does $\dfrac{6}{7\frac{1}{8}}$ exceed $\dfrac{6\frac{1}{7}}{8}$?

   SOLUTION:

   $$6 \div \frac{7}{8} = \frac{6}{1} \times \frac{8}{7} = \frac{48}{7} = 6\frac{6}{7}$$
   $$\frac{6}{7} \div 8 = \frac{6}{7} \times \frac{1}{8} = \frac{3}{28}$$
   $$6\frac{6}{7} = 6\frac{24}{28} \quad \text{L.C.D.} = 28$$
   $$- \frac{3}{28} = \frac{3}{28}$$
   $$\frac{}{6\frac{21}{28} = 6\frac{3}{4}} \quad (d)$$

   ANSWER: $6\frac{3}{4}$

7. SOLUTION:
   $$3\frac{1}{2} = 3\frac{12}{24} \text{ miles first week}$$
   $$1\frac{1}{4} = 1\ \frac{6}{24}$$
   $$1\frac{1}{6} = 1\ \frac{4}{24} \quad \text{L.C.D.} = 24$$
   $$2\frac{3}{8} = 2\ \frac{9}{24}$$
   $$\frac{}{7\frac{31}{24}} = 8\frac{7}{24} \text{ miles traveled first week}$$

   $$\frac{1}{4} = \frac{4}{16} \text{ miles 2nd week}$$
   $$\frac{3}{8} = \frac{6}{16}$$
   $$\frac{9}{16} = \frac{9}{16} \quad \text{L.C.D.} = 16$$
   $$3\frac{1}{16} = 3\frac{1}{16}$$
   $$2\frac{5}{8} = 2\frac{10}{16}$$
   $$3\frac{3}{16} = 3\frac{3}{16}$$
   $$\frac{}{8\frac{33}{16}} = 10\frac{1}{16} \text{ miles traveled 2nd week}$$
   $$(a)$$

   L.C.D. = 48
   $$10\frac{1}{16} = 9\frac{51}{48} \text{ miles 2nd week}$$
   $$-8\frac{7}{24} \quad 8\frac{14}{48} \text{ miles first week}$$
   $$\frac{}{1\frac{37}{48} \text{ miles more traveled 2nd week}}$$

   ANSWER: $1\frac{37}{48}$

8. SOLUTION:
   L.C.D. $= 4 \times 7 \times 11 = 308$
   $$\frac{1}{4} = \frac{77}{308} \text{ first man ate}$$
   $$\frac{2}{7} = \frac{88}{308} \text{ second man ate}$$
   $$\frac{3}{11} = \frac{84}{308} \text{ third man ate}$$
   $$\frac{}{\frac{249}{308} \text{ three men ate}}$$

   $$\frac{308}{308} = \text{ whole pie}$$
   $$- \frac{249}{308} =$$
   $$\frac{}{\frac{59}{308} = \text{ fourth man ate}} \quad (a)$$

   ANSWER: $\frac{59}{308}$

9. SOLUTION:
   $$\frac{1}{6} = \frac{4}{24} - \text{ A receives}$$
   $$+ \frac{1}{8} = \frac{3}{24} - \text{ B receives}$$
   $$\frac{}{\frac{7}{24}} \quad \text{A \& B receive}$$

   A gives $\frac{2}{3}$ to C
   $$\frac{1}{6} \times \frac{2}{3} = \frac{1}{9} \text{ to C}$$
   $$\frac{24}{24} = \text{ whole estate} \quad \text{L.C.D.} = 24$$
   $$- \frac{7}{24} = \text{ A \& B receive}$$
   $$\frac{}{\frac{17}{24} = \text{ C receives}}$$

   C has $\frac{17}{24}$
   $$\frac{1}{9} + \frac{17}{24} = \frac{8}{72} + \frac{51}{72} = \frac{59}{72}$$
   $$\frac{59}{72} \text{ C's final share}$$

   C gives $\frac{3}{4}$ to B
   $$\frac{59}{\underset{24}{72}} \times \frac{\overset{1}{3}}{4} = \frac{59}{96}$$

   B had $\frac{1}{8}$
   $$\frac{1}{8} + \frac{59}{96} = \frac{12}{96} + \frac{59}{96} = \frac{71}{96}$$
   $$\frac{71}{96} \text{ B's final share} \quad (b)$$

   ANSWER: $\frac{71}{96}$

10. SOLUTION:
    30 minutes — 15 minutes = 15 minutes
    more, B must be ahead of A
    $2\frac{3}{4}$ minutes + 1 minute (loss) = $3\frac{3}{4}$ minutes
    B gains over A each day
    15 minutes ÷ $3\frac{3}{4}$ minutes = $15 \div \frac{15}{4} =$
    $$\frac{15 \times 4}{15} = 4 \text{ days} \quad (b)$$

    ANSWER: It will take Clock B four days to
    be 30 min. ahead of Clock A.

DECIMALS

27. A decimal, which is a number with a decimal point (.), is actually a fraction the denominator of which is understood to be 10 or some power of 10.

a. The number of digits, or places, after a decimal point determines which power of 10 the denominator is. If there is one digit, the denominator is understood to be 10; if there are two digits, the denominator is understood to be 100, etc.

Example: $.3 = \frac{3}{10}$, $.57 = \frac{57}{100}$, $.643 = \frac{643}{1000}$.

b. The addition of zeros after a decimal point does not change the value of the decimal, and if there are zeros only after a decimal point, they may be removed without changing the value of the decimal.

Example: $.7 = .70 = .700$ and vice versa, $.700 = .70 = .7$

c. Since a decimal point is understood to exist after any whole number the addition of any number of zeros after such decimal point written in does not change the value of the number.

Example: $2 = 2.0 = 2.00$, etc.

d. If a decimal point already exists with digits following it, the addition of any number of zeros after such digits will not change the value of the decimal.

Example: $.53 = .530 = .5300$, etc.

ADDITION OF DECIMALS

28. The addition of decimals is the same as that of whole numbers with the added provision that the decimal points must be kept in a vertical line, one under the other. This determines the place of the decimal point in the answer.

Illustration: Add: 2.31, .037, 4, and 5.0017.
SOLUTION:
```
  2.3100
   .0370
  4.0000        (27c)
  5.0017
 -------
 11.3487
```
Answer: 11.3487

SUBTRACTION OF DECIMALS

29. The subtraction of decimals is the same as that of whole numbers with the added provision that, as in addition, the decimal points be kept in a vertical line, one under the other. This determines the place of the decimal point in the answer.

Illustration: Subtract 4.0037 from 15.3
SOLUTION:
```
  15.3000      (27d)
 - 4.0037
 --------
  11.2963
```
Answer: 11.2963

MULTIPLICATION OF DECIMALS

30. The multiplication of decimals is the same as that of whole numbers.

a. The number of decimal places in the product equals the sum of the decimal places in the multiplicand and in the multiplier.

b. If there are fewer places in the product than this sum, then a sufficient number of zeros must be added in front of the product to equal the number of places required, and a decimal point is written in front of the zeros.

Illustration: Multiply 2.372 by .012
SOLUTION:
```
   2.372   (3 decimal places)
 x  .012   (3 decimal places)
 -------
   4744
   2372
 -------
 .028464       (30b)
```
Answer: .028464

31. A decimal can be multiplied by a power of 10 by moving the decimal point to the *right* as many places as indicated by the power. If multiplied by 10, the decimal point is moved one place to the right; if multiplied by 100, the decimal point is moved two places to the right, etc.

Example:
$.235 \times 10 = 2.35$
$.235 \times 100 = 23.5$
$.235 \times 1000 = 235$ etc.

DIVISION OF DECIMALS

32. There are four types of division involving decimals:
    a. When the dividend only is a decimal.
    b. When the divisor only is a decimal.
    c. When both are decimals.
    d. When neither dividend nor divisor is a decimal.

33. A decimal can be cleared of its decimal point by multiplying it by a power of 10 which is indicated by the number of decimal places involved.
    Example: To clear 5.38 of its decimal point, it must be multiplied by 100. 5.38 x 100 = 538

34. When a divisor is thus multiplied by some power of 10, the dividend must be multiplied by a similar power of 10 in order to keep the value intact.

35. **TYPE A**
    When the dividend only is a decimal, the division is the same as that of whole numbers, except that a decimal point must be placed in the quotient exactly above that in the dividend.
    Illustration: Divide 12.864 by 32

    $$\begin{array}{r} .402 \\ 32\overline{)\ 12.864} \\ \underline{12\ 8} \\ 64 \\ \underline{64} \end{array}$$

    Answer: .402

36. **TYPE B**
    When the divisor only is a decimal, the divisor must be cleared of its decimal point and as many zeros must be added to the dividend as there were decimal places in the divisor. (33, 34)
    Illustration: Divide 211327 by 6.817
    SOLUTION:

    $$6.817\overline{)\ 211327} = 6817\begin{array}{r} 31000 \\ \overline{)\ 211327000} \\ \underline{20451} \\ 6817 \\ \underline{6817} \end{array}$$

    Answer: 31000

37. **TYPE C**
    When both divisor and dividend are decimals, the divisor must be cleared of its decimal, and the decimal point in the dividend must be moved to the right as many places as there were in the divisor. If there are not enough places in the dividend, zeros must be added to make up the difference.

    Illustration: Divide 2.62 by .131
    SOLUTION:

    $$.131\overline{)\ 2.62} = 131\begin{array}{r} 20 \\ \overline{)\ 2620} \\ \underline{262} \end{array} \quad (33, 31, 34)$$

    Answer: 20

38. **TYPE D**
    Neither the divisor nor the **dividend need be** a decimal and yet the problem **may involve** decimals. This occurs in two **cases:**
    a. When the dividend is a **smaller number** than the divisor.
    b. When it is required to work out a **division** to a certain number of decimal places.
    In either case, write in a decimal point after the dividend, add as many zeros as necessary, and place a decimal point in the quotient above that in the dividend.

    Illustration: Divide 7 by 50   (Case A)
    SOLUTION:

    $$50\begin{array}{r} .14 \\ \overline{)\ 7.00} \\ \underline{5\ 0} \\ 2\ 00 \\ \underline{2\ 00} \end{array} \quad (35)$$

    Answer: .14

    Illustration: How much is 155 divided by 40, carried out to 3 decimal places? (Case B)
    SOLUTION:

    $$40\begin{array}{r} 3.875 \\ \overline{)\ 155.000} \\ \underline{120} \\ 35\ 0 \\ \underline{32\ 0} \\ 3\ 00 \\ \underline{2\ 80} \\ 200 \end{array} \quad (35)$$

    Answer: 3.875

39. A decimal can be divided by a power of 10 by moving the decimal to the left as many places as indicated by the power. If divided by 10, the decimal point is moved one place; if divided by 100, the decimal point is moved two places, etc. If there are not enough places, add zeros in front of the number to make up the difference and add a decimal point.
    Example: .4 divided by 10 = .04
                   .4 divided by 100 = .004

CONVERSION OF FRACTIONS TO DECIMALS

40. A fraction can be changed to a decimal by dividing the numerator by the denominator and working out the division to as many decimal places as required.

Illustration: Change 5/11 to a decimal of 2 places.

$$\text{SOLUTION: } 5/11 = 11 \overline{)\begin{array}{r} .45\ ^5\!/_{11} \\ 5.00 \\ \underline{4.44} \\ 60 \\ \underline{55} \\ 5 \end{array}} \quad (27b)$$

Answer: .45 $^5\!/_{11}$

41. If the problem requires the fraction to be changed to the nearest decimal point, carry it out one place further. Then, if the last digit is 5 or more, add 1 to the digit before, if it less than 5, discard the last digit.

Illustration: What is 6/7 in decimal form to the nearest tenth?

$$\text{SOLUTION: } 6/7 \quad 7\overline{)\begin{array}{r} .85 \\ 6.00 \\ \underline{5\ 6} \\ 40 \\ \underline{35} \\ 5 \end{array}}$$

.85 to the nearest tenth = .9
Answer: .9

42. To clear fractions containing a decimal in either the numerator or the denominator, or in both, divide the numerator by the denominator.

Illustration: What is the value of 2.34/.6

$$\text{SOLUTION: } 2.34/.6 = .6\overline{)2.34} = 6\overline{)\begin{array}{r} 3.9 \\ 23.4 \\ \underline{18} \\ 5\ 4 \\ \underline{5\ 4} \end{array}}$$
(37)

Answer: 3.9

CONVERSION OF DECIMALS TO FRACTIONS

43 Since a decimal point indicates a denominator which is a power of 10, a decimal can be expressed as a fraction the numerator of which is the number itself and the denominator of which is the power indicated by the number of decimal places there were in the decimal.
Example: .3 = $^3\!/_{10}$,   .47 = $^{47}\!/_{100}$ (27a)

44. When the decimal is a mixed number, divide by the power of 10 indicated by its number of decimal places. The fraction does not count as a decimal place.

Illustration: Change .25⅓ to a fraction.
$$\begin{aligned} \text{SOLUTION: } .25\tfrac{1}{3} &= 25\tfrac{1}{3} \div 100 & (44) \\ &= {}^{76}\!/_3 \times {}^1\!/_{100} & (24) \\ &= {}^{76}\!/_{300} = {}^{19}\!/_{75} & (8) \end{aligned}$$
Answer: $^{19}\!/_{75}$

45. When to change decimals to fractions.
   a. When dealing with whole numbers, do not change the decimal.

Example: In the problem 12 x .14, it is better to keep the decimal. 12 x .14 = 1.68   (30)
   b. When dealing with fractions, change the decimal to a fraction.

Example: In the problem ⅗ x .17, it is best to change the decimal to a fraction.
$$\tfrac{3}{5} \times .17 = \tfrac{3}{5} \times {}^{17}\!/_{100} = {}^{51}\!/_{500} \quad (43, 16)$$

PROBLEMS INVOLVING DECIMALS

1. Add 37.03, 11.5627, 3.4005, 3423, and 1.141
   - (a) 3476.1342
   - (c) 3524.4322
   - (b) 3500
   - (d) 3424.1342.

2. Subtract 4.64324 from 7.
   - (a) 3.35676
   - (c) 2.45676
   - (b) 2.35676
   - (d) 2.36676.

3. Multiply 27.34 by 16.943
   - (a) 463.22162
   - (c) 462.52162
   - (b) 453.52162
   - (d) 462.53162

4. How much is 19.6 divided by 3.2 carried out to 3 decimal places.
   - (a) 6.125 (b) 6.124 (c) 6.123 (d) 5.123.

5. What is $\frac{5}{11}$ in decimal form? (To the nearest hundredth)
   - (a) .44 (b) .55 (c) .40 (d) .45.

6. What is .64⅔ in fraction form?
   - (a) $\frac{97}{120}$
   - (c) $\frac{97}{130}$
   - (b) $\frac{97}{150}$
   - (d) $\frac{98}{130}$.

7. What is the difference between ⅗ and ⅜ expressed decimally?
   - (a) .525 (b) .425 (c) .520 (d) .500.

8. If 314 clerks filed 6594 papers in 10 minutes, what is the number filed per minute by the average clerk?
   - (a) 2 (b) 2.4 (c) 2.1 (d) 2.5.

9. A man receives a monthly salary of $120 and saves .08⅓ of his earnings. How many months would it take him to save $1000?
   - (a) 90 (b) 80 (c) 85 (d) 100.

10. A man willed his property to his three sons,—to the youngest he gave $968.49, to the second 3.4 as much as to the youngest, and to the eldest 3.7 times as much as to the second. What was the value of his estate (to the nearest penny)?
    - (a) $16,450.50
    - (c) $16,444.90
    - (b) $16,444.55
    - (d) $16,444.96.

Correct Answers

1. a	3. a	5. d	7. a	9. d
2. b	4. a	6. b	8. c	10. d

NOW, CHECK YOUR METHODS WITH OUR SIMPLIFIED PROBLEM SOLUTIONS, WHICH FOLLOW DIRECTLY.

PROBLEM SOLUTIONS | Decimals

1. SOLUTION:
   Add:
   ```
      37.03
      11.5627
       3.4005
   3423.0000
       1.141
   ─────────
   3476.1342   (a)
   ```
   ANSWER: Sum = 3476.1342

2. SOLUTION:
   Subtract 4.64324 from 7
   ```
    7.00000
   −4.64324
   ─────────
    2.35676   (b)
   ```
   ANSWER: Difference = 2.35676

3. SOLUTION:
Multiply 27.34 by 16.943

$$
\begin{array}{r}
27.34 \\
\times\ 16.943 \\
\hline
8202 \\
109360 \\
2460600 \\
16404000 \\
27340000 \\
\hline
463.22162 \quad (a)
\end{array}
$$

ANSWER: Product = 463.22162

4. SOLUTION:
Divide 19.6 by 3.2 to 3 decimal places

$$
\begin{array}{r}
6.125 \quad (a) \\
3.2\,)\overline{19.6.000} \\
\underline{19\ 2} \\
4\ 0 \\
\underline{3\ 2} \\
80 \\
\underline{64} \\
160 \\
\underline{160}
\end{array}
$$

ANSWER Quotient = 6.125

5. SOLUTION:
$^5/_{11}$ in decimal form

$$
\begin{array}{r}
.45\ ^5/_{11} \quad (d) \\
11)\overline{5.00} \\
\underline{4\ 4} \\
60 \\
\underline{55} \\
5
\end{array}
$$

$^5/_{11}$ less than $\frac{1}{2}$ so drop it

ANSWER: Decimal = .45

6. SOLUTION:
.64⅔ in fraction form

$$.64\tfrac{2}{3} = \frac{64\frac{2}{3}}{100} = \frac{\frac{194}{3}}{100} = \frac{194}{3} \times \frac{1}{100} = \frac{194}{300} = \frac{97}{150} \quad (b)$$

ANSWER: .64⅔ = $\frac{97}{150}$ in fraction form

7. SOLUTION:
Difference between ⅗ and ⅞ expressed decimally

$\tfrac{7}{8} = 1.125$ $\tfrac{3}{5} = .60$

$$
\begin{array}{r}
1.125 \\
-\ \ .60 \\
\hline
.525 \quad (a)
\end{array}
$$

ANSWER: Difference = .525

8. SOLUTION:
6594 papers ÷ 314 clerks = 21 papers per clerk
21 papers ÷ 10 minutes = 2.1 papers per minute filed by average clerk   (c)

ANSWER: Average clerk filed 2.1 papers per minute

9. SOLUTION:

$$
\begin{array}{r}
\$120 \text{ monthly salary} \\
\times\ \ .08\tfrac{1}{3} \\
\hline
40 \\
9\ 60 \\
\hline
\$10.00 \text{ saved monthly}
\end{array}
$$

$1000 ÷ $10 = 100 months   (d)

ANSWER: Saved 100 months

10. SOLUTION:

$$
\begin{array}{r}
\$968.49 \\
\times\ 3.4 \\
\hline
387396 \\
2905470 \\
\hline
\$3292.866 \\
\times\ 3.7 \\
\hline
23050062 \\
98785980 \\
\hline
\$12183.6042
\end{array}
$$

$968.49 willed to youngest son

$3292.866 to second son = $3292.87

$12183.6042 to eldest son = $12,183.60

$$
\begin{array}{r}
\$968.49 \quad \text{youngest son} \\
3,292.87 \quad \text{second son} \\
\underline{12,183.60} \quad \text{eldest son} \\
\$16,444.96 \quad \text{value of estate} \quad (d)
\end{array}
$$

ANSWER: Value of estate = $16,444.96

PERCENTS

46. The per cent sign (%) is a symbol used to indicate percentage, but no operations can be performed with the number to which it is attached. For convenience, then, it is sometimes required to attach a per cent sign; but to perform operations with the number, it is necessary to remove the per cent sign.
a. In general, to add a % sign, multiply the number by 100.
Example: 3=300%
b. In general, to remove a % sign, divide the number by 100.
Example: 200%=2
c. A per cent may be expressed as a decimal or a fraction by dividing it by 100.
Example: 57%=.57   (39)
      9%=$^9/_{100}$ (1b)
d. A decimal may be expressed as a per cent by multiplying it by 100.
Example: .67=67%   (31)

47. To change a fraction or a mixed number to a per cent:
a. Multiply the fraction or mixed number by 100.
b. Reduce, if possible.
c. Add a % sign.

Illustration: Change $\frac{1}{7}$ to a per cent.
SOLUTION: $\frac{1}{7}$x100=$^{100}/_7$
      (16, 47a, 46a)
      =14$\frac{2}{7}$ (5, 47b)
    $\frac{1}{7}$=14$\frac{2}{7}$%   (47c)
Answer: 14$\frac{2}{7}$%
Illustration: Change 4$\frac{2}{3}$ to a per cent.
SOLUTION: 4$\frac{2}{3}$x100=$\frac{14}{3}$x100=$^{1400}/_3$
      (16, 47a)
     =466$\frac{2}{3}$
      (5, 47b)
  4$\frac{2}{3}$=466$\frac{2}{3}$% (47c)
Answer: 466$\frac{2}{3}$%

48. To remove a % sign attached to a decimal and to keep it as a decimal, divide the decimal by 100.
Example: .5%=.5÷100=.005   (39)

49. To remove a % sign attached to a decimal and to change the number to a fraction:
a. Divide the decimal by 100.
b. Change this result to a fraction.
c. Reduce, if necessary

Illustration: Change 15.05% to a fraction.
SOLUTION:
  15.05%=15.05÷100=.1505
      (39, 49a)
    =1505/10000
      (43, 49b)
    =301/2000
      (6, 49c)
Answer: 301/2000

50. To remove a % sign attached to a fraction or mixed number and to keep it as a fraction, divide the fraction or mixed number by 100.

Illustration: Change $\frac{3}{4}$% to a fraction.
SOLUTION: $\frac{3}{4}$%=$\frac{3}{4}$÷100=$\frac{3}{4}$ x 1/100
      (22)
    =3/400
Answer: 3/400

51. To remove a % sign attached to a fraction or mixed number and to change the number to a decimal:
a. Divide the fraction or mixed number by 100.
b. Change this result to a decimal.

Illustration: Change 3/5% to a decimal.
SOLUTION:
  3/5%=3/5÷100=3/5x1/100 (22, 51a)
      =3/500   (16)
      .006   (40, 51b)
  3/500=500$\overline{)3.000}$
Answer: .006

52. To remove a % sign attached to a decimal including a fraction and to keep it as a decimal, divide the decimal by 100.
Example: .5$\frac{1}{3}$%=.005$\frac{1}{3}$ (39)

53. To remove a % sign attached to a decimal including a fraction and to change the number to a fraction:
    a. Divide the decimal by 100.
    b. Change this result to a fraction.
    c. Clear this mixed fraction.
    d. Reduce, if necessary.

Illustration: change .14 1/6% to a fraction.
SOLUTION: .14 1/6% = .0014 1/6
$$(39, 53a)$$
$$= \frac{14\ 1/6}{10000}$$
$$(43, 53b)$$

$$= 14\ 1/6 \div 10000$$
$$(24, 53c)$$
$$= 85/6 \times 1/10000$$
$$(22)$$
$$= 85/60000$$
$$(16)$$
$$= 17/12000$$
$$(7, 53d)$$

Answer: 17/12000

53A. In a percentage problem, the whole is 100% (or 1).
    Example: If a problem involves 10% of a quantity, the rest of the quantity is 90%.

PERCENTAGE PROBLEMS

1. What per cent is 2 5/13?
   (a) 239 6/13% (c) 237 6/14%
   (b) 238 6/13% (d) 200 6/13%.

2. What is 5.37% in fraction form?
   (a) 537/10,000 (c) 537/1000
   (b) 5 37/10,000 (d) 5 37/100.

3. What is ¾% in decimal form?
   (a) .75 (b) 7.5 (c) .075 (d) .0075.

4. What is 2 3/7% in fraction form?
   (a) 18/700 (c) 17/1700
   (b) 17/800 (d) 17/700.

5. What per cent is 14% of 23%?
   (a) 60% (c) 60 20/23%
   (b) 61½% (d) 60 2/5%.

6. The entrance price to see an exhibition was reduced by 25%, but the daily attendance increased 30%. What was the effect of this on the daily receipts?
   (a) 2% increase (c) 2½% increase
   (b) 2% decrease (d) 2½% decrease.

7. A house valued at $4,750 is insured for 4/5 of its value at 1¼%. What is the amount of premium which must be paid?
   (a) $47.50 (c) $46.00
   (b) $47.00 (d) $48.50.

8. A certain family spends 30% of its income for food, 8% for clothing, 25% for shelter, 4% for recreation, 13% for education, and 5% for miscellaneous items. The weekly earnings are $50. What is the number of weeks it would take this family to save $1500?
   (a) 100 (b) 150 (c) 175 (d) 200.

9. On Monday a man deposited $360 in the bank. On Tuesday he deposited a sum 5% greater than the deposit of Monday; and on Wednesday he deposited a sum 4% greater than the sum of the first two deposits; on Thursday he withdrew 25% of the total deposit. How much did he have left in the bank?
   (a) $1130 (c) $1130.45
   (b) $1129.14 (d) $1142.50.

10. A man owned 50 shares of stock worth $75 each. The firm declared a dividend of 4%, payable in stock. How many shares did he then own?
   (a) 50 (b) 52 (c) 53 (d) 54.

Correct Answers				
1. b	3. d	5. c	7. a	9. b
2. a	4. d	6. d	8. d	10. b

PROBLEM SOLUTIONS   Percentage

1. $2\frac{5}{13}$ = what %
SOLUTION:
$2\frac{5}{13} = \frac{31}{13}$

$\quad\quad 2.38\frac{6}{13} = 238\frac{6}{13}\%$ (b)
13)31.00
$\quad$ 26
$\quad$ ——
$\quad$ 50
$\quad$ 39
$\quad$ ——
$\quad$ 110
$\quad$ 104
$\quad$ ——
$\quad$ 6

ANSWER: $2\frac{5}{13} = 238\frac{6}{13}\%$

2. 5.37% in fraction form
SOLUTION:

$5.37\% = .0537 = \frac{537}{10,000}$ (a)

ANSWER: $5.37\% = \frac{537}{10,000}$ in fraction form

3. $\frac{3}{4}\%$ in decimal form
SOLUTION: $\frac{3}{4}\% = \frac{3}{4} \div 100 = \frac{3}{400} = .0\frac{3}{4}$
$= .0075$
$\frac{3}{4}\% = .0075$ in decimal form   (d)

ANSWER: $\frac{3}{4}\% = .0075$ in decimal form

4. $2\frac{3}{7}\%$ in fraction form
SOLUTION:

$2\frac{3}{7}\% = \frac{17\%}{7} = \frac{17}{7} \times \frac{1}{100} = \frac{17}{700}$ (d)

ANSWER: $2\frac{3}{7}\% = \frac{17}{700}$ in fraction form

5. What % is 14% of 23%?
SOLUTION:

$\quad\quad\quad\quad .60\frac{20}{23} = 60\frac{20}{23}\%$ (c)
14% of 23% = 23.)14,00
$\quad\quad\quad\quad\quad$ 13 8
$\quad\quad\quad\quad\quad$ ——
$\quad\quad\quad\quad\quad$ 20

ANSWER: 14% of 23% = $60\frac{20}{23}\%$

6. SOLUTION:
100% − 25% = 75% entrance price
100% + 30% = 130% daily attendance
$\quad\quad$ 1.30
$\quad\times\ $ .75
$\quad$ ——
$\quad$ 650
$\quad$ 9100
$\quad$ ——
$\quad$ .9750 income

100.0% daily receipts
− 97.5% income
——
$\quad$ 2.5% or 2½ % decrease   (d)

ANSWER: Decrease of 2½ %

7. SOLUTION:
Value of house $4750. Insurance $\frac{4}{5}$ of value at
$1\frac{1}{4}\%$
$\quad\quad$ 950
$4\cancel{750} \times \frac{4}{\cancel{5}1} = \$3800$ insurance value

$\quad\quad\quad\quad\quad\quad\quad\quad$ 19
$\$3800 \times 1\frac{1}{4}\% = \$\cancel{3800} \times \frac{5}{\cancel{4}2} \times \frac{1}{\cancel{100}1} =$

$\frac{95}{2} = \$47\frac{1}{2} = \$47.50$ premium   (a)

ANSWER: Premium = $47.50

8. SOLUTION:
30% income spent
$\ $ 8%   "   "
25%   "   "
$\ $ 4%   "   "
13%   "   "
$\ $ 5%   "   "
——
85% income expenses
$\quad\quad$ "or"
30% + 8% + 25% + 4% + 13% + 5% =
85% expenses

$\quad$ 100% income $\quad\quad$ $50 weekly earnings
− $\ $ 85% expenses $\quad\quad\times$ .15
—— $\quad\quad\quad\quad\quad\quad\quad$ ——
$\quad$ 15% saves $\quad\quad\quad$ $7.50 saves weekly

$\quad\quad\quad\quad\quad\quad$ 2 00.weeks   (d)
$7.50)$1500,00 to save
$\quad\quad\quad$ 1500
$\quad\quad\quad$ ——
$\quad\quad\quad\quad\quad$ 00

ANSWER: 200 weeks to save $1500

9. SOLUTION:
Monday deposits $360
$360 \times 5\% = \$360 \times .05 = \$18.00$
$$+ \ 360.00$$
$$\overline{\$378.00}\ \text{Tuesday}$$

$378 Tuesday deposits
360 Monday deposits
$738 both days deposits
$\times \ .04$
$29.52
$+ \ 738.00$
$767.52 Wednesday deposits

$360   deposited Monday
378   deposited Tuesday
767.52   deposited Wednesday
$1505.52 Total deposits in bank

Withdrew 25% Thursday = ¼

$\$1505.52 \times \dfrac{1}{4} = \$376.38$ withdrew Thursday

$1505.52 (total) −$376.38 = $1129.14 left in bank   (b)

ANSWER: Left in bank $1129.14

10. SOLUTION:
$75 \times 50 = \$3750$ value of stock
$3750 value of stock
$\times \ .04$
$150.00 dividend

2 dividend shares
$75)\overline{\$150}$
150

50 shares owned
$+ \ 2$ shares dividend
52 shares then owned   (b)

ANSWER: Shares then owned = 52

FRACTIONAL AND MIXTURE PROBLEMS

54. When given the value of a fractional part of a quantity, to find the whole quantity, divide the given value by the fraction.

Illustration: If $60 = \frac{2}{3}$ of a number, what is the number?
SOLUTION: 60 = given value
$\frac{2}{3}$ = fraction
$60 \div \frac{2}{3} = 60 \times \frac{3}{2} = 90$ (22)
Answer: 90

55. When given the value of a decimal part of a quantity, to find the whole quantity, divide the given value by the decimal.

Illustration: If $50 = .125$ of a number, what is the number?
SOLUTION:
50 = given value
.125 = decimal
$50 \div .125 = .125 \overline{)50} = 125 \overline{)50000}$ (36)
Answer: 400

56. When given the value of a per cent part of a quantity, to find the whole quantity:
a. Change the per cent to a fraction or decimal.
b. Divide the given value by this fraction or decimal.

Illustration: If $40 = 30\%$ of a number, what is the number?
SOLUTION: $30\% = 30/100 = 3/10$
         (46c, 7, 56a)
$40 =$ given value
$40 \div 3/10 = 40 \times 10/3$
$= 400/3$ (22, 56b)
$= 133 \ 1/3$ (5)
Answer: 400/3 or 133 1/3

57. The principle of finding the whole when part is known is a very important feature in the solution of many types of problems. The three preceding paragraphs should be carefully studied and practised. The solution of fractional problems depends mainly on this principle.

Illustration: A and B competed in a race. It was discovered that $\frac{2}{3}$ of B's rate was equal to $\frac{3}{4}$ of A's rate. A's rate was 120 miles an hour. What was B's rate?
To Solve:
a. State all facts given.
b. Through substitution, establish a relation between A's and B's rates.
c. Solve to find B's rate.

SOLUTION: $\frac{2}{3}$ of B's rate $= \frac{3}{4}$ of A's rate (given)
A's rate $= 120$ (given) (57a)
$\frac{2}{3}$ of B's rate $= \frac{3}{4}$ of 120 (substitution) (57b)
$= 90$ (18, 19)
B's rate $= 90 \div \frac{2}{3}$ (54)
$= 90 \times \frac{3}{2}$ (22)
$= 135$ (18, 57c)
Answer: B's rate = 135 miles an hour.

58. To find what fractional part, or what per cent, one quantity is of another:
a. Divide the quantity following the word "is" by the quantity following the word "of."
b. Change this quotient to a per cent, if required.

Illustration: What per cent of $\frac{1}{2}$ is $\frac{3}{8}$?
SOLUTION: The quantity following the word "is" is $\frac{3}{8}$
The quantity following the word "of" is $\frac{1}{2}$
$\frac{3}{8} \div \frac{1}{2} = \frac{3}{8} \times 2 = \frac{3}{4}$
      (22, 18, 22b, 58a)
$\frac{3}{4} = 75\%$ (47, 58b)
Answer: $\frac{3}{8}$ is 75% of $\frac{1}{2}$

59. MIXTURE PROBLEMS. In a mixture problem, there are usually three items—the original mixture, the element which is added or removed, and the final mixture.

60. To solve mixture problems:
    a. Determine which element of the mixture will not change.
    b. Ascertain the exact amount of that element.
    c. Establish a relation between the amount of this stable element and the final mixture.
    d. Solve to find the final mixture.
    e. Subtract the original mixture from the final mixture to find the amount to be added.

Illustration: In a 20 gallon mixture of alcohol and water, there is 5% water. How much water must be added to make it 10% of the final mixture?

SOLUTION: In this problem, water is to be added. Therefore, the element which will not change is the alcohol. (60a)
Since there is 5% water, the amount of alcohol must be 95% of the original mixture. (53a)

95% of 20 gallons=.95x20
(19, 46c)
=19 gallons of alcohol
(30, 60b)
In the final mixture, there will be 10% water. Therefore, the alcohol will be 90% of the final mixture. (53a)
19 gallons of alcohol=90% of the final mixture (60c)
$19 = {}^{90}/_{100}$ of the final mixture. (46c, 56a)
$19 = {}^{9}/_{10}$ of the final mixture (7)
Therefore, final mixture$=19 \div {}^{9}/_{10}$ (56b)
$=19 \times {}^{1}/_{9}$ (22)
$=190/9$ (16)
$=21{}^{1}/_{9}$ gallons
(5, 60d)
The amount to be added$=21{}^{1}/_{9}-20$
(60e)
$=1{}^{1}/_{9}$ gallons
Answer: $1{}^{1}/_{9}$ gallons of water must be added.

61. When a mixture is made of two different grades of an article, to find the amount of each:
    a. Multiply the total mixture by its value to find the total value.
    b. Multiply the total mixture by the value of the lower grade.
    c. Subtract this product from the total value.
    d. Divide by the difference in the two grades to find the amount of the higher grade in the mixture.
    e. To find the amount of the lower grade in the mixture, simply subtract from the total mixture.

Illustration: How many pounds of 25¢ a lb. coffee have to be mixed with 40¢ a lb. coffee to make a mixture of 60 pounds worth 35¢ a pound?

SOLUTION: $60 \times 35¢ = \$21.00$—total value
(61a)
$60 \times 25¢ = \$15.00$ (61b)
$\$21.00 - \$15.00 = \$6.00$
(61c)
The difference in the two grades$=.40 - .25 = .15$
$\$6.00 \div .15 = 40$ (37, 61d)
$60 - 40 = 20$ (61e)
Answer: 40 pounds of the 40¢ a lb. coffee
20 pounds of the 25¢ a lb. coffee

There are several types of problems that are solved similarly to the above. Notice that there are two grades of a quantity, each having a different value. Of course, the problem can be solved by multiplying the total quantity by the value of either grade, but in order to avoid confusion, only the value of the lower grade is multiplied by the total quantity.

FRACTIONAL AND MIXTURE PROBLEMS

1. A bridge crosses a river which is 760 feet wide. One bank of the river holds $\frac{1}{5}$ of the bridge while the other holds $\frac{1}{6}$ of it. How long is the bridge?
(a) 1200 (b) 1000 (c) 1056 (d) 2000.

2. A man spent $^{15}/_{16}$ of his entire fortune in buying a house for $7500. How much money did he possess?
(a) $6000 (b) 6500 (c) $7000 (d) $8000.

3. What percent of $\frac{5}{6}$ is $\frac{3}{4}$?
(a) 75% (b) 60% (c) 80% (d) 90%.

4. A mixture of alcohol and water contains 16 quarts of which 7 quarts are alcohol. How many quarts of water must be added in order that $\frac{1}{3}$ of the resulting mixture shall be alcohol? (a) 6 (b) 7 (c) 5 (d) 4.

5. A man bequeaths his estate to his three sons. To the first, he gives $\frac{2}{7}$ of his entire estate; to the second, he gives 96 acres, and to the third the rest of the estate which is as much as the first two together. How large is the estate? (a) 450 acres (b) 448 acres (c) 452 acres (d) 500 acres.

6. There are some animals in a barnyard, consisting of chickens and cows. If the number of heads equals 36 and the number of feet equals 100, how many chickens are there?
(a) 20 (b) 21 (c) 22 (d) 23.

7. A typist earned $1350 in a given year which was $12\frac{1}{2}$% more than what she earned the year before. How much did she earn in the earlier year?
(a) $1200 (b) $1100 (c) $1300 (d) $1250.

8. How many pounds of 20¢ a lb. coffee must be blended with 25¢ a lb. coffee to make a mixture of 50 lbs. to be sold at 22¢ a pound?
(a) 28 (b) 32 (c) 30 (d) 31.

9. A man insures 80% of his property and pays a $2\frac{1}{2}$% premium which amounts to $34.80. What is the total value of his property?
(a) $1700 (b) $1800 (c) $1840 (d) $1740.

10. A manufacturer bought two grades of chairs, a total of 80 chairs for $240. If he paid $3.50 for the better grade and $2.25 for the other, how many of better grade did he buy?
(a) 46 (b) 48 (c) 45 (d) 42.

Correct Answers

(You'll learn more by writing your own answers before comparing them with these.)

1. a	3. d	5. b	7. a	9. d
2. d	4. c	6. c	8. c	10. b

PROBLEM SOLUTIONS — Fractional and Mixture

1. SOLUTION: L.C.D. = 30
$\frac{1}{5} + \frac{1}{6} = \frac{11}{30}$ of bridge held by both banks of river
$\frac{30}{30}$ = entire bridge $\frac{30}{30} - \frac{11}{30} = \frac{19}{30}$
part spanning river $\frac{19}{30}$ = 760 feet

760 ft. $\div \frac{19}{30} = \overset{40}{\cancel{760}} \times \frac{30}{\cancel{19}} = 1200$ feet (a)

ANSWER: Length of bridge = 1200 feet

2. SOLUTION:
$\frac{15}{16}$ = $7500 cost of house

$7500 \div \frac{15}{16} = \overset{500}{\cancel{\$7500}} \times \frac{16}{\cancel{15}} = \$8000$

possessed (d)

ANSWER: He possessed $8000

3. What percent of $\frac{5}{6}$ is $\frac{3}{4}$?
SOLUTION:

$$\frac{\frac{3}{4}}{\frac{5}{6}} = \frac{3}{4} \div \frac{5}{6} = \frac{3}{\underset{2}{4}} \times \frac{\overset{3}{6}}{5} = \frac{9}{10} = 90\% \quad \text{(d)}$$

ANSWER: $\frac{3}{4}$ is 90% of $\frac{5}{6}$

4. SOLUTION: Find the number of qts. in final mixture first.
$7 = \frac{1}{3} \times m$

$m = 7 \div \frac{1}{3} = 7 \times \frac{3}{1} = 21$ (final number of qts.)

Only water is to be added, so $W = 21 - 16 = 5$ (c)

ANSWER: 5

5. SOLUTION:
$\frac{2}{7}$ of the estate $+ 96$ acres $= \frac{1}{2}$ of the estate
96 acres $= \frac{1}{2} - \frac{2}{7}$ or $\frac{3}{14}$ of the estate

estate $= 96 \div \frac{3}{14} = \overset{32}{\cancel{96}} \times \frac{14}{\underset{1}{\cancel{3}}} = 448$ acre estate (b)

ANSWER: Estate = 448 acres

6. SOLUTION:
$100 \div 2 = 50$ possible heads of $2-$footed animals.
We know there are 36 heads
50 heads $-36 = 14$ heads of 4-footed cows
36 heads -14 heads $= 22$ of 2-footed chickens —(c)
PROOF: $22 \times 2 = 44$ ft. for 22 chickens
$14 \times 4 = \underline{56}$ ft. for 14 cows
$\overline{100}$ feet in all

ANSWER: 22 chickens

7. SOLUTION:
$12\frac{1}{2}\% = \frac{1}{8}$ more earned
$\frac{8}{8} + \frac{1}{8} = \frac{9}{8}$ then had
$\$1350 = \frac{9}{8}$ of previous year's salary
$\$1350 \div \frac{9}{8} = \$1350 \times \frac{8}{9} = \$1200$ earned earlier year (a)

ANSWER: Earned earlier year $1200

8. SOLUTION:
$50 \times 22\cancel{c} = \$11.00$ total value of coffee sold at 22¢ lb.
$50 \times 20\cancel{c} = \underline{\$10.00}$ value at 20¢ lb.
$\overline{\$1.00}$ difference

The difference in two grades $= 25¢ - 20¢ = 5¢$ or $\$.05$
$\$1.00 \div .05 = 20$ lb. of 25¢ coffee
50 pounds $- 20$ pounds $= 30$ pounds (c)

ANSWER: 30 lbs. of 20¢ coffee

9. SOLUTION:
$2\frac{1}{2}\%$ premium $= \$34.80$
$\$34.80 \div .025 = \$1392.$
80% of property $= \frac{4}{5}$
$\frac{4}{5} = \$1392$ ($\$1392 \div 4 = \$348$)
$\frac{1}{5} = \$348$
$\frac{5}{5} = 5 \times \$348 = \$1740$ total value of property (d)

ANSWER: Total value of property = $1740.

10. SOLUTION:
Total chairs bought $= 80$
Cost Price $= \$240$
Kinds of chairs—$3.50 for better grade
$2.25 for lesser grade
$\$3.50 - \$2.25 = \$1.25$ or $\$\frac{5}{4}$ more for $3.50 grade chair
Suggestion in book:
In order to avoid confusion by multiplying quantity by value of either grade, **use only value of lower grade multiplied by total quantity.** Therefore:

$\$2\frac{1}{4} \times 80 = \frac{\$9}{\underset{1}{4}} \times \overset{20}{\cancel{80}} = \$180$ for lower grade chairs

$\$240$ total cost of all chairs
$\underline{- \quad 180}$ cost lower grade chairs
$\$\ 60$ difference toward better grade chairs

$\$60 \div \$1\frac{1}{4} = \$60 \div \frac{\$5}{4} = \$\overset{12}{\cancel{60}} \times \frac{4}{\underset{1}{\cancel{5}}} = 48$ chairs of better grade (b)

ANSWER: He bought 48 of better grade chairs
PROOF: 80 chairs — 48 better grade chairs = 32 lesser grade chairs
$48 \times \$3.50 = \$168.00$
$32 \times \$2.25 = \underline{\quad 72.00}$
$\overline{\$240.00}$ spent

PROFIT AND LOSS

62. The following terms may be encountered in profit and loss problems:
   a. The cost price of an article is the price paid by a person who wishes to sell it again.
   b. There may be an allowance or trade discount on the cost price.
   c. The list price or marked price is the price at which the article is listed or marked to be sold.
   d. There may be a discount or series of discounts on the list price.
   e. The selling price or sales price is the price at which the article is finally sold.
   f. If the selling price is greater than the cost price, there has been a profit.
   g. If the selling price is lower than the cost price, there has been a loss.
   h. If the article is sold at the same price as the cost, there has been no loss or profit.
   i. Profit or loss may be based either on the cost price or on the selling price.
   j. Profit or loss may be stated in terms of dollars and cents, or in terms of per cent.
   k. Overhead expenses include such items as rent, salaries, etc. and may be added to the selling price.

63. To find the profit in terms of money, subtract the cost price from the selling price, or selling price—cost price=profit.
   Example: If an article costing $3.00 is sold for $5.00, the profit is $5.00—$3.00=$2.00

64. To find the loss in terms of money, subtract the selling price from the cost price, or, cost price—selling price=loss.
   Example: If an article costing $2.00 is sold for $1.50, the loss is $2.00—$1.50=$.50

65. If the profit or loss is expressed in terms of money, then
   a. Cost price+profit=selling price.
   b. Cost price—loss=selling price.
   Example: If the cost of an article is $2.50, and the profit is $1.50, then the selling price is $2.50+$1.50=$4.00   (65a)

Example: If the cost of an article is $3.00, and the loss is $1.20, then the selling price is $3.00—$1.20=$1.80

66. To find the selling price if the profit is expressed in per cent based on cost price:
   a. Multiply the cost price by the % profit to find the profit in terms of money.
   b. Add this product to the cost price.

Illustration: Find the selling price of an article costing $3.00 which was sold at a profit of 15% of the cost price.
SOLUTION: $3.00×15%=3.00×.15
                              (46c, 66a)
                    =$.45=Profit
                              (30)
          $3.00+$.45=$3.45
                              (65a, 66b)
Answer: The selling price is $3.45

67. To find the selling price if the loss is expressed in per cent based on cost price:
   a. Multiply the cost price by the % loss to find the loss in terms of money.
   b. Subtract this product from the cost price.

Illustration: If an article costing $2.00 is sold at a loss of 5% of the cost price, find the selling price.
SOLUTION: $2.00×5%=2.00×.05
                              (46c, 67a)
                    =$.10=loss   (30)
          $2.00—$.10=$1.90
                              (65b, 67b)
Answer: The selling price is $1.90

68. To find the cost price when given the selling price and the % profit based on the selling price:
   a. Multiply the selling price by the % profit to find the profit in terms of money.
   b. Subtract this product from the selling price.
   Illustration: If an article sells for $12.00 and there has been a profit of 10% of the selling price, what is the cost price?

SOLUTION: $\$12.00 \times 10\% = 12.00 \times .10$

(46c, 68a)

$= \$1.20 = $ profit

(30)

$\$12.00 - \$1.20 = \$10.80$

(68b)

Answer: Cost price $10.80

69. To find the cost price when given the selling price and the % loss based on the selling price:

a. Multiply the selling price by the % loss to find the loss in terms of money.
b. Add this product to the selling price.

Illustration: What is the cost price of an article selling for $2.00 on which there has been a loss of 6% of the selling price?

SOLUTION: $\$2.00 \times 6\% = 2.00 \times .06$

(46c, 69a)

$= \$.12 = $ loss

(30)

$\$2.00 + \$.12 = \$2.12$ (69b)

Answer: Cost price $= \$2.12$

70. To find the % profit based on cost price:
a. Find the profit in terms of money.
b. Divide the profit by the cost price.
c. Convert to a per cent.

Illustration: Find the % profit based on cost price of an article costing $2.50 and selling for $3.00

SOLUTION: $\$3.00 - \$2.50 = \$.50 = $ profit

(63, 70a)

$2.50 \overline{)\,.50} = 250 \overline{)50.00} = .20$

(37, 38, 70b)

$= 20\%$

(46d, 70c)

Answer: Profit $= 20\%$

71. To find the % loss based on cost price:
a. Find the loss in terms of money.
b. Divide the loss by the cost price.
c. Convert to a per cent.

Illustration: Find the % loss based on cost price of an article costing $5.00 and selling for $4.80.

SOLUTION: $\$5.00 - \$4.80 = \$.20 = $ loss

(64, 71a)

$5.00 \overline{)\,.20} = 500 \overline{)20.00} = .04$

(37, 38, 71b)

(46d, 71c)

$= 4\%$

Answer: Loss $= 4\%$

72. To find the % profit based on selling price:
a. Find the profit in terms of money.

b. Divide the profit by the selling price.
c. Convert to a per cent.

Illustration: Find the % profit based on the selling price of an article costing $2.50 and selling for $3.00.

SOLUTION:

$\$3.00 - \$2.50 = \$.50 = $ profit (63, 72a)

$3.00 \overline{)\,.50} = 300 \overline{)50.00} = .16\tfrac{2}{3}$

(37, 38, 72b)

$= 16\tfrac{2}{3}\%$

(46d, 72c)

Answer: Profit $= 16\tfrac{2}{3}\%$

73. To find the % loss based on selling price:
a. Find the loss in terms of money.
b. Divide the loss by the selling price.
c. Convert to a per cent.

Illustration: Find the % loss based on the selling price of an article costing $5.00 and selling for $4.80.

SOLUTION:

$\$5.00 - \$4.80 = \$.20 = $ loss (64, 73a)

$4.80 \overline{)\,.20} = 480 \overline{)20.00} = .04\tfrac{1}{6}$

(37, 38, 73b)

Answer: Loss $4\tfrac{1}{6}\%$

74. To find the cost price when given the selling price and the % profit based on the cost price:
a. Establish a relation between the selling price and the cost price.
b. Solve to find the cost price.

Illustration: An article is sold for $2.50 which is a 25% profit of the cost price. What is the cost price?

SOLUTION: Since the selling price represents the whole cost price plus 25% of the cost price,

$2.50 = 125\%$ of the cost price (74a, 53a)

$2.50 = {}^{125}\!/_{100}$ of the cost price (56a)

Cost price $= 2.50 \div {}^{125}\!/_{100}$

$= 2.50 \times {}^{100}\!/_{125}$ (22)

$= {}^{250}\!/_{125} = \$2.00$ (31, 74b)

Answer: Cost price $= \$2.00$

75. To find the selling price when given the profit based on the selling price.
a. Establish a relation between the selling price and the cost price.
b. Solve to find the selling price.

Illustration: A merchant buys an article for $27.00 and sells it at a profit of 10% of the selling price. What is the selling price?

SOLUTION:

$27.00 + \text{profit} = \text{selling price}$ (65a)

Since the profit is 10% of the selling price, the cost price must be 90% of the selling price.   (53a)

$27.00 = 90\%$ of the selling price   (75a)

$= {}^{9}\!\%_{00}$ of the selling price   (56a)

selling price $= 27.00 \times {}^{100}\!\%_{9}$ (56b, 24)

$= \$30.00$ (18, 75b)

Answer: Selling price $= \$30.00$

76. To find the selling price when given the % loss of the selling price:
   a. Establish a relation between the cost price and the selling price.
   b. Solve to find the selling price.

Illustration: Find the selling price of an article bought for $5.00 on which there is a 25% loss on the selling price.

SOLUTION:

$\$5.00 - \text{loss} = \text{selling price}$ (65b)

Since the loss is 25% of the selling price, the cost price must be 125% of the selling price.   (53a)

$5.00 = 125\%$ of the selling price.   (76a)

$5.00 = {}^{125}\!\%_{00}$ of the selling price   (56a)

selling price $= 5.00 \times {}^{100}\!\%_{125}$ (56b, 24)

$= \$4.00$ (18, 76b)

Answer: Selling price $= \$4.00$

77. TRADE DISCOUNTS — A trade discount, usually expressed in per cent, indicates the part that is to be deducted from the list price.

78. To find the selling price when given the list price and the % discount:
   a. Multiply the list price by the % discount to find the discount in terms of money.
   b. Subtract the discount from the list price.
   Illustration: The list price of an article is $20.00. There is a discount of 5%. What is the selling price?
   SOLUTION:
   $\$20.00 \times 5\% = 20.00 \times .05 = \$1.00 = \text{discount.}$ (46c, 30, 78a)
   $\$20.00 - \$1.00 = \$19.00$ (78b)
   Answer: Selling price $= \$19.00$

79. SERIES OF DISCOUNTS—There may be more than one discount to be deducted from the list price. These are called a discount series.

80. To find the selling price when given the list price and a discount series:
   a. Multiply the list price by the first % discount.
   b. Subtract this product from the list price.
   c. Multiply the remainder by the second discount.
   d. Subtract this product from the remainder.
   e. Continue the same procedure if there are more discounts.

Illustration: Find the selling price of an article listed at $10.00 on which there are discounts of 20% and 10%.
SOLUTION:
$\$10.00 \times 20\% = 10.00 \times .20 = \$2.00$ (46c, 30, 80a)
$\$10.00 - \$2.00 = \$8.00$ (80b)
$\$8.00 \times 10\% = 8.00 \times .10 = \$.80$ (46c, 30, 80c)
$\$8.00 - \$.80 = \$7.20$ (80d)
Answer: Selling price $= \$7.20$

81. Instead of deducting each discount individually, it is often more practicable to find the single equivalent discount first and then deduct. It does not matter in which order the discounts are taken.

82. To find the single equivalent discount of a discount series:
   a. Add the first two discounts.
   b. Multiply the first two discounts.
   c. Subtract this product from the sum to find the equivalent discount of the first two discounts.
   d. If there is a third discount, add the equivalent of the first two discounts to the third.
   e. Multiply the equivalent of the first two discounts by the third.
   f. Subtract this product from the sum to find the equivalent of the three discounts.
   g. Continue the same procedure if there are more discounts.
   Illustration: What is the single discount equivalent to the discount series 20%, 25%, and 10%?
   SOLUTION:
   $20\% + 25\% = .20 + .25 = .45$ (46c, 28, 82a)
   $20\% \times 25\% = .20 \times .25 = .0500$ (46c, 30, 82b)
   $.45 - .05 = .40$ (27b, 29, 82c)
   $.40 + 10\% = .40 + .10 = .50$ (46c, 28, 82d)
   $.40 \times 10\% = .40 \times .10 = .0400$ (46c, 30, 82e)
   $.50 - .04 = .46$ (27b, 29, 82b)
   $.46 = 46\%$ (46d)
   Answer: The single equivalent discount of the three discounts is 46%.

PROFIT AND LOSS PROBLEMS

1. A car cost a dealer $516. He wishes to mark it so that he may deduct 20% from the marked price and still make a profit of 25% of the cost. What is the list price?
(a) $806.25 (c) $800.00
(b) $805.25 (d) $805.00.

2. A dealer sells a set of furniture for $900 which is 80% more than he paid for it. At what price must he sell the same set to make 120% on the cost price?
(a) $1000 (c) $1200
(b) $1100 (d) $1250.

3. A man sells two houses for $2400 each. He makes 20% of the cost price on the first, but on the second he has a loss of 20% of the cost price. How much did he gain or lose by this transaction?
(a) $200 loss (c) $250 loss
(b) $200 gain (d) $250 gain.

4. A merchant sells a shipment of gloves at a profit of 16%. He invests the proceeds of this sale in a lot of women's dresses which he sells at a loss of 4% of the cost. He makes a net profit of $56.80. What was the cost of the gloves?
(a) $600 (c) $500
(b) $200 (d) $450.

5. After marking down a desk 20%, a dealer asked $40 for it. Being unable to sell it at this price, he gave another discount of 5% and still made $8. What was the percent above cost at which the desk was originally marked?
(a) 50% (c) 66⅔%
(b) 60% (d) 33⅓%.

6. If the cost of an article is $3.80, the profit being 20% of the cost and the selling expense 5% of the sales, what is the selling price?
(a) $5.00 (c) $4.50
(b) $4.40 (d) $4.80.

7. A company had been selling its pianos for $325, less 20% for cash. To increase its sales, it decided to allow an additional discount so that a piano could sell for $234. What was the second discount allowed?
(a) 70% (c) 9%
(b) 8% (d) 10%.

8. A manufacturer's list price is 40% above the cost of manufacture. He allows a trade discount of 10% from the list price. What is his per cent profit based on cost price?
(a) 25% (c) 28%
(b) 26% (d) 30%.

9. Assuming that the yearly depreciation value of a typewriter is 10%, what is closest to the original cost if the value at the end of the third year is $65.61?
(a) $60 (c) $80
(b) $70 (d) $90.

10. If a man buys an article at ¾ its value and sells it for 20% more than its value, what is his per cent profit based on cost?
(a) 50% (c) 70%
(b) 60% (d) 80%.

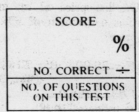

SCORE
%
NO. CORRECT ÷
NO. OF QUESTIONS ON THIS TEST

Correct Answers

(You'll learn more by writing your own answers before comparing them with these.)

1. a	3. a	5. c	7. d	9. d
2. b	4. c	6. d	8. b	10. b

PROBLEM SOLUTIONS Profit and Loss

1. SOLUTION:
   Cost of car = \$516   25% = ¼

   $$100\% - 20\% = \$516 + \left(\$516 \times \frac{1}{4} \right)$$

   (with 129 written above, \$516 crossed to show reduction)

   80% = \$516 + \$129 = \$645
   \$645 = 80% of list price
   List Price = \$645 ÷ 80% = \$645 ÷ $^{80}\!/_{100}$ =
   \$645 × $^{100}\!/_{80}$ = \$806.25

   ANSWER: \$806.25   (a)

2. SOLUTION:
   100% + 80% = 180% or $1\frac{4}{5} \times$ cost price
   equals selling price

   $$\$900 \div 1\tfrac{4}{5} = \$900 \times \frac{5}{9} = \$500 \text{ Cost Price}$$

   120% = $1\frac{1}{5}$

   $$\$500 \times 1\tfrac{1}{5} = \$500 \times \frac{6}{5} = \$600 \text{ to make}$$

   (with 100 written above \$500)

   120%
   \$600 + \$500 = \$1100 Selling Price   (b)

   ANSWER: \$1100 = Selling Price

3. SOLUTION:
   100% + 20% = 120% Selling Price on one house
   100% − 20% = 80% Selling Price on another house
   120% = $1\frac{1}{5}$
   80% = $\frac{4}{5}$
   120% = \$2400

   $$\$2400 \div 1\tfrac{1}{5} = \$2400 \div \tfrac{6}{5} = \$2400 \times \frac{5}{6}$$

   (with 400 written above \$2400)

   = \$2000 Cost
   \$2400 − \$2000 = \$400 profit on first house
   100% − 20% = 80% = $\frac{4}{5}$

   $$\$2400 \div \tfrac{4}{5} = \$2400 \times \frac{5}{4} = \$3000 \text{ Cost 2nd}$$

   (with 600 written above \$2400)

   house
   \$3000 − \$2400 = \$600 loss 2nd house
   \$600 loss − \$400 profit = \$200 loss   (a)

   ANSWER: Loss = \$200

4. SOLUTION:
   100% + 16% = 116% Selling Price at profit of 16%
   100% − 4% = 96% Selling Price at loss of 4%
   1.16 × .96 = 1.1136   1.1136 − 1.00 = .1136   .1136 = \$56.80
   \$56.80 ÷ .1136 = \$500 Cost   (c)

   ANSWER: Cost = \$500

5. SOLUTION:
   100% − 5% = 95% second discount
   \$40 × .95 = \$38.00 Selling Price
   100% − 20% = 80% first discount
    80% = \$40
   \$40 ÷ .80 = \$50 marked price
   \$38 − \$8 = \$30 cost
   \$50 − \$30 = \$20 marked up

   $$\$20 \div \$30 = \frac{20}{30} = \tfrac{2}{3} = 66\tfrac{2}{3}\% \quad (c)$$

   ANSWER: 66⅔% above original cost

6. SOLUTION:
   \$3.80 = cost   20% profit
   100% + 20% = 120% = $1\frac{1}{5}$ = $\frac{6}{5}$

   $$\$3.80 \times \frac{6}{5} = \$4.56$$

   (with .76 written above \$3.80)

   100% − 5% = 95%
   \$4.56 ÷ .95 = \$4.80 Selling Price   (d)

   ANSWER: Selling Price = \$4.80

7. SOLUTION
   \$325 × 20% = \$65.00 discount
   \$325 − \$65 = \$260 Selling Price
   \$260 − \$234 = \$26 second discount

   $$\$26 \div \$260 = \frac{26}{260} = \frac{1}{10} = 10\% \quad (d)$$

   ANSWER: Second discount allowed = 10%

8. SOLUTION:
   100% + 40% = 140% = 1.40
   1.40 × .10 = .14 = 14% trade discount
   140% − 14% = 126%
   126% − 100% = 26% profit   (b)

   ANSWER: Profit = 26%

9. SOLUTION:
    $100\% \times 10\% = 10\%$ $100\% - 10\% =$
    90% value at end of first year.
    $90\% \times 10\% = 9\%$
    $90\% - 9\% = 81\%$ value second year
    $81\% \times 10\% = 8.1\%$
    $81\% - 8.1\% = 72.9\%$ value third year
    $72.9\% = \$65.61$
    $\$65.61 \div .729 = \$90$ original cost   (d)

    ANSWER: Original cost = $90

10. SOLUTION:
    $100\% =$ original value
    $100\% \times \frac{3}{4} = 75\%$ cost
    $100\% + 20\% = 120\%$ Selling Price
    $120\% - 75\% = 45\%$ profit

    $45\% \div 75\% = \dfrac{45}{75} = \dfrac{3}{5} = 60\%$ (b)

    ANSWER: Per cent based on cost = 60%

INTEREST

83. Interest is the price paid for the use of money. There are three items considered in interest:
    1. The principal which is the amount of money bearing interest.
    2. The interest rate, expressed in per cent on an annual basis.
    3. The time, during which the principal is used.

84. Since the interest rate is an annual rate, the time must be expressed annually, too.
    a. If the time is given in years, or part of a year, do not change the figures given.
    b. If the time is given in months it should be expressed as a fraction, the numerator of which is the number of months given, and the denominator of which is 12.
    c. If the time is given in days, it should be expressed as a fraction, the numerator of which is the number of days given, and the denominator of which is 360. (Sometimes, it is required to find the exact interest, in which case 365 is the denominator.)
    d. If the time is given in terms of years and months, change it all to months and form a fraction, the numerator of which is the number of months, and the denominator of which is 12.
    e. If the time is given in terms of years, months, and days, or months and days, or years and days, change it all to days and form a fraction, the numerator of which is the number of days, and the denominator of which is 360 (or 365, if so required.) A month is considered as 30 days.

85. To find the interest when the three items are given:
    a. Change the rate of interest to a fraction.
    b. Express the time as a fractional part of a year.
    c. Multiply all three items.
    Illustration: Find the interest on $400 at at $2\frac{1}{4}\%$ for 3 months and 16 days.
    SOLUTION: $2\frac{1}{4}\% = \frac{9}{400}$ (50, 85a)
    3 months and 16 days $= \frac{106}{360}$
    of a year   (84e, 85b)

(30 days to a month)
$400 \times \frac{9}{400} \times \frac{106}{360}$
$= \frac{53}{20}$ (18, 85c)
$= \$2.65$ (38d)
Answer: Interest $2.65

86. If the interest, interest rate, and time are given, to find the principal:
    a. Change the interest rate to a fraction.
    b. Express the time as a fractional part of a year.
    c. Multiply the rate by the time.
    d. Divide the interest by this product.
    Illustration: What amount of money invested at 6% would receive interest of $18 over $1\frac{1}{2}$ years?
    SOLUTION: $6\% = \frac{6}{100}$ (46c, 86a)
        (84a, 86b)
    $1\frac{1}{2}$ years $= \frac{3}{2}$ years
    $6/100 \times 3/2 = 9/100$ (18, 86c)
    $\$18 \div 9/100 = 18 \times 100/9$
    $= \$200$ (86d, 22, 18)
    Answer: Amount$=\$200$

87. If the principal, time and interest are given, to find the rate:
    a. Change the time to a fractional part of a year.
    b. Multiply the principal by the time.
    c. Divide the interest by this product.
    d. Convert to a per cent.
    Illustration: At what interest rate should $300 be invested for 40 days to accrue $2 in interest?
    SOLUTION: 40 days $= \frac{40}{360}$ of a year
        (84e, 87a)
    $300 \times \frac{40}{360} = \frac{100}{3}$ (18, 87b)
    $\$2 \div 100/3 = 2 \times 3/100$
    $= 3/50$ (22, 18, 87c)
    $\frac{3}{50} = 6\%$ (47)
    Answer: Interest rate$=6\%$

88. If the principal, interest, and interest rate are given, to find the time (in years):
    a. Change the interest rate to a fraction (or decimal).

b. Multiply the principal by the rate.

c. Divide the interest by this product.

Illustration: Find the length of time for which $240 must be invested at 5% to accrue $16 in interest.

SOLUTION: 5%=.05   (46c, 88a)

        240x.05=12   (18, 88b)

        16÷12=1⅓   (88c)

Answer: Time=1⅓ years

COMPOUND INTEREST

89. Interest may be computed on a compound basis; that is, the interest at the end of a certain period (half year, full year, or whatever time stipulated) is added to the principal for the next period. The interest is then computed on the new increased principal, and for the next period, the interest is again computed on the new increased principal. Since the principal constantly increases, compound interest yields more than simple interest.

COMPOUND INTEREST RATE

90. Since the interest rate is an annual rate, it must be proportionately reduced if the interest is compounded on less than a yearly basis. In general, if the interest is computed for some fractional part of a year, use that same fractional part of the interest rate. Specifically:

a. If the interest is compounded annually, use the rate given.

b. If compounded semi-annually, use ½ the rate given.

c. If compounded quarterly, use ¼ the rate given, etc.

91. To find the compound interest when given the principal, the rate, and time period:

a. Determine the rate to be used, and change it to a decimal.

b. Multiply the principal by this rate to ascertain the interest for the first period.

c. Add the interest to the principal.

d. Multiply the new principal by the determined rate to find the interest for the second period.

e. Add this interest to form a new principal.

f. Continue the same procedure until all periods required have been accounted for.

g. Subtract the original principal from the final principal to find the compound interest.

Illustration: Find the amount that $200 will become if compounded semi-annually at 4% for 1½ years.

SOLUTION: Since it is to be compounded semi-annually for 1½ years, the interest will have to be computed 3 times, and the rate to be used is 2%=.02

        (90b, 46c, 91a)

Interest for the first period: $200x.02=$4   (30, 91b)

First new principal: $200+$4 =$204   (91c)

Interest for the second period: $204x.02=$4.08   (30, 91d)

Second new principal: $204+ $4.08=$208.08   (91e)

Interest for the third period: $208.08x.02=$4.1616

        (30, 91f)

Final principal: $208.08 $4.16=$212.24

Answer: $212.24

BANK DISCOUNTS

92. When a note is cashed by a bank in advance of its date of maturity, the bank deducts a discount from the principal and pays the rest to the depositor.

93. To find the bank discount:

a. Find the time between the date the note is deposited and its date of maturity, and express this time as a fractional part of a year.

b. Change the rate to a fraction.

c. Multiply the principal by the time and the rate to find the bank discount.

d. If required, subtract the bank discount from the original principal to find the amount the bank will pay the depositor.

Illustration: A $400 note drawn up on August 12, 1962 for 90 days is deposited at the bank on September 17, 1962. The bank charges a 6½ % discount on notes. How much will the depositor receive?

SOLUTION: From August 12, 1962, to September 17, 1962 is 36 days. This means that the note has 54 days to run.

    54 days=$^{54}/_{360}$ of a year

        (84c, 93a)

    6½ %=$^{13}/_{200}$ (50, 93b)

    $400x13/200x54/360= 39/10=$3.90

        (18, 38b, 93c)

    $400—$3.90=$396.10 (93d)

Answer: The depositor will receive $396.10

INTEREST PROBLEMS

1. Find the interest on $480 at 3½% for 2 months and 15 days.
   (a) $2.50 (c) $3.25
   (b) $3.50 (d) $4.00.

2. Find the length of time it would take $432 to yield $78.66 in interest at 4¾%.
   (a) 2 yrs. 10 mos. (c) 3 yrs. 10 mos.
   (b) 3 yrs. (d) 4 yrs.

3. A man wishes to borrow a certain sum of money for 120 days. He goes to a bank whose rate is 6%. They deduct $360 as discount. How much does the man borrow?
   (a) $5000 (c) $15,000
   (b) $10,550 (d) $18,000.

4. One sum of money is invested at 3% and a second sum, twice as large as the first, is invested at 2½%. The total interest is $448. How much is invested at 2½%?
   (a) $11,000 (c) $11,200
   (b) $11,100 (d) $11,300.

5. Mr. B borrowed $600 and at the end of 9 years and 6 months returned $856.50. What is the rate per cent?
   (a) 4½% (b) 5% (c) 6% (d) 7%.

6. A house costs $100,000. Incidental expenses and taxes amount to $3600 a year. What rent per month must the owner receive to clear 6% of his investment?
   (a) $600 (b) $650 (c) $800 (d) $850.

7. What is the compound interest on $600, compounded quarterly, at 6% for 9 months?
   (a) $27.38 (c) $27.41
   (b) $27.40 (d) $27.42.

8. A 90-day note was drawn up on April 16, 1974 and discounted at 6% on May 31, 1974. What was the face amount of the note if the depositor received $754.30?
   (a) $760 (b) $750 (c) $740 (d) $735.

9. What is the discount rate of a bank if a 60-day note for $320, discounted 45 days after being drawn, yields $319.40?
   (a) 4½% (b) 4% (c) 4¾% (d) 5%.

10. A 60-day note for $432 was drawn up on October 6, 1971. Some time later, it was deposited at a bank whose discount rate was 5¼% and the depositor received $430.74. When was it deposited?
    (a) November 15, 1971
    (b) October 15, 1971
    (c) December 15, 1971
    (d) January 15, 1972.

Correct Answers

| 1. b | 3. d | 5. a | 7. c | 9. a |
| 2. c | 4. c | 6. c | 8. a | 10. a |

NOW, CHECK YOUR METHODS WITH OUR

SIMPLIFIED PROBLEM SOLUTIONS, WHICH FOLLOW.

PROBLEM SOLUTIONS | Interest

1. SOLUTION:

2 months 15 days = 75 days or $\dfrac{75}{360}$ of year

$3\frac{1}{2}\% = \dfrac{7}{2}\% = \dfrac{7}{200}$

$\$480 \times \dfrac{7}{200} \times \dfrac{75}{360} = \dfrac{21}{6} = \$3.50$ Interest

$$\dfrac{\$3.50}{6)\overline{21.00}} \quad \text{(b)}$$

ANSWER: Interest = \$3.50

2. SOLUTION:

$\$432 \times 4\frac{3}{4}\% \quad 4\frac{3}{4}\% = \dfrac{19}{4}\%$

$\$432 \times \dfrac{19}{4}\% = \$432 \times \dfrac{19}{400} = \$20.52$

Interest 1 year
$78.66 Interest
$78.66 \div \$20.52 = 3.83\frac{1}{3}$ year $= 3\frac{5}{6}$ year

$\dfrac{5}{6} \times 12$ mo. = 10 mo. Therefore 3 years 10 months.   (c)

ANSWER: Time — 3 years 10 months

3. SOLUTION:

120 days $= \dfrac{120}{360}$ year $= \dfrac{1}{3}$ year

$\dfrac{1}{3} \times 6\% = \dfrac{1}{3} \times \dfrac{6}{100} = \dfrac{2}{100} = .02$

$\$360 \div .02 = \$18,000$ borrowed   (d)

ANSWER: Man borrowed \$18,000.

4. SOLUTION

Sum #1 at 3% = Interest on #1 = 3%
Sum #2 (twice as large) Sum #1
Sum #2 at 2½% = Interest Sum #2
5% + 3% = 8% on Interest #1 + Interest
#2 (2 × 2½% = 5% Interest)
8% = \$448

$\$448 \div \dfrac{8}{100} = \$448 \times \dfrac{100}{8} = \$5600$
Sum #1

$2 \times \$5600 = \$11,200$ or Sum #2

ANSWER: Invested 2½% = \$11,200 = sum
(c)

PROOF:

$\$5600 \times 3\% = \$5600 \times \dfrac{3}{100} = \$168.00$

Interest at 3%
$11,200 \times 2\frac{1}{2}\% = \$11,200 \times .025 = \$280$
$168 + \$280 = \$448$ Total Interest

5. SOLUTION:
$856.50 — \$600 = \$256.50
9 years 6 months = 9½ years

$\$256.50 \div 9\frac{1}{2} = \$256.50 \div \dfrac{19}{2} =$

$\$256.50 \times \dfrac{2}{19} = \dfrac{\$513.00}{19} = \$27$

$\dfrac{\$27}{600} = \dfrac{9}{200} = 4.5\% = 4\frac{1}{2}\%$ (a)

ANSWER: Rate per cent = 4½%

6. SOLUTION:
$100,000 \times 6\% = \$6000$ to receive on his investment for one year
$6000 + \$3600 = \$9600$ profit and expenses
$9600 \div 12 = \$800$ Rent per month   (c)

ANSWER: Rent per month — \$800.

7. Compound interest on \$600 — quarterly at 6% for 9 months
SOLUTION:
$600 at 6% for 9 months or $\frac{3}{4}$ year
$600 \times .06 \times \frac{1}{4} = \$9.00$ Interest for 1st quarter
$600 + \$9 = \$609$ due at end of 1st quarter
$609 \times .06 \times \frac{1}{4} = \$9.13\frac{1}{2}$ \$9.14 Interest 2nd quarter
$609 + \$9.14 = \$618.14$ due at end 2nd quarter
$618.14 \times .06 = \$37.0884 \times \frac{1}{4}$ \$9.2721 = \$9.27 Interest 3rd quarter
$6.18.14 + \$9.27 = \$627.41$ due end 3rd quarter
$9.00 + \$9.14 + \$9.27 = \$27.41$ compound Interest (c)

ANSWER: Interest compounded quarterly \$27.41

8. SOLUTION:

Discount $754.30 @ 6% on 90-day note,
April 16, 1974 to May 31, 1974
April 16 to April 30 = 14 days

May	31 days
	45 days = $\dfrac{45}{360}$ year

$$\frac{45}{360} \times \frac{6}{100} = \frac{3}{400} \text{ Interest}$$

Explanation

$$\left(\frac{\overset{9}{\cancel{45}}}{\underset{60}{\cancel{360}}} \times \frac{\overset{1}{\cancel{6}}}{\underset{20}{\cancel{100}}} = \frac{9}{1200} = \frac{3}{400} \right)$$

$$100\% - \frac{3}{400} = \frac{400}{400} - \frac{3}{400} = \frac{397}{400}$$

$$\$754.30 \div \frac{397}{400} = \$754.30 \times \frac{400}{397} = \$760 \quad (a)$$

ANSWER: Face amount of note = $760

9. SOLUTION:
60 days — 45 days = 15 days
$320 — $319.40 = $.60 Interest saved in 15 days.

$$\frac{.60}{320} \div \frac{15}{360} = \frac{\overset{.04}{\cancel{.60}}}{\underset{8}{\cancel{320}}} \times \frac{\overset{9}{\cancel{360}}}{\underset{1}{\cancel{15}}} = \frac{.36}{8} = 4\frac{1}{2}\%$$

discount rate   (a)

ANSWER: Discount rate = 4½%

10. SOLUTION:
60 day note for $432 drawn up on October 6, 1971

$$60 \text{ day note} = \frac{60}{360} = \frac{1}{6} \text{ year for note}$$

Discount rate = 5¼% received $430.74

$$5\frac{1}{4}\% = \frac{21\%}{4} = \frac{21}{400} \text{ discount rate}$$

$432 — $430.74 = $1.26 = interest charged by bank

$$\$1.26 \div \frac{21}{400} \div \$432 =$$

$$\$\overset{.06}{\cancel{1.26}} \times \frac{400}{\underset{1}{\cancel{21}}} \times \frac{1}{432} = \frac{24.00}{432} = \frac{24}{432} = \frac{1}{18} \text{ yr.}$$

$$\frac{1}{\underset{1}{\cancel{18}}} \times \overset{20}{\cancel{360}} = 20 \text{ days}$$

NOTE: Since the note was deposited 20 days before the date of maturity, the bank charged a discount which could be considered interest on the face value. The number of days between the date the note was drawn up and the time of deposit, added to the number of days from the date of deposit to the date of maturity must equal the full term of the note or 60 days.

60-day note — 20 days = 40 days after it was drawn up, it was deposited.

October 6, 1971 to

October 31, 1971 =	25 da. left in Oct.
November 15, 1971 = +	15 da. left in Nov.
	40 da.

Therefore 40 da. = Nov. 15 note deposited   (a)

ANSWER: Note deposited November 15, 1971

TAXATION

94. The following facts should be taken into consideration in taxation problems:
   a. Taxes may be expressed as a per cent or in terms of money based on a certain denomination.
   Example: The general tax rate for Unemployment Insurance in New York State is 2.7%. On the other hand, the realty tax in New York City for the fiscal year of 1963 was $4.27 per $100 of assessed property.
   b. A surtax is an additional tax besides the regular tax rate.

95. In taxation, there are usually three items involved: the amount taxable, henceforth called the base, the tax rate, and the tax itself.

96. To find the tax when given the base and the tax rate in per cent:
   a. Change the tax rate to a decimal.
   b. Multiply the base by the tax rate.

   Illustration: How much would be realized on $4000 if taxed 15%?
   SOLUTION: 15%=.15   (46c, 96a)
   $4000x.15=$600   (30, 96b)
   Answer: Tax=$600

97. To find the tax rate in % form when given the base and the tax:
   a. Divide the tax by the base.
   b. Convert to a per cent.

   Illustration: Find the tax rate at which $5600 would yield $784.
   SOLUTION: $784÷$5600=.14
                                   (38a, 97a)
                .14=14%   (46d, 97b)
   Answer: Tax rate=14%

98. To find the base when given the tax rate and the tax:
   a. Establish a relation between the tax and the base.
   b. Solve to find the base.

   Illustration: What amount of money taxed 3% would yield $75?

SOLUTION: $75=3% of the base   (98a)
            $75=3/100 of the base (46c)
            Base=75÷3/100   (56b)
                =75x100/3=$2500
                            (22, 18, 98b)
Answer: Base=$2500

99. When the tax rate is fixed and expressed in terms of money, take into consideration the denomination upon which it is based; that is, whether it is based on every $100, or $1000, etc.

100. To find the tax when given the base and the tax rate in terms of money:
   a. Divide the base by the denomination upon which the tax rate is based.
   b. Multiply this quotient by the tax rate.

   Illustration: If the tax rate is $3.60 per $1000, find the tax on $470,500.
   SOLUTION: $470,500÷1000=470.5
                            (38, 100a)
                $470.5x3.60=$1,693.80
   Answer: $1,693.80   (30,100b)

101. To find the tax rate based on a certain denomination when given the base and the tax derived:
   a. Divide the base by the denomination indicated.
   b. Divide the tax by this quotient.

   Illustration: Find the tax rate per $100 which would be required to raise $350,000 on $2,000,000 of taxable property.
   SOLUTION: $2,000,000÷100=20,000
                            (101a)
                $350,000÷20,000=$17.50
                            (38b, 101b)
   Answer: Tax rate=$17.50 per $100

102. Since a surtax is an additional tax besides the regular tax, to find the total tax:
   a. Change the regular tax rate to a decimal.
   b. Multiply the base by the regular tax rate.
   c. Change the surtax rate to a decimal.
   d. Multiply the base by the surtax rate.
   e. Add both taxes.

Illustration: Assuming that the tax rate is 2⅓% on liquors costing up to $3.00, and 3% on those costing from $3.00 to $6.00, and 3½% on those from $6.00 to $10.00, what would be the tax on a bottle costing $8.00 if there is a surtax of 5% on all liquors above $5.00?

SOLUTION: An $8.00 bottle falls within the category of $6.00 to $10. The tax rate on such a bottle is

3½%＝.035　　(51, 102a)

$8.00x.035＝.28　(30, 102b)

surtax rate＝5%＝.05

(46c, 102c)

$8.00x.05＝$.40　(30, 102d)

$.28+$.40＝$.68　(102e)

Answer: Total tax＝$.68

TAXATION PROBLEMS

1. Lodge A with 120 men is assessed $96.75. Lodge B with 160 members is assessed $85. How much more is the average for a member of Lodge A than for a member of Lodge B?
   (a) $.275 (b) $.375 (c) $.475 (d) $.35

2. What tax rate on a base of $3650 would raise $164.25?
   (a) 4% (b) 5% (c) 4½% (d) 5½%

3. If the tax rate is 3½% and the amount to be raised is $64.40, what is the base:
   (a) $1800 (b) $1840 (c) $1850 (d) $1860

4. What is the tax rate per $1000 if a base of $338,500 would yield $616.07?
   (a) $1.80 (b) $1.90 (c) $1.95 (d) $1.82

5. On what base would a tax rate of $2.51 per $100 yield $1689.23?
   (a) $67,000　(c) $67,350
   (b) $66,300　(d) $67,300

6. What is the premium on a $7200 policy at $.67 per 100?
   (a) $48.24　(c) $47.00
   (b) $48.20　(d) $49.00

7. A merchant who has debts of $43,250 has gone bankrupt and can pay off only 15¢ on the dollar. How much will his creditors receive?
   (a) $6487.50　(c) $6387.00
   (b) $6387.50　(d) $6287.00

8. A certain community needs $185,090.62 to cover its expenses. If its tax rate is $1.43 per $100 of assessed valuation, what must be the assessed value of its property?
   (a) $12,900,005　(c) $12,940,000
   (b) $12,943,400　(d) $12,840,535

9. A house is insured for 80% of its value at $\frac{5}{16}$%. The premium is $32.50. What is the total value of the house?
   (a) $11,500　(c) $13,000
   (b) $12,000　(d) $13,500

10. Assuming that the income tax law allows $500 personal exemption for single people and $200 for each dependent, and that the tax rates are 2½% on the first $2000 taxable income and 4½% on the next $3000 taxable income, what would be the income tax of Mr. Jones, single, who earns $5200 a year and has two dependents. There is a surtax of 3¼% on all net income, (net income after the personal exemption and dependency deductions have been made).
    (a) $280　　　(c) $290.25
    (b) $293.25　(d) $284.25

Correct Answers

1. a	3. b	5. d	7. a	9. c
2. c	4. d	6. a	8. b	10. b

PROBLEM SOLUTIONS — Taxation

1. SOLUTION:
   120 men assessed $96.75—Lodge A
   160 men assessed $85.00—Lodge B
   How much more is average for member Lodge
   A than for Lodge B?
   ($96.75 ÷ 120) — ($85.00 ÷ 160)
   $.806¼ — $.531¼ = $.275 (a)

   ANSWER: $.275 more for Lodge A member

2. SOLUTION:
   What tax rate on a base of $3650 would raise
   $164.25?

   $$?\% = \frac{\$\,164.25}{\$3650.00} = .04\tfrac{1}{2} = 4\tfrac{1}{2}\% \quad (c)$$

   ANSWER: Tax rate = 4½%

3. SOLUTION:
   Tax = 3½% Amount to be raised = $64.40
   Find base.

   $$\$64.40 \div 3\tfrac{1}{2}\% = \$64.40 \div \frac{7}{200}$$

   $$\frac{\overset{9.20}{\cancel{\$64.40}} \times 200}{\underset{1}{\cancel{7}}} = \$1840.00 \text{ base} \quad (b)$$

   ANSWER: Base = $1840

4. SOLUTION:
   Base of $338,500 yielded $616.07
   Find tax rate per $1000.

   $$\frac{\$338,500}{1000} = \$338.50$$

   $$\frac{\$616.070}{338.50} = \$1.82 \text{ tax rate per thousand} \quad (d)$$

   ANSWER: Tax rate per $1000 = $1.82

5. SOLUTION:
   Find base when tax rate of $2.51 per $100
   yields $1689.23.

   $$Rate = \frac{\$2.51}{100}$$

   $$\frac{\$1689.23 \times 100}{2.51} = \frac{\$168923}{2.51} = \$67,300$$
   base (d)

   ANSWER: Base $67,300

6. SOLUTION:
   Policy = $7200   Rate = $.67 per $100
   Find premium

   $$\frac{\$72\cancel{00}}{1\cancel{00}} \times .67 = \$48.24 \text{ premium} \quad (a)$$

   ANSWER: Premium = $48.24

7. SOLUTION:
   Debt = $43,250
   Pays .15 on $1.00

   $$\frac{\$43,250 \times .15}{1.00} = \$6487.50 \quad (a)$$

   ANSWER: Creditors receive $6487.50

8. SOLUTION:
   Community needs $185,090.62
   Tax = $1.43 per $100 assessed valuation
   Find assessed value of property

   $$\frac{\$185090.62}{1.43} \times 100 = \$12,943,400 \quad (b)$$

   Explanation (8th problem)
   $185090.62 × 100 = $18,509,062

   ```
                 $12943400
   1.43.)$18509062.00.
            143
            420
            286
           1349
           1287
            620
            572
            486
            429
            572
            572
   ```

   ANSWER: Assessed value of property = $12,943,400

9. SOLUTION:

   Insurance = 80% of value
   Rate = $\frac{5}{16}$%
   Premium = $32.50
   Find total value of house

   $$\$32.50 \div \tfrac{5}{16}\% = \$32.50 \times \frac{1600}{5} = \$10,400$$

   amt. for which house was insured.

   $10,400 \div \frac{80}{100} = 10,400 \times \frac{100}{80} =$
   $13,000 value of house   (c)

   ANSWER: Value of house = $13,000

10. SOLUTION:

   $500 single exemption, $200 each dependent
   Taxable income $5200

   Single exemption = $500
   2 dependents   = + 400
   _____
                 $900 deduction
                 $5200 salary
                  −900
                 _____
                 $4300 net income
   $4300 − $2000 = $2300

   1st $2000 at 2½ % = $ 50
      $2300 × 4½ % =   103.50
      $4300 × 3¼ % =   139.75
                    _____
                 $293.25 (Total
                    income tax)   (b)

   ANSWER: $293.25 Total income tax

RATIO AND PROPORTION

103. A ratio expresses the relationship between two (or more) quantities in terms of numbers. The mark used to indicate ratio is the colon (:) and is read as "is to".
Example: The ratio 2:3 is read "2 is to 3".

104. A ratio represents the function of division. Therefore, any ratio of two terms may be written as a fraction, and any fraction may be written as a ratio.
Example: $3:4 = \frac{3}{4}$
$5/6 = 5:6$

105. To simplify any complicated ratio of two terms containing fractions, decimals, or per cents:
a. Divide the first term by the second.
b. Convert to a ratio.
Illustration: Simplify the ratio $\frac{5}{6} : \frac{7}{8}$
SOLUTION: $\frac{5}{6} \div \frac{7}{8} = \frac{5}{6} \times \frac{8}{7} = \frac{20}{21}$
$$(22, 18, 105a)$$
$$\frac{20}{21} = 20:21 \qquad (103, 105b)$$

106. There are two main types of ratio problems:
a. Problems in which the ratio is given.
b. Problems in which the ratio is not given.

107. To solve problems in which the ratio is given:
a. Add the terms in the ratio.
b. Divide the total amount that is to be put into a ratio by this sum.
c. Multiply each term in the ratio by this quotient.
   Illustration: The sum of $360 is to be divided among three people according to the ratio 3:4:5. How much does each one receive?
   SOLUTION: $3+4+5 = 12$ (107a)
   $360 \div 12 = 30$ (107b)
   $30 \times 3 = 90$,
   $30 \times 4 = 120$,
   $30 \times 5 = 150$ (107c)
   Answer: The money is divided thus: $90, $120, $150

108. In problems in which the ratio is not given, there is a basic quantity with which all the others are compared.

109. To solve such problems:
a. Assign the ratio value of 1 to the basic quantity.
b. With 1 as a basis, compute the ratio values of the other quantities based on the facts given.
c. Form a ratio using the ratio values derived.
d. Add the terms in the ratio.
e. Divide the total by this sum.
f. Multiply each term in the ratio by this quotient.

Illustration: A man bought three houses. The first one cost ¼ more than the second, and the third ½ more than the second. He paid $30,000 for the three houses. How much did he pay for each?
SOLUTION: The basic house is the second one which has the ratio value of 1. (108, 109a)
The first house cost ¼ more than the second; therefore, its ratio value is 1¼. (109b)
The third house cost ½ more than the second; therefore, its ratio value is 1½. (109b)
Ratio of the costs $= 1\frac{1}{4} : 1 : 1\frac{1}{2}$ (109c)
$$1\frac{1}{4} + 1 + 1\frac{1}{2} = 15/4$$
$$(12, 109d)$$
$$\$30,000 \div 15/4 = \$8000$$
$$(22, 109e)$$
$$\$8000 \times 1\frac{1}{4} = \$10,000$$
$$\$8000 \times 1 = \$8000$$
$$\$8000 \times 1\frac{1}{2} = \$12,000 \quad (109f)$$
Answer: The first house cost $10,000
The second house cost $8,000
The third house cost $12,000

REVERSING THE RATIO

110. When a fractional part of one quantity is equal to a fractional part of a second quantity, the ratio of the fractions is the reverse of the ratio of the quantities.

111. To solve such problems:
   a. Find the ratio of the fractions.
   b. Reverse this ratio to find the ratio of the quantities.
   c. Add the terms in the ratio.
   d. Divide the total by this sum.
   e. Multiply each term in the ratio by this quotient.

   Illustration: A and B have $80 together and ½ of A's money is equal to ⅓ of B's money. How much has each?
   SOLUTION: Ratio of the fractions=½:⅓
   =3:5   (105, 111a)
   Ratio of A's money to B's
   money=5:3   (110, 111b)
   5+3=8   (111c)
   $80÷8=$10   (111d)
   $10×5=$50   A's money
   $10×3=$30   B's money
                              (111e)

   Answer: A has $50 and B has $30

PROBLEMS SIMILAR TO RATIO PROBLEMS

112. Problems which involve quantities bought at different prices are solved in a manner similar to that of ratio problems. In general, there are two types:
   a. Problems in which the quantity bought at each price is the same.
   b. Problems in which the quantities bought at each price are not the same.

113. To solve when the quantity bought at each price is the same.
   a. Add the various prices.
   b. Divide the total price by this sum to find the number bought at each price.
   c. If required, multiply each price by this quotient to find the amount spent for each quantity.

   Illustration: A man goes into a store and buys the same quantity of 50¢, 75¢, and $1.00 ties. Altogether, he spends $15.75. How many of each does he buy?
   SOLUTION: 50¢+75¢+$1.00=$2.25
                              (113a)
       $15.75÷$2.25=7 (37, 113b)
   Answer: He bought 7 of each

114. When the quantities bought at each price are not the same, there is a basic quantity with which all the others are compared. To solve such problems:
   a. Assign the value 1 to the basic quantity, and with this as a basis, compute the values of the other quantities based on the facts given.
   b. Multiply the prices by their respective values and add these products.
   c. Divide the total price by this sum.
   d. Multiply each of the values by this quotient to find the quantity bought at each price.
   e. If required to find the amount spent for each quantity, multiply each quantity by its respective price.

   Illustration: A man buys twice as many red pencils at 5¢ each as blue ones at 3¢ each, and three times as many yellow pencils at 10¢ each as blue ones. How many does he buy of each if he spends $8.60 altogether?
   SOLUTION: The basic quantity is the number of blue pencils which has a basic value of 1. There are twice as many red pencils as blue ones; therefore, the value of the number of red pencils is 2. There are three times as many yellow pencils as blue ones; therefore, the value of the number of yellow pencils is 3.
                              (114a)

   1 blue   @ .03—.03
   2 red   @ .05—.10
   3 yellow @ .10—.30
   _____
                  .43   (114b)
   $8.60÷.43=20   (37, 114c)
   Number of blue pencils   1×20=20
   Number of red pencils   2×20=40
   Number of yellow pencils 3×20=60 (114d)
   Answer: He bought 20 blue pencils, 40 red pencils, and 60 yellow pencils.

PROPORTION

115. a. A proportion indicates the equality of two (or more) ratios.
   Example: 2:4=5:10=6:12 is a proportion.
   b. If a proportion contains only four terms, the two outside terms are called the extremes, and the two inside terms are called the means.
   Example: In the proportion 2:3=4:6, 2 and 6 are the extremes, and 3 and 4 are the means.

c. In any proportion of four terms, the product of the means equals the product of the extremes.

d. The product of the extremes divided by one mean equals the other mean; the product of the means divided by one extreme equals the other extreme.

116. A proportion problem usually has one term unknown. To solve such problems:

a. Draw a diagram whenever possible to evaluate the proportion correctly.

b. Formulate the proportion very carefully according to the facts given. (If any term is misplaced, the solution will be incorrect.) Any symbol may be written in place of the missing term.

c. Determine by inspection whether the means or the extremes are known. Multiply the pair that has both terms given.

d. Divide this product by the third term given to find the unknown term.

Illustration: Two adjacent trees are 30 feet and 50 feet tall. The 30-foot tree casts a shadow of 12 feet. What length is the shadow cast by the 50-foot tree (given that the height and shadows are in proportion)?

SOLUTION:

tree 30′ | tree 50′ (116a)
shadow 12′ | shadow s

The proportion is:
The ratio of the heights of the trees = the ratio of the length of the shadows.
$30:50=12:s$ (116b)
The pair that has both terms given is the means.
$50\times12=600$ (116c)
$600\div30=20$ (115d, 116d)

Answer: The length of the shadow cast by the 50 foot tree is 20 feet

WEIGHTED AVERAGE PROBLEMS

117. Weighted average problems are included in this chapter because they are very similar in the manner of solution.

118. To obtain the average of quantities that are weighted:

a. Set up a table listing the quantities, their respective weights, and their respective values.

b. Multiply the value of each quantity by its respective weight.

c. Add up these products.

d. Add up the weights.

e. Divide the sum of the products by the sum of the weights.

Illustration: Assuming that the weights for the following subjects are: English 3, History 2, Mathematics 2, Foreign Languages 2, and Art 1—What would be the average of a student whose marks are: English 80, History 85, Algebra 84, Spanish 82, and Art 90?

SOLUTION:

Subject	Weight	Mark
English	3	80
History	2	85
Algebra	2	84
Spanish	2	82 (118a)
Art	1	90

English $3\times80=240$
History $2\times85=170$
Algebra $2\times84=168$
Spanish $2\times82=164$ (118b)
Art $1\times90=\ 90$
————
832 (118c)
Sum of the weights
$3+2+2+2+1=10$ (118d)
$832\div10=83.2$ (39, 118e)

Answer: Average=83.2

119. If the weights and the final average are given, but the value of one quantity is unknown, to find the unknown value:

a. Set up a table listing the quantities, their respective weights, and all the known values.

b. Add up the weights and multiply this sum by the final average.

c. Multiply each of the values by their respective weights and add up these products.

d. Subtract this sum from the product obtained in (b).

e. Divide this difference by the weight of the unknown value.

Illustration: To enter a certain college, an average of 80 is required. The weights are: English 3, Mathematics 2, History 2, and Foreign Languages 2. One student's marks are: English 82, Geometry 75, and French 78. What is the lowest mark he must attain in History to be able to enter?

SOLUTION:

Subject	Weight	Mark	
English	3	82	
Geometry	2	75	
French	2	78	
History	2	?	(119a)
	9		

$9 \times 80 = 720$ (119b)

English $3 \times 82 = 246$
Geometry $2 \times 75 = 150$
French $2 \times 78 = 156$

552

(119c)
$720 - 552 = 168$ (119d)
The missing mark is in History which has a weight of 2
$168 \div 2 = 84$ (119e)
Answer: He must attain at least 84 in History to be able to enter.

RATIO AND PROPORTION PROBLEMS

1. A certain pole casts a shadow 24 feet long. At the same time another pole 3 feet high casts a shadow 4 feet long. How high is the first pole (given that the heights and shadows are in proportion)?
   (a) 18 ft. (b) 19 ft. (c) 20 ft. (d) 21 ft.

2. If ¼ of A's money is equal to $\frac{2}{7}$ of B's money and their total wealth is $7500, how much money has B?
   (a) $3500 (b) $3600 (c) $3700 (d) $3800

3. Two homes cost $2600. One costs $\frac{3}{5}$ more than the other. How much is the higher priced one?
   (a) $1500 (b) $1600 (c) $1700 (d) $1800

4. A, B, and C invested $8000, $7500, and $6500 respectively. Their profits were to be divided according to the ratio of their investment. If B uses his share of the firm's profit of $825 to pay a personal debt of $230, how much will he have left?
   (a) $51.00 (b) $51.10 (c) $51.25 (d) $51.20

5. A man purchased an equal number of $3, $2, and 75¢ ties. He spent $40.25 for all the ties. How much of each did he buy?
   (a) 5 (b) 4 (c) 7 (d) 6

6. A boy purchased 5 times as many red pencils at 10¢ each as blue pencils at 5¢ each. He also purchased ½ as many 25¢ yellow pencils as blue ones. Altogether, he spent $27.00. What was the cost of the red pencils?
   (a) $20 (b) $19 (c) $18 (d) $17

7. An estate is divided among three heirs—A, B, and C—so that A has $\frac{5}{12}$ of the whole estate and B has twice as much as C. A has 56 acres more than C. How many acres are there in the entire estate?
   (a) 250 (b) 252 (c) 254 (d) 256

8. A pole 63 feet long was broken into two unequal parts so that $\frac{3}{5}$ of the longer piece equaled ¾ of the shorter piece. Find the length of longer piece.
   (a) 33 (b) 34 (c) 34½ (d) 35

9. What is the average of a student who received 90 in English, 84 in Algebra, 75 in French, and 76 in Music, if the subjects have the following weights: English 4, Algebra 3, French 3, and Music 1?
   (a) 81 (b) 81½ (c) 82 (d) 83

10. If the entrance requirement of a certain college is 82, what mark must a student have in Geometry (weight 2) to be able to enter if his other marks are English 88 (weight 3), Spanish 78 (weight 2), and History 80 (weight 2)?
    (a) 79 (b) 80 (c) 81 (d) 82

Correct Answers

1. a	3. b	5. c	7. b	9. d
2. a	4. c	6. a	8. d	10. a

PROBLEM SOLUTIONS — Ratio and Proportion

1. SOLUTION:

   Let h = height of 1st pole
   1st pole casts shadow 24′ long
   2nd pole 3 feet high casts
   shadow 4′ long.
   From the similar triangles we have the proportion:

   $$\frac{\text{shadow of small pole}}{\text{shadow of taller pole}} = \frac{\text{height of smaller pole}}{\text{height of taller pole}}$$

   ### ILLUSTRATIONS

   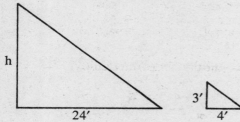

   4:24 : : 3:h
   24 × 3 = 4h
   72 = 4h
   18 = h
   h = 18 ft. height 1st pole   (a)

   ANSWER: Height of 1st pole = 18 ft.

2. SOLUTION:

   ¼ of A's money = ²⁄₇ of B's money
   Total wealth = $7500
   Find amount of B's money
   Find ratio of fractions

   $$\frac{1}{4} : \frac{2}{7} = \frac{7}{28} : \frac{8}{28} = \frac{7:8}{1}$$

   Sum of 7 + 8 = 15   (¹⁵⁄₁₅ = total wealth)
   $7500 ÷ 15 = $500   (¹⁄₁₅ of total wealth)
   $500 × 7 = $3500 = B's money (a) $4000 =
   A's money
   $500 × 8 = $4000
   Proof: $3500 + $4000 = $7500

   ANSWER: B's money = $3500

3. SOLUTION

   One basic house has ratio value of 1

   $$1 + \frac{3}{5} = \frac{8}{5} \text{ cost 2nd house}$$

   Find cost of 2nd house

   $$1 + \frac{8}{5} = \frac{5}{5} + \frac{8}{5} = \frac{13}{5}$$

   $$\frac{13}{5} = \$2600$$

   $$\frac{1}{5} = \$2600 \div 13 = \$200$$

   $$\frac{8}{5} = 8 \times \$200 = \$1600 \text{ Cost 2nd house}   (b)$$

   ANSWER: $1600 cost of higher price home

4. SOLUTION:

   $8000 invested by A
   $7500 invested by B $230 debt
   $6500 invested by C
   $8000 + $7500 + $6500 = $22,000 invested
   by all

   $$\frac{\$825 \times \$7500^{15}}{\$22000_{44}} = \$281.25$$

   $281.25 − 230.00 = $51.25 B has left   (c)

   ANSWER: B has left $51.25

5. SOLUTION:

   t = ties bought at each price
   3t = val. of $3.00 ties
   2t = val. of $2.00 ties
   ¾ t = val. of $0.75 ties
   3t + 2t + ¾ t = $40.25
   12t + 8t + 3t = $161.00
   23t = $161.00
   t =   7 ties of each kind   (c)

   PROOF: 7 × $3.00 = $21.00
          7 × $2.00 = $14.00
          7 × $ .75 = $ 5.25
          _____
                      $40.25

   ANSWER: He bought 7 ties of each kind

6. SOLUTION:

$5p$ = red pencils $5¢ = \frac{1}{2}$ of $10¢$
p = blue pencils
$\frac{1}{2}p$ = yellow pencils

$p(5¢) + 5p(10¢) + \frac{1}{2}p(25¢) = \$27.00$

$.05p + .50p + \frac{.25}{2}p = \$27.00$ (clear dem.

by multiplying all other terms by 2)

$.10p + 1.00p + .25p = \$54.00$

$\$1.35p = \$54.00$

$p = 40$ blue pencils

$5p = 200$ red pencils

red pencils @ .10

$200 \times .10 = \$20$ cost of red pencils   (a)

ANSWER: Cost of red pencils = $20

7. SOLUTION:

Estate divided among 3 heirs
A has $\frac{5}{12}$ of whole estate
B has twice as much as C
A has 56 acres more than C
Find the number of acres in estate

e = estate

$\frac{5e}{12}$ = A's estate

$\frac{5e}{12} - 56 = C$

$2\left(\frac{5e}{12} - 56\right) = B$

$\frac{5e}{12} + \left(\frac{5e}{12} - 56\right) + \left(\frac{10e}{12} - 112\right) = e$

$5e + 5e - 672 + 10e - 1344 = 12e$

$5e + 5e + 10e - 12e = 1344 + 672$

$8e = 2016$

$e = 252$ acres

ANSWER: Whole estate = 252 acres

8. SOLUTION:

Let x = No. of feet in longer part
$63 - x$ = No. of feet in shorter part (since their sum is 63)
The problem says that $\frac{3}{5}$ of the longer piece equals $\frac{3}{4}$ of the shorter, which gives us the equation:

$\frac{3}{5} \cdot x = \frac{3}{4}(63-x)$

Multiplying both sides by 20, the L.C.D.

$\overset{4}{\cancel{20}} \cdot \frac{3}{\cancel{5}} x = \overset{5}{\cancel{20}} \cdot \frac{3}{\cancel{4}}(63-x)$

$12x = 15(63-x)$

$12x = 945 - 15x$

$27x = 945$

$x = 35$ (d)

ANSWER: 35

9. SOLUTION:

Find student's average when

Subject	Grade	Weight
English	90	4
Algebra	84	3
French	75	3
Music	76	1

$(90 \times 4) + (84 \times 3) + (75 \times 3) + (76 \times 1)$

$360 + 252 + 225 + 76 = 913$

Weight = $4 + 3 + 3 + 1 = 11$

$913 \div 11 = 83$ average   (d)

ANSWER: Student's average = 83

10. SOLUTION:

Find student's mark in Geometry if

Subject	Weight	Mark
Geometry	2	?
English	3	88
Spanish	2	78
History	2	80

$2 + 3 + 2 + 2 = 9$ total weight given
Average requirement of college = 82
$82 \times$ total weight $9 = 738$
$(88 \times 3) + (78 \times 2) + (80 \times 2) =$
$264 + 156 + 160 = 580$
$738 - 580 = 158$
$158 \div 2$ (weight Geometry) $= 79$ Geometry Mark   (a)

ANSWER: Mark in Geometry must be 79

WORK PROBLEMS

120. a. In work problems, there are three items involved: the number of men working, the time, and the amount of work done.
   b. The number of men working is directly proportional to the amount of work done; that is, the more men on the job, the more the work that will be done, and vice versa.
   c. The number of men working is inversely proportional to the time; that is, the more men on the job, the less time it will take to finish it, and vice versa.
   d. The time expended on a job is directly proportional to the amount of work done; that is, the more time expended on a job, the more work that is done, and vice versa.

WORK AT EQUAL RATES

121. a. When given the time required by a number of men working at equal rates to complete a job, to find the time required by one man to do the complete job, multiply the number of men by their time.
   Example: If it takes 4 men working at equal rates 30 days to finish a job, then one man will take 30 x 4 or 120 days.
   b. When given the time required by one man to complete a job, to find the time required by a number of men working at equal rates to complete the same job, divide the time by the number of men.
   Example: If 1 man can do a job in 20 days, it will take 4 men working at equal rates 20÷4 or 5 days to finish the job.

122. To solve problems involving men who work at equal rates:
   a. Multiply the number of men by their time to find the time required by 1 man.
   b. Divide this time by the number of men required.
   Illustration: Four men can do a job in 48 days. How long will it take 3 men to finish the same job?

SOLUTION: One man can do the job in 48 × 4 or 192 days (121a, 122a) 3 men can do the job in 192÷3=64 days (121b, 122b)
Answer: It would take 3 men 64 days.

123. In some work problems, the rates, though unequal, can be equalized by comparison. To solve such problems:
   a. Determine from the facts given how many equal rates there are.
   b. Multiply the number of equal rates by the time given.
   c. Divide this by the number of equal rates.

Illustration: Three men can do a job in 12 days. Two of the men work twice as fast as the third. How long would it take one of the faster men to do the job himself?
SOLUTION: There are two fast men and one slow man; therefore, there are actually five slow men working at equal rates. (123a) 1 slow man will take 12×5 or 60 days (121a, 123b) 1 fast man= 2 slow men; therefore, he will take 60÷2 or 30 days to complete the job. (121b, 123c)
Answer: It will take 1 fast man 30 days to complete the job.

124. Unit time is time expressed in terms of 1 minute, 1 hour, 1 day, etc.

125. The rate at which a man works is the amount of work he can do in unit time.

126. If given the time it will take one man to do a job, then the reciprocal of the time is the part done in unit time.
   Example: If a man can do a job in 6 days, then he can do $\frac{1}{6}$ of the work in 1 day. (21a)

127. The reciprocal of the work done in unit time is the time it will take to do the complete job.
Example: If a man can do $\frac{3}{7}$ of the work in 1 day, then he can do the whole job in $\frac{7}{3}$ or $2\frac{1}{3}$ days.
(5, 21b)

128. If given the various times at which each of a number of men can complete a job, to find the time it will take to do the job if all work together:
a. Invert the time of each to find how much each can do in unit time.
b. Add these reciprocals to find what part all can do in unit time.
c. Invert this sum to find the time it will take all of them together.

Illustration: If it takes A 3 days to dig a certain ditch, whereas B can dig it in 6 days, and C in 12, how long would it take all three to do the job?

SOLUTION: A can do it in 3 days; therefore, he can do $\frac{1}{3}$ in one day. (126)
B can do it in 6 days; therefore, he can do $\frac{1}{6}$ in one day. (126)
C can do it in 12 days; therefore, he can do $\frac{1}{12}$ in one day. (126, 21a, 128a)
$\frac{1}{3}+\frac{1}{6}+\frac{1}{12}=\frac{7}{12}$ (12, 128b)
A, B, and C can do $\frac{7}{12}$ of the work in one day; therefore, it will take them $1\frac{2}{7}$ or $1\frac{5}{7}$ days to complete the job.
(21b, 127, 128c)
Answer: A, B, and C working together, can complete the job in $1\frac{5}{7}$ days.

129. If given the total time it requires a number of men, working together, to complete a job, and the times of all but one are known, to find the missing time:
a. Invert the given times to find how much each can do in unit time.
b. Add the reciprocals to find how much is done in unit time by those whose rates are known.
c. Subtract this sum from the reciprocal of the total time to find the missing rate.
d. Invert this rate to find the unknown time.

Illustration: A, B, and C can do a job in 2 days. B can do it in 5 days and C can do it in 4 days. How long would it take A to do it himself?
SOLUTION: B can do it in 5 days; therefore, he can do $\frac{1}{5}$ in one day.
(126)
C can do it in 4 days; therefore, he can do $\frac{1}{4}$ in one day.
(126, 21a, 129a)
$\frac{1}{5}+\frac{1}{4}=\frac{9}{20}$ (12, 129b)
The total time is 2 days; therefore, all can do $\frac{1}{2}$ in one day.
(126)
$\frac{1}{2}-\frac{9}{20}=\frac{1}{20}$ (14, 129c)
A can do $\frac{1}{20}$ in 1 day; therefore, he can do the whole job in 20 days. (127, 21b, 129d)
Answer: It will take A 20 days to complete the job himself.

130. In some work problems, certain values are given for the three factors—number of men working, the amount of work done, and the time. It is then usually required to find the changes that occur when one or two of the factors are given different values.

131. One of the best methods of solving such problems is by directly making the necessary cancellations, divisions and multiplications.
In this problem it is easily seen that more men will be required since more houses are to be built in a shorter time.
Illustration: If 60 men can build 4 houses in 12 months, how many men would be required to build 6 houses in 4 months?
SOLUTION: Since we must build 6 houses where before there were only 4 it should be clear that to accomplish this if the time factor remained the same, we would need $\frac{6}{4}$ of the number of men.
$$\frac{6\times60}{4}=90$$
And since we now utilize 4 months where previously we utilized 12 we see that we must increase the number of men threefold.
$$\frac{12\times90}{4}=270$$
Answer: 270 men will be needed to build 6 houses in 4 months.

TANK PROBLEMS

132. The solution of tank problems is similar to that of work problems. There is one added feature, and that is that the two actions of filling and emptying may go on at the same time.

133. If given the time it takes a pipe to fill or empty a tank, the reciprocal of the time will represent what part of the tank is filled or emptied in unit time.
Example: If it takes a pipe 4 minutes to fill a tank, then $\frac{1}{4}$ of the tank is filled in one minute.

134. If given the part of a tank that a part of a pipe or a combination of pipes can fill or empty in unit time invert the part to find the total time required to fill or empty the whole tank.
Example: If a pipe can fill $\frac{2}{5}$ of a tank in 1 minute, then it will take $\frac{5}{2}$ or $2\frac{1}{2}$ minutes to fill the entire tank.

135. To solve tank problems in which only one action is going on:
   a. Invert the time of each pipe to find how much each can do in unit time.
   b. Add the reciprocals to find how much all can do in unit time.
   c. Invert this sum to find the total time.

Illustration: Pipe A can fill a tank in 3 minutes whereas B can fill it in 4 minutes. How long would it take both pipes, working together, to fill it?

SOLUTION: Pipe A can fill it in 3 minutes; therefore, it can fill $\frac{1}{3}$ of the tank in one minute. (133)
Pipe B can fill it in 4 minutes; therefore, it can fill $\frac{1}{4}$ of the tank in one minute. (133, 135a)
$\frac{1}{3}+\frac{1}{4}=\frac{7}{12}$ (12, 135b)
Pipe A and pipe B can fill $\frac{7}{12}$ of the tank in one minute therefore, they can fill the tank in $\frac{12}{7}$ or $1\frac{5}{7}$ minutes. (134, 135c)

Answer: Pipes A and B, working together, can fill the tank in $1\frac{5}{7}$ minutes.

136. In problems in which both actions are going on, it must be determined (unless stated) which process is faster.
   a. If a combination of filling pipes can fill more of a tank in unit time than the emptying pipes, the tank will ultimately be filled, and vice versa.
   b. The amount that a pipe can fill or empty in unit time is its rate.

137. To determine which process is faster:
   a. Add up the rates of the filling pipes.
   b. Add up the rates of the emptying pipes.
   c. Find the L. C. D. of both sums and change them to fractions having the L. C. D. as denominator.
   d. The fraction with the greater numerator will indicate which process is faster.

Illustration: Pipes A and B can fill a tank in 2 and 6 hours respectively; pipes C and D can empty the same tank in 3 and 5 hours respectively. If all four pipes are working together, will the tank be ultimately filled or emptied?

SOLUTION: The rates of the filling pipes are $\frac{1}{2}$ and $\frac{1}{6}$ (133, 136)
$\frac{1}{2}+\frac{1}{6}=\frac{2}{3}$ (12, 137a)
The rates of the emptying pipes are $\frac{1}{3}$ and $\frac{1}{5}$ (133, 136)
$\frac{1}{3}+\frac{1}{5}=\frac{8}{15}$ (12, 137b)
The L. C. D. of $\frac{2}{3}$ and $\frac{8}{15}$ is 15 (11)
$\frac{2}{3}=\frac{10}{15}$, $\frac{8}{15}=\frac{8}{15}$ (12c, 137c)
$\frac{10}{15}$ is greater than $\frac{8}{15}$; therefore, the tank will ultimately be filled. (137d, 25a)

138. The difference between the sum of the filling rates and the sum of the emptying rates is the part of the tank that is actually being filled or emptied in unit time. The fraction representing the slower action is subtracted from the fraction representing the faster process.

139. To solve tank problems in which actions are going on:
   a. Invert the time of each filling pipe to find how much each can fill in unit time.
   b. Add the reciprocals to find how much of the tank all can fill in unit time.
   c. Invert the time of each emptying pipe to find how much each can empty in unit time.

d. Add the reciprocals to find how much of the tank all can empty in unit time.

e. If required, determine which process is faster and subtract the smaller fraction from the larger to find how much of the tank is actually filled or emptied in unit time.

f. Invert this difference to find the time it will take to either fill or empty the entire tank.

Illustration: A certain tank can be filled by pipes A and B in 4 and 5 minutes respectively. Another pipe C can empty it in 3 minutes. How long will it take to fill or empty the tank, if all three pipes are working together?

SOLUTION: Pipe A can fill the tank in 4 minutes; therefore, it can fill $\frac{1}{4}$ of the tank in 1 minute

(133)

Pipe B can fill the tank in 5 minutes; therefore, it can fill $\frac{1}{5}$ of the tank in 1 minute.

(133, 139b)

$\frac{1}{4} + \frac{1}{5} = \frac{9}{20}$ (12, 139a)

Pipes A and B can fill $\frac{9}{20}$ of the tank in 1 minute. Pipe C can empty the tank in 3 minutes; therefore it can empty $\frac{1}{3}$ of the tank in 1 minute

(133, 139c, d)

The L. C. D. of $\frac{9}{20}$ and $\frac{1}{3}$ is 60   (10, 137c)

$\frac{9}{20} = \frac{27}{60}, \frac{1}{3} = \frac{20}{60}$

(12c, 137c)

$\frac{27}{60} - \frac{20}{60} = \frac{7}{60}$

(14, 138, 139e)

Since $\frac{7}{60}$ of the tank is actually being filled every minute, it will take $\frac{60}{7}$ or $8\frac{4}{7}$ minutes to fill the entire tank.

Answer: It will take $8\frac{4}{7}$ minutes to fill the tank if all three pipes work together.

140. If it is required to find the time it will take to do a fraction of the work, multiply the total time by the fraction.

Example: If a job can be done in 64 minutes, then $\frac{3}{4}$ of the work can be done in $\frac{3}{4} \times 64$ or 48 minutes. If a tank can be filled in 48 minutes, then $\frac{2}{3}$ of the tank can be filled in $\frac{2}{3} \times 48$ or 32 minutes.

WORK AND TANK PROBLEMS

1. If clerk A can type 50 letters in 10 minutes, whereas clerk B can type only 40 letters in 10 minutes, in how many minutes can they type 360 letters together?
   (a) 35 (b) 38 (c) 39 (d) 40.

2. A and B can do a certain job in 4 days, B and C can do it in 6 days, and A, and C can do it in 8 days. How long would it take all three to do the job together?
   (a) 3 days   (c) $3\frac{9}{13}$ days
   (b) 4 days   (d) $3\frac{1}{2}$ days.

3. A tank which holds 400 gallons of water can be filled by one pipe in 15 minutes and emptied by another in 40 minutes. How long would it take to fill the tank if both pipes are open?
   (a) 20 minutes   (c) 23 minutes
   (b) 21 minutes   (d) 24 minutes.

4. A pool can be filled by pipes A, B, and C in 4, 5, and 6 minutes respectively and pipe D can empty the pool in 3 minutes. The pool being empty, pipes A and C are opened for 2 minutes. They are then closed and pipes B and D are opened. In how many minutes will the pool be entirely empty?
   (a) $6\frac{1}{4}$ minutes   (c) $6\frac{3}{4}$ minutes
   (b) $6\frac{1}{2}$ minutes   (d) 7 minutes.

5. Four men working together can dig a ditch in 42 days. They begin but one man works only half days. How long will it take to complete the job?
   (a) 48 days   (c) 43 days
   (b) 45 days   (d) 44 days.

6. A can do a job in 10 days whereas B takes 15 days to do it. A, B, and C can complete the same job in 5 days. All three start working, and after completing $\frac{1}{4}$ of their shares, A and B quit. How long will it take C to finish the job alone?
   (a) $22\frac{1}{2}$ days   (c) 16 days
   (b) 15 days   (d) 17 days.

7. If in 5 days a clerk can copy 125 pages, 36 lines each, 11 words to the line, how many pages of 30 lines each and 12 words to the line can he copy in 6 days?
   (a) 145 (b) 155 (c) 160 (d) 165.

8. A can do a piece of work in 9 days. B can do the job in 6 days and C can do the job in $\frac{3}{4}$ the time required by both A and B. A and B work together for 2 days; then C completes the job. How long did C work?
   (a) 2 days   (c) $2\frac{1}{5}$ days
   (b) $1\frac{1}{5}$ days   (d) $3\frac{1}{5}$ days.

9. A can do a job in 4 days. B assists him for 2 days and then both stop working. C who can do the work in 10 days, works 4 days and completes the job. How long would it take B to do the complete job himself?
   (a) 18 days   (c) 20 days
   (b) 19 days   (d) 21 days.

10. A tank is $\frac{3}{4}$ full. Pipe A can fill the tank in 12 minutes. Pipe B can empty it in 8 minutes. If both pipes are open, how long will it take to empty or fill the tank?
    (a) 14 minutes   (c) 16 minutes
    (b) 22 minutes   (d) 18 minutes.

Correct Answers

(You'll learn more by writing your own answers before comparing them with these.)

1. d	3. d	5. a	7. d	9. c
2. c	4. a	6. a	8. b	10. d

NOW, CHECK YOUR METHODS WITH OUR

SIMPLIFIED PROBLEM SOLUTIONS, WHICH FOLLOW.

PROBLEM SOLUTIONS   Work and Tank

1. SOLUTION:
   A—50 letters in 10 minutes
   B—40 letters in 10 minutes
   Find number minutes to type 360 letters together.
   A $= 50 \div 10 = 5$ letters per minute
   B $= 40 \div 10 = 4$ letters per minute
   5 letters $+$ 4 letters $=$ 9 letters per min.
   working together
   360 letters $\div$ 9 letters $=$ 40 minutes

   ANSWER: Type 360 letters together in 40 minutes

2. SOLUTION:
   A & B do the job in 4 days, or ¼ of the job in one day
   B & C do the job in 6 days, or ⅙ of the job in one day
   A & C do the job in 8 days, or ⅛ of the job in one day
   If A & B work ⅓ of day, then B and C work ⅓ of a day and A & C work ⅓ of a day, in one day they would accomplish:

   $$\left(\frac{1}{3}\times\frac{1}{4}\right)+\left(\frac{1}{3}\times\frac{1}{6}\right)+\left(\frac{1}{3}\times\frac{1}{8}\right)=$$

   $$\frac{1}{12}+\frac{1}{18}+\frac{1}{24}=\frac{6}{72}+\frac{4}{72}+\frac{3}{72}=\frac{13}{72}$$

   of the job
   But with only 2 men working at a time, they accomplish ⅔ of the fraction they would do if all worked together. $\frac{13}{72}\times\frac{3}{2}=\frac{13}{48}$ of the job

   if all worked, therefore the number of days required is $^{48}\!/_{13} = 3^9\!/_{13}$ (c)

   ANSWER: It would take 3⁹⁄₁₃ days working together

3. SOLUTION:
   Tank holds 400 gallons water. Can be filled in 15 minutes.
   Can be emptied in 40 minutes. $\frac{1}{15}$ in 1 min.
   $\frac{1}{40}$ in 1 min.

   L.C.D. $= 120$

$$\frac{1}{15}=\frac{8}{120}$$

$$-\frac{1}{40}=\frac{3}{120}$$

$$\frac{5}{120} \text{ of tank, filled in 1 min.}$$

Reverse fraction $=\dfrac{120}{5}=24$ min.   (d)

ANSWER: Takes 24 min. to fill tank.

4. SOLUTION:

	Fill A	Fill C	Entire tank Empties D	Entire tank Fills B
1 min.	¼	⅙	⅓	⅕
2 min.	2/4	2/6		

A $+$ C filled in 2 min.   L.C.D. $= 12$
$\frac{2}{4}+\frac{2}{6}=\frac{6}{12}+\frac{4}{12}=$
$\frac{10}{12}$ or ⅚ filled in 2 min.

D $-$ B $=$ empty pool in ? min. L.C.D. $= 15$
$\frac{1}{3}-\frac{1}{5}=\frac{5}{15}-\frac{3}{15}=\frac{2}{15}$ emptied in 1 min.
Invert the above difference to find the time it will take to empty the tank.
$\frac{2}{15}$ reversed $=\frac{15}{2}=7\frac{1}{2}$ min. to empty whole pool *but* we have only ⅚ of pool filled, therefore $\frac{5}{6}\times 7\frac{1}{2}$ min. $=\frac{5}{6}\times\frac{15}{2}=\frac{75}{12}$ or $6\frac{1}{4}$ min. to empty pool   (a)

ANSWER: 6¼ min.

5. SOLUTION
   The four men working together can dig a ditch in 42 days, therefore all working together finish $\frac{1}{42}$ of the job in one day. But with one man working only half-days, they accomplish only ⅞ as much work in one day (we assume they work at equal rates).

   Fraction of work done in one day is

$$\frac{\cancel{7}^{1}}{8}\times\frac{1}{\cancel{42}_{6}}=\frac{1}{48}$$

Therefore number of days required is $\dfrac{1}{\frac{1}{48}}$ or 48   (a)

ANSWER: 48 days

6. SOLUTION:
    $A + B + C = 5$ days all complete the job.
    Then all do $\frac{1}{5}$ of the work in 1 day.
    $A = 10$ days work or does $\frac{1}{10}$ of the job in 1 day; $\frac{5}{10}$ in 5 days
    $B = 15$ days work or $\frac{1}{15}$ of the job in 1 day; $\frac{5}{15}$ in 5 days.
    $\frac{5}{10} + \frac{5}{15} = \frac{15}{30} + \frac{10}{30} = \frac{25}{30}$ or $\frac{5}{6}$ of the job in 5 days. L.C.D. = 30
    Since A, B & C together finish job in 5 days, C does $1 - \frac{5}{6} = \frac{1}{6}$ of the job in 5 days or $\frac{1}{6} \div 5 = \frac{1}{6} \times \frac{1}{5} = \frac{1}{30}$ of the job in one day.
    After A and B quit, C has ¾ of the job to do.

$$\frac{3}{4} \div \frac{1}{30} = \frac{3}{\underset{2}{4}} \times \frac{\overset{15}{30}}{1} = \frac{45}{2} = 22\tfrac{1}{2} \quad \text{(a)}$$

ANSWER: 22½ days

7. SOLUTION:
    36 lines $\times$ 11 words = 396 words on each page
    125 pages $\times$ 396 words = 49,500 words in 5 days
    $49,500 \div 5 = 9,900$ words in 1 day
    12 words $\times$ 30 lines = 360 words on each page
    $9900 \div 360 = 27\tfrac{1}{2}$ pages in 1 day   (d)

ANSWER: Clerk can copy 165 pages in 6 days.

8. SOLUTION:
    $A = 9$ days $B = 6$ days $\frac{1}{9} + \frac{1}{6} = \frac{4}{36} + \frac{6}{36} = \frac{10}{36}$, 1 day's work for $A + B$
    (L.C.D. = 36)
    Therefore $A + B$ can do the whole job in $\frac{36}{10}$ days
    $\frac{10}{36} + \frac{10}{36} = \frac{20}{36}$, 2 day's work for $A + B$

It takes C $\dfrac{3}{\underset{1}{4}} \times \dfrac{\overset{9}{36}}{10} = \dfrac{27}{10}$ days to do job alone

or $\frac{10}{27}$ of job in 1 day
So $1 - \frac{20}{36}$ [A + B for 2 days] $= \frac{16}{36} = \frac{4}{9}$ of job for C to do alone

$$\frac{4}{9} \div \frac{10}{27} = \frac{4}{\underset{1}{9}} \times \frac{\overset{3}{27}}{\underset{5}{10}} = \frac{6}{5} = 1\tfrac{1}{5} \text{ days} \quad \text{(b)}$$

ANSWER: C works 1⅕ days

9. SOLUTION:
    C can do whole job alone in 10 days or $\frac{1}{10}$ of the job in one day.
    In the 4 days he worked alone, he did $4 \times \frac{1}{10}$ or $\frac{2}{5}$ of the job.

    A and B together did $1 - \frac{2}{5} = \frac{3}{5}$ of the job before quitting.
    A can do whole job in 4 days or $\frac{1}{4}$ of the job in one day, or $\frac{1}{2}$ of the job in two days he worked with B.
    B did $\frac{3}{5} - \frac{1}{2}$ or $\frac{1}{10}$ of the job in 2 days.
    In one day B would do $\frac{1}{2} \times \frac{1}{10}$ or $\frac{1}{20}$ of the job.
    Therefore, it would take B 20 days to complete job himself.   (c)

ANSWER: 20 days

10. SOLUTION:
    A can fill the tank in 12 min. or fill $\frac{1}{12}$ of the tank in 1 min.
    B can empty the tank in 8 min. or empty $\frac{1}{8}$ of the tank in 1 min.
    $\frac{1}{12} = \frac{2}{24}$ (fill) $\frac{1}{8} = \frac{3}{24}$ (empty) L.C.D. = 24
    $\frac{3}{24} - \frac{2}{24} = \frac{1}{24}$ (empty)
    It would take 24 min. to empty whole tank,

    but it is only ¾ full, therefore: $\dfrac{3}{\underset{1}{4}}$ of $\dfrac{\overset{6}{24}}{1}$ min. =

    18 min. to empty the tank   (d)

ANSWER: 18 min.

DISTANCE PROBLEMS

141. In distance problems, there are usually three items involved: the distance, the rate, and the time.
   a. To get the distance, multiply the rate by the time.
   Example: A man traveling 40 miles an hour for 3 hours, travels 40 × 3 or 120 miles.
   b. The rate is the distance traveled in unit time. To get the rate, divide the distance by the time.
   Example: If a car travels 100 miles in 4 hours, the rate is 100÷4 or 25 miles an hour.
   c. To get the time, divide the distance by the rate.
   Example: If a car travels 150 miles at the rate of 30 miles an hour, the time is 150÷30 or 5 hours.

COMBINED RATES

142. a. When two people or objects are traveling towards each other, then the rate at which they are approaching each other is the sum of their respective rates.
   b. When two people or objects are traveling in directly opposite directions, then the rate at which they are separating is the sum of their respective rates.

143. To solve problems involving combined rates:
   a. Determine which of the three factors is to be found.
   b. Combine the rates and find the unknown factor.
   Illustration: A and B are walking towards each other over a road 120 miles long. A walks at a rate of 6 miles an hour, and B walks at the rate of 4 miles an hour. How soon will they meet?
   SOLUTION: The factor to be found is the time. (143a)
   Time=distance÷rate (141c)
   Distance= 120 miles
   Rate=6+4=10 miles an hour (142a)
   Time=120÷10=12 hours (143b)
   Answer: They will meet in 12 hours.

Illustration: Joe and Sam are walking in straight opposite directions. Joe walks at the rate of 5 miles an hour, and Sam walks at the rate of 7 miles an hour. How far apart will they be at the end of 3 hours?
SOLUTION: The factor to be found is distance (143a)
Distance=time×rate (141a)
Time: 3 hours
Rate: 5+7=12 miles an hour (142b)
Distance: 12×3=36 miles (141a, 143b)
Answer: They will be 36 miles apart at the end of 3 hours.

144. To find the time it takes a faster person or object to catch up with a slower person or object:
   a. Determine how far ahead the slower person or object is.
   b. Subtract the slower rate from the faster rate to find the gain in rate per unit time.
   c. Divide the distance that has been gained by the difference in rates.
   Illustration: Two automobiles are traveling along the same straight road. The first one, which travels at the rate of 30 miles an hour, starts out 6 hours ahead of the second one which travels at the rate of 50 miles an hour. How long will it take the second one to catch up with the first one?
   SOLUTION: The first automobile starts out 6 hours ahead of the second. Its rate is 30 miles an hour. Therefore, it has traveled 6 × 30 or 180 miles. (141a, 144a) The second automobile travels at the rate of 50 miles an hour; therefore, its gain is 50—30 or 20 miles an hour. (144b) The second auto has to cover 180 miles; therefore, it will take 180÷20 or 9 hours to catch up with the first automobile. (141c, 144c)
   Answer: It will take the faster auto 9 hours to catch up with the slower one.

AVERAGE OF TWO RATES

145. In some problems, two or more rates have to be averaged. When the times are the same for two or more different rates, add the rates and divide by the number of rates.
Example: If a man travels for 2 hours at 30 miles an hour, at 40 miles an hour for the next 2 hours, and at 50 miles an hour for the next 2 hours, then his average rate for the 6 hours is $(30+40+50)\div3=40$ miles an hour.

146. When the times are not the same, but the distances are the same:
  a. Assume the distance to be a convenient length.
  b. Find the time at the first rate.
  c. Find the time at the second rate.
  d. Find the time at the third rate, if any.
  e. Add up all the distances and divide by the total time to find the average rate.
Illustration: A boy travels a certain distance at the rate of 20 miles an hour and returns at the rate of 30 miles an hour. What is his average rate for both trips?
SOLUTION: The distance is understood to be the same.
  Assume that it is 60 miles.
        (146a)
  The time for the first trip is $60\div20=3$ hours   (141c, 146e)
  The time for the second trip is $60\div30=2$ hours
        (141c, 146c)

The total distance is 120 miles. The total time is 5 hours. Average rate is $120\div5=24$ miles an hour   (141b, 146e)
Answer: The average rate is 24 miles an hour.

147. When the times are not the same and the distances are not the same:
  a. Find the time for the first distance.
  b. Find the time for the second distance.
  c. Find the time for the third distance, if any.
  d. Add up all the distances and divide by the total time to find the average rate.
Illustration: A man travels 100 miles at 20 miles an hour, 60 miles at 30 miles an hour, and 80 miles at 10 miles an hour. What is his average rate for the three trips?
SOLUTION: The time for the first trip is $100\div20=5$ hours
        (141c, 147a)
  The time for the second trip is $60\div30=2$ hours
        (141c, 147b)
  The time for the third trip is $80\div10=8$ hours
        (141c, 147c)
  The total distance is 240 miles. The total time is 15 hours. Average rate is $240\div15=16$ hours   (141, 147d)
Answer: The average rate for the three trips is 16 miles an hour.

DISTANCE PROBLEMS

1. A man can cover a distance of 360 miles in 12 hours by automobile and in 30 hours on foot. He starts out in his automobile, but breaks down on the way, and walks the rest of the distance spending twice as much time on foot as in the automobile. How long did the trip take?

2. Two cars driven by A and B respectively are 580 miles apart. They drive towards each other. A's car had traveled 20 miles an hour, 4 hours per day for 5 days when it met B's car. If B drove 3 hours a day for 5 days, what was B's rate of speed?

3. Two trains running on the same track travel at the rates of 25 and 30 miles an hour. If the first train starts out an hour earlier, how long will it take the second train to catch up with it?

4. Sam and Joe are on opposite sides of a circular lake which is 1260 feet in circumference. They walk around it starting at the same time and in the same direction. Sam walks at the rate of 50 yards a minute and Joe walks at the rate of 60 yards a minute. In how many minutes will Joe overtake Sam?

5. Two ships are 1550 miles apart sailing towards each other. One sails at the rate of 85 miles per day and the other at the rate of 65 miles per day. How far apart will they be at the end of 9 days?

6. A and B started towards each other at the same time from places 350 miles apart and met in 7 hours. If A's rate was 30 miles an hour, what was B's?

7. A man can travel a certain distance at the rate of 25 miles an hour by automobile. He walks back the same distance on foot at the rate of 10 miles an hour. What is his average rate for both trips?

8. A hiker travels 30 miles at 6 miles an hour, 20 miles at 10 miles an hour, and 15 miles at 5 miles an hour. What is his average rate for the complete distance?

9. A man travels 20 miles at 4 miles an hour, and another 60 miles in 6 hours. What is his average rate for both trips?

10. When an automobile travels 60 miles at the rate of 30 miles an hour, at what rate would it have to return in order to average 40 miles an hour for the round trip?

Correct Answers

(You'll learn more by writing your own answers before comparing them with these.)

1. 20 hours
2. 12 mi. per hr.
3. 5 hours
4. 21
5. 200 miles
6. 20 miles per hour
7. 14$\frac{2}{7}$ mi. per hr.
8. 6½ mi. per hr.
9. 7$\frac{3}{11}$ mi. per hr.
10. 60 mi. per hr.

NOW, CHECK YOUR METHODS WITH OUR

SIMPLIFIED PROBLEM SOLUTIONS, WHICH FOLLOW.

PROBLEM SOLUTIONS — Distance

1. SOLUTION:
360 mi. ÷ 12 hr. = 30 m.p.h. by car
360 mi. ÷ 30 hr. = 12 m.p.h. by foot
$\frac{1}{3}$ of each hr. by car; $\frac{2}{3}$ of each hr. on foot
$\frac{1}{3}$ of 30 mi. = 10 mi. by car
$\frac{2}{3}$ of 12 mi. = 8 mi. by foot
1 hr. = 10 mi. + 8 mi. = 18 mi.
360 ÷ 18 (mi. per hr.) = 20 hrs.

ANSWER: 20 hrs.

2. SOLUTION:
5 × 4 = 20 hr. = 5 da. A; 20 × 20 mi. = 400 miles = A
580 mi. − 400 mi. = 180 mi. left
5 × 3 hr. = 15 hr. B
180 mi. ÷ 15 = 12 mi. per hr. = B's rate of speed.

ANSWER: 12 mi. per hr.

3. SOLUTION:
30 mi. − 25 mi. = 5 mi. gain per 1 hr.
$\frac{25}{5}$ = 5 hrs.

ANSWER: 5 hrs.

4. SOLUTION:
60 yds. − 50 yds. = 10 yds. gain by Joe
1260 ft. ÷ 3 ft. = 420 yds.
420 yds. ÷ 10 yds. (gain) 42 min.
Divide by 2 because they are half the circumference apart
42 yds. ÷ 2 = 21 min. Joe overtook Sam

ANSWER: 21 min.

5. SOLUTION:
85 mi. × 9 da. = 765 mi.
65 mi. × 9 da. = 585 mi.
$\overline{1350}$
1550 mi. − 1350 = 200 miles apart at end of 9 days

ANSWER: 200 miles

6. SOLUTION:
30 mi. × 7 hrs. = 210 miles A's distance
350 total mi. − 210 = 140 miles B's distance
140 ÷ 7 hrs. = 20 mi. per hr. B's rate

ANSWER: 20 miles per hr.

7. SOLUTION:
Assume distance 50 mi. (suggested in solution for average of two rates, No. 146)
Time 1st rate $\frac{50 \text{ mi.}}{25 \text{ mi.}} = 2$ hrs. = 5
Time 2nd rate $\frac{50 \text{ mi.}}{10} = 5$ hrs.
5 hrs. + 2 hrs. = 7 hrs. total time
50 mi. + 50 mi. = 100 mi. total distance
100 mi. ÷ 7 hrs. = $\frac{100}{7}$ = $14\frac{2}{7}$ mi. per hr.

ANSWER: $14\frac{2}{7}$ mi. per hr.

8. SOLUTION:
30 miles + 20 miles + 15 miles = 65 miles
$\frac{30 \text{ mi.}}{6} = 5$ hrs. $\frac{20 \text{ mi.}}{10} = 2$ hrs. $\frac{15 \text{ mi.}}{5} = 3$ hrs.
5 hrs. + 2 hrs. + 3 hrs. = 10 hrs.
$\frac{65 \text{ mi.}}{10 \text{ hrs.}} = 6\frac{1}{2}$ mi. per hr.

ANSWER: $6\frac{1}{2}$ mi. per hr.

9. SOLUTION:
Distance = Rate × Time
Rate = Distance ÷ Time
Time = Distance ÷ Rate
20 mi. = 5 hrs. time for 1st part of trip
4 mi. = 6 hrs. (given) for 2nd part of trip
11 hrs. total time of trip
20 miles + 60 miles = 80 miles traveled
80 mi. ÷ 11 hrs. = $7\frac{3}{11}$ miles per hr.

ANSWER: $7\frac{3}{11}$ miles per hr.

10. SOLUTION
Travel 60 mi. in 2 hrs. (30 mi. per hr.)
120 miles (round trip)   40 mi. = 3 hrs.
3 hrs. − 2 hrs. = 1 hr. return trip
60 mi. = 1 hr. return trip

ANSWER: 60 mi. per hr.

GEOMETRIC FIGURES

TWO-DIMENSIONAL FIGURES

148. Four two-dimensional figures will be considered in this chapter: squares, rectangles, triangles, and circles.
    a. In a figure of two dimensions, the total space within the figure is called the area, which is expressed in square denominations.
    b. The length of the curved line enclosing the area is called the perimeter.
    c. The square of a number is that number multiplied by itself. The square of a number is indicated by placing the exponent 2 at the upper right of the number.
    Example: $3^2 = 3 \times 3 = 9$.
    d. The square root of a quantity is the number which, multiplied by itself, equals the quantity. The square root of a number is indicated by a radical sign ($\sqrt{}$).
    Example: $\sqrt{16} = 4$
    e. The cube of a number is that number multiplied by itself twice. The cube of a number is indicated by placing the exponent 3 at the upper right of the number.
    Example: $4^3 = 4 \times 4 \times 4 = 64$.
    f. An angle is formed when two lines meet.
    g. A right angle is formed when two lines meet perpendicularly. A right angle has 90 degrees.

SQUARES

149. A square is a figure of four equal sides meeting at right angles.

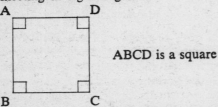

ABCD is a square

    a. The area of a square is equal to the square of the length of any side.
    Example: The area of a square one side of which is 6 inches = $6 \times 6 = 36$ square inches.
    (148a, c)

    b. If given the area of a square, then the length of one side equals the square root of the area.
    Example: If the area of a square is 49 square feet, then the length of one side = $\sqrt{49} = 7$ feet.
    c. The perimeter of a square equals one side multiplied by 4.
    Example: The perimeter of a square one side of which is 5 feet = $5 \times 4 = 20$ feet.

SQUARE ROOT

150. The square roots of small perfect squares are generally known, or may be discovered by trial and error. But to extract the square root of numbers that are not perfect squares, or which are large perfect squares, involves a process which should be carefully studied. If this operation is not familiar, it would be worthwhile to practice it as much as possible.

151. To extract the square root of a number:
    a. Write the number down, place an answer block at the right of it, and mark off every two digits from right to left. If the number is a decimal, start at the decimal point and mark off every two digits to the right and to the left of the decimal point. Any number of zeros may be written after a decimal point. Remember to write a decimal point in the answer block when it is reached in the process of extracting the square root.
    b. Determine the closest square root of the first group of digits the square of which will not exceed the group. Remember that the first group may have either one or two digits.
    c. Write this square root in the answer block.
    d. Write the square of this number below the first group and subtract.
    e. Copy down the next group of digits to form the next dividend.
    f. Double the number in the answer block and write it at the left a little space away from the dividend.

g. To this doubled number, annex a number (to form a divisor), which when multiplied by the divisor thus formed will give the nearest number to the dividend but not exceeding it.

h. Write this number (which has been attached) in the answer block. Notice that this number has been written in three places: 1. next to the doubled number, 2. underneath the divisor in order to multiply it, 3. in the answer block as part of the answer.

i. Write this same number underneath the divisor (145), multiply it by the divisor and place this product under the dividend.

j. Subtract, copy down the next group, if any, form a new divisor by doubling the entire number in the answer block, and continue in the same manner.

k. If, at any time, the divisor which is formed is larger than the dividend, write a zero in the answer block, add a zero to the divisor, and copy down the next group of digits.

Illustration: Find the square root of 91204.

SOLUTION:

```
9' 12' 04    |302
  9
602 | 12 04
  2 | 12 04
```

Illustration: Find the square root of 465432.06 to the nearest hundredth. (Work it out to three decimal places.)   (41)

SOLUTION:

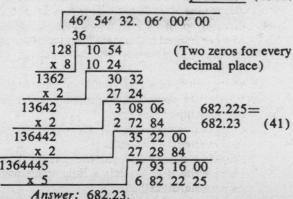

```
               )682.225  (151a)
  46' 54' 32. 06' 00' 00
  36
128 | 10 54        (Two zeros for every
x 8 | 10 24         decimal place)
1362 |   30 32
x 2  |   27 24
13642 |   3 08 06     682.225=
x 2   |   2 72 84     682.23   (41)
136442 |   35 22 00
x 2    |   27 28 84
1364445 |  7 93 16 00
x 5     |  6 82 22 25
```

Answer: 682.23.

RECTANGLES

152. A rectangle is a four-sided figure whose opposite sides are equal and meet at right angles. A rectangle has a length and a width.

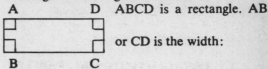

ABCD is a rectangle. AB or CD is the width:

AD or BC is the length.

a. The area of a rectangle equals the product of the length multiplied by the width.

Example: If the length of a rectangle is 6 feet and its width 4 feet, then the area=6×4=24 square feet.   (148a)

b. If given the area of a rectangle and one dimension, to find the other dimension, divide the area by the given dimension.

Example: If the area of a rectangle is 48 sq. feet and one dimension is 4 feet, then the other dimension=48÷4=12 ft.

c. The perimeter of a rectangle equals twice the sum of the length and the width.

Example: The perimeter of a rectangle whose length is 7 feet and width 3 feet equals 2×10=20 ft.

TRIANGLES

153. A triangle is a three-sided closed figure with three vertices.

ABD is a triangle whose vertices are A, B, and D.

a. The altitude of a triangle is a line drawn from a vertex perpendicular to the opposite side. The opposite side becomes a base.

Example: AC is an altitude; BD is the base corresponding to altitude AC.

b. The area of a triangle equals the product of ½ the base multiplied by the altitude.

Example: The area of a triangle who altitude is 5 inches and whose base is 12 inches. ½ × 60=30 square inches.   (148a)

c. A right triangle is a triangle containing a right angle. The sides enclosing the right angle are called the legs. The side opposite the right angle is called the hypotenuse. ABC is a right triangle. C is the right angle. Sides AC and BC are the legs. Side AB is the hypotenuse.

d. The area of a right triangle equals ½ the product of the legs. (One of the legs is actually an altitude.)
Example: If the legs of a right triangle are 7 and 8 inches, then the area=½ × 56=28 square inches.
e. In a right triangle, the square of the hypotenuse equals the sum of the squares of the legs. (Pythagorean Theorem)

154. To find the hypotenuse of a right triangle when given the legs:
   a. Square each leg.
   b. Add the squares.
   c. Extract the square root of this sum.
   Illustration: In a right triangle the legs are 6 inches and 8 inches. Find the hypotenuse.
   SOLUTION: $6^2=36$ $8^2=64$
                                    (148c, 154a)
   $36+64=100$ (154b)
   $\sqrt{100}=10$ (148d, 154c)
   Answer: The hypotenuse is 10 inches.

155. To find a leg when given the other leg and the hypotenuse of a right triangle.
   a. Square the hypotenuse and the given leg.
   b. Subtract the square of the leg from the square of the hypotenuse.
   c. Extract the square root of this difference.
   Illustration: One leg of a right triangle is 12 feet and the hypotenuse is 20 feet. Find the other leg.
   SOLUTION: $12^2=144$ $20^2=400$
                                        (148c, 155a)
   $400—144=256$ (155b)
   $\sqrt{256}=16$ (148d, 155c)
   Answer: The other leg is 16 feet.

CIRCLES

156. A circle is a closed, curved line every point of which is equally distant from the center of the circle.

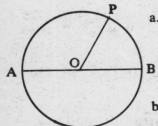

   a. The length of the curved line, or perimeter, of a circle is called the circumference.
   b. Any line drawn from the center (O) and terminating at the circumference is called a radius. OP is a radius. All radii are equal.

c. A line drawn through the center the extremities of which terminate at the circumference is called a diameter. A diameter is twice the length of any radius. AB is a diameter and is twice the length of OP.
d. In any circle, the ratio of the circumference to the diameter is equal to π (called "pi")=$2\frac{2}{7}$, 3.14, or to be more exact 3.1416. The problem will state which value to use: otherwise, express the answer in answer in terms of "pi." π
e. There are 360 degrees in a circle.
f. The circumference of a circle is equal to the product of the diameter multiplied by π.
   Example: The circumference of a circle whose diameter is 4 inches=4 π inches; or, if it is stated that π =$2\frac{2}{7}$, then the circumference =$4\times2\frac{2}{7}=\frac{88}{7}=12\frac{4}{7}$ inches.   (16, 5)
g. Since the diameter is twice the radius, it can be stated that the circumference equals twice the radius multiplied by π.
   Example: If the radius of a circle is 3 inches, then the circumference=6 π inches.
h. The diameter of a circle equals the circumference divided by π.
   Example: If the circumference of a circle is 11 inches, then the diameter (assuming that π=$2\frac{2}{7}$)=$11\div2\frac{2}{7}=3\frac{1}{2}$ inches.   (22, 18)
i. The area of a circle is equal to the radius squared multiplied by π.
   Example: If the radius of a circle is 6 inches, then the area= 36 π square inches (148a, c)

THREE DIMENSIONAL FIGURES

157. Of the three-dimensional figures, two will be considered: rectangular solids and cubes.
   a. In a three dimensional figure, the total space contained within the figure is called the volume which is expressed in cubic denominations.
   b. The total outside surface is called the surface area and it is expressed in square denominations.

158. A rectangular solid is a figure of three dimensions having six rectangular faces meeting each other at right angles. The three dimensions are length, width, and height.

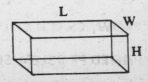

The figure at the left is a rectangular solid; "L" is the length, "W" is the width, and "H" is the height.

a. The volume of a rectangular solid is the product of the length, width, and height.

Example: The volume of a rectangular solid whose length is 6 ft., width 3 ft., and height 4 ft. $6 \times 3 \times 4 = 72$ cubic ft.

b. The surface area of a rectangular solid is equal to twice the sum of the areas of the three sides which do not face each other.

159. A cube is a rectangular solid whose sides and dimensions are all equal.

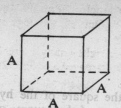

The figure at the left is a cube; the length, width, and height are all equal to "A".

a. The volume of a cube is equal to any dimensioned cubed.

Example: The volume of a cube whose height is 6 inches equals 6^3 $= 6 \times 6 \times 6 = 216$ cubic inches. (148e)

b. The surface area of a cube is equal to the area of any side multiplied by 6.

Example: The surface area of a cube whose length is 5 inches $= 5^2 \times 6 = 25 \times 6 = 150$ square inches.

PROBLEMS INVOLVING GEOMETRIC FIGURES

1. An automobile wheel has a diameter of 24 inches. How many revolutions will it make in covering 3 miles? ($\pi = 2\frac{2}{7}$).

2. A ladder 65 feet long is leaning against the wall. Its lower end is 25 feet away from the wall. How much further away will it be if the upper end is moved down 8 feet?

3. A circle graph shows that 30% of this year's immigrants are German, 28% are Spanish, 20% are English, 10% are miscellaneous, and the rest are French. How many degrees of the circle should be devoted to the French?

4. A square lot has a diagonal path cut through it. If the path is 40 yards long, what is the area of the lot?

5. If the cost of digging a trench is $2.12 a cubic yard, what would be the cost of digging a trench 2 yards by 5 yards by 4 yards?

6. How many boxes 3 inches by 4 inches by 5 inches can fit into a carton 3 feet by 4 feet by 5 feet?

7. The area of a rectangular garden is 60 square yards and the width is 5 yards. How much longer is the perimeter than the sum of both diagonals?

8. What is the area of a right triangle whose hypotenuse is 5 inches and one of its legs is 3 inches?

9. A box is 12 inches in width, 16 inches in length, and 6 inches in height. How many square inches of paper would be required to cover it on all sides?

10. Find the square foot of 534206 to the nearest tenth.

Correct Answers

1. 2520	6. 1728
2. 14 ft.	7. 8 yds.
3. 43.20°	8 6 sq. in.
4. 800 sq. yds.	9. 720 sq. in.
5. $84.80	10. 730.9

NOW, CHECK YOUR METHODS WITH OUR

SIMPLIFIED PROBLEM SOLUTIONS, WHICH FOLLOW

NECESSARY BACKGROUND

The following information is needed to understand solutions of problems in Chapters entitled: Geometric Figures, Algebra, First Plane Geometry Test.

An **angle** is the figure formed by two lines meeting at a point.

The point B is the **vertex** of the angle and the lines BA and BC are the **sides** of the angle.

ILLUSTRATION

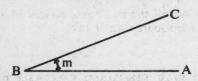

There are three common ways of naming an angle:
1. By a small letter or figure written within the angle, as ∠ m.
2. By the capital letter at its vertex ∠ B.
3. By three capital letters, the middle letter being the vertex letter, as ∠ ABC.

Kinds of angles:

When two straight lines intersect (cut each other), four angles are formed. If these four angles are equal, each angle is a **right angle** and contains 90°.

When one line forms a right angle with another line, the lines are **perpendicular** to each other.

An angle less than a right angle is an **acute angle.**

If the two sides of an angle extend in opposite directions forming a straight line, the angle is a **straight angle.**

ILLUSTRATIONS

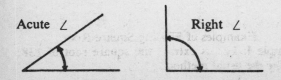

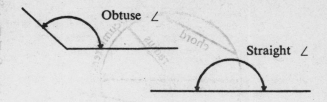

An angle greater than a right angle (90°) and less than a straight angle (180°) is an **obtuse angle.**

Kinds of triangles:

If a triangle has two equal sides, it is **isosceles.** If a triangle has its three sides equal, it is **equilateral.**

ILLUSTRATIONS

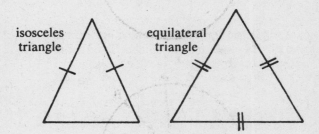

A **right triangle** is a triangle that has one right angle.

The sum of the angles of any triangle is 180 degrees.

A **circle** is a closed plane curve, all points of which are equidistant from a point within called the center.

A **chord** is a line segment connecting any two points on the circle.

A **radius** of a circle is a line segment connecting the center with any point on the circle.

A **diameter** is a chord passing through the center of the circle.

A **secant** is a chord extended in either one or both directions.

A **tangent** is a line touching a circle at one point and only one.

The **circumference** is the curved line bounding the circle.

An **arc** of a circle is any part of the circumference.

ILLUSTRATIONS

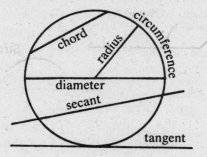

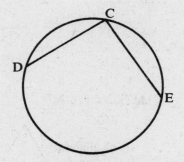

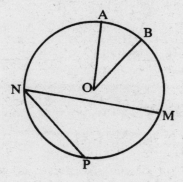

An angle is inscribed in an arc if its vertex is on the arc and its sides are chords joining the vertex to the end points of the arc. ∠ DCE is inscribed in arc DCE.

A **central angle,** as ∠ AOB in the figure, is an angle whose vertex is the center of the circle and whose sides are radii. A central angle is equal in degrees to (or has the same number of degrees as) its intercepted arc.

An **inscribed angle,** as ∠ MNP, is an angle whose vertex is on the circle and whose sides are chords.

PERFECT SQUARES AND SQUARE ROOTS

To square a number means to multiply the number by itself.

If we know the product of two equal numbers, one of these numbers is called the square root of the given product:

Since $12^2 = 144$, the square root of $144 = 12$. The symbol for square root is $\sqrt{}$; it is read "the square root of." $\sqrt{144} = 12$

It may mean any of the following:
a) What number multiplied by itself will give 144?
b) What number squared will give 144?
c) What number has been used twice as a factor to produce 144?
d) What is one of the two equal factors of 144?
e) What is the square root of 144?

METHOD FOR FINDING SQUARE ROOT

1. Locate the decimal point.
2. Mark off the digits in groups of two in both directions beginning at the decimal point.
3. Mark the decimal point for the answer just above the decimal point of the number whose square root is to be taken.
4. Find the largest perfect square contained in the left-hand group.
5. Place its square root in the answer. Subtract the perfect square from the first digit or pair of digits.
6. Bring down the next pair.
7. Double the partial answer.
8. Add a trial digit to the right of the doubled partial answer. Multiply this new number by the trial digit. Place the correct new digit in the answer.
9. Subtract the product.
10. Repeat Steps 6-9 as often as necessary.

You will notice that you get one digit in the answer for every group you marked off in the original number.

To find the square root of a fraction, extract the square of both the numerator and the denominator.

$$\sqrt{\frac{4}{9}} = \frac{2}{3} \qquad \sqrt{\frac{1}{16}} = \frac{1}{4}$$

Examples of Finding Square Root

Example I: Let us extract the square root of 138,-384 by the usual method.

1. The number must first be pointed off in groups of two figures each, beginning at the decimal point, which, in the case of a whole number, is at the right. The number of figures in the root will be the same as the number of groups so obtained.

$$\begin{array}{r} 3 \\ \sqrt{13'83'84} \\ 3^2 = 9 \\ \hline 483 \end{array}$$

2. The largest square less than 13 is 9
$$\sqrt{9} = 3$$

3. Place its square root in the answer.

4. Subtract the perfect square from the first digit or pair of digits.

5. Bring down the next pair.

6. To form our trial divisor, annex 0 to this root "3" (making 30) and multiply by 2. 483 ÷ 60 = 8. Multiplying the trial divisor 68 by 8, we obtain 544, which is too large.

$$\begin{array}{r} 3\ 7\ 2 \\ \sqrt{13'83'84} \\ 3 = 9 \\ \hline 483 \\ 7 \times 67 = 469 \\ \hline 1484 \\ 2 \times 742 = 1484 \end{array}$$

7. We then try multiplying 67 by 7. This is correct.

8. Add the trial digit to the right of the doubled partial answer. Place the new digit in the answer.

9. Subtract the product. Bring down the final group.

10. Annex 0 to the new root 37 and multiply by 2 for the trial divisor:
$$2 \times 370 = 740$$
$$1484 \div 740 = 2$$
Complete divisor $= 740 + 2$

Hence, the positive square root of 138,384 is 372.

Example II: Find the positive square root of 3 to the nearest hundredth.

$$\begin{array}{r} 1.\ 7\ 3\ 2 \\ \sqrt{3.00'00'00} \\ 1 \\ \hline \end{array}$$

$$\begin{array}{rr} 20 & 200 \\ 7 \times 27 = & 189 \\ \hline 340 & 1100 \\ 3 \times 343 = & 1029 \\ \hline 3460 & 7100 \\ 2 \times 3462 = & 6924 \end{array}$$

Hence, the positive square root of 3 is 1.73 to the nearest hundredth and 1.7 to the nearest tenth.

NOW, CHECK YOUR METHODS WITH OUR SIMPLIFIED PROBLEM SOLUTIONS, WHICH FOLLOW DIRECTLY.

PROBLEM SOLUTIONS — Geometry

1. SOLUTION:

Formula: Circumference of a circle $2\pi R$
Diameter 24 in. or 2 ft. $\pi = 22/7$
Radius ½ of 2 ft. = 1 ft.
3 miles = 5280 ft. × 3 = 15,840 ft.
$2\pi R$

$$2 \times 1 \text{ ft.} \times \frac{22}{7} = \frac{44}{7} \text{ ft. in one revolution}$$

$$\frac{15,840}{1} \div \frac{44}{7} = \frac{\overset{3960}{\cancel{15,840}}}{1} \times \frac{7}{\underset{11}{\cancel{44}}} = \frac{27,720}{11} = 2520$$

2520 revolutions will be made in covering 3 miles

ANSWER: 2520

2. SOLUTION:

Formula: In a right triangle: $c^2 = a^2 + b^2$
In a right triangle, the square of the hypotenuse equals the sum of the squares of the other two sides.
ladder = hypotenuse, c
ground = base, b
wall   = altitude, a
$$\sqrt{c^2 - b^2} = a$$
$$\sqrt{65^2 - 25^2}$$
$$\sqrt{4225 - 625} = \sqrt{3600} = 60 \text{ ft. wall}$$
60 ft. — 8 ft. = 52 ft. new altitude
$$\sqrt{c^2 - a^2} = b \qquad \sqrt{65^2 - 52^2} = b$$
$$\sqrt{4225 - 2704} = b$$
$$\sqrt{1521} = 39 \text{ ft. new base}$$
39 ft. — 25 ft. = 14 ft. moved farther from the wall

ILLUSTRATION

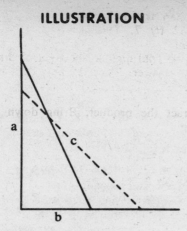

ANSWER: 14 ft.

3. SOLUTION:
30% = Germans
28% = Spanish
20% = English
10% = Miscellaneous
——
88%
? = French
——
100%

100%
− 88%
——
12% French
12% = .12
Circle = 360° × .12 = 43.20° French

ANSWER: 43.20° French

4. SOLUTION:
Path = hypotenuse 40 yds.
Formula: $c^2 = a^2 + b^2$
Since it is a square lot $c^2 = s^2 + s^2$ (both sides are equal)
$40^2 = s^2 + s^2$
$1600 = s^2 + s^2$
$1600 = 2s^2$
$800 = s^2$

ANSWER: 800 square yds.

5. SOLUTION:
Formula for volume = V = LWH
2 yd. × 5 yd. × 4 yd. = 40 cu. yd.
$2.12 × 40 = $84.80 cost of digging trench

ANSWER: $84.80

6. SOLUTION:
Formula for volume = V = LWH
3 ft. × 4 ft. × 5 ft. = 60 cu. ft. size of carton

$$\frac{1728 \times \cancel{60}}{\cancel{3} \times \cancel{4} \times \cancel{5}} = 1728 \text{ boxes}$$
1728 cu. in. = 1 cubic foot
Therefore 1728 boxes càn fit into the carton

ANSWER: 1728 boxes

7. SOLUTION:
Area of a rectangle = LW
Therefore area ÷ L = W   5 yds. given length
60 yds. ÷ 5 yds. = 12 yds. width
2 (5 yds. + 12 yds.) = 34 yards perimeter
Diagonals = the hypotenuse
Formula $a^2 + b^2 = c^2$
Therefore $12^2 + 5^2$ = hypotenuse or diagonal squared
$\sqrt{12^2 + 5^2} = \sqrt{144 + 25} = \sqrt{169} = 13$ yds. diag.
13 × 2 = 26, length of both diagonals
34 yds. − 26 yds. = 8 yds.   Perimeter longer than both diagonals.

ANSWER: 8 yds.

8. SOLUTION:
area of a triangle = ½ bh
In a right triangle $c^2 = a^2 + b^2$
$c^2 − b^2 = a^2$
$\sqrt{5^2 − 3^2}$
$\sqrt{25 − 9} = \sqrt{16} = 4$ inches other leg
3 × 4 = 12 sq. in ÷ 2 = 6 sq. in. area of triangle.

ANSWER: 6 sq. in.

9. SOLUTION:
Find area of each side and then add the three areas.
2(12 × 16) + 2(16 × 6) + 2(12 × 6)
384 sq. in. + 192 sq. in. + 144 sq. in. = 720 sq. in.

ANSWER: 720 sq. in.

10. SOLUTION See instructions for preceding problem for solutions in this chapter.
$$\begin{array}{r} 7\ 3\ 0\ .\ 8\ 8 \\ \sqrt{53'42'06'.00'00} \end{array}$$
7^2 = 49
——
442
3 × 143 = 429
——
130600
8 × 14608 = 116864
——
1373600
8 × 146168 = 1169344

ANSWER: 730.88 = 730.9 (nearest tenth)

SERIES

160. A series is a sequence of numbers based on a certain pattern. There are three main types of series:

   a. If each term in a series is being increased or diminished by the same number to form the next term, then it is an arithmetic series. The number being added or subtracted is called the difference.
   Example: 2, 4, 6, 8, 10 . . . is an arithmetic series in which the difference is 2.
   14, 11, 8, 5, 2 . . . is an arithmetic series in which the difference is 3.

   b. If each term of a series is being multiplied by the same number to form the next term, then it is a geometric series. The number multiplying each term is called the ratio.
   Example: 2, 6, 18, 54 . . . is a geometric series in which the ratio is 3.
   64, 16, 4, 1 . . . is a geometric series in which the ratio is $\frac{1}{4}$.

   c. If the series is neither arithmetic nor geometric, it is a miscellaneous series. Such a series may have each term a square or a cube, or the difference may be squares or cubes; or there may be a varied pattern in the series which must be determined by this pattern.

161. A series may be ascending, that is, the numbers increase; or descending, that is, the numbers decrease.

162. To determine whether the series is arithmetic;

   a. If the series is ascending, subtract the first term from the second, and the second from the third. If the difference is the same in both cases, the series is arithmetic.

   b. If the series is descending, subtract the second term from the first, and the third from the second. If the difference is the same in both cases, the series is arithmetic.

163. To determine whether the series is geometric, divide the second term by the first, and the third by the second. If the ratio is the same in both cases, the series is geometric.

164. What is usually required in a series problem is either to find the term following the last one given, or to find the term preceding the first one given. (Of course, it may be required to find a missing term.)

165. To solve a problem in which the series is arithmetic and ascending:

   a. Subtract the first term from the second to find the difference.

   b. To find the term following the last one given, add the difference to the last term.

   c. To find the term preceding the first one given, subtract the difference from the first term.
   Illustration: What number follows $16\frac{1}{3}$ in this series, 3, $6\frac{1}{3}$, $9\frac{2}{3}$, 13, $16\frac{1}{3}$. . . .
   SOLUTION: $6\frac{1}{3}-3=3\frac{1}{3}$ (162a, 165a)
   The difference is $3\frac{1}{3}$.
   $16\frac{1}{3}+3\frac{1}{3}=19\frac{2}{3}$ (12, 165b)
   Answer: The term following $16\frac{1}{3}$ is $19\frac{2}{3}$

166. To solve a problem in which the series is arithmetic and descending;

   a. Subtract the second term from the first to find the difference.

   b. To find the term following the last one given, subtract the difference from the last term.

   c. To find the term preceding the first one given, add the difference to the first term.
   Illustration: What number precedes 16 in this series, 16, $13\frac{1}{2}$, 11, $8\frac{1}{2}$, 6 . . .
   SOLUTION: $16-13\frac{1}{2}=2\frac{1}{2}$
   (162b, 166a)
   The difference is $2\frac{1}{2}$.
   $16+2\frac{1}{2}=18\frac{1}{2}$ (166c)
   Answer: The term preceding 16 is $18\frac{1}{2}$

167. To solve a problem in which the series is geometric:

   a. Divide the second term by the first to find the ratio.

   b. To find the term following the last one given, multiply the last term by the ratio.

   c. To find the term preceding the first one given, divide the first term by the ratio.
   Illustration: What number precedes the first term in this series, 8, 12, 18, 27. . . .

SOLUTION: $12 \div 8 = \frac{3}{2}$ The ratio is $\frac{3}{2}$.
(167a)
$8 \div \frac{3}{2} = \frac{16}{3}$ (22, 167c)
Answer: The term preceding the first term is $\frac{16}{3}$

168. If, after trial, a series is neither arithmetic or geometric, it must be one of a miscellaneous type. Test to see whether it is a series of squares or cubes or whether the difference is the square or the cube of the same number; or the same number may be first squared, then cubed, etc. (148e)

169. To find the last term of an arithmetic series:
   a. Subtract 1 from the number of terms.
   b. Multiply this by the difference.
   c. Add the first term to this product.
   Illustration: What is the 15th term in this series, 3, 7, 11, 15. . . .
   SOLUTION: Number of terms=15. Difference=4 (165a). First term=3. 15—1=14 (169a). $14 \times 4 = 56$ (169b). 56+3=59 (169c).
   Answer: The 15th term is 59

170. To find the sum of an arithmetic series:
   a. Divide the number of terms by 2.
   b. Multiply this quotient by the sum of the first term and the last term.

Illustration: What is the sum of 10 terms of an arithmetic series beginning with 3 and ending with 30?
SOLUTION: Number of terms=10. First term=3. Last term=30.
$10 \div 2 = 5$ (170a). $5 \times 33 = 165$ (170b)
Answer: The sum of 10 terms is 165

171. A straight series is an arithmetic series that either begins or ends with 1 in which the difference is 1.
   Example: 1, 2, 3, 4, 5, 6 . . . and 6, 5, 4, 3, 2, 1 are straight series.

172. To find the sum of a straight arithmetic series where the first term is 1:
   a. Add 1 to the highest term.
   b. Multiply this sum by the highest term.
   c. Divide this product by 2.

   Illustration: A pile of logs has 20 logs at the bottom, 19 in the next layer, 18 in the next, etc. and finally 1 at the top. How many logs are there in the pile?

   SOLUTION: Highest term=20. 20+1 =21   (172a)
   $21 \times 20 = 420$ (172b). $420 \div 2 = 210$
   Answer: There are 210 logs in the pile

PROBLEMS INVOLVING SERIES

1. What number follows the last term of this series: $2\frac{1}{2}$, $6\frac{3}{4}$, 11, $15\frac{1}{4}$ . . .

2. What number precedes the first term in this series: 4, $13\frac{1}{3}$, $44\frac{4}{9}$, $148\frac{4}{27}$ . . .

3. What is the 5th term in this series: 3, 5, 9, 17.

4. Find the missing term in this series: 3, 7, 18, 26, 37, 53, ___, 96.

5. In a lodge of 200 men, each man shakes the hand of every member once. How many hand shakes are there?

6. Assuming that a clock strikes once at 1 o'clock, twice at 2 o'clock, etc., how many times does it strike in 24 hours?

7. A man owes $2035. He arranges to make monthly payments, paying $40 the first month, and $5 more each succeeding month. How much does he still owe after 20 months?

8. A man saves $2 the first week, $4 the second week, $6 the third week, etc. How much does he save in a year?

9. A man walks along a road, going 10 yards the first minute, 12 yards the second minute, 14 yards the third, etc. How long is the road, if it takes him 12 minutes to cover it?

10. A depositor starts off a bank account with $5; the next week he deposits $10, the next $15, etc. What is his deposit on the 16th week?

Correct Answers

(You'll learn more by writing your own answers before comparing them with these.)

1. $19\frac{1}{2}$	5. 19,900	9. 252 yards
2. $1\frac{1}{5}$	6. 156	10. $80
3. 33	7. $285	
4. 64	8. $2756	

NOW, CHECK YOUR METHODS WITH OUR

SIMPLIFIED PROBLEM SOLUTIONS, WHICH FOLLOW.

PROBLEM SOLUTIONS	Series

Explanation of arithmetic progressions: a sequence of numbers each of which differs from the next preceding one by a fixed number called the common difference.

The numbers of the sequence are called the terms of the progression.

Let a = first term
    d = the common difference
    n = the number of terms considered
    L = nth or last term
    s = the sum of the sequence

We have by definition of an arithmetical progression:

$$a = \text{first term}$$
$$a + d = \text{second term}$$
$$a + 2d = \text{third term}$$
$$a + 3d = \text{fourth term}$$
$$. . .$$
$$a + (n-1)d = \text{nth term}$$
$$a + (n-1)d = L \text{ or last term}$$

Formula (arrived at algebraically with s = to the sum) for solving problems dealing with arithmetical

progression: $s = \dfrac{n}{2}(a + L)$

1. What number follows the last term of this series:
   2½, 6¾, 11, 15¼ . . .
   SOLUTION:
   Formula: $L = a + (n-1)d$
               $L = 2½ + (5-1)\,4¼$
               $L = 2½ + (4)\,4¼$
               $L = 2½ + 17$
               $L = 19½$

   a = first term, 2½
   n = number of terms, 5
   d = common difference, 4¼
   L = last term, 19½

   ANSWER: 19½

2. What number precedes the first term in this series:
   4, 13⅓, 44⁴⁄₉, 148⁴⁄₂₇ . . .
   This is a geometrical progression, which is a sequence of numbers in which the same quotient is obtained by dividing any term by the preceding term. The quotient is called the **ratio**.

SOLUTION: $13⅓ \div 4 = \dfrac{\overset{10}{\cancel{40}}}{3} \times \dfrac{1}{\underset{1}{\cancel{4}}} = \dfrac{10}{3}$

$= 3⅓$

3⅓ = ratio

$4 \div 3⅓ = \dfrac{4}{1} \times \dfrac{3}{10} = \dfrac{12}{10} = 1⅕$

ANSWER: Number preceding the first term is 1⅕.

3. What is the 5th term in this series:
   3, 5, 9, 17,—
   SOLUTION:
   Pattern: Double the difference between the two preceding terms in the series and then add this doubled difference to get the next term in the series.
   EXAMPLE:
   Term of series: 1st, 2nd, 3rd, 4th, 5th
   Numbers in series: 3   5   9 17 33
   Difference: 2   4   8 16

   ANSWER: 33 is the 5th term

4. Find the missing term in this series:
   3, 7, 18, 26, 37, 53, ____ , 96
   SOLUTION:
   Double the difference found by subtracting the first term from the second, add this to the next succeeding odd term, to get the next even term; continue this procedure of doubling the difference and adding until the desired term is obtained.

   All odd terms of the series are obtained by adding eleven to each preceding even term

   EXAMPLE:
   Term of series: 1st, 2nd, 3rd, 4th, 5th, 6th,
   Number in series: 3, 7, 18, 26, 37, 53,
   Difference: 4, 11, 8, 11, 16, 11,
                   7th, 8th
                   64, 96
                     32

   ANSWER: 64 is the missing term

5. SOLUTION:
   What is the number of combinations of 200 things taken 2 at a time: Each of 200 men shakes hands with each of the other 199, but A shaking hands with B is the same as B shaking hands with A (so we divide by 2)

   $$\frac{\overset{100}{\cancel{200}} \times 199}{\underset{1}{\cancel{2}}} = 19{,}900 \text{ handshakes}$$

   ANSWER: 19,900 handshakes

6. SOLUTION:
   Formula:

   $$s = \frac{n}{2}(a + L)$$

   $$s = \frac{\overset{6}{\cancel{12}}}{\underset{1}{\cancel{2}}}(1 + 12)$$

   $s = \text{sum}$
   $n = \text{no. of terms, 12}$
   $a = \text{first term, 1}$
   $L = \text{last term, 12}$

   $s = 6 \times 13 = 78$ No. of strikes in 12 hrs.

   ANSWER: Number of strikes in 24 hrs. is 2 $\times$ 78 = 156

7. SOLUTION:
   a) Formula for finding last term:
   $L = a + (n - 1)\ d$
   $L = 40 + (20 - 1)\ 5 =$
   $40 + (19 \times 5) =$
   $L = 40 + 95$
   $L = 135$

   $a = \text{1st term, 40}$
   $n = \text{no. of terms, 20}$
   $d = \text{com. diff., 5}$
   $L = \text{last no., } \mathbf{135}$
   $s = \text{sum}$

   b) Formula for finding the sum: $s = \dfrac{n}{2}(a + L)$

   $$s = \frac{\overset{10}{\cancel{20}}}{\underset{1}{\cancel{2}}}(40 + 135)$$

   $s = 10 \times 175$
   $s = \$1750$ paid after 20 payments
   $\$2035 - \$1750 = \$285$ he still owes

   ANSWER: $285

8. SOLUTION:
   a) Formula for finding last term:
   $L = a + (n - 1)\ d$ $a = \text{1st term, 2}$
   $L = 2 + (52 - 1)\ 2$ $n = \text{no. of terms, 52}$
   $L = 2 + (51 \times 2)$ $d = \text{com. diff., 2}$
                               $L = \text{last term, } \mathbf{104}$
   b) Formula for finding the sum:

   $$s = \frac{n}{2}(a + L)$$

   $$s = \frac{\overset{26}{\cancel{52}}}{\underset{1}{\cancel{2}}}(2 + 104)$$

   $s = 26 \times 106 = \$2756$ saved in a year

   ANSWER: $2756

9. SOLUTION:
   a) Formula for finding the last term:
   $L = a + (n - 1)\ d$
   $L = 10 + (12 - 1)\ 2$
   $L = 10 + (11 \times 2)$
   $L = 32$

   $a = \text{1st term, 10}$
   $n = \text{no. of terms, 12}$
   $d = \text{com. diff., 2}$
   $L = \text{last term, } \mathbf{32}$

   b) Formula for finding the sum:

   $$s = \frac{n}{2}(a + L)$$

   $$s = \frac{\overset{6}{\cancel{12}}}{\underset{1}{\cancel{2}}}(10 + 32)$$

   $s = 6 \times 42$
   $s = 252$ yds. covered in 12 min.

   ANSWER: 252 yards

10. SOLUTION:
    Formula for finding the last term:
    $L = a + (n - 1)\ d$
    $L = 5 + (16 - 1)\ 5$
    $L = 5 + (15 \times 5)$
    $L = 5 + 75 = \$80$ deposited

    $a = \text{1st term, \$5}$
    $n = \text{no. of terms, 16}$
    $d = \text{com. diff., 5}$
    $L = \text{last term, } \mathbf{80}$

    ANSWER: $80 deposited on the 16th week.

SYMBOLIC ARITHMETIC

173. Symbolic arithmetic is arithmetic expressed in terms of symbols and letters of the alphabet. Although in arithmetic the answers may be expressed by a number entirely different from those given in the problem, in symbolic arithmetic, the answer must be expressed in terms of the letters given. As in arithmetic, the letters may be added, subtracted, multiplied, or divided. Whatever operation would be performed in ordinary arithmetic, perform likewise in symbolic arithmetic.

ADDITION

174. In symbolic arithmetic, addition is expressed by plus (+) sign. The letters may be interchanged, although an alphabetic sequence is preferred.

  Example: The sum of a and b is $a + b$, or $b + a$. ($a + b$ is preferred)

  a. Two or more terms containing similar letters may be added.
  Example: $ab + 2ab = 3ab$.

  b. Where no sign exists a plus sign is understood. If the first term is plus, there is usually no sign written.

SUBTRACTION

175. Subtraction is indicated by a minus (—) sign. The first term in a subtraction is understood to be larger than the second, since in most of the problems you will be dealing with, the answer is positive. The letters may not be interchanged, and for that reason the wording should be carefully noticed.

  a. Two or more terms containing similar letters may be combined.
  Example: $-bc -3bc = -4bc$.

  b. If one term is + and a similar term is —, the result is zero.
  Example: $3ab - 3ab = 0$.

  c. Two or more similar terms may be combined according to their signs.
  Example: $2ab + 6ab - 3ab = 5ab$

176. Notice these different wordings which indicate subtraction:

  a. How much is "a" less "b"? *Answer:* a-b

  b. How much is "a" diminished by "b"? *Answer:* a-b

  c. How much is "b" subtracted from, or deducted from "a"? *Answer:* a-b

  d. If Joe has "a" dollars and Albert has "b" dollars, how much more money has Joe, assuming that he has more money?
  Answer: a-b dollars

MULTIPLICATION

177. In symbolic arithmetic, there are four different ways to indicate the multiplication of letters:

  a. By using the symbol "x". This is used when multiplying fractions.
  Example: $a/b \times c/d$

  b. By using a period mark written a little above the line. This symbol is used whenever an "x" occurs in the symbolic problem in order not to confuse it with the "x" of multiplication.
  Example: $a/b \cdot x/y$

  c. By using parentheses. These are used when groups of letters which are being added or subtracted are multiplied.
  Example: $a(b-c)$

  d. By simply placing the letters next to each other without using any symbol. The letters may be interchanged, although an alphabetic sequence is preferred.
  Example: "a" multiplied by "b" = ab, or ba. (ab is preferred.)

  e. A term multiplied by itself is equal to that term squared.
  Example: $a \times a = a^2$

  f. A term multiplied by 1 equals the term itself.
  Example: $ab \times 1 = ab$

178. As stated before, parentheses are used in some cases to indicate multiplication:

  a. If a letter is multiplied by the sum or difference of two or more letters, the latter group must be placed in parentheses to indicate multiplication by all parts of the group. The single letter may be placed in front of or behind the parentheses.

Example: "a" multiplied by "b—c" =
a(b—c) or (b—c)a.

b. If the sum or difference of letters is multiplied by another sum or difference of letters, then each group must be placed in parentheses. The groups may be interchanged.

Example: "a + b" multiplied by "c—d" =
(a+b) (c—d), or (c—d) (a+b)

DIVISION

179. Division, in symbolic arithmetic, is indicated by a fraction bar; the numerator is the dividend, and the denominator, the divisor. The letters may not be interchanged and, for that reason, the following wordings should be carefully studied:
a. How much is "a" divided
by "b"?   *Answer:* a/b
b. How many times is "a" contained in "b"?   *Answer:* b/a
c. If "a" is divided into "b" parts, how much is each part?   *Answer:* a/b

CANCELLATION

180. Cancellation, as in arithmetic, is a device to facilitate multiplication. If two similar letters or groups of letters (which are not being added or subtracted) are in the numerator and denominator of a fraction, they may be canceled.

Example: $\dfrac{ab}{b} = \dfrac{a\cancel{b}}{\cancel{b}} = a$

But in the fraction a-b the "b's" may not be canceled.
$$\frac{a-b}{b}$$

ADDITION AND SUBTRACTION OF FRACTIONS

181. Two or more fractions in letter form can be added or subtracted and expressed as a single term.
a. To find the L. C. D. of such fractions, multiply all the denominators. If the same denominator appears more than once, use it only once.
Example: The L.C.D. of a/b, c/d, and 2/d is bd.   (111e)
b. If both plus (+) signs and minus signs (—) are involved, keep these signs intact.

182. To add and subtract fractions:
a. Find the L.C.D.

b. Change each fraction to ones having the L.C.D. as the denominator.
c. Add and subtract the new numerators and place this sum over the L.C.D.
d. Reduce if possible.
Illustration:
Add a/b + c/d — 2/d
Solution:
L.C.D. = bd   (181a, 182a)
a/b=ad/bd, c/d = bc/bd
2/d = 2b/bd   (12d, 182b)
ad/bd + bc/bd — 2b/bd =
$$\frac{ad + bc - 2b}{bd}$$ (181b, 182c)

Answer: $\dfrac{ad + bc - 2b}{bd}$

CLEARING OF PARENTHESES

183. Multiplication as has been shown, is indicated in many cases by parentheses. These parentheses may be cleared, if necessary.
a. When one letter is multiplied by a group in parentheses, to clear parentheses, multiply each letter of the group inside the parentheses, by the letter outside, keeping the signs that were inside the parentheses.
Example: a(c—d) = ac — ad
b. When two groups of letters within parentheses are being multiplied, to clear the parentheses, make one group the multiplicand and the other the multiplier, and multiply the multiplicand by each term of the multiplier, keeping in mind that:
1. A plus sign × a plus sign = +
2. A minus sign × a minus sign = +
3. A minus sign × a plus sign = —
4. Where there is no sign, a plus sign is understood.
Example: (a—b) (a—b) =
a—b
a—b
$$a^2 - ab - ab + b^2$$
(177d, e)
$$a^2 - 2ab + b^2$$ (175a)

MULTIPLICATION OF FRACTIONS

184. The multiplication of symbolic fractions is performed in a manner similar to that of arithmetic fractions. Cancellation may be employed.

a. If a letter is multiplied by a fraction, multiply the numerator of the fraction by the letter. A letter has the denominator 1 understood.
Example:

S multiplied by $\dfrac{X}{M} = S/1 \cdot X/M$ (177b)

$$= SX/M$$

b. two or more fractions are being multiplied, multiply numerator by numerator, and denominator by denominator. Cancellation may be employed.

Example: $r \div b : v \div tr = rv \div vtr = v \div bt$

DIVISION OF FRACTIONS

185. To divide symbolic fractions, invert the second fraction and multiply. Cancellation may be employed.
Example:

$$S/T \div RS/BT = S/T \times BT/RS = B/R$$

RULES FOR ALGEBRA

Rules for signed numbers:

1. **Addition**—To add signed numbers whose signs are alike, find the sum of their absolute values and use the common sign.

   To add unlike signed numbers, find the difference between their absolute values and use the sign of the number with the larger absolute value.

2. **Subtraction**—To subtract signed numbers. mentally change the sign of the subtrahend and proceed as in algebraic addition.

3. **Multiplication**—To multiply two monomials:
   1) Multiply the coefficients;
   2) Give each letter in the product an exponent which is the sum of the exponents which that letter has in the original expressions. When two numbers having like signs are multiplied the product is positive. When two numbers having unlike signs are multiplied the product is negative.

4. **Division**—To divide one monomial by another:
   1) Divide the coefficients:
   2) Give each letter in the quotient an exponent which is the difference between the exponents of that letter in the dividend and the divisor. The quotient of two numbers with like signs is positive. The quotient of two numbers with unlike signs is negative.

DIRECTIONS FOR SOLVING PROBLEMS

1) Read the problem, and determine what number (or numbers) you are asked to find.

2) Represent the unknown number (or numbers) algebraically.
   a. If you are asked to find only one number. let some letter equal or represent it.
   b. If you are asked to find more than one number, then let some letter equal one of them; then represent each of the other numbers in terms of this letter.
   c. When possible, make a drawing to show steps a and b above, and the number relations of the problem.

3) From the condition of the problem—find two expressions that are equal. Then connect these two equal expressions by an equal sign, forming an equation.

4) Solve this equation for the unknown letter. If you are asked to find more than one number, do this from step 2b above.

5) Prove by seeing that your answer satisfies all the conditions of the problem.

FACTORS

When two or more numbers are multiplied together to form a product, the numbers multiplied are called **factors** of that product. For example, 3 and 5 are factors of 15, a and b are factors of ab, and x and x are factors of x^2. Every number is divisible by itself and 1. $15 \times 1 = 15$. $x(1) = x$. It is customary, however, to consider as factors **only whole numbers other than 1.** Numbers which have no factors, other than themselves and one, are said to be prime. The numbers 2, 3, 5, 7, 11, etc., are prime as are x, y, a, or any other literal number.

Find the factors of $3x^3 + 6x^2y + 9x^2z + 3x^2$.
Solution: A study of the terms of this polynomial shows that the monomial expression $3x^2$ is contained in each. $3x^2$, then, is one of the factors of the polynomial. The other factor may be obtained by dividing the given expression by the monomial factor already found.

$$\frac{3x^3 + 6x^2y + 9x^2z + 3x^2}{3x^2} = x + 2y + 3z + 1$$

We thus obtain the factors
$$3x^2 (x + 2y + 3z + 1)$$

RULE:
To find the factors of an expression which is the product of a monomial and a polynomial
1. Study the terms of the given expression to obtain the largest monomial factor common to them all.
2. Divide the expression mentally by this monomial to obtain the polynomial factor.
3. Indicate the product of the factors found.

Let us consider the product of the binomials $x - 2y$ and $3x + 4y$ in which the terms of one are respectively similar to those of the other. If the multiplication is performed in the usual way, it is seen that the first term of the product, $3x^2$, is obtained by multiplying the first terms of the binomials: namely, 3x and x. In like manner the last term of the product, $- 8y^2$, is obtained by multiplying the last terms of the binomials: namely, 4y and $- 2y$. The middle term of the product, $- 2xy$, is obtained by adding to the product of x and 4y the product of 3x and $-2y$. These are called **cross products.**

$$
\begin{array}{r}
3x + 4y \\
\underline{x - 2y} \\
3x^2 + 4xy \\
\underline{- 6xy - 8y^2} \\
3x^2 - 2xy - 8y^2
\end{array}
$$

Factors of Quadratic Trinomials

We see that the product of two binomials having similar terms is usually a trinomial. This trinomial always contains the squares of the letters involved and hence is called a quadratic trinomial (from the Latin word **quadratus,** meaning "square"). Find the factors of $x^2 - 6x + 8$.

From what we have just learned we know that the trinomial will factor into two binomials, so we write two parentheses next to each other (   ) (   ). What will be the first term in each binomial? They will have to be factors of x^2, so x and x. Likewise, the second term in each binomial will be factors of 8. Will they be 4 and 2, or 8 and 1? We will have to make our choice on the basis of the middle term of the trinomial. (x-4) (x-2) will be our choice. So $x^2 - 6x + 8 = (x - 4) (x - 2)$. Check by multiplying the factors.

Solving Quadratic Equations by Factoring

A **quadratic** equation is an equation which contains the second power of the unknown quantity, but no higher power. For example:
$x^2 - bx = c^2$; $x^2 = 9$; $2x^2 + 6x = 10$; $x^2 - 4x + 3 = 0$ are quadratic equations.

Quadratic equations as well as literal equations may often be solved by factoring. In many cases we require more advanced methods, which are explained later. But the method of solving by factoring, where it is possible, is shown by the following example:

Solve: $\quad\quad x^2 - 3x = 28$
Solution: $\quad x^2 - 3x - 28 = 0$
$\quad\quad\quad\quad\quad\quad\quad$ Transposing the 28.

$(x - 7) \ (x + 4) = 0 \quad$ factoring the left member.

$x - 7 = 0 \quad x + 4 = 0$
$\quad x = 7 \quad\quad x = -4$

By setting each factor equal to 0, we obtain two simple equations and solve each.

It is important for you to remember that **a quadratic equation always has two roots.** These roots may be equal. The equation above states that this product equals 0. No product can equal 0 unless one of the factors equals 0, but the product will equal 0 if any factor in it equals 0.

RULE: To solve a quadratic equation by factoring:
1. Transpose every term to the left member of the equation, thus making the right member 0.

2. Factor the left member.
3. Set each factor which contains the unknown quantity equal to 0, and solve the resulting simple equations.

The results obtained are the roots of the quadratic equation.

Solution of Complete Quadratic Equations by a Formula:

$ax^2 + bx + c = 0$ represents **any** complete quadratic equation, since a, b, c may have **any** numerical values. When a complete quadratic equation is arranged in this form, with descending powers of x in the left member, and with the right member 0, it is in standard form.

The roots of this equation in terms of coefficients a, b, and c are expressed by the formula:

$$x = \frac{-b \pm \sqrt{b^2 - 4ac}}{2a}$$

This is called the quadratic formula. This formula is of the greatest importance, since, as you know, not all quadratic equations can be factored. You should memorize this formula thoroughly.

The way in which this formula is used to solve quadratic equations is shown by the following:

Solve $2x^2 + x = 6$.

SOLUTION: Transpose every term to the left member as in the equation $ax^2 + bx + c = 0$
We obtain $\qquad 2x^2 + x - 6 = 0$
Then   a (the coefficient of x^2) = 2
         b (the coefficient of x) = 1
         c (the term without x) = −6
Substituting these values in the formula

$$x = \frac{-b \pm \sqrt{b^2 - 4\,ac}}{2a}$$

gives us $x = \dfrac{-1 \pm \sqrt{(1)^2 - 4 \cdot 2(-6)}}{2 \cdot 2}$

$$= \frac{-1 \pm \sqrt{1 + 48}}{4}$$

$$= \frac{-1 \pm 7}{4} = \frac{-1 + 7}{4} \text{ and } \frac{-1 - 7}{4}$$

$$= \frac{3}{2} \text{ and } - 2$$

(1) Write the equation in standard form.
(2) Write down the values of a, b, and c.
(3) Substitute these values in the formula.
(4) Perform all operations.
(5) Check each root.

RULE: Roots are sometimes the same.

ANGLE OF ELEVATION:

PC is a pole, standing on level ground. The sun casts a shadow, AC · 6. A line segment drawn from A (the end of the shadow) through P (the top of the pole) would be directed at the sun. The angle ($<$ CAP) is called the **angle of elevation** of the sun.

ILLUSTRATION

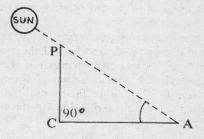

CONGRUENT TRIANGLES: Triangles whose vertices can be made to correspond so that lengths of corresponding sides and the measures of corresponding angles are equal.

Some problems involve Trigonometry. The following is a brief explanation to give you some knowledge of Trigonometry.

The word "trigonometry" is derived from two Greek words which mean "triangle measurement." It is that branch of mathematics which deals with the relations between the sides and the angles of triangles.

One of the main purposes of trigonometry is to obtain formulas by means of which distances and angles may be measured (indirectly). Trigonometry will enable you to compute the values of the unknown parts.

The value of the ratios of the sides of the right triangles depends upon the size of angle A and not upon the size of the right triangles. The values of these ratios change as angle A changes and for this reason are called **functions** of angle A.

ILLUSTRATION

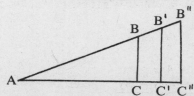

Trigonometric
functions of an
acute angle:

1. The **sine** of an acute angle of a right triangle is the ratio of the opposite leg to the hypotenuse.
2. The **cosine** of an acute angle of a right triangle is the ratio of the adjacent leg to the hypotenuse.
3. The **tangent** of an acute angle of a right triangle is the ratio of the opposite leg to the adjacent leg.

It is customary, in the study of trigonometry, to let the capital letters A, B, and C denote the angles of a right triangle, C being the right angle, and the small letters a, b, and c denote the corresponding opposite sides.

From the right $\triangle$ ABC,

the sine of $\angle$ A (written sin A) $= \dfrac{a}{c}$

the cosine of $\angle$ A (written cos A) $= \dfrac{b}{c}$

the tangent of $\angle$ A (written tan A) $= \dfrac{a}{b}$

In like manner, sin B $= \dfrac{b}{c}$; cos B $= \dfrac{a}{c}$;

tan B $= \dfrac{b}{a}$

ILLUSTRATION

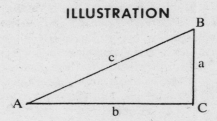

Given the tangent of an angle you can find the measure of an angle by consulting a "Table of Trigonometric Functions." Conversely, given the measures of an angle you can find the tangent of the angle.

Proceed the same way when given the sine of an angle or the cosine of an angle.

ALGEBRA PROBLEMS

1. Reduce to lowest terms $\dfrac{X-4}{X^2-X-12}$

   Answers:

   (1) $\dfrac{x}{x+3}$ (2) $\dfrac{3x}{x-3}$ (3) $\dfrac{1}{x+3}$ (4) $\dfrac{x}{3x+3}$

2. Find the logarithm of 1.516
   - (1) 1807
   - (2) 1.0879
   - (3) 0.1759
   - (4) 1.1870

3. Find the positive geometric mean between 2 and 32
   (1) 12   (2) 8   (3) 14   (4) 16

4. The first term of an arithmetic progression is 3 and the sixth term is 23. The common difference is
   (1) 6   (2) 8   (3) 4   (4) 2

5. The sum of the infinite series 6, 3, 1 ½, — is
   (1) 10   (2) 11   (3) 12   (4) 13

6. A leg of an isosceles triangle is 16 and a base angle is 64°. The altitude on the base (to the nearest integer) is
   (1) 10   (2) 12   (3) 14   (4) 16

7. A solution of salt water is 12% salt. Another solution is 4% salt. How many pounds of the second solution must be added to 24 pounds of the first solution to make a 10% solution?
   (1) 8   (2) 10   (3) 12   (4) 16

8. If the roots of a quadratic equation are real and equal, the discriminant of the equation is
   (1) greater than 0   (3) equal to 0
   (2) less than 0   (4) impossible to determine

9. The sum of the first 16 terms of the series 1, 3, 5—is
   (1) 240   (2) 266   (3) 256   (4) 650

10. A geometric mean between two numbers is 8. If one of the numbers is 2, the other is
    (1) 26   (2) 28   (3) 30   (4) 32

11. Find, correct to the nearest degree, the smaller acute angle of the right triangle whose legs are 14 and 20.
    (1) 25°   (2) 30°   (3) 35°   (4) 40°

12. In slight stretching of elastic bodies, the stretch varies directly as the force. If a spring is stretched 1 inch by a force of 25 pounds, the amount of stretch produced by a 15-pound force is
    (1) 3/5   (2) 1/8   (3) 6/8   (4) 15/50

13. The first term of an arithmetic progression is 5 and the second term is 7; the sum of the first 10 terms is
    (1) 120   (2) 130   (3) 140   (4) 150

14. If 2 and 54 are the first and fourth terms respectively of a geometric progression, the *second* and *third* terms are
    (1) 6, 8   (2) 6, 18   (3) 8, 24   (4) 12, 36

15. When a dealer heard that the price of a certain product was about to advance $3 per barrel, he bought a number of barrels of this product for $300. Had he bought at the new price, he would have obtained 5 barrels fewer for the same money. How many barrels did he buy?
    (1) 25   (2) 30   (3) 35   (4) 40

16. A number of men agree to contribute equally toward a $14 fund. Later four more men joined the group, causing the individual contributions to be 40 cents less. How many men were originally in the group?
    (1) 3   (2) 8   (3) 10   (4) 14

17. Given: $y = \dfrac{1-x}{x^2}$. Indicate whether each of the statements below is true or false.
    (1) If x is a positive number greater than 1, then y is negative.
    (2) If x is less than O, y is positive.
    (3) if x is greater than O, but less than 1, y is positive.
    (4) As x increases, y decreases.

18. The roots of the equation $x^2 + 16 = 0$.
    (1) real and equal
    (2) real and unequal
    (3) imaginary

19. The graph of the equation $2x^2 - 3y^2 = 5$ is
    (1) a circle   (2) an ellipse   (3) a hyperbola

20. The sum of the roots of the quadratic equation is $2x^2 - 4x - 5 = 0$
    (1) -4 (2) 2   (3) -2 (4) 4

21. If the parcel post rate is p cents for the first pound and a cents for each additional pound, express in cents the cost of sending a package of n pounds where n is an integer greater than 1.
    (1) $p + a(n-1)$ (3) $np - a$
    (2) $p + (n-a)1$ (4) $p - a(n-1)$

22. Two geometric means between 3 and 192 are
    (1) 12 and 48   (3) 16 and 52
    (2) 14 and 50   (4) 10 and 62

23. The 31st term of the progression 3, 7, 11—is
    (1) 121   (2) 123   (3) 137   (4) 86

24. To the nearest degree, the elevation of the sun when an 8-foot vertical pole casts a shadow 10 feet long is
    (1) 46°   (2) 18°   (3) 80°   (4) 39°

25. The sum of the infinite geometric progression whose first term is 2 and whose ratio is 2/3 is
    (1) 6   (2) 8   (3) 10   (4) 9

26. If the discriminant of a quadratic equation is -49, the roots are:
    (1) imaginary
    (2) real and unequal
    (3) real and equal

27. The graph of the equation $2x^2 - 2y^2 = 15$ is
    (1) a circle   (2) an ellipse   (3) a hyperbola

28. Each of the expressions in parts (1)-(5) is equivalent to two of the four choices given. Write in the space to the right of the question the numbers (1) through (5) and after each indicate the correct choices by writing two of the letters a, b, c and d.

(1) $(x^2)^{-3}$ equals (a) x^{-6}, (b) $\dfrac{1}{(x^2)^3}$, (c) x^{-8}, (d) $\dfrac{1}{\sqrt[3]{x^2}}$

(2) $.000027$ equals (a) $\dfrac{27}{1000000}$, (b) 2.7×10^{-6}, (c) $(.003)^3$, (d) 2.7×10^{-5}

(3) $\dfrac{1 - \dfrac{1}{a}}{1 - \dfrac{1}{a^2}}$ equals (a) $\dfrac{1}{1 + \dfrac{1}{a}}$, (b) $\dfrac{1}{1 - \dfrac{1}{a}}$, (c) $\dfrac{a}{a+1}$, (d) $\dfrac{1}{a+1}$

(4) $(2^x)(4^x)$ equals (a) 8^x, (b) 8^{2x}, (c) 2^{3x}, (d) 4^{3x}

(5) Log $10x^2$ equals (a) $2 \log 10x$, (b) $20 \log x$, (c) $\log 5x + \log 2x$, (d) $1 + 2 \log x$

29. A man was r years old m years ago. His age b years from now would be expressed by
    (1) $r + m + b$ (3) $m + r - b$
    (2) $r - m + b$ (4) $b + m - r$

30. If x varies directly as y^2 and if $x = 9$ when $y = 2$, what is the value of x when $y = 8$?
    (1) 168   (2) 144   (3) 966   (4) 130

31. At a point 20 feet from the base of a flagpole the angle of elevation to its top is 58°. To the nearest foot, the height of the flagpole is, in feet,
    (1) 26   (2) 28   (3) 24   (4) 32

32. The 13th term of the progression 7, 4, 1, ...is
    (1) 28   (2) -28 (3) 29   (4) -29

33. Using the formula: $A = P(1 + rt)$, find A when $P = 500$, $r = .03$ and $t = 15$.
    (1) 720   (2) 725   (3) 625   (4) 800

34. If r varies directly as s and if $r = 3$ when $s = 8$, find r when $s = 12$.
    (1) 4½   (2) 5   (3) 6   (4) 7½

35. Solve for x the equation $\sqrt{x+2}=3$
    (1) 6   (2) 7   (3) 8   (4) 9

36. The positive root of the equation: $2x^2-3x-2=0$ is
    (1) 1 (2) 2 (3) 3 (4) 4

37. The hypotenuse of a right triangle is 12 and one of the acute angles is 28°. To the nearest tenth, the longer leg of the triangle is
    (1) 8.4   (2) 10.8   (3) 10.6   (4) 14.8

38. The roots of the equation $2x^2-8x+3=0$ are
    (1) equal and rational
    (2) unequal and rational
    (3) unequal and irrational

39. The straight line $y=mx$ and the circle $x^2+y^2=9$, when drawn on the same set of axes,
    (1) intersect regardless of what value m may have
    (2) may be tangent
    (3) may not intersect

40. If log r + log s=log t, then
    (1) log (r + s) = log t
    (2) r + s = t
    (3) rs = t

Correct Answers

(You'll learn more by writing your own answers before comparing them with these.)

1. 3	12. 1	23. 2	30. 2
2. 3	13. 3	24. 4	31. 4
3. 2	14. 2	25. 1	32. 4
4. 3	15. 1	26. 1	33. 2
5. 3	16. 3	27. 3	34. 1
6. 3	17. all true	28. (1) ab	35. 2
7. 1	18. 3	(2) ad	36. 2
8. 3	19. 3	(3) ac	37. 3
9. 3	20. 2	(4) ac	38. 3
10. 4	21. 1	(5) cd	39. 1
11. 3.	22. 1	29. 1	40. 3

PROBLEM SOLUTIONS   Algebra

1. Reduce to lowest terms:
$$\frac{x-4}{x^2-x-12}$$

SOLUTION:
Factoring $x^2-x-12=$
$$(x-4)(x+3)$$

$$\frac{\overset{1}{\cancel{x-4}}}{\underset{1}{\cancel{(x-4)}}(x+3)}=\frac{1}{x+3} \qquad \text{(No. 3 answer)}$$

ANSWER: $\dfrac{1}{x+3}$

2. Find the logarithm of 1.516.
Explanation:
We must consider two parts of the logarithm of a number, the characteristic and the mantissa.
a. The characteristic is the integral part of a logarithm and is numerically equal to the number of digits between the line and the decimal point.

Ex.

Number	2|659.4	0.7|82	0.0006|5
Characteristic	3	−1	−4

SOLUTION:
So write down the given number and draw a vertical line just to the right of the first non-zero digit

1\|,516 characteristic 0

It is positive if the decimal point is to the right of the line and negative if it is to the left, e.g.

Number:	2|659.4	0.7|82
Characteristic:	3	−1

b. The mantissa is independent of the position of the decimal point. The tables of logarithms contain only the mantissas.

	(Mantissa)
For example, 1516 =	.1807
151.6 =	.1807
1.516 =	.1807

To find log of 1.516, find the mantissas from log tables for 1510 and 1520; they are 1790 and 1818. The difference between these two mantissas is 28. Since 1516 is .6

of the interval from 1510 to 1520, by principle of proportional parts, we add to 1790:

$$.6 \times 28 = 16.8 = 17$$

$$10 \left\{ 6 \left\{ \begin{array}{l} 1510 = .1790 \\ 17 \\ 1516 = .1807 \\ 1520 = .1818 \end{array} \right. 28 \right.$$

Hence log 1.516 = 0.1807

ANSWER: 0.1807

(Answer No. 1 most nearly correct)

3. Explanation of Geometrical means: The first and last terms of a geometrical progression are called the **extremes,** while the remaining terms are called the geometrical **means.** To insert "n" geometrical means between **two** given numbers is to find a geometrical progression of $n + 2$ terms having the two given numbers for extremes.

$$\dfrac{\text{Extreme } 2}{\text{mean } \quad x} = \dfrac{x \quad \text{mean}}{32 \quad \text{extreme}}$$

SOLUTION: According to proportion
2:x :: x:32   (product of the means = the
$x^2 = 64$ product of the extremes)
$x = 8$

ANSWER: 8   (No. 2 answer)

4. Explanation of Arithmetical progression. An arithmetical progression is a sequence of numbers each of which differs from the next preceding one by a **fixed number** called the common difference.

Ex. 1,2,3, . . . ,   2,4,6, . . .

However, the formulas for finding the sum and the last term cannot be used unless the common difference is a fixed number.

The numbers of the sequence are called the terms of the progression.

Let d = the common difference
n = the number of terms considered
L = nth or last term
s = the sum of the sequence

We have by definition of an arithmetical progression:

a = first term
$a + d$ = second term
$a + 2d$ = third term
$a + 3d$ = fourth term
. . .

$$a + (n-1)\, d = \text{nth term}$$

Formula (arrived at algebraically with s = the sum of the terms) for solving problems dealing with arithmetical progressions.

$$s = \dfrac{n}{2}\,(a + L)$$

SOLUTION: Use formula for last term.
$a + d\,(n-1) = L$
$3 + d\,(5) = 23$ (where 23 = L)
$5d = 20$ (sub. 3 from ea. side; a = first term = 3)
$d = 4$, common difference   (divide ea. side by 5)

n = no. of terms, 6
d = com. diff., 4 (No. 3 answer)

ANSWER: 4

5. SOLUTION:

Formula: $s = \dfrac{a}{1 - r}$ (this is true only for an infinite [non-ending] geometric series when the ratio lies between -1 and 1)

$$s = \dfrac{6}{1 - \frac{1}{2}} = \dfrac{6}{\frac{1}{2}} = 6 \times 2 = 12$$

a = 1st term, 6
r = com. ratio, ½
s = sum

ANSWER: 12   (No. 3 answer)

6. EXPLANATION:

The sine of an angle is an important ratio. In any right triangle the sine (abbreviated sin) of either acute angle is the ratio of the leg opposite the angle to the hypotenuse.

SOLUTION:

Formula: $\sin 64° = \dfrac{\text{opposite side}}{\text{hypotenuse}}$

sin of < 64° = .8988 (according to table)
16 = hypotenuse
Let x = opposite side

$$\dfrac{x}{16} = .8988$$

$x = .8988 \times 16$
$x = 14.3708$ or 14 opposite side

(No. 3 answer)

ILLUSTRATION

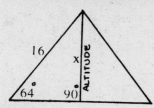

ANSWER: 14

7. SOLUTION: lbs. of salt in 1st sol. + lbs. of salt in 2nd sol. = lbs. of salt in mixture.

Let x = number of lbs. for 2nd solution
12% = .12   4% = .04   10% = .10
.12 (24 lb.) + .04 (x) = .10 (24 + x)
$$2.88 + .04x = 2.4 + .10x$$
$$.48 = .06x \quad \text{(multiply both sides by 100)}$$
$$48 = 6x$$
$$8 = x$$
(No. 1 answer)

ANSWER: 8 pounds

8. SOLUTION:
The formula for solving a quadratic equation is:
$$x = \frac{-b \pm \sqrt{b^2 - 4ac}}{2a}$$

The discriminant is the radicand $b^2 - 4ac$. When the roots are real and equal, the discriminant is zero; e.g. (x + 2) (x + 2) = 0
$$x = -2$$
$$x = -2$$

$$x^2 + 4x + 4 = 0 \quad a = 1$$
$$\sqrt{16 - 16} = 0 \quad b = 4$$
$$c = 4$$

Or when $b^2 - 4ac = 0$ your roots are real and equal to 0.
(No. 3 answer)

ANSWER: equal to zero

9. SOLUTION:

Formula: $s = \frac{n}{2}(a + L)$ a = 1

Must solve for last term first:
n = no. of terms, 16
d = com. diff., 2
$$L = a + d(n - 1) \quad L = \text{last term}, \quad 31$$
$$L = 1 + 2(15)$$
$$L = 31$$

$$s = \frac{n}{2}(a + L)$$

$$s = \frac{\overset{8}{\cancel{16}}}{\underset{1}{\cancel{2}}}(1 + 31)$$

$$s = 8(32)$$
$$s = 256 \qquad \text{(No. 3 answer)}$$

ANSWER: 256

10. See No. 3 of preceding section for explanation of geometrical means.
SOLUTION: 8 = geometric mean
2 = one number
x = other number

then $\dfrac{2}{8} = \dfrac{8}{x}$
$$64 = 2x$$
$$32 = x \text{ or the other number}$$
(No. 4 answer)

ANSWER: 32

11. Explanation: In any right triangle the tangent (abbreviated tan) of either acute angle is the ratio of the length of the leg opposite the angle to the length of the leg adjacent to the angle.
SOLUTION:
14 and 20 are legs
$$\tan \angle m = \frac{\text{opp. side}}{\text{adj. side}}$$

$$\tan \angle m = \frac{14}{20}$$

$$\frac{14}{20} = .7$$

ILLUSTRATION

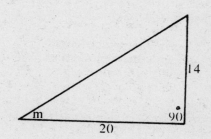

Angle which has a tangent equal to .7 is 35°
Therefore, tan 35° = .7 (according to table)
$$\angle m = 35° \qquad \text{No. 3 answer)}$$

ANSWER: 35°

12. SOLUTION:

Solve by using direct proportion
x = amount of stretch

$$\frac{15}{25} = \frac{x}{1''}$$

$$25x = 15 \text{ in.}$$

$$x = \frac{15}{25} = \frac{3}{5}$$ (No. 1 answer)

ANSWER: $\frac{3}{5}$

13. SOLUTION:

Formula: $s = \frac{n}{2}(a + L)$

Must solve for last term:

Formula: $L = a + d(n - 1)$
$$L = 5 + 2(9)$$
$$L = 23$$

a = 1st term, 5
n = no. of terms, 10
d = com. diff., 2
L = last term, **23**
s = sum

Therefore: $s = \frac{n}{2}(a + L)$

$$s = \frac{\overset{5}{\cancel{10}}}{\underset{1}{\cancel{2}}}(5 + 23)$$

$$s = 5 \times 28$$

$$s = 140$$ (No. 3 answer)

ANSWER: **140**

14. SOLUTION:

Let r be the common ratio (or the number by which each term is multiplied to get the next)

2 = 1st term (extreme)
2r = 2nd term (means)
$2r^2$ = 3rd term (means)
54 = 4th term (extreme)

Product of the extremes equals the product of the means.

$$2r(2r^2) = 108$$
$$4r^3 = 108 \quad \text{(divide by 4)}$$
$$r^3 = 27$$
$$r = 3$$

$2 \times 3 = 6$ 2nd term
$2 \times 9 = 18$ 3rd term (No. 2 answer)

ANSWER: **6, 18**

15. SOLUTION:

Let x = present cost per barrel
x + 3 = advanced price

$$\frac{\$300}{x} = \frac{\$300}{x + 3} + 5 \quad \text{(clear denominators)}$$

(300x cancel on both sides Cancel both denom. first

$$\frac{\cancel{300x} + 900}{\cancel{x(x+3)}} = \frac{\cancel{300x} + 5(x)(x + 3)}{\cancel{x(x+3)}}$$

$$900 = 5x^2 + 15x$$
(divide by 5)
$$180 = x^2 + 3x$$

factors for: $x^2 + 3x - 180 = 0$
$$(x + 15)(x - 12) = 0$$
$$-15 = x \text{ (neg. sol. is of no value)}$$
$$+12 = x \text{ (present price per barrel)}$$

$$\frac{\$300}{\$12} = 25 \text{ barrels}$$

ANSWER: **25 barrels** (No. 1 answer)

16. SOLUTION:

Let x = No. of men originally in group.
x + 4 = No. of men after 4 joined group.

$\frac{14}{x}$ = contributions per person

$$\frac{14}{x} - .40 = \frac{14}{x + 4}$$

$$14x + 56 - .40x(x + 4) = 14x$$
$$56 - .4x^2 - 1.6x = 0$$
$$.4x^2 + 1.6x - 56 = 0 \quad \text{(Multiply by 10)}$$
$$4x^2 + 16x - 560 = 0 \quad \text{(Divide by 4)}$$
$$x^2 + 4x - 140 = 0$$
$$(x + 14)(x - 10) = 0$$
$$x = -14 \text{ (No. of men can't be negative)}$$
$$x = 10, \text{ number of men}$$

ANSWER: **10 men** (No. 3 answer)

17. $y = \dfrac{1 - x}{x^2}$

SOLUTION:

1) As soon as the value of x is greater than 1, the law of signs for subtraction would make the numerator a negative number. x^2 is always positive. In dividing this negative by a positive denominator, the value of y is negative.

2) Using the above reasoning and having x as a negative number, the numerator becomes a positive number. The rest follows.

3) In this case, the numerator is a positive quantity and again the result of division is a positive quotient.

4) The denominator, as divisor, increases while numerator decreases, making the quotient constantly smaller.

Therefore: all answers are true.

ANSWER: all true

18. SOLUTION:

$$x^2 + 16 = 0$$
$$x^2 = -16$$

$$x = i\sqrt{-16} = i\sqrt{-1} \times \sqrt{16} \qquad (-1 = i^2)$$
$$x = i\sqrt{16}$$
$$x = \pm 4i \text{ (an imaginary number)}$$
(No. 3 answer)

ANSWER: an imaginary number

19. $2x^2 - 3y^2 = 5$

SOLUTION:
Dividing by 5, we have the standard form
Standard form for hyperbola is:

$$\frac{x^2}{a^2} - \frac{y^2}{b^2} = 1$$

$$\frac{2x^2}{5} - \frac{3y^2}{5} = 1 \text{ or } \frac{x^2}{5/2} - \frac{y^2}{5/3} = 1$$
(No. 3 answer)

ANSWER: A hyperbola

20. $2x^2 - 4x - 5 = 0$

Solution of a complete quadratic equation by a formula

$ax^2 + bx + c = 0$ represents **any** complete quadratic equation since a, b, c may have any numerical value. The roots of this equation in terms of coefficients a, b, and c are expressed by the formula:

$$x = \frac{-b \pm \sqrt{b^2 - 4ac}}{2a}$$

a (the coefficient of x^2) = 2
b (the coefficient of x) = −4
c (the constant term without x) = −5

$$x = \frac{4 \pm \sqrt{(4)^2 - 4 \times 2(-5)}}{2 \times 2}$$

$$x = \frac{4 \pm \sqrt{16 + 40}}{4} =$$

$$x = \frac{4 \pm 2\sqrt{14}}{4} = 1 \pm \tfrac{1}{2}\sqrt{14}$$

$$(1 + \tfrac{1}{2}\sqrt{14}) + (1 - \tfrac{1}{2}\sqrt{14}) = 2$$

ANSWER: 2   (No. 2 answer)

21. SOLUTION:

$p + a(n - 1)$

n is greater than 1, so express additional pounds (after the first) as n − 1. Express "a" as additional cost which we multiply by additional pounds in order to find increased rate.
(No. 1 answer)

ANSWER: $p + a(n - 1)$

22. See No. 3, of preceding section for explanation of geometrical means

Solution: 3 = first term (extreme)
3r = second term (means)
$3r^2$ = third term
192 = fourth term

$$\frac{3}{3r} = \frac{3r^2}{192}$$
$$576 = 9r^3$$
$$64 = r^3$$
$$4 = r$$

3×4 = second term, 12
3×4^2 = third term, 48
(No. 1 answer)

ANSWER: 12 and 48

23. SOLUTION:

Formula $L = a + d(n - 1)$
a = 1st term, 3
d = common difference, 4
n = no. of terms, 31
L = last term
L = 3 + 4(30)
L = 3 + 120
L = 123 (No. 2 answer)

ANSWER: 123

24. See No. 11 of preceding section for explanation of tangent.

SOLUTION: 8 ft. and 10 ft. are legs

$$\tan \angle A = \frac{\text{opposite side}}{\text{adjacent side}}$$

$$\tan A = \frac{8}{10} = .8$$

ILLUSTRATION

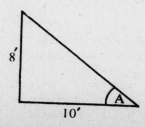

angle which has a tangent equal to .8 is 39°
(No. 4 answer)

ANSWER: ∠ of elevation is 39°

25. SOLUTION:
Formula for the sum of an infinite geometric progression is

$$s = \frac{a}{1-r} \quad (\text{when} -1 < r < 1)$$

a = 1st term, 2
r = ratio, ⅔

$$s = \frac{2}{1-\frac{2}{3}} = \frac{2}{\frac{1}{3}} = 2 \times 3 = 6$$

$$s = 6 \qquad (\text{No. 1 answer})$$

ANSWER: 6

26. SOLUTION:

Formula $\quad x = \dfrac{-b \pm \sqrt{b^2 - 4ac}}{2a}$

The discriminant = $b^2 - 4ac$
When $b^2 - 4ac$ is negative your roots are imaginary.
Radical of a negative number is imaginary $\sqrt{-49}$; 49 is negative, therefore roots are imaginary. (No. 1 answer)

ANSWER: Imaginary

27. SOLUTION:
In working with plotting geometric figures on a graph, one must consider the x-axis and y-axis as fitting into the formula for a hyperbola.
Proof for the derivation of this formula is obtained in any book on analytic geometry. It is stated here that the equation for a hyperbola is in the form of:

$$\frac{x^2}{a^2} + \frac{y^2}{b^2} = 1 \text{ or}$$
$$b^2x^2 + a^2y^2 = a^2b^2$$

Formula for the circle becomes $x^2 + y^2 = r^2$ where the center is at the origin or zero.
Equations for the circle whose center is at (h, k).
Example: No. 1 $(x - h)^2 + (y - k)^2 = r^2$
Example: No. 2 $(x - 2)^2 + (y - 4)^2 = r^2$
In any case, to have a circle, the coefficients of x^2 and y^2 must be equal (including sign.)
Note: See No. 19 of preceding chapter for examples for hyperbola
Therefore, $2x^2 - 2y^2 = 15$

$$\frac{x^2}{\frac{15}{2}} - \frac{y^2}{\frac{15}{2}} = 1, \text{ therefore a hyperbola}$$

(No. 3 answer)

ANSWER: a hyperbola

28. SOLUTION:
1) $(x^2)^{-3}$ equals (a) x^{-6} (answer a)

$\quad (x^2)^{-3}$ equals (b) $\dfrac{1}{(x^2)^3}$ (answer b)

because any factor of the numerator may be transferred to the denominator or vice versa, if the sign of the exponent of the factor is changed.

ANSWER: (ab)

2) $.000027 = $ (d) answer 2.7×10^{-5}

$\quad .000027 = $ (a) answer $\dfrac{27}{1,000,000}$

ANSWER: (ad)

3)

$$\frac{1 - \dfrac{1}{a}}{1 - \dfrac{1}{a^2}} = \frac{\dfrac{a-1}{a}}{\dfrac{a^2-1}{a^2}}$$

$$\frac{\cancel{a-1}}{\cancel{a}} \times \frac{\cancel{a^2}^{\,a}}{\cancel{(a-1)}(a+1)} = \frac{a}{a+1}$$

(answer c)

ANSWER: $\dfrac{a}{a+1}$ **(ac)**

$$\frac{1 - \dfrac{1}{a}}{1 - \dfrac{1}{a^2}} = \frac{(a-1)}{a} \times \frac{\cancel{a^2}^{\,a}}{\cancel{a^2-1}\,_{a+1}} = \frac{a}{a+1}$$

$$\frac{a \times \dfrac{1}{a}}{(a+1) \times \dfrac{1}{a}} = \frac{1}{\dfrac{a}{a} + \dfrac{1}{a}} = \frac{1}{1 + \dfrac{1}{a}}$$

(answer a)

ANSWER: $\dfrac{1}{1 + \dfrac{1}{a}}$

4) $(2^x)(4^x) = 8^x$ (answer a)
$\quad (2^x)(2^2)^x = 2^x + {}^{2x} = 2^{3x}$ (answer c)

ANSWER: 8x or 2^{3x} (ac)

5) $\text{Log } 10 \text{ } x^2 = \text{Log } (10 \cdot x^2)$
$\text{Log } 10 + \text{Log } x^2$
$1 + 2 \text{ Log } x$ (answer d)

ANSWER: $1 + 2$ Log x

$\text{Log } 10x^2 = \text{Log } (5x \cdot 2x)$
$\text{Log } 5x + \text{Log } 2x$ (answer c)

ANSWER: Log 5x + Log 2x   (cd)

29. SOLUTION:
r = age m years ago
r + m = age now
(r + m) + b = age b years from now or r + m + b = age b years from now   (No. 1 Answer)

ANSWER: r + m + b

30. x varies directly as y^2
SOLUTION: Formula for direct variation

$$\frac{x}{x^1} = \frac{y^2}{(y^1)^2}$$
$x = 9$
$y = 2$
$$\frac{9}{x} = \frac{2^2}{8^2}$$
$9(8)^2 = 2^2x$
$9(64) = 4x$ (divide by 4)
$9(16) = x$
$144 = x$ (No. 2 answer)

ANSWER: 144

31. SOLUTION:

$$\tan \angle A = \frac{\text{opposite side}}{\text{adjacent side}} = \frac{x}{20}$$

$$\tan 58° = \frac{x}{20}$$

$\tan 58° = 1.6003$ (according to table)
$x = 20 \tan 58°$ or
$x = 20(1.6003) = 32.0060$ ft. or
    32 ft.   (No. 4 answer)

ANSWER: 32

32. SOLUTION:
Formula:
$L = a + d(n - 1)$ a = 1st term, 7
$L = 7 + (-3)(12)$ d = com. dif., — 3
$L = -29$ n = no. of terms, 13
                  L = last term, — 29

ANSWER: —29   (No. 4 answer)

33. SOLUTION:
Formula $A = P(1 + rt)$
$A = 500 [1 + .03(15)]$
$A = 500 (1 + .45)$
$A = 500 \times 1.45 = 725$
(No. 2 answer)

ANSWER: 725

34. SOLUTION:
r varies directly as s

$$\frac{r}{r^1} = \frac{s}{s^1}$$
$$\frac{3}{r^1} = \frac{8}{12}$$
$36 = 8r^1$
$r^1 = 4\frac{1}{2}$ (No. 1 answer)

ANSWER: 4½

35. SOLUTION:
Solve for x
$\sqrt{x + 2} = 3$
$\sqrt{(x + 2)^2} = 3^2$
$x + 2 = 9$
$x = 9 - 2 = 7$ (No. 2 answer)

ANSWER: 7

36. SOLUTION:
See page xx for rule for solving a quadratic equation by factoring.
$2x^2 - 3x - 2 = 0$
$(2x + 1)(x - 2) = 0$
$x = 2$ (No. 2 answer)

ANSWER: 2

37. SOLUTION:

Sum of angles of any triangle $= 180°$
Given: one acute angle is $28°$

$28° + 90° = 118°$
$180° - 118° = 62°$ in $\angle$ opp. longer leg

$\sin 62° = .8829$ (according to table)

$$\frac{\text{opposite side}}{\text{hypotenuse}} = \sin 62°$$

ILLUSTRATION

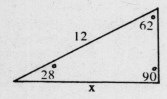

then $\dfrac{x}{12} = \sin 62°$ or $.8829$

$x = 12 \times .8829$
$x = 10.6$ (No. 3 answer)

ANSWER: 10.6

38. SOLUTION:

Discriminant $b^2 - 4ac = 40$;
therefore roots are unequal and irrational
because $\sqrt{40}$ is an irrational number

(No. 3 answer)

ANSWER: roots are unequal and irrational

39. SOLUTION:

Straight line $y = mx$
circle $x^2 + y^2 = 9$

When drawn on the same set of axes they intersect regardless of what value "m" may have because circle has center at origin and radius 3.

ILLUSTRATION

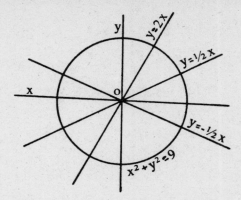

intercepts are $y = x = \pm 3$
They have to intersect because the line $y = mx$, passes through the origin. The pt. $(0,0)$ lies on any line of the form $y = mx$ (no constant term)

(No. 1 answer)

ANSWER: intersect regardless of what value m may have.

40. SOLUTION:

If $\text{Log } r + \text{Log } s = \text{Log } t$
then $rs = t$ because

Logarithm of a product is equal to the sum of the logs of the factors

$\text{Log } r + \text{Log } s = \text{Log } t$
$\text{Log } (r \times s) = \text{Log } t$
$rs = t$

Example: $r \times s = t$
$4 \times 3 = 12$
$\text{Log } 4 = 0.6021$
$\text{Log } 3 = \underline{0.4771}$
$\text{Log } 12 = 1.0792$ (according to log table)

(No. 3 answer)

ANSWER: $rs = t$

PLANE GEOMETRY

1. In parallelogram ABCD, angle B is twice as large as angle A. How many degrees are there in angle A?

2. In right triangle ABC, altitude CD is drawn to hypotenuse AB. If angle A contains 32°, how many degrees are there in angle BCD?

3. How many degrees are there in each angle of a regular polygon of 8 sides?

4. Angle ABC, formed by diameter AB and chord BC of a circle, contains 30°. If the diameter of the circle is 10, find chord AC.

5. A line parallel to base AB of triangle ABC intersects the sides AC and BC at points D and E respectively. If CD=4, DA=6 and CE=8, find EB.

6. The area of a triangle is 24. If one side of the triangle is 12, find the altitude drawn to that side.

7. Find the ratio of the areas of two similar polygons whose corresponding sides are in the ratio 2:3.

8. The area of a circle is 49π. Find its circumference. (Answer may be left in terms of π.)

9. Find the area of a square circumscribed about a circle whose radius is 10.

10. In triangle ABC, angle C=90°, BC=3, AC =4; find angle A correct to the *nearest degree*.
Directions (questions 11-17) — If the blank in each statement is filled by one of the words *always, sometimes* or *never*, the resulting statement will be true. Select the word that will correctly complete each statement and write the word at the right.

11. Triangles that have equal bases and equal altitudes are .... congruent.

12. If angle B of triangle ABC contains 95°, then it is .... possible to determine which is the longest side of the triangle.

13. The altitude and the median are drawn from the same vertex of a triangle. The altitude is .... greater than the median.

14. The center of the circle which is circumscribed about a triangle .... lies inside the triangle.

15. If the perpendiculars drawn from the center of a circle upon two chords are equal, then the minor arcs subtended by these chords are .... equal.

16 Tangents drawn from an external point to a circle .... make equal angles with the chord joining the points of tangency.

17. If the dimensions of a rectangle are doubled, then its area is .... doubled.
Directions (questions 18-20) — Indicate the correct answer to *each* question by writing in the space to the right of the question the letter a, b, c or d.

18. Two angles that are both equal and supplementary are
(a) adjacent,   (c) right,
(b) acute,   (d) obtuse.

19. The mid-point of the hypotenuse of a right triangle is the point of intersection of
(a) the three medians,
(b) the bisectors of the three angles,
(c) the perpendicular bisectors of the three sides,
(d) the three altitudes.

20. If the bases of a trapezoid are b and b', then the median of the trapezoid, in terms of b and b', is (a) 1/2 bb', (b) 1/2 (b+b'), (c) b+b', (d) (b+b')

Correct Answers			
1. 60°	6. 4	11. sometimes	16. always
2. 32°	7. 4:9	12. always	17. never
3. 135°	8. 14π	13. never	18. c
4. 5	9. 400	14. sometimes	19. c
5. 12	10. 37°	15. always	20. b

NECESSARY BACKGROUND

If two lines are cut by a third line, AB, called a transversal, the angles are named as follows: ∠ 2 and ∠ 4 are called interior angles on the same side of the transversal; also ∠ 1 and ∠ 3. ∠ 1 and ∠ 4 are called alternate-interior angles; also ∠ 2 and ∠ 3.

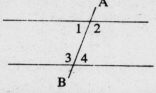

If the two lines which are cut by the transversal are parallel lines (everywhere equidistant) then we have the theorems:

Alternate-interior angles are equal
$1 = ∠ 4$ and $∠ 2 = ∠ 3$

Interior angles on the same side of the transversal are supplementary (their sum is 180°)
∠ 2 and ∠ 4 are supplementary
∠ 1 and ∠ 3 are supplementary

PROBLEM SOLUTIONS   Plane Geometry 1

1. SOLUTION:
Given: ABCD
$∠ B = 2 × ∠ A$
Prove: number of degrees in ∠ A.

ILLUSTRATION

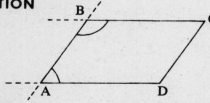

Statements:		Reasons:
BC and AD are // lines	1.	Opp. sides of a parallelogram are parallel
$A + B = 180°$	2.	When // lines are cut by a transversal, interior ∠s on same side of transversal are supp.
$A + 2 ∠ A = 180°$	3.	Substitution
$3 ∠ A = 180°$	4.	Equals divided by equals, quotients are equal.
$∠ A = 60°$		

ANSWER: 60°

2. SOLUTION:
Given: Rt. △ with Alt. CD
$C = 90°$; $A = 32°$
Prove: Number of degrees in BCD

ILLUSTRATION

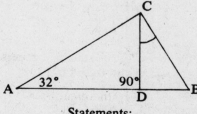

Statements:
1) $∠ A + ∠ B + ∠ C = 180°$
2) $∠ C = 90°$
3) $∠ A + ∠ B = 90°$
4) $∠ + ∠ BCD + ∠ CDB = 180°$
5) $∠ CDB = 90°$
6) $∠ B + ∠ BCD = 90°$
7) $∠ A + ∠ B = ∠ B + ∠ BCD$
8) $∠ A = ∠ BCD$
9) $∠ A = 32°$
10) $∠ BCD = 32°$

Reasons

1) Sum of ∠s of △ = 180°
2) Given
3) equals sub. from equals differences are equal
4) Same as #1
5) Alt. is drawn ⊥ to side from opp. vertex
6) Same as #3
7) Quantities equal to the same quantities are equal to each other
8) equals sub. from equals differences are equal
9) Given
10) Substitution

ANSWER: 32°

3. Any eight-sided figure can be divided into six triangles as shown in figure. The sum of the angles of each of these triangles is 180°. Therefore the sum of the interior angles of the eight-sided figure is 6 (180°) or 1080°. In a regular polygon, the angles are all equal, so here each is ⅛ of the total or ⅛ (1080°) = 135°

ILLUSTRATION

SOLUTION:
Each interior angle of a regular polyon of "n" sides contains:

Formula: $\dfrac{180\,(n-2)}{n}$

$$\dfrac{180\,(8-2)}{8} = \dfrac{1080}{8} = 135°$$

ANSWER: 135°

4. SOLUTION:
Given: Circle with chords CB and AC; diameter AB = 10
∠ ABC = 30°
Prove: Length of chord AC

ILLUSTRATION

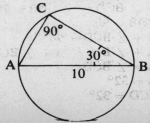

Statements:

1) AB is diameter
2) arc AB is a semicircle = 180°
3) ∠ C = ½ of arc AB
4) ∠ C = 90°
5) AB = 10 = hypotenuse
6) AC = 5 = ½ of hypotenuse

Reasons:

1) Given
2) A semicircle is an arc that is half a circle
3) An inscribed ∠ = in degrees to ½ of its intercepted arc
4) An ∠ inscribed in a semicircle is a right ∠
5) Def. of hypotenuse
6) In a 30°, 60°, 90° rt. △ , side opp. 30° = ½ hypotenuse.

ANSWER: 5

5. SOLUTION:
Given: △ ABC
DE // AB
AD = 6; DC = 4
CE = 8
Prove: Length of EB

ILLUSTRATION

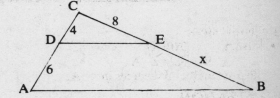

Statements:

1) $\dfrac{AD}{CD} = \dfrac{EB}{CE}$

2) $\dfrac{6}{4} = \dfrac{x}{8}$

3) 4x = 48

4) x = 12

Reasons:

1) If a line is // to one side of a △ and intersects the other 2 sides, it divides 2 sides proportionally.
2) Substitution
3) Product of means = product of extremes
4) Equals divided by equals, quotients are equal.

ANSWER: 12

6. SOLUTION:
Formula for area of a triangle:
$A = \frac{1}{2}B \cdot h$ Let x = altitude
$24 = \frac{1}{2} \cdot 12 \cdot x$ or height
$24 = 6x$
$4 = x$ Altitude = 4

ILLUSTRATION

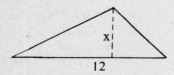

ANSWER: 4

7. SOLUTION:
The area of two similar polygons have the same ratio as the squares of any two corresponding sides.

$$\frac{2^2}{3^2} = \frac{4}{9}$$

The corresponding areas are in ratio 4:9

ANSWER: 4:9

8. SOLUTION:
Area of a circle = πr^2
Formula $A = \pi r^2$
        $C = 2\pi r$

$A = \pi r^2$ $C = 2\pi r$
$A = \pi \times 48$ $C = 2\pi \times 7$
$\pi r^2 = 49\pi$ $C = 14\pi$
$r^2 = 49$ Circumference = 14π
$r = 7$

ANSWER: 14π

9. SOLUTION:
Area of a square circum-
scribed about a circle = d^2 $d = 2r$
                   $r = 10$ $d = 20$
             $20 \times 20 = 400$

ILLUSTRATION

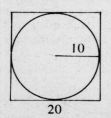

ANSWER: 400

10. SOLUTION:
The tangent of an acute angle of a right triangle is the ratio of the opposite leg to the adjacent.

$$\tan \quad A = \frac{opp.}{adj.} = \frac{3}{4} = .75$$

$A = 37°$ (value from angle whose tan is .75)

ILLUSTRATION

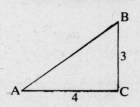

ANSWER: 37°

11. SOLUTION:
If two triangles have the three sides of one equal to the three sides of the other, the triangles are congruent. But with only equal bases and equal altitudes, they are **sometimes** congruent because the other two corresponding sides are not always equal.

ILLUSTRATIONS

$a = a' = a''$ and $b = b' = b''$

ANSWER: sometimes

12. SOLUTION:

If angle B of triangle ABC contains 95°, then it is possible **always** to determine which is the longest side of the △

Reason—If one angle of △ is greater than a second ∠, the side opp. the first ∠ is greater than the side opp. the second ∠; ∠ B is the greatest ∠ possible because the △ is obtuse. Side b opp. 95° ∠ must be the longest side.

ILLUSTRATION

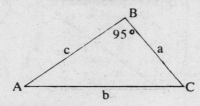

ANSWER: always

13. SOLUTION:

A median of a triangle is a line segment joining any vertex to the midpoint of the opposite side. An altitude of a triangle is a perpendicular line segment from any vertex to the opposite side.

ILLUSTRATIONS

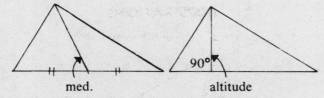

med.   altitude

Altitude is never greater than the median because it is a ⊥ which is the shortest distance from a point to a line.

ANSWER: never

14. SOLUTION:

The center of a circle which is circumscribed about a triangle **sometimes** lies inside the triangle.

This does not hold when △ is a rt. △ or an obtuse △

ILLUSTRATIONS

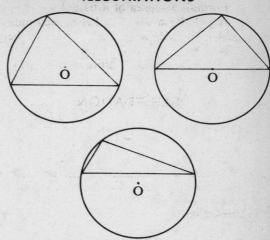

ANSWER: Sometimes

15. SOLUTION:

A chord is a line segment connecting any two points on the circle. In a circle or in equal circles equal chords are equidistant from the center. So the minor arcs subtended by these chords are always equal

ILLUSTRATION

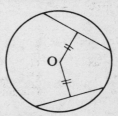

ANSWER: Always

16. SOLUTION:

The tangents to a circle from an external point are equal. Form an isosceles triangle with the chord connecting pts. of tangency; two equal sides have equal angles opposite them.

ILLUSTRATION

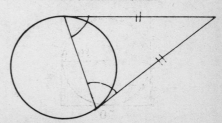

ANSWER: Always

17. SOLUTION:
If the dimensions of a rectangle are doubled, then its area never doubled because its area becomes four times as much
Example: A = LW
A = 5x4 = 20
A = 10x8 = 80
A = 20x16 = 320
A = 40x32 = 1280

ANSWER: Never

18. SOLUTION:
Two angles are supplementary when their sum is a straight angle; since both are equal both are right angles or 90°.

ILLUSTRATION

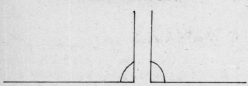

ANSWER: Right angle

19. SOLUTION:
The midpoint on the hypotenuse of a right triangle is equidistant from the vertices of the triangle; therefore, the perpendicular bisectors of the three sides meet there. The angle bisectors and medians always meet at points **within** the triangle. The two legs themselves are two of the altitudes and meet at the vertex of the rt. △

ILLUSTRATION

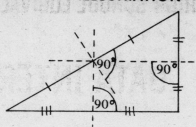

ANSWER: the perpendicular bisectors of the three sides.

20. SOLUTION:
The median of a trapezoid is equal to one half the sum of the bases.

ILLUSTRATION

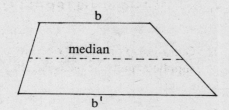

ANSWER: median = ½ (b + b′)

DATA INTERPRETATION

The ability to read and interpret graphs, charts and tables is an important test-taking skill. What's more, it is one of those skills that can be sharpened by study and drill. This chapter provides just the kind of practice you need to score high on the graph and table questions that are likely to appear on your test. It gives tips for attacking this type of question, a sampling of the kinds of questions you can expect, and detailed solutions for self-evaluation and self-help.

TIPS ON INTERPRETING GRAPHIC MATERIALS

1. Get a grasp of the data before you start. Check dates, kinds of information supplied, units of measure, etc.

2. Do the easier questions first, those that can be answered by observation alone. Then turn to those questions that require calculating. There are usually some easy questions in each set and they count just as much as the more difficult ones in determining your score.

3. Visualize rather than calculate answers wherever possible. When dealing with averages, for example, imagine a line between the highest and lowest readings given in the particular graph or chart. Since the average of any group of numbers must fall somewhere between the highest and lowest points, establishing a visual midpoint can save valuable time.

4. Use the edge of your answer sheet or your pencil to help you read line and bar graphs or tables more accurately.

5. Rephrase questions that seem to stump you at first. Change verbal problems into mathematical ones or vice versa to see if you can get a better grasp of the situation.

6. Work with round numbers where possible. Often questions do not require exact answers and you can arrive at the correct answer faster and more easily by using approximate numbers.

7. Work with the smallest possible units. It is a waste of time to convert readings to fractional parts of a million and then try to work with the resulting huge numbers. If a table concerns population in millions, for example, calculate as follows:

    2 units + 1½ units = 3½ units.

    If each unit = 2 million, then 3½ × 2 million = 7 million

8. Do your figuring as neatly as possible so that you can refer to it if necessary. Calculations from a previous question in the set may save valuable time in answering subsequent questions on the same data.

9. Make certain that the answer you choose is in the same terms as the question; for example, dollars, millions, tons, miles. Pay particular attention to problems involving percentages. Remember that to change a number to a percentage you must multiply by 100. Thus, .049 × 100 = 4.9% while .49 × 100 = 49%.

10. Work only with the information stated or implied in the data presented. Attempting to bring outside knowledge to bear in answering a particular question may only lead you astray.

TEST I. DATA INTERPRETATION

TIME: 35 Minutes. 25 Questions.

DIRECTIONS: This test consists of data presented in graphic form followed by questions based on the information contained in the graph, chart or table shown. After studying the data given, choose the best answer for each question and blacken the corresponding space on the answer sheet. Answer each group of questions solely on the basis of the information given or implied in the data preceding it.

Explanations of the key points behind these questions appear with the answers at the end of this test.

Questions 1 to 17

In the table that follows lettered entries have been substituted for some of the numbers. In answering the questions about the lettered entries, you are to compute the number that should be in the space where the lettered entry appears. In those questions which concern tokens, consider the worth of a token as 35 cents.

DAILY FARE REPORT

Date: 3/12/76   Booth No. S-50

Name: John Brown
Time: From 7 A.M. to 3 P.M.

Name: Mary Smith
Time: From 3 P.M. to 11 P.M.

TURNSTILES

TURN-STILE	OPENING READING	CLOSING READING	DIFFER-ENCE	OPENING READING	CLOSING READING	DIFFER-ENCE
1	5123	5410	287	5410	6019	609
2	3442	Entry F	839	4281	4683	402
3	8951	9404	453	Entry G	9757	353
4	7663	8265	602	8265	8588	Entry H

Totals: Entry I — 27360 — 2181 | 27360 — Entry J — 1687

Total Fares 2181	Total Fares 1687
Deduct: Slugs, Foreign Coins 12	Deduct: Slugs, Foreign Coins Entry K
Deduct: Test Rings-Turnstile # 0	Deduct: Test Rings-Turnstile #3 3
Net Fares 2169	Net Fares 1680
(a) Net Fares at Token Value Entry L	(a) Net Fares at Token Value $588.00
Token Reserve at Start 4200	Token Reserve at Start 5000
Add: Tokens Received 2200	Add: Tokens Received Entry M
Deduct: Tokens Transferred Out 1400	Deduct: Tokens Transferred Out 0
Total Token Reserve Entry N	Total Token Reserve 6450
Deduct: Total Reserve at End 4330	Deduct: Total Reserve at End 5674
No. of Reserve Tokens Sold 670	No. of Reserve Tokens Sold Entry O
(b) Value of Reserve Tokens Sold Entry P	(b) Value of Reserve Tokens Sold $271.60
Net Amount Due: (a) + (b) $993.65	Net Amount Due: (a) + (b) Entry Q

1. Entry F for Brown's tour of duty should be a closing reading of
   (A) 2603   (B) 3873   (C) 4281   (D) 4671

2. Entry G for Smith's tour of duty should be an opening reading of
   (A) 8642   (B) 3932   (C) 9404   (D) 9857

3. Entry H for Smith's tour of duty should be a difference of
   (A) 303   (B) 323   (C) 344   (D) 402

4. Entry I for Brown's tour of duty should be a total of
   (A) 24299   (B) 25179   (C) 26288   (D) 27168

5. Entry J for Smith's tour of duty should be a total of
   (A) 28036   (B) 29047   (C) 29556   (D) 30437

6. Entry K for Smith's tour of duty should indicate that the number of slugs and foreign coins is
   (A) 0   (B) 2   (C) 4   (D) 7

7. Entry L for Brown's tour of duty should indicate that the net fares at token value amount to
   (A) $493.80   (B) $542.25   (C) $650.70   (D) $759.15

8. Entry M for Smith's tour of duty should indicate that the tokens received number
   (A) 674   (B) 1000   (C) 1200   (D) 1450

9. Entry N for Brown's tour of duty should indicate a total token reserve of
   (A) 670   (B) 5000   (C) 6400   (D) 7800

10. Entry O for Smith's tour of duty should indicate that the number of reserve tokens sold was
    (A) 776   (B) 1450   (C) 3250   (D) 12124

11. Entry P for Brown's tour of duty should indicate that the value of reserve tokens sold should be
    (A) $210.00   (B) $234.50   (C) $490.00   (D) $523.35

12. Entry Q for Smith's tour of duty should indicate that the net amount due is
    (A) $859.60   (B) $478.30   (C) $317.10   (D) $270.90

13. The number of passengers using Turnstile No. 2 from 7 A.M. to 11 P.M. is
    (A) 1241   (B) 839   (C) 402   (D) 287

14. The turnstile showing the greatest use from 7 A.M. to 3 P.M. is

(A) No. 1   (B) No. 2   (C) No. 3   (D) No. 4

15. The total fares for all turnstiles from 7 A.M. to 11 P.M. amounted to

(A) 1687   (B) 2181   (C) 3868   (D) 4275

16. The total net fares from 7 A.M. to 11 P.M. amounted to

(A) 1680   (B) 2169   (C) 3849   (D) 3868

17. Net fares at token value from 7 A.M. to 11 P.M. amounted to

(A) $993.65   (B) $588.00   (C) $1353.80   (D) $1347.15

Questions 18 to 22

Questions 18 to 22 are based on the chart of HOURLY TURNSTILE READINGS shown below. Refer to this chart when answering these questions.

HOURLY TURNSTILE READINGS					
TURNSTILE NO.	7:00 AM	8:00 AM	9:00 AM	10:00 AM	11:00 AM
1	37111	37905	38342	38451	38485
2	78432	79013	79152	79237	79306
3	45555	45921	45989	46143	46233
4	89954	90063	90121	90242	90299

18. The total number of passengers using Turnstile No. 1 from 7:00 A.M. to 11:00 A.M. is

(A) 580   (B) 794   (C) 1374   (D) 1594

19. The turnstile which registered the largest number of fares from 7:00 A.M. to 8:00 A.M. is

(A) No. 1   (B) No. 2   (C) No. 3   (D) No. 4

20. The total number of passengers using all four turnstiles between 10:00 A.M. and 11:00 A.M. is

(A) 57   (B) 250   (C) 396   (D) 3271

21. Turnstile No. 4 registered the highest number of passengers between

(A) 7:00 A.M. and 8:00 A.M.   (B) 8:00 A.M. and 9:00 A.M.
(C) 9:00 A.M. and 10:00 A.M.   (D) 10:00 A.M. and 11:00 A.M.

22. The turnstile which registered the lowest number of passengers between 8:00 A.M. and 9:00 A.M. is

(A) No. 1   (B) No. 2   (C) No. 3   (D) No. 4

Questions 23 to 25

In the graph below, the lines labeled "A" and "B" represent the cumulative progress in the work of two file clerks, each of whom was given 500 consecutively numbered applications to file in the proper cabinets over a five-day work week. Answer questions 23 to 25 solely upon the data provided in the graph.

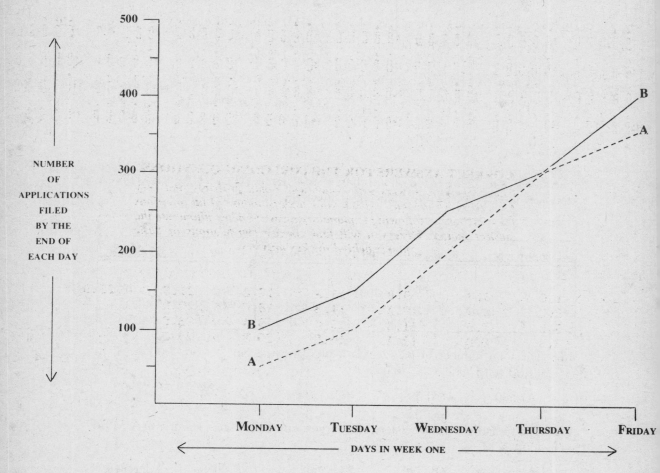

23. The day during which the largest number of applications was filed by both clerks was
(A) Monday
(B) Tuesday
(C) Wednesday
(D) Friday

24. At the end of the second day, the percentage of applications still to be filed was
(A) 25%
(B) 50%
(C) 66%
(D) 75%

25. Assuming that the production pattern is the same the following week as the week shown in the chart, the day on which the file clerks will finish this assignment will be
(A) Monday
(B) Tuesday
(C) Wednesday
(D) Friday

CONSOLIDATE YOUR KEY ANSWERS HERE

Practice using Answer Sheets. Make ONE mark for each answer. Additional and stray marks may be counted as mistakes. In making corrections erase errors COMPLETELY. Make glossy black marks. To arrive at an accurate estimate of your ability and progress, we suggest that you cover the Correct Answers with a sheet of white paper while you are taking this test.

CORRECT ANSWERS FOR THE FOREGOING QUESTIONS.

Check our key answers with your own. You'll probably find very few errors. In any case, check your understanding of all questions by studying the following explanatory answers. They illuminate the subject matter. Here you will find concise clarifications of basic points behind the key answers.

1.C	5.B	9.B	13.A	17.D	21.C	25.B
2.C	6.C	10.A	14.B	18.C	22.D	
3.B	7.D	11.B	15.C	19.A	23.C	
4.B	8.D	12.A	16.C	20.B	24.D	

TEST I. EXPLANATORY ANSWERS

The core of the Question and Answer Method ... getting help when and where you need it. Even if you were able to write correct key answers for the preceding questions, the following explanations illuminate fundamental facts, ideas, and principles which just might crop up in the form of questions on future tests.

1. **(C)** It is possible to answer this question by careful reading of the two reports shown, without any computation at all. John Brown's report covers Turnstiles 1, 2, 3, and 4 from 7 AM to 3 PM, and Mary Smith's report covers the same Turnstiles from 3 PM to 11PM. Therefore, the Closing Reading for Turnstile 2 on John Brown's report (Entry F) will be the same figure as the Opening Reading for Turnstile 2 on Mary Smith's report.

   To compute the Closing Reading, simply add the Difference shown for Turnstile 2 to the Opening Reading given:
   $$3442 + 839 = 4281$$

2. **(C)** As in Question 1, this figure can be supplied by simply reading the report. The Opening Reading for Turnstile 3 (Entry G) on Mary Smith's report will be the same as the Closing Reading for Turnstile 3 on John Brown's report.

   To compute the Opening Reading, subtract the Difference (or number of turns made) from the Closing Reading given:
   $$9757 - 353 = 9404$$

3. **(B)**

       8588 Closing Reading
     −8265 Opening Reading
        323 Difference or Entry H

4. **(B)** Entry I is the sum of all opening Readings

       5123
       3442
       8951
       7663
      25179

5. **(B)** Entry J is the sum of all closing readings

       6019
       4683
       9757
       8588
      29047

6. **(C)** The difference between Total Fares and Net Fares = 1687 − 1680 = 7
Since Test Rings = 3, the remainder of the difference must be made up of
Slugs and Foreign Coins.

> 7 Difference between Total Fares and Net Fares
> −3 Test Rings
> ‾‾‾‾‾‾‾‾‾‾‾
> 4 Slugs and Foreign Coins

7. **(D)**
> 2169 Net Fares
> × .35 Token Value
> ‾‾‾‾‾‾‾‾‾‾‾
> $759.15 Net Fares at Token Value or Entry L

8. **(D)** Since no tokens were transferred out, Mary Smith's Total Token
Reserve = Tokens at Start + Tokens Received.

> 6450 Total Token Reserve
> −5000 Token Reserve at Start
> ‾‾‾‾‾‾‾‾‾‾‾
> 1450 Tokens Received or Entry M

9. **(B)**
> 4200 Token Reserve at Start
> +2200 Tokens Received
> ‾‾‾‾‾‾‾‾‾‾‾
> 6400
> −1400 Tokens transferred Out
> ‾‾‾‾‾‾‾‾‾‾‾
> 5000 Total Token Reserve or Entry N

10. **(A)**
> 6450 Total Token Reserve
> −5674 Total Reserve at End
> ‾‾‾‾‾‾‾‾‾‾‾
> 776 No. of Reserve Tokens Sold or Entry O

11. **(B)**
> 670 No. of Reserve Tokens Sold
> ×.35 Value of Each Token
> ‾‾‾‾‾‾‾‾‾‾‾
> $234.50 Value of Reserve Tokens Sold or Entry P

12. **(A)**
> 588.00 Net Fares at Token Value (a)
> +271.60 Value of Reserve Tokens Sold (b)
> ‾‾‾‾‾‾‾‾‾‾‾
> $ 859.60 Net Amount Due

13. **(A)** The Difference between the Opening Reading and the Closing Reading for each Turnstile = the number of times the Turnstile has turned or the number of passengers who have passed through the Turnstile. Therefore, the total number of passengers using Turnstile 2 = Number of Passengers (Difference) from 7 AM to 3 PM + Number of Passengers (Difference) from 3 PM to 11 PM.

$$839 + 402 = 1241$$

14. **(B)** Examination of the chart shows that Turnstile 2 had a Difference (which is the number of turns made or the number of passengers using the turnstile) of 839 between Opening and Closing Readings. This is greater than the Difference shown for Turnstiles 1, 3, or 4.

15. **(C)**   2181 Total Fares 7 AM to 3 PM
            + 1687 Total Fares 3 PM to 11 PM
            3868 Total Fares 7 AM to 11 PM

16. **(C)**   2169 Net Fares 7 AM to 3 PM
            + 1680 Net Fares 3 PM to 11 PM
            3849 Total Net Fares 7 AM to 11 PM

17. **(D)**   2169 Net Fares 7 AM to 3 PM
            + 1680 Net Fares 3 PM to 11 PM
            3849 Total Net Fares 7 AM to 11 PM
            ×   .35 Value of Tokens
        $1347.15 Net Fares at Token Value 7 AM to 11 PM

18. **(C)**   To find the total number of passengers using Turnstile No. 1 from 7 AM to 11 AM, subtract the 7 AM reading at Turnstile 1 from the 11 AM reading at Turnstile 1:

    38485 11 AM Reading
    − 37111 7 AM Reading
        1374 Total Number of Passengers using Turnstile No. 1

19. **(A)**   To find the number of fares registered between 7 AM and 8 AM, subtract the 7 AM Reading from the 8 AM Reading for each Turnstile. Then compare the results to see which is the greatest.

    Turnstile 1   37905 8 AM Reading
                    − 37111 7 AM Reading
                       794 Number of fares registered

    Turnstile 2   79013 8 AM Reading
                    − 78432 7 AM Reading
                       581 Number of Fares Registered

    Turnstile 3   45921 8 AM Reading
                    − 45555 7 AM Reading
                       366 Number of Fares Registered

    Turnstile 4   90063 8 AM Reading
                    − 89954 7 AM Reading
                       109 Number of Fares Registered

20. **(B)**   To find the number of passengers using all turnstiles from 10 AM to 11 AM, subtract the 10 AM reading from the 11 AM reading for each turnstile, then add the resulting figures.

    Turnstile 1   38485 11 AM Reading
                    − 38451 10 AM Reading
                        34 Passengers Registered

    Turnstile 2   79306 11 AM Reading
                    − 79237 10 AM Reading
                        69 Passengers Registered

Turnstile 3   46233 11 AM Reading
              −46143 10 AM Reading
                   90 Passengers Registered

Turnstile 4   90299 11 AM Reading
              −90242 10 AM Reading
                   57 Passengers Registered

34 + 69 + 90 + 57 = 250 Total number of passengers using all turnstiles between 10 and 11 AM.

21. **(C)** To find the number of passengers registered per hour, subtract the earlier reading from the latter reading as follows:

90063 8 AM Reading
−89954 7 AM Reading
    109 Number of Passengers between 7 AM and 8 AM

90121 9 AM Reading
−90063 8 AM Reading
    58 Number of Passengers between 8 AM and 9 AM

90242 10 AM Reading
−90121 9 AM Reading
   121 Number of Passengers between 9 AM and 10 AM

90299 11 AM Reading
−90242 10 AM Reading
    57 Number of Passengers between 10 AM and 11 AM

Comparison of the resulting figures shows that the greatest number of passengers at Turnstile 4 was registered between 9 AM and 10 AM.

22. **(D)** Find the number of passengers for each Turnstile by subtracting the 8 AM Reading from the 9 AM Reading, then compare the results to see which is lowest.

Turnstile 1   38342 9 AM Reading
              −37905 8 AM Reading
                  437 Passengers between 8 AM and 9 AM

Turnstile 2   79152 9 AM Reading
              −79013 8 AM Reading
                  139 Passengers between 8 AM and 9 AM

Turnstile 3   45989 9 AM Reading
              −45921 8 AM Reading
                   68 Passengers between 8 AM and 9 AM

Turnstile 4   90121 9 AM Reading
              −90063 8 AM Reading
                   58 Passengers between 8 AM and 9 AM

Turnstile 4, with only 58 passengers registered, had the lowest number of passengers between 8 AM and 9 AM.

23. **(C)** The progress of Clerk A is as follows:

    Mon.   1 to 50 =   50 Applications Filed
    Tues.   50 to 100 =   50
    Wed. 100 to 200 = 100
    Thur. 200 to 300 = 100
    Fri.   300 to 350 =   50

    The progress of Clerk B is as follows:
    Mon.   1 to 100 = 100 Applications Filed
    Tues. 100 to 150 =   50
    Wed. 150 to 250 = 100
    Thur. 250 to 300 =   50
    Fri.   300 to 400 = 100

    Combined Totals of Applications Filed by both clerks =
    Mon.   50 + 100 = 150
    Tues. 50 +   50 = 100
    Wed. 100 + 100 = 200
    Thur. 100 +   50 = 150
    Fri.   50 + 100 = 150

    Therefore, the largest number of applications filed by both clerks was 200 applications, which were filed on Wednesday.

24. **(D)** Using the calculations above, it can be seen that by the end of the second day, Clerks A and B had filed 150 + 100 or 250 applications. Since they each had 500 applications to file, there are 1000 applications to be filed.

    1000 − 250 = 750 applications still to be filed after second day

    $\dfrac{750}{1000}$ = .75 or 75% of applications still to be filed.

25. **(B)** Using the calculations made above, it can be seen that the two clerks filed 750 applications from Monday to Friday
    $$(150 + 100 + 200 + 150 + 150 = 750)$$

    1000 − 750 = 250 applications left to be filed in the following week.

    At the rate of 100 to 150 applications filed per day, they will finish the job on Tuesday of the following week.

PART SEVEN

Another Exam...Another Chance

7

A NOTE ABOUT TEST TIMES.

The time allotted for each Test in each Examination in this book is based on a careful analysis of all the information now available. The time we allot for each test, therefore, merely suggests in a general way approximately how much time you should expend on each subject when you take the actual Exam. We have not, in every case, provided precisely the number of questions you will actually get on the examination. It's just not possible to know what the examiners will finally decide to do for every Test in the Examination. It might be a good idea to jot down your "running" time for each Test, and make comparisons later on. If you find that you're working faster, you may assume you're making progress. Remember, we have timed each Test uniformly. If you follow all our directions, your scores will all be comparable.

HIGH SCHOOL EQUIVALENCY DIPLOMA TESTS

FINAL VERISIMILAR EXAMINATION

Testing your assimilation of the contents of this book. Hopefully, we are also proving your new-found ability to score high on the exam to come. Each of the included subjects is, in our judgment, likely to appear on your exam. You should be able to do equally well on all of them.

Allow about 6 hours for this Examination.
That's approximately how much time you'll have on the actual exam. Keep a record of your time, especially if you want to break up this practice into several convenient sessions. Then you'll be able to simulate actual exam conditions.

Correct answers for all the questions in all the Tests of this Exam appear at the end of the Exam.

ANALYSIS AND TIMETABLE: VERISIMILAR EXAMINATION III.

This table is both an analysis of the exam that follows and a priceless preview of the actual test. Look it over carefully and use it well. Since it lists both subjects and times, it points up not only what to study, but also how much time to spend on each topic. Making the most of your study time adds valuable points to your examination score.

WRITING SKILLS		**SCIENCE**	
Spelling	7 min.	Interpretation of Science Readings	60 min.
English Grammar and Usage	18 min.		
Effectiveness of Expression	15 min.	Science Information	30 min.
Logic and Organization	5 min.		
		READING SKILLS	
		Interpretation of Literary Materials	30 min.
SOCIAL STUDIES		Interpretation of Prose	60 min.
Interpretation of Social Studies Readings	60 min.		
		MATHEMATICS	
Social Studies Knowledge	30 min.	General Mathematical Ability	40 min.
		Graph Interpretation	5 min.

ANSWER SHEET FOR VERISIMILAR EXAMINATION III.

Consolidate your key answers here just as you would do on the actual exam. Using this type of Answer Sheet will provide valuable practice. Tear it out along the indicated lines and mark it up correctly. Use a No. 2 (medium) pencil. Make only ONE mark for each answer. Additional and stray marks may be counted as mistakes. In making corrections erase errors COMPLETELY. Make glossy black marks.

TEST I. SPELLING

TEST II. ENGLISH GRAMMAR AND USAGE

TEST III. ENGLISH GRAMMAR AND USAGE

TEST IV. EFFECTIVENESS OF EXPRESSION

TEST V. LOGIC AND ORGANIZATION

TEST VI. INTERPRETATION OF SOCIAL STUDIES READINGS

Reading Passage I

Reading Passage II

Reading Passage III

Reading Passage IV

Reading Passage V

TEST VII. SOCIAL STUDIES KNOWLEDGE

TEST VIII. INTERPRETATION OF SCIENCE READINGS

Reading Passage I

Reading Passage II

Reading Passage III

A B C D E   A B C D E   A B C D E   A B C D E   A B C D E   A B C D E   A B C D E   A B C D E
1 ☐☐☐☐☐   2 ☐☐☐☐☐   3 ☐☐☐☐☐   4 ☐☐☐☐☐   5 ☐☐☐☐☐   6 ☐☐☐☐☐   7 ☐☐☐☐☐   8 ☐☐☐☐☐

A B C D E   A B C D E   A B C D E   A B C D E   A B C D E   A B C D E   A B C D E   A B C D E
9 ☐☐☐☐☐ 10 ☐☐☐☐☐ 11 ☐☐☐☐☐ 12 ☐☐☐☐☐ 13 ☐☐☐☐☐ 14 ☐☐☐☐☐ 15 ☐☐☐☐☐ 16 ☐☐☐☐☐

TEST IX. SCIENCE INFORMATION

A B C D E   A B C D E   A B C D E   A B C D E   A B C D E   A B C D E   A B C D E   A B C D E
1 ☐☐☐☐☐   2 ☐☐☐☐☐   3 ☐☐☐☐☐   4 ☐☐☐☐☐   5 ☐☐☐☐☐   6 ☐☐☐☐☐   7 ☐☐☐☐☐   8 ☐☐☐☐☐

A B C D E   A B C D E   A B C D E   A B C D E   A B C D E   A B C D E   A B C D E   A B C D E
9 ☐☐☐☐☐ 10 ☐☐☐☐☐ 11 ☐☐☐☐☐ 12 ☐☐☐☐☐ 13 ☐☐☐☐☐ 14 ☐☐☐☐☐ 15 ☐☐☐☐☐ 16 ☐☐☐☐☐

A B C D E   A B C D E   A B C D E   A B C D E   A B C D E   A B C D E   A B C D E   A B C D E
17 ☐☐☐☐☐ 18 ☐☐☐☐☐ 19 ☐☐☐☐☐ 20 ☐☐☐☐☐ 21 ☐☐☐☐☐ 22 ☐☐☐☐☐ 23 ☐☐☐☐☐ 24 ☐☐☐☐☐

TEST X. INTERPRETATION OF LITERARY MATERIALS

A B C D E   A B C D E   A B C D E   A B C D E   A B C D E   A B C D E   A B C D E   A B C D E
1 ☐☐☐☐☐   2 ☐☐☐☐☐   3 ☐☐☐☐☐   4 ☐☐☐☐☐   5 ☐☐☐☐☐   6 ☐☐☐☐☐   7 ☐☐☐☐☐   8 ☐☐☐☐☐

A B C D E   A B C D E   A B C D E   A B C D E   A B C D E   A B C D E   A B C D E   A B C D E
9 ☐☐☐☐☐ 10 ☐☐☐☐☐ 11 ☐☐☐☐☐ 12 ☐☐☐☐☐ 13 ☐☐☐☐☐ 14 ☐☐☐☐☐ 15 ☐☐☐☐☐ 16 ☐☐☐☐☐

A B C D E   A B C D E   A B C D E   A B C D E   A B C D E   A B C D E   A B C D E   A B C D E
17 ☐☐☐☐☐ 18 ☐☐☐☐☐ 19 ☐☐☐☐☐ 20 ☐☐☐☐☐ 21 ☐☐☐☐☐ 22 ☐☐☐☐☐ 23 ☐☐☐☐☐ 24 ☐☐☐☐☐

TEST XI. INTERPRETATION OF PROSE

A B C D E   A B C D E   A B C D E   A B C D E   A B C D E   A B C D E   A B C D E   A B C D E
1 ☐☐☐☐☐   2 ☐☐☐☐☐   3 ☐☐☐☐☐   4 ☐☐☐☐☐   5 ☐☐☐☐☐   6 ☐☐☐☐☐   7 ☐☐☐☐☐   8 ☐☐☐☐☐

A B C D E   A B C D E   A B C D E   A B C D E   A B C D E   A B C D E   A B C D E   A B C D E
9 ☐☐☐☐☐ 10 ☐☐☐☐☐ 11 ☐☐☐☐☐ 12 ☐☐☐☐☐ 13 ☐☐☐☐☐ 14 ☐☐☐☐☐ 15 ☐-☐-☐ 16 ☐☐☐☐☐

A B C D E   A B C D E   A B C D E   A B C D E   A B C D E   A B C D E   A B C D E   A B C D E
17 ☐☐☐☐☐ 18 ☐☐☐☐☐ 19 ☐☐☐☐☐ 20 ☐☐☐☐☐ 21 ☐☐☐☐☐ 22 ☐☐☐☐☐ 23 ☐☐☐☐☐ 24 ☐☐☐☐☐

A B C D E   A B C D E   A B C D E   A B C D E   A B C D E   A B C D E   A B C D E   A B C D E
25 ☐☐☐☐☐ 26 ☐☐☐☐☐ 27 ☐☐☐☐☐ 28 ☐☐☐☐☐ 29 ☐☐☐☐☐ 30 ☐☐☐☐☐ 31 ☐☐☐☐☐ 32 ☐☐☐☐☐

TEST XII. GENERAL MATHEMATICAL ABILITY

A B C D E   A B C D E   A B C D E   A B C D E   A B C D E   A B C D E   A B C D E   A B C D E
1 ☐☐☐☐☐   2 ☐☐☐☐☐   3 ☐☐☐☐☐   4 ☐☐☐☐☐   5 ☐☐☐☐☐   6 ☐☐☐☐☐   7 ☐☐☐☐☐   8 ☐☐☐☐☐

A B C D E   A B C D E   A B C D E   A B C D E   A B C D E   A B C D E   A B C D E   A B C D E
9 ☐☐☐☐☐ 10 ☐☐☐☐☐ 11 ☐☐☐☐☐ 12 ☐☐☐☐☐ 13 ☐☐☐☐☐ 14 ☐☐☐☐☐ 15 ☐☐☐☐☐ 16 ☐☐☐☐☐

A B C D E   A B C D E   A B C D E   A B C D E   A B C D E   A B C D E   A B C D E   A B C D E
17 ☐☐☐☐☐ 18 ☐☐☐☐☐ 19 ☐☐☐☐☐ 20 ☐☐☐☐☐ 21 ☐☐☐☐☐ 22 ☐☐☐☐☐ 23 ☐☐☐☐☐ 24 ☐☐☐☐☐

A B C D E   A B C D E   A B C D E   A B C D E   A B C D E   A B C D E   A B C D E   A B C D E
25 ☐☐☐☐☐ 26 ☐☐☐☐☐ 27 ☐☐☐☐☐ 28 ☐☐☐☐☐ 29 ☐☐☐☐☐ 30 ☐☐☐☐☐ 31 ☐☐☐☐☐ 32 ☐☐☐☐☐

TEST XIII. GRAPH INTERPRETATION

A B C D E   A B C D E   A B C D E   A B C D E   A B C D E   A B C D E   A B C D E   A B C D E
1 ☐☐☐☐☐   2 ☐☐☐☐☐   3 ☐☐☐☐☐   4 ☐☐☐☐☐   5 ☐☐☐☐☐   6 ☐☐☐☐☐   7 ☐☐☐☐☐   8 ☐☐☐☐☐

PART I. THE WRITING SKILLS TEST

TIME: 45 Minutes. 82 Questions.

TEST I. SPELLING

TIME: 7 Minutes. 14 Questions.

DIRECTIONS: In each of the following groups one word may be misspelled. For each group select the one misspelled word. If you think all four words in the group are correctly spelled, mark the answer E.

1. (A) calender   (B) maintenance
   (C) analyze   (D) indefinite
   (E) none wrong

2. (A) laboratory (B) occasionally
   (C) profiscient (D) previously
   (E) none wrong

3. (A) ambitious   (B) accomodate
   (C) approximately (D) ledger
   (E) none wrong

4. (A) pronunciation (B) inteligent
   (C) associated   (D) voucher
   (E) none wrong

5. (A) expenditure (B) abbreviation
   (C) neurotic   (D) ridecule
   (E) none wrong

6. (A) anonymus   (B) personnel
   (C) municipality (D) appropriation
   (E) none wrong

7. (A) battallion   (B) accordance
   (C) annoyance   (D) opponent
   (E) none wrong

8. (A) proportion   (B) indebtedness
   (C) statistics   (D) parallal
   (E) none wrong

9. (A) community   (B) association
   (C) cooperation (D) conscientious
   (E) none wrong

10. (A) acknowledge (B) incessent
    (C) definition (D) beneficial
    (E) none wrong

11. (A) occurrence (B) guarrante
    (C) deceive   (D) accuracy
    (E) none wrong

12. (A) partial   (B) business
    (C) through   (D) comission
    (E) none wrong

13. (A) accounts   (B) financial
    (C) reciept   (D) answer
    (E) none wrong

14. (A) except   (B) conection
    (C) altogether (D) credentials
    (E) none wrong

END OF TEST

Go on to do the following Test in this Examination, just as you would be expected to do on the actual exam. You will find correct answers for the entire Examination following the last question. Check your answers carefully after you have completed the whole Examination.

TEST II. ENGLISH GRAMMAR AND USAGE

TIME: 9 Minutes. 15 Questions.

DIRECTIONS: *This is a test of standard written English. The rules may differ from everyday spoken English. Many of the following sentences contain grammar, usage, word choice, and idiom that would be incorrect in written composition. Some sentences are correct. No sentence has more than one error. Any error in a sentence will be underlined and lettered; all other parts of the sentence are correct and cannot be changed. If the sentence has an error, choose the underlined part that is incorrect, and mark that letter on your answer sheet. If there is no error, mark E on your answer sheet.*

1. He had a large amount of friends until he lost all his
         A   B   C   D
   money. No error.
          E

2. John said, that he would transfer to another school
       A   B
   at the end of the year. No error.
       C   D   E

3. Would you agree to Parsons having full control of the
         A   B   C
   operation? No error.
       D   E

4. "Your's is not to question why!" she declaimed
      A   B   C
   from the stage. No error.
       D   E

5. She was promoted because she had made less errors than
        A   B   C
   the other secretary. No error.
       D   E

6. I would appreciate your treating me as if I was your
         A   B   C   D
   brother. No error.
       E

7. The teacher asked three of us, Dan, Edward and I, to
                            ‾‾‾‾‾‾
                              A   B̅
   carry the plants down to the cafeteria. No error.
   ‾‾‾‾   ‾‾‾‾   ‾‾‾‾‾‾‾
     C   D   E

8. Here, Jane, bring this note to the office. No error.
   ‾‾‾‾   ‾‾‾‾   ‾‾   ‾‾‾   ‾‾‾‾‾‾‾
     A   B   C   D   E

9. Being that she was a newcomer to our organization, Rose
   ‾‾‾‾‾‾‾‾   ‾‾‾‾‾‾‾‾   ‾‾‾‾‾‾‾‾‾‾‾‾
      A   B   C
   was shy. No error.
   ‾‾‾   ‾‾‾‾‾‾‾
    D   E

10. My father, along with hundreds of other workers,
              ‾‾‾‾‾‾‾‾‾‾   ‾‾‾‾‾‾‾‾‾‾‾‾‾‾
                  A   B
    have been on strike since New Year's Day. No error.
    ‾‾‾‾‾‾‾‾   ‾‾‾‾‾‾‾‾‾‾‾‾‾   ‾‾‾‾‾‾‾
       C   D   E

11. The constant rise of prices and wages bring about
        ‾‾‾‾‾‾‾   ‾‾‾‾‾‾   ‾‾‾‾‾
           A   B   C
    inflation. No error.
    ‾‾‾‾‾‾‾‾   ‾‾‾‾‾‾‾
       D   E

12. That was the same identical damaged article that was
                 ‾‾‾‾‾‾‾‾‾‾‾‾‾ ‾‾‾‾‾‾‾   ‾‾‾‾
                      A   B   C
    returned to the store last month. No error.
                        ‾‾‾‾‾‾‾‾‾‾   ‾‾‾‾‾‾‾
                            D   E

13. If I weren't dressed in this uniform, I wouldn't feel so
        ‾‾‾‾‾‾   ‾‾‾‾‾‾‾‾‾   ‾‾‾‾‾‾‾‾
          A   B   C
    conspicuous. No error.
    ‾‾‾‾‾‾‾‾‾‾‾ ‾‾‾‾‾‾‾
        D   E

14. It was not quite clear whether it was his friend or him
       ‾‾‾‾‾‾‾‾‾‾   ‾‾‾‾‾‾‾   ‾‾‾
          A   B   C
    who had requested the favor. No error.
        ‾‾‾‾‾‾‾‾‾‾‾‾‾   ‾‾‾‾‾‾‾
             D   E

15. After he had paid the fee and saw the pictures, he was
              ‾‾‾‾‾‾‾‾   ‾‾‾   ‾‾‾‾‾‾‾‾
                 A   B   C
    quite satisfied. No error.
    ‾‾‾‾‾   ‾‾‾‾‾‾‾
      D   E

END OF TEST

TEST III. ENGLISH GRAMMAR AND USAGE

TIME: 9 Minutes. 15 Questions.

DIRECTIONS: *This is a test of standard written English. The rules may differ from everyday spoken English. Many of the following sentences contain grammar, usage, word choice, and idiom that would be incorrect in written composition. Some sentences are correct. No sentence has more than one error. Any error in a sentence will be underlined and lettered; all other parts of the sentence are correct and cannot be changed. If the sentence has an error, choose the underlined part that is incorrect, and mark that letter on your answer sheet. If there is no error, mark* E *on your answer sheet.*

1. Why should we give him our books, when he had extras
   A   B   C
   why did he refuse to share them with us? No error.
   D   E

2. Jack likes all sports: tennis, basketball, football, and etc.
   A   B   C   D
   No error.
   E

3. That Bill's reasoning was fallacious was soon apparent
   A   B   C
   to all. No error.
   D   E

4. Neither John nor his children is likely to attend the
   A   B   C
   ceremonies. No error.
   D   E

5. He will give the message to whoever opens the door.
   A   B   C   D
   No error.
   E

6. The boy, as well as his mother, desperately need help.
   A   B   C   D
   No error.
   E

7. Because he <u>has always been</u> popular and <u>with abundant</u>
                A   B

   <u>wealth</u>, he <u>thoroughly</u> enjoyed his <u>college years</u>. <u>No error.</u>
     B   C   D   E

8. <u>Having studied</u> your report carefully, I <u>am convinced that</u>
        A   B

   <u>neither</u> of your solutions <u>are</u> correct. <u>No error.</u>
     C   D   E

9. If he is successful in his attempt <u>to cross</u> the lake, he
                                    A

   <u>will have swum</u> a <u>distance</u> of <u>twelve miles</u>. <u>No error.</u>
       B   C   D   E

10. <u>In spite of</u> his youth, <u>no faster</u> runner than <u>him</u>
         A   B   C

    <u>will be found</u> in our school. <u>No error.</u>
        D   E

11. <u>Because of</u> the poor lighting, they <u>mistakenly supposed</u>
        A   B

    the <u>intruder</u> to be <u>I</u>. <u>No error.</u>
        C   D E

12. <u>None of the</u> <u>diplomats</u> at the conference was able either
        A   B

    <u>to comprehend</u> or <u>solve</u> the problem. <u>No error.</u>
         C   D   E

13. It was <u>agreed</u> by a majority of the signers of the <u>compact</u>
          A   B

    that truth <u>as well as</u> justice was to be <u>there</u> rule of life.
              C   D

    <u>No error.</u>
      E

14. Everybody was <u>up</u> early on Monday <u>because</u> our <u>local</u>
                A   B   C

    store was having <u>it's</u> annual sale. <u>No error.</u>
             D   E

15. A careful driver <u>watches</u> the road and goes <u>slowly</u> or
                A   B

    quickly <u>depending upon</u> the condition of the road, the
          C   D

    <u>visibility</u>, and the traffic. <u>No error.</u>
                            E

TEST IV. EFFECTIVENESS OF EXPRESSION

TIME: 15 Minutes. 30 Questions.

DIRECTIONS: A sentence is given in which one part is underlined. Following the sentence are five choices. The first (A) choice simply repeats the underlined part. The subsequent four choices suggest other ways to express the underlined part of the original sentence. If you think that the underlined part is correct as it stands, write the answer A. If you believe that the underlined part is incorrect, select from among the other choices (B or C or D or E) the one you think is correct. Grammar, sentence structure, word usage, and punctuation are to be considered in your decision, and the original meaning of the sentence must be retained.

1. I feel as though I was being borne bodily through the air.
   (A) as though I was being borne
   (B) as though I was being born
   (C) like I was being borne
   (D) like as though I was being borne
   (E) as though I were being borne

2. Honor as well as profit are to be gained by this work.
   (A) Honor as well as profit are to be gained by this work.
   (B) Honor as well as profit is to be gained by this work.
   (C) Honor in addition to profit are to be gained by this work.
   (D) Honor, as well as profit, are to be gained by this work.
   (E) Honor also profit is to be gained by this work.

3. He was neither in favor of or opposed to the plan.
   (A) He was neither in favor of or opposed to the plan.
   (B) He was not in favor of or opposed to the plan.
   (C) He was neither in favor of the plan or opposed to it.
   (D) He was neither in favor of the plan or opposed to the plan.
   (E) He was neither in favor of nor opposed to the plan.

4. I don't do well in those kinds of tests.
   (A) I don't do well in those kinds of tests.
   (B) I don't do well in those kind of tests.
   (C) I don't do good in those kinds of tests.
   (D) I don't do good in those kind of tests.
   (E) I don't do good in tests like those.

5. We were amazed to see the amount of people waiting in line at Macy's.
   (A) amount of people waiting in line at Macy's.
   (B) number of people waiting in line at Macy's.
   (C) amount of persons waiting in line at Macy's.
   (D) amount of people waiting in line at Macys.
   (E) amount of people waiting at Macy's in line.

6. Whoever the gods wish to destroy, they first make mad.
   (A) Whoever   (C) Whomever
   (B) Whoever,   (D) Whomever,
         (E) Whosoever

7. She is one of those girls who are always complaining.
   (A) who are   (C) whom are
   (B) who is   (D) whom is
         (E) whose

8. We buy only cherry plums since we like those kind best.
   (A) those kind   (C) that kind
   (B) these kind   (D) that kinds
         (E) them kind

9. Making friends is more rewarding than to be antisocial.

   (A) to be antisocial
   (B) us being anti-social
   (C) being anti social
   (D) to be anti-social
   (E) being antisocial

10. Jerry Cruncher was very aggravated by his wife's praying.

   (A) very aggravated
   (B) quite aggravated
   (C) much annoyed
   (D) very much aggravated
   (E) very agitated

11. They invited my whole family to the cookout —my father, my mother, my sister and I.

   (A) my sister and I.
   (B) my sister and me.
   (C) I and my sister.
   (D) me and my sister.
   (E) both my sister and I.

12. Having raked the beach for hours, the search for the lost ring was abandoned.

   (A) Having raked the beach.
   (B) Having the beach raked.
   (C) After we had raked the beach.
   (D) Having raked, the beach.
   (E) Raking the beach.

13. Her brother never has and never will be dependable.

   (A) never has
   (B) hardly never has
   (C) never had
   (D) not ever has
   (E) never has been

14. My brother is making chicken for dinner tonight, and I don't want to miss it.

   (A) miss it.
   (B) miss tonight.
   (C) miss the chicken.
   (D) miss my mother.
   (E) miss the dinner.

15. His tone clearly implied that he was bitterly disappointed.

   (A) clearly implied.
   (B) clearly inferred.
   (C) inferred clearly.
   (D) implied a clear inference.
   (E) made a clear implication.

16. Now kick your feet in the water like Gregory just did.

   (A) like Gregory just did.
   (B) as Gregory just did.
   (C) like Gregory just done.
   (D) as Gregory just done.
   (E) like Gregory's.

17. Macy's sells merchandise of equal quality and having a lower price.

   (A) having a lower price.
   (B) having lower prices.
   (C) having lower price.
   (D) has a lower price.
   (E) with a lower price.

18. After I had sucked the lemon, the apple tasted sweetly.

   (A) tasted sweetly.
   (B) tasted sweet.
   (C) tasted sweetened.
   (D) tastes sweetly.
   (E) had a taste that was sweet.

19. The reason Frank is going to Arizona is because he needs a dry climate.

   (A) is because he needs.
   (B) is that he needs.
   (C) is because he needed.
   (D) is on account of he needs.
   (E) is that he has a need for.

20. We can't <u>assist but one</u> of you at a time, so try to be patient.

    (A) We can't assist but one.
    (B) We can assist but one.
    (C) We can't assist only one.
    (D) We can't only assist one.
    (E) We can assist not one.

21. If you <u>would have been prompt</u>, we might have arrived in time for the first act.

    (A) If you would have been prompt.
    (B) If you were to have been prompt.
    (C) If you would've been prompt.
    (D) If you had been prompt.
    (E) If you'd of been prompt.

22. <u>After he graduated high school</u>, he went to Dartmouth.

    (A) After he graduated high school.
    (B) When he graduated high school.
    (C) After he had graduated from high school.
    (D) After he graduated from high school.
    (E) Having graduated high school.

23. The recurrence of identical sounds, <u>help to awaken</u> the emotions.

    (A) help to awaken.
    (B) help to wake up.
    (C) will help to have awakened.
    (D) assist in awakening.
    (E) helps to awaken.

24. Oliver Wendell Holmes decided to become a writer <u>being that</u> his father was a successful author.

    (A) being that.
    (B) on account of.
    (C) since.
    (D) in view of.
    (E) in that.

25. Nothing would satisfy him <u>but that</u> I bow to his wishes.

    (A) but that.
    (B) although that.
    (C) when that.
    (D) that.
    (E) but.

26. <u>Let's you and me</u> settle the matter between ourselves.

    (A) Let's you and me.
    (B) Let's I and you.
    (C) Let's both of us.
    (D) Let's me and you.
    (E) Let you and me.

27. <u>If you would have considered</u> all the alternatives, you would have chosen another course.

    (A) If you would have considered.
    (B) If you would've considered.
    (C) If you considered.
    (D) If you had considered.
    (E) If you have considered.

28. <u>Due to</u> the mechanic's carelessness, forty lives were lost.

    (A) Due to.
    (B) As to.
    (C) Because of.
    (D) In view of.
    (E) Seeing that it was.

29. The climate of Israel is somewhat <u>like California</u>.

    (A) like California.
    (B) like California's.
    (C) as California.
    (D) as California's.
    (E) similar to California.

30. By 2 o'clock, the child <u>will have lain</u> in his bed for ten solid hours.

    (A) will have lain.
    (B) will have lied.
    (C) will have laid.
    (D) will have lay.
    (E) will be laying.

END OF TEST

Go on to do the following Test in this Examination, just as you would be expected to do on the actual exam. You will find correct answers for the entire Examination following the last question. Check your answers carefully after you have completed the whole Examination.

TEST V. LOGIC AND ORGANIZATION

TIME: 5 Minutes. 8 Questions.

DIRECTIONS: This test consists of brief passages in which each sentence is numbered. Following each passage are questions which refer to the numbered sentences in the passage. Answer each question by choosing the best alternative (A,B,C,D, or E) and blacken the space corresponding to your choice on the Answer Sheet provided.

Explanations of the key points behind these questions appear with the answers at the end of this test. The explanatory answers provide just the help you need to strengthen your ability to meet and master this type of question.

[1]In the course of the larger social movements of the twentieth century, what is being done to and for children is especially magnetic. [2]This is true not only for child welfare today but also for the entire social, since today's children will take their places in it as adults. [3]The treatment of children is a forecast, prophecy and prediction of social change. [4]Nevertheless, those are true because in the status and nurture of the child are expressed the values of the future. [5]It is appropriate, therefore, to consider what changes are taking place in the ideas and conceptions about childhood. [6]It is important to see where the movement is going and what ideas and conceptions are guiding it. [7]The rate of progress of this movement largely depresses the progress of civilization.

1. The word *magnetic* in sentence 1 should be

    (A) left as it is
    (B) changed to *pathetic*
    (C) changed to *tolerant*
    (D) changed to *infantile*
    (E) changed to *significant*

2. The meaning of sentence 2 would be clearest if

    (A) the sentence were left as it is
    (B) *life in the future* were added after *social*
    (C) *currently* were added after *welfare*
    (D) the part after *places* were omitted
    (E) *This is true* were omitted

3. Sentence 3 would be most improved if

    (A) it were left as it is
    (B) *of children* were omitted
    (C) the part after *prediction* were omitted
    (D) *prophecy and prediction* were omitted
    (E) *The treatment of* were changed to *How we treat*

S3616

4. Sentence 4 should begin

(A) as it begins now
(B) with *Nevertheless, this is true*
(C) with *This is true*

(D) with *Those are true*
(E) with *Notwithstanding, these are true*

5. In sentence 5, the phrase *taking place* is best

(A) left as it is
(B) changed to *taking off*
(C) changed to *flying by*

(D) changed to *taken*
(E) changed to *are flown to places*

6. Sentence 6 is best placed

(A) where it is now
(B) before sentence 1
(C) after sentence 7

(D) after sentence 6
(E) after sentence 2

7. The word *depresses* in sentence 7 is best

(A) left as it is
(B) changed to *depression*
(C) changed to *determines*

(D) changed to *determination*
(E) changed to *deterring*

8. If the passage is to be divided into two paragraphs, the second paragraph should begin with

(A) sentence 3
(B) sentence 2
(C) sentence 6

(D) sentence 7
(E) sentence 5

END OF PART

Go on to the following Test in the next Part of this Examination, just as you would be expected to do on the actual exam. If you have any available time use it to make sure that you have marked your Answer Sheet properly for this Part. Correct Answers for all Parts of this Exam follow the last question. Derive your scores only after completing the entire Exam.

PART II. THE SOCIAL STUDIES TEST

TIME: 90 Minutes. 57 Questions.

TEST VI. INTERPRETATION OF SOCIAL STUDIES READINGS

TIME: 60 Minutes. 37 Questions.

DIRECTIONS: Read each passage to get the general idea. Then reread the passage more carefully to answer the questions based on the passage. For each question read all choices carefully. Then select the answer you consider correct or most nearly correct. Blacken the answer space corresponding to your best choice, just as you would do on the actual examination.

To explain exactly how to answer this type of social studies question we show you a social studies passage and sample questions. The correct answers are: S1 = A; S2 = D

Sample:

It is not always necessary to travel great distances to foreign lands to bring back interesting and valuable scientific results. Right here in the United States there are treasures to be sought which in a few years may be past obtaining. The frontier is gone but even today there are areas of no inconsiderable magnitude practically unexplored; and one need not even go so far as our newer West, for, though they are becoming scarce, little-explored regions still exist along the Atlantic seaboard and in the Mississippi Valley. Among the treasures today sought by expeditions from museums and universities are photographs of native wild birds and recordings of their voices — particularly of birds which, because of the development of civilization, are becoming rare.

S1. The writer points out that the Atlantic states provide
A. a rich field for scientific investigation
B. a high level of civilization
C. opportunities for travel
D. great museums and universities.

S2. The writer mentions museum expeditions sent out to
A. create bird sanctuaries
B. domesticate wild birds
C. kill and retrieve birds for exhibits
D. take pictures of rare birds.

Reading Passage I

In the consistent development of our previous efforts toward the saving and safeguarding of our national life, I have continued to recognize three related steps. The first is relief because the primary concern of any Government dominated by the humane ideals of democracy is the simple principle that in a land of resources no one should be permitted to starve. Relief was and continues to be our first consideration. It calls for large expenditures and will continue in modified form to do so for a long time to come. We may as well recognize that fact. Relief comes from the paralysis that arose as the after-effect of that unfortunate decade characterized by a mad chase for unearned riches, and an unwillingness of leaders in almost every walk of life to look beyond their own schemes and speculations.

In our administration of relief we followed two principles: first, that direct giving should, wherever possible, be supplemented by provision for useful and remunerative work and, second that where families in their existing surroundings will in all human probability never find an opportunity for full self-maintenance, happiness and enjoyment, we shall try to give them a new chance in new surroundings.

The second step was recovery, and it is sufficient for me to ask each and every one of you to compare the situation in agriculture and in industry today with what is was fifteen months ago.

At the same time, we have recognized the necessity of reform and reconstruction-reform because much of our trouble today and in the past few years has been due to lack of understanding of the elementary principles of justice and fairness by those in whom leadership in business and finance was placed, reconstruction because the new conditions in our economy as well as old but neglected conditions had to be corrected.

1. The proposals mentioned in this passage suggest that this government is slightly
   (A) theocratic   (C) socialistic
   (B) autocratic   (D) plutocratic.

2. This program is intended to
   (A) bring the economy to a halt
   (B) put the economy onto its feet again
   (C) increase exports into foreign countries
   (D) help the small businessman.

3. These measures will create
   (A) budgetary deficit
   (B) budgetary surplus
   (C) balanced budget
   (D) unbalanced budget

4. The speaker states in the first paragraph that in order to obtain relief, it will be necessary to
   (A) levy more taxes
   (B) stop importing foreign goods
   (C) increase governmental spending for a long time to come
   (D) stop wasting natural resources.

5. For a government dominated by humane ideals, the primary concern should be that
   (A) one is innocent until proven guilty
   (B) freedom to worship as one pleases will never be denied
   (C) in a land of resources no one will starve
   (D) our natural resources will not be misused.

6. By "relief," the author hopes to provide
   (A) useful and remunerative work as well as new, more enjoyable surroundings
   (B) higher wages
   (C) more vacations and a shortening of the working day
   (D) better housing for low income families.

7. According to this article, leaders in the field of business and finance
   (A) are hard-working and industrious
   (B) do not understand elementary principles of justice and fairness
   (C) are paid more than they are worth
   (D) ought to become more patriotic.

8. Reconstruction is necessary because
   (A) many buildings were bombed during the war
   (B) the South lost the Civil War
   (C) nothing else worked
   (D) conditions in our economic life had to be corrected.

9. The author of this speech is
   (A) Franklin D. Roosevelt
   (B) Karl Marx
   (C) Abraham Lincoln
   (D) Dwight D. Eisenhower.

Reading Passage II

Europe has a set of primary interests which to us have none or a very remote relation. Hence she must be engaged in frequent controversies, the causes of which are essentially foreign to our concerns. Hence, therefore, it must be unwise in us to implicate ourselves by artificial ties in the ordinary vicissitudes of her politics or the ordinary combinations and collisions of her friendships or enmities.

Our detached and distant situation invites and enables us to pursue a different course. If we remain one people, under an efficient government, the period is not far off when we may defy material injury from external annoyance; when we may take such an attitude as will cause the neutrality we may at any time resolve upon to be scrupulously respected; when belligerent nations under the impossibility of making acquisitions upon us will not lightly hazard giving us provocation; when we may choose peace or war, as our interest, guided by justice, shall counsel.

Why forego the advantages of so peculiar a situation? Why quit our own to stand on foreign ground? Why by interweaving our destiny with that of any part of Europe, entangle our peace and prosperity in the toils of European amition, rivalship, interest, humor or caprice.

1. Our interests and those of Europe are
   (A) very similar
   (B) quite divergent
   (C) chiefly concerned with trade
   (D) not mentioned in the above article.

2. The author is advocating a policy of
   (A) free-trade
   (B) aggressive neutralism
   (C) isolationism
   (D) anschluss.

3. According to the author, the state of European politics is
   (A) peaceful
   (B) to be used as an example for America to follow
   (C) on the verge of decadence and collapse
   (D) uncertain and unpredictable.

4. The best course for America to follow would be to
   (A) build up an army strong enough to withstand any attack from Europe
   (B) remain a unified people under an efficient government and avoid European involvement
   (C) try and play one European state off against another
   (D) deal with all European nations regardless of political conditions.

5. At the time this article was written, the chief obstacle in closer American-European relations was
   (A) the Atlantic Ocean
   (B) a difference in religion
   (C) a difference of languages
   (D) the Revolutionary War.

Reading Passage III

The duties of all public officers are, or at least admit of being made, so plain and simple that men of intelligence may readily qualify themselves for their performance; and I cannot but believe that more is lost by the long continuance of men in office than is generally to be gained by their experience. I submit, therefore, to your consideration whether the efficiency of the Government would not be promoted and official industry and integrity better secured by a general extension of the law which limits appointments to four years.

In a country where offices are created solely for the benefit of the people no one man has any more intrinsic right to official station than another. Offices were not established to give support to particular men at the public expense. No individual wrong is, therefore, done by removal, since neither appointment to nor continuance in office is a matter of right. The incumbent became an officer with a view to public benefits, and when these require his removal they are not to be sacrificed to private interests. It is the people, and they alone who have a right to complain when a bad officer is substituted for a good one. He who is removed has the same means of obtaining a living that is enjoyed by the millions who never held office. The proposed limitation would destroy the idea of property now so generally connected with official station, and although individual distress may be sometimes produced, it would by promoting that rotation which constitutes a leading principle in the republican creed, give healthful action to the system.

1. A fitting title for this selection is

   (A) Rotation in Public Office
   (B) Longer Terms for Public Officials
   (C) Corruption in Government
   (D) Government for the People.

2. The duties of public office are

   (A) strenuous   (C) arduous and difficult
   (B) dull and boring (D) plain and simple

3. Who are allowed to hold public office?

   (A) college graduates
   (B) all citizens
   (C) persons owning property
   (D) persons who voted in the previous election.

4. Political offices were created

   (A) to support particular men at the public expense
   (B) in the Constitution of the United States
   (C) for the benefit of the people
   (D) for politicians.

5. The author can be considered a (an)

   (A) anarchist   (C) democrat
   (B) monarchist   (D) liberal

6. The chief duty of an official is to

   (A) pass laws
   (B) serve his constituents
   (C) consult with the President
   (D) investigate graft in government

7. According to the author, the idea of "property" connected with public office

   (A) promotes a high class of officials
   (B) is neither good nor bad
   (C) is good for our economy
   (D) eliminates many worthy candidates.

8. The author is writing against

   (A) excessively long tenure of office
   (B) graft among public officials
   (C) nepotism
   (D) older officials in government.

9. The author of this selection is

   (A) John Adams
   (B) Andrew Jackson
   (C) Franklin D. Roosevelt
   (D) Abraham Lincoln.

Reading Passage IV

Fate has brought it about that America is at the center, no longer on the edges, of Western civilization. In this fact resides the American destiny. We can deny the fact and refuse our destiny. If we do, Western civilization, which is the glory of our world, will become a disorganized and decaying fringe around the Soviet Union and the emergent people of Asia. But if we comprehend our destiny we shall become equal to it.

For America is now called to do what the founders and the pioneers always believed was the American task: to make the New World a place where the ancient faith can flourish anew. To ask whether the American nation will rise to this occasion and be equal to its destiny is to ask whether Americans have the will to live.

The American idea is a hope and a pledge of fulfillment. It is founded upon an image of man and of his place in the universe, of his reason and his will, his knowledge of good and evil, his hope of a higher and a natural law which is above all governments, and indeed above all particular laws: this tradition descends to Americana from the Mediterranean world of the ancient Greeks, Hebrews and Romans. The Atlantic is now the Mediterranean sea of this culture and this faith.

1. The best title for this article is
   (A) The American Destiny
   (B) The Mediterranean and the Atlantic
   (C) The New America
   (D) The Greeks and the Americans.

2. The center of Western civilization is now located
   (A) around the Mediterranean
   (B) in the United States
   (C) in England
   (D) in Greece and Rome.

3. If America refuses its destiny, Western civilization will
   (A) continue its rapid advance
   (B) be inferior to that of Africa's in the near future
   (C) be surpassed and discarded by Russia and other Asiatic countries
   (D) not be affected either way.

4. According to the original founders, America's task was to enable the ancient faith to
   (A) be reborn
   (B) die out peacefully

   (C) grow into something new and different
   (D) be completely forgotten.

5. America's failing to fulfill her task is tantamount to saying that America
   (A) has no competent leaders
   (B) will lose the next conflict with Russia
   (C) needs a better education system
   (D) has no desire to exist.

6. The American idea
   (A) is basically for all people
   (B) is embodied in the Bill of Rights
   (C) came down to us from the Greeks, Romans, and Hebrews
   (D) developed over our three hundred year history.

7. The Greeks and Romans regarded the Mediterranean in much the same way that Western civilization regards the
   (A) Great Lakes
   (B) Gulf of Mexico
   (C) Panama Canal
   (D) Atlantic Ocean.

Reading Passage V

You tell me that law is above freedom of utterance. And I reply that you can have no wise laws nor free enforcement of wise laws until there is free expression of the wisdom of the people — and, alas their folly with it. But if there is freedom, folly will die of its own poison. That is the history of the race. You say that freedom of utterance is not for time of stress, and I reply with the sad truth that only in time of stress is freedom of utterance in danger. No one questions it in calm days, because it is not needed. And the reverse is true also; only when free utterance is suppressed is it needed, and when it is needed, it is most vital to justice. Peace is good. But if you are interested in peace through force and without discussion, that is to say, free utterance decently and in order — your interest in justice is slight. And peace without justice is tyranny. This state today is in more danger from suppression than from violence, because, in the end, suppression leads to violence. Violence is the child of suppression. Whoever pleads for justice helps to keep the peace; and whoever tramples upon the plea for justice, temperately made in the name of peace, only outrages peace and kills something fine in the heart of man which was put there when we got our manhood. When that is killed, brute meets brute on each side of the line.

1. Wise laws are dependent upon
   (A) judicious legislators
   (B) an enlightened population
   (C) freedom of expression
   (D) the amount of corruption in government.

2. The greatest threat to free expression is during
   (A) a depression
   (B) a critical period
   (C) an election campaign
   (D) prosperity.

3. Just as clouds precede the rain, suppression leads to
   (A) prejudice
   (B) violence
   (C) dictatorship
   (D) anarchy.

4. When times are peaceful
   (A) there is bound to be graft in government
   (B) people don't care about freedom of speech
   (C) freedom of expression is never questioned
   (D) freedom of speech is in serious danger.

5. When peace is brought about with the use of force
   (A) it will last a long time
   (B) it is lacking justice
   (C) it won't be democratic
   (D) there will be the need for a constant police force.

6. "With freedom of expression, there will be much folly as well as wisdom." According to the author
   (A) this statement is not true
   (B) only with true freedom will wisdom survive and folly be exposed.
   (C) censorship is needed to weed out the folly
   (D) this statement is true only in times of stress.

7. Our freedom is protected in the
   (A) first amendment to the Constitution
   (B) Declaration of Independence
   (C) Magna Carta
   (D) thirteenth amendment to the Constitution.

END OF TEST

TEST VII. SOCIAL STUDIES KNOWLEDGE

TIME: 30 Minutes. 20 Questions.

DIRECTIONS: *For each of the following questions, select the choice which best answers the question or completes the statement.*

1. The first three Articles of the Constitution of the United States of America represent a principle in government known as
   (A) separation of powers
   (B) guarantee of civil rights
   (C) limitation of central authority
   (D) elasticity.

2. Rules pertaining to the display and use of the United States flag are determined by
   (A) joint resolution of Congress
   (B) local custom
   (C) state legislation
   (D) Presidential order.

3. Authors such as Ida M Tarbell, Upton Sinclair and Samuel H. Adams were identified as
   (A) abolitionists   (B) anti-Federalists
   (C) realists   (D) muckrakers.

4. The words, " . . . secure the blessings of liberty to ourselves and our posterity" are part of the
   (A) United States Constitution
   (B) United Nations Charter
   (C) Magna Carta
   (D) Declaration of Independence.

5. Coal mining is an important industry in all of the following states except
   (A) West Virginia   (B) Kentucky
   (C) Idaho   (D) Illinois.

6. The shortest and most direct air route from New York to Moscow is over
   (A) North Pole   (B) Alaska
   (C) Iceland   (D) the Azores.

7. All of the following slogans are correctly associated except
   (A) "Square Deal"—Herbert Hoover
   (B) "New Deal"—Franklin D. Roosevelt
   (C) "New Freedom"—Woodrow Wilson
   (D) "Fair Deal"—Harry S. Truman.

8. Petroleum was first produced in the United States in
   (A) Pennsylvania   (B) Texas
   (C) Oklahoma   (D) California.

9. Abraham Lincoln gained wide publicity through his debates on the slavery issue with
   (A) Henry Clay   (B) John Calhoun
   (C) Stephen Douglas   (D) Jefferson Davis.

10. The largest area of new territory was acquired by the United States under the Presidency of
    (A) Thomas Jefferson
    (B) James Polk
    (C) Theodore Roosevelt
    (D) Andrew Johnson.

11. The country whose neutrality was violated by German forces during both World Wars I and II was
    (A) Netherlands   (B) Denmark
    (C) Norway   (D) Belgium.

12. Of the following, the pair in which the items are incorrectly associated is
    (A) American Red Cross—Clara Barton
    (B) Penal reform—John Stuart Mill
    (C) Salvation Army—William Booth
    (D) Women's Rights—Emmeline Pankhurst.

13. Which one of the following groups consists of foreign visitors who wrote books delineating the character of American society?
    (A) Mary Antin—Andrew Carnegie—Allan Nevins
    (B) James Bryce—Alexis deTocqueville—Frances Trollope
    (C) Hamlin Garland — Marquis James — Jacob Riis
    (D) Edward Bok — Merle Curti — Carl C. Jensen.

14. Which one of the following is paired correctly with a book which he wrote?
    (A) Theodore Dreiser—Babbitt
    (B) Jack London—Theory of the Leisure Class
    (C) O. E. Rolvaag—Son of the Middle Border
    (D) Lincoln Steffens—The Shame of the Cities.

15. Which one of the following statements is true of the legislative process under the British Parliamentary System?
    (A) The House of Lords may delay money bills up to two years
    (B) Bills go through the House of Lords in much the same fashion as through the House of Commons
    (C) The House of Lords can debate bills initiated in the House of Commons, but may not amend them
    (D) The committee system of law-making has given way to open and direct debate of cabinet-sponsored measures.

16. The North raised most of its revenue for financing the Civil War by
    (A) levying the first United States income tax
    (B) increasing customs duties
    (C) borrowing through the sale of bonds
    (D) issuing greenbacks.

17. The decade of largest European immigration into the United States was
    (A) 1881-1890   (C) 1911-1920
    (B) 1901-1910   (D) 1921-1930

18. The Twenty-second Amendment
    (A) limited the President's term of office to eight years
    (B) limited the President to two terms plus any part of an unexpired term
    (C) expressly exempted the incumbent President from its provisions
    (D) designated the Speaker of the House as next to the Vice-President in the line of presidential succession.

19. The Constitution of the United States provides that the salary of a justice of the Supreme Court may *not* be
    (A) taxed
    (B) changed during a justice's term of office
    (C) reduced during a justice's term of office
    (D) unequal as compared with another justice's salary.

20. As a result of the decision in Marbury vs. Madison the
    (A) original jurisdiction of the Supreme Court was enlarged
    (B) appellate jurisdiction of the Supreme Court was enlarged
    (C) original jurisdiction of the Supreme Court was left unchanged
    (D) appellate jurisdiction of the Supreme Court was curtailed.

END OF PART

Go on to the following Test in the next Part of this Examination, just as you would be expected to do on the actual exam. If you have any available time use it to make sure that you have marked your Answer Sheet properly for this Part. Correct Answers for all Parts of this Exam follow the last question. Derive your scores only after completing the entire Exam.

PART III. THE SCIENCE TEST

TIME: 90 Minutes. 58 Questions.

TEST VIII. INTERPRETATION OF SCIENCE READINGS

TIME: 60 Minutes. 38 Questions.

This test places a special emphasis on scientific vocabulary and ability to pay close attention to detail and logic. It consists of a selection of passages from the field of natural sciences at the high school level and a number of questions testing a person's ability to comprehend and to interpret the content of each passage.

DIRECTIONS: Read each passage to get the general idea. Then reread the passage more carefully to answer the questions based on the passage. For each question read all choices carefully. Then select the answer you consider correct or most nearly correct. Blacken the answer space corresponding to your best choice, just as you would do on the actual examination.

To show you exactly how to answer this type of natural science question, we give you a representative natural science passage and suggest that you answer the two sample questions based on it. The correct answers are: S1=D; S2=C.

Sample: Influenza travels exactly as fast as man. In oxcart days its progress was slow. In 1918 man could girdle the globe in eight weeks, and that is exactly the time it took influenza to complete its encirclement of the earth. Today, by jet, man moves at higher speed. This modern speed makes influenza's advent unpredictable from day to day. It all means that our control over the disease must be proportionately swifter.

S1. The title below that best expresses the ideas of this paragraph is:
A. Influenza Around the World
B. Influenza Epidemic of 1918
C. Unpredictability of Influenza
D. The Effect of Speed on the Spread of Influenza.

S2. The author states that more adequate control of influenza is necessary nowadays because
A. it may occur at any time
B. it may occur anywhere
C. man carries it about more quickly
D. germs can travel as fast as an airplane.

Correct answers for these questions appear at the end of this examination, together with the answers to all the other tests.

Reading Passage I

As the world's population grows, the part played by man in influencing plant life becomes increasingly greater. In old and densely populated countries, as in central Europe, man determines almost wholly what shall grow and what shall not grow. In such regions, the influence of man on plant life is in large measure a beneficial one. Laws, often centuries old, protect plants of economic value and preserve soil fertility. In newly settled countries the situation is unfortunately quite the reverse. The pioneer's life is too strenuous for him to think of posterity.

Some years ago Mt. Mitchell, the highest summit east of the Mississippi, was covered with a magnificent forest. A lumber company was given full rights to fell the trees. Those not cut down were crushed. The mountain was left a wasted area where fire would rage and erosion complete the destruction. There was no stopping the devastating foresting of the company, for the contract had been given. Under a more enlightened civilization this could not have happened. The denuding of Mt. Mitchell is a minor chapter in the destruction of lands in the United States; and this country is by no means the only sufferer. China, India, Egypt, and East Africa all have their thousands of square miles of wasteland, the result of man's indifference to the future.

Deforestation, grazing, and poor farming are the chief causes of the destruction of land fertility. Wasteful cutting of timber is the first step. Grazing then follows lumbering in bringing about ruin. The Caribbean slopes of northern Venezuela are barren wastes owing first to ruthless cutting of forests and then to destructive grazing. Hordes of goats have roamed these slopes until only a few thorny acacias and cacti remain. Erosion completed the devastation. What is there illustrated on a small scale is the story of vast areas in China and India, countries where famines are of regular occurrence.

Man is not wholly to blame, for Nature is often merciless. In parts of India and China, plant life, when left undisturbed by man, cannot cope with either the disastrous floods of wet seasons or the destructive winds of the dry season. Man has learned much; prudent land management has been the policy of the Chinese people since 2700 B. C., but even they have not learned enough.

When the American forestry service was in its infancy, it met with much opposition from legislators who loudly claimed that the protected land would in one season yield a crop of cabbages of more value than all the timber on it.

Herein lay the fallacy, that one season's crop is all that need be thought of. Nature, through the years, adjusts crops to the soil and to the climate. Forests usually occur where precipitation exceeds evaporation. If the reverse is true, grasslands are found; and where evaporation is still greater, desert or scrub vegetation alone survives. The phytogeographic map of a country is very similar to the climatic map based on rainfall, evaporation, and temperature. Man ignores this natural adjustment of crops and strives for one "bumper" crop in a single season; he may produce it, but "year in and year out the yield of the grassland is certain, that of the planted fields, never."

Man is learning; he sprays his trees with insecticides and fungicides; he imports ladybugs to destroy aphids; he irrigates, fertilizes, and rotates his crops; but he is still indifferent to many of the consequences of his short-sighted policies. The great dust storms of the western United States are proof of this indifference.

In spite of the evidence to be had from this country, the people of other countries, still in the pioneer stage, farm as wastefully as did our own pioneers. In the interiors of Central and South American Republics natives fell superb forest trees and leave them to rot in order to obtain virgin soil for cultivation. Where the land is hillside, it readily washes and after one or two seasons is unfit for crops. So the frontier farmer pushes back into the primeval forest, moving his hut as he goes, and fells more monarchs to lay bare another patch of ground for his plantings to support his family. Valuable timber which will require a century to replace is destroyed and the land laid waste to produce what could be supplied for a pittance.

How badly man can err in his handling of land is shown by the draining of extensive swamp areas, which to the uninformed would seem to be a very good thing to do. One of the first effects of the drainage is the lowering of the water-table, which may bring about the death of the dominant species and leave to another species the possession of the soil, even when the difference in water level is little more than an inch. Frequently, bog country will yield marketable crops of cranberries and blueberries but, if drained, neither these nor any other economic plant will grow on the fallow soil. Swamps and marshes have their drawbacks but also their virtues. When drained they may leave waste land the surface of which rapidly erodes to be then blown away in dust blizzards disastrous to both man and wild beasts.

1. The best title for this passage might be

    (A) How to Increase Soil Productivity
    (B) Conservation of Natural Resources
    (C) Man's Effect on Soil
    (D) Soil Conditions and Plant Growth.

2. A policy of good management is sometimes upset by

    (A) the indifference of man
    (B) centuries-old laws
    (C) floods and winds
    (D) grazing animals.

3. Areas in which the total amounts of rain and snow falling on the ground are greater than that which is evaporated will support

    (A) forests
    (B) grasslands
    (C) scrub vegetation
    (D) no plants

4. Pioneers do not have a long range view on soil problems since they

    (A) are not protected by laws
    (B) live under averse conditions
    (C) use poor methods of farming
    (D) must protect themselves from famine.

5. Phytogeographic maps are those that show

    (A) areas of grassland
    (B) areas of bumper crops
    (C) areas of similar climate
    (D) areas of similar plants.

6. The basic cause of frequent famines in China and India is probably due to

    (A) allowing animals to roam wild
    (B) drainage of swamps
    (C) over-grazing of the land
    (D) destruction of forests.

7. With a growing world population the increased need for soil for food production might be met by

    (A) draining unproductive swamp areas
    (B) legislating against excess lumbering
    (C) trying to raise bumper crops each year
    (D) irrigating desert areas.

8. What is meant by "the yield of the grasslands is certain; that of the planted field, never" is that

    (A) it is impossible to get more than one bumper crop from any one cultivated area
    (B) crops, planted in former grasslands will not give good yields
    (C) through the indifference of man, dust blizzards have occurred in former grasslands
    (D) if man does not interfere, plants will grow in the most suitable environment.

9. The first act of prudent land management might be to

    (A) prohibit drainage of swamps
    (B) use irrigation and crop rotation in planted areas
    (C) increase use of fertilizers
    (D) prohibit excessive forest lumbering.

10. The results of good land management may usually be found in

    (A) heavily populated areas
    (B) areas not given over to grazing
    (C) underdeveloped areas
    (D) ancient civilizations.

11. Long-range programs of soil management are possible only in

    (A) young nations
    (B) ancient civilizations
    (C) those nations with an agricultural economy
    (D) those nations which want it.

Reading Passage II

Of all the physical changes that have been and are now taking place on the surface of the earth, the sea and its shores have been the scene of the greatest stability. The dry land has seen the rise, the decline, and even the disappearance of vast hordes of various types and forms within times comparatively recent, geologically speaking; but life in the sea is today virtually what it was when many of the forms now extinct on land had not yet been evolved. Also, it may be parenthetically stated here, the marine habitat has been biologically the most important in the evolution and development of life on this planet. Its rhythmic influence can still be traced in those animals whose ancestors have long since left that realm to abide far from their primary haunts. For it is now generally held as an accepted fact that the shore area of an ancient sea was the birthplace of life.

Still, despite the primitive conditions still maintained in the sea, its shore inhabitants show an amazing diversity; while their adaptive characters are perhaps not exceeded in refinement by those that distinguish the dwellers of dry land. Why is this diversity manifest? We must look for an answer into the physical factors obtaining in that extremely slender zone surrounding the continents, marked by the rise and fall of the tides.

It will be noticed by the most casual observer that on any given seashore the area exposed between the tide marks may be roughly divided into a number of levels each characterized by a certain assemblage of animals. Thus in proceeding from high—to low-water mark, new forms constantly become predominant while other forms gradually drop out. Now, provided that the character of the substratum does not change, these differences in the types of animals are determined almost exlusively by the duration of time that the individual forms may remain exposed to the air without harm. Indeed, so regularly does the tidal rhythm act on certain animals (the barnacles, for instance), that certain species have come to require a definite period of exposure in order to maintain themselves, and will die out if kept continuously submerged. Although there are some forms that actually require periodic exposure, the number of species inhabiting the shore that are able to endure exposure every twelve hours, when the tide falls, is comparatively few.

With the alternate rise and fall of the tides, the successive areas of the tidal zone are subjected to force of wave-impact. In certain regions the waves often break with considerable force. Consequently, wave-shock has had a profound influence on the structure and habits of shore animals. It is characteristic of most shore animals that they shun definitely exposed places, and seek shelter in nooks and crannies and such refuges as are offered under stones and seaweed; particularly is this true of those forms living on rock and other firm foundations. Many of these have a marked capacity to cling closely to the substratum; some, such as anemones and certain snails, although without the grasping organs of higher animals, have special powers of adhesion; others, such as sponges and sea squirts, remain permanently fixed, and if torn loose from their base are incapable of forming a new attachment. But perhaps the most significant method of solving the problem presented by the surf has been in the adaptation of body-form to minimize friction. This is strikingly displayed in the fact that seashore animals are essentially flattened forms. Thus, in the typically shore forms the sponges are of the encrusting type, the non-burrowing worms are leaflike, the snails and other mollusks are squat forms and are without the spines and other ornate extensions such as are often produced on the shells of many mollusks in deeper and quieter waters. The same influence is no less marked in the case of the crustaceans; the flattening is either lateral, as in the amphipods, or dorso-ventral, as in the isopods and crabs.

In sandy regions, because of the unstable nature of substratum, no such means of attachment as indicated in the foregoing paragraph will suffice to maintain the animals in their almost ceaseless battle with the billows. Most of them must perforce depend on their ability quickly to penetrate into the sand for safety. Some forms endowed with less celerity, such as the sand dollars, are so constructed that their bodies offer no more resistance to wave impact than does a flat pebble.

Temperature, also, is a not inconsiderable factor among those physical forces constantly operating to produce a diversity of forms among seashore animals. At a comparatively shallow depth in the sea, there is small fluctuation of temperatures; and life there exists in surroundings of serene stability; but as the shore is approached, the influence of the sun becomes more and more manifest and the variation is greater. This variation becomes greatest between the tide marks where, because of the very shallow depths and the fresh water from the land, this area is subjected to wide changes in both temperature and salinity.

Nor is a highly competitive mode of life without its bearing on structure as well as habits. In this phase of their struggle for existence, the animals of both the sea and the shore have become possessed of weapons for offense and defense that are correspondingly varied.

Although the life in the sea has been generally considered and treated as separate and distinct from the more familiar life on land, that supposition has no real basis in fact. Life on this planet is one vast unit, depending for its existence chiefly on the same sources of supply. That portion of animal life living in the sea, notwithstanding its strangeness and unfamiliarity, may be considered as but the aquatic fringe of the life on land. It is supported largely by materials washed into the sea, which are no longer available for the support of land animals. Perhaps we have been misled in these considerations of sea life because of the fact that approximately three times as many major types of animals inhabit salt water as live on the land: of the major *types* of animals no fewer than ten are exclusively marine, that is to say, nearly half again as many as land-dwelling types together. A further interesting fact is that despite the greater variety in the form and structure of sea animals about three fourths of all known *kinds* of animals live on the land, while only one fourth lives in the sea. In this connection it is noteworthy that sea life becomes scarcer with increasing distance from land; toward the middle of the oceans it disappears almost completely. For example, the central south Pacific is a region more barren than is any desert area on land. Indeed, no life of any kind has been found in the surface water, and there seems to be none on the bottom.

Sea animals are largest and most abundant on those shores receiving the most copious rainfall. Particularly is this true on the most rugged and colder coasts where it may be assumed that the material from the land finds its way to the sea unaltered and in greater quantities.

1. The best title for this passage might be
   (A) Between the Tides
   (B) Seashore Life
   (C) The Tides
   (D) The Seashore.

2. Of the following adaptations, the one that would enable an organism to live on a sandy beach is
   (A) the ability to move rapidly
   (B) the ability to burrow deeply
   (C) a flattened shape
   (D) spiny extensions of the shell.

3. The absence of living things in mid-ocean might be due to
   (A) lack of rainfall in mid-ocean
   (B) the distance from material washed into the sea
   (C) larger animals feeding on smaller ones which must live near the land
   (D) insufficient dissolved oxygen.

4. A greater variety of living things exists on a rocky shore than on a sandy beach because
   (A) rocks offer a better foothold than sand

   (B) sandy areas are continually being washed by the surf
   (C) temperature changes are less drastic in rocky areas
   (D) the water in rock pools is less salty.

5. Organisms found living at the high-tide mark are adapted to
   (A) maintain themselves in the air for a long time
   (B) offer no resistance to wave impact
   (C) remain permanently fixed to the substratum
   (D) burrow in the ground.

6. The author holds that living things in the sea represent the aquatic fringe of life on land. This is so because
   (A) there are relatively fewer marine forms of animals than there are land-living forms
   (B) there is greater variety among land-living forms
   (C) marine animals ultimately depend upon material from the land
   (D) there are three times as many kinds of animals on land than there are in the sea.

7. A biologist walking along the shore at the low-tide line would not easily find many live animals since

   (A) their flattened shapes make them indistinguishable
   (B) they are washed back and forth by the waves
   (C) they burrow deeply
   (D) they move rapidly.

8. The intent of the author in the last paragraph is to show that

   (A) the temperature and salinity of the sea determine the variety among shore animals
   (B) marine animals are vastly different from terrestrial organisms
   (C) colder areas can support more living things than warm areas
   (D) marine forms have the same problems as terrestrial animals.

9. A scientist wishing to study a great variety of living things would do well to hunt for them

   (A) in shallow waters
   (B) on a rocky seashore
   (C) on a sandy seashore
   (D) on any shore between the tide lines.

10. The most primitive forms of living things in the evolutionary scale are to be found in the sea because

   (A) the influence of the sea is found in land animals
   (B) the sea is relatively stable
   (C) many forms have become extinct on land
   (D) land animals are supposed to have evolved from sea organisms.

11. The author suggests that any area on the shore bounded by the high and low tide lines

   (A) has a greater variety of physical factors than area of similar size any other place
   (B) has a greater variety of living things than any other area of similar size
   (C) can be used to explain the great variations among living things
   (D) can be used to explain the adaptations that are found among living things.

12. Some organisms can withstand wave shock by

   (A) periodic exposures to air
   (B) hiding under stones
   (C) moving out to deep water
   (D) forming new attachments to the substratum.

13. Commercial fishing vessels would find their greatest catch in

   (A) mid-ocean
   (B) off cold land areas
   (C) off warm, moist land areas
   (D) off areas with great rainfall.

14. The greatest variations among shore animals are adaptations to

   (A) changing temperatures
   (B) variations in sub-stratum
   (C) minimize friction
   (D) alterations in salinity.

15. The fact that there is a greater number of kinds of animals living on land than in the sea might be related to the fact that

   (A) water does not show as great extremes in temperature as land does
   (B) evolution has proceeded at a faster pace on land than on the sea
   (C) aquatic animals depend for food upon that which is no longer needed by land animals
   (D) land animals live in a great variety of environments.

16. Live barnacles might be found on the bottom of a rowboat beached for some time just above the low-tide line since

   (A) they require alternate periods of immersion in the sea
   (B) they are protected from the impact of the waves
   (C) they require extremes of temperatures afforded by the beach
   (D) they are incapable of forming new attachments.

Reading Passage III

Recent scientific discoveries are throwing new light on the basic nature of viruses and on the possible nature of cancer, genes and even life itself. These discoveries are providing evidence for relationships between these four subjects which indicate that one may be dependent upon another to an extent not fully appreciated heretofore. Too often one works and thinks within too narrow a range and hence fails to recognize the significance of certain facts for other areas. Sometimes the important new ideas and subsequent fundamental discoveries come from the borderline areas between two well-established fields of investigation. This will result in the synthesis of new ideas regarding viruses, cancer, genes and life. These ideas in turn will result in the doing of new experiments which may provide the basis for fundamental discoveries in these fields.

There is no doubt that of the four topics, life is the one most people would consider to be of the greatest importance. However, life means different things to different people and it is in reality difficult to define just what we mean by life. There is no difficulty in recognizing an agent as living so long as we contemplate structures like a man, a dog or even a bacterium, and at the other extreme a piece of iron or glass or an atom of hydrogen or a molecule of water. The ability to grow or reproduce and to change or mutate has long been regarded as a special property characteristic of living agents along with the ability to respond to external stimuli. These are properties not shared by bits of iron or glass or even by a molecule of hemoglobin. Now if viruses had not been discovered, all would have been well. The organisms of the biologists would have ranged from the largest of animals all the way down to the smallest of the bacteria which are about 200 millimicrons. There would have been a definite beak with respect to size: the largest molecules known to the chemist were less than 20 millimicrons in size. Thus life and living agents would have been represented by those structures which possessed the ability to reproduce themselves and to mutate and were about ten times larger than the largest known molecule. This would have provided a comfortable area of separation between living and non-living things.

Then came the discovery of the viruses. These infectious, disease-producing agents are characterized by their small size, by their ability to grow or reproduce within specific living cells, and by their ability to change or mutate during reproduction. This was enough to convince most people that viruses were merely still smaller living organisms. When the sizes of different viruses were determined, it was found that some were actually smaller than certain protein molecules. When the first virus was isolated in the form of a crystallizable material it was found to be a nucleoprotein. It was found to possess all the usual properties associated with protein molecules yet was larger than any molecule previously described. Here was a molecule that possessed the ability to reproduce itself and to mutate. The distinction between living and non-living things seemed to be tottering. The gap in size between 20 and 200 millimicrons has been filled in completely by the viruses, with some actual overlapping at both ends. Some large viruses are larger than some living organisms, and some small viruses are actually smaller than certain protein molecules.

Let us consider the relationships between genes and viruses since both are related to life. Both genes and viruses seem to be nucleoproteins and both reproduce only within specific living cells. Both possess the ability to mutate. Although viruses generally reproduce many times within a given cell, some situations are known in which they appear to reproduce only once with each cell division. Genes usually reproduce once with each cell division, but here also the rate can be changed. Actually the similarities between genes and viruses are so remarkable that viruses were referred to as "naked genes" or "genes on the loose."

Despite the fact that today viruses are known to cause cancer in animals and in certain plants there exists a great reluctance to accept viruses as being of importance in human cancer. Basic biological phenomena generally do not differ strikingly as one goes from one species to another. It should be recognized that cancer is a biological problem and not a problem that is unique for man. Cancer originates when a normal cell suddenly becomes a cancer cell which multiplies widely and without apparent restraint. Cancer may originate in many different kinds of cells, but the cancer cell usually continues to carry certain traits of the cell of origin. The transformation of a normal cell into a cancer cell may have more than one kind of a cause, but there is good reason to consider the relationships that exist between viruses and cancer.

Since it has not been proved that human cancer, as generally experienced, is infectious, many persons believe that because viruses are infectious agents they cannot possibly be of importance in human cancer. However, viruses can mutate and examples are known in which a virus that never kills its host can mutate to form a new strain of virus that always kills its host. It does not seem unreasonable to assume that an innocuous latent virus might mutate to form a strain that causes cancer. Certainly the experimental evidence now available is consistent with the idea that viruses as we know them today, could be causative agents of most, if not all cancers, including cancers in man.

1. People were convinced that viruses were small living organisms, because viruses

   (A) are disease producing
   (B) reproduce within living cells
   (C) could be grown on artificial media
   (D) consist of nucleoproteins.

2. Scientists very often do not apply the facts learned in one subject area to a related field of investigation because

   (A) the borderline areas are too close to both to give separate facts
   (B) scientists work in a very narrow range of experimentation
   (C) new ideas are synthesized only as a result of new experimentation
   (D) fundamental discoveries are based upon finding close relationships in related sciences.

3. Before the discovery of viruses, it might have been possible to distinguish living things from non-living things by the fact that

   (A) animate objects can mutate
   (B) non-living substances cannot reproduce themselves
   (C) responses to external stimuli are characteristic of living things
   (D) living things were greater than 20 millimicrons in size.

4. The size of viruses is presently known to be

   (A) between 20 and 200 millimicrons
   (B) smaller than any bacterium
   (C) larger than any protein molecule
   (D) larger than most nucleoproteins.

5. That genes and viruses seem to be related might be shown by the fact that

   (A) both are ultramicroscopic
   (B) each can mutate but once in a cell
   (C) each reproduces but once in a cell
   (D) both appear to have the same chemical structure.

6. Viruses were called "genes on the loose" because they

   (A) seem to wander at will within cells
   (B) like genes, seem to be able to mutate
   (C) seemed to be genes without cells
   (D) could loosen genes from cells.

7. Cancer should be considered to be a biological problem rather than a medical one because

   (A) viruses are known to cause cancers in animals
   (B) at present, human cancer is not believed to be contagious
   (C) there are many known causes for the transformation of a normal cell to a cancer cell
   (D) results of experiments on plants and animals do not vary greatly from species to species.

8. The possibility that a virus causing human cancer may appear might be due to

   (A) the fact that viruses have been known to mutate
   (B) a cancer-immune individual might lose his immunity
   (C) the fact that reproduction of human cancer cells might be due to a genetic factor
   (D) the fact that man is host to many viruses.

9. The best title for this passage might be

   (A) New Light on the Cause of Cancer
   (B) The Newest Theory on the Nature of Viruses
   (C) Viruses, Genes, Cancer and Life
   (D) On the Nature of Life.

10. It is quite possible that viruses unknown today, may be discovered by scientists in the future, since

   (A) viruses have been known to mutate
   (B) the crystalline structure of viruses can be changed
   (C) viruses have been known that cause cancer in animals
   (D) viruses must reproduce only within a specific cell.

11. Which of the following might not be a basis for the writer's last sentence?

   (A) Genes and viruses are both known to mutate.
   (B) Cancer is a universal phenomenon among living things.
   (C) Viruses are infectious while cancer is not.
   (D) Viruses may stimulate a normal cell to change to a cancer cell.

END OF TEST

TEST IX. SCIENCE INFORMATION

TIME: 30 Minutes. 20 Questions.

DIRECTIONS: For each of the following questions, select the choice which best answers the question or completes the statement.

Correct answers for these questions appear at the end of this examination, together with the answers to all the other tests.

1. Of the following, the part of a ship which gives it stability by lowering the center of gravity is the
   (A) bulkhead
   (B) anchor
   (C) keel
   (D) prow.

2. A wax begonia often turns reddish in a classroom because
   (A) it is not receiving enough sunlight
   (B) the soil is too rich
   (C) the soil is too dry
   (D) it is receiving too much sunlight.

3. Ringworm is caused by a(n)
   (A) alga
   (B) bacterium
   (C) fungus
   (D) protozoan.

4. Of the following, the most important function performed for man by the bee is to
   (A) produce beeswax
   (B) pollinate plants
   (C) produce honey
   (D) destroy harmful insects.

5. Nitrogen-fixing bacteria are found in nodules on the roots of the
   (A) beet
   (B) carrot
   (C) potato
   (D) clover.

6. Of the following animals, the one which is most closely related to the extinct dinosaur is the
   (A) sloth
   (B) elephant
   (C) lizard
   (D) whale.

7. The process which is responsible for the continuous removal of carbon dioxide from the atmosphere is
   (A) respiration
   (B) metabolism
   (C) oxidation
   (D) photosynthesis.

8. Bacilli are bacteria that are shaped like
   (A) chains of beads
   (B) isolated spheres
   (C) rods
   (D) spirals.

9. Among the following, the invertebrate is the
   (A) dinosaur
   (B) pigeon
   (C) python
   (D) starfish.

10. Saliva contains an enzyme which acts on
    (A) carbohydrates
    (B) minerals
    (C) proteins
    (D) vitamins.

11. The biologist who probably first used the term "cell" was
    (A) Hooke
    (B) Leeuwenhoek
    (C) Browne
    (D) Schleiden.

12. The term "tetrad" in genetics and cytology refers to a grouping of
    (A) genes
    (B) chromosomes
    (C) gametes
    (D) cells.

13. The taxonomic group just larger than a genus is the
 (A) phylum
 (B) order
 (C) family
 (D) class.

14. The botanical family to which the sweet pea belongs is the
 (A) Compositae
 (B) Rosaceae
 (C) Umbelliferae
 (D) Leguminosae.

15. Kelp belongs to the phylum
 (A) Thallophyta
 (B) Bryophyta
 (C) Pteridophyta
 (D) Spermatophyta.

16. Paramecium belongs to the class
 (A) Sarcodina
 (B) Mastigophora
 (C) Ciliata
 (D) Sporozoa.

17. Of the following groups of plants, the one in which the gametophyte generation is most reduced is the
 (A) thallophytes
 (B) bryophytes
 (C) pteridophytes
 (D) spermatophytes.

18. Scouring rushes and horsetails are most closely related to which one of the following?
 (A) mosses
 (B) mushrooms
 (C) ferns
 (D) grasses.

19. Of the following, the group of fish which have no true bones are the
 (A) teleosts
 (B) ganoids
 (C) elasmobranchs
 (D) dipnoids.

20. Flowering plants with parallel-veined leaves have in their seeds
 (A) no cotyledons
 (B) one cotyledon
 (C) two cotyledons
 (D) many cotyledons.

END OF PART

Go on to the following Test in the next Part of this Examination, just as you would be expected to do on the actual exam. If you have any available time use it to make sure that you have marked your Answer Sheet properly for this Part. Correct Answers for all Parts of this Exam follow the last question. Derive your scores only after completing the entire Exam.

PART IV. THE READING SKILLS TEST

TIME: 90 Minutes. 47 Questions.

TEST X. INTERPRETATION OF LITERARY MATERIALS

TIME: 30 Minutes. 17 Questions.

DIRECTIONS: Below each of the literary passages you will find one or more incomplete statements about the passage of prose, poetry, or drama. Each "stem" is followed by four or five "foils." Read each passage slowly, visualizing the plot, setting, action, characters, meaning, tone, and style. Re-read the passage before answering each question. From the emotions and attitudes expressed, choose the BEST "foil." Blacken the corresponding space on the answer sheet.

Correct answers for these questions appear at the end of this examination, together with the answers to all the other tests.

Fiction Passage I.

He felt strong enough to clear out the whole office single-handed. His body ached to do something, to rush out and revel in violence. All the indignities of his life enraged him . . . Could he ask the cashier privately for an advance? No, the cashier was no good, no damn good: he wouldn't give an advance . . . He knew where he would meet the boys: Leonard and O'Halloran and Nosey Flynn. The barometer of his emotional nature was set for a spell of riot.

His imagination had so abstracted him that his name was called twice before he answered. Mr. Alleyne and Miss Delacour were standing outside the counter and all the clerks had turned round in anticipation of something. The man got up from his desk. Mr. Alleyne began a tirade of abuse, saying that two letters were missing. The man answered that he knew nothing about them, that he had made a faithful copy. The tirade continued: It was so bitter and violent that the man could hardly restrain his fist from descending upon the head of the manikin before him:

"I know nothing about any other two letters," he said stupidly.

"You—know—nothing. Of course you know nothing," said Mr. Alleyne. "Tell me," he added, first glancing for approval to the lady beside him, "do you take me for a fool? Do you think me an utter fool?"

The man glanced from the lady's face to the little egg-shaped head and back again; and, almost before he was aware of it, his tongue had found a felicitous moment:

"I don't think, sir," he said, "that that's a fair question to put to me."

There was a pause in the very breathing of the clerks. Every one was astounded (the author of the witticism no less than his neighbors) and Miss Delacour, who was a stout, amiable person, began to smile broadly. Mr. Alleyne flushed to the hue of a wild rose and his mouth twitched with a dwarf's passion. He shook his fist in the man's face till it seemed to vibrate like the knob of some electric machine:

"You impertinent ruffian! You impertinent ruffian! I'll make short work of you! Wait till you see! You'll apologize to me for your impertinence or you'll quit the office instanter! You'll quit this, I'm telling you, or you'll apologize to me!"

He stood in a doorway opposite the office watching to see if the cashier would come out alone. All the clerks passed out and finally the cashier came out with the chief clerk. It was no use trying to say a word to him when was with the chief clerk. The man felt that his position was bad enough. He had been obliged to offer an abject apology to Mr. Alleyne for his impertinence but he knew what a hornet's nest the office would be for him. He could remember the way in which Mr. Alleyne had hounded little Peake out of the office in order to make room for his own nephew. He felt savage and thirsty and revengeful, annoyed with himself and with every one else. Mr. Alleyne would never give him an hour's rest; his life would be a hell to him. He had made a proper fool of himself this time. Could he not keep his tongue in his cheek? But they had never pulled together from the first, he and Mr. Alleyne, ever since the day Mr. Alleyne had overheard him mimicking his North of Ireland accent to amuse Higgins and Miss Parker; that had been the beginning of it. He might have tried Higgins for the money, but sure Higgins never had anything for himself. A man with two establishments to keep up, of course he couldn't . . .

—James Joyce, "Counterparts"

1. The unnamed man who is the main character of the story

   (A) is a happy and peaceful person
   (B) is interested in getting a loan of money
   (C) loves Miss Delacour, but has not been able to tell her
   (D) likes Mr. Alleyne but believes he loses his temper too easily

2. Because he looked at Miss Delacour for approval, it is obvious that Mr. Alleyne

   (A) is jealous of his clerk
   (B) was unaware she was in the room
   (C) is a show-off
   (D) is embarrassed to be yelling in front of a lady

3. When the author compares the man's emotional nature to a barometer, he is using

   (A) an apostrophe
   (B) a metaphor
   (C) a quotation
   (D) a colloquialism

4. "Seemed to vibrate like the knob of some electric machine" is an example of

   (A) a simile
   (B) a metaphor
   (C) a metonym
   (D) a cliché

5. The man knows that sooner or later

   (A) he will receive a promotion and a good raise in pay
   (B) Mr. Alleyne will hound him out of his job
   (C) Mr. Alleyne will be fired and he will take his place
   (D) Mr. Alleyne will apologize to him for his rudeness

6. The mood of the main character at the end of the selection is that of

   (A) deep humility
   (B) frustration and anger
   (C) exhaustion
   (D) bliss mixed with sorrow

Poetry Passage II.

1 For thee I shall not die,
2   Woman high of fame and name;
3 Foolish men thou mayest slay,
4   I and they are not the same.

5 Why should I expire
6   For the fire of any eye,
7 Slender waist or swan-like limb,
8   Is't for them that I should die?

9 The round breasts, the fresh skin,
10   Cheeks crimson, hair so long and rich;
11 Indeed, indeed, I shall not die,
12   Please God, not I, for any such.

13 The golden hair, the forehead thin,
14   The chaste mien, the gracious ease,
15 The rounded heel, the languid tone,
16   Fools alone find death from these.

17 Thy sharp wit, thy perfect calm,
18   Thy thin palm like foam of sea;
19 Thy white neck, thy blue eye,
20   I shall not die for thee.

21 Woman, graceful as the swan,
22   A wise man did nurture me,
23 Little palm, white neck, bright eye,
24   I shall not die for thee.

—David Hyde, "I Shall Not Die For Thee"

7. The poet thinks the woman is

(A) beautiful
(B) nagging
(C) ugly
(D) haughty

8. "A wise man did nurture me" implies

(A) a wise man was the poet's father
(B) the wise man was once her love
(C) the poet has been taught that it is foolish to suffer for love
(D) he is going against the wise man's advice

9. The first line of the first stanza is an example of

(A) paradox
(B) trimeter

(C) tetrameter
(D) anapestic foot

10. Which of the following lines is an example of the trochaic tetrameter?

(A) second line, second stanza
(B) first line, fourth stanza
(C) first line, third stanza
(D) second line, first stanza

11. When the poet writes "Thy thin palm like foam of sea," he is using

(A) hyperbole
(B) an apostrophe
(C) a simile
(D) a metaphor

Dramatic Passage

(Enter Hastings.)

Hastings. My dear friend, how have you managed with your mother? I hope you have amused her with pretending love for your cousin, and that you are willing to be reconciled at last? Our horses will be refreshed in a short time, and we shall soon be ready to set off.

Tony. And here's something to bear your charges by the way. *(Giving the casket)* Your sweetheart's jewels. Keep them, and hang those, I say, that would rob you of one of them.

Hastings. But how have you procured them from your mother?

Tony. Ask me no questions, and I'll tell you no fibs. I procured them by the rule of thumb. If I had not a key to every drawer in mother's bureau, how could I go to the alehouse so often as I do? An honest man may rob himself of his own at any time.

Hastings. Thousands do it every day. But to be plain with you; Miss Neville is endeavouring to procure them from her aunt this very instant. If she succeeds, it will be the most delicate way at least of obtaining them.

Tony. Well, keep them, till you know how it will be. But I know how it will be well enough; she'd as soon part with the only sound tooth in her head.

Hastings. But I dread the effects of her resentment, when she finds she has lost them.

Tony. Never you mind her resentment, leave me to manage that. I don't value her resentment the bounce of a cracker. Zounds!

(Exit Hastings.)

(Tony, Mrs. Hardcastle, Miss Neville)

Mrs. Hardcastle. Indeed, Constance, you amaze me. Such a girl as you want jewels? It will be time enough for jewels, my dear, twenty years hence, when your beauty begins to want repairs.

Miss Neville. But what will repair beauty at forty, will certainly improve it at twenty, Madam.

Mrs. Hardcastle. Yours, my dear, can admit of none. That natural blush is beyond a thousand ornaments. Besides, child, jewels are quite out at present. Don't you see half the ladies of our acquaintance, my Lady Kill-day-light, and Mrs. Crump, and the rest of them, carry their jewels to town, and bring nothing but Paste and Marcasites back?

Miss Neville. But who knows, Madam, but somebody that shall be nameless would like me best with all my little finery about me?

Mrs. Hardcastle. Consult your glass, my dear, and then see, if with such a pair of eyes, you want any better sparklers. What do you think, Tony, my dear, does your Cousin Con want any jewels, in your eyes, to set off her beauty?

Tony. That's as thereafter may be.

Miss Neville.   My dear aunt, if you knew how it would oblige me.

Mrs. Hardcastle.   A parcel of old-fashioned rose and table-cut things. They would make you like the court of King Solomon at a puppet-show. Besides, I believe I can't readily come at them. They may be missing, for aught I know to the contrary.

Tony (apart to Mrs. Hardcastle).   Then why don't you tell her so at once, as she's so longing for them. Tell her they're lost. It's the only way to quiet her. Say they're lost, and call me to bear witness.

Mrs. Hardcastle (apart to Tony).   You know, my dear, I'm only keeping them for you. So if I say they're gone, you'll bear me witness, will you? He! he! he!

Tony.   Never fear me. Ecod! I'll say I saw them taken out with my own eyes.

Miss Neville.   I desire them but for a day, Madam. Just to be permitted to shew them as relicks, and then they may be lock'd up again.

Mrs. Hardcastle.   To be plain with you, my dear Constance, if I could find them, you should have them. They're missing, I assure you. Lost, for aught I know; but we must have patience wherever they are.

Miss Neville.   I'll not believe it; this is but a shallow pretence to deny me. I know they're too valuable to be so slightly kept, and as you are to answer for the loss.

Mrs. Hardcastle.   Don't be alarm'd, Constance. If they be lost, I must restore an equivalent. But my son knows they are missing, and not to be found.

Tony.   That I can bear witness to. They are missing, and not to be found. I'll take my oath on't.

Mrs. Hardcastle.   You must learn resignation, my dear; for tho' we lost our fortune, yet we should not lose our patience. See me, how calm I am.

Miss Neville.   Ay, people are generally calm at the misfortunes of others.

Mrs. Hardcastle.   Now, I wonder a girl of your good sense should waste a thought upon such trumpery. We shall soon find them; and, in the mean time, you shall make use of my garnets till your jewels be found.

Miss Neville.   I detest garnets.

Mrs. Hardcastle.   The most becoming things in the world to set off a clear complexion. You have often seen how well they look upon me. You shall have them.

Miss Neville.   I dislike them of all things. You shan't stir.—Was ever any thing so provoking—to mislay my own jewels, and force me to wear her trumpery.

Tony.   Don't be a fool. If she gives you the garnets, take what you can get. The jewels are your own already. I have stolen them out of her bureau, and she does not know it. Fly to your spark, he'll tell you more of the matter. Leave me to manage her.

Miss Neville.   My dear cousin.

Mrs. Hardcastle.   Confusion! thieves! robbers! We are cheated, plundered, broke open, undone.

Tony. What's the matter, what's the matter, mama? I hope nothing has happened to any of the good family!

Mrs. Hardcastle. We are robbed. My bureau has been broke open, the jewels taken out, and I'm undone.

Tony. Oh! Is that all? Ha! ha! ha! By the laws, I never saw it better acted in my life. Ecod, I thought you was ruin'd in earnest, ha, ha, ha.

Mrs. Hardcastle. Why, boy, I am ruin'd in earnest. My bureau has been broke open, and all taken away.

Tony. Stick to that; ha, ha, ha! stick to that. I'll bear witness, you know, call me to bear witness.

Mrs. Hardcastle. It tell you, Tony, by all that's precious, the jewels are gone, and I shall be ruin'd for ever.

Tony. Sure I know they're gone, and I am to say so.

Mrs. Hardcastle. My dearest Tony, but hear me. They're gone, I say.

Tony. By the laws, mama, you make me for to laugh, ha! ha! I know who took them well enough, ha! ha! ha!

Mrs. Hardcastle. Was there ever such a blockhead, that can't tell the difference between jest and earnest. I tell you I'm not in jest, booby.

Tony. That's right, that's right: You must be in a bitter passion, and then nobody will suspect either of us. I'll bear witness that they are gone.

Mrs. Hardcastle. Was there ever such a cross-grain'd brute, that won't hear me! Can you bear witness that you're no better than a fool? Was ever poor woman so beset with fools on one hand, and thieves on the other?

Tony. I can bear witness to that.

Mrs. Hardcastle. Bear witness again, you blockhead you, and I'll turn you out of the room directly. My poor niece, what will become of her! Do you laugh, you unfeeling brute, as if you enjoyed my distress?

Tony. I can bear witness to that.

Mrs. Hardcastle. Do you insult me, monster? I'll teach you to vex your mother, I will.

Tony. I can bear witness to that.

(He runs off, she follows him.)

—Richard Sheridan, *She Stoops to Conquer*

12. The jewels were in the possession of Mrs. Hardcastle until

(A) they were lost
(B) Tony stole them
(C) Mrs. Hardcastle gave them to their rightful owner
(D) Hastings bought them

13. Mrs. Hardcastle says that the jewels

(A) do not belong to Miss Neville
(B) have been sold
(C) are not as fine as Constance's blush and eyes
(D) cannot compare with her son Tony

14. Mrs. Hardcastle believes that

    (A) Tony should not ever get his hands on the jewels
    (B) jewels should be worn only by older women
    (C) jewels are always in fashion
    (D) Miss Neville should marry Hastings

15. When Mrs. Hardcastle discovers that the jewels are really missing, she

    (A) becomes very happy
    (B) accuses Tony of taking them
    (C) is shocked
    (D) calls for the police

16. Mr. Hastings

    (A) hates Tony
    (B) persuades Mrs. Hardcastle to part with the jewels peacefully
    (C) plans to run off with Miss Neville
    (D) refuses to take the jewels from Tony

17. It is obvious from Hastings' first speech and from Mrs. Hardcastle's attitude that

    (A) she thinks Miss Neville would be a poor wife for anyone
    (B) Tony is deeply in love with Constance
    (C) Tony wants the jewels because he needs money to spend in the ale-house
    (D) she wishes Tony to marry Miss Neville

END OF TEST

Go on to do the following Test in this Examination, just as you would be expected to do on the actual exam. You will find correct answers for the entire Examination following the last question. Check your answers carefully after you have completed the whole Examination.

TEST XI. INTERPRETATION OF PROSE

TIME: 60 Minutes. 30 Questions.

This test is based on a selection of passages, both prose and verse. The questions emphasize knowledge and special abilities not frequently needed in ordinary reading. The abilities to interpret figures of speech, to cope with unusual sentence structure and word meaning, and to recognize mood and purpose are often tested, as is an understanding of literary forms.

DIRECTIONS: Below each of the following passages of literature you will find one or more incomplete statements about the passage. Each statement is followed by five words or expressions. Select the word or expression that most satisfactorily completes each statement in accordance with the direct or implied meaning of each passage.

Correct answers for these questions appear at the end of this examination, together with the answers to all the other tests.

Reading Passage 1

The modern biographer's task becomes one of discovering the "dynamics" of the personality he is studying rather than allowing the reader to deduce that personality from documents. If he achieves a reasonable likeness, he need not fear too much that the unearthing of still more material will alter the picture he has drawn; it should add dimension to it, but not change its lineaments appreciably. After all, he has had more than enough material to permit him to reach conclusions and to paint his portrait. With this abundance of material he can select moments of high drama and find episodes to illustrate character that make for vividness. In any event, biographers, I think, must recognize that the writing of a life may not be as "scientific" or as "definite" as we have pretended. Biography partakes of a large part of the subjective side of man, and we must remember that those who walked abroad in our time may have one appearance for us—but will seem quite different to posterity.

1. The title below that best expresses the ideas of this passage is
    (A) the dynamic personality
    (B) the growing popularity of biography
    (C) the scientific biography
    (D) a verdict of posterity
    (E) an approach to biography.

2. According to the author, which is the real task of the modern biographer?

    (A) interpreting the character revealed to him by the study of the presently available data
    (B) viewing the life of the subject in the biographer's own image
    (C) leaving to the reader the task of interpreting the character from contradictory evidence
    (D) collecting facts and setting them down in chronological order
    (E) being willing to wait until all the facts on his subject have been uncovered.

Reading Passage II

Acting, like much writing, is probably a compensation for and release from the strain of some profound maladjustment of the psyche. The actor lives most intensely by proxy. He has to be somebody else to be himself. But it is all done openly and for our delight. The dangerous man, the enemy of non-attachment or any other wise way of life, is the born actor who has never found his way into the Theater, who never uses a stage door, who does not take a call and then wipe the paint off his face. It is the intrusion of this temperament into political life, in which at this day it most emphatically does not belong, that works half the mischief in the world. In every country you may see them rise, the actors who will not use the Theater, and always they bring down disaster from the angry gods who like to see mountebanks in their proper place.

3. The title below that best expresses the ideas of this passage is
    (A) the influence of the theater
    (B) the tensions of theatrical life
    (C) the dangers of nonprofessional acting
    (D) the importance of makeup in the theater
    (E) the place for mountebanks.

4. Which best describes the author's attitude toward professional actors?
    (A) sneering
    (B) jealous
    (C) spiteful
    (D) detached
    (E) understanding.

5. According to the author, much of the world's trouble is caused by
    (A) theatergoers
    (B) underpaid actors

    (C) biographers of actors
    (D) performing politicians
    (E) angry gods.

6. According to the passage, the professional actor
    (A) relives his part offstage
    (B) releases his tensions onstage
    (C) becomes mentally unbalanced
    (D) is difficult to get along with
    (E) is unsuited for politics.

7. As used in line 6, the word "Theater" means the
    (A) original Shakespearean theater
    (B) legitimate stage
    (C) every-day actions of man
    (D) political arena
    (E) theater of war.

Reading Passage III

The Mideast lives amid vanished glories, present prejudices and future fears. Scrabble in its soil with a hoe and you will find relics of empires long, long gone—birthplaces of civilizations that have waxed and wanted—and monuments to religions almost as old as recorded history.

From the Nile to the Euphrates, where transworld air routes now cover much the same trails as the plodding camel caravans of the past, Man—persistent, passionate, prejudiced—carries on the age-old plot of the human drama. All has altered, yet nothing has changed in the Middle East since centuries before Christ.

Palmyra, the caravan city of Queen Zenobia, is now a magnificent but melancholy reminder of the dreams of men long dead. Baalbek, where even the gods of yesterday have died, is but a tourist attraction, though today no tourists come. The Pyramids themselves, grandiose monuments to man's eternal hope of immortality, are scuffed and wrinkled now—cosmetically patched against the inexorability of the centuries.

Yet, essentially nothing has changed. Man and his emotions, Man and his ignorance and knowledge, Man in his pride, Man at war with other men, sets the scene and dominates the stage of the turbulent Middle East.

8. The title below that best expresses the ideas of this passage is
   (A) the old vs. the new
   (B) the appeal of the Pyramids
   (C) the unchanging Mideast
   (D) new routes to the Mideast
   (E) the birthplace of empires.

9. According to the passage, problems in the Middle East have been due to the
   (A) waning of civilization
   (B) lack of tourist trade
   (C) collapse of former civilizations
   (D) disappearance of belief in immortality
   (E) weaknesses of man.

10. The passage suggests that
    (A) man's nature does not change
    (B) man will eventually triumph over ignorance

    (C) man's destiny has changed
    (D) man's nature has improved in the last thousand years
    (E) man's prejudices against others will gradually disappear.

11. The passage suggests that men of the ancient Middle East were
    (A) irreligious   (B) vain
    C) melancholy   (D) poor
    E) unimaginative

12. The reader may conclude from the passage that ancient civilizations
    (A) existed before Christianity
    (B) embraced one God
    (C) relied upon agriculture as their industry
    (D) were interested in the drama
    (E) were democratic in the nature.

Reading Passage IV

Readers in the past seem to have been more patient than the readers of today. There were few diversions, and they had more time to read novels of a length that seems to us now inordinate. It may be that they were not irritated by the digressions and irrelevances that interrupted the narration. But some of the novels that suffer from these defects are among the greatest that have ever been written. It is deplorable that on this account they should be less and less read.

13. The title below that best expresses the ideas of this passage is
    (A) defects of today's novels
    (B) novel reading then and now
    (C) the great novel
    (D) the impatient reader of novels
    (E) decline in education.

14. The author implies that
    (A) authors of the past did not use narration to any extent
    (B) great novels are usually long
    (C) digressions and irrelevances are characteristic of modern novels
    (D) readers of the past were more capable
    (E) people today have more pastimes than formerly.

Reading Passage V

A legendary island in the Atlantic Ocean beyond the Pillars of Hercules was first mentioned by Plato in the *Timaeus*. Atlantis was a fabulously beautiful and prosperous land, the seat of an empire nine thousand years before Solon. Its inhabitants overran part of Europe and Africa, Athens alone being able to defy them. Because of the impiety of its people, the island was destroyed by an earthquake and inundation. The legend may have existed before Plato and may have sprung from the concept of Homer's Elysium. The possibility that such an island once existed has caused much speculation, resulting in a theory that pre-Columbian civilizations in America were established by colonists from the lost island.

15. The title below that best expresses the ideas of this passage is
    (A) a persistent myth
    (B) Geography according to Plato
    (C) the first discoverers of America
    (D) buried civilizations
    (E) a labor of Hercules.

    (C) were a religious and superstitious people
    (D) used the name Columbus for America
    (E) left no recorded evidence of this existence.

16. According to the passage, we may most safely conclude that the inhabitants of Atlantis
    (A) were known personally to Homer
    (B) were ruled by Plato

17. According to the legend, Atlantis was destroyed because of the inhabitants
    (A) failed to obtain an adequate food supply
    (B) failed to conquer Greece
    (C) failed to respect their Gods
    (D) believed in Homer's Elysium
    (E) had become too prosperous.

Reading Passage VI

A large number of Shakespeare's soliloquies must be considered as representing thought, not speech. They are to make the audience understand what is passing through the mind of the character, not what under the circumstances he would have said aloud. A maiden would not say aloud Juliet's speech, "Gallop apace, you fiery-footed steeds," which represents the secret passion of her body and soul. And her soliloquy when she takes the drug also represented her thoughts; it was not spoken in reality. The dramatist is compelled to put into words and the actress to speak it—but to add to it gesture or great changes in the voice or outward show is to mistake altogether the idea of the dramatist.

18. The title below that best expresses the ideas of this passage is
    (A) gesture and changes in the voice
    (B) the difficulties of Shakespearean actors
    (C) misunderstanding Shakespearean plays
    (D) revealing thought through the soliloquy
    (E) unfolding the plot through the sililoquy.

19. The writer assumes that
    (A) actors have used poor enunciation
    (B) *Romeo and Juliet* is the most popular play by Shakespeare
    (C) his readers are familiar with Shakespeare's plays

    (D) many people dislike Shakespeare
    (E) Shakespeare is only for "highbrows."

20. Which statement can be made on the basis of the passage?
    (A) the role of Juliet is more difficult than other roles
    (B) The role of Juliet is only one example of the point made
    (C) audiences have no feeling for characterization
    (D) Shakespeare was an incompetent dramatist in some respects
    (E) there are too many soliloquies in Shakespeare's plays.

Reading Passage VII

By the words *public duty* I do not necessarily mean *official* duty, although it may include that. I mean simply that constant and active practical participation in the details of politics without which upon the part of the most intelligent citizens, the conduct of public affairs falls under the control of selfish and ignorant or crafty and venal men. I mean that personal attention—which, as it must be incessant, is often wearisome and even repulsive—to the details of politics, attendance at meetings, service upon committees, care and trouble and expense of many kinds, patient endurance of rebuffs, chagrins, ridicules, disappointments, defeats—in a word, all those duties and services which, when selfishly and meanly performed, stigmatize a man as a mere politician but whose constant, honorable, intelligent and vigilant performance is the gradual building, stone by stone and layer by layer, of that temple of self-restrained liberty which all generous souls mean that our government should be.

21. The title below that best expresses the ideas of the paragraph is

    (A) the public duty of intelligent men
    (B) the evils of indifference
    (C) characteristics of the mere politician
    (D) the ideal democracy
    (E) true patriotism.

22. The maintenance of the American democratic ideal depends upon

    (A) a highly educated body of citizens
    (B) unification of political parties
    (C) absence of dissenting ideas
    (D) an easily lead minority
    (E) alert sharing of civic responsibility.

23. Which one of the following statements best expresses an idea found in the passage?

    (A) constant and active participation in politics perpetuates the democratic ideal
    (B) personal attention of officeholders insures American democratic principles
    (C) genuine public spirit demands personal secrifice
    (D) *public duty* is synonymous with official duty
    (E) American liberty is based on constant legislation.

Reading Passage VIII

The reclamation of a worn-out farm, thanks to modern conservation, is no longer so rare an event as to be particularly earth-shaking. But when a whole river valley, some 330 square miles, is transformed from an erosion of mud and a pollution-ridden area into one of the most beautiful, healthful and prosperous places to live in America, that is news!

In March, 1945, some farmers, sportsmen and townspeople, all living in the Brandywine Valley of Delaware and southeastern Pennsylvania, got together to take a good look at their land. Out of that meeting grew a conservation program that stands as the finest example of land reclamation and watershed protection in the country.

Best of all, the highly successful program of the Brandywine Valley Association is one that can be copied in every section needing it, and they are legion, for river valleys have always been Americans' favorite home locations.

24. The title below that best expresses the ideas of this passage is

    (A) worn-out farms
    (B) enterprising farmers
    (C) a lesson in civic action
    (D) America's favorite homes
    (E) the inhabitants of Brandywine Valley.

25. The writer indicates that

    (A) this was a state project
    (B) a committee did all the work
    (C) such programs as this are common
    (D) this program would work everywhere
    (E) many areas need such programs as this.

26. The initial meeting was probably the result of a desire to

    (A) improve the land
    (B) publicize the valley
    (C) rebuild farm buildings
    (D) improve the view of the valley
    (E) be the first to reclaim an entire valley.

Reading Passage IX

Nevertheless, there is such a voluble hue and cry about the abysmal state of culture in the United States by well-meaning, sincere critics that I would like to present some evidence to the contrary. One is tempted to remind these critics that no country has ever achieved the complete integration of *haute culture* into the warp and woof of its everyday life. In the wishful memories of those who moon over the passed glories of Shakespeare's England, it is seldom called to mind that bearbaiting was far more popular than any of Master Shakespeare's presentations. Who cares to remember that the same Rome that found a Juvenal proclaiming *mens sana in corpore sano* also watch an Emperor Trajan celebrate his victory over Decebalus of Dacis in 106 A.D. with no fewer than 5,000 pairs of gladiators matched to the death? And this in the name of amusement!

27. The title below that best expresses the ideas of this passage is
    (A) the hue and cry of the critics
    (B) reflections on culture
    (C) dangers in contemporary criticism
    (D) the world's amusements
    (E) everyday life.

28. The paragraph preceding this passage most probably discussed
    (A) the increased interest of Americans in public affairs
    (B) the popularity of Shakespeare during his lifetime

    (C) the interest of Americans in the arts
    (D) the duties of a literary critic
    (E) Juvenal's contributions to poetry.

29. According to the passage, those who criticize the level of culture in America are:
    (A) amusing   (B) outspoken
    (C) unappreciated   (D) sarcastic
    (E) popular

30. The author's attitude toward culture is essentially
    (A) despairing   (B) realistic
    (C) distorted   (D) uncritical
    (E) childish

END OF PART

Go on to the following Test in the next Part of this Examination, just as you would be expected to do on the actual exam. If you have any available time use it to make sure that you have marked your Answer Sheet properly for this Part. Correct Answers for all Parts of this Exam follow the last question. Derive your scores only after completing the entire Exam.

PART V. THE MATHEMATICS TEST

TIME: 45 Minutes. 36 Questions.

TEST XII. GENERAL MATHEMATICAL ABILITY

TIME: 40 Minutes. 30 Questions.

DIRECTIONS: Study each of the following problems and work out your answers in the blank space at the right. Below each problem you will find a number of suggested answers. Select the one that you have figured out to be right and mark its letter on the answer sheet. In the sample questions provided, the correct answers are: S1 = A; S2 = C.

Correct and explanatory answers are provided at the end of the exam. After you have completed the entire exam, read the explanations carefully. They'll reinforce your strengths and pinpoint your weaknesses so that you know just what to study to raise your score.

1. Assuming that the series will continue in the same pattern, the next number in the series 3, 5, 11, 29 . . . . is:
   (A) 41 (B) 47
   (C) 65 (D) 83

2. DCCXLIX in Roman numerals represents the number:
   (A) 749 (B) 764
   (C) 1249 (D) 1264

3. If the total area of a picture measuring 10 inches by 12 inches plus a matting of uniform width surrounding the picture is 224 square inches, the width of the matting is:
   (A) 2 inches (B) 2 $\frac{6}{11}$ inches
   (C) 3 inches (D) 4 inches

4. The net price of a $25 item after successive discounts of 20% and 30% is:
   (A) $11.00 (B) $12.50
   (C) $14.00 (D) $19.00

5. The cost of 63 inches of ribbon at $.12 per yard is:
   (A) $.20 (B) $.21
   (C) $.22 (D) $.23

6. If 1½ cups of cereal are used with 4½ cups of water, the amount of water needed with ¾ of a cup of cereal is:
   (A) 2 cups (B) 2⅛ cups
   (C) 2¼ cups (D) 2½ cups

7. Under certain conditions, sound travels at about 1100 ft. per second. If 88 ft. per second is approximately equivalent to 60 miles per hour, the speed of sound, under the above conditions, is, of the following, closest to:
   (A) 730 miles per hour
   (B) 740 miles per hour
   (C) 750 miles per hour
   (D) 760 miles per hour

8. If one angle of a triangle is three times a second angle and the third angle is 20 degrees more than the second angle, the second angle is (in degrees):
   (A) 32 (B) 34
   (C) 40 (D) 50

9. Assuming that on a blueprint ¼ inch equals
12 inches, the actual length in feet of a steel
bar represented on the blueprint by a line
3⅜ inches long is:
(A) 3⅜   (B) 6¾
(C) 12½   (D) 13½

10. If Mrs. Jones bought 3¾ yards of dacron at
$1.16 per yard and 4⅔ yards of velvet at
$3.87 per yard, the amount of change she
receives from $25 is:
(A) $2.12   (B) $2.28
(C) $2.59   (D) $2.63

11. The water level of a swimming pool, 75 feet
by 42 feet, is to be raised four inches. The
number of gallons of water needed for this is:
(A) 140   (B) 7,854.5
(C) 31,500   (D) 94,500

12. If shipping charges to a certain point are 62
cents for the first five ounces and 8 cents for
each additional ounce, the weight of a package for which the charges are $1.66 is:
(A) 13 ounces   (B) 1⅛ pounds
(C) 1¼ pounds   (D) 1½ pounds

13. If 15 cans of food are needed for seven men
for two days, the number of cans needed for
four men for seven days is:
(A) 15   (B) 20
(C) 25   (D) 30

14. The total saving in purchasing 30 13-cent
ice cream pops for a class party at a reduced
rate of $1.38 per dozen is:
(A) $.35   (B) $.40
(C) $.45   (D) $.50

15. A candy recipe calls for, among other things,
1½ cups of sugar and ¾ of a cup of boiling
water. Mary wants to use this recipe, but has
only one cup of sugar. How much boiling
water should she use?
(A) ¼ cup   (B) ⅓ cup
(C) ½ cup   (D) ⅝ cup

16. In a 3-hour examination of 350 questions,
there are 50 mathematics problems. If twice
as much time should be allowed for each
problem as for each of the other questions,
how many minutes should be spent on the
mathematical problems?
(A) 45 minutes   (B) 52 minutes
(C) 60 minutes   (D) 72 minutes

17. A rectangular picture measures 4½" by
6¾". If the picture is proportionally enlarged so that the shorter side is 7½", what
will be the length of the longer side?
(A) 9¾"   (B) 11¼"
(C) 13½"   (D) 20¼"

18. A typewriter was listed at $120.00 and was
bought for $96.00. What was the rate of
discount?
(A) 16⅔%   (B) 20%
(C) 24%   (D) 25%

19. In two hours, the minute hand of a clock ro-
tates through an angle of
(A) 90°   (B) 180°
(C) 360°   (D) 720°

20. Assuming that the following series will continue in the same pattern, the next number
in the series 2, 6, 14, 30, 62, ... is
(A) 96   (B) 126
(C) 186   (D) 216

21. An individual intelligence test is administered
to John A when he is 10 years 8 months old.
His recorded M.A. is 160 months. What I.Q.
should be recorded?
(A) 80   (B) 125
(C) 128   (D) 160

22. When it is noon at prime meridian on the
equator, what time is it at 75° north latitude
on this meridian?
(A) 12 N.   (B) 3 P.M.
(C) 5 P.M.   (D) 7 A.M.

23. A carpenter needs boards for 4 shelves, each 2'9" long, and ½" thick. How many feet of board should he buy?
    (A) 11   (B) 11⅛
    (C) 13   (D) 15½

24. CMXLIX in Roman numerals is the equivalent of
    (A) 449   (B) 949
    (C) 969   (D) 1149 .

25. If you subtract —1 from +1 the result will be
    (A) —2   (B) 0
    (C) 1   (D) 2

26. Of the following, the one which is the equivalent of 2⅓ is
    (A) ⅓ of 2   (C) ⅔ of 1
    (B) 2 and ⅓ of 1   (D) 2 and ⅓ of 2

27. A man bought a TV set that was listed at $160. He was given successive discounts of 20% and 10% The price he paid was
    (A) $112.00   (C) $119.60
    (B) $115.20   (D) $129.60

28. The total length of fencing needed to enclose a rectangular area 46 feet by 34 feet is
    (A) 26 yards 1 foot   (C) 52 yards 2 feet
    (B) 26⅔ yards   (D) 53⅓ yards

29. Mr. Jones' income for a year is $15,000. He pays $2250 for income taxes. The percent of his income that he pays for income taxes is
    (A) 9   (C) 15
    (B) 12   (D) 22

30. Of the following, the one that is NOT a meaning of ⅔ is
    (A) 1 of the 3 equal parts of 2
    (B) 2 of the 3 equal parts of 1
    (C) 2 divided by 3
    (D) a ratio of 3 to 2

END OF TEST

Go on to do the following Test in this Examination, just as you would be expected to do on the actual exam. You will find correct answers for the entire Examination following the last question. Check your answers carefully after you have completed the whole Examination.

TEST XIII. GRAPH INTERPRETATION

TIME: 5 Minutes. 6 Questions.

DIRECTIONS: Read each test question carefully. Each one refers to the following graph, and is to be answered solely on that basis. Select the best answer among the given choices and blacken the proper space on the answer sheet.

Correct and explanatory answers are provided at the end of the exam. After you have completed the entire exam, read the explanations carefully. They'll reinforce your strengths and pinpoint your weaknesses so that you know just what to study to raise your score.

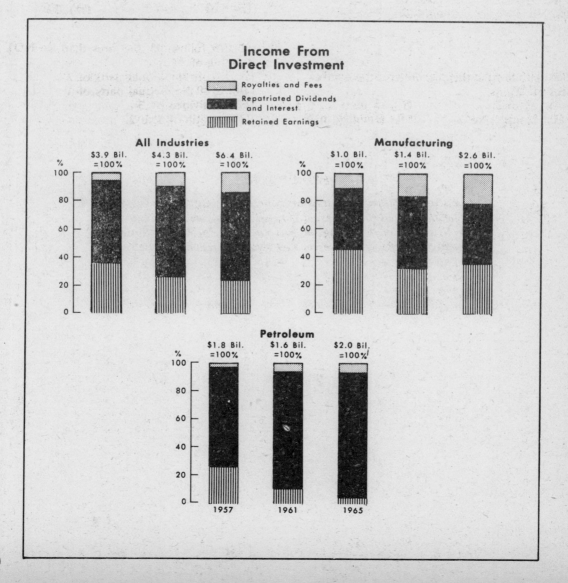

1. The manufacturing and petroleum industries accounted for what percent of income from direct investment in all industries in 1961?

    (A) 40%   (B) 50%
    (C) 60%   (D) 70%
    (E) cannot be determined from the given information

2. In 1957, how much was classified as "Retained Earnings" in the combined Petroleum and Manufacturing industries?

    (A) $400 million   (B) $450 million
    (C) $520 million   (D) $630 million
                (E) $900 million

3. The greatest percent increase of income was seen in

    (A) the manufacturing industry between 1957 and 1961
    (B) the manufacturing industry between 1961 and 1965
    (C) the petroleum industry between 1957 and 1961
    (D) the petroleum industry between 1961 and 1965
    (E) the combined statistics for all industries between 1957 and 1965

4. Which of the following does *not* represent an *increase?*

    (A) Royalties and fees in the manufacturing industry, 1961-1965
    (B) Repatriated dividends and interest in the petroleum industry, 1961-1965
    (C) Retained earnings in all industries, 1957-1961
    (D) Royalties and fees in the petroleum industry, 1957-1961
    (E) Repatriated dividends and interest in all industries, 1957-1965

5. Which represents the greatest amount?

    (A) Retained earnings in all industries in 1957
    (B) Total income from direct investment in manufacturing in 1957
    (C) Total retained earnings in the petroleum industry for all three years
    (D) Repatriated dividends and interest from manufacturing in 1965
    (E) Royalties and fees for all industries in 1965

6. How many degrees of a "pie" chart would be occupied by the manufacturing industry if the whole pie were to represent income from direct investment in 1961 for all industries?

    (A) 96°   (B) 107°
    (C) 117°   (D) 124°
                (E) 145°

END OF EXAMINATION

Now that you have completed the last Test in this Examination, use your available time to make sure that you have written in your answers correctly on the Answer Sheet. Then, after your time is up, check your answers with the Correct Answers we have provided for you. Derive your scores for each Test Category and determine where you are weak so as to plan your study accordingly.

CORRECT ANSWERS FOR VERISIMILAR EXAMINATION III.

TEST I. SPELLING

1.E	3.B	5.D	7.A	9.E	11.B	13.C
2.C	4.B	6.A	8.D	10.B	12.D	14.B

TEST II. ENGLISH GRAMMAR AND USAGE

1.B	3.B	5.B	7.B	9.A	11.C	13.E	15.B
2.A	4.A	6.D	8.B	10.C	12.A	14.C	

TEST III. ENGLISH GRAMMAR AND USAGE

1.B	3.E	5.E	7.B	9.E	11.D	13.D	15.E
2.D	4.C	6.D	8.D	10.C	12.E	14.D	

TEST IV. EFFECTIVENESS OF EXPRESSION

1.E	5.B	9.E	13.E	17.D	21.D	25.A	29.B
2.B	6.C	10.C	14.E	18.B	22.C	26.A	30.A
3.E	7.A	11.B	15.A	19.B	23.E	27.D	
4.A	8.C	12.C	16.B	20.B	24.C	28.C	

TEST V. LOGIC AND ORGANIZATION

1.E	2.B	3.D	4.C	5.A	6.A	7.C	8.E

TEST V. EXPLANATORY ANSWERS

1. **(E)** *Diction*. "Magnetic" is an adjective that means powerfully attractive. "Significant," an adjective that means full of meaning, most correctly completes sentence 1.

2. **(B)** *Clarification*. "Social" as it stands now is an adjective modifying nothing. The addition of "life in the future" provides a noun for "social" and clarifies the meaning of sentence 2.

3. **(D)** *Economy*. The nouns, "forecast, prophecy and prediction," mean essentially the same thing. Thus the sentence is improved by omitting "prophecy and prediction."

4. **(C)** *Sentence relationship*. Sentence 4 refers explicitly to sentence 3. Beginning sentence 4 with "This is" correctly links the two sentences together.

5. **(A)** *Diction*. "Taking place" is another way of saying "occurring." It is therefore the correct verb for sentence 5.

6. **(A)** *Ordering*. Sentence 6 as it stands fits into the flow of thought of the passage.

533

534 / High School Equivalency Diploma Tests

7. **(C)** *Diction*. The verb, "depress," is defined as to press down or to sadden. The verb, "determine," which is defined as to be the deciding factor in or to set limits to, correctly completes sentence 7.

8. **(E)** *Paragraphing*. Sentence 5 introduces the "changes taking place" in the concepts elaborated upon in the first five sentences. It thus introduces the second paragraph of the passage.

TEST VI. INTERPRETATION OF SOCIAL STUDIES READINGS

Reading Passage I

1.C	3.A	5.C	7.B	9.A
2.B	4.C	6.A	8.D	

Reading Passage II

1.B	2.C	3.D	4.B	5.A

Reading Passage III

1.A	3.B	5.C	7.D	9.B
2.D	4.C	6.B	8.A	

Reading Passage IV

1.A	2.B	3.C	4.A	5.D	6.C	7.D

Reading Passage V

1.C	2.B	3.B	4.C	5.B	6.B	7.A

TEST VII. SOCIAL STUDIES KNOWLEDGE

1.A	4.A	7.A	10.A	13.B	16.C	19.C
2.A	5.C	8.A	11.D	14.D	17.B	20.D
3.D	6.C	9.C	12.B	15.B	18.C	

TEST VIII. INTERPRETATION OF SCIENCE READING

Reading Passage I

1.C	3.A	5.D	7.B	9.D	11.C
2.C	4.B	6.D	8.D	10.A	

Reading Passage II

1.B	3.B	5.A	7.D	9.D	11.A	13.D	15.B
2.A	4.B	6.C	8.D	10.B	12.A	14.C	16.A

Reading Passage III

1.B	3.D	5.D	7.D	9.C	11.C
2.B	4.A	6.B	8.A	10.A	

TEST IX. SCIENCE INFORMATION

1.C	4.B	7.D	10.A	13.C	16.C	19.C
2.D	5.D	8.C	11.A	14.D	17.D	20.B
3.C	6.C	9.D	12.B	15.A	18.C	

TEST X. INTERPRETATION OF LITERARY MATERIALS

1.B	4.A	7.A	10.D	13.C	16.C
2.C	5.B	8.C	11.C	14.B	17.D
3.B	6.B	9.C	12.B	15.C	

TEST XI. INTERPRETATION OF PROSE

1.E	5.D	9.E	13.B	17.C	21.A	25.E	29.B
2.A	6.B	10.A	14.E	18.D	22.E	26.A	30.B
3.C	7.B	11.B	15.A	19.C	23.C	27.B	
4.E	8.C	12.A	16.E	20.B	24.C	28.C	

TEST XII. GENERAL MATHEMATICAL ABILITY

1.D	5.B	9.D	13.D	17.B	21.B	25.D	29.C
2.A	6.C	10.C	14.C	18.B	22.A	26.B	30.D
3.A	7.C	11.B	15.C	19.D	23.A	27.B	
4.C	8.A	12.B	16.A	20.B	24.B	28.D	

TEST XII. EXPLANATORY ANSWERS

1. SOLUTION:
   1) Series: 3, 5, 11, 29, —
      Triple the difference between the two preceding terms in the series and then add this tripled difference to get the next term in the series.

EXAMPLE

Term of series:	1st	2nd	3rd	4th	5th
Number in series:	3	5	11	29	**83**
Difference		2	6	18	54

ANSWER: 83 (D)

2. SOLUTION: The following principles apply for the Roman numeration system.

(1) Repetition: If two adjacent symbols are alike, each symbol names the same number and the numbers named are to be added.

(2) Addition: If two numerals are not alike, one must name a smaller number than the other. If the numeral for the smaller number is written to the right of the other numeral, the smaller number is to be added.

(3) Subtraction: If the numeral for the smaller number of a pair of numerals appears to the left of the other numeral, the smaller number is to be subtracted.

DCCXLIX = 749 (A)

PROOF

$$D = 500$$
$$CC = 200$$
$$XL = 40$$
$$IX = \underline{9}$$
$$749$$

3. SOLUTION:
   3) $12'' \times 10'' = 120''$
   224 sq. in. — 120 sq. in. = 104 sq. in.
   $2(10 \cdot x) + 2(12 \cdot x) + 4x^2 = 104$
   $20x + 24x + 4x^2 = 104$
   $4x^2 + 44x - 104 = 0$ (divide by 4)
   $x^2 + 11x - 26 = 0$ (quadratic equation factoring) $(x + 13)(x - 2) = 0$ (a)

ANSWER: x = 2 (A)

Explanation of factoring in Example 3 If the product of two factors = 0, then at least one of the factors must be zero.

ILLUSTRATION

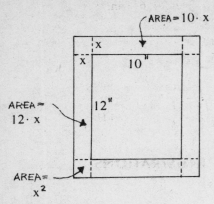

AREA = 10 · x

x

x   10"

AREA ≈ 12 · x   12"

AREA = x^2

EXAMPLE

If $a \cdot b = 0$, then either $a = 0$, or $b = 0$ or both. The two factors above, $x + 13$ and $x - 2$, are like the a and b above.
If $x - 2 = 0$, then $x = 2$ (answer)
If $x + 13 = 0$, then $x = -13$.
The second solution must be discarded (being negative) since it doesn't fit the conditions of the problem.

4. SOLUTION:
$25 \times .20 = 5.00 first discount
$25 - $5 = 20.00
$20 \times .30 = 6.00 second discount
$20 - $6 = 14.00 Net Price

ANSWER: $14   (C)

5. SOLUTION:
36 inches = 1 yard
63 inches ÷ 36 = 1¾ yards

$.12 \times 1¾ = $.12 \times \dfrac{7}{4} = \dfrac{.84}{4} = $.21$ Cost of

ribbon

ANSWER: $.21   (B)

6. SOLUTION:
1½c : 4½c :: ¾c : x

$\dfrac{3}{2}x = \dfrac{9}{2} \cdot \dfrac{3}{4}$

$x = \dfrac{9}{2} \cdot \dfrac{3}{4} \cdot \dfrac{2}{3}$

$x = \dfrac{9}{4}$ or 2¼ cups water

ANSWER: 2¼   (C)

7. SOLUTION:
Sound travels 1100 ft. per sec.
88 ft. per sec. = 60 mi. per hr.

$$\dfrac{1100 \text{ ft./sec.}}{88 \text{ ft./sec.}} = \dfrac{x \text{ mi./hr.}}{60 \text{ mi./hr.}}$$

$$x = \dfrac{\overset{15}{\cancel{88}} \cdot \overset{50}{\cancel{1100}}}{\underset{22}{\cancel{88}}} = 750 \text{ mi./hr.}$$

ANSWER: 750   (C)

8. SOLUTION:
x = angle 2
$3x$ = angle 1
$x + 20$ = angle 3
$x + 3x + x + 20° = 180°$
$5x = 180° - 20°$
$5x = 160°$
$x = 32°$

ANSWER: 32   (A)

9. SOLUTION:
On blueprint ¼ in. = 12 in. or 1 ft.

$3⅜ \div ¼ = \dfrac{27}{8} \div ¼$

$\dfrac{27}{\underset{2}{\cancel{8}}} \times \dfrac{\overset{1}{\cancel{4}}}{1} = \dfrac{27}{2} = 13½$ length in feet

ANSWER: 13½   (D)

10. SOLUTION:
$1.16 \times 3¾ = $1.16 \times {}^{15}\!/_4 = $ 4.35$ cost—dacron
$3.87 \times 4⅔ = $3.87 \times {}^{14}\!/_3 = 18.06 cost—velvet
$ 4.35 + $18.06 = 22.41
$25.00 - $22.41 = 2.59 change

ANSWER: $2.59   (C)

11. SOLUTION:
The volume of water to be added (4 in. = ⅓ ft.)

$$75 \times \overset{14}{\cancel{42}} \times \dfrac{1}{\underset{1}{\cancel{3}}} = 1050 \text{ cu. ft.}$$

Since there are 7.4805 gal. in a cu. ft. then
$1050 \times 7.4805 = 7854.5$ gal.

ANSWER: 7854.5   (B)

12. SOLUTION:

$1.66 — $.62 = $1.04 charge for additional
weight over 5 ozs.
$1.04 ÷ $.08 = 13 ounces additional
13 oz. + 5 oz. = 18 oz.
16 oz. = 1 pound
18 oz. ÷ 16 oz. = 1⅛ pounds

ANSWER: 1⅛ pounds (B)

13. SOLUTION:

First find number of cans each man needs for one day.
$^{15}/_7$ = no. of cans each man needs for 2 days.
$^{15}/_7 \times ½ = {}^{15}/_{14}$ no. of cans each man needs for 1 day.
Then, the no. of cans needed by 4 men for 7 days
$^{15}/_{14} \times 7 \times 4 = 30$ cans

ANSWER: 30 (D)

14. SOLUTION:

$30 \times $.13 = $3.90 cost for 30 pops
$30 ÷ 12 = 2½ doz.
$1.38 \times 2½ = $3.45 cost by doz.
$3.90 — $3.45 = $.45 saving

ANSWER: $.45 (C)

15. SOLUTION:

1½ cups sugar   ¾ cup boiling water
Has only 1 cup sugar
Let x = boiling water   ¾c : x :: 1½c : 1
$$\frac{¾}{1½} = \frac{x}{1}$$
$^3/_2 x = ¾$
$x = ¾ \cdot ⅔ = ½$ cup

ANSWER: ½ cup (C)

16. SOLUTION: Let x = number of minutes on each non-math question
50 math questions   3 hr. = 180 min.
350 ques. — 50 math. = 300 other ques.
$2(50x) + 300x = 180$ min.
$100x + 300x = 180$ min.
$400x = 180$ min.
$$x = \frac{180}{400} = \frac{9}{20}$$ min. on

each non-math problem
Each math. problem takes $2 \cdot (^9/_{20}) = {}^9/_{10}$ min.
$50 \cdot {}^9/_{10}$ min. = 45 min.

ANSWER: 45 min. (A)

17. SOLUTION:

Let x = longer side
4½ in. : 7½ in. :: 6¾ in. : x
$$\frac{4½}{7½} = \frac{6¾}{x}$$
$$\frac{9}{2}x = \frac{15}{2} \cdot \frac{27}{4}$$
$$x = \frac{15}{2} \cdot \frac{27}{4} \cdot \frac{2}{9} = \frac{45}{4} = 11¼$$

ILLUSTRATIONS

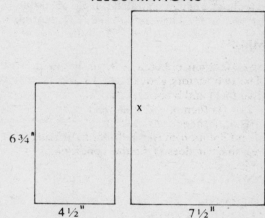

ANSWER: 11¼ (B)

18. SOLUTION:

$120 — $96 = $24 discount
$$\frac{$24}{$120} = \frac{4}{20} = \frac{1}{5} = 20\% \text{ Rate of discount}$$

ANSWER: 20% (B)

19. SOLUTION:

1 hr. = 360°   360° = clock circle
2 hr. = 2 × 360° = 720°   minute hand rotates.

ANSWER: 720° (D)

20. SOLUTION:

Series 2, 6, 14, 30, 62,—
Double the difference found by subtracting first term from second term; add this doubled difference to get the next term in the series.

Terms of series:	1st	2nd	3rd	4th	5th	6th
Numbers in series:	2,	6,	14,	30,	62	**126**
Difference:		4	8	16	32	64

ANSWER: 126 (B)

21. SOLUTION:
Mental Age = MA = 160 mo.
Chronological Age = CA = 10 yr. 8 mo.
  10 yr. 8 mo. = 128 mo. CA
$$\frac{160 \text{ mo.}}{128 \text{ mo.}} = 1.25 \qquad 1.25 \times 100 = 125$$
  I.Q.
        (Mult. by 100 because I.Q
        is like a %)

ANSWER: 125   (B)

22. SOLUTION:
Same time anywhere on the same meridian, therefore it would be noon at 75° N. latitude when it is noon at prime meridian on the equator.

ANSWER: 12M or noon   (A)

23. SOLUTION:
2'9" long = $2\frac{9}{12}$ = $2\frac{3}{4}$ ft.
$4 \times 2\frac{3}{4}$ ft. = $\frac{4}{1} \times 11\frac{1}{4}$ = $\frac{44}{4}$ = 11 ft.

ANSWER: 11 ft.   (A)

24. SOLUTION:
CMXLIX
See page xx
for explanation of
Roman numerals.

$$\begin{array}{r} 1000 - 100 = 900 \\ 50 - 10 = 40 \\ 10 - 1 = 9 \\ \hline 949 \end{array}$$

ANSWER: 949   (B)

25. SOLUTION:
Subtract −1 from +1
$$\begin{array}{l} +1 \\ -1(+1) \text{ change signs} \\ +2 \end{array}$$
Think: what number must be added to − 1 to give + 1?

ANSWER: 2   (D)

26. SOLUTION:
A) $\frac{1}{5}$ of 2 = $\frac{2}{5}$ B) 2 and $\frac{1}{5}$ of 1 = $2\frac{1}{5}$
C) $\frac{2}{5}$ of 1 = $\frac{2}{5}$ D) 2 and $\frac{1}{5}$ of 2 = $2\frac{2}{5}$

ANSWER: 2 and $\frac{1}{5}$ of 1   (B)

27. SOLUTION:
$160 List Price   Successive disc.
              of 20% and 10%
$160 × 20% = $160 × $\frac{1}{5}$ = $32 1st disc.
$160 − $32 = $128
$128 × 10% = $128 × $\frac{1}{10}$ = $12.80 2nd disc.
$128 − $12.80 = $115.20 Cost Price

ANSWER: $115.20   (B)

28. SOLUTION:
Find Perimeter
2 equal sides 2 × 46' = 92'   2 sides
2 equal sides 2 × 34' = 68'   2 sides
                        160' perimeter
  160' ÷ 3 = $53\frac{1}{3}$ yards

ILLUSTRATION

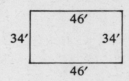

ANSWER: $53\frac{1}{3}$ yards   (D)

29. SOLUTION
Find % of income
$15,000 = yearly income
$ 2250 = income taxes (yearly)
$$\frac{\$2250}{15000} = \frac{3}{20} = 15\% \text{ of income for income taxes}$$

ANSWER: 15%   (C)

30. SOLUTION:
A = 1 of the 3 equal parts of 2 = $\frac{2}{3}$
B = 2 of the 3 equal parts of 1 = $\frac{2}{3}$
C = 2 divided by 3 = $\frac{2}{3}$
D = a ratio of 3 to 2 = $\frac{3}{2}$ = $1\frac{1}{2}$ Answer because it is not $\frac{2}{3}$

ANSWER: A ratio of 3 to 2   (D)

TEST XIII. GRAPH INTERPRETATION

1.D   2.E   3.B   4.C   5.A   6.C

TEST XIII. EXPLANATORY ANSWERS

1. **(D)** 1.6 billion + 1.4 billion = 3 billion. 3 billion is about 70% of 4.3 billion.

2. **(E)** 25% of 1.8 billion + 45% of 1 billion = 900 million.

3. **(B)** 2.6 billion minus 1.4 billion = 1.2 billion.

4. **(C)** 1957: 35% of 3.9 billion = 1 billion, 365 million. 1961: 30% of 4.3 billion = 1 billion, 290 million.

5. **(A)** 35% of 3.9 billion = 1 billion, 365 million. This exceeds the amount of each of the other choices.

6. **(C)** $\frac{1.4}{4.3}$ times 360 degrees = approx. 117 degrees.

HIGH SCHOOL EQUIVALENCY DIPLOMA TESTS

ARCO BOOKS FOR MORE HELP

Now what? You've read and studied the whole book, and there's still time before you take the test. You're probably better prepared than most of your competitors, but you may feel insecure about one or more of the probable test subjects.

Perhaps you've discovered that you are weak in language, verbal ability or mathematics. Why flounder and fail when help is so easily available? Why not brush up in the privacy of your own home with one of these books?

And why not consider the other opportunities open to you? Look over the list and make plans for your future. Start studying for other tests *now*. You can then pick and choose your *ideal* position, instead of settling for the first *ordinary* job that comes along.

Each of the following books was created under the same expert editorial supervision that produced the excellent book you are now using. Though we only list titles and prices, you can be sure that each book performs a real service, and keeps you from fumbling and from failure. Whatever your goal. . . Civil Service, Trade License, Teaching, Professional License, Scholarships, Entrance to the School of your choice. . .you can achieve it through the proven Question and Answer Method.

S3556

GED PREPARATION

Comprehensive Math Review for the High School
Equivalency Diploma Test, McDonough 03420-3 4.00
High School Equivalency Diploma Tests, Turner 00110-0 5.00
Preliminary Arithmetic for the High School Equivalency
Diploma Test 02165-9 4.00
Preliminary Practice for the High School Equivalency
Diploma Test 01441-3 4.00
Preparation for the Spanish High School Equivalency
Diploma (Preparacion Para El Exam De Equivalencia
De La Escuela Superior—En Espanol) 02618-9 6.00
Step-By-Step Guide to Correct English, Pulaski 03402-5 3.95

General Education Development Series

Correctness and Effectiveness of Expression (English HSEDT),
Castellano, Guercio & Seitz 03688-5 4.00
General Mathematical Ability (Mathematics HSEDT),
Castellano, Guercio & Seitz 03689-3 4.00
Reading Interpretation in Social Sciences, Natural Sciences,
and Literature (Reading HSEDT), Castellano, Guercio & Seitz.. 03690-7 4.00
Teacher's Manual for the GED Series, ... 03692-3 2.50

COLLEGE BOARD ACHIEVEMENT TESTS

American History and Social Studies Achievement Test,
Altman 01722-8 1.45
Chemistry Achievement Test, Spector & Weiss .... LR 01261-7 4.50
College Board Achievement Test: Biology, Solomon 04094-7 3.95
College Board Achievement Test: Chemistry, Solomon 04101-3 3.95
English Composition Achievement Test .... 01247-1 .95
French Achievement Teest, Biezunski & Boisrond 01668-X 1.45
German Achievement Test, Greiner 01698-1 1.45
Latin Achievement Test 01743-0 1.45
Mathematics: Level I Achievement Test, Bramson 03847-0 3.00
Mathematics: Level II Achievement Test, Bramson .... 01456-3 .95
Physics Achievement Test, Bruenn 01265-X 1.95
Spanish Achievement Test, Jassey 01741-4 1.45

ARCO COLLEGE CREDIT TEST-TUTORS

American History: CLEP and AP Subject Examination, Woloch ...03804-7 4.95

PROFESSIONAL CAREER EXAM SERIES

Action Guide for Executive Job Seekers and Employers, Uris ... 01787-2 3.95
Automobile Mechanic Certification Tests, Sharp 03809-8 6.00
Bar Exams 01124-6 5.00
The C.P.A. Exam: Accounting by the "Parallel Point"
Method, Lipscomb 02020-2 15.00
Certificate in Data Processing Examination, Morrison 04032-7 12.00
Certified General Automobile Mechanic, Turner 02900-5 6.00
Computer Programmer, Luftig 01232-3 6.00
Computers and Automation, Brown 01745-7 5.00
Dental Admission Test, Arco Editorial Board 04293-1 6.00
Graduate Management Admission Test 03926-4 6.00
Graduate Record Examination Aptitude 00824-5 5.00
Health Insurance Agent (Hospital, Accident, Health, Life) 02153-5 5.00
How a Computer System Works, Brown & Workman 03424-6 5.95
How to Become a Successful Model, Krem 03625-7 5.00
How to Get Into Medical and Dental School,
Shugar, Shugar & Bauman 02523-9 4.00
How to Make Money in Music, Harris & Farrar 04089-0 5.95
The Installation and Servicing of Domestic
Oil Burners, Mitchell & Mitchell 00437-1 10.00
Insurance Agent and Broker 02149-7 6.00
Law School Admission Test, Turner 00840-7 5.00
Life Insurance Agent 02343-0 6.00
Medical College Admission Test, Turner 04289-3 6.00
Miller Analogies Test—1400 Analogy Questions 01114-9 4.00
The 1977-78 Airline Guide to Stewardess and
Steward Careers, Morton 04350-4 5.95
Notary Public 00180-1 6.00
Nursing School Entrance Examinations, Turner 01202-1 6.00
Oil Burner Installer 00096-1 6.00
The Official 1976-77 Guide to Airline Careers, Morton 03955-8 5.95
Playground and Recreation Director's Handbook 01096-7 6.00
Principles of Data Processing 04268-0 7.50
Quizzer for Students of Education, Walton 01447-4 4.00
Real Estate License Examination, Gladstone 03755-5 6.00
Refrigeration License Manual, Harfenist 02726-6 10.00
Resumes for Job Hunters, Shykind 03961-2 4.00

Resumes That Get Jobs, revised edition, Resume Service 03909-4 3.00
Security Representatives' Examinations, Stefano 01934-4 5.00
Simplify Legal Writing, Biskind 03801-2 5.00
Spanish for Nurses and Allied Health Science Students,
Hernandez-Miyares & Alba 04127-7 10.00
Stationary Engineer and Fireman 00070-8 6.00
The Test of English as a Foreign
Language (TOEFL), Moreno, Babin & Scallon 02944-7 6.00
Veterinary College Admissions 04147-1 6.00
Your Resume—Key to a Better Job, Corwen 03733-4 4.00

ADVANCED GRE SERIES

Biology: Advanced Test for the G.R.E., Miller 04310-5 4.95
Business: Advanced Test for the G.R.E., Berman,
Malea & Yearwood 01599-3 4.95
Chemistry: Advanced Test for the G.R.E., Weiss 01069-X 4.95
Economics: Advanced Test for the G.R.E., Zabrenski &
Heydari-Darafshian 01557-8 4.95
Education: Advanced Test for the G.R.E., Beckoff 01223-4 4.95
Engineering: Advanced Test for the G.R.E., Ingham & Nesbitt .. 01604-3 4.95
French: Advanced Test for the G.R.E., Dethierry 01070-3 3.95
Geography: Advanced Test for the G.R.E., White 01710-4 3.95
Geology: Advanced Test for the G.R.E., Dolgoff 01071-1 3.95
History: Advanced Test for the G.R.E., Smith 01072-X 4.95
Literature: Advanced Test for the G.R.E. 01073-8 3.95
Mathematics: Advanced Test for the G.R.E., Bramson 04264-8 4.95
Music: Advanced Test for the G.R.E., Murphy 01471-7 3.95
Philosophy: Advanced Test for the G.R.E., Steiner 01472-5 3.95
Physical Education: Advanced Test for the G.R.E., Rubinger 01609-4 3.95
Physics: Advanced Test for the G.R.E., Bruenn 01074-6 4.95
Political Science: Advanced Test for the G.R.E.,
Meador & Stewart 01459-8 3.95
Psychology: Advanced Test for the G.R.E., Millman & Nisbett ... 01145-9 4.95
Sociology: Advanced Test for the G.R.E., Reddan 01444-X 4.95
Spanish: Advanced Test for the G.R.E., Jassey 01075-4 3.95
Speech: Advanced Test for the G.R.E., Graham 01526-8 3.95

CIVIL SERVICE AND GENERAL TEST PREPARATION

LR—Library Reinforced Binding

Plumber—Plumber's Helper	00517-3	6.00
Police Administration and Criminal Investigation	00565-3	6.00
Police Administrative Aide, Turner	02345-7	5.00
Police Officer—Patrolman P.D, Murray	00019-8	6.00
Police Science Advancement—Police Promotion Course	02636-7	10.00
Policewoman	00062-7	6.00
Post Office Clerk-Carrier	00021-X	5.00
Post Office Motor Vehicle Operator	01162-9	4.00
Postal Inspector	00194-1	5.00
Postal Promotion Foreman—Supervisor	00538-6	6.00
Postal Service Officer	01658-2	5.00
Postmaster	01522-5	5.00
Practice for Civil Service Promotion	00023-6	6.00
Practice for Clerical, Typing and Stenographic Tests	04324-5	6.00
Principal Clerk—Stenographer	01523-3	8.00
Probation and Parole Officer	04203-6	8.00
Professional and Administrative Career Examination (PACE)	03653-2	6.00
Professional Careers Test	01543-8	6.00
Professional Trainee—Administrative Aide	01183-1	5.00
Public Health Sanitarian, Coyne	00985-3	8.00
Railroad Clerk	00067-8	4.00
Railroad Porter	00128-3	4.00
Real Estate Assessor—Appraiser—Manager	00563-7	8.00
Resident Building Superintendent	00068-6	5.00
Road Car Inspector (T.A.), Turner	03743-1	8.00
Sanitation Foreman (Foreman & Asst. Foreman)	01958-1	6.00
Sanitation Man	00025-2	4.00
School Crossing Guard	00611-0	4.00
Securing and Protecting Your Rights in Civil Service, Resnicoff	02714-2	4.95
Senior Clerical Series	01173-4	6.00
Senior Clerk—Stenographer	01797-X	6.00
Senior File Clerk, Turner	00124-0	5.00
Senior and Supervising Parking Enforcement Agent, Turner	03737-7	6.00
Senior Typist	03870-5	6.00
Sergeant, P.D.	00026-0	10.00
Shop Clerk, Turner	03684-2	6.00
Social Supervisor	04190-0	8.00
Staff Attendant	00828-8	4.00
Staff Positions: Senior Administrative Associate and Assistant	03490-4	6.00
State Trooper	00078-3	6.00
Statistician—Statistical Clerk	00058-9	5.00
Stenographer—Typist (Practical Preparation)	00147-X	5.00
Stenographer—U.S. Government Positions GS 2-7	04309-1	8.00
Storekeeper—Stockman (Senior Storekeeper)	01691-4	6.00
Structural Apprentice, Turner	00177-1	5.00
Structure Maintainer Trainee, Groups A to E, Turner	03683-4	6.00
Supervising Clerk (Income Maintenance)	02879-3	5.00
Supervising Clerk—Stenographer	04309-1	8.00
Supervision Course	01590-X	5.00
Surface Line Dispatcher	00140-2	6.00
Tabulating Machine Operator (IBM)	00781-8	4.00
Taking Tests and Scoring High, Honig	01347-8	4.00
Telephone Maintainer: New York City Transit Authority	03742-3	5.00
Telephone Operator	00033-3	8.00
Test Your Vocational Aptitude, Asta & Bernbach	03606-0	6.00
Towerman (Municipal Subway System)	00157-7	5.00
Trackman (Municipal Subways), Turner	00075-9	5.00
Track Foreman: New York City Transit Authority	03739-3	6.00
Traffic Control Agent	03421-1	5.00
Train Dispatcher	00158-5	5.00
Transit Patrolman	00092-9	5.00
Transit Sergeant—Lieutenant	00161-5	4.00
Treasury Enforcement Agent	00131-3	8.00
U.S. Professional Mid-Level Positions Grades GS-9 Through GS-12	02036-9	6.00
U.S. Summer Jobs, Turner	02480-1	4.00
Ventilation and Drainage Maintainer: New York City Transit Authority, Turner	03741-5	6.00
Vocabulary Builder and Guide to Verbal Tests	00535-1	4.00
Vocabulary, Spelling and Grammar	00077-5	4.00
Welder	01374-5	5.00
X-Ray Technician	01122-X	4.00

MILITARY EXAMINATION SERIES

Practice for Army Classification and Placement (ASVAB)	03845-4	6.00
Practice for the Armed Forces Tests	00063-5	6.00
Practice for the Navy's Basic Test Battery	01300-1	5.00
Practice for Air Force Placement Tests	04270-2	6.00
Practice for Officer Candidate Tests	01304-4	6.00
Tests for Women the Armed Forces	03821-7	6.00
U.S. Service Academies	01544-6	6.00

HIGH SCHOOL AND COLLEGE PREPARATION

American College Testing Program Exams	00694-3	5.00
Arco Arithmetic Q & A Review, Turner	02351-1	4.00
Better Business English, Classen	04287-7	2.95
Catholic High School Entrance Examination	00987-X	5.00
The College Board's Examination, McDonough & Hansen	02623-5	5.00
College By Mail, Jensen	02592-1	4.00
College Entrance Tests, Turner	01858-5	5.00
College-Level Examination Program (CLEP), Turner	04150-1	6.00
College Scholarships	00569-6	2.00
The Easy Way to Better Grades, Froe & Froe	03352-5	1.50
Elements of Debate, Klopf & McCroskey	01901-8	4.00
Encyclopedia of English, Zeiger	00655-X	2.50
English Grammar: 1,000 Steps	02012-1	4.00
English Grammar and Usage for Test-Takers, Turner	04014-9	5.00
Good English with Ease, Beckoff	00859-8	3.00
Good English with Ease, revised edition, Beckoff	03911-6	4.00
Guide to Financial Aids for Students in Arts and Sciences for Graduate and Professional Study, Searles & Scott	02496-8	3.95
High School Entrance and Scholarship Tests, Turner	00666-8	4.00
High School Entrance Examinations—Special Public and Private High Schools	02143-8	5.00
How to Obtain Money for College, Lever	03932-9	5.00
How to Prepare Your College Application, Kussin & Kussin	01310-9	2.00
How to Use a Pocket Calculator, Mullish	04072-6	3.95
How to Write Reports, Papers, Theses, Articles, Riebel	02391-0	5.00
Letter-Perfect: The Accurate Secretary, Gilson	04038-6	6.00
Mastering General Mathematics, McDonough	03732-6	5.00
New York State Regents Scholarship	00400-2	5.00
Organization and Outlining, Peirce	02425-9	4.95
Practice for Scholastic Aptitude Tests	04303-2	1.50
Scholastic Aptitude Tests	04341-5	5.00
Scoring High on the PSAT-NMSQT, Turner	00413-4	4.00
Scoring High on Reading Tests	00731-1	5.00
Summaries of the Occupational Outlook Handbook	04328-8	3.95
Triple Your Reading Speed, Cutler	02083-0	4.00
Typing for Everyone, Levine	02212-4 E	3.95

GENERAL INTEREST BOOKS

How To Start A Typing Service In Your Own Home, Wilbanks ... 02608-1 5.00
How to Win Success in the Mail Order Business 02897-1 4.00
How to Write Successful Business Letters, Riebel 02290-6 5.00
Jazz Piano: Ragtime to Rock Jazz, Stormen 03828-4 3.95
Magic for All, Dunn 03827-6 2.50
Magic of the Masters, Delvin 04132-3 4.95
Mathematical Puzzles, Games, And Fallacies, Lamb 04092-0 1.95
Mixed Marriage Between Jew and Christian, Silver .... LR 04046-7 1.95
Modern Police Service Encyclopedia, Salottolo 02389-9 8.00
100 Classic Houdini Tricks You Can Do, Dunninger 03617-6 2.25
141 Magic Tricks, Ripley & Spina 03252-9 1.95
Out of the Past: The Istanbul Grand Bazaar, Berry 03778-4 14.95
Popular Piano Self-Taught, Stormen 00429-0 4.00
Profitable Telephone Sales Operations, Steckel 03649-4 15.00
Prospect of Scotland, Hannavy 03726-1 10.00
The Psychology of Witchcraft, Ravensdale & Morgan 03501-3 10.00
Secrets of the Sea, Mallan 03922-1 2.00
Test Your Own Mental Health, Gladstone 04186-2 5.95
Trading with China, Mobius & Simmel .... LR 02908-0 4.95

Treasure Hunter's Guide (How and Where to Find It) 01806-2 5.95
Understanding Investments and Mutual Funds, Potts 02713-4 8.95
Victorian Public Houses, Spiller 02711-8 10.00
Wake Up and Write, revised edition, Manners 04093-9 2.95
Warriors of the Plains, Taylor 03447-5 15.00
The World of Big Bands, Jackson 04168-4 12.95
You Can See the World in 40 Days, Waggoner 04040-8 10.95

CHILDREN'S BOOKS

Let's Explore Mathematics—Book 1, Marsh 01511-X 2.45
Let's Explore Mathematics—Book 2, Marsh 01512-8 2.45
Let's Explore Mathematics—Book 3, Marsh 01513-6 2.45
Let's Explore Mathematics—Book 4, Marsh 01824-0 2.45
Teacher's Guide: Children Explore Mathematics, Marsh 02077-6 3.00

ARCO TAX GUIDES

Confidential Official IRS Tax Audit Guide 03837-3 3.95
Your Federal Income Tax Annual 1978 .... 00865-2 1.25

AUTOMOTIVE

Arco Motor Vehicle Dictionary: English and Spanish, Lima ....LR 01927-1 5.00
Auto Repair Frauds, Engel .... LR 03763-6 8.95
Auto Repairs You Can Make, Weissler 03957-4 3.95
British Sports Cars Since the War, Watkins 03390-8 6.95
Car Care, Editors of Mechanix Illustrated .... LR 01918-2 4.95
Car Service Data, Seale 03357-6 6.95
The Complete Book of Minibikes and Minicycles, Engel ...LR 02733-9 7.95
The Complete Book of Mobile Home Living, Engel .... LR 02896-3 5.95
The Complete Book of Motor Camping (Revised), Engel 02916-1 2.95
The Complete Book of Trailering, Engel 02715-0 2.95
Famous Old Cars, Bowman .... LR 00597-1 3.50
The Fastest Men in the World—On Wheels 03305-3 5.95
Fiat 1899-1972, Sedgwick 03306-1 14.95
Grand Prix Cars of the 3-Litre Formula, Pritchard 04211-7 12.95
Hot Rod Handbook, Hochman .... LR 00602-1 3.95
How to Beat Police Radar . . . and Do It Legally, Power ....LR 04317-2 5.95
How to Customize Cars and Rods, Barris & Thoms ....LR 01151-3 3.95
The Incredible A. J. Foyt, Engel .... LR 02195-0 6.95
Karting, Smith .... LR 01939-5 6.95
Learning to Drive, Stevenson .... LR 03373-8 5.95
Mario Andretti—The Man Who Can Win Any Kind of Race .... LR 02193-4 4.95

Maserati: A History, Pritchard 04000-9 14.95
Motocourse 1976-77, Carter 04177-3 21.95
Motorcycle Panorama, Holliday 03647-8 7.95
Motorcycle Pioneers, Partridge 04035-1 8.95
Motorcycle Racing Champions, Whyte 03910-8 7.95
The New Book of Motorcycles, Arctander .... LR 01813-5 3.50
The New Guide to Motorcycling, Cutter ....LR 02732-0 7.95
The New How To Build Hot Rods, Jaderquist ....LR 00553-X 4.95
Oldtime Steam Cars, Bentley .... LR 02073-3 3.50
132 of the Most Unusual Cars That Ever Ran at
   Indianapolis, Engel & Editors of Auto Racing Magazine ..... LR 02194-2 4.95
The Porsche 911 Story, Frere 03964-7 15.00
The Racer's and Driver's Reader, Harding & Ionicus 02689-8 6.95
Racing Car Oddities, Nye 03724-5 8.95
The Racing Driver's Manual, Gardner 03458-0 8.50
The Racing Porsches, Frere 02972-2 15.00
Racing to Win—Wood Brothers Style, Engel 02886-6 5.95
Rolls-Royce—The History of the Car, Bennett 03619-2 19.95
Vintage and Veteran Cars, Hendry 03326-6 4.95
The World's Most Powerful Road Racing Cars, Ludvigsen &
   Editors of Auto Racing Magazine 03304-5 5.95

ASTROLOGY, HANDWRITING, HYPNOSIS, OCCULT ARTS, AND PALMISTRY

The Astrologer's Manual, Green 04200-1 6.95
Astrology, Davison 01128-9   .95
Astrology Dial-A-Scope, Wade 02393-7 3.50
An Astrology Guide to Your Sex Life, Robson 01628-0   .95
Biorhythm: A Personal Science, Gittelson 03415-7 8.95
The Book of Charms and Talismans, Sepharial 02010-5   .95
The Book of Fortune Telling, Fabia 03603-6 3.95
Cheiro's Book of Fate and Fortune, Cheiro 02507-7 5.95
Cheiro's Book of Numbers, Cheiro 01170-X 1.50
Cheiro's Language of the Hand, Cheiro 01780-5 1.95
Cheiro's Palmistry for All, Cheiro 01194-7   .95
Cheiro's When Were You Born, Cheiro 01168-8   .95
The Complete Guide to Palmistry, Psychos 01133-5   .95
Everything You Want to Know About Astrology,
   Numerology, How to Win, Zolar 02656-1   .95

Everything You Want to Know About Black Magic,
   Revelations by Zolar, Metaphysical Astrology,
   Mediumship, Crystal Gazing, Zolar 02658-8   .95
Everything You Want to Know About Dreams, Lucky
   Numbers, Omens, Oils and Incense, Zolar 02600-6 1.50
Everything You Want to Know About Fortune Telling
   With Cards, Karma System, Gypsy System,
   Professional System, Palmistry, Zolar 02659-6   .95
Everything You Want to Know About Hypnotism,
   Psychic Powers, Telepathy, E.S.P., Zolar 02662-6   .95
Everything You Want to Know About Nature's Mysteries,
   The Prophets, Nostradamus, Tea Leaf Reading,
   Herbs, Candle Burning, Zolar 02661-8   .95
Everything 36-copy prepack, Zolar 02924-2 34.20
Guide to Personality Through Your Handwriting, Marcuse 01339-7 1.45

7101